COLOR LINES

COLOR LINES

THE TROUBLED DREAMS OF RACIAL HARMONY IN AN AMERICAN TOWN

MIKE KELLY

WILLIAM MORROW AND COMPANY, INC. NEW YORK

Library of Congress Cataloging-in-Publication Data

Kelly, Mike, 1953-
    Color lines: the troubled dreams of racial harmony in an American town / Mike Kelly.—
1st ed.
        p.   cm.
    Includes bibliographical references and index.
    ISBN 0-688-11795-3
    1. Teaneck (N.J.)—Race relations.   2. Police shooting—New Jersey—Teaneck.   I. Title.
F144.T23K45   1995
305.8'00979421—dc20   95-13172   CIP

Printed in the United States of America

First Edition

1 2 3 4 5 6 7 8 9 10

BOOK DESIGN BY JESSICA SHATAN

FOR JUDY
WITH LOVE

AUTHOR'S NOTE

This is the story of one American town, one death, and one trial, all of which found themselves stirred and heated by the unpredictable fires of racial politics. Research is based, in part, on the reflections and memories of more than 250 people, some of whom were interviewed more than a dozen times, as well as on my own observations of many of the events described in these pages. To tell this story, I have selected a window of time—September 1989 to August 1992—and framed the narrative around a handful of people of diverse backgrounds who were touched in personal ways by the events and were willing to share their thoughts and feelings extensively and honestly.

When a person speaking is dead, I have relied on the recollections of people who claim to have heard the conversation. When only one person was present at an event, I have indicated as much in the manuscript. In some instances when a person's unspoken thoughts are described, those thoughts were reconstructed later in interviews with me.

Additional research—some of it to corroborate elements of the personal accounts by those interviewed—is based on some ten thousand pages of documents, including the transcripts of two grand juries and of court hearings not held in public but obtained later. Other materials include videotapes of Teaneck events made by television stations, private citizens, and Teaneck High School, of the trial, and of autopsy tests by prosecutors, files from defense lawyers and from the attorney general of New Jersey, court documents, newspaper and magazine accounts, and an extensive analysis of census and other demographic data of Teaneck that were compiled with the help of the Bergen County Department of Economic Planning, the U.S. Census Bureau, the New Jersey Department of Education, the New Jersey State Police, the Bergen County Prosecutor's Office, the Teaneck Police Department, the Teaneck town manager's office, the Teaneck school district, and various Bergen County real estate agents. Dialogue and other quoted statements are taken from transcripts of grand jury testimony, trial testimony, video recordings of events, sworn statements to the police, transcripts of police radio calls, interviews with the person who is speaking, or my own recording and observations of events.

Any recounting of history necessarily requires the blending of opposing viewpoints in the hope of fashioning a balanced, accurate portrait. To some extent such efforts inevitably are captive of the foibles of memory, as well as the eccentricities and passion that govern one's point of view and depth of emotion. When I found some accounts to be untruthful or incapable of being proved, I omitted them. In a few cases, where the truth in some accounts was later questioned, I reported those challenges because they were important to the story. I have tried to present as much of this variety as possible, some of it contradictory, in the hope of documenting the complexity of emotions that continue to surface in Teaneck. Such variety of perspectives is the power of this story. It is also the heart of its mystery.

CONTENTS

Part IV   TRIALS

The problem of the twentieth century is the problem of the color line.

—W.E.B. Du Bois

All politics is local.

—Tip O'Neill

PROLOGUE

I still keep the rock that hit me in the head. It is my guidepost, my compass point, the welt on my memory of the day this journey began.

To write about race is to navigate a swampy minefield of private lives and public history. Few of us can approach it casually, and without the burden of memory, yet few can run from it forever. For all its discomfort, race remains a subject we ponder relentlessly, often subconsciously, a social and moral laser beam that shines into our prisms of perception and shapes and colors our pictures of life in a way few other subjects can. It lurks just under the surface of political debates over schools, housing, and welfare. It provides a subtext to almost every story about crime, and it still hovers as an unspoken theme on the fringes of American sports. It is the reason so many whites (and blacks) count colors: how many blacks in Congress, how many blacks in the L. L. Bean catalog, how many black families on the block, how many black murderers, how many black voters. Few aspects of American life are tabulated so carefully.

But ultimately race is not just social arithmetic or a news story in which "issues" are framed in thirty-second sound bites or painted in street corner anger. Inevitably race is personal. And in the clear sunlight of a spring day in 1990, race became personal for me in a way it never had.

A rock struck me in the head. It was thrown by a teenager in a crowd outside the police station in the town I call home, Teaneck, New Jersey.

I stood that day in the midst of what was later called a racial incident, carried there by my job as a newspaper columnist. The previous night a police officer had shot and killed a teenager, and now I had a story to write, perplexing and troublesome. The cop was white; the kid was black. In my gut I sensed that this was no ordinary shooting, that the magnifying powers of race would bend and focus this story in a way that would take it far beyond the lives of a cop and a kid and the .32-caliber bullet that drew them together.

The rock came from behind, so unexpectedly that I didn't know what hit me until I looked down at the macadam and spotted the rectangular chunk of brown stone no bigger than a Milky Way candy bar. I picked it up and spun around, my coat flying open. I wanted to fight. I wanted to run. I felt like a fool. I looked up and met a collective stare—blank, angry, and distant. Looking at me were about a hundred students from Teaneck High School, mostly male, all but a handful of them black.

How odd, I thought. This wasn't happening in a dank city of hardship, where racial lines are as wide as avenues. It was afternoon in the New Jersey suburbs, the land of Volvo station wagons and pink dogwoods, of weed-free lawns and garage sales. My town was less than five miles from the anxious pace of Manhattan. Safe, I thought.

It was April 11, 1990. The buds on the oaks and maples by the police station were popping their red and green heads. Across the parking lot, seemingly oblivious of the black students by the police station, parents walked their children into the town library to return borrowed books. A warm southern breeze had kicked up, tossing a swirl of crusty leftover autumn leaves by the curb. Overhead, puffs of cumulus clouds glided across the azure sky. In the air I smelled a faint trace of fecund soil that had just broken free of winter's frost. The American flag flapped lightly on a pole outside the town hall, which, like the adjacent police station and library, had a dignified colonial brick motif. Two centuries before, George Washington had marched along a road not far from this spot at the head of his retreating army, accompanied by Thomas Paine, who was at work on the essay that contains the line "These are the times that try men's souls."

On this day few phrases seemed more appropriate. The teenager had been shot after having been chased into a backyard. His lifeless body was sprawled on the wet grass between an iris garden and the budding yellow crown of a forsythia bush. He was sixteen years old, and police said he had a silver .22-caliber pistol in his coat pocket when he died. Black witnesses said that the boy's hands were raised in surrender and he was unarmed.

As a columnist for the *Bergen Record*, a daily newspaper in northern New Jersey, I studied the news that morning, wondering what the shooting meant for Teaneck and where the truth lay in the conflicting accounts. I also knew the timing couldn't be worse, or the setting more ironic. Teaneck, green and ordered, didn't seem to hide from race; a quarter of its thirty-eight thousand residents were black. But now, as I looked into the eyes of the students outside the police station, something seemed out of character. Had the racial whirlwinds I had read about elsewhere, as the 1980s gave way to the 1990s, touched down now in Teaneck?

Twenty-five years after the civil rights movement, America's national journey toward racial harmony seemed stalled in confusion at a crossroads. Like the students who marched to the police station that April afternoon, the anger I saw on both sides of America's racial fence seemed deeper, tied more to frustration at promises unfulfilled than at old wrongs that still needed to be righted. The datelines no longer carried the moral clarity of Selma and Montgomery. New datelines had given birth to new and murkier questions, more complicated personalities.

In Miami the year before, riots had broken out after a police officer shot and killed a man on a motorcycle. The cop said the man tried to run him down; protesters called it brutality. Closer to home, in Brooklyn a gang of whites had murdered a black teenager whose only transgression was to venture into their neighborhood to look at a used car. The Rodney King beating and the riots in South Central Los Angeles were still more than a year off. But as race relations soured in other American communities, I believed Teaneck would be spared. Years before, professors and politicians had labeled it a model town. But now outside the police station I wondered if it was on the verge of becoming just another racial dateline, that despite past achievements, the portrait was still incomplete.

As a journalist I had rarely written about my town, often finding my subjects elsewhere and viewing Teaneck as a refuge to return to, not a mystery to explore. Yet on this day I knew I had to be here. I grabbed a notebook and got in the car.

I had driven first to the high school, majestic and brick, resembling a Tudor castle, a place that advertised itself as regularly sending students to the Ivy League and with a faculty that had one of the highest concentrations of Ph.D.'s at any public high school in the nation. Inscribed in Latin on the concrete front steps was the school's motto, *Mentem Colere et Personem Meliorare*—"To enrich the mind and improve the character." By a window in the main office sat a desk used by Abraham Lincoln when he was a young Illinois legislator. But today this was no bastion of academics. A volatile power seemed to have taken over. Many classes had been canceled or disrupted by fire alarms. Clumps of black youths stood outside, talking loudly about what they termed rampant racism in town. White students gathered in quiet knots if they were at school at all. On a nearby wall someone had hung a hand-scrawled paper sign: ONE BLACK LIFE TODAY, ALL BLACKS TO-MORROW.

I approached a circle of black students, but a young man, who had graduated a few years before and returned that day when he heard students had walked out of class, blocked my path and announced that blacks should not talk to white journalists. "We will talk to each other and determine the truth," he said. "Then we will tell you."

I left for the shooting scene, awash now in media examination. It was a wellspring of rumor, but it was also the setting for a tragic incongruity for Teaneck: The backyard where the teenager was shot was across the street from the town's first elementary school to be integrated twenty-five years before.

In the eight years I had lived in Teaneck, I had assumed that the town found harmony in its diversity. But that day I discovered undercurrents to the town's life that had been either consigned to secrecy or just ignored: that some black students, for instance, felt the police singled them out for harassment; that, in turn, some police officers had worried in private for the last several years about reports of more black kids carrying guns. I learned that the teenager who had been killed was a member of a gang called the Violators. Months earlier I had noticed the gang's name in graffiti and had made a mental note to check it out. I wished I had.

When I arrived at my last stop, the police station, I wondered if some of the students gathered outside in bandannas, baggy jeans, and hooded sweatshirts were members of this gang. I approached a cluster and asked if anyone knew about the Violators. "A gang?" one boy asked, seeming childlike beneath a stony glare and his mocking tone. "It wasn't no gang. They were just friends."

"Why did they call themselves the Violators?" I asked.

"It was just a name."

I turned to walk away, and it was then I became the target for the rock. No one laughed. No one asked if I was hurt. I put my hand to the back of my scalp; I wasn't bleeding. I left, suddenly fearful yet also summoned to the office by a deadline and the need to sort through a notebook that had grown thick with strands of stories and impressions that didn't tie neatly together. As I walked off the elevator and into the newsroom, a colleague took me aside to pass on a sentiment that became a prelude to the rhetoric ahead: "I know this: If that kid was white, he would never have been shot."

"Dunno," I mumbled, wondering as much about my answer as about what prompted such thoughts from my colleague.

At my desk the phone rang. It was an old friend, whose children attended the same Catholic grammar school as my daughters. He wanted to tell me about the cop who had pulled the trigger; already he had heard rumors that the officer was being portrayed by blacks as a racist. "Nothing could be farther from the truth," my friend said. "This guy is compassionate, a family man and a devout Catholic." My friend described having been with the officer only a month before at a lighthearted dinner party when the conversation had drifted to the dangers police face as more criminals get their hands on guns. My friend explained how the cop had listened in silence, then said: "I don't like guns. I don't like wearing them. I don't like having them."

My friend's voice softened. "This cop's not a thug. There are some guys on the police force who I could see going after a black kid. Not him."

"So what do you make of all this then?" I asked.

My friend was silent a few seconds.

"I don't know."

I phoned a neighbor. We had lived side by side for eight years. We talked about baseball, politics, the weather, our lawns. But we never talked about race and our different skin colors.

"What do you think?" I asked, amazed afterward at how naïve this must have sounded.

"I'm hearing all sorts of things," he said. He wondered if the confrontation that led to the shooting had begun with some sort of police harassment.

"The cops don't like the kids congregating," he told me. "And if you're black and drive a nice car, they'll stop you for no reason. I know many black parents who talk about this all the time."

He mentioned a young man who claimed to have been stopped a half dozen times. I recognized the name. It was that of the man who had been at the high school hours earlier, telling students not to talk to the white media.

I was no stranger to writing about race and its passions. A decade before I had chronicled the exploits of the Ku Klux Klan in the South, once watching a cross burning on a small patch of dusty farmland outside Decatur, Alabama, as solemn white men in white robes gathered with their shotguns and their misguided piety. Years later I had marveled at the pride Jesse Jackson stirred in a forlorn Newark neighborhood during a campaign stop. I had also briefly followed Al Sharpton as he tried to transform a teenager named Tawana Brawley into a martyr. The man's brazen salesmanship had shocked me then. But so had his ability to touch a chord in blacks that few whites could understand.

What was unfolding in Teaneck, however, was different. A fatal gunshot had changed the town and opened racial fissures that many assumed had been healed long before or had never existed. In time I discovered that the angry sentiments of that day in April 1990 went far beyond a single shooting.

The larger story, I discovered, had begun long before.

PART I

PROMISED LAND

ONE

TURF

SEPTEMBER 6, 1989

On the first day of another school year Batron* Johnson took a bite from a cheeseburger and washed it down with chocolate milk. It was lunchtime at Teaneck High School, and Batron had grabbed the seat he usually took at the corner table in the cafeteria. As he looked back on the moment later, he remembered he had made his selections as much by reflex and habit as anything else, and he felt good doing that. Batron loved the first day of a school year, with its new faces and new clothes and new reputations. No matter what had taken place in the past, the day always stirred in him a sense of uncomplicated hope and renewed possibility about the months ahead. Yet he also sought sanctuary in the memory of old habits. Batron liked that, too, when he pondered it: something old, something new.

He gazed across the cafeteria, filling up now with students. Over his shoulder the room's high windows framed a blue northern sky that hinted at the crisp autumn weather ahead but was still splashed in spots with the heavy oatmeal clouds of summer's humidity. Batron

*Pronounced bah-TRON.

pictured the faces of new girls he had seen in the morning biology and English classes. Nice, he thought, and smiled to himself.

He was no longer a freshman. Not just another black kid in the high school. He had a reputation as a fighter, as a leader, tough and loyal to his friends. If you were in a fight, you'd want Batron Johnson there. And Batron liked that feeling. He didn't run, didn't need to. He could hold his own with anybody. He was proud of that. He was a sophomore now. Getting to be a man, with a man's stout shoulders, thick forearms, and meaty hands. Except for some extra weight on his waist, he had the unmovable, fire plug look of a football nose tackle, the guy who played the middle of the line and stopped lumbering fullbacks. His eyes, mahogany and deep, could switch in a flash from playful mirth to stony anger, depending on the moment and the mood.

There had been too many angry moments over the summer, too many turf fights—"beefs" Batron called them—with kids from Englewood and Hackensack. The white kids in Teaneck hardly knew about this. Or if they knew, Batron figured, they didn't care. This was a black thing—black on black, never blacks attacking whites or whites going after blacks. In Teaneck it was a black kid's unofficial rite of passage. When you reached puberty, you learned your turf and how to use your fists against boys with your skin color.

Batron knew something had changed in this rite. Older guys talked of how fights in the sixties had pitted one boy against another. Now the kids fought in gangs. Sometimes it was an argument over a girl. Sometimes it was a need to build a reputation—"rep."

Punks loved rep. And Batron loved taking care of punks. A couple of punches usually did it. But mostly the fights were over turf and protecting your own boys. "My boys," said Batron. He loved the sound of it.

And he loved the feel of turf. Batron's turf was his town, Teaneck. Anybody who came here was on his turf, his neighborhood. He fought for his Teaneck. Likewise, the black kids from Englewood and Hackensack—the towns that bordered Teaneck to the east and west like bread on a sandwich—fought for their turf. At times, Batron told himself, it made no sense, this tradition of black kids fighting over their reps and bragging rights to invisible borders. Yet it made all the sense in the world. It was about respect. And for a black kid in suburban Teaneck in 1989, respect was a red Corvette with a new coat of wax. People noticed.

On your turf *you* set the rules; anyplace else you were on foreign soil. Teaneck kids didn't go to Englewood or Hackensack. "The

Woods" and "The Hack" were how Batron and his pals termed their rival towns. Hackensack and Englewood punks were simply not supposed to come to Teaneck, "The Neck." If they did, it was an unspoken challenge to fight. That summer Batron had learned how to watch his back when he walked alone. But mostly he learned to stay with his group.

Today, in the school cafeteria, all that seemed far off. He felt safe.

On this day, in Brooklyn, a white boy named Joey Fama was being arraigned for murdering a sixteen-year-old black youth named Yusuf Hawkins, who had ventured into the white, Italian neighborhood of Bensonhurst to look at a car for sale. Batron had thought much about Yusuf Hawkins in the last few weeks. Like Hawkins, Batron was sixteen. Batron's mother sometimes told him about problems blacks had had with white folks when she was growing up in North Carolina. She mentioned the Klan and the unspoken rule that black boys did not look at white girls. To Batron the stories seemed like tales from another age. Yusuf Hawkins was different. He was alone, on someone else's turf, surrounded by a gang of whites when he was shot. His was the first racial death that Batron had spent much time thinking about. Just the same, Batron felt distant from that violence and apart from its victim. Yusuf Hawkins might have been black, but he lived miles away, in Brooklyn. Besides, if Batron got into trouble, it was never with whites. And he rarely walked alone anymore.

Batron looked up from his place in the cafeteria corner, his back to the wall so he could see everyone. It was shortly after noon, and the room was filling with old friends and old smells. Burger smells. French fries. Milk. Dusty books. Fresh wax on floors.

Steve walked in and dropped into a seat. Batron called him Bruiser, and Steve had his own nickname for Batron: Bubba. The two looked so alike, with powerful shoulders and arms, that they might have passed for brothers. Batron looked up, smiled again. Chuckie and Tyrone were sitting down. The boys had known one another since elementary school, and last year with some other friends they took a collective name. A gang name: Baddy Boys.

Batron liked the sound. The name automatically bestowed a reputation. He could have used the gang's help when he was jumped on a winter night eight months before by some boys from Paterson who were cruising Teaneck in a car, looking for a fight. It was after that fight that Batron and the others decided to call themselves Baddy Boys. As a sign of their new status, the Baddies adopted a dress code: baggy black jeans and "hoodies," hooded sweatshirts. Their trademark, though, was hats, navy blue Boston Red Sox baseball caps with a red B. The Baddies wore the hats constantly, usually backward. If anybody else in school wore a Boston hat, the Baddies usually took it. And nobody complained. Or if anyone did, Batron didn't hear.

But now the name was gone. Over the summer the Baddies had taken a new name: Violators.

The name had come to them on a hot July night when the group gathered in a local park to share a bottle of Old English, a malt liquor. One of the rap deejays on a local radio station had used the name. Batron and the others heard it and liked the name better than Baddy Boys. *Violators*. *V-I-O-L-A-T-O-R-S*. That night in the park an older boy visiting from New York City chuckled at the sight of a group of fifteen- and sixteen-year-old suburban black kids, trying to make a name for themselves.

"Hey, you guys are always violating," the boy joked. "You're a bunch of violators."

Perfect. Yes. It was as if an electrical charge had swept through each of them. The name stuck. It sounded menacing. Not just bad and boyish, like a bunch of pranksters who wore Boston Red Sox caps. No, this was a serious name. No messing around. No jokes. Just the sort of rep Batron wanted.

Violators.

Even the graffiti looked good. Big, bubble letters, painted on cement walls. That morning one of them—Zeke—started carving the name into desks at the high school or in the bathroom stalls. Where was Zeke now? Batron wondered. It was lunchtime, and he wasn't here. And the others too. Otis and Phil?

Yeah, Phillip Pannell. Batron had known Phil since the second grade. As thick and round-faced as Batron was, Phil was tall and lanky, with a thin face. He had played freshman football the year before, and the kids said he loved the game's rough blocking and tackling. Off the field he never ran from a fight. He had a big heart and a big sense of humor. Batron loved being with him, loved the Nintendo games the two played for hours in Phil's house, loved the jokes they played on each other.

Batron had seen Phil that morning in English class and now wanted to ask him about the new girls he had seen. Batron remembered one new girl with long dark hair and a light honey complexion. Maybe Phil knew who she was.

Batron looked across the table at Steve.

"Where's Phil?"

Steve shrugged.

No matter, Batron thought. They'd catch each other later, maybe for a slice at Jerry's Pizza. Batron lifted the cheeseburger again for a bite. He followed up with a french fry and gulped the rest of the chocolate milk. Felt good, he thought. Good to be past the summer. Good to be back on his school turf. Good to have a rep.

Lost in the thought for a moment, he heard another boy's voice rising over the cafeteria jumble. It was one of the younger guys, a pilot fish who liked to hang with the Violators.

"Yo!"

"Huh?"

Batron looked up. Instantly he knew something was wrong. The boy was out of breath, worried, talking fast over the cafeteria churn.

"Yo, Phil is getting jumped outside by Hackensack! Phil and Otis and Zeke."

Outside, by the football stadium, Muziki Stewart—Zeke—was the first to see them coming. Trouble, he figured. Hackensack boys on Teaneck turf.

"Damn, it's a whole lot of new motherfuckers coming to school today," Zeke mumbled. He paused a few seconds, then mumbled again, "We're in for some shit."

That day for lunch Muziki had stayed outside with some of the other Violators. Otis was there. So were Gary and Rasjus and Ed and Phil Pannell. At Teaneck High School lunchtime was free time. You could leave the campus or stay inside.

Zeke and the boys had headed for the concrete steps of the school stadium, down the front lawn from the Tudor turrets of the high school and through a grove of oaks and maples. The stadium had no seats or chairs, only a set of large concrete steps, leading from the cinder track to the trees. At football games or graduation the steps were choked with spectators. At lunch it was home to anyone who wanted to relax. A place to chill out, Zeke knew. No teachers or administrators. The cops usually stayed away too.

Zeke bought a pineapple soda from one of the concession trucks that flocked to the school at lunch hour. He lit a cigarette. The other boys sipped sodas or munched on cookies. Phil bit into a bagel.

Phil and Zeke were dressed as brothers. Blue, baggy jeans and red hoodies. The only difference was the footwear. Zeke wore heavy black combat boots. Phil wore black Reeboks.

Zeke faced the football field. To his right he could hear the hum of traffic on Route 4, beyond the stadium and another line of trees. To his left and across a street sat a neighborhood of fifty-year-old Tudor houses, owned mostly by white families with six-figure incomes and pool memberships and vacations for which they needed passports. It was a professional neighborhood, accustomed to the daytime silence of suburbia that comes when almost everyone is out of the home, making something of his or her life.

The dozen Hackensack boys, all black, walked through the quiet streets and headed for the stadium. Even near the high school, where almost half the students were black, Asian, or Hispanic, this neighborhood rarely saw what was about to happen. Most of Teaneck High's black students walked north when they left school, primarily because most blacks in Teaneck lived on the northeast side of town. To the south, especially the area immediately outside the high school door, it was white and upper middle class.

Zeke looked over his shoulder at the Hackensack crew. He turned to his left and looked at Phil Pannell.

"I don't know any of them," Zeke said.

None of the other Violators recognized them. Someone asked, "Who are they?"

"We'll soon find out."

The Hackensack gang strutted into the stadium, passing through a gate in the chain-link fence. One picked up a fallen tree branch and carried it like a club. Others clenched their fists.

Phil Pannell turned to Zeke, stood up, and whispered, "Yo, I'm ready, man."

Zeke got up. "Yo, I'm ready too."

The two had fought side by side before, mostly petty fistfights against guys in Hackensack or Englewood. Zeke felt Pannell grab the back of his hooded sweatshirt and tug. Phil had done that before in other fights, and in return Zeke tugged at the back of Phil's hoodie. "Whatever happens," Zeke said. "Let's stay close."

The Violators all were standing in a line at the top of the stadium steps. The leader of the Hackensack crew walked to the end, to one of the Violators farthest from Zeke and Phil.

"Yo, who's got a beef? Who's got a beef? You got a beef?"

He stopped at each Violator, one at a time, repeating the question.

Zeke and Phil were last. As the Hackensack kid approached, Phil took a half step back. Zeke put down his soda can, jabbed a cigarette between his teeth, and took a drag.

The Hackensack kid looked up at Zeke. "Who's got—"

He never got the last word out. Zeke blew smoke in his face and followed with a quick, hard right.

Zeke's fist caught the Hackensack kid in the nose. Zeke thought he drew some blood, but he couldn't tell. The boy staggered, but not enough to fall down the steps. Phil followed with a punch, but it wasn't enough to stop the others. The Violators were outnumbered; eleven on six. They ran out of the stadium and onto the lawn, scattering beneath the leafy tree canopy, bolting toward the flagpole and the steps to the high school.

Zeke heard screaming now. He threw another punch. From the side a fist caught him in the cheek squarely and hard. He never saw it coming. He staggered a second, then flailed at the boy who had socked him. Otis grabbed a tree branch and started swinging, back and forth, not connecting but trying to fend off several attackers.

Phil took a hit in the back with a branch and another in the side of the head. He ran for a door on the side of the school. Zeke, trying to fight off two kids, saw the Teaneck police cars arriving, lights flashing.

The gang from Hackensack ran.

———

Batron was running too.

In the cafeteria the word "fight" slashed through the easy mood like a fire alarm. He left his burger on his tray and headed for the cafeteria door. For some reason, perhaps instinct, perhaps fear, he grabbed a chair and carried it to the door, then discarded it as he ran into the hall.

The boy who delivered the message had said only that the fight was by the stadium, and Batron couldn't have been in a worse position to help. The cafeteria was on the opposite side of the school. He turned left in the hall, made another left, and vaulted down two sets of the stairs and through steel doors to the first floor. He sprinted along a hallway, hooked a left by the auto shop, and darted down another hallway, through two more sets of double doors, past a set of lockers, an attendance office, and classrooms. Batron, out of breath and trotting, ran into Jimmy Davis, who was Phil's cousin and a marginal Violator, and Sean Honegan, another friend. Seconds before, Jimmy and Sean had seen Phil, bleeding and woozy, stagger through the outside door and slump against a locker, mumbling about being hit with a branch. By the time Batron arrived, Phil had gotten back on his feet and gone outside.

Batron listened to Jimmy and Sean and bolted through the door. Phil was in the backseat of the police car now. An officer closed the door. "Taking them to the station to give statements," one student said. Batron nodded and looked again at his friend in the car, still bleeding from the cut over his eye.

Damn, Batron thought. Shoulda been there. Coulda stopped it. Coulda helped the Violators hold their own.

He went to class. But all afternoon, as he sat through math and social studies, his thoughts wandered to the stadium. By the time the final bell rang, word had been passed: "Get to a meeting at Mackel Park." The Violators would hold a council.

Mackel Park was Violators' turf. It was here, near the basketball court, only a few months before that they had taken their name. If anybody noticed that the park was across from a funeral home, nobody cared. The Violators were bulletproof. If they bled, as Phil had that afternoon, it was supposed to be only temporary. In the end the Violators usually won. Batron expected that.

For their council they bought a bottle of Old English. The boys called it a 40, a reference to the forty ounces each bottle held. By 3:00 P.M. most of them were at Mackel, gathered around the swings.

Zeke retold the story of the fight. So did Otis. The group laughed when they heard he had swung a tree branch like some sort of comic book warrior. Phil mentioned how someone from Hackensack with another tree branch had bashed him in the back and clubbed him over the head. His back ached badly now. The boys passed around the Old English.

The sun was still high in the southwestern sky when they left the park, walked past the fire station, and dropped into another favorite spot, Jerry's Pizza. Batron grabbed a table. The others followed. It was time, Batron thought, to go over the list of Hackensack boys who attacked.

"How about Khalid?" somebody asked.

"Yeah. I saw him," someone else answered.

"Okay. How about Sweat and Tyra and Derek and Johnson?"

"Yeah. Saw them too."

That day the Violators came up with the names of eleven Hackensack boys. Gonna get them all, Batron thought. Gonna settle this beef. Soon.

———

In Teaneck it had been a relatively quiet week except for the fight at the high school. Most of the world's troubles seemed across the border. Or if crime came to town, it seemed to have been brought in by outsiders.

Shortly after 8:00 P.M. on the following Monday a twenty-three-year-old man from Brooklyn, Richard Decambre, walked up to four black men on a street corner in Englewood, a few hundred yards over the line from Teaneck. Decambre asked for directions to Teaneck and was told to head west, up the hill. He took a few steps and turned back, as if unsure of where he was.

If anybody had noticed anything suspicious about Decambre, he didn't say. One of the four men on the corner started to walk away. Decambre followed. The man turned, and Decambre pulled a .32-caliber automatic pistol from his belt, shoved it in the man's ribs, and demanded his gold ring, his watch, and the cash in his pocket.

The heist took only a few seconds. Decambre jogged west now on Forest Avenue, toward Teaneck. The man who had been robbed of his ring, watch, and fifty dollars in cash shouted and took a few steps in pursuit. Decambre spun around, raised his pistol, and fired.

He missed. And took off.

The man who had been robbed ran to a phone to call police, and within a few minutes an alarm was broadcast for a "Jamaican male wearing a white shirt and blue pants, armed with a handgun."

To the cops it looked at first glance like a quick hit by a lone drug user in search of money to feed his habit. But in the suburbs when drug users turned to thievery, they usually didn't carry guns. Even more seldom did they fire a shot. In Teaneck, any time cops in neighboring Englewood broadcast a warning about a crime in the black neighborhood, it was reason to take notice. In recent years the boundary between Englewood's and Teaneck's black neighborhoods had blurred. If a robber found a mark in Englewood, especially in the black section, it was a safe bet he might try his luck over the border in Teaneck.

That night Teaneck Police Officer Gary Spath was working the four to midnight shift. Around 8:00 P.M. he stopped at police headquarters to check in with his supervisor. As he walked by the radio room on the first floor, he heard the call from Englewood and the description of the robbery suspect; Jamaican male, with a gun. Spath paused and listened. He looked trim in his navy blue uniform pants and sky blue shirt, perhaps a little thin and, with his hairline receding.

Spath liked being a cop, most of the time anyway. His dad had been a Teaneck detective, and Gary, the youngest of four children, born and raised in Teaneck, was carrying on the family tradition. At twenty-eight he was known to his superiors as an energetic cop; he had made his mistakes, but friends noticed he had an instinct for the job and didn't have to be told to respond to an emergency call. He liked being involved and had the citations to back up his reputation too. In six years as a cop he had seven commendations.

The voice on the radio had changed. Another Teaneck officer, Walter "Andy" Haase, was calling from his radio car. Haase had listened to the Englewood cops on the radio and had already talked to a witness who had tried to chase the robber. The robber fled Englewood over a pedestrian footbridge, the witness told Haase. The bridge crossed from a poor black section of Englewood over an old but congested four-lane highway, Route 4, and dropped into the middle of one of Teaneck's white neighborhoods, Phelps Manor. In the 1980s there had been a string of burglaries there, usually by black drug addicts who sneaked in for quick hits. Among some white homeowners the burglars were a constant worry, one reason why the burglar alarm business was booming in the area. Some whites had even begun to wonder aloud if they had made a mistake living so close to a poorer black enclave where crime seemed prevalent. Burglars would hit houses and escape to Englewood. If they had cars, they could zip onto Route 4, disappear over the George Washington Bridge, and be in New York City in ten minutes.

Still listening to the radio, Spath turned to a lieutenant and laid down a matter-of-fact challenge: "Let's go get this guy."

Spath knew the territory. If the robber got into Phelps Manor, he could lose the cops amid the maze of winding streets. If the man had a gun, as witnesses reported, who knew what might happen? Spath turned from the radio room, walked past a bookcase that held the department's trophies, and headed outside to his patrol car. It was 8:20 P.M. and not quite dark yet.

Spath needed only two minutes to reach Phelps Manor. He knew where to go: the footbridge by Phelps Road. From there a man on foot had only three choices. Spath turned on Minell Place, across from the Mediterranean Deli, where he was known as a regular customer on coffee breaks.

At one end of Minell Place a three-story apartment building sits on the corner like a fortress to protect the quiet, tree-lined neighborhood of single-family houses that wind to the east. Spath drove a block and spotted a man with no apparent destination.

Spath felt scared—at least, the feeling of fear would remain with him later when he looked back several years later and reflected on the day. He pulled his car to the curb, got out, drew his revolver, and yelled, "Drop the gun. Drop the gun."

The man seemed startled. He was fifty feet from Spath now. He tossed a dark object into a yard, turned, and started to run. On instinct Spath took off. He had done this before, but there is no set game plan. The most dangerous moment in police work comes when a lone cop confronts an armed suspect. The police academy can teach tactics and pursuit—what to say, how to react, what to do and not do—but when you're on a residential street at dusk, facing a man who may have a gun, there is no textbook you can turn to for answers. And if the suspect has thrown something on a lawn, how do you know what it was? His gun? His loot? What?

The man sprinted a half block on Minell Place. Spath kept shouting, "Halt! Drop the gun. Halt."

The man stopped.

Spath stopped.

The man whipped around. They were face-to-face now. From ten feet away Spath approached slowly. He could see the man's hands: no weapon. The man suddenly spun and ran. Again Spath's instincts took over. He sprinted several steps, reached, lunged.

And landed.

It was a classic open-field tackle, as if Spath were a defensive back and the man a wide receiver. The man stumbled to the pavement, with Spath's arms around him.

Other cops were arriving. One headed up the street to the lawn where the man had tossed something and found a .32-caliber automatic pistol. In another car the robbery victim from Englewood pulled up. Yes, it was the man who robbed him, he said, a positive ID.

Spath and the other officers took the suspect to the Teaneck police station. He was from Brooklyn, and he insisted he had done nothing illegal. The cops searched him just the same, and in the man's underwear they found a fat gold ring and a wad of money that matched the amount that had been stolen.

———

It was a proud moment for Spath, and over the following days two lieutenants in the Teaneck police headquarters sat down at typewriters and wrote letters recommending him for a special commendation. "Spath coupled his training, experience, and his instincts with a total disregard for his own personal safety," wrote one of them, Lieutenant Warren White.

Three weeks later, on September 27, Chief Bryan Burke made it official: Spath was to get his eighth commendation from the Teaneck department. What's more, the chief announced he would nominate Spath for a special award from the Bergen County Chiefs Association, the most prestigious honor Spath had ever received. In his commendation letter, Chief Burke paid tribute to his young officer's "keen observations and professional demeanor." He noted that Spath had managed to chase the man and eventually to wrestle him to the ground "without injury to the public or yourself." And in the final sentence of his letter the chief alluded to the most dangerous aspect of Spath's deed: approaching a man who might have had a gun, yet remaining calm enough to hold his fire. "It is especially gratifying to me," wrote Burke, "that this incident was handled as it was."

TWO

"WE ALL LIVE
IN A VERY
SPECIAL TOWN"

Even before there was a town called Teaneck, there was a dividing line. It was a rocky ridge, a three-mile-long spine of shale that rose slowly out of the salt marshes to the south and split the forest of red oaks, maples, beeches, and yellow pines that covered most of the six square miles of Jersey piedmont that eventually became Teaneck. The ridge also split people, in this case a tribe of Leni-Lenape Indians. To the west of the ridge, where the Hackensack River widened and wound its way to Newark Bay and the Atlantic Ocean, one clan of Leni-Lenapes had set up a small village. On the eastern side, by the edge of the reedy marshes and meandering streams of black water in the western shadow of the Palisades cliffs that separate the marsh basin from the Hudson River, another clan had set up camp. The ridge was not high, perhaps no more than 150 feet in the days before bulldozers carved roads and shaped neighborhoods from its thick groves of trees, ravines, and rock outcroppings. But it was enough of a barrier to separate families, commerce, and friendships. Crossing it was a major excursion over ancient tribal paths.

By the middle of the twentieth century, as the craggy ridge that once separated the Leni-Lenapes had gradually been smoothed, Teaneck no longer seemed dominated by barriers. To the outside world, it stood for an ideal: a community that sought to erase the social, cultural, political, and religious lines that separate people, one of the few suburban communities in America that actively sought to open its doors to people of different colors and faiths. By the 1970s Teaneck was bragging about its singular stamp on American history: the first town in the nation to vote to integrate its schools through busing.

When that school integration experiment began in 1964 and when it was cemented by the 1965 election of a pro-busing slate to the school board, it was a proud moment for Teaneck. The school buses rolled only weeks after Congress passed the federal Civil Rights Act that banned discrimination in voting, jobs, and public accommodations. Just as the federal government and Lyndon Johnson's Great Society agenda were attempting to do for a sometimes reluctant nation, so Teaneck was trying to correct old ills and meet new challenges. In many ways it was a profound transformation from what the town had been.

In 1905, a decade after Teaneck had been formally incorporated, it was home to only 1,222 people, all but two dozen of them white and many still bearing the names of the German and Dutch colonial settlers who had carved the first farms into Teaneck's meadows and hills before the American Revolution. At the start of the Great Depression only 66 blacks lived among Teaneck's 16,513 residents. By World War II the town's population had swollen to 25,275, but its only 202 blacks made up less than 1 percent of the population. Whatever its racial makeup, the town's wholesome, efficient appearance so impressed the federal government that after the war Teaneck was selected as the setting for a photo exhibit to be shown to liberated peoples in Europe and Japan to demonstrate how democracy worked in a quintessential American town.

The model town image stuck, and in the 1950s, as millions of Americans left the concrete confines of cities for the lawns of suburbia, Teaneck was transformed in a way that few other suburbs were. The town had consciously decided not to bar its doors to heretofore unwanted minorities. Some towns in northern New Jersey made no secret of their disdain for Jews and blacks, even going so far as to allow deeds to homes to include clauses specifically barring the sale to anyone who wasn't Christian or white or encouraging realtors to designate the town as "closed"—a real estate codeword that meant Jews and nonwhites were unwanted. Teaneck welcomed everyone. The first to come were Jews, many of them armed with professional degrees and white-collar jobs in Manhattan. On their heels came a new black middle class, with small businesses, professorships, practices in law or medicine, or prominent spots in entertainment or athletics. One of the most conspicuous was Elston Howard, who broke the color line in another bastion of white America, the New York Yankees. Still, even an athlete as successful as Howard met with mixed reactions even in Teaneck. When he tried to move from the largely black neighborhood on the town's northeast side to a mostly white section with larger houses, white homeowners there complained.

By 1960 the town's black population had quadrupled. Blacks made up only 4 percent, about 1,665 of the town's 42,085 residents. Nonetheless it was the unmistakable start of an inevitable trend. Black families had found a suburban home in Teaneck, though there was not always an easy transition. Many blacks still recalled how Teaneck's WASP leaders in the 1940s had been so worried about black families moving from nearby Englewood (where for decades a black neighborhood provided homes for the servants at the mansions of such luminaries as Charles Lindbergh and Gloria Swanson) that they established a tree-filled park as a buffer zone.

As more blacks moved into Teaneck's northeast neighborhoods in the early 1960s, some real estate agents, at least one of whom was black, tried to set off panic selling by white families. The process, known as blockbusting, was a well-known tactic among blacks and other ethnic minorities who had been barred from white neighborhoods. For blacks, it had positive effects: It gave them an entry into previously exempt turfs. For whites, however, blockbusting was tumultuous, causing many to sell their homes below market value merely as a misguided precaution against the neighborhood's losing its market value. When blockbusting came to Teaneck, however, large numbers of whites on the northeast side of town formed groups to fight it. Some were resigned to welcoming blacks into their neighborhood, if not always willingly, and they put up Not for Sale signs on their front lawns as a message that they would not be pushed out by the fear tactics of realtors.

But as much as Teaneck seemed to be more open than most suburbs to integration, it soon faced an unfortunate side effect of such integration: schools that were becoming segregated. Teaneck had built six elementary schools to handle its postwar baby boom migration, each one in a distinct neighborhood. The system was a throwback to small-town America, with children walking to school and often heading home for lunch. By the early 1960s there was one obvious snag. Because black families were clustered in one section of town, the northeast, half the students at the elementary school there were black. With other Teaneck schools virtually all white, school officials and other town leaders figured it was only a matter of time before civil rights lawyers filed a lawsuit to desegregate the schools. With one eye on its collective conscience to do what was right and another on the legal realities coming from the U.S. Supreme Court and its landmark 1954 ruling that outlawed segregated schools, Teaneck decided to head off federal intervention and voluntarily integrate its schools with a new device that had been rarely used: busing. To promote this experiment, a new political coalition of blacks, Jews, and other liberal whites, many with strong ties to progressive Protestant movements, was formed by Teaneck's first Jewish mayor, Matthew Feldman, a tightly muscled Jersey City–born liquor salesman who had once been an amateur boxer and a hand-to-hand combat instructor for the U.S. Army during World War II. The charismatic Feldman was a natural leader, not to mention a glib talker with a nickname to match—Matty the Mensch. Each day at dawn he went to his synagogue to pray, but he was not the sort of man to back away from a confrontation and turn the other cheek. At parties Feldman often told stories of his riding to the towns around Teaneck in the 1930s from his Jewish neighborhood in Jersey City to pick fights with German-Americans who attended Nazi Bund rallies. To hear Feldman tell it, he never lost a fight.

In Teaneck he didn't lose either. Feldman cajoled his opponents and skillfully molded his supporters into a strong voting bloc. His chief ally and architect of the busing plan was the town's school superintendent, Harvey Scribner, who later became chancellor of New York City's schools. Scribner and Feldman both were regarded as men ahead of their times, as Teaneck embraced integration and formally desegregated its schools. By 1970, while surrounding towns remained largely white, 14 percent of Teaneck's residents were black, welcomed in part by the well-publicized town vote to integrate its schools. By 1990, 26 percent of Teaneck's residents were black. The town that singer Pat Boone had called home in the 1950s became home to millionaire baseball star Dave Winfield in the 1980s. The town that had been home to several prominent pro-Nazi Bund members who were targets of Feldman's anger in the 1930s was governed in the 1980s by a black mayor.

━━━━━

In all, 567 individual municipalities had carved out space in New Jersey, the vast majority occupying only a few square miles of land. And while home rule and the number of small towns had the advantage of allowing citizens greater access to government, they also had a disadvantage that few New Jersey politicians were willing to talk about: segregation. By the 1980s the state, 120 miles long and 90 miles wide, was anchored by four desperately poor, fading industrial cities— Paterson, Newark, Jersey City, and Camden—that seemed like malignant polyps along New Jersey's spine. The cities were primarily black, the suburbs mostly white. But such racial lines were fortified by stark economic disparities. New Jersey was one of the richest states in America, with a per capita income second only to Connecticut's. But most of New Jersey's wealth was suburban; four of America's twenty-five richest counties were in the state. At the same time, two of its largest cities—Newark and Paterson—were ranked among the five poorest in the United States.

The economic and racial differences between the suburbs and the cities were most apparent in the most vulnerable of places, schools. With their high concentration of wealth and their reliance on home rule and local property taxes, New Jersey's suburbs became the sites of some of the best public schools in America. The cities were another story. School dropout rates in Newark and Jersey City routinely were above 50 percent. Math and reading test scores were light-years behind those in the suburbs. By the nineties a study by Harvard University found that New Jersey had the fourth highest rate of school segregation in America. Mississippi and Alabama—long considered the last bastions of Jim Crow segregation—were no longer among the five worst states. Northern states, with their gaps between poor and black industrial cities and middle-class and white suburbs, now held the distinction of becoming the most intensely segregated.

Teaneck watched these developments in New Jersey and elsewhere with a certain amount of I-told-you-so pride. Amid the largely white suburban landscape in New Jersey and across America, Teaneck bragged about itself with all the swagger of a champion boxer and even fashioned a public relations effort to promote its racial and ethnic distinction. The town saw itself as a self-proclaimed bulwark of middle-class diversity, with a tolerance for progressive politics rarely found outside cities. While much of New Jersey's suburbs was bedrock Republican, Teaneck was a liberal Democratic oasis. In 1972 George McGovern won there.

By 1990 realtors were marketing the town as a "Little United Nations." One local legend was that Teaneck was the place all the liberals on Manhattan's Upper West Side moved to when they got married, had kids, and wanted a backyard for the barbecue and a volleyball net. Another tale that drew on the crazy-quilt nature of the town's social fabric depicted Teaneck as having the highest concentration of psychological therapists in the Western Hemisphere. Certainly it was home to one of the most diverse sets of eating establishments, from Indian to southern soul food to Chinese kosher. Bookstores featured sections on black studies, Judaism, and feminism. It was not uncommon to see Muslim women, covered head to toe in traditional robes, walking on the same street with Orthodox Jews in long black coats and black, broad-brimmed hats. The place celebrated its diversity. Schools were assembling a "global multicultural curriculum." The high school had turned over a portion of a library to build a "cultural hub," with rooms designated for the Holocaust and for African, Asian, Hispanic, and European studies.

Until the 1970s America's suburbs were largely off limits to blacks, no matter how wealthy they were; while 12 percent of Americans were black in 1970, only 6 percent of suburbanites were black. By 1980 the black share of suburbia had increased by 40 percent, and Teaneck had become a well-regarded magnet for a growing black professional middle class of lawyers, doctors, bankers, professors, entertainers, and media executives, who, like their white counterparts, wanted to escape the cities to towns such as Evanston, Illinois, and Shaker Heights, Ohio. In 1990 it wasn't uncommon to find blacks in Teaneck driving eighty-thousand-dollar Mercedes sedans, joining tennis clubs, and sending their children to prep schools.

The rest of the town was an ethnic vegetable soup, from the older Germans, Italians, and Irish to the new American immigrants from the Philippines, Korea, the Caribbean, Latin America, and India. In all, more than four dozen nationalities lived in Teaneck. There were seven synagogues, portions of three Catholic parishes, and a dozen Protestant congregations, among them three Lutheran and two Episcopal. And those were just the mainstream religions. For those in search of something different, there was a Baha'i Center, an Ethical Culture Society, a Christian Science Reading Room, and a mosque.

Through it all the town had managed to maintain a secure place on that barometer of suburban pride property values, which remained high. Teaneck was not like other towns, where blacks moved in and within a few years whites moved out and the values of homes plummeted. In 1990 the average house in Teaneck sold for almost two hundred thousand dollars.

Beneath such successes, however, the town's best intentions toward integration were strained by persistent divisions. Like the ridge that once divided the Leni-Lenapes, Teaneck's social landscape was essentially divided by railroad tracks. To the east of the tracks, in the northeast corner of town, nine of ten residents were black. To the west nine of every ten people were white. Most of Teaneck's low-income families were black, except for small pockets of poorer whites to the south. Muslims and Asian Indians clustered in the southeast end of town, not far from the site of the old Leni-Lenape encampment, where a gleaming new mosque now stood. Orthodox Jews clustered in the northwest section within walking distance of synagogues. "A community of communities" was how the town's first black mayor, Bernard Brooks, described Teaneck in the late 1980s. His words were both a compliment and a criticism; many diverse groups managed to coexist within Teaneck's borders, but all too often they kept their distance from one another.

There were exceptions, of course. And on a humid Sunday afternoon in May 1989, in Votee Park—a ten-acre piece of land where the old dividing ridge flattened—the modern tribes that now made Teaneck their home gathered together. The organizers called it Diversity Day, and it was as unlikely an event as you might expect to find in any American suburb.

What blossomed in Votee Park was the quintessential American ethnic melting pot and a celebration of Teaneck's best intentions. Or as the local weekly newspaper, the *Suburbanite*, editorialized:

While we could stick our heads in the sand and say the township's vision of racial and cultural diversity has been an easy road to hoe, that would miss the point. Invariably, when people hold different values, worship different gods and speak in different tongues, there will be some measure of friction. That friction is the spark of American genius. Still if left untended, the sparks of diversity can all too quickly become the inferno of racial bias and cultural bigotry. In Teaneck, a firm commitment to this American genius has been tended, and democracy flourishes. On May 21, the people of Teaneck will gather to celebrate Diversity Day. Imagine it— people, young and old, celebrating the many contributions of their neighbors of all colors, cultures, races, religions. Out in New York Harbor, the Lady of Liberty will undoubtedly be breaking a broad smile.

The event was planned with all the attention to political correctness that Teaneck had become known for in trying to accommodate its various ethnic constituencies. Diversity Day was scheduled for a Sunday in part so Jewish residents who observed the Sabbath on Saturday could come. But the festivities didn't begin until 1:00 P.M. so as not to interfere with Christian services, especially those at black churches, which tended to run past noon. As for the participants, it was as if someone invited a portion of the United Nations General Assembly or assembled a cast for an ethnically balanced television ad. The entertainment began with black and white eighth graders from the Thomas Jefferson Middle School performing a skit entitled "Escape from Apartheid." Next came a Filipino dance troupe, a Jewish women's chorus performing Israeli folk songs, gospel singers from several churches, and then a musical group that played songs from the Andes Mountains and other parts of South America. Children in costumes representing some thirty countries held a parade. Local restaurants set up food booths where people could sample African American soul food, Japanese sushi, kosher pizza, and burgers from an American barbecue. There were also displays by the Afro-American Association, the Jewish War Veterans, the National Association of Negro Business and Professional Women, synagogues, the Seventh-Day Adventists, the local Baha'i center, the local chapters of the National Organization for Women and Mothers Against Drunk Driving, the garden club, the Teaneck police, the volunteer ambulance corps, a language institute, and a battered-women's group called Shelter Our Sisters.

In the crowd that day a man named Arthur Gardner marveled at the town he now called home. Gardner, six feet four and possessed of a powerful baritone that rolled easily across an athletic field or off the walls of a gymnasium, taught physical education and coached football at Teaneck High School. He had grown up in the South of Jim Crow laws and segregated schools, in the tiny village of Georgetown on South Carolina's coast, the son of a harbor pilot who guided ships over the tricky shoals, the great-grandson of a former slave who had escaped from his Confederate masters and fought in the Civil War for the Union Army. When the war ended, Gardner's great-grandfather returned to South Carolina and took a new surname that celebrated his ability to grow corn and wheat in the sandy soil: Gardner. In Teaneck, Art Gardner each year kept his great-grandfather's tradition by planting a vegetable garden that was the marvel of the neighborhood.

Gardner had never shared a classroom with a white student until he left South Carolina and drove north to become a teacher, first in Paterson and then in Teaneck. In South Carolina blacks lived separate and unequal lives amid whites. Separate neighborhoods. Separate churches. Separate schools. Separate careers.

Each summer in his teenage years Gardner headed up the South Carolina coast to Myrtle Beach and a job in one of the hotels. He started as a busboy and graduated to waiter, mastering the resort city's most important rule: White folks came first. The Myrtle Beach hotels were set up for the enjoyment of whites. If blacks ventured onto the properties, it was to work at menial jobs. White men were always called sir and women ma'am. As for the black help, Gardner learned a rule about them too: they never spoke their minds. If they did, they could lose their jobs.

On a July afternoon in the late 1950s Gardner was taught a new lesson about crossing racial boundaries. One of the waitresses at the hotel where he worked was a white college girl from Boston. She and Art talked frequently on the job, though Gardner remembers never feeling comfortable about it. In all his earlier years he had never really spoken on equal terms with a white woman. In South Carolina befriending white women was a way to find yourself making a trip to prison or becoming a target of the Klan. Art was intrigued by the white girl, yet he feared the consequences. What's more, he didn't know what to tell her, fearing that her feelings might be hurt if he explained that Boston's rules about white girls' talking to black men were more progressive than South Carolina's. He did what most black men in the South did when it came to white women: He tried to keep his distance.

One Sunday afternoon he could not, however. It was his day off, and Art decided to take a bus into town from the hotel. Each hotel not only housed its workers in dormitories—separate for blacks and whites, of course—but provided bus service to town. Art took a seat, and when the bus pulled up to the white workers' dormitory, the girl got on. With a wide smile and a carefree air, she sat next to Art.

Art kept up his friendly front, but he knew the gravity of the situation. In South Carolina it was rare for a black man to speak to a white woman. It was something of a social earthquake for a black man and a white woman to sit together on a bus. Gardner knew all eyes were on him, yet he couldn't bring himself to say anything. Oblivious, she proceeded to talk about the weather, the customers, her errands in town—everything but what was so painfully obvious to Gardner.

The ride lasted only fifteen minutes, but for Art it seemed fifteen hours. He got off and started to walk away. At that point he noticed that one of the older black women on the bus, a maid who had worked at the hotel for years, had taken the white girl aside.

"Now don't you go talking to Arthur here," the maid said.

"Why?" The girl seemed perplexed.

"Down here white girls don't talk to black boys. You could get Arthur in a heap of trouble. You don't want that, do you?"

The girl's smile vanished. She nodded. Art saw her eyes lower. She seemed fearful and ashamed all at once. She apologized, then walked away. After that the two rarely spoke.

Back in Georgetown, Art was luckier than most of his friends, in part because of his size. After high school and a hitch in the navy, he took his six-foot-four, 240-pound frame to the all-black Allen State College and its football team, where he gained a reputation as a ferocious defensive tackle. It was 1964, and while Art was unaware of the integration movement in Teaneck, he was certainly aware of what was happening in the South. In Columbia, home of both Allen State and the all-white University of South Carolina, the civil rights movement that was starting to gain strength in the South and capture the attention of the rest of the nation seemed remote. The Confederate flag fluttered atop the State Capitol in Columbia. A few blocks away blacks were still barred from sitting in the same restaurants with whites. Gardner heard that black college students from other states had walked into restaurants near their homes and demanded service. In a few cases the students had succeeded in changing customs. Art read the news accounts of civil rights activists. He was astonished by their personal courage yet angry that a century after the Civil War and the end of slavery the South continued to be a land of roadblocks and rules that kept blacks down and away from even the most basic of privileges such as sitting in an air-conditioned luncheonette and ordering a Coke.

On an especially hot afternoon in August, Gardner and two other teammates felt hungry.

"Let's go on down to the luncheonette," one of them suggested.

"Why not?" Gardner said.

The three drove to town and sauntered into the luncheonette. The three or four customers, all of them white, hardly seemed to notice as the three students took seats at the counter. And waited.

The manager walked up. "We don't serve colored here," he said.

"Why not?"

The manager paused. "We don't." He waited a few more seconds. "Now don't y'all be making trouble. Okay?"

That day Gardner and his teammates left the luncheonette without being served. In the days ahead Gardner decided he would never again be afraid to cross boundaries, no matter how humiliating or difficult or fearsome.

Like many other blacks in the decades after World War II, Gardner traded the South for the North almost as soon as he could, in hope of a better job and a friendlier welcome. In the northern New Jersey city of Paterson, where he taught gym in mostly black and Hispanic schools, Gardner met a white Jewish woman, Susan Drabkin, who had just returned from a stint in Panama with the Peace Corps. On one of their first dates Susan took him to Teaneck and taught him a basic lesson in how northern segregation worked. As the two sat in a Friendly's ice cream shop on Teaneck's northeast end, Susan turned to Art and proclaimed, "This is the black side of town."

She then pointed west. Across the railroad tracks, she said, was the white side. That day, a little surprised, Art laughed. Even in the North there were lines between races. It was just a little more subtle.

Not long afterward he and Susan crossed a substantial boundary: interracial marriage. Although they found holes in Teaneck's integration image, they decided to call the town home. "I wanted our children to grow up in a place where they would not feel different," Art often told friends, citing the sprinkling of other interracial couples who lived in the town.

Gardner was keenly aware of divisions in his new town, but he saw Susan and him as able to melt them. And so, after marrying, Art and Susan went house hunting. Instead of opting for the safe confines of Teaneck's black neighborhood, where interracial couples gravitated, the Gardners chose a colonial house on Teaneck's northeast side, on a block with a large number of Orthodox Jewish families. It was, as Art became fond of saying, a way of breaking the mold, but it was not easy. In those first years he was often mistaken for a maintenance man or, ironically, a gardener, not a homeowner. Years later he still bore the scars, quietly. Beneath his broad smile a fire burned in Art Gardner.

On Diversity Day, May 21, 1989, Gardner had walked down the hill from his house and crossed the railroad tracks that ran through Teaneck. On the other side, in the park, he found more breaking of molds, with blacks and whites and Asians and Hispanics, Jews and Christians and Muslims, all together, mixing, talking to one another, applauding one another's skits and music. As the sun began to set behind the trees and he turned to walk home, Art smiled and told himself, "It's a great day."

Across the Hudson, in New York City, the races seemed to be growing apart. The year before, the city had been fixated on the Tawana

Brawley case, in which a black teenage girl had falsely accused a group of white men of raping her. The month before, in Manhattan's Central Park, a white female investment banker on a morning jog had been brutally raped and left for dead by a gang of black teenagers, one of whom smashed her face with a brick. The attack on the woman who came to be known as the Central Park Jogger had spawned a new term for black teenage gang violence: wilding. But to Teaneck, such violence—and the vocabulary that accompanied it—were remarkably foreign. On Diversity Day Teaneck seemed blessed. By 7:00 P.M., when the last tribute sounded and the last door prize was drawn, the event was being hailed as a huge success. Even the weather had held up. In towns to the south and north on that Sunday, thunderstorms had punctuated the afternoon; in Teaneck the sun had shone all day.

As darkness closed in on the park and the day's organizers cleaned up after the participants and visitors had trickled away, the festive mood vanished. A few hundred yards beyond the band shell where the Diversity Day music had been performed, a group of black teens had gathered at the park's basketball court. Around 7:30 P.M. an argument broke out. Some of the Teaneck players didn't want outsiders on their turf. Three players who had come to Teaneck from New York City had been standing on the side of the court. A Teaneck youth pushed a New Yorker, who pushed back. Someone threw a punch, someone answered it. A fight was on.

The New Yorkers ran, and some twenty youths from Teaneck were on their heels. At the northern end of the park, near the tennis courts and beyond the Little League baseball diamond, the Teaneck kids caught up to the New Yorkers, with at least one of the Teaneck youths swinging a baseball bat. Two of the three New Yorkers ended up in the hospital, and the next day some police and town officials had a term for the fight: wilding.

In Teaneck the term was as welcome as a tax increase. *Wilding? Here?*

One of the most accomplished detectives in the Teaneck Police Department, Lieutenant Jack Terhune, tried to downplay the similarity of the fight in Teaneck to New York City's wilding. He was a smart cop, one of the few anywhere who had gone to prep school before going on to college and to graduate school, where he completed a master's degree. When Terhune joined the police force in Teaneck, he was following a long family tradition of service. Terhune could trace his roots in Bergen County

back nine generations to the Dutch settlers who farmed the area before
the English arrived. In the mid-nineteenth century, his great-great-great
grandfather and great-great gandfather each had been sheriff of Bergen
County and went on to become county freeholders. On the Teaneck force
Terhune parlayed his sharp instincts into quick promotions. His colleagues said he would probably become chief if he stayed out of trouble.
Certainly he had the brains and the exemplary record.

In public he spoke confidently, was not at all shy. So when he offered an
opinion on any aspect of crime, people in Teaneck tended to listen. And
Jack Terhune was quick to offer some thoughts on the Diversity Day fight.
"I think they just happened to be there and decided to pick on this group
from New York," he said of the Teaneck kids. "We don't have any evidence to indicate there was any organized gang activity or wilding. I don't
see any motive. I don't see any indication that there was a fight over a ball
or something. I would have to characterize it as an unprovoked attack."

Terhune had seen something like this before. From his youth he
could remember that kids in Teaneck often squared off in fights. In
the late 1950s the gangs called themselves the Ashacks and the Vikings—their members all white. In the late 1960s the first black gang
was formed, the Family. But Terhune did not see any of the gangs as
contributing to the crime rate. The kids joined because they yearned
for a sense of belonging, he said. And if a fight broke out, the weapon
of choice was generally a fist.

Terhune's boss, Chief Bryan Burke, saw no reason to sound an alarm
either. He was not comfortable with the term "wilding," but he was
sure of one thing. The Teaneck kids "were a group of well-known
troublemakers," said Burke. "We are in the process of running down
a few more to charge."

What Burke and Terhune didn't know was that a group of Teaneck
High School students were in the park and watching the fight after
Diversity Day. The Baddy Boys, soon to be the Violators, were fast
learning old lessons of fighting over turf. That day the Baddy Boys kept
their distance; the argument was between older boys.

But the Baddies were hardly keeping quiet. That spring they had
begun to flex their muscles, and only a week before Diversity Day one
of them found himself in trouble. Phillip Pannell and a friend had
jumped one of their rivals and sent him to the hospital. Pannell had
been arrested before for vandalizing a school, but this was something
new. For the first time his record listed a crime of violence: aggravated
assault.

He was fifteen, a high school freshman.

Frank Hall, the Teaneck mayor, sensed there was a lesson to be learned in the news of the fight after Diversity Day. But what? Hall, who had been in politics longer than any other elected official in Teaneck, was the last remaining member of the coalition that had brought integration to the town in the mid-1960s. Short and barrel-chested, with piercing eyes and wisps of hair that seemed perpetually out of place, Hall was an engineer with the company that had built the Three Mile Island nuclear reactor. As a young marine in World War II he had been wounded on Guam and had been evacuated from Iwo Jima after going into shell shock. Indeed, only one man in his company of three hundred came out of the war without being wounded or killed. Like many soldiers who survived the brutality of combat that killed so many of their buddies, Hall yearned to give something back when he returned to civilian life, if for no other reason than to compensate for his luck. After eight years of night courses at what was then known as Fairleigh Dickinson College and establishing himself in his career, he decided to venture into politics in Teaneck, first as a volunteer in an election campaign, later as a key adviser to the integration coalition led by Matty Feldman. Hall believed wholeheartedly in integration, especially in the ideals that his political hero John F. Kennedy espoused. And so he felt it entirely natural for him to board a bus in Teaneck on a humid August morning in 1963 and ride to Washington, D.C., to march and listen to the Reverend Martin Luther King, Jr., declare, "I have a dream." Hall was troubled by something that day, however. He was one of the few whites from Teaneck to make the trip. He remembers wondering where all his fellow progressives were that day. He never got an answer.

In the days after the 1989 Diversity Day events, Hall studied the police reports for clues to the fighting. A few years before he had divorced and moved to an apartment on the northeast side of town. His living-room windows looked out on Teaneck Road and across to a municipal parking lot where teenagers often gathered on warm nights, sometimes on cold nights too. Down the block stood Carl's Corner, a tavern that catered mostly to blacks. Two blocks in the opposite direction was a liquor store, another hangout with a mostly black clientele.

Hall watched the ebb and flow of the social tides on his street and in other places of his town and wondered whether these were natural growing pains or the town's delicate social fabric was separating in a way that would be difficult to mend. One of his daughters briefly dated a black man. Hall had no problem with that. What bothered him were the stories his daughter relayed to him: that occasionally the car she and her date were in was pulled over for no apparent reason by Teaneck police. She said the cops told her they were performing routine checks. Hall worried about this pattern but decided not to say anything to the police. Maybe his daughter exaggerated. Maybe not. Anyway, she had stopped dating the black man. When she rode with white male friends, the cops never pulled her over.

Outside his window Hall noticed increased numbers of black youths on the street, sometimes until midnight. He wondered where their parents were or if their parents wondered where their children were. He made a mental note to discuss this at a council meeting, but the time never seemed right. Must be careful when talking about race in public, he thought, especially if the discussion combined those two flammatory ingredients: race and crime. At the high school Hall heard stories that black students were often in fights. And if there was a fight in town, it was usually blacks kids fighting other black kids.

Now there were reports of this wilding. Hall was troubled. "I'd hate to dismiss it as an isolated incident," he told a newspaper reporter who asked him about it. "Let's find out the kids who did this, and let's get to the cause. But I hardly think it's wilding or that kind of thing."

Frank Hall did not get his "cause" for months.

━━━━━━━━

What Hall was experiencing was something common in the lives of many in Teaneck. The churn, as some called it, was usually a private experience, one of those secrets that are brought out only with trusted friends. But often driven by news reports of crime or trouble—and race—it was real.

To live in Teaneck was to worry. And by the late 1980s much of the worry revolved around issues of skin color.

Eleven days before Diversity Day the chairwoman of the group that was sponsoring the celebration, Loretta Weinberg, walked into Teaneck's council chambers and announced she was concerned about several recent anti-Semitic and racist incidents. Weinberg had grown up in Los Angeles. In the 1960s she moved East, first from California to an apartment in New York City and then, after marriage and the births of a daughter and a son, to Teaneck. By 1989 she was head of the Teaneck civic group known variously as the Advisory Board on Community Relations or the Community Relations Advisory Board. The latter name was popular among critics, who liked to refer to the group by its unofficial acronym, CRAB. But the board was held in high regard by supporters, as one of the few groups in town that actively recruited members of every ethnic group in an attempt to discuss racial and ethnic problems in an evenhanded, honest manner. On the night she entered the council chamber, though, Weinberg raised some of the most disturbing questions that Teaneck had heard in years, in public anyway.

Well aware she might incur some wrath from her neighbors, Weinberg cited three recent examples of bigotry. There had long been an unspoken agreement among some in town not to discuss such matters in public for fear that Teaneck's reputation might be eroded or be viewed negatively. As Skip Denhem, the black assistant school superintendent, said in the months ahead when the media descended on the town, "There are a lot of people out there who want to see Teaneck fail." Denhem's view was not uncommon in Teaneck, and for some, it was the catalyst for weaving a protective cocoon, an image that sought to cast Teaneck as a racial model.

At this meeting, however, Weinberg decided she had enough of history and image preserving. A few weeks before, someone had scrawled swastikas in shaving cream on the home of an Indian family. Months before that, a two-foot swastika had been burned into the front lawn of a Jewish family. Lastly, students at a local yeshiva for Orthodox Jewish children had been called kikes and other racial slurs as they walked down a Teaneck sidewalk. At the microphone and facing Mayor Frank Hall and the six-member council, Weinberg seemed in part to be sounding a warning, in part pleading for help. "We all live in a very special town," she said. "We do not believe these incidents should be kept quiet. In this town we don't tolerate this behavior."

The council members nodded in agreement. None of them was surprised by what Weinberg had to say. Like Weinberg, Mayor Hall also worried. Were these isolated incidents? Or did they reveal something being torn in the town? The council promised to look into the problem, but two days later the police chief, Bryan Burke, tried to downplay Weinberg's concerns. "There's not an increase," he said. "We're dealing with kids' pranks and kids' ways of getting at somebody. They know it upsets people or else they wouldn't do it."

The town seemed perplexed by the increasing number of fights between black teenagers. For all its attention to integration, Teaneck had never been able to face publicly questions of black-on-black violence and crime. The fighting between black teens raised a whole new dimension because it seemed to have no reason behind it. Black teens were not necessarily trying to rob each other or burglarize each other's houses. They just wanted to hurt each other, often in the most ironic of settings. Which is why the story of a fight after the lip sync concert in 1988 seemed so odd.

The concert took place on a Friday evening in late March, and it was sponsored by Art Gardner's pride and joy at the high school, the Black Youth Organization. Years before, Gardner had noticed that black students had no organization to promote their heritage. He believed that a black student group would instill pride and provide a way of doing good deeds at the school and in the community.

The group performed plays by black authors. It delivered turkeys at Thanksgiving and Christmas to poor residents, black and white. It organized discussions of black history. The lip sync concert was to be one of the group's most venturesome efforts, an attempt to fill the high school auditorium and raise money to expand the group's programs. As for the talent, lip-synching, or the mimicking of recordings, was meant to be humorous. Gardner hoped the evening would be one of laughter.

And it was. The performers, almost all of them black, lip-synched songs by rap artists for the mostly black audience. Nothing wrong there, Art Gardner figured. Good to have black students together, enjoying one another, laughing.

The concert ended, the doors opened, and the audience walked into the cold March air. Outside were some five hundred black students, many from Hackensack and Englewood. Some had come to Teaneck High School that night for the concert. Others, however, had come to settle beefs or start them. A fight broke out by the steps on the north side of the school. Another broke out by the flagpole between the main door and the football stadium, another in the street by Route 4. And still another seemed to be brewing when two teens parked their Jeep in a no-parking zone and other teens tried to block them in.

That night Teaneck High School had hired two off-duty police officers and kept several administrators on the scene for the concert. But as the fight swelled and a thousand students in the auditorium mixed with five hundred outside, a call for help went out. Officers from Teaneck as well as surrounding towns sped to the scene, their lights flashing atop squad cars. This time they had a new weapon.

The Bergen County police had kept an attack dog unit for years but had rarely used it for crowd control. The dogs were often a curiosity, an adornment at parades and fairs, with children walking up and petting them. On this night, when the dogs were brought out to control the black students outside Teaneck's high school, they took on a whole new meaning.

Art Gardner was troubled by the fighting between black students. But the dogs touched a part of his memory he thought he had buried long before. "There're only two places that I've seen dogs and children, and that's in the South and in South Africa," he said that night. "The children were scared off by the dogs."

Gardner's deeper worry was that black students were fighting one another more, causing more trouble than he had seen in his fifteen years at Teaneck High School. He didn't know why. The high school stopped holding basketball games at night, scheduling them instead during the afternoon. Another staple of high school life—the Friday night dance—was also curtailed. The reason: too much fighting between black Teaneck students and rivals from Hackensack and Englewood. As with so many decisions that involved race and violence, though, this strategy was rarely discussed publicly.

But of all the assorted skirmishes and fights in recent years, one stood out for the ferocity of its participants and for its ominous warning signs. Actually it was a series of brawls, all taking place in September 1988 during a weeklong carnival at St. Anastasia's Catholic Church. The first fight began with two black girls, then spread to almost a hundred teenagers, grouped on a street between the church and its school. The next night it was the boys' turn: Englewood versus Teaneck, with more than fifty youths on each side. When police separated the groups, they found something they had never found before at one of these turf battles. Tossed under a car was a Mini-14 semiautomatic assault rifle.

Batron Johnson and the others were there that night. They were not yet going by the name Violators; still calling themselves the Baddy Boys, they thought that the turf battle with Englewood was for the older crowd—"old heads," as some put it. At the carnival, though, the Baddy Boys learned a lesson that they kept with them in the months ahead. "Always stay together," Zeke explained. "Be ready." That night he was carrying a .32-caliber pistol.

The rest of the gang, including Batron, ran from the carnival, chased by a dozen Englewood kids. At Batron's home on Summit Avenue, his mother, Lelia Johnson, heard the Baddies rush through the front door and lock it behind them.

She got up and walked into the room. "What's wrong?" she asked that night.

Batron told her some boys were chasing him and his friends. She was stunned, and her voice shifted into that mix of worry and anger that parents employ when their children seem to tell incredible tales that, if true, are disturbing and, if false, are annoying.

"Who's running after you?" she demanded.

"Those boys from Englewood," said Batron. "They're trying to beat us up."

Lelia Johnson looked in her son's brown eyes and caught a glimpse of something she had not seen in him for years: fear.

———

Bill Crain had heard the stories about fighting, though he had yet to hear of the Baddy Boys. More important perhaps, he was painfully aware of the implications.

School violence was not something Teaneck wanted to be known for, especially now. He was also aware of what school violence did to school enrollment, especially in an integrated student body. Whites fled, but they were not alone. Black students were leaving too. By 1989 more than 50 percent of the white students of high school age in Teaneck were being sent to private schools, usually yeshivas or Catholic high schools. Among black students the trend was just as worrisome: More than 30 percent of blacks who were eligible to attend the high school had enrolled in private institutions. And while many whites cited religion as their reason for enrolling in parochial high schools, the blacks cited another problem: the fear of black-on-black violence and the peer pressure not to "act white" and perform well academically.

As much as he wanted his family to live in an integrated town, Crain knew what race mixing had done to many other towns across America. The pattern was as predictable as the prejudice it sought to overcome. For a few years whites held on to a majority of the population. But gradually the numbers started to change as white families moved out and black families replaced them. Social scientists had even coined a phrase to describe this movement: white flight. And if the modern history of American race relations was known for anything besides violence, it was the tradition of white flight.

In Teaneck, ever since the block busting and integration campaign of the 1960s, officials had kept careful tabs on white flight. The town formed committees with names such as Teaneck Together or the Teaneck Housing Information Center to counter efforts by real estate agents in other towns who steered black home buyers only to Teaneck. The groups also promoted the town's combination of diversity and middle-class stability nationwide, often to corporations that transferred executives to the New York City area. The concept stemmed from recognizing a harsh reality: that to be a model for the nation and buck the trend toward white flight, Teaneck had to work hard to invite in more whites. But even the town's former manager, Werner Schmid, acknowledged that the motives of some whites could be viewed as racist. "The whole idea of a balanced community," he said, "is fraught with racism, because for many whites it means they fear other whites will move out and they will be the last to leave." For many in Teaneck, balancing meant maintaining a stable white population.

In general, Teaneck's efforts paid off. The town's median income was 20 percent higher than the nation's. Equally important in the eyes of town leaders, income in Teaneck had kept pace with other wealthy and white towns in Bergen County. Even marketing experts found Teaneck an inviting place, giving it high marks as a community whose residents regularly used disposable income to buy exercise equipment, go out to dinner, or take expensive vacations, all measuring rods of a town's middle-class strength. By the late 1980s, however, Teaneck was obsessed with another phenomenon that was a direct consequence of white flight and had everything to do with the sort of social balancing act that the town had embraced a quarter century before. There was even a name for this: tipping.

Among those who study integration trends, tipping describes the point at which whites essentially give up on a town, the point at which the town has such a large number of black families that new white families stop moving in. In its crudest terms, the town is no longer viewed by whites as a "white town."

The pattern of white flight and the concern over tipping began in cities in the mid-1950s as large numbers of black families left the segregated South and integrated northern cities. In the 1960s, as blacks began their slow push into suburbs, the pattern continued. The process of tipping generally took about ten years. Black families moved in. When their number approached 35 percent of the population, the balance tipped and whites fled in large numbers.

There were, of course, notable exceptions. Shaker Heights, Ohio, was one town that managed to stem white flight. So was Oak Park, Illinois. And Evanston, Illinois. And Montclair, New Jersey. In each case social scientists found a common denominator to success. Whites stayed—or at least delayed leaving—if the town maintained a top-of-the-line public school system, free of violence and with a consistent stream of graduates to top colleges.

In the spring of 1988 Bill Crain, another Los Angeles native who had moved east, decided he wanted to give something back to his town. He ran for the Teaneck school board and was elected overwhelmingly, testimony to the strength of his ideas and the friendships he had molded during years of coaching his sons and others in baseball, football, and basketball leagues. He was, in many ways, a perfect man for the job. He was an educator—the head of the psychology department at the City College of New York—with degrees from Harvard and the University of Chicago. His two sons and one daughter all went to the public schools. And he was well grounded in an understanding of the kind of multicultural issues that Teaneck was grappling with. Bill Crain may have had a WASPish name, but his family tree had roots in several cultures. In California, his Anglo grandfather married a Mexican woman who was part Native American. As a boy he never had to go far from home to learn the pain and troubles to fit into American society for those with nonwhite skin colors and with ethnic heritages that were not rooted in northern Europe. All he had to do was listen to stories of his grandmother and the prejudice she had felt in 1930s California.

Crain wore his empathy for society's underdogs and outcasts as a badge of personal pride. At first meetings he frequently seemed shy and occasionally withdrawn, a tall man who seemed to carry himself in a permanent hunch, even on his daily jogs around Votee Park. But when the subject moved him, he was unafraid to speak up, often eloquently and often as a lone dissenter among a majority that opposed him. When he was a youth, his family had moved to the suburbs of Orange County, to the south of Los Angeles. In the late 1950s the area was known for three things—orange groves, Disneyland, and staunch anticommunism—and for one of the most enduring political personalities of the twentieth century, Richard Nixon. Crain, the valedictorian of his high school class, was deeply upset by what he saw as the cultural and social pressure by the anti-Communist crowd against anything remotely progressive, and he quickly became known as something of a free spirit, who followed his own conscience and bucked the trend.

When Crain settled into his seat on the school board in the summer of 1988, the Teaneck district was facing one of its most difficult decisions yet: whether to spend $24.6 million to remodel several older

schools with shiny new classroom wings, upgrade the high school football field and the track, add fine arts classrooms and multimedia cen-
ters, and construct an indoor swimming pool next to a junior high
school. At the heart of the debate was that old, unspoken concern for
racial balance and Teaneck's sustained attempts to make its schools
attractive to white students. This time there was a new twist, though.

The slow trickle of white students from the high school had resulted
in some odd finger pointing. Instead of taking a hard look at why
students left and at whether violence might be a factor, many in Teaneck seemed to be blaming the newest group of white immigrants for
the white flight: Orthodox Jews. For Teaneck, few things could have
been more ironic.

In the 1940s, when Jews began to escape city neighborhoods, Teaneck was one of the first suburban towns in America to open its doors.
By 1970 roughly a third of the town's thirty-eight thousand residents
were Jewish. But only 2 percent ascribed to Judaism's strictest standards of eating only kosher food, of not driving cars or using electrical
appliances on the Sabbath, and of attending Jewish-only schools. Most
members of Teaneck's Jewish community had followed the postwar
trend and dropped many of the old customs. Indeed, many credited
the high standards of Teaneck's public schools to the high expectations
of well-educated Jewish families who flocked to the town.

During the 1980s Teaneck's liberal Jews did some soul-searching.
The Orthodox community in the town had grown to 10 percent. You
didn't need a math degree to figure out how this would affect the
schools. In many cases Orthodox families, often with four and five
children, were moving in and buying homes from older, liberal Jews
who had settled Teaneck in the 1950s and whose kids had grown and
left the nest. On census reports the overall racial balance of the town
remained stable on the surface, with white families replacing older,
white families who moved upon retirement, breaking the tradition of
white flight. In Teaneck it was a healthy cycle, many believed—except
for one worrisome snag for whites who were committed to integration
in the public schools: Few Orthodox families sent their children to
public schools.

In most towns the customs and traditions of 10 percent of the residents probably wouldn't mean much. In Teaneck it dominated many
conversations among whites about public schools. Teaneck's school
superintendent, Harold Morris, remembers feeling some measure of
shock after he arrived in town in 1986. After a school meeting he had

stopped at Louie's Charcoal Pit for a late-night snack with three white women, all of them Jewish and politically liberal, all of them well educated and upper middle class, all parents who wanted their children to attend the public schools. That night they spoke highly of the town's public schools, but the conversation eventually took an ugly turn. "The Orthodox are wrecking the town," one woman said. "Why did they have to come here?"

Morris had never heard such a blatant expression of dislike of Jews from fellow Jews. To do so was to risk being called anti-Semitic. Indeed, in 1975 a councilman who was Jewish but not Orthodox, Martin Cramer, had tried to encourage a public discussion about his worries that Orthodox Jews moving into town might tip the racial balance in public schools. He may as well have been wearing the white robes of the Ku Klux Klan when he opened his mouth. He was publicly denounced in his own synagogue, and on election day he was voted out of office. There would be no anti-Semites in Teaneck, no, sir. Not in public anyway. Years later more than a few in Teaneck said Cramer was right.

Unlike Catholics, who did not feel as compelled by their religious tradition to educate their children only in parochial schools, Orthodox Jews consider it a solemn spiritual duty. Among some in Teaneck this was regarded as traitorous. By settling in the town, Orthodox Jews stabilized its overall racial balance—roughly 70 percent white to 30 percent black and Hispanic—but by taking white students out of the school system, they moved the balance at the public schools toward a 50–50 ratio of black and white students, a ratio that made some whites uncomfortable. It was the tipping point. Black families had an entirely different view—that it didn't matter. But it was rarely discussed. Few whites blamed the two hundred white Catholic families that sent their children to parochial schools. Instead Orthodox Jews became the target of blame for the tipping point Teaneck feared it was reaching. And Teaneck knew the hard facts about tipping. It had only to look across the border to Englewood.

Teaneck did not want to become Englewood. In the 1940s, Teaneck had established a park to act as a buffer between its northeast neighborhood, then almost all white, and Englewood's poor black neighborhood just over the line. Roads to link Englewood with Teaneck had been mapped out to be cut through the trees. But Teaneck's leaders suddenly put a stop to that. They named the entire area Argonne Park, after the thick French forest that rebuffed invaders for centuries. Today, amid the weeds and brush and under the tall oaks and flowing maples, you can still find curbs and sewer lines that were cut into the forest but never used.

For all its worries about becoming another Englewood, Teaneck was fundamentally different from its eastern neighbor. Like Teaneck, Englewood had two distinct sides to its town, but in Englewood the dividing lines were not set just by race. Class also played a major role. On Englewood's East Hill, which rolled up and over the Palisades to the Hudson River, stood a series of lavish mansions. In the basin, at the bottom of the hill and across another set of railroad tracks, sat the black neighborhood. In the 1920s the black servants for the mansions lived there. In 1967, in the midst of the turmoil that swept American cities, local blacks had staged a riot of their own over poor housing conditions and a lack of jobs. By the 1980s Englewood's black neighborhood was still an enclave for the poor, though more government-subsidized housing had been built there. If black residents had aspirations to leave town, often they wanted to move to Teaneck, where the homes for black residents were more modern, where there was a stable black middle class, where they assumed there was no hill for white folks and no bottomland for blacks.

Teaneck's whites had a far different view. Despite the clear differences of class in the towns, white Teaneck residents looked at Englewood's public schools with a sense of foreboding. In the late 1960s Englewood's public schools were almost evenly balanced between black and white students. By 1989, however, nine of every ten students were black. At the high school there were fewer than twenty white students in an enrollment of more than a thousand.

Teaneck had long embraced a strategy to stem white flight in its own public schools: Keep the standards high and whites would stay. When the school authorities proposed in 1989 to spend $24.6 million on school upgrades, there was more at stake than deciding how to improve the chemistry lab or what color to paint the classrooms in the new wing of the elementary school or how many lanes the proposed indoor pool might have.

Bill Crain sensed all this. In his mind Teaneck was special, not so much because it had succeeded in finding the solution to integration but because it believed in deliberately trying to avoid the suburban, homogeneous mold. When his sons, Tom and Adam, played sports, Crain had followed their teams to other suburban schools and listened in amazement and disgust to the prejudice with which some white teams and their white supporters greeted Teaneck's integrated teams.

Crain wanted none of that for his family. That was why he moved to Teaneck when he thought his neighborhood on Manhattan's Upper West Side had become too dangerous to raise children in.

Crain had often heard that good public schools were at the heart of stopping white flight. But it took money to maintain a world-class school system that consistently dispatched graduates to Harvard, Yale, Duke, and Johns Hopkins. And when Crain studied Teaneck's $24.6 million plan to upgrade its schools, he was deeply bothered.

All during the summer of 1989 he examined the pros and cons. And by fall he had made up his mind. The plan, he concluded, was too expensive, especially for older Teaneck residents whose incomes had leveled off. A family with a house assessed at $225,000—the town's average—would have to pay an additional $213 in property taxes each year for twenty years, all this while Teaneck's school enrollment seemed to be leveling off or sinking. When the day came for the eight-member school board to vote on whether to allow the spending plan to be put to a town-wide referendum, there was immense pressure from school officials for the board to vote unanimously. The idea was to send a unified message to the community: This plan is good.

Crain was the only board member to vote no. Several days later his phone rang at home. It was an old friend, a supporter in his campaign. The woman told Crain she believed she needed to express her dismay over his vote and the message it might send to the community that the school board was divided on the spending plan. Crain listened politely and tried to convince the woman that he had voted his conscience, that the plan was too expensive.

She could not be swayed. Before hanging up, she left this thought with Crain: "If the town votes down this plan, I want you to know you'll be responsible for more white flight and turning this town into Englewood."

On December 12, 1989, after months of campaigning, including a demonstration down Teaneck's main business district by supporters who carried signs that proclaimed HELP OUR SCHOOLS, IMPROVE OUR COMMUNITY and chanted, "Two, four, six, eight, fix our schools and make them great," the $24.6 million budget plan was rejected by Teaneck's voters, with some of the strongest opposition coming from older whites who no longer had children in the schools and from Orthodox Jews. The final tally wasn't even close: 1,420 in favor to 5,202 against. Bill Crain, despite feeling sure of his vote, still worried. His town seemed torn in a way that seemed far more serious than a school budget plan.

On an otherwise quiet afternoon in the same fall of 1989, two white
women held a brief conversation about race relations in Teaneck. One
of them, Dorothy Marcus, was well trained in the language and codes
of race after years of civil rights jobs that had begun in the South in
1954, when she'd graduated from college a month after the Supreme
Court released its landmark school desegregation decision, *Brown* v.
Board of Education. Marcus, who went to an all-girls Baptist college in
Winston-Salem, North Carolina, and planned to become a Christian
missionary, was galvanized by the budding civil rights movement. She
vent to work with a liberal Baptist civil rights group in Raleigh, North
Carolina, and never looked back. Over the years she held civil rights
obs in Philadelphia and Michigan. By the 1970s she had married a
lack man and bought a house on Teaneck's northeast side. As a white
oman who ventured between black and white cultures, she under-
:ood all too well the language of race and how coded phrases often
ere like fingerprints on a doorknob at a crime scene, clues to
omething more complicated.

   That day in 1989 Marcus's friend spoke first. Something was trou-
ling her about the high school. It wasn't the caliber of the teachers,
the curriculum, or even the age of the building. Like Marcus, she was
the mother of a high school student, a boy. Marcus's daughter had
been in the same play group with the boy when the children were
preschoolers. The two families had drifted apart, primarily because
they lived on different sides of the tracks—Marcus on the black side,
her friend on the white side. But Marcus remembered the woman as
thoughtful. Certainly she had never displayed any hostile feelings toward blacks, and Marcus knew her as someone who had tried to raise
her children to treat everyone fairly.

   That was why the woman was troubled. And as she began to quote
her son, Marcus could see why. "There are three groups at the high
school," the son had told his mother. "There are the white kids, and
there are the black kids who live in white neighborhoods. And then
there are the niggers that none of us want to have anything to do
with."

   The "niggers," the woman quoted her son as saying, lived at the
northeast end of town. They were usually among some of the worst
students. If there was trouble, he assumed they were usually at its
center.

THREE

THE BOY IN
THE RED PARKA

On the north side of Teaneck High School, facing a concrete overpass that crosses a highway, stands one of the town's most enduring ironies. It is a doorway, ordinary in every way except for a nickname that seems more suited to schools of the Jim Crow South than a self-proclaimed model of integration in the North. Students call it the black door.

The door received its nickname in the late 1950s, when all but a handful of the black students at Teaneck High School lived on the northeast side of town. When black students left school to walk home each afternoon, most passed through the door to get to the two-lane concrete bridge that took them over Route 4 into their neighborhoods. Hence the name: black door. No one takes credit for the name, but legends point to whites as the source, with blacks quietly going along. Over the years school officials and teachers tried to ignore the name and even condemn it in some cases, but it stuck, cemented into the social geography by habit and the undeniable fact that most of Teaneck's black students walked in one direction to go home and most whites in another.

By the fall of 1989 the black door had taken on a different meaning. To many black students, the door had evolved into a source of pride, in the same way that some black ghettos, such as New York City's Harlem, or some black colleges, such as Alabama's Tuskegee Institute, had become testimony to black survival and bonding even though they had been created in part out of prejudice and segregation. The door was a gathering place for black students, their turf. Some white students avoided it, if only to stay out of the way of trouble and avoid occasional taunts from walking a gauntlet of black students who resented someone crossing their line.

The Violators had adopted the black door as their turf by the first week of October 1989. It had been a month since their fight with the Hackensack gang, and they were looking for revenge. On the first Wednesday in October they got it.

The day before, October 3, Phillip Pannell had turned sixteen. On Wednesday, as the last school bell sounded for the day, the Violators headed through the black door and gathered as usual by the concrete bridge. Batron Johnson eased himself onto the ledge and let his feet dangle. The gentle Indian summer sun warmed the concrete, and it felt good to sit for a few minutes as the stream of students passed or collected in clumps of two or three to talk. Phillip Pannell followed Batron up on the ledge. His long legs reached almost to the sidewalk. Phillip was taller than Batron even though Batron was a few months older. Phillip was almost five feet ten, but much thinner than Batron. The two friends waited for a few minutes, looking for Steve, Ed, Tyrone, and Chuckie: the Violators. They walked to school together, met between classes, ate at the same cafeteria table, escorted one another home.

Phillip's back still ached from the fight with the Hackensack boys. At home recently his mother, Thelma Pannell, had nudged him as she often did in a playful manner, and he winced. "My back, Ma," he told her. "My back. Those boys hit me hard."

Phillip didn't know it then, but the sharp pains that jabbed at his back were the result of a cracked vertebra. He found some comfort in his soreness, though. That fall he did not try out for the school football team, even though he'd had a promising season the year before. He told several friends that his back was too sore to play. But as much as he loved the game, Phillip loved hanging out with his friends more. If there was any solace in not playing football, perhaps he found it in the red San Francisco 49ers parka that he wore each day.

Batron looked up and noticed a familiar face by the black door, a boy taller than Batron, muscular, with several chains around his neck and a gold tooth.

Batron turned to Pannell. "Phil, ain't that the kid from Hackensack?"

Pannell lifted his head. Batron watched as Pannell examined the boy, who was now talking with a Teaneck girl on the opposite curb.

"That kid there," Batron said, "talking to that girl. That the kid from Hackensack who jumped you on the first day of school?"

Pannell paused. "Yeah," he said slowly.

"All right. We're gonna go over there and get him."

Batron didn't wait for a response. He jumped off the ledge and strode across the street, balling his meaty right hand into a fist. The Hackensack boy's back was turned. Later Batron remembered being focused only on the kid, the hate rising through almost every cell of his body. Perfect opportunity, Batron thought. Anyway, if the situation had been reversed and Batron had been alone in Hackensack, he figured the Hackensack boys would do the same to him.

He aimed for the boy's head, cocking his arm.

Wham.

Batron's fist slammed into the back of the boy's head, and the boy staggered forward and tried to run. He stumbled and scrambled down a slight grade toward the rear parking lot of the high school. Pannell and the other Violators were there now, kicking, swinging, stomping. Another Hackensack boy ran up, but he too was pummeled. Batron got in several more solid whacks, then saw Phillip land several punches. Good, Batron thought. One of the Hackensack boys lost a gold tooth. The other's face was swollen.

And the Violators ran.

Teachers and school administrators were on the scene quickly. The police were on their way too. Batron, Phillip, and the other Violators sprinted over the concrete overpass, then turned right into a grove of trees—"the trails" Batron called them. The trees were a buffer the town had set up for the residential neighborhoods to absorb the highway noise. The town called it the green strip, and it was one of Teaneck's proud trademarks to the outside world. While other towns allowed gas stations and malls to dot the edge of Route 4, Teaneck kept its portion green and tree-lined. Real estate agents loved it too. When prospective homeowners drove from New York City, Teaneck's green strip stood out in bucolic invitation.

Today it was an escape route. The Violators knew these woods well. When they were younger, they rode their bicycles there, creating twisting dirt bike courses, laced with moguls and banked turns. Batron and Phillip ran with the others down a path that took them out of sight of the police and school administrators and spilled onto Teaneck Road near a nursing home that Pannell's father had worked at briefly. From there it was only a short jog past St. Anastasia's grammar school and into their neighborhood. Ten minutes after Batron threw the first punch, the Violators were at Chuckie's house.

The boys checked for bruises. None. Tomorrow they probably would be in trouble at school, but Batron was more worried about what might happen today. For every action there is a reaction. It was a basic fact of physics. In the world of the Violators it was a way of life.

———

At Teaneck High the police were taking down names, and within minutes they had identified most of the fighters. More than a dozen witnesses had seen the fight. The Hackensack boys were cooperating with names too.

In his second-floor office overlooking the football stadium, the Teaneck High School principal James DeLaney heard a name that bothered him deeply. The group that had attacked the Hackensack boys was a gang: the Violators.

DeLaney had come to Teaneck High School in the early 1960s, as integration was experiencing its first labor pains. He had taught biology, transferred to administrative duties, and eventually landed the principal's job. Over the years he had dealt with other attempts to form gangs. In the early weeks of this school year he had seen some Violators' graffiti in a bathroom. He had also heard rumors about a new gang being formed, but he hadn't yet made the connection between the bathroom graffiti and the gang. Now it was all too clear. A gang and its name, Violators, had been linked to something the school could not tolerate: violence.

A few blocks away, at the Teaneck police station, detectives in the second-floor office of the juvenile bureau studied the names they had written down. There would be arrests, but there was no need to rush. The police could find the Violators easily enough—at school. As much as the Violators saw their studies as an intrusion, they also saw school as a home base and social outlet. A few days later police picked up Batron, Phillip, and three other Violators.

When detectives spoke to the Violators, the story of revenge for an earlier fight emerged. Nothing surprising there. Teaneck's police were familiar with the turf wars. But this time one of the cops noticed something seemed out of place. When asked where he lived, Phillip Pannell had not given an address in Teaneck, as police expected. He said he had a new home, Reis Avenue in Englewood, several hundred yards over the Teaneck line. If Phillip no longer lived in Teaneck, why was he at Teaneck High School? Englewood kids went to the high school in Englewood. It was the law. Days later police told school officials about the boy who lived over the border.

Yes, Phillip Pannell had a new home in a new town, but, except for that mention to the police, he wasn't talking much about it, even to close friends like Batron.

Batron noticed a sadness in his friend that he had not seen before, but this time he knew why. Phillip's moods seemed to rise and sink with his father's adventures.

Even though he was still married to Phillip's mother and living in the family home, Phillip David Pannell could not fulfill one basic requirement of parenthood: financial support. Thelma Pannell had gone to court the year before and persuaded a judge to order her husband to contribute $257 a week. But after a year Pannell couldn't come up with that sum on his own.

Seven days before the Violators took out their revenge on the Hackensack boys outside the black door, and six days before Phillip's sixteenth birthday, his father landed in the Bergen County jail. If he couldn't make his child support payments by himself, the Bergen County sheriff would see he did it. Pannell was placed in a special work-release program that automatically took part of his weekly paycheck and passed it back to his family.

Phillip David Pannell was born on February 3, 1951, on a farm in the rolling piedmont between Virginia's Blue Ridge Mountains and its coastal tidewater. His hometown, Gretna, was at the hub of two Civil War–era roads. On one road the Pannells could drive an hour to Appomattox, where the Old South of slavery had come to its crashing end with the surrender of the Confederate Army. On the other road it took only an hour to reach the old Confederate capital of Richmond.

But if the Pannells felt any particular connection to the Civil War or to the brutal slavery that fueled it, they didn't say. They had inherited the postwar lot of millions of blacks, sharecropping on white-owned land, with many mouths to feed and too many dreams that seemed to go wanting. The civil rights movement that blossomed as the children grew seemed as remote as the Civil War.

Phillip David Pannell was the second youngest in a family of eight children, three girls and five boys. His father, Ben Charles Pannell, worked the rolling Virginia fields, coaxing tobacco, wheat, and corn from the soil until he died from a stroke in 1980 at the age of sixty-five. Pannell's mother, Jessie Mae Pannell, had died when he was two and only two months after she had given birth to her youngest child, a son. For years Pannell told friends and police that she had been poisoned, but no one had ever been charged with her murder.

The children all worked the farm, perhaps the reason none of them went into farming as an adult. Even in the 1950s, when American agriculture had embraced technology, tobacco farming in the South was still the domain of sharecropping families that often tilled the rich black soil by hand or with the help of rusty tractors or mules. After the harvest most of the profits went to pay the landowner for rent. It was a cyclical system of plantings and harvests, with earnings siphoned away. After World War II that system began to change, and the great northern migration began for thousands of southern black families, including the Pannells of Gretna, Virginia. Four of the Pannell children sought refuge in northern industrial jobs. One brother, Russell Charles, became a trucker and moved to Englewood. Another sister, Bennie Jean, also moved to Englewood for a factory job. Two other brothers, Billy and Edward Charles, moved to Newark and drove trucks.

Phillip David Pannell dropped out of high school a year before graduation. He headed to Vermont and a stint on a construction crew with the federal Job Corps. Two years later he drifted southward to New Jersey and met a young woman with a familiar face.

Thelma Mae Monroe had also grown up in Virginia's tobacco country in a small town called Long Island about twenty miles from Gretna. Her parents were also tobacco sharecroppers with a large family. The Monroes had ten children, evenly split between boys and girls. Thelma and her twin sister were the eldest girls. Her mother's maiden name was Pannell, but she was not related to Phillip's family. Among blacks in tidewater Virginia, Pannell was not an uncommon name. Also, like Pannell, Thelma dropped out of high school a year shy of graduation. She was seventeen and in search of something to do with her time, and up north in Englewood, her aunt, Molly Dickerson, needed baby-sitting help. Thelma Monroe decided to give it a try. She wanted to escape the farm, but she figured she could always return. If she could find a better life, that would be fine too.

Monroe had known Phillip David Pannell in Virginia. He was two years older than she and often stopped by the Monroe farm to visit her older brothers. So when Phillip Pannell and Thelma Monroe found their way to Englewood, it was only natural that they visited each other. Within a year they had begun dating. Pannell was working as a meat cutter. Monroe took a job as a seamstress in an embroidery factory. Among its specialties, the factory produced Dutch windmill shoulder patches for the Teaneck Police Department. Monroe sewed the patchs' silver edges.

In early 1973 Monroe became pregnant, and just after 1:30 A.M. on Wednesday, October 3, she gave birth to a son at Englewood Hospital. Marriage didn't come until four months later—on February 3, 1974, Phillip David Pannell's twenty-first birthday. Thelma was 20.

Thelma named her new son Phillip, after his father. But this son was no junior. His mother chose Clinton as a middle name after one of her favorite uncles who had moved from Virginia to the Bronx. In later years she rarely called her son by his first name. To her, the boy was Clinton, and the name rolled off her tongue long and slowly *Clinnnn-tonnn*.

Ten months later the Pannells were renting the top floor of a house in Englewood near Argonne Park that Teaneck once used as a buffer against black migration. On a humid day Thelma Pannell walked onto the front lawn and looked up. She gasped and froze. Phillip's crib was next to an open window, and he had managed to lift himself up, pop open the screen, and crawl onto a portion of the roof that extended over the first floor. The roof was pitched, and Phillip seemed unaware of the danger The boy was clearly proud of himself. But if he moved too much, he would roll off. She told neighbors to gather under the ledge and catch the boy if he rolled. Then she headed upstairs and ran to the open window.

"Come on, baby. Come on to me," she called out. "Come to Ma. Come on, baby."

Her son crawled back to her that day, but not before he paused and looked out on the world as if it were his to explore. Years later, her memory of the day was centered not on the danger her son faced but on how sure he seemed of himself on the ledge.

In those early days the entire family seemed sure of itself. Pannell was working regularly as a meat cutter, Thelma Pannell at the embroidery factory. By 1977 they had become, on paper anyway, the quintessential American family: two parents, a son, and now a daughter, Natasha, born that January. They had also scraped together enough money to buy a $45,000 house in Teaneck. The monthly mortgage bill was steep for them—$769, including taxes—but with two salaries they could manage. When the family moved from its rented digs in Englewood over the border and up the hill to an eight-room Cape Cod on Circle Drive on Teaneck's northeast side of town, they seemed well on their way to the quiet middle-class comfort of Little League and children's bicycles and backyard barbecues. They even had a live-in baby-sitter, an elderly woman who was a friend of the family and offered to watch the Pannell children while their parents worked.

"I loved Teaneck," Thelma Pannell said years later. It was only after she had moved in that she learned that her town considered itself a model of integration. For the Pannells, Teaneck offered something more basic: a home on a quiet street.

But the family's stability would not last.

———

For Phillip David Pannell, Phillip senior, the trouble that eventually tore apart his family and landed him in the Bergen County jail in the fall of 1989 had begun years before, with drugs.

Just after 5:00 P.M. on January 27, 1983, David Bowman, a detective with the Englewood Police Department, got a call from one of his reliable street sources that a man named Phil Pannell had been at a neighborhood gin mill, Cassie's Tavern, and had left, bragging that he would return with cocaine. Pannell, the source told Bowman, would be traveling from his home in Teaneck, probably within a half hour.

In a police report written later Bowman described how he and another Englewood detective, Sergeant Ted Chapman, headed for the Teaneck line in an unmarked car and parked at a spot not far from Cassie's Tavern. They knew Pannell as one of the bar's regulars; they also knew his 1979 silver Ford pickup truck and didn't have to wait long for it.

Fifteen minutes later the detectives spotted the truck and turned on a flashing light. Pannell pulled over, and before the detectives could get out, he opened his door and walked toward them. The cops told Pannell to empty his pockets, and he did, removing a plastic bag with two grams of marijuana and two small brown jars, one with a white powdery residue and the other with a white powder. Together the jars held about eight tenths of a gram of cocaine.

That night Pannell was charged with two counts of drug possession. But in 1983 at least Phillip David Pannell seemed like a good candidate to go clean. He was thirty-two, married, the father of a son, who had recently celebrated his tenth birthday, and a six-year-old daughter, who had just started first grade. Pannell was sorry for his crime. He seemed stable and owned a home and helped support his wife and children with a solid job, earning eleven dollars an hour. The judge saw no reason to throw Pannell in jail for what might have been a momentary lapse in judgment while trying to impress his friends at a local bar. In his report on October 18, 1983, the judge ended with this notation: "Such a person is a good candidate to divert from the criminal justice system." He gave Pannell the customary slap on the wrist for first-time drug offenders: probation, with regular urine tests.

Three weeks later Pannell was in trouble again.

What Phillip D. Pannell hadn't told the judge or the probation officers was that he had begun snorting cocaine the year before and smoking marijuana. Drug use, coupled with regular trips to a variety of neighborhood bars, had become a drain on the family finances. He soon turned to burglary.

Around 10:00 P.M. on November 11, 1983, Englewood cops again noticed Pannell behind the wheel of his pickup. The truck, police said in their reports, was swerving back and forth, a sign that a drunk might be behind the wheel. When they stopped Pannell, police not only discovered he was drunk but found one of the oddest caches of stolen merchandise they had ever stumbled upon: several boxes of steaks from a meat-packer where Pannell had worked until recently. Total value: five hundred dollars.

The arrest cemented a fact of life that was becoming all too clear to police: Phillip David Pannell seemed to be leading two lives. He owned a home, had a growing family, and worked at a meat-packing plant close to Teaneck. He sang in the choir at a local Baptist church and moonlighted occasionally as a landscaper or a janitor. But he was also fighting a private war with alcohol and drugs—and stealing to support his habits.

Pannell apologized for taking the steaks. He was so convincing that his old boss wrote the judge a letter asking for leniency. Pannell himself told probation officers that he intended to go straight. "I am guilty," he said in a probation report to the court. "I am working steady. I am sorry for what has happened. I made a mistake, and I have embarrassed my family. I plead with the Court to place me on probation so I can continue to provide and care for my family."

It took almost a year for the case to wind its way through the Bergen County court system. By then investigators again had judged Pannell to be a man to be trusted. Prosecutors decided to drop the charge of stealing meat, but with one familiar condition: Pannell would be placed on probation for three years and had to submit to regular drug tests. He agreed, and on January 7, 1985—almost two years after his first drug arrest—the papers landed on the desk of one of Bergen County's most experienced judges, Charles R. DiGisi.

It was DiGisi's task to approve Pannell's probation. Pannell seemed on the way to putting his life together, according to a report submitted by prosecutors. Anyway, the jails were overcrowded with men who had done far worse. DiGisi signed off on the plea bargain. Phillip David Pannell went free again.

Eight months later, on August 30, 1985, he was arrested once more, charged this time with burglarizing a tire dealership where he moon-lighted as a janitor with his brother and brother-in-law. But this time Pannell had a new partner, his eleven-year-old son.

It was the first time young Phillip had ever been taken to a police station. He wasn't charged that night; cops turned him over to his mother even though they suspected the boy had been a lookout for his father. Once again the court system treated Phillip senior with all the tenderness of a first-time offender. Three months later the burglary charge was downgraded to a disorderly person's offense, and he was put on probation. He paid a $250 fine, plus $25 in court fees, and was free to return to his home, his family, and his job—what was left of them anyway. Pannell now had another problem he didn't tell proba-tion investigators about: He could not hold a job.

———

It's never easy to measure when the problems of adults begin to affect a boy's outlook on life and himself. Some psychologists say children sense problems between their parents in early infancy and develop elaborate protective habits to shield themselves or send a message of pain in the hope that the parents will change. Others contend that it takes years for a child's pain to set in. Most agree, however, that es-pecially by the time a child reaches the delicate threshold of puberty and the teenage years, the marriage problems of parents not only dom-inate homelife but shape the child's outlook on the future.

According to Thelma Pannell, the problems in her marriage began soon after the family moved to Teaneck. Back then the difficulties seemed small: minor arguments about money or about her husband wanting to go out by himself. The problems persisted, however. The arguments grew in frequency and fervor. She found herself alone more and more in the evenings, having to shoulder a greater share of the parenting load. Add to this mix a father who flirts with alcoholism and drug abuse and is habitually arrested, and you have the emotional framework for young Phillip Clinton Pannell's world in 1986. He was about to turn thirteen, when on an August night, almost a year to the day after his father had taken him on a botched burglary to the tire warehouse, young Phillip stormed out of the house and told his mother he was going to kill himself.

Thelma Pannell had become more protective of him in those years. Even his friends, Chuckie and Batron, noticed that she often hugged her son and whispered that she didn't "want anything bad to happen" to him.

Phillip would laugh. Then he might tease his mother or tickle her and then give her a playful hug and his own attempt at reassurance: "Ah, Mom, don't worry."

The night he ran out of his house, Phillip was bare-chested and wore only shorts and sneakers. It was 9:20 P.M., and Thelma Pannell was settling down to watch television and prepare for work the next day at the embroidery factory. Her son wanted to go out with his friends. She countered that it was too late. He pointed to the clock. It wasn't even ten yet. Anyway, he was just going up the block to Teaneck Road and Mackel Park. No, she said.

When her son stormed out, threatening suicide, she waited twenty minutes for him to return before telephoning the Teaneck police. Several cars were dispatched, but there was no sign of the boy in the shorts and sneakers.

In the annals of juvenile crime this would not amount to much, even in suburban Teaneck. Phillip returned home four hours later, at one-twenty the next morning. His mother phoned the police, who took a report. The next day a detective from the juvenile bureau visited the house and recommended that mother and son contact a crisis intervention social worker. They never did.

━━━━

Four months later, on New Year's Day 1987, Teaneck's police heard again from Thelma Pannell. This time the problem wasn't her son. It was her husband. She claimed he had sexually assaulted her.

When the cops arrived, they found the formula of personal anger and alcohol that often fuels these sorts of spats, especially on New Year's Day. But this time Thelma Pannell added something else: Besides beating her and attempting to rape her, she told police that "he put some kind of pill in my drink."

Since losing his meat cutter's job a few years back, Phillip David Pannell had drifted from paycheck to paycheck. For a while he worked in the laundry at Englewood Hospital, earning $175 a week. He also put in time as a maintenance man at the Teaneck Nursing Home for

$200 a week, and he worked on a garbage truck at $450 a week. He even joined the Teamsters, with dues of $18 a month, so he could drive the garbage truck or get another trucking job. During slow weeks Pannell hooked on with a construction company or worked landscaping jobs on his own. He was, by his own admission, a survivor. He had earned only $18,892 in 1983, the first year he was arrested. Five years later he was making $28,000. Including Thelma Pannell's job at the embroidery factory, the family income hovered around $44,000. Measured solely by the cold statistics of financial records, the Pannells were solidly middle-class.

After their fight on New Year's Day 1987, life calmed somewhat. At least there were no calls to police. But increasingly Pannell was not working, partly because of the slowdown in construction jobs resulting from the national recession that was beginning to cut its swath through New Jersey's middle class. Increasingly the family budget was being supported by Thelma Pannell's factory job. And Pannell was drinking again.

On July 3, 1988, Thelma Pannell went to court to bar her husband from the home. Eight weeks later, just before the Labor Day weekend and the start of another school year, she went to court again with a demand for child support. A month later, after social workers had analyzed the family finances and lawyers had prepared the necessary court motions, a family court judge ordered Phillip David Pannell to pay $257 a week to support his family.

Four months later, right after New Year's Day 1989, Thelma Pannell was on the phone to the Teaneck police again, claiming her husband had threatened to kill her. Her husband, she said, was living several blocks away and, during a boozy visit one evening, had slapped her.

Police arrested Pannell that night, and prosecutors announced they would take his case to a grand jury, a serious step that could result in a trial and a jail sentence. In the interim he went back on the street, still drinking. Thelma Pannell feared being alone and told friends she was concerned what might happen the next time her husband showed up at the door in a drunken fit. It might be a good idea, she told friends and family, to have some protection.

A friend offered her a silver Italian-made Mondial starter's pistol, no bigger than her palm. The pistol couldn't fire bullets, but it made plenty of noise—enough to scare anyone. She took the gun and placed it in a box on a shelf in her bedroom closet.

Protection. In the early months of 1989 young Phillip Clinton Pannell also had begun to understand the importance of the word in his Teaneck neighborhood. If he was afraid of his father, he wasn't saying. Phillip worried about protecting himself from other gangs. Each night groups of black teens gathered along the side of Teaneck Road or in nearby parking lots near Popeyes chicken or the Carvel ice-cream stand. In the spring of 1989 police noted that the boy in the red San Francisco 49ers parka had become a regular, even on school nights.

At police headquarters in the spring of 1989 young Phillip was building a thick file. Besides the arrests for school vandalism and assault, he was suspected of pulling fire alarms along Teaneck's main business district and in the high school.

All these were warning signs of a teenager gradually descending the ladder of worsening criminal behavior. In July 1989 police received the most ominous warning yet. Phillip had found a way to combine violence with theft. Not even his father had done that.

It was just after seven-thirty in the evening on July 13 when young Pannell and another boy, Melvin, walked into the Star International Grocery Store on Teaneck Road. Phillip started playing the Tiger Road video game near the front of the store. Midway through, he slammed the machine, broke open the coin box, and grabbed a handful of quarters.

From behind the counter, the store owner, Khaiser Krazvi, screamed at him to stop. Phillip kept pounding the coin box on the video game. Krazvi reached for a telephone to call police, but Phillip's friend, Melvin, leaped over the counter and ripped the phone off the wall. Phillip fled with a handful of coins. Melvin grabbed two boxes of candy.

Within days Teaneck police arrested both boys. In juvenile court the two received a warning that if they continued with this behavior, they would end up in a state juvenile prison and were ordered to report to a probation officer who was to monitor their behavior.

As the Teaneck police were getting to know young Phillip, what stuck in their minds was the way his mother handled his arrests. She didn't try to defend her son as an angel. When police called, Thelma Pannell instinctively knew what they were telling her: that her son was on a downward slide. "I always said this about Thelma," said Teaneck Sergeant Robert Adomilli. "She never said, 'Not my kid.' She knew she had a problem with him."

But one remark by Thelma Pannell stayed with Adomilli, an unsettling reminder of what life must have been like behind the doors of the Pannell home. After Phillip had been arrested for school vandalism, his mother approached Adomilli at police headquarters. She shook her head and muttered, "It's all on me, and I don't get no help."

She went on to say how she worried whether she would be able to discipline Phillip, that he seemed to be even more uncontrollable than before. She also mentioned that her husband wasn't giving her enough child support and she was having trouble making ends meet. By the end of July 1989 Pannell was supposed to have delivered more than thirteen thousand dollars to his family. He had managed only half.

One evening in August, Pannell dropped by the house on Circle Driveway. Young Phillip sat outside on the steps that night with his friend Chuckie, listening as his parents' conversation grew loud and angry. Chuckie studied his friend and noticed Phillip's demeanor had changed. Gone was the confident, happy-go-lucky personality. The boy Chuckie saw that night was silent and sullen.

After his father had stormed out, Phillip continued to sit in silence, then walked off to spend a few hours on Teaneck Road with the newly named Violators.

The group was not known for introspection. If anything, Phillip, Batron, Chuckie, and the other Violators prided themselves in living for the moment and for their turf. But that month they were stunned by the news of the death of Yusuf Hawkins in Brooklyn, and in one of the few times any of them remember, Chuckie and Batron found themselves in a discussion with Phillip and the other Violators about what it meant to be a young black male living in a world of unexpected violence. The boys had gathered by the steps of St. Anastasia's Catholic Church. When someone mentioned Yusuf's death, they grew somber. The Violators had discussed many things—girls, fights, parents, teachers, sports, the cops, other gangs—but never death. Chuckie remembers someone asking what it felt like to die.

"Dunno," someone else said.

Another boy mentioned how unjust Yusuf's death seemed. The boys grew silent again.

It felt all right to be together. Chuckie. Phil. Batron. Steve . . . The Violators. They were bigger now. Soon they'd be sophomores. The summer had been a time of maturing. But it had also been a time of fear. There had been minor fistfights. Certainly nothing like the fights after the carnival the previous fall. There had also been lots of staring and posing when the cars with the Hackensack and Englewood kids cruised Teaneck Road. It was almost as if everyone were sizing up everyone else. What's more, the Violators had heard new talk on the street. Some kids now carried knives; some even had guns.

As the Violators sat on the concrete steps of the church that evening, the turf squabbles that they spent so much time and energy on seemed a galaxy away. Cars and buses passed, a steady symphony of machines on Teaneck Road. A few adults who had worked late were walking home, men with their ties off, women with their hair limp. After a few minutes one of the boys spoke. "One of us is going to get killed."

Chuckie agreed. The thought had been on his mind. But he had kept it to himself, not wanting to risk being laughed at. The boys no longer walked alone, not even in Teaneck. To do so was to invite a carload of boys from another town to jump them. Batron had been caught alone a few times. So had Phil. Even as a group they rarely went to the McDonald's in Englewood.

Chuckie thought: Someone will either get hurt or shot. He figured it might be him.

Or Phil.

Jim DeLaney knew something had to be done. As principal of Teaneck High School, he had dealt with his share of tough kids over the years. But if this was truly a gang or even just a bunch of suburban kids trying to flex their muscles, DeLaney knew it had to be disbanded quickly. Within days he had the names of the Violators. No surprises here. He knew Batron and Phillip and Steve and Chuckie. Young kids, for sure, but also the kind who were not afraid to make trouble, especially Phillip.

Phillip had become what teachers and administrators call a chronic discipline problem. He was also a kid with potential. He would cut classes one day, attend all of them the next. In one class he would wear his baseball hat backward and fool around, totally oblivious of a teacher's pleading for him to stop. In another class he would raise his hand and answer questions thoughtfully. He would go weeks without doing any homework; then, one day, he would arrive with every assignment completed.

DeLaney knew Phillip was no dummy. "He was the kind of kid who people got upset about," the principal remembered. "He was smart enough to do the work, but he wasn't hooked into any aspects of school. This place was social for him. This was his place where he met the kids."

DeLaney had spotted the boy's good and bad qualities within the first weeks of school. Phillip was a leader. He was popular, outspoken, gregarious. He wasn't a nasty kid, but he had a temper and seemed to be one of those kids who backed up what they said. "He initiated actions," DeLaney said. "When you have kids who always get into trouble, you always have a few kids who are in the second row watching and then the kids in the first row doing. Phillip was always a doer. He didn't lay back and watch. He wasn't real careful." He was, DeLaney thought, one of those kids you'd like to capture and turn around.

If he works in a school long enough, around different types of kids, a school administrator or teacher learns how to talk to students, even the silent ones. With some he can crack jokes. Some respond better to a firm one-on-one tough-guy approach. Others appreciate the fatherly or motherly soft touch. Still others react best to strict rules and regulations.

The Violators were different, DeLaney noticed. "It was just a very close-knit, almost impregnable group," he said later. "I always sensed from these kids that they always listened. They were not what I would call disrespectful unless we were in a big confrontation. But at the same time they had a different agenda."

The high school prided itself on its diversity and trying to blend students of different colors and economic groups. At times this involved the most scrupulous counting: how many black and white cheerleaders, how many blacks on the tennis team, how many white basketball players. But often there was no easy mixing. How, for example, do you force the black kids who congregate at one cafeteria table to join the white kids at another? How do you place more black kids in honors classes when whites consistently make better grades? How do you convince more whites to try out for the basketball and football teams? A decade before, the school had formed a task force of teachers and social workers to examine the challenge posed by the lower academic achievements of most black students. The school thought it might hire more black teachers. But no long-term plan was settled upon. The problem was far from being solved at Teaneck High.

The Violators posed an additional problem. The group was so tight that even other black students couldn't seem to penetrate it. The Violators walked to school together. They met between classes and conferred and walked one another to class. They ate together at lunch. Afterward they walked home. Some, like Phillip, had played sports the year before but had given it up for the group. And if something was happening in school—a fight or a prank—the Violators knew about it before anyone else. The word was passed between members as if each of them had a cellular telephone.

"A very intense communication system," DeLaney noted. "With other groups you mingle in and out, back and forth. These kids always seemed to be together. All the time. Whether it was because they were frightened and afraid and felt they needed to stay together because someone was after them—I don't know. They always seemed to be together."

And they always seemed to be in trouble. DeLaney had been receiving reports from the police department about students who fought on weekends or were just hanging out on street corners. In those first weeks of school in the fall of 1989 the names of the Violators were an almost permanent fixture of those reports.

DeLaney figured it was time to sit down and talk. On a Tuesday, six days after the October 1989 revenge fight against the Hackensack crew, the Violators were gathered in a room on the first floor of Teaneck High School. It was 5:00 P.M., and the school was quiet except for the rustle of janitors and the occasional student or teacher passing through the halls on the way to football practice or another activity. DeLaney had summoned the Violators with their parents, in the hope of heading off more trouble. He wanted the parents involved. DeLaney did not want to mince words on this day. He also wanted to send a message. Draw the line, he thought.

DeLancy and two assistant principals arranged chairs in a circle. The room had been chosen with great care. It was on the north side of the high school, so if parents wanted to see where the fight had taken place, they had only to walk a few yards. DeLaney wanted the circle so the discussion could flow back and forth, from students and parents to administrators. If this was only a lecture from him, he figured the chances of success were nil. But if he could convince the parents to speak up and if students volunteered to explain why they fought so much, perhaps something might be done.

DeLaney walked in, and what he saw did not fill him with hope. It was Phillip Pannell. He was in a chair, slouched, legs out, his body language screaming out, "I don't care."

It was a pose DeLaney was familiar with. Phillip wore the standard clothes of an urban tough: baggy jeans, a hooded sweatshirt, a baseball cap worn backward. But inside, he had changed too. He seemed to exhibit a contempt for authority. It was as if he had awakened each day and planned his moves by the lifestyle shown on a rap music video, not by the suburban values of Teaneck.

Phillip was not alone. DeLaney had seen the changes in students, especially blacks. In the 1960s black students in Teaneck were primarily from middle-class families, whose parents were often educated and married. By the 1980s DeLaney noticed a profound shift in the black families that came to Teaneck, in their economic classes, family stability, and educational backgrounds. Many were working-class and could barely afford the move. DeLaney surmised that the 1980s decay of cities, especially New York City, had driven many black families to try almost anything to escape the drugs and crime that controlled city streets. Some moved in with relatives in Teaneck. Others were stretching the budget beyond the breaking point.

DeLaney observed something even more worrisome. Whereas the black families who had come to Teaneck in the 1960s were intact, many of these families escaping the cities had been fragmented by divorce. More students were being raised by single mothers. Others had no parents on the scene at all and were classified by the school as being on "affidavit status," meaning that they were being raised by grandparents or aunts. The chief guidance counselor, Jay Wolff, noticed the increase in troubled kids from troubled families and wondered about the consequences. So did the gym teacher, Art Gardner. Gardner could remember that only a few years before, if he had reprimanded a student for wandering the halls between classes, he would likely get an embarrassed, respectful answer, as well as an obedient response. It was what he had come to expect in Teaneck, where middle-class values translated into respect for teachers. Now, Gardner thought, if he disciplined a student, he might be met with a deep, hair-trigger anger. As a black man himself Gardner could empathize with any anger that was carried deep within. But why such anger coming from kids who lived in the suburbs? "They see discipline as a challenge to them," Gardner said, his voice rising to mimic the kids' anger. "A few just say, 'Fuck you, man. Don't hassle me.'"

And now there was this gang, the Violators, and actual violence. As the Violators gathered that day, DeLaney studied each of them. He saw looks of concern from parents. Batron's mother, Lelia Johnson, eight months pregnant with another child, had come. So had her new husband. Good, DeLaney thought. Chuckie's mother and grandmother showed up, as had Steven's mother and Phil Pannell's mother. More good signs. DeLaney began, then momentarily paused as another parent arrived. Pannell's father walked in. He was late, but DeLaney was gratified he was there just the same.

The principal talked first about the revenge fight at the high school the previous week. He told what he knew, noting that it was not isolated but seemed to be one of a series of fights with students from Hackensack and Englewood. He also reviewed his plan for disciplining the students. Each would be placed immediately on academic and social probation. Their schoolwork would be reviewed each week, and they would be barred from all after-school activities, such as athletic events, for six months. And if the fighting continued, he warned, each student would be suspended for ten days.

The parents nodded. They did not seem to be objecting to what DeLaney said. Another good sign. At least he wouldn't have to convince them of the need for action. He had learned that when parents expressed disbelief at their child's behavior, it was often out of a sense of denial about the child's need for discipline and occasionally a reluctance to get involved. But when parents nodded in agreement, it was often because they faced the same problems at home and were already trying to solve them.

DeLaney moved on to the most important point of the meeting. He mentioned the name Violators. This, he saw, surprised parents.

Batron's mother was one of the first to speak. "I've never heard that word in my house before. Never."

Others nodded.

DeLaney said that he had heard the Violators had become a gang, that they had fought together.

Chuckie laughed. "Oh, wow, we're not no gang. We got the name off the radio."

Lelia Johnson was angry. She knew that if the name became well known, the Violators would be immediately linked to any trouble in town. It was, as she saw it, an invitation to trouble. She was disappointed in the boys. Days later, when they gathered at her house, she brought up the subject. "Why would you label yourselves?" she asked. "That's the worst thing you could have done." One of the boys muttered an answer, almost sheepishly: "We just thought it was something to do."

Jim DeLaney wondered what the boys sitting before him were thinking. Except for Chuckie's explanation of where the Violators got their name, few had spoken except for a brief "yes" or "no." The one thing DeLaney had learned to distrust was a student's silence. The boys were respectful, and he thought they were putting on a good show for their parents. But he did not trust them. The meeting lasted more than an hour. DeLaney shook hands with each boy as the group left. And then he thought: It's not over.

A few days later DeLaney followed up with a two-page letter to parents of each gang member, again warning that the Violators or any gang would not be tolerated at the high school. "I encourage you to work with us to be sure that the sad events of recent weeks are in the past and that the future will focus on quality education," he wrote. He went on to thank the parents and ended with a plea of sorts: "We need to work together to maintain a peaceful, positive environment in school and in the community."

DeLaney figured he could count on the parents for some sort of help. This was a cooperative group, he thought. One parent seemed especially troubled. Thelma Pannell had mentioned to him that her son had been uncontrollable in recent months. She didn't go into details, but she mentioned she had been considering taking some drastic action, perhaps even placing Phillip in a detention home for troubled youths.

DeLaney had known Thelma Pannell somewhat but not well. As he spoke to the group, he sensed she was searching for help, wondering perhaps if detention might put her son on the right track. This was no fleeting question or idle threat from her, DeLaney thought. He wondered how bad things were in that home.

What DeLaney didn't know was that the Pannells left the meeting in different directions. Thelma Pannell went home with her son to her new place in Englewood. Her husband went back to the county jail.

━━━━━

The Bergen County jail, built for 450 men and home to almost twice that many, sits low and ungainly on the banks of the Hackensack River. Here, barely a half mile south of the Teaneck border, the river bends west, then north again, and narrows. Barges with oil and gravel still make the fifteen mile trip from Newark Bay to the Hess oil tank farm and the Raia concrete factory, but it's never easy. The ocean tides muscle into this part of the river, dumping silt and choking the channel. The water is part salt, part fresh, a merging of fresh river water that drains from the Ramapo Mountains to the north and salty river water that gets its start in the Atlantic Ocean from the south.

The county's politicians put the jail at this point in the river primarily because no one wanted the marshy land for anything else. To build anything substantial on the waterlogged ground, you needed to pound pilings into the bedrock, sometimes to a depth of a hundred feet or more. And then, after you built, there were the tides to deal with. If the moon was full and the tide ran strong, the Hackensack overflowed its banks, flooding River Street in front of the jail with a foot of water. On those days the jail was even more isolated than it usually is.

Phillip David Pannell's new address was the jail, but unlike most prisoners, he was able to come and go, to merge with the outside world by day and return to the world of convicts and cellblocks and guards at night. He was in a work-release program, and the goal in his case was to allow him to continue working but to supervise him and funnel a portion of his wages to his wife and children.

Pannell entered the program on September 26, 1989. He lasted five weeks before he was in trouble. On the day after Halloween—November 1, All Saints' Day and three weeks after the meeting with Jim DeLaney at the high school—guards put Pannell in a full-time lockup and suspended him from work-release privileges for eight days. He had been returning to the jail drunk. Equally bad, he had not been turning in his paychecks.

What the guards didn't know is that Pannell didn't have a paycheck to turn in. He hadn't been working. On most days, as soon as he left the jail in the morning, he headed to a liquor store for a bottle.

———

Only a few days after the October 10 meeting with the Violators and their parents, Jim DeLaney heard more disturbing news about sophomore Phillip Clinton Pannell. The school district's attendance office had received information from the Teaneck police that Pannell was no longer living in Teaneck. DeLaney was asked to check it out.

DeLaney was no stranger to this sort of problem. With its reputation for college prep courses and its history of sending students on to top colleges, Teaneck was a magnet for children from other towns who wanted a better education, particularly black students from poor schools in New York City or Newark or Paterson. In recent years Teaneck had discovered black students taking buses from the Bronx and enrolling at the high school by using the addresses of aunts or grandmothers in Teaneck. In some cases, students like Pannell moved over the border to Englewood, yet tried to remain in Teaneck High School.

As painful as it was to order a student out of a school, it was against school regulations to allow those from other towns to attend school without paying out-of-town tuitions of more than eight thousand dollars. But in some cases the attendance office was a little too zealous and mistakes were made. This could be just a mix-up. Rather than confront the Pannells, DeLaney decided to send a letter.

On October 25, 1989, he wrote to the old address on Circle Drive-way in Teaneck, noting that "our attendance office has informed us that you no longer reside" there. DeLaney asked the Pannells for proof that they still lived in Teaneck. He told them he would like to hear from them in a week. He never got an answer.

After Halloween—only days after her husband had been taken off his work-release program—Thelma Pannell received a telephone call at the house on Reis Avenue in Englewood she now called home. It was a girlfriend's place, and she had moved there when she left Circle Driveway in Teaneck. She figured it was a temporary stopover until she found something else. But on the phone now was the Teaneck school district with something more pressing. Her son could no longer go to Teaneck High School.

On Monday, November 13, Phil Pannell left Teaneck High School for the last time. On Wednesday, November 22, the day before Thanksgiving, he was officially taken off the rolls. Batron Johnson remembered his friend's explanation. "Yo," he said, "I got kicked out."

———

On Thanksgiving Phillip's dad was granted a furlough from the county jail to visit his family. He stopped by the house on Reis Avenue, but just after 7:00 P.M. he was at Holy Name Hospital in Teaneck being treated for a gash in his head.

Pannell had left the family around 6:00 P.M. and was visiting friends in an apartment on the other side of Teaneck. He was drinking. By 6:58 P.M. three Teaneck police officers had been dispatched to the apartment after tenants complained of fighting. The cops found Phillip David Pannell bleeding from his forehead. All he would tell them was that a twenty-two-year-old woman in the apartment had picked up an ashtray and hit him in the head with it. That night, with one of the Teaneck police investigators, Wayne Blanco, taking notes, Pannell said he would not press charges against the woman. Pannell "considered it a family matter," Blanco reported.

Pannell headed back to the Bergen County jail that night to sleep. Six days later, on November 29, he was in trouble again. At 10:32 P.M. he walked up to the jail entrance used by work-release prisoners. He was six hours past his curfew. He also smelled as if he had taken a bath in a tub of beer. Pannell told guards that he had been working overtime and that he had telephoned ahead to let them know. Guards could not find any note that he had called. As for his drunkenness, Pannell told the guards, "I had a couple of beers."

The guards ordered him to take a Breathalyzer test, which measures the amount of alcohol in the body. Within a few minutes the verdict was in: Phillip Pannell was legally, as well as obviously, drunk.

TWO DAYS LATER

Her son had been out of school almost two weeks. Thelma Pannell decided it was time he went to class. It was December 1, as good a time as any for a new beginning. That morning Thelma Pannell drove Phillip to Dwight Morrow High School, the public high school in Englewood. She parked the car, walked him into the guidance office, and took a seat.

She didn't know that she and her son were being watched. Soon after Phillip opened the car door, word spread among Englewood students that he had arrived, wearing a black hooded sweatshirt and the red San Francisco 49ers parka.

He was tracked to the guidance office, and as he sat there with his mother, a steady stream of Englewood students strolled by to get a look.

That day the Englewood students began planning a welcome for Phillip Clinton Pannell. Some of them had even heard a week before that he had left Teaneck High School and might be transferring to Englewood. "Everybody was waiting," said Englewood student Livingston Douglas.

Phillip Pannell had a reputation in Englewood, but it was remarkably different from the image he fashioned in Teaneck as a fighter with heart. "He was a punk," said Englewood's Oshia Cason. "He can't fight. He was lots of talk. Some people say he has heart. He'll be tough around his friends. But get him alone, and he's not tough at all."

There was turf to consider too. "He fought us," Cason said, "and he thinks he can come to school here?"

Phillip's mother said good-bye and left for work at the embroidery factory. She had already called ahead and told her boss she would be late; he didn't object. Phillip stayed and talked to William Mack, a guidance counselor and basketball coach who took pride in his rapport with students.

Mack, also black, took a look at the young man in the chair across from his desk. Here was a suburban rapper wannabe if ever there was one, Mack thought. Pannell wore baggy jeans, slung low on his rear end. He had no shirt, just a black hoodie under a red 49ers parka. His face was etched with a look of terminal boredom.

"Why did you leave Teaneck High School?" Mack asked.

It was a standard question, one that Mack made a point of asking all new students, if for no other reason than to startle them with his directness. In this case, however, Mack got one of the oddest answers.

"I couldn't get along with the kids," Pannell said.

Mack was puzzled and made a mental note to check it out. "Most of the time they tell you lies anyway," he said. Anyway, Mack had a more pressing problem. Pannell had no transcripts of his grades or courses he had taken in Teaneck. Nor did he have his health records. Pannell could go to class without his transcripts, but not without checking whether he had all his shots. After a thirty-minute, largely one-way chat Mack sent Pannell to the nurse's office.

Pannell walked out of Mack's office and into the stark gaze of two Englewood students, Tyrone and Darryl.

"Who you looking at?" Pannell asked.

Tyrone swung at Pannell's nose. Darryl followed with a hook to Pannell's temple. Pannell staggered, then ran for the nurse's office.

A phone rang in an office on the other side of the building. Principal Richard Segall picked up the receiver. Come quickly, a voice told him. Kids are banging on the door of the nurse's office. They want to beat up a new student.

Segall ran the hundred yards of hallway to the nurse's office in less than a minute. As he arrived, Tyrone was jumping and punching the air, his face twisted in anger. "I'm going to kill him," he yelled, pointing through the windows at Pannell. "Why are you allowing him in the school? He's got no business here. I'm going to get that muthafucker."

Segall walked into the nurse's office. Before him on a cot, looking scared and hunched, sat the target of Tyrone's fist-swinging, screaming anger. Phil Pannell dabbed the blood on his nose and looked up as Segall closed the door behind him.

"What the hell kind of school you have here?" Pannell barked.

Segall paused, listened.

Pannell kept going: "The kids are out to get me. What are you going to do to protect me? I've only been here a day. The kids won't even give me a chance. What kind of school do you have here?"

Segall let Pannell go home that day. At least that's where Pannell said he was heading. After lunch, as if drawn like a homing pigeon,

Phil Pannell was outside Teaneck High School, near the black door. He sent word inside to tell Batron Johnson he wanted to speak to him.

Within minutes Batron was downstairs by a gym door. He motioned for Phillip to step inside. "What's up?" Batron asked, glad to see his friend again.

"They tried to jump me, man."

Batron could feel his fist tighten, the anger boiling up. He said nothing, and Phil kept talking. "I just had a fight. They jumped me."

Batron nodded. "So what's up?" he asked. "You want us to come down there and we can just take care of it?"

Phillip shook his head. He didn't want Batron or any of the Violators coming to Englewood. A few minutes later Batron turned and walked back inside, assuming that Phillip wanted to take care of the problem himself.

As Phillip walked away from Teaneck High School, he was spotted by an administrator, who phoned police. Five days later the Teaneck police filed charges against Pannell: trespassing on school property.

THE SAME DAY

Across the Hackensack River from Teaneck, in the county jail, Phillip's father told a jail alcoholism counselor, Charles Griffin, that his drinking had gotten out of hand and he wanted help to cure it. Griffin noted in a report that Pannell described "a past history of alcohol abuse which has caused some hardship within his family."

Griffin recommended that Pannell be allowed to go out for treatment for alcoholism.

THREE DAYS LATER

Phillip Clinton Pannell returned to Dwight Morrow High School in Englewood, but not to attend classes. Richard Segall wanted to speak with him.

The principal had asked his staff to check into Phillip Pannell's background, and what they uncovered alarmed him and called for a face-to-face discussion. Pannell was described as an "enforcer" for the Violators. Like James DeLaney, his counterpart at Teaneck High

School, Segall was shocked when he heard of the gang's name and reputation.

When Pannell walked into Segall's office, he seemed aloof and quietly cocky, certainly not the fearful teenager in the nurse's office. Segall had checked Pannell's report cards. There were some uneven grades, but Segall noticed that Pannell did not fit the profile of most troublemakers. Pannell had a few Cs and even a B or two. Potential, Segall thought.

He asked Pannell if he planned to return to class.

"How am I gonna be safe?" Pannell shot back. "How can I go to class if I'm always afraid someone is outside waiting to jump me?"

Segall figured he would try some straight talk, with a backhanded appeal to Pannell's ego. "You can't have it both ways," he said. "You can't be an enforcer with a group in Teaneck and come over here and expect that people won't care. You have to make a choice. You are in a unique position to reduce the violence. You can be a hero here."

Pannell listened. Segall thought he seemed polite, attentive. When Segall stopped, Pannell seemed to ponder the challenge. *You can be a hero here.*

"Yeah," said Pannell. "That sounds like a good idea."

Segall gazed across the table. He sensed that he wasn't connecting, that Pannell appeared to be listening but didn't really believe anything he was being told. Segall suspected the worst: The sullen young man before him had no intention of turning his life around.

Nor did Pannell have any intention of returning to class. He left that day. Richard Segall never saw him again.

CHRISTMAS

Thelma Pannell had worn out her welcome at her girlfriend's home in Englewood. She had to move. And there was the other problem of her husband being in jail and not paying child support. Finally there was the problem of what to do about her son. He wasn't in school. It had been almost two months since he had last gone to school in Teaneck.

But first there was Christmas to celebrate. A few weeks before, Thelma Pannell drove to a store in Paterson and selected her son's present: a new parka, made in South Korea by a company called Master of Down. It was knee-length, with a nylon lining, a flannel exterior, deep pockets, and a hood trimmed with brown rabbit fur. Most important was the color. Red was the color her son loved.

Thelma Pannell laid eighty dollars on the counter and walked out with the parka in a bag. This Christmas the boy she called Clinton would be happy. That much she was sure of.

FOUR

THE COP

For the last day of 1989, a Sunday, the *Bergen Record* published the usual boilerplate assortment of end-of-the-year stories. In the newspaper business New Year's Eve is a sleeper, a day when there are few major news stories and much of the paper is devoted to articles that assess the year just past and predict the one ahead. This day was special for other reasons. Not only were a new year and a new decade about to begin but it was a time of distinctive political upheaval as well. In Europe the old, rusty Iron Curtain was crumbling. In the White House President George Bush was beginning to face a daunting recession that eventually was to overwhelm him. In New Jersey Governor Tom Kean, a cherubic, widely popular Republican, well known for his progressive views on race relations and education as well as his blue-blood family tree that included several ancestors who had signed the Declaration of Independence, was about to leave office after serving his limit of two terms. About to take his place was Jim Florio, a scrappy, bare-knuckle Democratic congressman from Camden who was as different from Kean as a heavy metal rock band is from a string quartet. If Kean was soft-spoken and prone to polite debate, Florio's style was brassy and confrontational. Two months before, Florio had triumphed over his conservative Republican challenger, Congressman James Courter, by the third-highest margin in state history. Brooklyn-born, a former boxer, and a high school dropout who went on to earn his high school equivalency diploma in the Navy and other degrees from Columbia University and Rutgers Law School, Florio had distinguished himself as one of the most active members of Congress in the post-Watergate years. His specialty was the environment, and his crowning achievement after sixteen years in the House of Representatives was the superfund bill, which set aside millions to clean up toxic dumps and other hazardous waste sites. As 1989 ended, politicians throughout New Jersey hoped that Florio would kindle a renewed burst of vitality in state government that had seemed to wane during Kean's final year. For his part, Florio wasted no time. He was already working on the inaugural speech that he was to deliver in two weeks. In it he planned to lay out his vision for uniting Jersey's predominantly white suburbs with its poorer, largely black cities. The new governor also had spent much of December assembling his cabinet. Of all the political insiders, policy wonks, and lawyers Florio had managed to attract, one man stood out: Robert Del Tufo, the new state attorney general.

Del Tufo had a considerable reputation for independence and political savvy from his days as the U.S. attorney in New Jersey and one of the chief prosecutors in the Abscam investigation into political fraud. Florio was proud of luring Del Tufo back to government. For attorney general, Florio wanted someone with experience and sound judgment. With his Yale law degree and years as a political confidant to New Jersey's Democrats, Del Tufo seemed the man.

On the last day of the year, though, such weighty issues were not even mentioned in the newspaper. The *Record*'s front page was a mix of stories about flaws in college entrance exams, an obscure legal skirmish over a stained glass window at a local church, and the establishment of a day care center for AIDS patients. Atop page 3 was a story about the weather. At the bottom, for those whose thoughts might be fixed on champagne and party hats, were two hundred words of advice under the headline DRINKING TONIGHT? CALL A CAB.

Teaneck was mentioned once that day in the *Record*. In the community news section the letters to the editor contained a glowing tribute to several Teaneck police officers, including one of the youngest, Gary Spath.

Spath had turned twenty-nine six weeks before and been a cop for only six and a half years. But he had earned eight commendations for competence and bravery, including the award the previous September for tackling the man with the gun. As important, Spath was earning a

reputation as one of the department's more sensitive officers, one unafraid to go beyond the standard rules of the job and offer advice,
consolation, or friendship. It was a characteristic not required of police
officers, but such a quality was not lost on Teaneck's police brass.
Captain Donald Giannone remembers Spath as the sort of cop who
readily dug into his pocket for spare change to help a homeless man
pay for a bus ride.

That day in the *Record* the headline on the 165-word letter to the
editor told much about Spath and the reputation he had built among
his admirers: TEANECK POLICE OFFICERS AGAIN DEMONSTRATE SKILL,
COMPASSION. Significant, too, was the letter's author, Paul Steven Ostrow. Like Spath, Ostrow was a child of Teaneck, raised in the town
in the years after integration had been embraced as an ideal. He was
proud of his roots and had stayed close to them. He had gone to
college in town, at the Teaneck campus of Fairleigh Dickinson University, and married a woman who had grown up in Teaneck. Paul's
wife, Ricki, had graduated from Teaneck High School with Spath's
older sister. When the Ostrows married and began their search for a
place to raise a family, it had been only natural for them to turn to
Teaneck and a home within walking distance of the public high school,
the library, and their synagogue. "It was," Paul often said, "a place
where I feel comfortable."

Ostrow was not a police officer; his skill was the most basic in business: sales. After several years of trading jewelry in Manhattan, Ostrow
had taken a job selling office supplies on the Jersey side of the Hudson. In only a few years he had become one of the most adept at
his company in finding new clients in the rigorously competitive
malls, main streets, and back roads of suburbia. But Ostrow's real
love was not selling pens and paper clips. It was Teaneck. And if
anybody could qualify as the town's unofficial salesman, it was Paul
Steven Ostrow.

To enter into a conversation with him was to take a journey into
the current state of affairs in the town he cherished, usually with an
accent on the passionately positive. In his view, Teaneck was special
because of its racial and ethnic diversity, because of the classic brick
and wood designs of its houses, because of its friendly people, and
because of its multitude of services. There was little to worry about,
he would tell you. He sang the praises of the library, the swimming
pool, the parks, the recreation leagues, the public schools, even the
shops. Paul Ostrow loved it all, and each time he took a stroll down

Cedar Lane with its array of delicatessens, drugstores, and gift shops, he drank in the variety like a man who had been shipwrecked for years on a desert island and suddenly had been transported back to modern suburban America and into one of its model towns.

If it was ice cream you wanted, Ostrow would point you to Bischoff's. There may have been better places in northern New Jersey to find a hot fudge sundae or a sugar cone, but not to Ostrow. Even the duke of Windsor placed orders for Bischoff's hand-packed rum raisin when he was staying in New York City. Want to go to a movie? Ostrow would stridently tell you to stay away from the multiplex joints on the highways or at the malls. Go to the Cedar Lane Cinema, he insisted. "Great popcorn." Want to play volleyball? Ostrow would practically order you to join the local swim club, where he presided over weekend volleyball games the way Ed Sullivan presided over his variety show. Want to read a best-seller? Ostrow knew where to find it at the library. And if the book was out, he might even call the library himself to put it on reserve for you.

Ostrow made a point of attending as many concerts in town as he could. On Saturdays and Sundays he tried to drive by Votee Park to take in a Little League or soccer game. And if he needed something, he looked for it in town. From wine to a computer, Paul Ostrow was able to find it all in Teaneck. It was important, he said, "to patronize local businesses."

If Ostrow had one priority in his municipal passion, however, it was the Teaneck volunteer ambulance corps. He had joined the corps when he was in high school in the 1960s in part because he harbored dreams of becoming a doctor. His dream took a detour, but not his love for ambulances, and he learned to drive a rig and administer basic first aid. Indeed, the ambulance corps combined much of what Paul Ostrow was about: a love for his town and a burning desire to give something back. By 1989 he had risen to become the corps president.

Ostrow kept a police radio by his bed to monitor nighttime calls. On his belt during his daytime rounds selling office supplies, he wore a portable radio in case someone needed an ambulance and he could take time away from his job to respond. On the floor of his car he kept a portable emergency flashing light that he could place on the dashboard as he sped to a call.

It was on one of these emergency calls a few weeks before New Year's Eve that Ostrow linked up with Gary Spath. A sixty-year-old woman had collapsed. The woman's husband, a psychiatrist, had come home late in the afternoon and found his wife's body in the den, her lunch half eaten on a nearby table and the television on. He phoned the police, who in turn put out a call for an ambulance.

Spath was the first officer on the scene, and after checking the woman's pulse and other vital signs, he realized there was nothing he could do. The woman seemed to have collapsed hours earlier, probably while watching a midday soap opera and munching on a sandwich. On Spath's heels was Ostrow with an ambulance rig and a squad of paramedics who swarmed around the woman. They tried to revive her, but were not having any luck.

As the paramedics worked, Spath turned to the woman's husband and took him into another room. Ostrow looked up and noticed Spath with his hand on the man's shoulder. As a sergeant arrived, Spath momentarily stepped aside to discuss who would call for the medical examiner to perform an autopsy, then turned his attention to the husband again. Spath gently explained that because the man's wife had died unexpectedly, an autopsy would have to be performed. Then Spath had a question: Could he call any relatives for the man?

Ostrow noticed Spath's voice. It was soft, not at all the matter-of-fact Joe Friday–cop style that so many hard-boiled officers adopted. There was none of the stiff by-the-book legal terminology. Spath helped the man to a chair in another room so he wouldn't have to watch the paramedics work on his wife, then asked if he could make him a drink.

After twenty minutes the ambulance workers placed the woman's body on a stretcher. They were about to walk out to the ambulance and head to the emergency room at Holy Name Hospital when the husband uttered a request: Could he have his wife's wedding ring? Spath nodded, then left the room with Ostrow. Spath fetched a bar of soap to rub on the woman's left ring finger, removed the wedding band, and brought it to the man. A few minutes later the ambulance workers carried the woman's body out, and Spath's sergeant left. Spath stayed behind so the man wouldn't be alone.

In his years with the ambulance corps Ostrow had seen many cops go to great lengths to help people who had just lost family members. But something about Spath was different, Ostrow remembered. It was almost as if Spath had stepped out of his police uniform into the role of a counselor.

For Ostrow, it had been quite a day. Earlier he had found himself at the side of another Teaneck police officer who revived a sixty-two-year-old man who had a heart attack. But Spath's soft touch was especially exemplary. When Ostrow sat down later that evening to write a letter to the editor of the *Record* about the police, he lavished praise on him. Spath, he wrote, was "not only extremely professional" but "unusually caring and compassionate" in an emergency. "Once again," Ostrow concluded, "we have witnessed in these situations examples of why our corps and our community are proud of our emergency services personnel."

Gary Spath was the sort of police officer that Paul Ostrow valued as one of Teaneck's hidden assets. To Ostrow, Spath was friendly, smiling, a seemingly lighthearted guy who always had a quick joke. When Spath drove by and stopped his police cruiser, he invariably greeted Paul Ostrow with the Hebrew word for peace, *shalom.* But just as important to Ostrow, Spath knew Teaneck and appreciated it. His roots were planted firmly there. In Gary Spath, Paul Ostrow saw the best of Teaneck.

━━━━━

Gary Guertin Spath came into the world on the cusp of social and political change that was about to sweep America as the Eisenhower years gave way to the sixties. He was born on Sunday, November 17, 1960, almost two weeks after John Fitzgerald Kennedy slipped past Richard Nixon to become America's thirty-fifth President. He was the youngest of four children, two girls and two boys, all raised by a mother and father who had both grown up in Teaneck and now lived in a two-story house with a dalmatian named Lady, a garage full of bats, balls, and bicycles, and a schedule that revolved around school and sports.

Gary's father, George, had served with the Marines as a boot camp drill instructor but had returned to Teaneck in 1956 and signed on with the township's police force. He never left his Marine roots far behind, however. When George Spath put on a suit jacket, he often wore on his lapel a small pin of the Marine globe-and-anchor insignia. As he rose through the police department and became a detective in the juvenile bureau, Spath was known as a cop who was tough but fair. He pulled no punches, played no games. Yet for all his by-the-book style, he also was known for reaching out to parents in an attempt to steer a wayward son or daughter onto a straight path. You could count on Detective George Spath, even when dealing with teenagers, to show up in a pressed shirt, a suit or sport jacket and slacks, and a subdued tie. To some in town, he was not just Teaneck's best-known juvenile detective but its best-dressed cop as well. With Detective

Spath, nothing seemed out of place, including ambition. The town's manager, Werner Schmid, found him to be that rare breed of officer who was absolutely content with the job he had. "George never wanted to be chief," said Schmid. "He wanted to be the juvenile officer." When Spath's youngest son came to his father and mentioned that he wanted to join the force, George Spath had this advice: "Gary, if you want to be a police officer, make sure you want it from the heart."

Gary's mother, Elaine, later referred to her son as an "all-American boy." As much as such a statement was grounded in a mother's unabashed love for her son, in many ways it was not an exaggeration. Elaine Andreana Spath had found Teaneck to be a quintessential all-American town. She was graduated from Teaneck High School in 1950, a year after the U.S. Army had dubbed the town a model American community and produced a photo exhibit about town life for postwar Japan and Europe. Years later, at her thirty-fifth high school reunion at Teaneck's Inwood Manor Restaurant, she wrote in the program, "We were blessed to have had our youth in that place, at that time. So much so that I'm still here." She was a teacher's aide in special education classes, working with some of the same black kids who later joined the Violators.

The Spath family home, a Dutch colonial, was nestled in a neighborhood whose street names evoked a sense of traditional roots that harkened back to the days when Elaine Andreana, whose yearbook dubbed her "Personality," met George Spath. If *Father Knows Best* or any of the other family-oriented television shows that were popular during the fifties and sixties needed a model area they should have come to the Spaths'. They lived on Trafalgar Street, named after the cape on the southwest coast of Spain where Lord Nelson's British warships shattered Napoleon's French fleet in 1805. A block away was Sussex Road. Down the street was Wellington Gate. It was a place of wide lawns, tall oaks, thick hedges, and people whose names often had a title, as in doctor, professor, lawyer, or, in a few cases, chairman of the board. By the 1980s it was not uncommon for houses there to sell for three hundred thousand dollars and more, primarily because the formerly WASP enclave had become one of the most sought-after neighborhoods for Teaneck's growing population of Orthodox Jews.

With its sweeping roof and manicured shrubs, the Spath house was much like the neighborhood around it: well kept, tasteful, a quiet blend of suburban class. It had one feature, however, that no other house nearby could boast: On the front lawn, proud and tall, stood a flagpole.

The flagpole was a silent but stout testimony to what the neighborhood had become by 1990: an embodiment of the American dream and one of Teaneck's brightest examples of achievement and stability. In the ten blocks surrounding Spath's boyhood home, an area of some 328 families, unemployment in 1990 was only 1.7 percent. But as low as that figure was, a census statistic underscored the economic stability of the neighborhood: Not one man who was eligible for a job was out of work. Family income averaged almost $130,000, and 75 percent of the children went to private schools. Three of every four adults had gone to college. Thirty-four percent of those had gone on to graduate school. Marriages and families were as solid as the brick houses that lined the streets; only 6 percent of the children were being raised by single parents.

The most striking characteristic of the area, however, was skin color. Spath's home was located in the middle of Teaneck's northwest area, where only 6 percent of the residents were black. His immediate neighborhood was even whiter. Of the 992 people who lived in the ten surrounding blocks, only 43, or about 3.9 percent, were black.

These blacks were from eleven families. And if you needed a barometer of black success in the suburbs, it was here. They included doctors, lawyers, and investment bankers. But if anything (besides the color of their skin) caused them to stand apart from their white counterparts, it was the stability of their families. These black families were even more intact than the white families that lived around them. Every black family in Spath's area was headed by a mother and a father. Not a single black child was being raised by a single parent. What's more, every black adult had a college degree, and none was among the 3 percent of the residents in the area receiving some form of welfare. In Gary Spath's neighborhood welfare was as rare as an unkempt lawn, but when it *was* doled out, the recipients were usually white, not black.

To find the most severe cases of hardship among black families, you needed to walk east from Spath's neighborhood, down the hill and across the railroad tracks, across Votee Park, over the old ridge that had once divided Indian clans, and into a neighborhood around Mackel Park and a street called Circle Driveway, the neighborhood where Phillip Clinton Pannell grew up.

By 1990 this had become the section of Teaneck where the poorest, least stable black families lived. It was not a neighborhood mired in poverty. Far from it. The average house sold for $167,000, and the average family earned $49,019—both measures of economic viability that might be cause for rejoicing in other American towns. But in

Teaneck such statistics hid problems. House prices in Pannell's neighborhood were almost $60,000 less than in white areas; average family incomes were almost $100,000 less. Even those differences did not reveal the trouble that had emerged. Though Teaneck's northeast side was home to hundreds of black families that were solidly middleclass—as the statistics on house prices and family incomes showed—it also held increasing numbers of black families that were struggling. If you wanted to find clusters of poverty, the ten blocks surrounding the Pannell house was a place to look. In all Teaneck, only 153 families had incomes below the poverty level of $20,000, but almost 40 percent of those families lived in Pannell's neighborhood. Here 15 percent of the children were being raised in poverty, and 11 percent of the men were unemployed. Only 6 percent of the children here attended private schools.

The single most telling characteristic of Phillip Pannell's neighborhood was again skin color. Much like Spath's neighborhood, here you could find the most obvious evidence of how Teaneck was integrated but divided: Blacks and whites shared the same town zip code, but many lived in neighborhoods that were segregated. Of the 1,696 persons who lived in the ten blocks surrounding Pannell's home, only 9 percent were white, and most of them were either elderly or Hispanic. Of the 152 whites who lived in that area, only 33 were children.

More telling, however, were the fissures that ran through families. In Pannell's neighborhood was the stark evidence of how black family life, even in the suburbs, was following the national trend toward turmoil and discord, with children raised by single parents or other relatives. Of all the single mothers in Teaneck with kids under five years old, 40 percent lived in Pannell's neighborhood. Overall almost 20 percent of the children in that area were being raised by single parents. In addition, the area housed a rising number of children being raised by other relatives because their parents were in jail, on drugs, or on the run. By 1990 the number of children in Pannell's area with no parents on the scene had reached 33 percent. Add in the number of kids raised by single parents, and you had a perfect equation for social turmoil. More than half the children in Phillip Pannell's neighborhood lived in broken homes.

Including Phillip Pannell.

———

Gary Spath crossed Teaneck's racial tracks one summer. Spath loved baseball. But like much in Teaneck, baseball was framed by lines of color and ethnicity. In the mid-1970s, when Spath was a teenager and Teaneck's journey with integration was more than a decade old, the town had three youth baseball leagues. On the western side of town the Western League attracted mostly Orthodox Jewish players. As a result, the league did not schedule games on Saturdays, the Jewish Sabbath. In the southern end of town, a mostly white, working-class enclave, Teaneck's Southern League was regarded in the 1960s and early 1970s as the domain of white players. Black players were all too rare, compared with their numbers in the town. If black youths played baseball, they usually joined the Teaneck Baseball Organization, the baseball league formed by black and white residents who were angry in part that the Southern League did not seem to welcome blacks.

It was in this new league that Gary Spath found a team to play for, a Babe Ruth squad for teenagers. He was one of only two white players, and his coach that summer was a man who had played a role in helping to form the new league, Fred Greene.

Greene had a unique history. He was Teaneck's first black police officer, hired in 1962. By the mid-1970s he had a reputation for working with Teaneck's black youths and others who seemed disenfranchised by the cultural changes that swept America in the late 1960s, even forming a special squad of cops outside the more formal confines of the department's juvenile squad. Greene and the other cops on the so-called special squad dressed in jeans and T-shirts and spent their days hanging out in pizza joints and parks, trying to forge lines of communication between cops and kids. On his own time Greene even set up a special program called Pieces of Africa, which encouraged black teenagers to examine their history and roots.

But if Fred Greene was known for anything, it was for a habit he developed that amazed and occasionally angered his fellow officers. He rarely carried a gun. "Makes for all sorts of problems," Greene said later. "Anyway, I find I don't need it. I can handle most situations by defusing the anger."

Greene grew up in Teaneck, on a street that bordered the old Argonne Park buffer zone. His home was on the Englewood side of the park, the last Teaneck street before the Englewood border. Here the high, arching trees were so plentiful and thick that they seemed to hover over the neighborhood of wood-frame homes like a leafy cocoon, separating it from the rest of Teaneck. But no buffer of trees could stop Greene from trying to join Teaneck life. His classmates nicknamed him Night Rain and predicted in his yearbook that he was "sure to become a great mechanical engineer." Greene's love was sports, though. In high school he played football, the center on an otherwise all-white team and one of only two black students at Teaneck High School. "I never had a black person in any class," Greene said. Thirty years later he still got angry when he recalled how a quarterback made jokes about his "nigger's butt" as Greene hiked the ball through his legs.

As the only black police officer in the early 1960s in the midst of the town's struggle with school desegregation, Greene learned how to walk the fine line between loyalty to his job and his fellow officers and his ideals. He also knew the price of speaking out, which he did occasionally to voice his concerns about the lack of recreation and other opportunities for black youths. One night, when he returned home from his shift at the police station, he found that every shrub he had recently planted in his front yard had been pulled out. Greene never found out who did it.

The experience taught him much about Teaneck. Despite the town's progressive leanings, it was still home to some who resented outspoken blacks, even on subjects as seemingly benign as recreation. The experience also taught Greene how painful it could be to cross the boundary from one world to another.

For this reason, Fred Greene came to admire his sixteen-year-old baseball player named Gary Spath, who wanted to play baseball so badly that he was willing to buck the trend in the town even in the 1970s and join an all-black team. Spath was not the star of the team. Far from it. But he was quick, with good hands. Greene noted one other thing: If Spath had any problems playing with an all-black team, he certainly never showed it. The boy from the white side of town fitted in easily with the black players. "He played as hard as anybody and never mentioned he was a white guy," Greene said. "I loved him. He was like a son to me."

That summer Spath divided his time between the baseball field and the classroom. If his talent was sports, his difficulty was academics. After nine years in Teaneck's public schools, Spath's parents enrolled him at the all-male Bergen Catholic High School in 1976, one of the most academically rigorous parochial schools in Bergen County. By the following spring, the end of his sophomore year, Spath had flunked biology and Spanish and ranked 263d in a class of 265. On his report card he did not have any final grades higher than 73.

It was the beginning of a pattern of academic ups and downs that was to follow him. His junior year Spath didn't fail any courses, but his 67 average was barely above passing. His class rank wasn't much better either. Spath's class had shrunk, due in part to some students flunking out. Still, he was ranked at the bottom: 251 out of 252 classmates. In his final year, with the pressure of graduation and college looming, Spath's grades improved. During his first semester of his senior year Spath recorded a 78 average. By the end of the second semester his grades had inched into the eighties.

At Bergen Catholic, Spath played varsity soccer and varsity baseball, as well as intramural football, basketball, volleyball, and street hockey. Outside sports, his most notable achievement was being chosen the school's delegate to the American Legion–sponsored Boys State conference. In his yearbook he listed his interests as waterskiing, sailing, and the shore. As for after-school predictions, the yearbook listed two: "Gary plans to enter the business field and live a long life."

His path to adulthood quickly took a rocky turn. In the fall of 1979 Spath's parents sent him to Springfield College, a small school in western Massachusetts known mostly for training gym teachers. Over the next ten months Spath enrolled in sixteen courses. He flunked five, was given Ds in four others, recorded two "incompletes," and withdrew outright from two more (tackle football and water stunts and diving). His only above-average grade—a B+—came in racquetball. His next highest grade—a C+—came in American art of the twentieth century. By the following June he was back in Teaneck, officially listed in the Springfield College records as "withdrawn." He never went back.

How Gary Spath decided to became a police officer is a combination of pragmatism, family ties, and Teaneck roots, say friends and family. In the months after college he worked a variety of jobs, from waiting tables in restaurants to helping his brother as a cruise director on ocean liners. He liked the idea of working on cruise ships so much that he briefly considered going into it as a career. But by 1982 he was engaged to a Teaneck resident, Nancy Campbell, a dental technician whose relatives owned a popular Teaneck bar, the Wigwam, where police and nurses from Holy Name Hospital often gathered for beers after work. Not long after Spath had joined the Teaneck Police Department, Spath carpooled home one evening with one of his sergeants, Robert Adomilli.

Adomilli liked Spath, especially the young cop's sense of humor. This was no shy rookie, Adomilli thought. As they drove home, he turned to Spath to ask, "Hey, Gary, how come you became a police officer?"

Adomilli, a juvenile officer who knew Spath's father, figured the son wanted to follow in his father's footsteps. But Spath said it wasn't that his father had lured him into police work as much as his own need for stability.

"I'll tell you," Spath told Adomilli. "I could have been a cruise director or I could have taken this. But, Bob, to tell you the truth, I'm getting married, and the job of a cruise director is for a single guy. It's not the job for a married guy. Since I was getting married, this is the job I decided on. I like it. It's a great job."

To become a Teaneck police officer in 1982, you needed to meet two requirements: You had to pass a civil service exam and you had to live in the town. Spath met both. In March he was appointed to the force; two weeks later, on April 5, 1982, he was sent to the police academy for three months of training. That day Teaneck appointed another resident to its police force, Wayne Blanco. Eight years older than Spath, Blanco did not know Spath before heading to the academy, but three months later the two officers stood together at graduation. Spath ranked thirtieth and Blanco thirty-first in a class of forty police recruits from towns in northern New Jersey. Years later Spath cited as one of his memories of the academy the day that an instructor took a piece of chalk and wrote a phone number on a blackboard and advised the new recruits that if they were ever in trouble, they should dial it. It was the phone number of a lawyer who had built a reputation for getting cops out of trouble. Spath didn't know the lawyer's name at the time, but he jotted down the phone number in a notebook—Robert Galantucci. It was eight years before Gary Spath had to make that call.

Gary Spath never had much of a chance to work side by side with his father. A few months after he completed his studies at the police academy and was sworn in as a probationary officer, George Spath retired. He had served twenty-six years with the Teaneck Police Department, nineteen of them as a juvenile officer.

In 1982 rookies spent an entire year as probationary officers, working with veterans on such things as how to handle accident calls, how to use the radio, and what shortcuts to take across town in emergencies. It was a time to learn the ropes and settle into the routine of police work. Spath's personal life, meanwhile, also was settling down. Eleven months after he had graduated from the police academy, Spath and Nancy Campbell married. It was no ordinary affair. The story made the *Bergen Record*.

Gary and Nancy had reserved St. Anastasia's Catholic Church for a May 28, 1983, nuptial mass and the Knights of Columbus hall in nearby Dumont for a reception. Three days before the wedding Nancy wound up in Holy Name Hospital with the double whammy of mononucleosis and hepatitis. Rather than cancel, Gary and Nancy went ahead with the ceremony. Instead of going to the church, Nancy donned her floor-length white satin wedding dress and took the elevator from her hospital bed to the hospital chapel for a small ceremony with two dozen friends, relatives, and nurses, then returned to her hospital bed.

A month later Spath completed his one-year probation as a police officer and was formally named to the force. Six weeks after that he earned his first commendation.

The incident did not require extraordinary bravery. If anything, it was routine. Nonetheless it demonstrated the sort of diligence that Spath's friends later said was a centerpiece of his daily police work.

Spath was on patrol near the Englewood border when a car with a black man at the wheel passed by. Spath thought the man looked suspicious and radioed headquarters with the numbers on the license plate. The desk officer punched the numbers into the computerized listing of outstanding warrants and bulletins. The car was listed as stolen. Spath called for help, then made the arrest. In his commendation letter two weeks later, Chief Bryan Burke noted that Spath's "dedication and professionalism prove you to be a credit to the department and the community at large."

Over the next seven years there were seven other commendations and citations from the department or the police union, not to mention a stack of letters from private citizens praising Spath's police work. For stopping a car with stolen plates in March 1984, Spath was cited for his "keen sense of observation and quick response." After calling an ambulance and a fire truck in October 1984 to rescue a woman whose car had skidded on leaves and crashed, Spath received a letter from the woman's husband praising his "excellent training and the manner" in which he had taken care of the injured wife. For tailing a suspicious car and then helping cops from the neighboring town of Bogota catch two armed robbery suspects in October 1986, he was singled out for his "extraordinary degree of professional initiative and streetwise patrol." For helping another officer in March 1987 rescue a man who tried to commit suicide by sitting in a garage with his car engine running, Spath was cited for his "rapid response and professional treatment." For comforting three young black women on a Teaneck street corner in November 1987 and then helping catch the four black men who had driven off with their purses, Teaneck's chief commended Spath for "a job well done."

The accumulation of citations and letters did not go unnoticed in the northern New Jersey police community. On March 30, 1988, Spath was nominated for the New Jersey Honor Legion, a fraternity of police officers who had demonstrated an extensive record of bravery and good service. Later that year Gary Spath had another first in his career as a cop: His picture made the newspapers. It was only a small item, a three-by-four-inch photograph in the weekly *Suburbanite*. Spath wore a satin baseball jacket and a cabbie's hat, and his name was misspelled as "Spaeth," but the photo said much about the kind of reputation Spath was building in the department. It showed Spath with three other Teaneck officers volunteering to pass out free Christmas turkeys to needy residents, in this case a black woman. The woman had a wide smile as she grasped the turkey in her arms. So did Gary Spath.

Spath's supervisor on the midnight shift during this time was his old baseball coach, Fred Greene, who had been promoted to lieutenant and worked a desk job at police headquarters. Unlike some of the other sergeants and lieutenants, Greene fancied himself as part cop, part counselor. It was an attitude he had kept from his days on the special youth squad. Greene let it be known that he welcomed officers who wanted to stop by his tiny, cluttered office just off the main radio room and chat about problems in their personal lives or on their jobs. With his meaty hands and a voice that was barely audible at times, Greene hardly portrayed the image of a tough cop. He could be tough when he wanted to—his stint on the county narcotics squad was proof of that—but his style was soft-touch, fatherly. Spath knocked on his door on more than one occasion with a common complaint.

If Teaneck cops were bothered in the 1980s, it usually wasn't about crime or the dangers they faced. The primary topic of conversation in Teaneck's police headquarters was police rules. Cops called it the quota system.

Each officer who patrolled the streets had to write at least two traffic tickets a day. For those on the daytime shifts, when Teaneck's streets were clogged with drivers, writing two tickets a day might not be much of a problem. But on the midnight shift, when traffic dwindled to almost nothing, forcing cops to meet a ticket quota was akin to forcing a beachfront shop to sell the same amount of suntan lotion in the winter as in the summer. For those officers who did not write the minimum amount of tickets, there were reprimands from the chief as well as punishments that included the docking of overtime pay. The quota system forced patrol officers to face this sad fact of life: If they needed to write a quick ticket, the best place to find a car with a broken taillight, a malfunctioning muffler, or an expired inspection sticker was in Teaneck's poor neighborhoods. And those neighborhoods were mostly black.

"All the cops knew this," said one officer. "When we wrote tickets, many of us just went to the black side of town." And in time some black residents came to feel singled out for harassment from police stopping them for what seemed to be no reason at all except to find something wrong. Some black residents even had a term for these road checks: "DWB"—driving while black.

Black residents weren't the only critics of the quota system. In a study of the Teaneck Police Department in 1984 the National Conference of Christians and Jews described the ticket quota system as "demeaning" and "counterproductive" for police officers and the community. As for Chief Bryan Burke, who promoted the system as a way of improving police productivity, the conference delivered a one-word assessment that spoke volumes about the rift he created in his department and, in later years, in the community as well: "inaccessible."

It was left to officers like Fred Greene to be accessible. Greene remembers Spath tapping on the door on more than one occasion after his shift and asking to talk for a few minutes. In those conversations Greene saw how his former baseball player had grown. To Greene, here was a young cop who understood that his job involved much more than carrying a badge and a gun, that it was a social contract with the community. Spath wondered why ticket quotas had been imposed and how officers could form a bond with a community while they were trapped in a bureaucratic vise whose purpose was not so much to protect as to search out those residents who had violated the smallest of traffic laws. Greene also sensed that ticket quotas alone were not the source of all that troubled the young officer. There were sides to Gary Spath that Greene could not see or touch. "There were many nights when Gary would come down and sit and talk after his shift was over," Greene said. "It was the pressures he felt. Sometimes he would cry, and I would just want to hug him."

Luis Torres also caught glimpses of a troubled side of Gary Spath.

By 1989 he believed he knew the source of the trouble. It was the gun that Spath carried.

Torres, who had arrived in Teaneck on something of a lark, had become the town's first Hispanic police officer. Born in Puerto Rico and raised in Spanish Harlem, Torres and his wife, Alma, had grown tired of cramped city apartments and a lifestyle hemmed in by the fear of drugs and crime. One summer Sunday in 1977 they drove into the Jersey suburbs for a look at what they had been told was the good life. They crossed the George Washington Bridge and pointed their car west on Route 4, weaving through the traffic and admiring the landscape. After several miles Torres eased the car off the highway and onto a shady street. A sign told them they were in Teaneck.

Luis and Alma Torres had never heard of Teaneck, but they stopped anyway at the first real estate office they saw and asked to look at a house. In some ways the stop was a test. They wanted to see how two Hispanics would be welcomed in what they assumed was another typical white suburb. That day a real estate agent showed them a two-story colonial on Teaneck's south end; Luis and Alma Torres liked it so much they asked to buy it. As they sat in the real estate office an hour later drawing up the papers, Torres gingerly asked the sales agent if the town welcomed Hispanics.

"Haven't you heard of Teaneck?" the agent responded. "We welcome everyone here."

Torres had been working as a security guard for Macy's in Manhattan but was gradually feeling bored. He had served in the Navy and believed he had many more talents than that required to check whether the teenage girls in the changing rooms were stealing prom dresses or the shoppers with the large bags were trying to slip in an extra pair of shoes. A year after they had moved into Teaneck, Alma Torres suggested he take the civil service test and apply for a job at the Teaneck Police Department. A year after that Luis Torres was in a police uniform.

He was lonely the first few years. Most of the other cops were white men who had grown up in Teaneck and spent many a Saturday night chugging Budweiser beers at the local Moose Lodge. A Puerto Rican American who had grown up in Harlem didn't exactly fit in. Another thing he noticed: No cop ever invited him or his wife to his home to socialize.

But then Luis Torres met Gary Spath. He was different. He hadn't become hardened by the job to the point where he was just going through the motions. Torres found a colleague who approached work with a sense of morality, wanting to leave the streets he patrolled a better place. One more thing: Gary Spath had no problem inviting a Hispanic family to his home.

The two fitted well. As a kid Torres had searched the Harlem libraries for novels by Truman Capote and others who were popular in the 1960s. He didn't just want to grow up knowing his Latino culture; he wanted to experience as many other cultures as he could. In Spath he found something of a conversational soul mate. The two worked the midnight shift, and in those quiet hours after the bars had closed and before the sun rose a few hours later, Torres and Spath would each grab a cup of coffee and park their patrol cars next to each other in the dark of Votee Park or another isolated spot and discuss everything from God to cops.

"I liked that he was genuine," Torres said later. "He was down-to-earth. There were no put-ons. I could be natural. You could talk to him about anything. And he was fun. The guy always seemed to be in a good mood. Always lively. I very rarely saw him down, depressed, or anything."

On their days off Spath and Torres occasionally went fishing. Sometimes they helped each other with remodeling on their houses and carpooling to a local hardware store. But as much as Torres had found a kindred spirit in Spath, he also discovered that one subject seemed off limits: the question of when a cop should draw his gun. Torres somehow knew that guns bothered Spath. He heard the nervous, anguished tone in his young friend's voice, especially the way it trailed off when Torres tried to broach the subject. To Torres, a police pistol was the ultimate form of street power. By 1989 he had pulled his gun two times during his career, but he had never come close to firing it and had felt bad afterward that he'd had to reach for it. He knew that once cops drew their guns, they set in motion a series of events that sometimes were hard to stop. "Out there you can take a life," Torres said.

But Torres never felt he could talk about this to his friend. He feared insulting Spath, feared treading on his pride, feared that Spath might stop talking to him. "It was one of those subjects like sex," Torres said. "If you talk to him about it, you just find he would skirt the issue, and so you avoid it and go on and talk about something else."

One day, Torres promised himself, he would break the silence with his friend and have that conversation about guns and the subject police officers called deadly force.

As the winter of 1990 spilled into spring, Gary Spath sat down with Bart Aslin, a Catholic priest who had become a close friend. Red-haired, muscular, and the owner of a pickup truck, Aslin hardly fitted the image of a sedate suburban priest. In his office hung a poster of Irish poets. On his office floor most days you could find a basketball rolling around. Before he was ordained, Aslin had been a firefighter in Linden, a lunch-pail, shot-and-beer city just south of Newark that was home to such highways as U.S. Route 1 and the New Jersey Turnpike as well as for the world's largest oil refinery and more than two hundred oil tanks that punctuated the low marshlandlike giant steel tree stumps. After graduating from the seminary and being ordained a dea-con as the first step toward priesthood, Aslin was assigned to a parish in a town that adjoined Teaneck where Spath had moved with his wife.

Spath and Aslin found they had much in common. Both liked to go fishing. Both were approaching their thirties. Both loved sports. And both enjoyed poking fun at each other. Aslin chided Spath that cops hung out too much in doughnut shops; Spath came right back with jokes about firefighters spending most of their days sleeping in a fire-house. If Spath seemed quiet about anything at first, it was his spiritual life; he initially struck Aslin as the sort of Catholic who was polite but not overly revealing of his religious side. Nonetheless Aslin sensed Spath wanted to grow spiritually, that being a Catholic was more than going to mass on Sunday and tossing a few dollars into the collection basket. The day Aslin was leaving for another parish, Spath had plans to go to a New York Giants football game. First he stopped by the church to say good-bye. Aslin took it as a sign that Spath wanted to stay in touch, and they did. Aslin was impressed. It was rare for a young man to confide in a priest, rarer still for him to invite a priest to dinner.

But Spath did just that. One evening in February 1990, when Aslin dropped by Spath's home for dinner, the two friends found themselves alone for a few minutes. Nancy Spath was upstairs putting their chil-dren to bed, and Spath sat down with Aslin in the living room.

Spath mentioned he was having some doubts about his career as a cop. It wasn't the Teaneck department as much as the nature of the job and the attitudes of some colleagues, said Aslin in recalling the conversation. The ideals of young recruits to help people and solve big social problems, Spath said, become dissipated by the day-to-day or-deal of patrolling streets and then fighting a system of bureaucratic rules that required a cop to worry about whether he had creased his pants correctly or if he had filled out every blank space on an accident report. "He saw people become hardened with the job," Aslin recalled. "They entered with good intentions, but sooner or later it just becomes a job to you."

Spath told Aslin he didn't want that for himself. If he could, Spath said he might even leave Teaneck's police force.

Aslin asked what he would do.

Spath mentioned transferring to a department in a smaller town in one of the more sedate communities in northern Bergen County where police work was less demanding and left more time to build relationships with people in the community. His real love, Spath said, was working with kids. He enjoyed his stints as a volunteer coach in the church basketball leagues. If he could, he would love to teach gym and to coach full-time.

Aslin noticed how Spath brightened and became animated whenever he talked about working with kids. Police work, on the other hand, was solitary and confrontational. Despite what you hear about police camaraderie, much of the job is lonely: one cop, in one car, chasing one call at a time and never establishing much of a connection with people. To make it worse, the streets were getting more dangerous. There were more fights, more confrontations. Police work in the suburbs was no longer a comfortable ride to a pension.

Aslin agreed. His two brothers were cops; he knew what Spath was talking about. But as the priest listened, he sensed Spath was bothered by more than just ordinary job hassles and stymied ideals. When Spath talked about the new dangers, Aslin mentioned a cop who'd had to fire his gun in the line of duty and was never the same afterward. He had started drinking and was eventually arrested for drunk driving.

Spath seemed to listen intently as Aslin told the story. When the priest finished, Spath spoke of his own worries. "My biggest fear," he said, "is that someday I'll have to shoot somebody. I don't know if I could handle that."

FIVE

"THIS TOWN IS A POWDER KEG"

On an otherwise nondescript Thursday in January, three weeks into 1990, a group of Teaneck's priests, ministers, and rabbis gathered at noon around a lone circular table under the gold and crystal chandelier in the center of the banquet hall in Teaneck's Jewish Community Center. Along the eastern wall, a row of stained glass windows kindled a glow of warmth, intimacy, and lightness. Thin winter sunlight bathed the lavender and yellow windows in pastels, giving the illusion, to anyone who wondered, that the temperature outside had not actually sunk to twenty-five degrees.

In many communities the mere thought of Catholics sitting down with Episcopalians for any meal was considered the modern ecumenical equivalent of Jesus' miracle of the loaves and fishes. Add to that Teaneck's mix of Reform and Conservative rabbis, not to mention an Ethical Culture leader and an occasional visit from a Muslim imam or even an Orthodox rabbi (who may have believed his Reform and Conservative Jewish brethren were not practicing their religion as they should because they drove automobiles on the Sabbath or allowed women to sit with men in the synagogue), and you had as wide a collection of religious views as could be gathered in almost any room in America. The aim of these meetings was not to hold a theological debate. Instead the group consciously sought to put aside, at least for an hour, the hot-button differences of their religions and build bonds of friendship. The conversations were part gossip, part shoptalk, part fence building between men and women whose theological differences were as wide and deep as the heavens but whose common link was the spiritual care and feeding of their town. It was rare that anyone spoke of anything controversial.

On this day one man in the group had a message on his mind that he wanted to pass along, but he wasn't sure if he could find the right words. Amandus "Mandy" Derr, the pastor of Teaneck's Grace Lutheran Church, had been bothered for months about what he was hearing in the town he had come to twenty years earlier to take over what had then been a struggling congregation. On the western edge of Teaneck, Grace Church seemed apart from the town's hub, taking up a woody corner where the land sloped into the Hackensack River and the first Dutch colonists had planted corn and barley. But in some ways the church's location made it an apt spot to gauge Teaneck's cultural tides. To the south sat the Teaneck campus of Fairleigh Dickinson University. To the east and north were Teaneck's wealthiest neighborhoods, overwhelmingly white and heavily Jewish. In the middle stood Derr's church, a congregation of old Germans and new arrivals. In 1970, when he took over, there was only one black family among the hundred families who regularly worshiped in Grace's pews. By 1990 the congregation had grown to three hundred families, including fourteen black and six Hispanic families. The ratio hardly came close to matching the demographics of town, but Derr considered it a small victory. In Teaneck he sensed the races weren't mixing as well as the town proclaimed they were to the outside world. Anything he could do to bring people together was a plus.

Derr's ancestors had landed at William Penn's English Quaker colony of Pennsylvania nine generations before, at about the same time as the Dutch were drifting across the Hudson River from New Amsterdam and carving farms into the rocky glens and low hills of what came to be, among other towns, Teaneck. You might even say that keeping tabs on the social and cultural pulse of any community Mandy Derr lived in was fused into his family soul; his own Lutheran ancestors had sought refuge in Quaker Pennsylvania from one of Europe's fratricidal wars between Protestants and Catholics. Derr was proud of his ability to listen to people, not only what was spoken from their lips but what weighed on their hearts and minds.

Tall and still boyish as he approached his forty-first birthday, Derr had grown up in Hanover, Pennsylvania, a hamlet outside Wilkes-

Barre. The town was located at the epicenter of the state's hilly an-
thracite coal–mining country. It was also bedrock Lutheran country.
Some locals joked that there were more Lutherans than trees. Actually
there was truth in the line. The hills were coated with layer upon layer
of culm, the largely infertile, gray, gravellike material that is left behind
after coal has been separated from the dirt and rock dug out of mines.
Little except weeds grew in the fields of culm.

Derr's father was a plumber; his grandfathers were miners. His great-
grandfather, a Union Army sergeant, fought alongside Pennsylvania
dairy farmers and coal miners against Robert E. Lee's Confederate
regiments at Gettysburg. Derr's grandmother kept his sword at home
as a link to the past. As another link, all the firstborn sons in the Derr
family were given the name Amandus, the German masculine version
of Amanda, which translates into "one who should be loved." But
Amandus Derr generally went by his nickname, Mandy, which he politely reminded friends was not a girl's name but in fact had come
from strong, masculine German Lutheran roots.

In high school Mandy had amassed such a record of high grades and
test scores that Princeton University offered him a full scholarship. No
one from his hard, muscular neighborhood of Lutheran coal miners
and Slovak factory workers had ever gone to Princeton—certainly not
on a scholarship. But before graduation, much to the dismay of his
teachers and friends, Derr turned down Princeton University for a
chance to go to a Lutheran seminary and become a minister.

He came to Teaneck partly by accident, invited initially as a college
assistant to an older pastor during the summer of 1970. Two springs
before, in April 1968, when Martin Luther King, Jr., was killed by a
sniper's bullet in Memphis, Tennessee, Derr, a college sophomore, had
been in Brooklyn's Bedford-Stuyvesant neighborhood, working with a
Lutheran youth outreach project. The experience of watching at first
hand the anguish of black residents in the days after the King assassination taught him much about the American dilemma of race and
the divisions in the nation's polyglot cultures. In integrated Teaneck,
where he was named full-time pastor in 1973 at the age of twenty-
three, he learned how whites and blacks spoke in code about race, how
the messages from people's mouths often barely hinted at the realities
in their hearts. Mandy Derr found confusion, anger, and dismay in
people's hearts over the racial lines that were being drawn in his town
over the years. He wondered what would come of it.

Derr's church with its seventy-foot-high wooden cross stood across the street from a Jewish neighborhood. As Derr learned, the cross was something of a smack in the face by the older German members of his church, a tit-for-tat religious retort to the neighborhood's complaints against the expansion years before of Grace Church and the occasional objection to the broadcasting of religious hymns on Grace's bell carillon. One old Lutheran hymn in particular, "Glories of Your Name Are Spoken," had the same tune as the old Nazi anthem "Deütschland über Alles." Derr, who did not recognize the similarities of the tunes, was in his office one day, listening to the soft, rhythmic bells when the phone rang with a Jewish neighbor protesting the music and its link to the Nazis. Derr immediately shut off the tape of the bells and never allowed that hymn to be played again. Even in Teaneck, Derr learned sadly, Jews and Lutherans with German roots occasionally angered one another, perpetuating hurts from the old country.

As the new decade began, he was hearing more about hurts, old and new. Actually the buzz had begun more than a year before, at the end of 1988, when Teaneck's business community decided to change the Christmas decorations along Cedar Lane. The silver bells that were put up on light poles for years had become worn-looking, and one of the merchants solicited contributions for a new set of decorations that might appeal to Christians as well as Jews. When Derr first heard of the idea, he liked it, thinking that it would be a true testimony to the town's ability to forge alliances. What went up on the light poles was a series of blue banners, each with a white snowflake and the message "Teaneck Wishes You Season's Greetings."

That was supposed to be the message anyway. As Derr quickly learned from irate members of his congregation, the greeting was actually divided: TEANECK WISHES YOU on banners on one side of the street and SEASON'S GREETINGS on banners on the other. And because the town's maintenance workers had made a mistake in putting the banners on the poles, the message read backward: "SEASON'S GREETINGS TEANECK WISHES YOU." In Derr's church, some interpreted this as a Jewish plot. Hebrew was written right to left—"backward." How else could such a mistake have been made? Or so the story went.

What's more, Derr was told, the snowflakes on the banners faintly resembled the Star of David. Derr examined the banners and could find no resemblance. The snowflakes didn't even have six points, as the Star of David did, but the story persisted. Finally there was the matter of the color of the banners: blue and white. Derr was told by another of the conspiracy theorists in his congregation that blue and white were the colors of the Israeli flag, as well as traditional Hanukkah colors. It was more evidence of a Jewish takeover of the town. Or so the story went.

By the holiday season of 1989 some members of Derr's church were upset again, this time over the news that Jewish residents had erected a menorah on the town green outside the police station. Each year the town traditionally put up Christmas lights on one of the large evergreens that stood outside the town hall and police headquarters. For several years, beginning in the mid-1980s, a committee of Jewish residents had asked to erect a menorah too, to celebrate Hanukkah. Teaneck's political leaders resisted the idea. Even some Jewish groups criticized it, fearing it might insult Christians during the Christmas season. But in 1989, after the Supreme Court had ruled in a similar case that towns with Christmas decorations on municipal property had to accommodate other religions, a menorah was lighted on Teaneck's green. In public anyway, Teaneck celebrated the event. In private, as Mandy Derr learned, too many agonized over it.

"People felt something had been taken from them," Derr said. "People didn't seem all that happy living with each other. You'd talk to the town officials, and they'd say, 'Oh, it's a wonderful town. We all get along.' But it was like a veneer on top of a cesspool."

In the social waters beneath Teaneck's surface, Derr found resentment from all corners of town, much of it linked to race, ethnicity, and religion. Some members of the black Baptist church on Teaneck's northeast side resented the difficulty it had in obtaining a variance to cut down several trees and expand its parking lot, claiming that an Orthodox Jewish congregation seemed to have no problem converting what was once a private home into a synagogue. Some black residents claimed that the expansion of a soccer field at Votee Park was a blatant catering to Jewish residents. The reason: Large numbers of children who played soccer were Jewish. Or so the story went.

In the fall of 1989 Derr heard too many white residents speaking (privately, of course) of how important it was to upgrade the schools with $24.6 million to stem white flight. There were also disturbing complaints from some in his congregation whenever a black boy was seen on the northwest side of town. Derr heard police had even been called and that cops regularly targeted carloads of blacks. Or so the story went. Derr himself had seen police pull over a car with a black driver and some black passengers. He had wondered if the police had a legitimate reason to make the stop or if this was just one of the checks he had heard about. At the same time he was becoming more concerned about stories police told him about the increased number of fights between black youths. He was told of the black door at the high school and how black and white students often gravitated toward different sports, different clubs, even different cafeterias. Was this evidence of a model town? Derr wondered. But he was especially worried about violence. He had tried to raise the subject of black-on-black fighting at the clergy council meeting in the fall of 1989. He stopped, however, when one of his colleagues said that some of his remarks—and the notion of whites discussing black-on-black violence—seemed racist.

On the night before Halloween 1989—"Mischief Night"—a Jewish man volunteered to guard his synagogue on Queen Anne Road. As a group of three boys—one Hispanic, one black, and one white—walked by with a carton of eggs, the man in front of the synagogue pulled out a .357 magnum revolver, pointed it at the boys, and was heard to proclaim in his best Clint Eastwood voice, "Go ahead. Make my day."

The boys walked on, not tossing an egg or an epithet. But they went home and told their parents, who in turn called the police, who then arrested the Eastwood wannabe and charged him with carrying a handgun in public.

Again, Mandy Derr wondered about the implications. Why would a Jewish man carry a pistol to defend his synagogue? What kinds of fears prompted him to do that? Was this man a loner trying to prove how tough he was or did he reflect something deeper and wider?

Derr watched this odd series of events and listened to the smattering of racial and ethnic musings for years. He wondered what they meant. Was there something about Teaneck's multicultural landscape that caused this sort of cultural buzz to emerge? Derr didn't know, but one thing disturbed him even more. Whenever there were difficulties of this kind, people often recalled the years of 1964 and 1965 and the efforts to integrate schools. Back then, as the coalition led by Mayor Feldman pushed for voluntary desegregation of Teaneck's schools, some opponents had grumbled that the troubles in Teaneck had begun when Jews moved into town in large numbers after World War II. After that, blacks arrived and Teaneck had left its homogeneous WASP roots on history's compost pile. Mandy Derr discovered that even in 1990 there were still some in Teaneck who hadn't got over that. What had happened a quarter century before was hailed in public as a model for the nation. In private far too many residents found the model riddled with problems. "People said if the town wasn't integrated, we would have none of these troubles now," Derr said.

With the anger over the Christmas decorations on his mind—and the disturbing suspicions of a Jewish conspiracy—Derr believed it was time to speak up. He had tried in his church to soothe people's ruffled feelings, even walking into the main aisle after one service to dispel the rumors about a Jewish plot to do away with Christmas decorations along Cedar Lane. As his fellow clergy gathered that Thursday in January for their monthly meeting in the Jewish Community Center, Derr decided to relay his concerns to Teaneck's priests, ministers, and rabbis if for no other reason than to share his worries. As the group finished its lunch, Derr saw an opening. He mentioned the resentment over the decorations, the instances of fighting by black youths, and the general sense he had that people in Teaneck seemed on edge about too many racial and ethnic issues. Then he launched a warning. "This town," said Derr, "is a powder keg."

The table hardly took time to ponder what he said. From one minister, Derr heard a quick "nah." From another, he heard, "Oh, you're overreacting."

Mandy Derr hoped he was.

Two weeks before the clergy council meeting the telephone rang in the guidance department at Dwight Morrow High School in Englewood. The guidance counselor, William Mack, picked up the receiver and heard a voice he had not heard in a month. "Mr. Mack? It's Phillip Pannell."

Pannell had never returned to class at Dwight Morrow after his fight outside the nurse's office on December 1 and after he talked to Principal Richard Segall. The school sent letters to Pannell's home that he was not attending classes, but Thelma Pannell never received them. Her son, she surmised later, simply intercepted the mail before she could read it.

Bill Mack held the telephone to his ear and wondered why Pannell was calling him. Phillip got right to the point. He wanted to transfer to a county high school that specialized in vocational training, such as carpentry, auto mechanics, restaurant cooking, and landscaping. Mack sensed that Phillip didn't want to attend the vocational high school to learn a trade as much as to escape the high school in Englewood.

"Is there a problem?" Mack asked.

"I don't know if I can get along at your school," Pannell answered. "I have a problem fighting. I was in a fight. I can't go to school there."

Mack waited.

The young voice on the phone was clearly troubled, maybe a little scared. But Mack also knew that Pannell was not facing up to his responsibilities. Students didn't merely walk into the county vocational high school whenever they wanted. The vocational school had a reputation for taking students who were not academic stars in such subjects as calculus or chemistry, but it had rigorous standards for students accepted into its technical programs. Most students were accepted in the ninth grade and only if they expressed interest in pursuing a technical career. Bergen Tech, as the school was called, did not want to take on another school's troublemakers. Transfers were rare.

Mack explained this to Pannell and brought up another point: Pannell had not even attended classes at Dwight Morrow. Why should the Dwight Morrow principal recommend that he be allowed to transfer to the vocational school? What's more, the city of Englewood would have to pay money for Pannell's bus to Bergen Tech as well as his tuition. Why should Englewood trust Pannell to attend classes at Bergen Tech? Mack suggested that Pannell return to class at Dwight Morrow and build a record of solid attendance and high grades. At the same time, the counselor said, Pannell could fill out an application for Bergen Tech. Maybe something could be worked out, but he couldn't guarantee it. Pannell had to take some responsibility, too.

The next morning Pannell walked into the guidance office. Mack handed the young man an application, then again tried to encourage him to return to class at Dwight Morrow while the application was processed. Pannell listened quietly, nodding, but not answering except to say "Uh-uh" or "yes."

"It was like pulling teeth to get him to talk," Mack said later.

It was also the last time Bill Mack saw Phillip Pannell.

What Phillip didn't say to Mack that day is that he had seen his father a few days before for the first time in two months. Phillip David Pannell was in trouble again at the county jail. Guards noted that he once again didn't have a paycheck. The senior Pannell explained that he hadn't been able to work that week; the mix of cold January sleet and snow had put a damper on work at the construction company. The guards warned Pannell to tell them when the weather was so bad that he couldn't work. They suspected he spent too many days lifting a beer in a bar rather than a shovel at a construction site. But they decided to give him another chance. Pannell said he had to go to a house closing. He and his wife were selling their Cape Cod on Circle Driveway in Teaneck.

Pannell returned to the jail in the midafternoon after the closing. Guards then gave him permission to go to an alcohol rehabilitation counseling session that he had enrolled in the month before. He was told to be back at the jail no later than 11:00 P.M. By the next morning he had still not come back, and guards issued a warrant for his arrest. They also phoned the construction firm where he had said he worked each day.

The firm's supervisor said Pannell had been fired the day before. He hadn't shown up for work for weeks.

That night Pannell got drunk. He also found his son in Englewood. Pannell had heard about the fights his son had gotten into at Dwight Morrow and how he spent his free time wandering around Teaneck and Englewood. Go back to school, the father told his son. Stop fighting.

The meeting was brief—that is, what Pannell can recall of it from his alcohol fog. As his son walked off to spend the evening with his mother, Pannell walked back toward Teaneck and the house on Circle Driveway that was no longer his. The doors and windows were all locked, so he went to the back door and broke a windowpane. He reached in, unlocked the door, and stepped inside.

Two days later the Bergen County Sheriff's Department received the formal warrant to arrest Pannell. Two detectives were sent to find him. They first checked an apartment on Forest Avenue in Teaneck: nothing. Next they checked a Chinese restaurant in Englewood: no sign of Pannell. Then they headed to the house on Circle Driveway.

As they looked in the windows, the place seemed empty. But the broken pane on the back door seemed suspicious. The detectives stepped into the house. Almost immediately they started coughing from the smell of natural gas. They phoned the fire department and Teaneck's police and also located the gas leak, a pilot light that had gone out on the basement water heater.

The house appeared empty, and the detectives walked upstairs to open windows and let in fresh air. As they reached a bedroom on the second floor, they heard an odd shuffling sound. It seemed to be coming from behind a closet, in a crawl space under the roof. The detectives opened the closet, then removed a panel that led to the crawl space.

Inside, they saw a familiar face. Phillip David Pannell came out without a struggle.

A WEEK LATER

Young Phillip Pannell got into a fight.

It was a Tuesday, two days before Mandy Derr spoke to the Teaneck Clergy Council. Pannell was in Teaneck again. Ever since he left Teaneck High School two months before, his pattern had remained the same. He awoke in the morning and told his mother he was going to school in Englewood. Instead he walked or hitchhiked the two miles into Teaneck, visited the Mediterranean Deli at noon to grab a soda or a sandwich, and tried to connect with some old classmates or members of the Violators as they walked from the high school for lunch. If he didn't see them at the deli, young Phillip drifted up the hill to the school, where he slowly strolled on the streets outside, trying to signal Batron or Chuckie or another of the Violators.

On Tuesday afternoon, January 23, when Teaneck High School's basketball team played a home game, a group of black teenagers from Hackensack High School showed up and picked a fight with one of Pannell's newest friends, an eighteen-year-old Teaneck student named Shariff. Pannell had not quit the Violators or disassociated himself from his younger friends. But after he moved to Englewood and was spending more time on the streets, he found himself with boys who were a year or two older. He was comfortable with them and felt protected somewhat. They, in turn, liked his humor and willingness to use his fists.

That day Shariff was beaten badly with a pipe by a Hackensack gang and had to be taken to Holy Name Hospital. Pannell didn't go home for dinner that night. He stayed in Teaneck and went to Holy Name to check on Shariff. Around 10:00 P.M. Pannell left the hospital with three more new friends: Sean, Tyrone, and Leslie. As they walked north on Teaneck Road, a black two-door Mazda 626 with a sunroof pulled over.

Behind the wheel sat Malik, one of the few boys Pannell knew with a car. He motioned for Pannell and the others to get in. As they settled into the seats, the five teenagers started to talk about what the Hackensack gang had done to Shariff. They ought to get revenge quickly this time and not wait. One of the boys suggested driving into Hackensack. This time the group had weapons besides their fists to fight with: a hammer, a crowbar, a bat, and a set of brass knuckles with a seven-inch knife attached.

Malik swung the car around and pointed it toward Hackensack.

Tuesday nights in January in downtown Hackensack are not the most inviting times for taking a walk in the fresh air. But that night Aaron Johnson had a bus to catch back to Passaic, an industrial town on the fringe of Paterson, about ten miles away. Johnson, twenty-one and unemployed, had no knowledge of the rivalries between Teaneck and Hackensack, nor did he care. He had taken the B-20 bus from Passaic to Hackensack to visit an old girlfriend, Monique. Around 10:15 P.M. he left Monique's house and walked two blocks to a bus stop and its Plexiglas shelter. No other pedestrians had ventured out in this cold weather. Cars were almost as scarce.

Johnson was alone in the bus stop and took a seat on the bench to await the B-20. Within minutes the black Mazda with the five guys from Teaneck passed.

Inside the car the boys looked into the bus stop and thought they recognized the face. Malik drove past, made a U-turn, and came back for another look.

"Let's stop," someone said. Malik pulled up to the curb by the bus stop and opened the door. Tyrone grabbed the bat. Leslie took the crowbar. Malik carried the hammer. Sean wrapped his fingers around the brass-knuckle knife. Phillip's hands were empty. He made a fist.

Malik led the group into the bus stop and sat down on the bench next to Aaron Johnson. "You from Hackensack?" Malik asked.

Johnson said no.

Malik persisted. He didn't believe Johnson, and his voice started to rise, his words dripping out in angry bursts. What you mean you're not from Hackensack? You're here in Hackensack, aren't you?

Johnson shook his head and told the group no. He had barely mouthed the words when the first fist smashed into the side of his face. Phillip Pannell threw the punch, and it staggered Johnson. He began to get up off the bench, and Malik swung the hammer. It glanced off Johnson's head. Johnson balled his fist and swung at one of the boys; he missed. He ran out of the bus stop, across the street and a set of railroad tracks. He figured he would find a safe haven if he could make it to Monique's house. But just over the railroad tracks, the Teaneck boys caught him. Johnson's jacket was half off, and Leslie swung the crowbar and hit Johnson in the back. Sean jabbed with the knife, sinking the blade into Johnson's right bicep. Johnson turned and tried to run, but after a few steps Sean caught him again with the knife, jabbing again. This time the blade hit Johnson in the back of the neck.

Sean looked at his hands. Blood all over his palm and his fingers.

Johnson ran another block to Monique's house and banged on the door. Monique called for an ambulance, and twenty minutes later Johnson was rolled into the emergency room at Hackensack Medical Center. The knife wounds were not deep, but doctors kept him overnight anyway.

It didn't take local police long to piece together the identities of one of the attackers. After he got out of the hospital, Aaron Johnson looked through a book of mug shots and identified Sean. When the police arrested him, he gave up the names of the others.

It took another week for the police to track down Phillip Pannell. At the time he was the only one of the attackers not living in Teaneck. Also odd, police thought, was the fact that Sean had no idea what Phillip's last name was. To him Phillip was just "Phil," a kid who hung out with the group. But in January 1990 there weren't many teenage boys named Phillip who wore red parkas and were quick with their fists. Police tracked down Pannell's Englewood address, phoned him, and asked him to come into the Englewood juvenile bureau to be picked up by the Hackensack police and questioned. When he arrived, Pannell walked in with his mother.

It had been a hard winter for Thelma Pannell. Her husband's work-release program wasn't providing the sort of child support payments she hoped for. Only a few days before, she had discovered her son had not been going to school. And now there was the matter of this fight in Hackensack. In the second-floor juvenile bureau at Englewood's police headquarters, Thelma Pannell slumped in a chair and looked around the room as detectives filled out papers on her son and what he had done. Of all the trouble her son had been in, this seemed the worst. This time someone had been stabbed and had been sent to the hospital.

She complained how hard it was trying to raise a son without a father. And then, to no one in particular, she muttered, "If he keeps this up, he's gonna end up dead."

———

Batron Johnson wondered where Phil had been. He hadn't seen his friend since New Year's Eve, when they had gone to a party on the northeast side of Teaneck. That night the party had been quiet. The boys mostly sat on a sofa listening to music and watching television until the lighted ball dropped in Times Square. Phillip dodged questions about school and his homelife. "It's okay," he told Batron on several occasions. As they left, they promised to see each other more in the days ahead. Batron heard that Phillip visited Teaneck High and the Mediterranean Deli, but the two always seemed to miss each other. As January ended, it was getting to the point where sightings of Phillip were something of a conversation starter among the Violators or other teenagers. Phillip looked different, carried himself differently now, and kept his own schedule. Often, when Batron spoke about Phillip to one of the Violators, it usually sparked a question: What's going on with Phillip?

On Teaneck Road Phillip Pannell's red parka was now a fixture, so much so that police wondered what the young man was doing with so much time on his hands. In the juvenile bureau at Teaneck police headquarters, Sergeant Robert Adomilli heard disturbing reports about the group that called itself the Violators. He was reluctant to overstate the danger and assume that an urban gang had started a farm team in Teaneck. But he wanted to be careful just the same. Adomilli knew Teaneck teenagers flirted with gang membership from time to time. He had been a cop long enough to remember the Ashacks and the Vikings.

Adomilli telephoned some police contacts in other towns, including Bergenfield, where many black teenagers from Teaneck congregated on weekends at a roller rink. Aside from some graffiti, there wasn't much to go on.

Like the police, Batron Johnson's mother noticed Phillip hanging out more on Teaneck Road. He had changed. That much was apparent. His clothes seemed shabby, his jeans baggier, his walk more sullen. He was often alone.

Lelia Johnson had first seen the change the summer before, as the boys prepared for the start of their sophomore year at Teaneck High School. Phillip came by the house less often. And when he did, his baseball hat was perched sideways on his head, his sneakers were open and untied. He looked sloppy. One day she decided to find out why.

"What's going on?" she asked Phillip, hoping for a glimpse into a boy who was troubled but unable to put his concerns into words.

"Nah," he said. "I'm all right."

Later she took Batron aside. "Batron, what's wrong with Phillip?"

"I don't know, Mommy," Batron answered. "His mom and dad ain't getting along well. He has problems at home."

Lelia Johnson didn't think much of it then and soon forgot about her concerns in part because she didn't see Phillip much anymore. She also knew his parents had been having trouble for years.

But as the winter of 1990 hardened and January slipped into February, Lelia Johnson again saw Phillip on Teaneck Road. He was not with Batron or any of the boys. Chuckie wasn't around. Nor was Steven or Otis. The new group with Phillip seemed older, tougher.

"Who are these people Phillip is hanging out with?" she asked Batron.

"Mommy, I don't even know those kids myself."

But Batron had heard something he didn't volunteer that day to his mother. Phillip Pannell had a new nickname: Philly Blunt.

Batron hadn't seen Phillip in weeks. But Batron knew that "Philly Blunt" was street slang for a large marijuana joint, made by taking the tobacco out of a cigar and refilling it with marijuana. Before Phillip left Teaneck High School, the hardest drug he or the other Violators had ever tried was malt liquor. Batron wondered if Phillip's new friends were introducing him to new highs that corresponded to his new nickname.

In Englewood Thelma Pannell decided it was time to move again. She found a small apartment in a tan building on Park Avenue in River Edge. It was a quiet street, far from the street fighting of Teaneck and Englewood that seemed to follow her son. The only noise came from the train tracks that ran behind the apartment house on a piece of fallow land between Park Avenue and the Hackensack River.

She also placed a call to the Newark office of the Job Corps. If her son wasn't going to school in Englewood or Teaneck—or to Bergen Technical High School—perhaps he would straighten out in the Job Corps. Besides, she felt in her gut that she needed to get her son away. He seemed almost uncontrollable now. And without a father around the house, it was difficult for a single mother to put the clamps on a sixteen-year-old boy.

A few weeks before, Lelia Johnson had come to Thelma Pannell and mentioned she had seen Phillip on Teaneck Road with a group of older, sloppier-looking boys. She said she hadn't recognized any of Phillip's new friends and wondered who the boys were. Thelma Pannell didn't seem surprised.

"He is hanging out with kids I don't know," she said.

Thelma's concerns deepened when she took her son one day into downtown Englewood to fetch some empty cardboard boxes from one of the stores. She needed the boxes for packing clothes and other items in preparation for the move to River Edge. As she drove into Englewood on Palisade Avenue, she saw a pile of boxes outside a drugstore.

She also noticed three boys eyeing her car, but she didn't think much of it until she asked her son to get out of the car and get several boxes.

"Ma, those boys over there are gonna jump me," Phillip said.

She had never heard so much fear in her son's voice. She spun around in the driver's seat and looked at him. Phillip didn't take his eyes off the three boys who now walked along the sidewalk by the boxes and glared at the Pannells. Thelma Pannell looked back at the boys, then got angry.

"Come on, boy," she told her son. "Stop acting stupid. Go on and get those boxes."

Phillip opened the car door and slowly got out. Across the street, on the sidewalk, the boys stopped. As Phillip stepped off the curb to cross Palisade Avenue and head for the pile of boxes, the three boys made their move. One rushed in and pushed Phillip, knocking him back. Another pushed him from behind. The third tried to shove him into a car.

Cars stopped and honked their horns. Thelma Pannell got out. Phillip was wearing his new red parka. She reached for a sleeve, pulled him back to her car, and shoved him into the passenger seat, calling him by his middle name. "CLINTON! CLIN-TON."

The three boys followed.

"Don't hit my mother's car," Phillip screamed.

"Come on, Clint, they ain't gonna hit my car," Thelma Pannell yelled.

"Ma, you don't know these guys."

She looked at the boys. Her son was right. She didn't know these boys.

The boys stopped, looking inside the car at Phillip. Finally one spoke. "Phil, we not gonna hit your mother's car. We respect your mother. We'll get you later."

Thelma Pannell glared at the boys. "My son is not meeting nobody nowhere," she shouted. "You kids should be home, somewhere off the streets."

And she drove off. She would get her boxes somewhere else. As soon as she could, she reminded herself to call the Job Corps again and ask if her son's application could be sped up.

━━━━━

Several weeks later, on the last Saturday in February, Gary Spath was working the evening shift. Around 7:30 P.M. he got a call that a woman had been drinking almost all afternoon at Carl's Corner. She was now drunk and belligerent. She also had her five-year-old son with her.

There were more than a dozen bars in Teaneck, many with special reputations and unique clienteles. Carl's Corner, on the northeast end of Teaneck Road, was a magnet for working-class blacks.

Spath parked his police cruiser at the curb. A few patrons were standing outside, and one of them motioned to him. As soon as he stepped inside, he saw the short, stocky sandy-haired woman. She was loudly berating several patrons around the bar. She was also white—unusual for Carl's. Her son sat sullenly nearby. If the woman was aware he was there, she didn't seem to care.

Spath felt a spurt of anger and sympathy. The woman was saying loudly that she had been waiting for hours for her boyfriend to meet her and give her some money. Spath decided it was time for her to leave; he walked up and asked her to come to police headquarters with the boy.

He didn't arrest her; there was no need to. Back at headquarters Spath took the woman and her son to the juvenile bureau to talk with Sergeant Adomilli. Seated at a long table in the middle of the bureau, the woman related her story: no husband, little money, and too much booze. Adomilli turned and looked across the room. Spath was at another table, playing with the boy. Adomilli thought the boy, blond and thin, looked a bit like Spath's son.

Adomilli turned back to the woman, who was in her late twenties. She was too drunk to go home right away. He asked if he could call a family member to take her and her son home. She said she had no one. Adomilli then told her that he thought it would be best if he called in a social worker from the state Division of Youth and Family Services. He said he didn't like to do this, but he wanted to play it safe. He suspected the woman might be a prostitute.

"Hey, listen"—Adomilli began to explain why he wanted to call a social worker—"this is a rough deal for you. We understand that. But this ain't the best life for this kid now."

The woman started to cry. From the corner the boy giggled. Spath rolled a toy car around the desk. The boy laughed. Spath picked him up, tickled him.

The woman gazed at the cop and her son for a silent moment, then turned back to Adomilli. "This is what my son needs," she told him. "My son needs more like this instead of seeing what he sees all the time. He needs more of a man around the house. There is no man in my life."

Adomilli picked up the phone to call the social worker.

"I know you have to do what you have to do," the woman said. "I hate to lose my son."

Adomilli paused. "Maybe you'll get your problems squared away. That doesn't mean you're going to lose your son."

"But I know how DYFS works," the woman said.

Adomilli frowned and sat silently for a few seconds more. "We gotta do what we got to do," he said.

Thirty minutes later the DYFS caseworker arrived. The woman repeated her story, but the verdict was the same: For at least a few nights, it would be best to place the boy in a foster home until DYFS could check on whether she was competent to care for him.

There was one problem. It was Saturday night, and placement in a foster family would have to wait until Monday. The caseworker explained there were several temporary homes the boy could be sent to. She promised it wouldn't be too traumatic and took out some forms to fill out.

Adomilli felt someone walk up behind him. He turned. It was Spath. "Hey, Sarge," Spath said, "can I talk to you?"

Spath motioned to the hall and walked out. Adomilli got up and followed. "What's up?" Adomilli asked as the door closed.

Spath seemed anxious, expectant. "Not for nothing," he said, "but do you think it would be possible for me to take this kid home?"

"What?" Adomilli looked into Spath's eyes, wondering if he was serious.

Spath spoke before the sergeant could say another word. "It's the weekend and they're only gonna put the boy in a temporary home anyway and on Monday he would have to go for this hearing that they have to go for. Do you think it would be possible?"

Adomilli was still stunned. "What would your wife say?"

Spath was ready for the question. "I already checked with her. She said it would be okay."

"Jesus, Gary, I'll tell ya the truth, I don't know. I've never heard . . ." Adomilli paused, then added: "I've never had anybody ask me that before or even considered it. I really don't know."

Spath looked back, and Adomilli now had no doubt the young cop was serious.

"Is it possible?" Spath pleaded. "Could you find out?"

Adomilli pondered the question. It seemed like a sincere request. Anyway, there was no harm in asking.

"All I'll do is ask the DYFS worker," Adomilli said. "The most she can say is no. What could she say?"

Spath nodded. "It's only a temporary home," he said. "It's not like I'd be screwing something up here."

Adomilli opened the door to the juvenile office and asked the caseworker to step into the hall. He presented Spath's suggestion but the caseworker shook her head from side to side as he mouthed the words.

Adomilli persisted.

Spath was not a bachelor with a one-room apartment, a pull-out sofa, and an empty refrigerator, he explained. He was married with a son and a daughter and a two-story colonial house in River Edge. Anyway, it was Saturday night, almost ten o'clock. Finding a temporary foster home at this hour would be difficult, if not impossible. Why not make it easy on the boy?

The caseworker pondered the idea. She said she couldn't make the decision herself. She had to make a call. She also needed the mother's permission to send the boy home with someone else, even a police officer.

As the mother of the little boy heard Spath's request, she brightened. She was also sobering up. "I have no problem with that," she said, looking again at Spath and her son as they rolled a toy car again atop the table. "What do I know what to do with a kid? What do I know what to do with a boy? This is what a man does when he plays with his son."

Thirty minutes later Spath walked out the door hand in hand with the boy. Adomilli sent the mother home with two detectives and forgot about it until a few days later, when he ran into Spath at police headquarters. Spath was ebullient. The boy had had a wonderful time and stayed several days beyond the weekend—such a good time that Spath and his wife were asking if they could even adopt the boy or become his foster parents.

"That's a big thing you're talking about," he told Spath. "You got a family already. You really need another kid?"

Spath nodded. He was displaying the same look of passion and concern that Adomilli had seen when Spath suggested he take the boy home. Adomilli smiled. He felt glad there were cops like Gary Spath in the Teaneck police force. This was what police work was all about: people.

The story of how Spath volunteered to take the boy home for the weekend and then talked of adopting him or becoming a foster father circulated around the police department in the next week. In some ways it was more moving than the stories of cops catching criminals. This was more than a story of routine bravery; this was a cop offering a piece of himself and his home to solve, for at least one night, a small problem of a small corner of America's underside. But this time there were no letters of commendations, no awards. And so four days later Officer Phil Lavigne, a friend of Spath's, wrote a letter to the Teaneck township manager, Jack Hadge:

> I feel the need to write to you simply to tell of a good deed that will go by mostly unnoticed as do many others. We as police officers have the opportunity to come in contact with many people.
>
> Unfortunately [in] most of these contacts we find the people at their worst, and when children are involved it makes the job harder. I don't believe there is an officer out there that doesn't put the extra effort into the job when a child is involved. It has always saddened me when I must handle a job with a child that has been injured, lost or stuck in the middle of a family crisis. You never forget the look in the eyes of a child, it stays with you forever. Having a son of my own, you feel for them even more. This is why I am compelled to write to you. It pertains to a brother officer.

Lavigne went on to describe how Spath had walked into Carl's Corner and found the drunken woman and her son, how he had returned to police headquarters with them, how no relatives could be found, how the DYFS caseworker had been called in, and how Spath had finally taken the boy to his own home. Spath, he said, quickly grew attached to the boy—so much so that he told Lavigne the next day that he and his wife talked about adopting him if a good home could not be found. But Spath had become frustrated, Lavigne wrote. After caseworkers had picked up the boy, Spath telephoned to check on his whereabouts and deliver a few toys. Lavigne finished his letter:

> They told Gary that he would not be allowed to see nor know where the boy was placed. I have known Gary for over ten years and have never seen him this frustrated and upset as on this day. As police officers it is our job to uphold the laws and to protect and serve the public. At times, this can be very frustrating, as we are limited to what we can do. Gary felt this frustration, but felt he needed to do more and he did just that. I myself felt for this little guy, so young, so alone, so confused, among a group of men he didn't know, yet knew they were there to protect him, to make

things better. My thoughts drifted to my own son. I prayed that he would never meet such a fate but if he did may there be a Gary Spath out there for him. I do not know where the boy is today, nor do I know what had happened to him prior to our meeting. But I do know that the time he spent with the Spath family will be cherished and greatly missed. We hope he does well. Officer Spath and his family have truly lived up to the standards of decent human beings. And Officer Spath has gone above and beyond the call of duty. No saying is more truly spoken than to say that Officer Spath is an officer who PROTECTS AND SERVES. I am proud to work by his side. In closing I would like to thank you for taking the time to read this letter. I hope it will help you understand our job from a point of view which is often hard to experience.

Several Weeks Later

In another town young Phillip Pannell confided in one of his closest friends one of his most troubling concerns: the breakup of his family. Some of the Violators knew Phillip was having trouble at home, but he rarely acknowledged it and certainly never talked about it at length. One reason is that other boys had troubles too. But Phillip seemed especially closed up. Batron tried to coax him to talk. So had Steven and Chuckie. Phillip either answered with a few words or changed the subject. Or, as he had done in recent months, he didn't come around as much as he once did. He was with his new friends.

After a party one evening Phillip found himself walking home with Muziki, one of the original Violators. The two had known each other since first grade, and Muziki had been something of a fixture at the Pannell dinner table during some of those intervening years when his own family had fractured and split and he had divided his time between his mother and grandmother. "My dad," said Muziki, "was gone before I even came."

The Pannells had treated Muziki like a son. And he had secretly envied Phillip for the family he had. To Muziki the Pannells had been everything his own family wasn't: a mother, a father, a brother, and a sister. On the surface at least it seemed like the model family Muziki longed for.

It was after midnight when Phillip and Muziki walked along Liberty Road, on the border of Teaneck and Englewood. It still hadn't snowed that winter, so there were no icy embankments to navigate. The party the two had attended had been at a home near the Teaneck Armory. Phillip was still living with his mother and sister in Englewood, and Muziki offered to walk with him to make sure no one from Englewood jumped him.

They headed south for a few blocks and didn't see more than one or two cars. Muziki felt safe. He sensed Phillip did too. The road darkened as they passed an old horse farm and Muziki remembered how the Pannell family house on Circle Driveway in Teaneck had been the scene of so many afternoons of fun with video games or bicycle rides. It was such a shame, he thought, that Pannell was living in another town, another neighborhood, with a whole new set of fears. He felt Phillip was thinking the same thing.

"Damn," said Muziki, breaking the silence. "Why'd you have to move?"

Phillip paused for a few seconds. "If it was up to me," he finally said, "none of this shit would have happened. I had to move, man. I had no control. I couldn't help it. I just . . ."

Phillip's voice trailed off. Then he caught himself. "We had to, I guess."

Muziki sensed his friend wanted to talk. A few years before, when Phillip's mother and father first started having problems, Phillip had occasionally confided in Muziki. But usually Muziki had had to take the first step. As the two boys rounded a bend, Muziki spotted a flat rock the size of a bench not far from a streetlight. Muziki sat down. Pannell huddled next to him.

At that moment, as Muziki looked at his friend, he felt that the two of them seemed oddly vulnerable. They sat in silence for a few minutes, their hands jammed into their pockets of their coats and trying to ward off the damp winter air. It was like we were little boys again, Muziki thought. He decided it was time to broach the difficult subject of Phillip's father.

"What's up with big Phil?" Muziki asked. "How's he doing? I haven't seen him in awhile."

He had heard a rumor that Phillip's father was in jail. He had also heard that Phillip's mother couldn't make payments on the house on Circle Driveway and had had to sell it.

Phillip said that his father hadn't been keeping up with his child support. But the embarrassing admission seemed to make him defensive. "Yo, man, my father does what he can for me," he said, his voice toughening. "He does what he can for me, you know?"

Muziki knew. He remembered Pannell as a kind man when he wasn't drinking. Muziki did not think he was the sort of father who would walk out on his wife and children.

"I haven't seen him in awhile," Phillip said. "But I talk to him, you know? My parents are not together no more. And now we're living in Englewood. I don't like this no more. I don't like this type of life no more."

He told Muziki that his mother had a new boyfriend. That lone fact seemed to put the heaviest, most intractable damper on the possibility of his parents' reuniting and resurrecting the family life they had once tried to have. He turned to Muziki and spoke softly. "I can't believe this, man. I can't believe this. I wish stuff was back the same as it was."

A MONTH LATER

Phillip Pannell moved to River Edge with his mother and sister. It was not a difficult move and did not require too much packing. The family had moved to Englewood only a few months before.

But at some point during the transfer of boxes, Phillip happened to open a box he found on a shelf in his mother's closet. Inside, he found a silver starter's pistol.

Phillip put the gun in the pocket of his red parka. From now on, he told friends, if anybody tried to jump him on his trek from his new home to his old turf in Teaneck, he would have some protection.

SIX

MOURNING DOVE

The auditorium at Teaneck's Benjamin Franklin Middle School swelled with civic pride. On the first Sunday in April 1990—April 1— 350 of Teaneck's citizens, many wearing their town spirit like fresh carnations in their lapels, gathered to pay homage to two men, one white and the other black. If anyone wondered about the ironic choice of April Fool's Day to honor Matthew Feldman, the leader of Teaneck's integration effort in the 1960s, and one of his key allies in the black community, Judge Isaac McNatt, no one dwelled on it.

It had been a quarter century since the beginning of Teaneck's heady quest for racial harmony. But now the white man who had led that effort, Matty Feldman, seemed cast as a graying visitor from another time, not unlike a once-great ballplayer who is honored on old-timers' day to remind the fans of what he did years before. Feldman was no longer the muscular man he had been, no longer swirling with energy as he strutted into council meetings with proposed ordinances or into newspaper offices to drop off press releases that announced his latest idea, however whimsical. He was still active in politics as a New Jersey state senator and was about to join other Democratic liberals in pushing through Governor Jim Florio's $2.8 billion increase in the state income tax, the largest in New Jersey history and, said some Republicans, the largest single state tax increase in the history of the United

States. But on that evening more than a few in the audience noticed that Feldman had slipped a bit. This was one of the few public appearances he had made in months, and at seventy-one he was thinner, less bouncy in his walk, suffering from a weakened heart that often caused him to tire easily. As a politician he was no longer setting an agenda from his perch in the state senate chambers in Trenton; even he acknowledged that on occasion when he stopped to reflect with friends. He was looking to pass his torch.

Still, in Teaneck no politician had emerged who could assume Feldman's grand style, the backslapping way in which he built coalitions with blacks and whites, his appeal-to-the-heart rhetoric. If there was a small-town Tip O'Neill, Matty Feldman was it. More than once in the old days, when asked why he took a controversial stand on race, Feldman reached for a simple explanation that spoke volumes: "Because it was right." In the 1990s few in America—and in Teaneck—spoke with such fundamental idealism about race. Yet few understood that to succeed, one had to build coalitions, not fences of separation.

That year some of Teaneck's political establishment, including Feldman, looked to Paul Ostrow, the president of the ambulance corps, as a new leader to carry on Feldman's legacy. Ostrow had run for Teaneck's council two years before and lost. But he had not given up. That spring he was running again, and he felt a special kinship to Feldman. The year before, when Feldman suffered a heart attack, Ostrow had performed CPR on Feldman as one of the ambulance crew that took him to the hospital. "I want," Ostrow told friends often, "to make this town better for my children and let them experience the kinds of things I experienced when I grew up here." That included the sense of the peaceful mixing of races. Of all his experiences in his high school years in Teaneck, Ostrow spoke most fondly about the town's ability to bring together peacefully all sorts of different people.

He saw himself as a man who could cross boundaries and create the same coalitions that Matty Feldman had fashioned as a younger man. As he took his seat with his wife on the center aisle, some twenty rows from the stage—a position selected so he could be far enough back to observe the speeches as well as the crowd reaction—Ostrow wondered if he was up to the job. He knew Teaneck had changed in recent years. There was the nagging trickle of white flight and the perplexing fights between black teenagers. He feared, as did many whites, that young white families were no longer looking as much to the town as a place to move to as they had. At the high school whites dominated the honors courses, by a ratio of ten to one in some cases; blacks dominated the remedial and special education classes—as well as suspensions for disciplinary problems. The basketball team was mostly black; the drama club was mostly white. Was Teaneck separating from within, even within its schools? If so, why? The questions popped into Ostrow's mind almost every day now. But if there were solutions, they seemed murky and difficult to define. There were no longer the clear 1960s goals that Matty Feldman had pursued so relentlessly. It was 1990, and race had become complicated.

Ostrow noted that the crowd in the auditorium was mixed, and there were lots of familiar faces of all races. But in looking at the black residents who attended, Ostrow saw something that unsettled him. Most of the blacks were older, veterans of the 1960s migration from New York City to Teaneck. Where were the younger blacks who had moved in since then?

Seated several rows away from Ostrow that evening was Frank Hall, Teaneck's mayor. Hall, elected to the council in 1966 and undefeated in every election since then, was the last link on the Teaneck council to the Feldman coalition of the 1960s. Hall did not possess Feldman's rhetorical gifts or his arm-on-the-shoulder ability to make people feel good about joining alliances they might not ordinarily join. For that reason, Hall did not evoke the same spirit, even though he shared many of Feldman's liberal principles. Hall, along with Bill Crain of the Teaneck school board, had already lent his name in support of a March Against Racist Violence that was scheduled for the following Sunday, April 8, in Newark to commemorate the twenty-second anniversary of the assassination of Martin Luther King and the twenty-fifth anniversary of King's protest march across the Alabama countryside, from Selma to Montgomery. As a measure of how much times had changed, Matty Feldman's name wasn't among the forty-five members of Congress, state legislators, and other political leaders who were listed as official supporters of the march.

If Hall's forte was not in organizing or attending rallies, his strength—and occasionally his Achilles' heel—was his ability to master details. He could cite the footnotes of an obscure rule in the town building code; he could also cite past insults from political rivals. Few details on the social and political landscape of Teaneck escaped his eye—probably the reason why he was able to survive so long in local politics. He was a man who measured well.

And this was an evening to measure success. Here, amid the best of Teaneck, success was something to behold. Black lawyers and businessmen parked their Acuras and Mercurys in the parking lot and walked into an auditorium to sit next to white lawyers and business-men who drove their own Acuras and Mercurys. Few blacks and whites socialized outside this sort of venue, and indeed, when they went home, there was a strong likelihood that blacks went to "their" side of town and whites to "theirs." In Teaneck separateness in small neigh-borhoods under the larger, town-wide umbrella of integration had be-come an accepted fact of life. With few exceptions, the races lived separately, and that was why events such as this were important. Much like the town's Diversity Day a year before, it was not only a chance to celebrate but an opportunity to mix and to remind one another of what the town was trying to be.

As Martin Lasky, one of the organizers, pointed out, this was what Teaneck was all about: blacks and whites coming together within its borders. Even the cosponsors of the event, the Bergen County chapter of the National Association for the Advancement of Colored People and the Palisades Council of B'nai B'rith, underscored the theme of Teaneck as a racial crossroads. Here were Jews and blacks together again, as they had been in Alabama and in Teaneck in 1965. And here in Teaneck a Jew, Matthew Feldman, was being honored with a black, Isaac McNatt. Their joint award "for lifetime services in the advance-ment of equality and human rights for all people" was named after Martin Luther King, Jr., and King's ally in the civil rights movement Rabbi Abraham Joshua Heschel. In the 1990s such a celebration of mixing had become a rare event anywhere in America, a harkening back to three decades before, when blacks and Jews joined hands in the turbulent integration campaigns of the South and more peacefully in northern towns, such as Teaneck.

That evening Benjamin Hooks, the national director of the NAACP, attended the ceremony along with Seymour Reich, the president of B'nai B'rith International. "Let this community of Teaneck and the leadership of Judge Isaac McNatt and Matthew Feldman serve as an example that we Jews and African-Americans can achieve much to-gether when we link arms," said Reich. Hooks had a similar message. He knew Teaneck and the ideals it tried to put into practice. He also knew there were problems. As he looked out over the gathering and spoke, his message was simple: Stay together; keep trying; remember your common bond.

George Powell, the president of the Bergen County NAACP and the master of ceremonies that night, listened to Hooks's and Reich's words and felt a surge of inspiration. When Powell and his wife decided to moved to Teaneck in 1970, the house they liked best was on the white side of the railroad tracks. When the owner learned that Powell was black, the house suddenly was taken off the market. Powell, a rising executive with the Philip Morris tobacco company, had spent enough time as a salesman in the South to smell even the most subtle forms of bigotry. He filed suit. Teaneck members of the Bergen County Fair Housing Council set up a picket line. The owner put the house back on the market, and the Powells moved in a few months later.

The years in Teaneck since then had mostly pleased Powell. The town wasn't perfect, but he figured it was better than most places. As he stood at the podium and looked into the crowd, he spotted a man he had become friendly with, Teaneck's police chief, Bryan Burke. The two couldn't have been more different—and not only in color. Burke, the son of an assistant sports editor of *The New York Times*, had anchored his life in Teaneck; Powell was a world traveler. Yet when Burke needed advice in dealing with the black community, he had gotten in the habit of picking up a telephone and calling George Powell.

Powell respected the chief for reaching out and decided it was time to point out how much he appreciated the police department's efforts to establish lines of communication with the black community. "Chief Burke's office is always open," Powell said.

It was time for closing remarks, and Powell paused, scanning again the audience of blacks and Jews. The thought occurred to him that in another week Christians and Jews would be celebrating some of their most solemn holidays. Passover and Holy Week. He also realized that in most cases—he was an exception—blacks still lived in their own neighborhoods and whites lived in theirs. Rarely did they visit each other. He decided to make an appeal to everyone's soul. "When we leave here," he said, "and go to our respective homes, especially at this time of our respective holidays, it would be nice to extend the invitation to brothers of different faiths to visit each other's homes."

The following week the local black newspaper, the *Connection*, editorialized that "from start to finish, the event was everything one might expect and left those in attendance with warm feelings."

———

On the Sunday before, two miles away in the town of River Edge, the phone had rung in the police station at 7:43 P.M.

The man on the phone was calling to report that he had heard a series of six consecutive gunshots coming from a field near the Hackensack River, the railroad tracks, and Park Avenue. A patrol car was dispatched but couldn't find—or hear—anything, and a report was filed away.

River Edge police did not know that evening, but a mother and two children had recently moved into an apartment building on Park Avenue that looked out on the railroad tracks. It was the third home in less than eight months for Thelma Pannell and her daughter and son. She hoped this would last for a while.

━━━━━

On March 30, 1990, four members of the town's League of Women Voters had signed a letter that was mailed to forty-six people in Teaneck. They had been carefully selected, the names broken down evenly by race, religion, sex, class, profession, and ethnicity.

For Dorothy Marcus, the letter was the culmination of three months of work. She had left her job in Manhattan at the United Church of Christ after the entire office had moved to Cleveland and Marcus had decided not to go. She was in her mid-fifties, her daughter was ready to graduate from high school, and her husband had been dead for several years. She was looking for a new direction to apply her talents, and she vowed to use the time between jobs to ponder her next career move. Also, she had a bad foot that needed an operation. Recovering from that would keep her at home for weeks anyway.

Over the winter Marcus had found herself returning to her old labor of love: race relations. It had been years since she had actively worked in the field, but she was never far away, her antenna having been well tuned in her youth to the coded vocabulary of race relations and how even the small chatting of ordinary people on street corners or on the telephone could reflect deep fears. Her conversation months before in which her old friend had noted that high school students had referred to poor black students as "niggers" still bothered her.

She called together three women and voiced her concerns. She then went to a meeting of the League of Women Voters and suggested the league take up the question of race relations in Teaneck. It agreed, and a month later Marcus mailed her letters, the words chosen so as not to inflame anyone's passion as much as to spark an honest, respectful discussion.

"Dear Friends," the letter said. "Responding to concerns expressed recently from many quarters about race relations in Teaneck, especially in the schools, the League of Women Voters is planning a program to explore these concerns and to see what we as a community can do to improve race relations."

Marcus ended by suggesting a meeting date that seemed to fall perfectly between the busy Passover and Easter holidays. It was April 12.

━━━━

Phillip Pannell's gun had bullets. It could fire too.

The gun originally was an eight-shot starter's pistol that fired blanks. But now it had been retooled to hold eight .22-caliber bullets. It was a crude job, to be sure. The cylinder—capped by the manufacturer at one end like the bottom of a soup can—had been sawed off and hollowed out. So had the barrel. Bullets could now be placed in the cylinder and fired through the barrel.

The Violators laughed when they heard about the new piece of protection Phillip carried. On a Saturday afternoon in late March several members of the gang, including Muziki, gathered in the home in Teaneck of one of Phillip's new friends, Leslie Johnson who was not related to Batron. Phillip was supposed to drop by but was visiting relatives in Newark.

"Phil's got a gun," one of the boys said.

Muziki was surprised. He had been away at a state reform school, the result of too many fights and too many arrests. He hadn't seen Phillip since the two had talked in the frigid midnight air the month before, and he knew Phillip feared walking the streets of Englewood alone. Even Muziki had briefly carried a .45 semiautomatic the year before, but he had never used it in a fight. And he had never thought Phillip would carry a gun.

"Oh, what? Phil's got a gun?" Muziki asked. "What's it look like?"

The others laughed, slapped their knees, as they described the converted starter's pistol.

"Bullets hang out of the thing," someone said.

"It looks like a piece of shit," said another boy.

"It's beat-up and old-looking" was another comment.

But it could fire bullets; that much Muziki learned. Pannell had told the Violators he had fired his gun in the woods near his house; a few others had seen him also fire it in Mackel Park in Teaneck.

"It sounds," said someone, "like a BB gun."

They laughed again.

━━━━

The rumor floated through Teaneck like spring pollen, noticeable to some, ignored by others. One of the Violators was said to be carrying a gun. Or if not the Violators, one of the black kids who was always in trouble.

At the high school Principal Jim DeLaney first heard the rumor in the fall, after the series of fights with the gangs from Hackensack. But as rumors go, this one seemed fuzzier than most. When he heard it again in the spring, the rumor seemed more urgent.

"We figured," he said, "that someone might get hurt. We figured it would be one of the kids shooting another kid."

In the police juvenile bureau Bob Adomilli first heard the rumor in 1988, after a fight at the St. Anastasia carnival. The rumor persisted as the fighting grew more common in 1989 and into the early months of 1990. But like DeLaney, Adomilli was unable to connect a specific person to a gun, though one name kept coming up: Violators. It was mostly talk, though. And how much stock do you put in street talk? Adomilli did not have to be reminded of how police work was changing in the 1990s, that since the introduction of crack cocaine in America in the mid-1980s violent crime had spread and more teenagers found ways to obtain handguns.

"We heard this stuff all the time," Adomilli said. "This guy has something. This guy has a knife. This guy has a gun."

If it was true, Adomilli shared DeLaney's fear. "We felt that if it comes down to somebody getting shot, it's going to be a kid shooting a kid."

Fred Greene had not seen Gary Spath in months. Greene had retired from the police force in 1988, but the two remained in touch. Greene still lived in his family's old house on the edge of Argonne Park, and in his retirement he had begun to take care of injured or abandoned animals.

It was not so much a career as a hobby. And it was not uncommon to find a raccoon that had been hit by a car or a lonesome, lost kitten in one of the homemade cages in Greene's tree-covered backyard. In his basement, which served as an office and storage room for photos, computers, clothes, and books, Greene continued to counsel cops through emotional injuries. On almost any day you might find a Teaneck patrol car in his driveway and an officer in the basement unloading his frustrations.

Spath dropped by a few times to talk about himself. One afternoon in the first week of April 1990 Spath came with another problem. As the young officer turned off the engine of his white Chevrolet Caprice patrol car, Greene smiled and noticed Spath was holding something in his hand.

It was a mourning dove. Spath had found it by the side of a road and wanted to know if Greene could care for it. Greene took the bird in his thick hands and examined it.

The mourning dove had a broken wing.

THE SAME WEEK

The phone rang at the embroidery factory in Fairview where Thelma Pannell worked. On the line was a man from the Job Corps office in Newark. He was sorry to bother her at work, but he wanted her to have the good news. Her son, Phillip, had been accepted into a Job Corps program in Buffalo that provided electrical training for teenage boys who were not making it in high school. There was also a spot in a Job Corps program in South Jersey. But Phillip's mother said no to that. She wanted him as far away from Teaneck as he could be. "I didn't want him to come back," she said. All Phillip needed before he went with the Job Corps was a doctor's physical, the man said. He could be gone in a few weeks. She made a mental note to herself to tell Phillip to get his physical before Easter.

Thelma Pannell hung up the phone and smiled to herself. She suddenly felt lighter, as if a burdensome, wet blanket had been lifted from the place where she stored her worries about her son. For the first time in months she felt good about her son and his future.

Finally.

PART II

DELIVERANCE

SEVEN

THIS DIFFERENT
NIGHT

On Tuesday, April 10, 1990, the first day of Passover and the third day of Easter Holy Week, the morning sun blinked warm and golden from behind soupy gray clouds. By afternoon the clouds blotted out the sun, and a cold, intermittent drizzle began to fall. On the calendar it was spring, but the roller-coaster weather was wet testimony that winter still had not loosened its grip. That morning Phillip Clinton Pannell slept late in the back bedroom of his family's apartment in River Edge. After getting out of bed each morning, Phillip usually left the apartment, promising his mother to fill out job applications at local stores. But he never could seem to find a job.

Phillip's daily routine was a point of tension. Thelma Pannell wanted her son in school, but he refused, fearing another fight. "He didn't want to go to school," said his sister, Natasha. "He didn't want to talk about it with my mother either." His mother thought Phillip did not tell her much about his comings and goings because she would remind him how much she feared for him. One evening, weeks before, she had even dreamed he had gotten into a fight and died.

"Clint," she told her son afterward, "I had a nightmare like I went to your funeral." He answered the way he usually did: "Oh, Mom, don't worry about me. I ain't gonna get in no trouble. I'm gonna be all right."

By April she had resigned herself to hoping Phillip's appointment to the Job Corps would come through soon. In the meantime, she worried about the boy with too much time on his hands, and each morning she left him with a commandment that wasn't always followed: "You come home before I get home." On April 10 she planned to get home before six.

Except for the fight in January, Phillip had managed to remain trouble-free. To get into the Job Corps, he had to have a clean record. If he had any responsibilities, it was keeping to his court-imposed schedule to visit his probation officer in Hackensack once a week. On April 10 his probation visit was scheduled for 1:00 P.M. Before that he planned to fill out another grocery store application.

Thelma Pannell was running late that morning and didn't stop by Phillip's room to say good-bye and give her son her usual playful nudge in his leg to wake him.

Natasha went to the door of Phillip's room. "Mommy says come right home after probation," she called out. Natasha watched Phillip roll over.

"Uh-huh," he answered.

And then he went back to sleep.

———

It is impossible to go back and find an independent version of everything that took place on April 10, as, say, researchers have done to some extent at Dealey Plaza in Dallas, with the home movie shot by Abraham Zapruder on November 22, 1963, when President John F. Kennedy was assassinated. Little about the events of April 10 in Teaneck comes to us from the antiseptic realm of scientific objectivity. Certainly nothing comes from an unbiased lens of a movie camera. Most of what we know of the day has been percolated through the perspectives of many, much of it shaped and edited by the imperfections of personal memory.

In the lives of Phillip Clinton Pannell and Gary Spath—indeed, of all Teaneck—the truth and meaning of what happened that day and in the weeks thereafter were filtered through the hearts and minds and consciences of scores of people. Like spokes on a bicycle wheel, the accounts came from all points on the emotional and interpretative compass, yet all were aimed at one moment that became a crucial hub in the history of the town. Many who looked at the same event that day—or said they did—came to believe in accounts that seemed contradictory. Some ended up settling for a personal truth that was framed by their own righteousness. Often what was believed became a matter of faith in whoever was telling the story, his or her background, and even his or her skin color.

———

A few hours after his mother left, Phillip was up and dressed. He put on white sweatpants, black Reebok high-top sneakers, and a plain white extralarge T-shirt. He also put on two more layers that he could remove if he had to: an extralarge black hooded sweatshirt and the red parka his mother had given him for Christmas. On his head he wore a red baseball cap with a University of Georgia bulldog insignia. In the pockets of the parka he carried a crumpled five-dollar bill that had been ripped near the picture of Abraham Lincoln, two quarters, a dime, a Trojan lubricated condom, a tube of Vaseline wild cherry lip therapy, a book of matches from a Teaneck real estate agency, a plastic membership card to a video store with the message "Enjoy movies every day," a black Magic Marker, a plastic key chain from a business school with the message "Have the vision to look ahead," an audiocassette of a Seventh-Day Adventists' meeting over which radio rap music had been taped, and a crumpled piece of a desk calendar, dated February 20, with yet another printed sentiment: "It takes no time to break something; it takes time to fix it."

Phillip also carried a three-page job application. He had picked it up from a Foodtown supermarket a few days before, scribbling "4/ /90," but leaving the exact date blank. The application asked him to give his age, his address, whether he had a criminal record, and the name of his guardian. In each case Phillip answered falsely.

In thin, jagged handwriting that tilted slightly to the left because he wrote with his left hand, he jotted that he still lived in Englewood (not River Edge), that he was seventeen (he was really sixteen), and that he did not have a criminal record even though he was making regular visits to a probation officer. Perhaps the oddest notation came under the heading of "Person to be notified in case of accident or emergency"—his guardian. Phillip did not list his mother; he put down his mother's twin sister, Dale Monroe of Englewood.

He went on to note that he was applying for "stock or putting the carts in order," that he would take five dollars an hour. Under "Experience, skills, or qualifications which you feel especially fit you for work with this company," he wrote nothing. On the third page of the application he took a short test of his computing skills with ten math questions. In each case, two or three grocery items were listed along with a total price; Pannell was asked to compute the price of a single item. He got four of the ten correct.

That morning he also carried the silver pistol. In recent weeks friends had sometimes seen him with the palm-size pistol in the parka's inside breast pocket, but lately Phillip had kept the gun in the left outside pocket, where the flannel lining was already coated with crumb-size pieces of silver that flaked off the pistol. Phillip had carried the gun regularly for weeks. But he told friends he usually tried to bring it home and return it to its place in the box each evening in case his mother might discover it was missing.

Sometime around midmorning he left the apartment.

The Same Day

Gary Spath wanted to fish. His friend Father Bart Aslin had a day off and had asked Spath to go fishing off the Jersey shore. Baseball was Spath's favorite sport, but if he couldn't throw a ball around, casting a line into the Atlantic Ocean was a beautiful way to spend the day.

Spath told other officers he was looking forward to the trip, but when the date came, he was unable to take the day off or switch shifts with another officer. As usual, he would be on the job at 4:00 P.M.

Noon

Phillip Pannell waited by the back parking lot of the Mediterranean Deli. Up the hill, at Teaneck High School, three members of the Violators jumped into the black Mazda that had carried Pannell and four others to Hackensack three months earlier for the assault on Aaron Johnson at the bus stop. It was the same driver too: Malik. That January night he had swung a hammer at Aaron Johnson and was now on probation. He pointed the Mazda down the hill toward the deli. Along for the ride was another veteran of the January assault, Leslie (the crowbar user), as well as Steven, one of the original Violators. As Malik swung the car into the rear parking lot of the deli, the boys saw a familiar red parka. The Mazda ground to a halt.

Phil was standing by the rear door of the deli with another Violator, Ed, who had been in the gang fight with the Hackensack boys on the first day of school. At 1:00 P.M. Phil, Ed, and Leslie had appointments to see probation officers in Hackensack. Malik offered them a lift but couldn't wait to bring them home.

The visit to the probation department didn't take more than forty-five minutes. Phil, Ed, and Leslie caught a bus back to Teaneck. Ed went home. By 3:00 P.M. Phil and Leslie were in Leslie's house, trans-fixed by a Nintendo game.

3:45 P.M.

Gary Spath walked into Teaneck police headquarters and saw a familiar face. Spath normally worked four to midnight, and now his classmate from the police academy, Wayne Blanco, had joined the shift too. Blanco had been assigned for several months to a squad of plainclothes officers that tracked burglars but had returned to patrol duties the day before. Blanco was given car 11; Spath took car 9. Both were assigned to the northeast side of town.

In Teaneck so far it had been a quiet day. Blanco needed a jolt of caffeine, and when he eased his patrol car out of the driveway of police headquarters, he headed for a diner and ordered coffee to go. He then cruised to the western edge of town and the Fairleigh Dickinson cam-pus, where he parked next to another officer, Steve Librie, and talked.

In police work, chatting among officers is as common as writing tickets. It's nearly a requirement of the job, especially in the suburbs, where most cops ride alone, with only radios to keep them company between calls. The stress of the job, not to mention the boredom, almost forces them to seek out one another, sometimes just to exchange scuttlebutt about the latest regulation from the brass or to unload frustrations about the job and the toll on their families. In Teaneck there are several choice spots for police chats, usually out of the way of watchful supervisors but not so far off that an officer can't respond quickly to a radio call.

Spath cruised by Teaneck High School and pulled his patrol car into the rear parking lot, where he found one of his soul mates on the force, Officer Phil Lavigne. The week before, Spath had spent a day at the police shooting range, taking his pistol-shooting test. He scored 90 out of a possible 100, a fact noted by other officers who had joked with him about the 78.4 he had recorded at the target range only the pre-vious spring.

Lavigne looked across at Spath. It was now going on 4:30 P.M., barely thirty minutes into the shift. Spath seemed a bit downcast and mentioned he had wanted to spend the day fishing but couldn't arrange it. Perhaps prompted by Spath's yearning to cast a line in the water or just the faint signals of spring, the two officers talked of how they couldn't wait to take their families on vacation. Spath mentioned his children, then talked about the young boy he'd found two months before at Carl's Corner.

Lavigne realized that Spath was still bothered and a little hurt that he had been unable to see or even send presents to the boy after that weekend in February. Spath often wondered where the boy was and how he was doing, and in recent weeks he had volunteered to work with another youth—this one a black teenager named Franklin Robinson, who hoped to become a boxer. Spath had told Robinson he would help him get into shape and arranged to meet the teenager the next day at a local basketball court for some one-on-one. Spath didn't know it then, but Robinson was a distant cousin of Phillip Pannell's.

Lavigne asked if Spath had any plans for dinner later. Spath said no. Lavigne thought of the meal his wife cooked every Tuesday, chicken fricassee. "Why don't you drop over the house?" Lavigne asked. "Anytime after six."

4 P.M.

The Nintendo game over, Phillip and Leslie went for a walk. Leslie suggested they head over to the Wash Board Laundromat; he wanted to say hello to a girl he knew there.

The boys walked slowly as they headed north on Teaneck Road. Pannell was a half foot taller, but Leslie was broader in the shoulders. After a few blocks they ran into Steven riding a new Diamond Back mountain bike.

If you're a teenager in Teaneck, there aren't many businesses that will allow you to hang out. On Cedar Lane in the 1960s Spath's father had earned a reputation for chasing kids "off the corner" by a newsstand and candy shop. By the 1980s the Mediterranean Deli was one site where high school students congregated. Another spot, on the northeastern side of town, was the Wash Board, if for no other reason than the fact even teenagers had to wash clothes sometimes.

That day a girl the boys called Tomisha was doing a load of whites and colors. She was tall and popular with the crowd that hung out with Phil, Leslie, and Steven. The boys spent almost forty minutes with her, then headed back outside and southward on Teaneck Road

with no firm destination. As with so much of Phil's comings and goings
in those months, the one-mile stretch of Teaneck Road between his
old neighborhood around Circle Driveway and the William Cullen
Bryant Elementary School was something of a large playground where
he might meet any one of a score of friends.

The boys walked two blocks south and noticed a circle of boys and
girls on Howland Avenue: a fight.

Two boys, Jayson and Willie, were air boxing, posing, circling, pushing, trash talking, and occasionally landing a jab or two. Leslie looked
across Teaneck Road. Two of the Violators were there: Rasjus and
another veteran of the January assault, Shariff. Like Leslie, Rasjus and
Shariff had left school at noon. But instead of going to the probation officer, they had gone home to spend a few hours in front of
a television set before heading out to Teaneck Road. On this day
Rasjus wore a red Kansas City Chiefs parka, a red baseball hat,
and gray sweatpants. He could have almost passed for his friend Phil
Pannell.

Phil, Leslie, and Steven dodged the Teaneck Road traffic. The group
around the two fighters was yelling now, louder with each swing or
feint, egging them on. According to Steve, the fight seemed like a joke
one minute, then quickly turned serious.

More kids were there now. The crowd grew louder. It was hard to
determine what the fight was about. Someone explained Jayson was
tired of being teased. Someone else said Willie was just trying to prove
how tough he was. No one seemed in command.

Jayson landed a punch, then Willie. Then a door opened at a house
across the street. It was a man, leaning out and yelling, "Get off the
street! . . . Stop that fighting. . . . I'm gonna call the police if you kids
don't knock it off."

As if on cue, the group started to move slowly, northward, across a
vacant lot, through an opening in a wooden stockade fence, and into
a parking lot for a building that once housed the Friendly's Ice Cream
store, but had been converted into a store that sold day-old Wonder
bread products at discount prices. The group had grown to a dozen
kids. As soon as everyone was in the parking lot, Jayson and Willie
started swinging again.

5:08 P.M.

The phone rang at the dispatcher's desk in police headquarters. A woman was calling. Kids were fighting behind the Wonder bread store, she said. Please send an officer.

The dispatcher looked over the list of officers assigned to the northeast end. In Teaneck's police force the dispatcher usually doesn't call an officer by name on the radio. Each officer is summoned by a number that corresponds to the car he is assigned to. Blanco, in car 11, was simply "eleven." Spath was "nine." The dispatcher reached for the radio microphone.

"Eleven and nine?"

Blanco was finishing his coffee and his chat with officer Librie, more than a mile from the Wonder bread store. Spath, meanwhile, was heading into Teaneck's northeastern neighborhoods.

Blanco answered first: "Eleven."

A second later Spath responded: "Nine."

"Check in the parking lot behind the Wonder bread for kids fighting and another group watching," the dispatcher said.

Such a radio request from the dispatcher is routine. Also common is the lack of back-and-forth conversation with the dispatcher. In most cases a cop gets an order from the dispatcher and hears it once, no questions asked, no comments suggested. If the officer wonders how many kids are in the group, whether the weapons are fists, knives, rocks, pipes, or guns, or whether the kids are twelve or eighteen—all questions that might make a difference in how he responds—he doesn't usually get much help over the radio. The idea among police is to keep radio banter to a minimum, in part because so many civilians listen in. The problem is that cops often arrive at the scene of a potentially explosive situation with very little information to make their judgments.

Blanco's sign-off was standard. He said, "Eleven," and put his car in gear. "Nine on," said Spath. He didn't know how far Blanco had to travel or if it mattered. Spath turned onto Amsterdam Avenue, which took him to a spot on Teaneck Road directly across from the Wonder bread store.

Spath saw ten to fifteen kids. He figured the average age was about fifteen. Most were black males. He recognized a few faces. Spath knew Rasjus and his red parka. Spath had arrested him a few months before for robbery. He also recognized Shariff; he was lighter-skinned than

Rasjus and had a faint mustache. Spath also knew Rasjus and Shariff were involved with the Violators. Spath knew of the gang only from what he had heard from other cops, but the description was consistently the same: young black males, trying to make a name for themselves.

On this day, if there were fists being thrown, they weren't hurting anyone. Spath noticed two kids who seemed to have squared off. He pulled into the parking lot, braked, opened the door, and stepped out.

"Okay," Spath said, "what's going on?"

The kids turned. "Nothing," said Jayson.

"Just chilling," another voice answered.

Spath told the group they were on private property. "Why don't you get away from the store?" he asked.

The group started walking slowly north. Spath sat in the patrol car another five minutes. The kids seemed unorganized, certainly not with any purpose or place to go. He spotted a heavyset boy, perhaps fourteen, on a mountain bike. Spath didn't know the boy's name, but he remembered having seen him before on Teaneck Road with large groups of kids. He reached for the radio and called police headquarters. Willie picked up a rock and threw it at Jayson and missed, but if Spath saw this, he didn't take it seriously.

"Just chilling," Spath told the dispatcher.

"They're gone, Gary?" the dispatcher asked.

"They said they were just chilling."

The dispatcher signed off. "Okay. Just chilling. Ten-four."

"We may be back," Spath added. "They're splitting up into two different groups. They're all from around here. The, uh, a couple of the Violators. You know, Shariff."

Spath made a note of the time on the activity report he carried in his patrol car. It was 5:15 P.M.

———

Shariff looked at the officer in the car. He knew the face, not the name. "Everybody just moved," said Shariff, describing the scene later. "Everybody moved on."

Most of the group, including Phil Pannell, headed to another parking lot, a block north, behind the Jobber auto parts store. Shariff and Rasjus cut away and walked out to Teaneck Road to pop into the Caribbean luncheonette for a bag of potato chips, then headed back to the group.

Blanco never made it to the Wonder bread parking lot. He was halfway there when he heard Spath say on the radio that the kids were moving on. Blanco headed for Goodman's hardware store, north of Votee Park and by the railroad tracks, to have an extra key made for his patrol car. As he walked out of Goodman's with the new key, Spath pulled up across the street to say hello.

"Let's go down the street and talk," Blanco yelled back.

He motioned to a parking lot, another favorite spot for police chats. Spath made a U-turn and followed Blanco into the lot. The two had barely had a chance to utter more than a sentence or two before their radios jumped to life again.

5:22 P.M.

At the William Cullen Bryant Elementary School teachers and aides were getting set to dismiss children from the after-school program. As parents trickled in, a teacher looked out a window and across the street to the Jobber auto parts store, then dialed the police.

"Hi," the woman said when the dispatcher answered, "there's a gang fight in, um, across the street from Bryant."

"What do you mean, a gang fight?" the dispatcher asked.

"Well," the woman answered, "there's like seven . . . eight . . . ten people all fighting."

"Do they have any weapons?" the dispatcher asked.

"Like, well, I'm in school right now, and I can't tell, and the parents are coming in."

The dispatcher reached again for the radio.

The intersection of Tryon Avenue and Teaneck Road is one of the busiest in town. On one corner sits the Bryant Elementary School. On another corner is a small strip mall with a video store, a Christian bookstore, and the Wash Board Laundromat. On the third corner is an apartment house. On the fourth corner, in a no-nonsense one-story, white cinder-block building, is the Jobber auto parts store. Spath and Blanco arrived at almost the same time.

The group had grown larger now. Four girls had joined, as well as six more boys. The center of attraction, however, was still the two fighters, Jayson and Willie. At least one of the boys, Steven, spotted

Spath in his car and wondered if the police officer was following the group. One of the girls, Tomisha, who had walked from the Wash Board, noticed the group moving on. "Someone," she later explained, "said the police were coming."

Another of the boys, Delano, laughed as Leslie called out that the tall, stout Blanco looked as if he could pass for the rotund John Goodman who plays Roseanne's husband on her television comedy show. Delano looked to Blanco for a reaction and found none. The cop just asked the kids to keep moving.

Blanco guessed that Spath, in driving down the block on the other side of the auto parts store, had told the kids to keep moving north, toward the Bryant School. As he sat in his car at the auto parts store, some of the kids passed in front of him and started to cross the street. Others still milled about in the parking lot.

Blanco rolled down the window. "Fellas," he called out, "do me a favor, you know? Go somewhere else. No more fighting, all right?"

"Yeah," someone answered.

Just before he walked through the Jobber parking lot and saw Blanco, Rasjus recognized Spath. The officer was talking to Shariff.

Shariff was angry. He heard Spath tell the group to move on. It was the same command he had heard numerous times from police officers, especially when a group of black kids congregated. It was time, Shariff figured, to answer.

"I'm just walking home," Shariff yelled back. "You're harassing me."

Shariff says Spath got out of his car. "You want to see harassment?" Shariff remembers Spath saying.

Shariff said later that Spath walked over and checked his pockets. Spath said he never did any such thing. It would not be the only time on this day that the police version of what happened was entirely different from the kids'.

5:30 P.M.

Spath pulled into the Jobber parking lot and parked next to Blanco. The kids were moving into the Bryant School playground and a neighborhood of mostly black families in small brick Cape Cod houses. The group now numbered almost twenty kids. In recent years groups of mostly black kids had become a sore spot in community relations, either with their fighting or milling about stores or blocking traffic.

The police response, however, was the same as in the 1960s, when Spath's father and other cops had confronted large groups of white kids: Move on.

Spath looked at Blanco in his car. Their shift wasn't even two hours old yet, and already they had responded to two complaints about kids fighting. Spath started to mention how he had planned to go fishing, but he was interrupted by a driver rolling down the window of a car slowing on Tryon Avenue.

"There's a fight at Tryon Park."

It was 5:40 P.M.

―――――

Tryon Park sits square and green in the midst of Teaneck's largest black neighborhood. Approached from the east, along Intervale Road, the park looks almost like an amphitheater, with a grassy slope that leads into three basketball courts. Beyond that are five acres of softball diamonds, children's swings, a wading pool, and grassy fields, all surrounded by a ring of oak and maple trees.

For years a concrete wall sat atop the grassy slope at the northwest end of the park. It seemed to have no purpose other than to stymie erosion, but teenagers saw it as a grandstand of sorts and often sat on it to watch the basketball games or hid behind it, out of sight of police. On almost every night in the summer, you could count on a police car dropping by to order the kids off the wall. Finally Teaneck solved the problem: It knocked down the wall.

The lights that shone on the basketball courts represented another sort of Teaneck solution, this one slightly more positive. In 1968 black high school students staged a protest march on Teaneck Road, complaining, among other things, of a lack of recreational facilities. Teaneck looked to Tryon Park, a centerpiece of black recreation, for the solution and installed lights for the basketball courts.

On this day, April 10, it was still too cold for the night basketball games to begin. A few boys—Jonathan, Jabbar, Tyrell, and Corey— were playing on one court as Phil Pannell and the others walked up.

The group was larger now, including two kids from Englewood. Except for the punches thrown by Jayson and Willie, the kids were in a playful mood. Around 5:30 P.M. a light rain had begun to dot the macadam courts. Phillip, Leslie, and Rasjus milled around the grassy area in the middle of the park, air boxing with each other and laughing. Steven left to shoot baskets. The original fighters, Jayson and Willie, still had not buried their beef. A few of the others teased Willie. "They were telling Willie that Jayson licked him, and so Willie was getting aggravated," said Delano.

Willie took a swing at Jayson. And Jayson answered with a swing at Willie. Then another. Jayson was getting to Willie now, landing punches, pummeling him, pushing him. Willie's brother, Carl, watched the fight worsen. He stepped forward and clocked Jayson in the right eye, staggering him. Several kids gathered around to look at Jayson's eye.

Someone yelled the police were coming.

———

After he had pulled out of the Jobber parking lot, Spath headed east on Tryon Road for several hundred yards, then made a left into a neighborhood of houses that ringed Tryon Park. He slowly cruised the perimeter of the park, eyeing the kids. "They were just milling around in the basketball court," he said later, "goofing around and shooting some hoops, no problem, no fight."

Blanco took a different route and cut into a driveway into the park that work crews use. The driveway wound past a brick building with toilets, past three cedar trees and a wading pool. Blanco headed across a grass field that led to the basketball courts.

And drove onto the courts.

The kids were angry now. Who was this cop driving his car on the basketball court? Why did he do this anyway?

Steven turned as the car rolled farther onto the black macadam. "What the—?"

The cop was getting out of the car.

"Get out of the park," Steven recalls him saying.

On an adjacent court Jon watched the police car roll onto the first court and the cop asking, "Is there a disturbance going on here?"

The kids on the first court shook their heads. Someone said, "No."

The cop drove to the middle court.

"And then he was starting to get out of his car," Jon said, "but he didn't. He closed the door and got back in."

Jon watched the cop drive farther onto the courts and again ask, "Is there a disturbance here?"

Again someone said, "No."

The cop explained that someone had complained of fighting. "He kept driving on the court," said Jon, "and then he got so far we couldn't play no more."

"There were punches being thrown," Blanco said later, explaining why he had driven onto the basketball courts. "Yes. The combatants never touched each other, but they were throwing punches at each other."

Blanco said he opened his car door, put his left foot on the pavement, and stood up.

"I started to get out of the car and called one of the kids over," Blanco said. "He looked like he was maybe thirteen years old. He had a T-shirt on."

It was Willie.

"Where do you live?" Blanco asked.

"Teaneck."

Blanco asked the boy's name.

Willie said later he gave Blanco a phony name.

"Do you have an address?"

The boy pointed in a southerly direction, at no house in particular.

Blanco looked at him. "You got to knock this off. You're going to get arrested for fighting, you know."

From his spot on the street Spath watched Blanco. There seemed to be no ringleaders, no apparent plans for passing the time. A few kids started to leave the park. Others walked farther into the grassy field. Spath noticed Shariff and Rasjus.

Blanco was going to get out and talk to more kids, but the radio was summoning him and Spath again.

It was a 10-27: police radio code for a car accident. The dispatcher named an intersection with more than its share of fender benders. Spath made a notation on his activity sheet. It was 5:45 P.M.

When the cops drove off, Jabbar was the first to see a gun. Some of the kids were walking up the grassy hill, heading back to the Bryant School playground. Jabbar, who was fourteen, knew most of the kids but had not been with the group on its slow trek earlier along Teaneck Road. He had gone home right after school, dropped his books, and run out the door to meet his friend Shawn, who lived with his grandmother on Intervale Road. Shawn and Jabbar grabbed a basketball and headed for Tryon Park, where they ran into the larger group.

As the other boys and girls sauntered away, Jabbar walked toward the center of the park, to a spot where the ground rises slightly. Steve and Rasjus and Shariff were there. And Phil.

The boys were laughing. Jabbar figured someone had told a joke.

One of the boys playfully pushed another. From a distance it could have appeared that the boys were dancing, as they feinted toward each other, then backed away. Phil fell behind Jabbar while the other three stayed in front, and out of the corner of his eye Jabbar noticed a glimmer of silver behind him, as if a camera strobe had flashed.

Phil was laughing more now, and Jabbar turned instinctively. He saw the flash of silver in Phil's hand.

Phil had come closer now and held the gun to Jabbar's head for a second or two, then shoved it back in his pocket. He kept laughing.

Over the next ten minutes that Phillip Pannell stayed in the park, he took out his gun at least two more times. A boy named Durell said later he watched as Phillip pulled the pistol from an inside pocket and playfully appeared to shoot Leslie, saying, "Pow," and then shoved the gun into the left outside pocket.

In all, nine children later said they had seen some sort of gun that day. Not all of them saw Phillip's, though. The group of teenagers who walked through Teaneck's northeast neighborhoods on April 10, 1990, carried an odd array of firepower. Besides Phillip's converted starter's pistol, Leslie had a .32-caliber revolver tucked into his belt, and two boys from Englewood pocketed pistols, their calibers unknown. Shariff had a BB gun, which he was passing around, first to a boy named Bernie, then to Phillip, then back to Shariff. That day Bernie ended up shooting a fourteen-year-old girl named Melissa in the leg with the BB gun.

"We were all playing around," she said later to a grand jury. "It was just a plastic gun." When Shariff retrieved his BB gun, he approached thirteen-year-old Sylvia and some of the other girls, telling them to quiet down and stop laughing. If they didn't, Sylvia said later, he threatened to shoot them "in the butt." Whatever the threat, though, neither Sylvia nor any of the other girls left. In the days ahead the teenagers who spoke about this day painted a playful scene when they spoke about the guns to the police and others, as if the guns were something to joke about. Guns were enough of a rarity for the teenagers to stop and take notice and even be curious about. But the weaponry apparently was not enough to cause anyone to feel uneasy enough to leave or tell the police or his or her parents.

A fifteen-year-old named Gail happened to be watching Phillip when, she says, he reached into his jacket, pulled out the silver gun, and pointed it into the air. "I didn't see him point it at anybody," she recalled. "I just saw it. I didn't look at it after I saw it." Gail walked out of the park with the other girls. Melissa, Sylvia, Joey, and Tomisha.

"He had a gun with him," Gail said she told the girls. "I don't know what he did with it."

As Gail remembered, no one said anything.

━━━━━━

Rasjus was not shocked to see Phillip's gun. Two weeks before, on Teaneck Road, Phil had told Rasjus about his fears of being jumped as he spent more time alone on the streets without the Violators. Rasjus had heard some of the Violators talking about Phillip's new piece and how it had been converted. He asked Phil if he had the gun.

Phil nodded and opened the left pocket of his parka. Rasjus gazed in and saw the silver barrel. Rasjus asked if Phil had fired it. Phil nodded again and said that he had been alone one weeknight on Teaneck Road, waiting for a bus to take him to River Edge. A car passed with some Hackensack kids and slowed. Rasjus says Phillip told him he had drawn the gun, pointed it at the car, and pulled the trigger once. The car drove away. Phil's shot missed.

Rasjus says Phil told him something else: Sometimes Phil gave his gun to Leslie.

On one of those occasions, several weeks before April 10, Delano saw Leslie with the gun. Delano, who was sixteen years old, was walking his dog one afternoon when Leslie walked up with Phillip and another boy named Jamil who was carrying his own weapon that day, a BB gun. Leslie showed Delano the silver pistol. Delano thought he saw some rust on it. "He was just showing it to us, saying it probably didn't work, and Jamil was making jokes," Delano said. "He said that it probably would blow up in your hand."

He also remembered Phillip making a request to Leslie that day. "Keep that thing from me," said Phillip. But he took back his gun.

━━━━━━

Phillip had a name for his gun. He called it "my tool." Leslie says he saw Phillip with the silver pistol at least twice. In each case Phillip was at Tryon Park, playing basketball. The first time Leslie noticed a bulge in the left outside pocket of Phillip's coat and asked about it. "I brought the tool in my pocket," Phillip told him. "See, I told you I had it."

On April 10, however, Phillip was worried. He was watching the time and told several friends that he wanted to get home before his mother did so he could return the silver pistol to its hiding place.

"I don't want her to know I have it," he said.

6:10 P.M.

As the group slowly walked from Tryon Park, Michelle saw the BB gun. She says Phillip Pannell had it at that point. She does not know how he came to have it, nor does anyone else. The kids were now winding up the grassy hill onto a cul-de-sac called Gramercy Place. At the end a path led from the street through a chain-link fence onto the grassy field around Bryant School. On Gramercy the kids lined up in three groups. At the front were the girls. Several feet behind were Jonathan, Jabbar, and some of the younger boys. A few feet behind them came the Violators—Leslie, Phil, Shariff, and Steven. Rasjus had borrowed Steven's bike to ride home for a sandwich. At the end of the block the groups converged, slowly, like an accordion.

Michelle remembers seeing Phil draw the black BB gun and point it at Melissa's leg and laugh. Jabbar turned, and Michelle saw Phil point the gun at Jabbar's head and laugh again. She heard Jabbar laugh too.

And she heard Shariff say, "Pass me the BB."

"Phil passed the gun to Shariff," says Michelle.

As the group stepped into the Bryant schoolyard, Shariff started to walk away.

Halfway up Gramercy Place, as the pavement flattened and led to the schoolyard, Leslie saw Jon go over to a garbage can by the curb and grab a bottle. The boys had been throwing dirt balls at one another. Jon raised the bottle as if he meant to throw it at Leslie.

Leslie turned. He saw Phil reach into his left outside pocket and pull out the gun—"a little silver twenty-two revolver, with a brown handle with a crack in the back of it," Leslie said afterward.

Phil held the gun out, its barrel toward the ground. Jon still held the bottle. According to Leslie, Phil paused with the gun in his left hand. Jon was silent, and Leslie heard Phil say mockingly, "Do you think that bottle could handle this gun?"

"No," said Jon.

"You better not mess with him," Phil said. "I got this tool."

Jon put the bottle down, and Phil returned the gun to his pocket.

Someone laughed. As the boys walked toward the chain-link fence, the laughing grew louder. Someone yelled that the gun was a fake.

Leslie walked over to Phil. "Lemme see the gun," Leslie said. "That's how people get shot."

Leslie says Phil reached into his pocket. Leslie took the gun, popped open the cylinder, then took off his baseball cap and turned the gun upside down, its barrel skyward. The bullets fell into the cap. He snapped the cylinder shut and handed the unloaded gun back to Phil. Phil put the gun in another pocket inside his parka. Leslie scooped up the eight bullets and handed them to Phil, who put the bullets in his left outside pocket.

Leslie now noticed a house and a black man, tall, with the beginnings of a beard, opening the door, walking out, and standing at the bottom of the front steps as the boys walked by. Leslie figured he was going to do yard work.

Going into the schoolyard a few minutes later, Melissa found herself walking next to Phil Pannell. He turned to her, worried and somber. "He always said that he was always in trouble with the police," Melissa said later. Phillip was talking about not wanting to be arrested again or picked up for even the smallest of reasons. "They told him if he did," she said, "he would get put in detention, or something, because he was on probation."

A fifteen-year-old girl named Joey waited with Michelle and Melissa as the other boys walked up with Leslie and Phillip. The girls, who had gone up Gramercy ahead of the boys, stood by the chain-link fence at the end of the cul-de-sac. Jon passed by, then Jabbar, then Shariff and Jamil and the others. Joey heard someone say, "Oh, man, it's a fake. It's a fake."

Another boy chuckled and said: "Yeah, it is."

Joey wondered for a moment what they were talking about. Phil looked Joey in the eye. He was close to her now, no more than five inches away. "I was talking to Michelle at the time," said Joey afterward, "and then I looked over, and he had a gun, but I don't know if it was real or fake. I'm not sure about guns, but I did see a gun."

It was silver, she said, with a brown handle. She saw Phil reach with his right hand across his chest into an inside pocket on the left side of his red parka. He drew the gun, she said, and in one, almost nonchalant motion shoved it into the waistband of his sweatpants.

"No one thought it was a big deal," Joey remembered.

6:15 P.M.

Norman Brew saw the gun too. He thought it was a big deal. Brew, fifty years old, tall, African-born, had just arrived home on Gramercy

Place from his inspector's job with the New York City Health Department. He had a busy night planned; his list of things to do included getting his wife and eleven-year-old daughter to choir rehearsal and meeting a banker at the house to discuss refinancing his mortgage. If he had time, he also wanted to slip out to buy a new stereo.

Forty-five minutes earlier, as his wife tried to pull into the driveway from work, a group of seven boys and five girls had walked past, momentarily blocking her path. Brew, who had lived on Gramercy since 1971, had stood inside the glass storm door of his house and wondered about the group; his eyes went to two boys in red parkas. The group seemed headed from the Bryant School playground to Tryon Park, but their slow gait seemed to indicate they were headed nowhere in particular. As the group passed, in the direction of Tryon Park, one of the boys nonchalantly tossed a potato chip bag and a napkin on Brew's front lawn.

Brew felt himself getting angry. He was a proper man, fastidious, protective of his home and his family. His daughter would never toss garbage on someone's lawn. He decided not to say anything.

Now, however, the group that had tossed the potato chip bag was coming back up the street toward the Bryant School. Brew again was inside his storm door. Two of the boys cut across a neighbor's lawn, and Brew watched the boys play fighting. He figured if anyone in the group tossed more garbage on the lawn, he would walk outside and order them to pick it up.

The group passed, with the girls several paces ahead and the boys lagging behind. As the last two boys passed in front of his driveway, Brew saw a boy in white sweatpants, a red baseball cap, and a red parka reach into a pocket. Brew studied the boy for a second. The boy laughed and, with his right hand, pulled out a gun. Brew then saw the boy place his left hand in his left outside pocket and withdraw what seemed to be bullets.

Brew watched the boy bring his left hand up to the gun, as if loading it, then point the gun at the head of the boy next to him. That boy darted across the street to a garbage can, reached inside, and picked something up, as if he were going to throw it.

Brew had seen enough. He recalls thinking at that moment of his daughter and also what he later called his "civic duty to alert the authorities if I see something wrong."

He went inside and dialed the police.

6:16 P.M.

The caller seemed nervous and rushed. He spoke with a slight accent. He didn't give his name when the dispatcher at Teaneck police headquarters answered the phone.

"Ah . . . a bunch of boys in the Bryant School park or schoolyard. There is one with a red jacket on. I think he has a gun in his pocket. Check him out please."

The dispatcher asked the caller to stay on the line. "Sir, don't hang up yet," the dispatcher pleaded. "I need a little more information. What is he wearing?"

The caller paused, said, "I don't . . . ," then expanded on the description he gave moments before: "A red jacket and a red hat. It's a bunch of them. He is the only one with a red jacket on."

"All right," said the dispatcher. "They're in the back of the school, in the playground?"

"Yes."

"Ah, what street's that on?" the dispatcher asked.

"Ah, Bryant School is the one on Teaneck Road and Tryon."

"Okay."

The dispatcher radioed first for Blanco. He was three blocks from the Bryant School, sitting in his cruiser and filling out a report on an accident between a van and a car. No one was hurt, but plenty of metal was bent and twisted. It would take awhile to write up everything.

"Out of service," Blanco answered when the dispatcher asked if he was available.

The dispatcher called for Spath. "Bryant School playground, on a group of kids," the dispatcher began. "One in particular wearing a red jacket and red cap. Uh. Anonymous caller believes that that youngster has a gun in his pocket. Uh, he saw the weapon. He's not sure from a distance if it's a toy or real."

Spath heard the terms "red jacket" and "red baseball hat" and had a feeling he knew who it was. But he couldn't remember the name. He reached for his radio. "I got that," he said. "That's the—what's his name?"

Spath paused, then called Blanco on the radio, using a nickname that cops had bestowed on Blanco as a tribute to his girth. "Meat? What's that guy's name?" Spath asked.

Blanco had an idea too. Even though he was working on his report, he had been listening to the radio. When he heard the description red jacket and red hat, a name flashed through his mind: Rasjus Jackson.

"Jackson," Blanco blurted into the radio.

Spath hit the accelerator. He took a back street, skirted the perimeter of the park, and spotted a boy on a bicycle heading up Gramercy Place and toward the Bryant School playground. The boy wore a red jacket. It was Rasjus Jackson.

Spath reached for the radio again. "You sure that was in the Bryant schoolyard?" he asked.

The dispatcher came back on the air. "That's what they gave us. Bryant School playground, at Teaneck and Tryon Road."

"All right," Spath answered. "I got him walking up Gramercy now, at the dead end. I'm gonna stop him."

"Okay," the dispatcher said. "The backup will be a minute."

Spath lay back, slowly following the red-jacketed Jackson as he approached the dead end and the narrow opening in the chain-link fence.

Norman Brew had been waiting inside his front door since phoning the police. The boy with the gun was in the playground now and was standing by the corner of the school. Two of the boy's friends sat nearby on a box.

Three minutes passed.

Brew looked out and saw another boy in a red jacket on his street, this one riding a bicycle. He passed Brew's house and headed toward the schoolyard. Brew looked down the block and saw a police car that appeared to be following the boy on the bike. Brew was concerned now. The cop was going after the wrong boy. As the patrol car reached his driveway, Brew opened the door and stepped out.

Spath heard a tap on the side window. His eyes had been locked on the boy and the bicycle. Spath looked up and saw a tall black man with a beard: Norman Brew.

"Did you call us?" Spath asked.

"Yes," Brew said.

Spath eyed the man for a second. He was tall, middle-aged, black, with glasses. "He seemed very nervous, very concerned," Spath recalled. "He mentioned something about a gun to the head. He mentioned his daughter. I took it to mean the gun was pointed at the head of his daughter."

Later Brew insisted he never said or meant any such thing.

"Are you sure it was a gun?" Spath asked.

Spath remembers Brew saying, "Yes, I saw it. He pulled it out right in front of my daughter."

Spath pointed toward the boy on the bicycle in the red parka, Rasjus Jackson. "Is this the person you saw with the gun?" he asked.

Brew shook his head. "No, that's not him."

Spath looked into the schoolyard and saw another boy in a red jacket who was walking away: Shariff. Spath reached for his radio. "All right," said Spath to the police dispatcher. "There's another guy I can see in the play yard wearing a red jacket and a red cap."

"Okay," the dispatcher cut in. "That's the one I believe the caller was, uh, reporting, the one in the playground, red jacket, red cap."

Brew cut in. "No. No. No," he remembers telling Spath. Brew pointed into the schoolyard, to a third boy with a red jacket: Phillip Pannell.

"Do you see the guy with the red hat, the red jacket, and the white pants?" Brew asked Spath.

The boy was standing by the corner of the school, sixty yards away.

Spath put the radio microphone to his lips again. "All right," he told the dispatcher, "there's a guy wearing a red jacket, and the third guy is wearing a red jacket and a red hat and has got white pants on. I'm gonna try and make my way over there. Get someone else up there 'cause it looks like he might be, uh, offing this thing," discarding it.

For Spath, there was one additional problem. Gramercy Place was a dead end. He was blocked. He slammed the patrol car into reverse and backed down Gramercy Place.

Norman Brew wondered about what had just unfolded. The police officer had not asked him anything about the gun—its color or size. He hadn't even asked which pocket of the boy's jacket the gun was in. Indeed, he hadn't even asked Norman Brew his name.

Brew turned. The empty potato chip bag was still on the grass. He picked it up, walked up his driveway, and placed the bag in a garbage can. He then walked back to the curb to watch the schoolyard, the boy in the red jacket, and the cop who just left.

████████

Rasjus felt the cop behind him as he rode Steve's bicycle up Gramercy Place. Rasjus had left his friends at the park fifteen minutes earlier to pedal to his home several blocks away and grab a bite to eat. Rasjus did not live with his mother and father; his father was gone, and his mother had sent him to live with relatives.

Rasjus walked in, talked briefly to his aunt and uncle, played with his cousin for a minute or two, then headed for the refrigerator. He had not been home all day. He made himself a sausage sandwich, took a bite, then wrapped the rest of the sandwich and put it in the pocket of his red parka.

On Gramercy Place Rasjus looked back at the police cruiser and saw a face he knew, Gary Spath. He remembers Spath reaching for the radio.

Rasjus pedaled to the end of Gramercy Place and passed through the opening in the chain-link fence to the schoolyard. The girls and a few boys stood nearby, looking at Jayson's eye, which was swelling up badly from all the punches he had taken in his fight with Willie, including a sucker punch from Willie a few moments before.

Rasjus heard someone say, "Lemme see," as Jayson paused and covered his eye with his palm. "Lemme see."

"Oh, wow," someone else said.

Rasjus saw Leslie and Phil across the macadam playground. Leslie was sitting on a box by the school building. Phil was standing with his back to Rasjus.

Rasjus looked back at Gary Spath.

It had been an afternoon of dodging cops, and Rasjus didn't feel good about the scene now. "Keep going," he told the group.

Shariff saw Rasjus coming. He also saw the police car with Spath and was worried. Shariff, also wearing a red jacket, was standing by a door to the school. Phil and Leslie were a few yards away.

Rasjus handed the bicycle to Steve, then walked across the school-yard, repeating what he had said to the group that had lingered by the chain-link fence: "Walk . . . walk."

Shariff, with the BB gun in his pocket, turned and started to walk away from the school back toward Teaneck Road and ran into Sylvia.

"Get ghost," said Shariff, using the street term to leave. "Get ghost."

———

Like Shariff, Dexter St. Hillaire worried about the scene unfolding before him. He sat on the schoolyard swings with a friend, Calvin Dixon, sharing a beer and talking.

St. Hillaire had moved recently and wanted to check whether he had received any mail at his old apartment in a mustard-colored house on Intervale Road, but that could wait. The two men, both twenty-nine, saw the kids walk through the opening in the chain-link fence.

They saw Willie punch Jayson. And now as some of the kids gathered around Jayson to look at his eye, Dexter looked through the fence and saw the police car slowly rolling up Gramercy Place. He saw a boy in a red jacket ride a bicycle through the fence opening. The police car stopped and seemed to be waiting for something.

A thought flashed through St. Hillaire's mind: Maybe the cop is waiting to see if the kids are fighting. St. Hillaire figured he ought to warn the kids.

"Y'all better leave," he called out. "Y'all better leave the schoolyard because the cop is watching y'all."

St. Hilaire says some of the kids turned, saw the police car, and started to walk away, toward the school.

Blanco was cruising the edge of Tryon Park now. He spotted Spath's car as it backed down Gramercy and picked up his radio microphone. "Behind you, Gary."

Because Gramercy was a cul-de-sac, Spath was taking a roundabout route to the Bryant School: down a block, a right turn on Tryon Avenue, and past the schoolyard field. Spath had several choices: He could either drive into the school's main parking lot or drive out to Teaneck Road and surprise the boys from behind. Or he could cut across the grassy schoolyard.

Spath jumped the curb on Tryon Avenue, gunned the engine, and drove across the two hundred yards of grass. It was the quickest way to get there, Spath thought.

Blanco followed.

6:20 P.M.

"Look. Look at this." Steve saw the police cars driven by Spath and Blanco rolling over the grass toward him and the others by the school, side by side, like automotive cavalry. He turned to Phil and Leslie. "What are they doing?"

Phil started to sidestep, southbound, toward Teaneck Road. Shariff was ahead of him. Leslie, pulling on his yellow hooded sweatshirt, slowly backed up the other way, looking for an escape route.

It was too late.

▬▬▬

As he drove the two hundred yards across the grass toward the school, Spath says he didn't take his eyes off the boy in the red jacket and white sweatpants. His mind raced: First move the kids to the wall; then conduct a search. He weighed other possibilities. "I was concerned that the individual described with the white pants, the red jacket, and the red hat may have given the gun to someone else," he said. "I tried to keep an eye on anybody looking suspicious or trying to walk away from the general area."

But the boy in the red jacket was moving now, sidestepping, to the left, toward Teaneck Road. Shariff was heading that way too. And now a third boy, wearing a yellow sweatshirt, was trying to walk away in another direction. Spath watched for a split second and remembers thinking that the yellow sweatshirt's name was Martiz. He had arrested someone by that name before.

The police cars needed less than ten seconds to cross the two hundred yards from Tryon Avenue to the school. The boys, numbering about a dozen, were closer to the school, and the girls, only about six, were about fifteen yards away, milling on the playground by a large white circle painted on the macadam. Spath and Blanco stopped at the edge of a ten-foot-wide sidewalk that rimmed the school. A second later they popped out of their cars, pistols in hand.

"Freeze," Blanco called out.

The kids looked at the police, some in surprise, some fearful, a few angry. Steve heard someone—he thought it was Rasjus—yell, "Hey, there's little kids out here. You gonna point guns at little kids?"

"Up against the wall," Spath answered. "I mean, everybody."

Spath noticed Blanco seemed to be focusing on the boy in the red jacket with the white sweatpants. Spath waved his pistol at the girls, motioning them with a jerk of his head to join the boys. "Come on, let's go," he said.

A girl spoke up. "Why? What did we do?"

"Come on," Spath repeated. "Let's go. Over by the wall."

The kid in the hooded yellow sweatshirt seemed to be backing up, trying to slip away.

"You too!" Spath yelled.

The other kids were turning right, left, and moving, to the side, backing up, toward the wall.

All except Phillip Pannell.

He took a step toward Wayne Blanco and stretched out his arms, palms up.

Spath remembers Pannell yelling, "What's going on?"

Steven remembers Pannell saying: "Hey, you know, what's this all about? What did we do? You guys have no right—"

Everyone who heard him remembers Pannell stopping in mid-sentence.

Blanco figured that the boy in the red jacket coming toward him now, arms flailing and yelling, was trying to escape past a chain-link fence surrounding the Bryant School parking lot. Blanco moved to his left, toward the fence.

The boy stopped.

Blanco stepped toward the boy. With his right hand, he pointed his .357 magnum at the boy, holding it at waist level. He says he reached out with his left hand and patted the boy's coat, running his hand first down the right side, then the left. In the left outside pocket he felt something heavy. A barrel. A cylinder. A handle.

A gun, Blanco remembers thinking.

Blanco says he looked in the boy's eyes. It was only a fraction of a second, but it told Blanco everything he needed to know: The gun was real.

The boy spun to his left. And ran.

Blanco reached for the boy's jacket. And missed.

"Gary!" Blanco remembers yelling. "He's got a gun."

No one, not even Gary Spath, saw Blanco touch the boy in red, much less pat him down in some sort of quick frisk. Spath was looking the other way, at the boy in the yellow hoodie. None of the eighteen kids on the scene said they saw Blanco's pat-down either. Nor did any of the adults.

Norman Brew watched the confrontation unfold across the playground. He says the police never even got close to the boy in red before he ran. Across Tryon Avenue, about two hundred yards away, Calvin Dixon's mother, Ellen, looked out her kitchen window. Her grandchildren lived in the neighborhood across the playground. When they came to visit her, as they did almost every day, Dixon would leave her house and help them cross Tryon Avenue. From her window she watched the teenagers on the playground. Her grandchildren weren't there, and she was about to leave her window perch when she saw the police cars racing across the grass toward the kids. As the cops got out of their cars and she saw they had guns in their hands, Dixon muttered to herself, "You fool. Don't shoot them kids."

She says the larger of the two cops moved toward the kids, in particular a boy in a red jacket. But the officer got only within a few yards of the boy before the boy ran.

From the next room Calvin's brother, Melvin, heard his mother yell as the police cars stopped. He walked into the kitchen and looked out the window. He too saw the boy in red run before the cop got close enough to conduct a frisk.

From his seat on the children's swings, Dexter St. Hillaire never saw the frisk either. And no one heard Blanco yell, "He's got a gun," either—except one other person.

Gary Spath wasn't looking at Blanco. But when he heard the warning "He's got a gun," he says he spun toward the voice and saw the boy in red running toward him. Spath, pistol still in his right hand, moved a step to cut the boy off, but he was too late.

The boy bobbed and weaved, then slipped and fell as he reached a corner of the school, by an alley. The pavement was still wet from the earlier drizzle. He went down but caught himself with his hands. Spath paused, then reached out and managed to touch the boy's red coat. But he couldn't get a grip on the coat.

Pannell took off.

———

There is no foolproof procedure for cops to follow when chasing a suspect on foot. Do they sprint? Do they get on the radio and call for help? Do they back off, get the suspect's name, and track him down later? The answers to those questions depend on the time of day, the terrain, the potential danger, and the suspect.

But first another decision has to be made: Why try to apprehend the suspect in the first place? At the police academy cops are taught that almost every decision and action to stop someone should be governed by the concept called probable cause. In order to search a suspect, you must have probable cause that the person is doing something illegal. The same concept is at work when an officer pulls over a car. Was the driver speeding? Did the cop notice a broken taillight?

Gary Spath never saw Pannell's gun. Neither did Wayne Blanco. But Spath had a witness, Norman Brew, telling him that the boy had a gun. Under the rules of probable cause that was enough to approach the boy. What was more, Blanco said he frisked the young man and felt a gun—and communicated his finding to Spath. That, too, was probable cause. But a foot chase and the decision to pursue someone pell-mell—similar to a car chase—add another element to the situation. Police label that a judgment call.

As Pannell sprinted from his grasp, Spath had a split second to decide what to do. Cops who go through such an experience say afterward that they become entirely focused, shut out outside sounds, and act on instinct. The heartbeat doubles, and the mouth turns to cotton. Whatever the decision made, it is then often filtered through a series of emotions that have little to do with police work but everything to do with being human. There is the cop's personal pride and the desire to make an arrest and not look foolish. There is anger at a suspect for not obeying an order. Finally there is the cop's training and the unspoken rule that police should never give up a chase, especially if the suspect is carrying a gun.

Spath chose the most dangerous and unpredictable option, but one that is entirely common among cops in that situation. Gun in hand, he ran after the boy.

——

The driveway behind the Bryant School was built mostly for fire trucks or its more frequent customers—school maintenance workers and children walking to the playground. On one side of the alley is the school, on the other, an eight-foot-high chain-link fence.

Pannell sprinted the first 50 feet, turned right by the edge of the fence, headed across a patch of worn grass near the school, a sidewalk, and a curb, and found himself on Intervale Road. To his left, 150 feet away, he could see Teaneck Road and the rush-hour traffic passing on the wet pavement. To his right, Intervale Road ran flat and straight, past modest split-levels and other houses for one block to Tryon Park. In front of Pannell was a two-story duplex house that had been preserved with mustard-colored aluminum siding. To the left of the house, separated by a narrow piece of dirt where grass had trouble growing because of the shade, was a gas station. To the right was a side yard that ran the entire length of the house, from a hedge by the front curb to a stockade fence at the back property line. In front of the fence a forsythia bush had begun to bloom. Beyond the bush an iris garden lay dormant.

Pannell headed into the yard.

Spath stayed with Pannell, step for step—and then some. The twenty-nine-year-old still maintained the athletic build of a teenager, at five feet ten, 165 pounds, and most of his speed from his days as a baseball player and soccer wing. As Pannell skirted off the curb and onto Intervale Road, he looked over his shoulder; Spath recalled later that he saw a flash of surprise in Pannell's eyes. Spath felt the boy didn't think the cop could stay with him.

Blanco was at least thirty feet behind. Taller and more heavyset, Blanco was not the athlete Spath was. He lost sight of the boy and Spath as the two turned on the driveway. He too ran with his gun in hand.

As his legs churned, Spath says he kept up a steady litany of commands: "Freeze . . . stop . . . halt . . . freeze . . . stop . . . halt."

Blanco says he added one more: "Freeze or we'll shoot."

Across Intervale Road, witnesses say, Pannell jumped through a hole in the hedge. Spath followed.

Pannell ran another twenty feet into the yard, then slowed and stopped and turned.

Spath thought: The boy is plunging his left hand into the left outside pocket of his red parka, going for the gun. The boy is starting to turn. Yes, he's really turning, spinning, fast now.

Spath remembers thinking of the boy's gun. He hadn't seen it, but he was sure it was there. Blanco had told him. And if the boy had a gun and was reaching for it . . .

"I was immediately concerned that he was reaching for the gun, and that he was going to shoot me."

Spath says he raised his pistol to shoulder level, arms outstretched in the point-shoulder position he had been taught at the police academy. He wrapped both hands around the handle. He squeezed the trigger once. And missed.

Across the street Jennifer Bradley and Melvin DeBerry watched.

Bradley saw the cop shoot, heard the sharp pop of the Ruger .357 magnum cut through the evening sounds of drizzle and the whoosh of rush-hour tires on Teaneck Road. It was almost as if a slow-motion film were running and she were in a front-row seat.

Bradley, twenty-nine, and her neighbor Melvin DeBerry, a thirty-four-year-old warehouse clerk, had been strolling home along the sidewalk on Intervale Road after picking up some beer and wine at a liquor store when they saw the boy in the red jacket sprint out of the Bryant School driveway and cut across their path. Next came the cops: a skinny one first, gun in hand, then a heftier one.

Bradley knew the boy's name was Phillip. She had seen him before in the neighborhood. He jumped the hedge across the street. The skinny cop was in the street now. DeBerry says he instinctively put up his hand to stop Bradley on the sidewalk. "Jennifer, hold it," he said. "Slow up."

DeBerry says he'd barely finished the words when the skinny cop fired.

Bradley thought the boy seemed to wobble. She recalls him turning, facing the cops, his hands raised, palms out, at ear level. She remembers him yelling something, but she couldn't make it out. She assumed he was wounded.

DeBerry thought the boy was hit. He figured the bullet struck just as he reached the hedge, thrusting him through and causing him to stumble, and turn and face the officer. The boy, said DeBerry, did a 360-degree clockwise turn. The boy seemed frightened, and DeBerry recalls him shouting, "Hold it! I'm going to stop. Okay, okay, okay."

The boy's hands, according to DeBerry, were raised to shoulder height, his palms out and empty.

DeBerry, by instinct, started to duck behind a tree and tried to pull Jennifer Bradley back. But she lunged forward, screaming, "Don't shoot . . . don't shoot . . . don't shoot."

Two houses away, by her front porch, Dorothy Robinson heard the shot, then someone screaming, "Don't shoot!"

She looked across the street, a hundred feet away. She saw a flash of brown fur on the hood of Pannell's red parka and thought of her grandson Shawn, who she thought was playing basketball at the park.

Robinson, a private-duty nurse who takes care of patients in their homes, arrived home from her shift around 4:30 P.M. She drank a beer, read the newspaper, then walked outside around 6:10 P.M. to visit a sick neighbor a few doors away. She had reached the end of her front walk when she heard the shot and turned. The cops were in the street. A boy was in the yard next to the mustard-colored house.

"I saw this kid on the inside of the yard at Nineteen Intervale," she said, "and he had his hands up, not high, but up to his shoulder. And then I heard two of my neighbors. They were screaming, 'Don't shoot.' "

And then she noticed the boy's jacket. "I call it a bomber jacket," she said. "All the kids wear the jacket with that fur lining, and from where he was, I thought it was my grandson, because he has one of those jackets, and all I saw was the fur and his, you know, the little face, and I immediately started to run."

———

Blanco had stepped off the curb and was on Intervale Road. The boy had jumped the hedge and had gone into the yard. So had Spath. Blanco wondered for a fraction of a second why they had jumped; there were plenty of holes in the hedge to walk through.

Blanco says the boy didn't put his hands up, didn't yell anything either. "We were screaming at him, 'Stop, stop, we'll shoot!' " Blanco said. "He stopped, put his—this is all like simultaneously—put his left hand in his left outer pocket and turned."

Blanco insisted that the boy kept his hand in his pocket as he turned his shoulder toward Spath. But the boy didn't turn around far enough to face the officers fully. Blanco saw Spath hold his pistol at waist level, fire, and miss.

Blanco says the boy then took his hand from his pocket, turned his back on the officers, and kept running to the back of the yard, toward the stockade fence.

———

From his perch on the swings at the Bryant School playground, Dexter St. Hillaire saw the boy in the red jacket bolt from the cops. St. Hillaire ran, too—first down the driveway, then around the fence by the school.

He heard the first shot but couldn't tell which officer had fired. The thin officer, he said, was on the sidewalk; the heftier one was in the middle of Intervale Road. St. Hillaire looked past the officers into the yard by the mustard-colored house. He saw the boy in red and heard Jennifer Bradley scream, "Don't shoot!" He says the boy's hands were raised, to his ears, palms out. St. Hillaire says the boy turned, faced the officers, fell to his knees, and yelled, "Don't shoot."

And then, St. Hillaire recalls, the boy got up and started to run toward the back of the yard.

AFTER THE FIRST SHOT

Jennifer Bradley insists she saw the skinny cop roll-dive on the grass. She is the only witness who claims this.

She says Phillip was only a few feet away from the cop, his hands up and yelling something she couldn't understand. Phillip seemed to be trying to get his balance. The boy's back was to the officers.

Her companion remembers the scene differently. After the first shot, Melvin DeBerry says, the boy turned and faced the officers. The boy seemed to be spinning, off-balance. The boy's hands, DeBerry recalled, were thrust in front of him, palms out, chest high, as if trying to signal a stop.

A second shot was fired.

DeBerry saw the bullet slam into the boy, pushing him on his back, near the fence. DeBerry says the skinny cop fired the second shot.

Bradley thought the heftier cop pulled the trigger. Phillip, she says, had his hands up.

———

After the first shot Spath saw the boy take his hand from his pocket and keep running. Spath yelled, "Halt!"

Five seconds passed, maybe ten. As he tried to piece it together later, Spath wasn't sure of the time lapse, although he remembers it as only a matter of seconds.

Spath saw the boy run farther into the backyard. He says the boy stopped, put his left hand into his left outer pocket again, and turned his shoulder toward him. It was the same motion as before. Fast. A split second.

Spath says he felt the same fear that had caused him to fire the first shot. The boy was reaching for a gun, Spath thought. "He was going to shoot me," he said.

Spath squeezed the trigger again. This time the boy went down.

———

Melvin DeBerry ran across the street. So did Jennifer Bradley.

"What the fuck you shoot him for?" Bradley remembers yelling. "Why you do that? Why you have to do that? You don't have to shoot no more."

Dorothy Robinson couldn't see the boy in the jacket, but when she heard the second shot, she was already running across the street. My grandson, she thought. She leaped over the hedge and looked. She expected to find the boy only a few feet beyond the midpoint in the lawn where she had seen him when the first shot went off. But he was in the back now. He must have run, she thought.

She saw the figure lying on his back, his hands still open, his head tilted to the left, his left leg folded under him. His head was pointed toward the fence, near a log that had been discarded under the forsythia bush. The boy appeared to be lifeless.

The heftier officer was standing near the boy's head. The skinny one was several feet away, by the fence. Robinson ran to the boy's feet and realized that her worst fears were unfounded: The boy was not her grandson. Robinson's nurse's training then surfaced. "Let me try to administer CPR," she said.

The heavier officer turned to her. "No," he said. "Get back."

Robinson backed up a few feet and noticed the skinny officer. He had been silent, but now he looked up at his heavier partner.

"What the fuck did we do?" she heard the skinny one say, throwing up his hands and slapping his head. "Look at the shit we're in now." With that, she says, the skinny officer threw his radio against the fence.

Melvin DeBerry says the thin officer walked in circles after he threw his walkie-talkie. The officer, DeBerry said, pounded his head with his hands, one of which still held his pistol.

Dexter St. Hillaire was in the yard now. He says the skinny cop threw his gun as well as his radio against the fence. St. Hillaire saw the bulkier officer hold the boy's head in his hands, check the boy's pulse, then look up at his skinny partner. "We fucked up," St. Hillaire remembers the heavy officer saying. "What do we do?"

DeBerry has yet another version. The big cop was standing by the boy's head. He looked at his partner. "You fucked up," DeBerry heard the big cop say to the skinny one. "What the fuck you doing?"

Minutes later more of the neighbors trickled out of their homes and ringed the yard, edging closer, trying to get a look. Melvin DeBerry heard the big cop tell the crowd to get back and remembers someone calling out, "Why we got to get back? Why you kill the kid?"

DeBerry remembers the big cop's answer: "He got a gun."

THE POLICE VERSION

Gary Spath says he didn't curse at all. Neither did Wayne Blanco. The boy, say Spath and Blanco, went down when Spath fired the second shot.

As the officers approached the body, "We were still yelling at him," Spath remembered. "Don't move. . . . Keep your hands where we can see them."

The boy was on the ground. He wasn't moving as he lay on his back, his hands outside his pockets. Blanco, kept his pistol aimed at the boy and yelled repeatedly, "Don't move."

The cops were shoulder to shoulder as they neared the body. Blanco moved to the boy's head, knelt, and checked his carotid artery for a pulse. Spath knelt and felt the boy's wrist for a pulse.

Nothing.

Blanco fished inside the left outside pocket of the boy's parka. At the bottom Blanco found a gun, silver, with a brown handle. He looked at the gun for a second, then stuffed the gun into his right back pants pocket. Spath was still kneeling, and Blanco looked up. Spath was pale, silent.

"I think he's dead," Blanco remembers saying. He reached for his walkie-talkie and turned to one of the neighbors. "Where are we?" he asked someone in the crowd.

"Nineteen Intervale."

Blanco pressed a button on the walkie-talkie. "Nineteen Intervale," Blanco told the headquarters dispatcher. "I need an ambulance. Rear yard."

■■■■

It had been two minutes, thirteen seconds since the last radio transmission, when Blanco's and Spath's patrol cars pulled out of Gramercy Place and raced across the field to confront the kids. The dispatcher put out a call to other patrol cars. Blanco cut in again. "You guys better send the chief up there too, all right? We got shots fired."

"We gathered that," the dispatcher said. "What is the situation?"

"A kid's been shot. He does have a weapon," Blanco said. "A guy on Gramercy reports the guy threatened his daughter with the gun. We have the gun. This is a possible forty-four." In police radio code, "44" means death.

The crowd was getting larger now. Some people were screaming at the cops. *"Why did you shoot? Why did you kill him?"* Some believed Blanco had done the shooting. One black teenage boy ran up and spit in Blanco's face. Spath thought of his car and Blanco's still sitting at the Bryant School, doors open, engines running. He pressed the button on his radio and summoned the dispatcher.

"We got two police cars in the rear of Bryant," Spath said. "If somebody can, get a check on them. They're probably gonna go over there and do something to the cars."

Spath signed off and says he threw his radio against the fence at this point.

"I threw it because I was disgusted," he said later. "I couldn't believe what had happened. I was disgusted. I was frustrated. This guy put me in a situation where I was forced to shoot him and take his life."

EIGHT

BITTER HERBS

In Hebrew *Seder* means "order," and the Passover meal that bears its name is nothing less than an orchestrated feast that follows an age-old script and aims to evoke for modern Jews the story of their ancestors' exodus from Egyptian slavery. It is an evening of storytelling and symbolism, with the youngest child beginning the recital of the Passover story by asking, "Why is this night different from all other nights?"

Art Gardner had been raised as a Baptist, but as a black man whose ancestors had been slaves and whose childhood in segregated South Carolina had caused him to embark on his own exodus northward, he found much symbolism in the annual Seder meal prepared by his Jewish wife, Susan. On April 10 Gardner's schedule was full. That afternoon he conducted a practice for his son's Little League baseball team. It had been raining off and on all day, but Gardner, who had volunteered to coach, wanted the boys to get in as much hitting and fielding as possible. Sunset was not until almost seven, but it had become so overcast and rainy that Gardner decided to call it quits. Anyway, there was Susan's Seder meal to get home to. In deference to Jewish tradition, she liked to begin just after sunset. Gardner checked his watch. It was after 6:00 P.M.

Two players needed rides home. One boy lived on the southern end of Teaneck two miles away; the other on Teaneck's northeast side, on

Intervale Road. Gardner started his car. It would be easier if he headed first to the southern end. The trip took less than twenty minutes, and by six-thirty Gardner was in rush-hour traffic heading to Teaneck's north end. He passed the Bryant School and signaled to turn right.

And stopped.

Before him, blocking the street, were an ambulance and several police cars parked at odd angles. On the sidewalk he could see twenty to thirty people. He pulled over to the curb by the school, dropped off the other boy, and turned to his son, Jerry. "Stay in the car, son. Don't come out."

In the rear of the yard next to a house Gardner saw paramedics hovering over a body on the grass. His eye was drawn to a Teaneck police officer in navy blue pants and light blue uniform shirt standing by the curb. The man was thin and balding and seemed unusually frail for a cop, Gardner thought. The cop stood with his hands folded in front of him. His head was down.

Across the yard, by a driveway, Gardner heard voices, loud, angry, and coming closer. He turned.

"He shot the brotha. *He shot the brotha.*"

It was a black kid shouting, his voice rising with each syllable as he strutted up to Gardner, the boy's fingers poking the air for emphasis. Gardner recognized the boy from one of his gym classes at Teaneck High.

"*BRAAAAA-tha.*"

Confused for a second, Gardner looked into the backyard. He turned back to the boy.

"Who?" Gardner asked.

The boy's face rippled in anger. His finger pointed at the thin cop standing by the sidewalk, head down. "Him," the boy said. "That bald-headed white muthafucker shot him."

Gardner looked into the backyard. He noticed a red coat. He turned to look again at the slender policeman standing now with two other officers. Gardner did not recognize him, but with every word from the crowd, the officer seemed to stoop even more. This guy, thought Gardner, looks awfully sorry for what's he's done.

Gardner heard more shouting. It was other black kids now. "*Let's get that muthafucker.*"

A group of teenage boys bolted out of the yard and headed toward the thin cop. Gardner stepped onto the sidewalk, between the boys and the cop, and raised his right hand in the universal sign for stop.

"Fellas," he boomed, "hold it. *Hold it!*"

The group stopped. Most knew Gardner from the high school and respected him. And if they didn't know him, Gardner's six-foot-four, 230-pound presence, not to mention his booming voice, was enough to get their attention.

"Fellas, don't do anything stupid. Now you go on back."

The boys turned, still yelling and cursing, and walked back to the driveway, twenty feet away. Gardner gazed back at the cops to see if they were safe. The thin one didn't say anything. One of the other officers, who had once played football at Teaneck High School for Gardner, looked up. "Thank you, Mr. Gardner."

Another officer took the thin cop by the arm and guided him across the street to a patrol car.

Still waiting in his father's car and watching the scene before him, Gardner's son, Jerry, listened as the crowd near the sidewalk started to discuss the incident.

"Shot in the back," someone said.

"The boy wasn't moving," said someone else.

Art Gardner looked again at the paramedics in the yard. They were lifting the boy with the red coat and placing him on a stretcher. He seemed limp. Gardner heard someone mention that the boy's name was Phil Pannell. Gardner knew Phillip, but as the stretcher went by, he couldn't see the boy's face; it was covered by an oxygen mask.

The street was crowded, but Gardner felt suddenly alone, almost distant for a brief second or two amid the noise and the rustle of men in police uniforms, of paramedics with stretchers and stethoscopes, and residents with their angry vocabulary. Gardner walked back to his car, feeling the press of time. Susan would be wondering where he was and why he wasn't home for the Seder. He paused before leaving and took in the scene. Here, thought Gardner, a police officer felt compelled to draw his gun and fire it at a teenager. Here now paramedics struggled to save the boy's life. We try to take a life on one hand, Gardner thought. On the other, we try to save it.

On Passover.

—————

The boy wasn't breathing. His heart wasn't beating.

Officer Phillip Lavigne pulled the stretcher into the ambulance and leaned over the boy and pushed on his chest—once, then again and again and again. Among those who know first aid, this process is called cardiopulmonary resuscitation. To the general public, the name has been reduced to three letters: CPR. The process—essentially a steady pushing against the chest—is a crude but often effective way to jump-start the heart and lungs of someone who for all practical purposes is dead or close to it.

Almost by instinct, Lavigne pumped. He knew shots had been fired, and he figured his friend Gary had pulled the trigger. Minutes earlier Lavigne had been home, eating his wife's dinner of chicken fricassee. He had expected Spath to walk in, but after he took off his gun belt and sat down at the table, he heard a brief exchange of messages on his portable radio about a gun at the Bryant School. He kept eating; the call was not in his patrol sector. But the more he listened, the more concerned he became. When he heard Spath's voice say the suspect might be "offing" the gun, he put down his fork, strapped on his gun belt, headed out the door, and climbed back into his patrol car.

When Lavigne arrived on Intervale Road, he saw Spath heading toward a patrol car with a sergeant. The nearby crowd was screaming. Spath, who looked pale, got into the passenger seat. Lavigne walked over to the car and noted that Spath's holster was empty. He studied his friend for a second. Spath wasn't talking and was staring ahead, a glazed look in his eyes. Lavigne wondered if Spath knew what was going on. He seemed in shock.

Lavigne walked across the street to the stretcher with the boy on it. A woman paramedic was trying to perform CPR but was having trouble keeping up the pace. Lavigne asked to take over.

He kept pumping as the stretcher was lifted into the ambulance. The doors closed, and the ambulance started to move. Lavigne, swaying and starting to lose his balance as he stood over the body, felt a hand grasp the back of his gun belt and steady him.

It was Officer Wayne Blanco on the ambulance seat behind him. Lavigne kept pumping. The boy did not respond.

No one spoke.

———

Spath was hardly speaking either. On the way to the hospital Sergeant Fred Ahearn steered the patrol car through the traffic. The two-mile trip took only eight minutes, Ahearn figured when he recounted the scene later. Spath mumbled a few phrases under his breath, one of which stood out clearly to Ahearn.

"I took a life," Spath said. "What will God say and what will my family do?"

Two miles away, at the home of his in-laws, Paul Ostrow had finished the Seder meal with his family. He felt full. It had been a joyous evening. Paul's wife, Ricki, was there, as were their son, Michael, and daughter, Lauren. Afterward Ostrow picked up the portable radio that he used to monitor ambulance calls. He had turned it off during dinner, not wanting to be disturbed during such a solemn meal. He pressed a button.

Odd, he thought.

On the radio police were talking about calling in the county prosecutor. An officer said that he had notified the chief. Another officer asked if other police departments had been called.

For what? Ostrow wondered.

He went to the telephone and dialed the ambulance corps headquarters. No answer.

He dialed police headquarters on a special line that is used mainly by ambulance volunteers and other emergency workers.

"What's going on?" he asked when the dispatcher picked up.

"We had an incident involving a weapon." Ostrow could tell much from the tone of her voice. She was terse, matter-of-fact. Ostrow took it as a signal that he shouldn't be tying up the line. He hung up and dialed the ambulance headquarters again. By this time one of the paramedics had returned.

"So what happened?" asked Ostrow.

"One of the cops shot and killed a kid."

Ostrow was stunned. "Who?"

"Gary," the paramedic said.

"Which Gary?" said Ostrow.

"Gary Spath."

"Gary Spath?" Ostrow barked. "What happened?"

"There was a report of young kids toying with a gun or pointing it at others."

Ostrow set down the phone and turned to his wife. "Gary Spath just shot and killed a kid."

The words hung there for a moment. They were almost surreal, Ostrow remembered. As quickly as he said them, a scene flashed into his mind. He thought back four months to that day in December when he had watched Gary Spath comfort the husband who had found his wife dead at home. Ostrow recalled the letter of praise for Spath he had sent to the newspaper. "Extremely professional," the letter had said. "Unusually caring and compassionate."

Ostrow looked out the window. It was dark and raining now, and he wondered: Why were kids out in the rain at the dinner hour?

In her apartment in River Edge Thelma Pannell wondered where her son was. It was now almost seven and she hadn't heard from him.

Earlier, around 4:30 P.M., as she drove home from the embroidery factory, she instinctively headed north on Teaneck Road to look for Phillip, near the Wonder bread store, the Jobber auto parts, the Bryant School, or Tryon Park. She knew most of his hangouts. But in recent weeks he had stayed out of trouble and seemed to be turning away from his bad habits. After several blocks Thelma Pannell turned off Teaneck Road and took another route home. She remembered how Phillip often felt strange when she pulled up in her car to take him home. Sometimes, she says, he chided her afterward: "Ma, don't embarrass me in front of my friends." That day she decided she would cut him some slack.

In her apartment she stood at the mirror in her room, brushing her hair. She heard heavy footsteps on the stairs leading to the apartment door from the first floor. Natasha opened the door. It was Steven and two other boys, but no Phillip.

Thelma Pannell walked out. One of the boys, Kyle, seemed out of breath. Another boy, Michael, who was older than the other two, spoke first. "Mrs. Pannell, Phil got shot. I think he's gonna be all right."

She looked at the three boys standing in her kitchen.

"By whom?" she asked.

Kyle answered, "By a cop."

"Why?" she asked, not waiting for an answer. She asked where her son was.

"At Holy Name Hospital."

She turned to Natasha and told her to fetch some of Phillip's clothes. He might need a clean set. Natasha went to Phillip's bedroom, opened a drawer, and took out a white T-shirt with a race car imprinted on it. It was one of her brother's favorites.

Thelma Pannell went to her car. With her daughter in the passenger seat, she drove past the grocery store where her son had told her he had picked up a job application. As she reached Teaneck, she pulled over to the curb. She put her head on the wheel and started to cry.

"I just know he's dead," she told her daughter.

Phillip Pannell was declared dead at 7:08 P.M.

The official pronouncement by a physician merely underscored what seemed to be a foregone conclusion. From the moment the bullet slammed into him from behind, Pannell never regained consciousness. At Holy Name Hospital's emergency room, where Pannell was brought around 6:30 P.M., four doctors were summoned to try to revive him. As he lay on bed number eight in the emergency room, the doctors and nurses quickly hooked up intravenous lines and inserted tubes into each side of his chest to expand what they suspected was a collapsed lung. When a surgeon arrived, he slit open Pannell's left side and performed a thoracotomy. It was a desperate attempt to repair any damaged organs and massage Pannell's heart into beating again. But it was too late. The chest cavity was filled with blood.

The first bullet from Spath's revolver had missed Pannell, but the second was as deadly a shot as could be, slamming into his back, a fraction of an inch below his left shoulder blade, a few inches to the left of his backbone. From there the bullet passed through Pannell's rib cage on a diagonal and ripped into his aorta, his heart, and his lungs before coming to rest under his skin to the right of his sternum. Doctors could even see the bullet protruding from the skin like some enlarged boil.

Spath arrived at the hospital emergency room shortly before Pannell. Sergeant Ahearn told doctors that Spath had been involved in a shooting and was emotionally upset, possibly in shock. Doctors led Spath to a small examining room set aside for women who have been raped or who are pregnant and in the throes of unexpected labor pains. Spath took a seat in a chair. A few minutes later Blanco and Lavigne came into the room.

Spath was leaning forward, his elbows on his knees, his head down. The room was stuffy, and Lavigne looked down at his friend, then bent down and unbuckled Spath's gun belt and took it off. He unbuttoned Spath's shirt and removed his bulletproof vest, found a wet rag, and started wiping his friend's neck and face.

"Hang in there," Lavigne said. "It's going to be okay. We'll get through this."

Spath looked up and shook his head. "I wish I wasn't married or had any kids," he said.

Spath turned toward Blanco. "Was it real?" Spath asked.

Blanco reached into his right rear pants pocket and pulled out the silver revolver he had found on Pannell. He held up the gun a moment for Spath to see.

"Yeah," said Blanco, "it's real."

Spath didn't respond.

Minutes later Blanco walked into the hallway and ran into Chief Burke, who asked, "What happened?"

Blanco ticked off the basics of the story: the call on the radio about a gun, the drive across the grassy schoolyard, Blanco's frisk of the boy in the red coat, his shout to Spath that the boy had a gun, the chase, the shouts of "halt" by the officers, the boy turning, and the two shots by Spath.

Burke asked to see Pannell's gun. Blanco again plunged his hand into his back pocket and pulled out the silver revolver. He held it before the chief with two fingers. Burke looked at the gun, his eyes especially drawn to the chamber and the variety of long and short bullets protruding from it. He said nothing. But after other versions of the shooting later emerged, the chief noted something different about the story Blanco had told him. Blanco had never mentioned that Pannell put his left hand in his pocket to draw the gun.

Burke asked where Spath was. Blanco pointed to the door to the ob-gyn room.

Spath was still sitting in the chair, his head down. Burke propped himself up on the examining table.

"What happened?" the chief asked.

Spath turned toward the chief. "Do you want me to tell you now or after I throw up?" he asked.

Burke asked everyone else to leave the room. Only he, Spath, and Sergeant Ahearn remained.

"What happened?" Burke asked again.

Spath seemed upset. The anger that had flickered moments before had disappeared. His voice was barely audible now. "I don't know," he said.

"I have to know what's going on," Burke said, "to determine how to conduct the investigation."

Spath didn't answer.

In the hallway now Lieutenant Patrick Hogan found himself alone with Blanco. "What happened?" Hogan asked.

Blanco again went through the story, beginning with the radio call and the dash across the schoolyard. He said that he had frisked Pannell, that Pannell had darted away, and that he and Spath had followed him. In this version, Blanco added that Spath was faster and was closer to Pannell. And from the way Blanco described the first shot, it was Hogan's impression that Blanco thought Spath was firing a warning shot at the boy.

Hogan was puzzled. Warning shots were illegal. But he also knew Blanco had recovered a pistol from the boy's pocket. So the boy was armed and potentially dangerous. But why fire a warning shot?

The boy had turned toward Spath, said Blanco, describing the motion as a "threatening move." But Hogan figured it was one thing to turn toward a police officer in what could be perceived as a threatening way; it was something else to turn with a gun in one's hands. If a fugitive turned and pointed a gun, an officer would be justified in firing a shot in self-defense. To turn with one's hands empty was an entirely different matter.

Blanco had not mentioned whether the boy had the gun in his hands or, for that matter, if he was pointing the gun at Spath in some kind of attempt to outdraw the officers.

It was an obvious point, Hogan thought, a basic piece of the investigative puzzle that could shed light on whether Spath's shooting was justified or not. Hogan wasted no time asking about it. "Did the kid ever have the weapon in his hand?"

"No," said Blanco. "He never put his hand in his pocket. He just moved toward it."

Hogan was not satisfied. He asked Blanco if Pannell's hand ever made it into the pocket.

"The hand," said Blanco, "never got into the pocket."

———

The phone was ringing as Batron Johnson walked in the door. He answered with his standard greeting: "Yo."

The greeting usually was returned in kind, but this time the voice on the other end of the line was loud and hysterical. It was a friend named Mike. "Phil got shot. *Phil got shot!*"

Batron could think of only one thing: Mike was playing some sort of sick joke.

"Stop playing," Batron said.

But Mike's voice grew even louder. "No, for real. *Phil got shot. Phil got shot.*"

"Meet me on the corner," Batron said. He slammed down the phone, grabbed his coat, and headed for the front door.

Minutes later Mike walked up, still repeating his earlier message. "Phil got shot." He didn't say how, and Batron didn't think to ask.

Mike said Phil had been taken to Holy Name Hospital. Batron figured that was a good sign. "Let's go to the hospital," he said.

The two boys first linked up with Chuckie, who had been sick most of the day with the flu and was lying in bed watching *Jeopardy* on television when Mike phoned. It was raining again as the three boys reached Teaneck Road and started to walk the half mile to the hospital.

He'll be okay, Batron said to himself. He'll be all right.

"I hope he just got shot in the leg," said Chuckie, thinking that Phil was only wounded.

Mike said he'd heard Phil was shot in the shoulder. Chuckie wondered for a second if Phil might be paralyzed. Just as quickly another thought flashed before him. "He could die from that," Chuckie said.

The boys looked at one another for a moment, then spotted another boy, Raheem, already running toward the hospital. They started to run too.

Captain Tom Pierson's phone rang just after seven. He was home in Fort Lee that night, wondering how his wife was doing. She was one of only a handful of female ambulance technicians in the old industrial city of Paterson and was working until eleven. As he listened to the voice on the phone, Pierson knew he too would be up late.

An officer at Fort Lee police headquarters was calling to explain that a cop in Teaneck had shot a kid. Could Pierson get to Holy Name?

Pierson was in his twenty-fifth year on the Fort Lee police force, but in the last few years he had become a counselor to cops and firefighters who needed a helping hand during traumatic moments. It was a vocation he had come to painfully. In 1966 his partner had been gunned down in a motel near the George Washington Bridge while checking out a report of a robbery. Pierson had been off that night, and only years later did he realize how deeply his partner's murder had affected him. Initially Pierson had felt guilty for not being with his partner. He was angry at the man who pulled the trigger yet also terrified for himself. In the years afterward he noticed how no one had ever asked him how he felt and what sorts of troubles may have afflicted him. Pierson eventually realized he was keeping too many of his feelings bottled up. He was a decorated cop, cited numerous times for bravery. He also was an occasional instructor at the county police academy, with a specialty in pursuit and SWAT team tactics. But if the police were well schooled in chasing suspects and firing weapons, Pierson came to realize they learned almost nothing about how to deal with the emotional trauma of seeing people die and possibly having to take a life in the line of duty.

With the help of a Catholic priest, Pierson formed a group of counselors for cops and firefighters. The group's first test came in 1988, when it counseled Hackensack firefighters after five members of the department were killed in a building collapse. The call from Teaneck, though, was Pierson's first request to counsel an officer who had shot someone. He threw on a white golf jacket and headed for the hospital.

The rules of counseling cops are not etched in stone, but Pierson knew he had to establish quickly that he was not there to judge the officer. From his own years on the force, he knew it was not uncommon for cops to feel defensive about themselves and what they do. The nature of police work causes this, Pierson explained, even more so than the emotional makeup of cops. Most police work involves having to administer hundreds of laws, usually against people who believe they are as innocent as newborn infants. If a cop doesn't follow every footnote of every procedure in something as routine as writing a traffic ticket, he not only has to answer to an angry citizen (and perhaps a high-priced lawyer) but has his chief breathing down his neck too. When a cop shoots someone, said Pierson, he feels as if he's on trial even if he never enters a courtroom.

As he walked into the hospital ob-gyn room where Spath was sitting alone, Pierson figured he'd better establish his ground rules. "Do you know who I am?" he asked.

Spath nodded. "You taught me when I was at the academy."

Pierson couldn't remember Spath's face or name. He looked for a brief moment at the officer before him, slumped, shirt open, clearly hurting.

"I don't want to know exactly what happened," Pierson said. "I'm not here for that purpose. I'm here because I went through a bad incident myself. I don't want to know about your incident. I don't want to hear if you did it justifiably or not, whether you're guilty or something went wrong. Let's talk about how you're feeling right now."

"I feel like shit," said Spath. "My God, I killed a kid."

Spath gazed back at Pierson, eye to eye. A good sign, Pierson thought. Eye contact is a quick, usually accurate way to assess the person who is talking. If the cop had been looking away from him, Pierson would be suspicious.

"I responded to a gun call and I got there and I thought this kid was drawing a weapon, and I pulled the trigger. And I'll never be right again."

Spath started to sob.

Pierson walked across the four feet of floor that separated them and put his hand on Spath's shoulder. "It's okay," Pierson said. "You're allowed to feel this way, and what you're going through right now, you're going to go through a lot more of this shit. This is what happens every time it happens because we're good people and we really feel it."

"I don't know what I'm going to do now," Spath muttered. "I just don't know what I'm gonna do."

He kept repeating the sentence. Pierson let the young cop keep talking.

"There was no other way," Spath said finally. "I had to do it."

"Okay," said Pierson. "I can accept that. I know that. And you're going to start feeling guilty later on. Maybe you could have or maybe you shouldn't have."

Spath said, "If only I hadn't gone on the call. If I only hadn't responded. It wasn't even my call. I just went to help."

Pierson suspected Spath was in shock. He had seen it before with the firefighters in Hackensack. A person who is traumatized slips into a back-and-forth, Ping-Pong set of emotions, first not believing what has happened, then sobbing at the realization.

"Look," said Pierson, "you're not going to understand what's going on now. It's gonna hurt you, and you are going to be interviewed. You are going to be interrogated. All you've got to do is tell the truth and know that people out there are supporting you and they've been there before."

Spath was silent. Pierson wondered if the officer was starting to insulate himself—another common occurrence after trauma. He put his arm around Spath and hugged him slightly. The gesture seemed to bring Spath back from whatever he was thinking.

"Thank you," Spath said. "Oh, my God. What's going to happen to my family? What's going to happen to my wife?"

———

Down the hall, in the otherwise empty emergency room, Thelma Pannell rubbed her son's arms and legs as he lay on a bed. Phillip seemed asleep, his mouth slightly ajar. She picked grass out of his hair. His skin, somewhat warm when she first was brought into the emergency room, was turning cold.

Phillip's sister, Natasha, called her brother by his middle name, repeating, "Clinton, I love you. I love you."

A Catholic priest from the hospital approached and led them in a short prayer. Thelma Pannell tried to focus her thoughts on God, but her mind raced. Why did they shoot him in the back? she thought.

As she left the hospital, she decided she would not return to River Edge that night. Instead she drove to her aunt's house in Engle-wood. She didn't want to be alone. Her husband was still in the county jail.

———

Pierson looked up. The door opened, and another officer poked his head into the ob-gyn room.

"There are a lot of people outside," the cop said, explaining that the driveway outside the hospital was choked with kids, cops, and reporters.

"Where's Gary going now?" Pierson asked.

"Back to the station," the officer said.

Pierson asked if he could bring Spath out the front door without having to walk through a gauntlet of people and reporters. The officer nodded, and Pierson handed Spath his white golf jacket for a disguise. As the two men walked out the front door of the hospital, Pierson figured they probably appeared to be just another pair of visitors.

Back at the police station Pierson took Spath into the basement locker room. On the wall heading downstairs a bumper sticker depicted an American flag with the promise "These colors don't run." Beyond the steel lockers, near the shower with its eternally dripping water, Spath took a seat amid the arrangement of old sofas and cushioned chairs that the police had collected over the years. Upstairs, witnesses paraded past the front desk and up to the second-floor detectives' bureau. Reporters and residents gathered on the front lawn. One by one cops walked down the stairs to the basement.

Pierson worried about how the other Teaneck cops might treat Spath. It was a delicate moment, and Pierson knew officers' reactions could run the gamut. Some might be too boisterous and shout, "Hey, good shooting, another dirtbag bites the dust." Others might ignore Spath completely, thinking he wanted to be alone in his silence. Neither extreme would be good for Spath, Pierson figured.

"Hey, Gary, we're with you," Pierson remembers one officer saying.

Another strutted by and rubbed Spath's shoulder. "Hey, Gary, you did the right thing." Another walked up and bear-hugged Spath.

Pierson stood across the room and watched the scene. More officers were arriving now, each one trying to touch Spath or whisper a gentle word of encouragement.

If only people realized, Pierson said to himself, we're not cops first. We're human beings first.

———

"Fuck the cops."

"Fuck 'em all."

Batron Johnson heard the shouting as he rounded the corner of the hospital driveway.

"Fuck the police. They killed our brother. We gonna get 'em back."

Batron stopped, looked around, confused. Steve was already there. So were Rasjus and Shariff and some of the other Violators. Batron saw Phillip's mother, as she was rolled out in a wheelchair, crying. By the hospital's glass doors, a cluster of police stood guard and talked quietly among themselves. Batron didn't need to be told. Phil was dead.

Someone hugged Batron. He didn't know who. He walked into the group. It seemed that everyone was trying to talk at once. One boy would shout something to no one in particular. Another would answer. Then a girl would continue the thought. Batron heard:

"He was shot in the back. . . ."

"His hands were up. . . ."

"He was yelling, 'don't shoot.' "

"The cops just blew him away. . . ."

"Shot in the back. *Shot in the back. Shot in the back.*"

Batron grabbed Chuckie and started to walk back up the driveway.

"I don't believe this is happening," Batron said as they reached Teaneck Road.

"I know," said Chuckie.

A police car passed, then another. On the sidewalk other teenagers who had been at the hospital were walking north. As the group approached the Mediterranean Deli, someone picked up a rock and threw it at a police car.

The rock bounced off the car's fender and skipped along the pavement. The car kept going.

———

For Lelia Johnson, it had been a night of prayer. A Baptist by birth, she had converted to the Jehovah's Witnesses in her twenties. On Tuesday, April 10, as Jews sat down to Seder meals to commemorate the Passover, the Jehovah's Witnesses celebrated one of their most solemn rituals, the Lord's Last Evening Meal, in which members of the congregation symbolically pass bread and wine to one another in much the same fashion that Christians believe Jesus did with his apostles at the Last Supper.

She was home by 9:30 P.M., and as she walked in the door, her husband, Edward, announced that Phillip Pannell had been shot, that the phone had been ringing all night, and that Batron had left in a rush. She spun around and headed out the door for her car. She wanted her son with her, not wandering the streets by himself or with his friends.

She pointed her brown Toyota Corolla south on Teaneck Road and within a half mile found Batron, Chuckie, Steven, and another boy. Lelia Johnson made a U-turn and told the boys to get in.

"Phillip is dead, Mommy," Batron announced as he slid into the seat beside her.

She looked at her son. He was upset, angry, ready to cry. "What do you mean," she asked, "Phillip is dead?"

"He was shot in the back," Batron said, his voice rising.

"Shot by who? What are you talking about?"

"By a police officer."

She shook her head back and forth. "I don't understand."

Batron told her that he did not know much but that the shooting had taken place on Intervale. His mother drove north. She wanted to go to the scene herself.

Intervale Road was still crowded when Lelia Johnson turned off Teaneck Road. TV news crews were already on the scene. Police officers milled around the yard by the mustard-colored house as a few detectives in sport coats examined the area and took measurements. Lelia Johnson noticed how silent the cops seemed. None of them seemed to be talking with the neighbors who stood in the street.

She parked and walked up to a customer she knew from the beauty salon, a woman named Mabel.

"The kid had his hands up," Mabel said.

Again Lelia Johnson couldn't believe what she was hearing. "What do you mean, he had his hands up in the air?"

"He shot the kid in the back," Mabel said.

"Why did he shoot him in the back?"

"He was running," said Mabel.

"Why was he running?"

"Somebody said that he had a gun," Mabel answered.

"What was he doing with a gun?"

Mabel was silent. The other adults who had inched closer as the two women talked also were silent. A few shook their heads as Lelia Johnson looked around at them for an answer. She thought: What *was* he doing with a gun?

Mabel broke the brief silence. "I don't believe that this happened in Teaneck."

Lelia Johnson nodded. She wouldn't have been surprised if it happened in Englewood or across the Hudson in New York City. But Teaneck? The thought seemed shocking, preposterous to her as she stood in the night air. Teaneck, she thought, was supposed to be safe, certainly as safe a place as she could find to raise her son.

She looked up the street at the crowd across from the house.

"Pigs!" someone shouted at the police.

Others in the crowd began to shout. *"Fuckin' cops . . . racists . . . you did it on purpose."*

She felt a tap on her shoulder. It was Batron. "Mommy, let's go."

Back home Batron walked in the door and headed up the stairs to his bedroom. It was barely 10:00 P.M. He lay down on the bed and flicked on the radio.

Batron kept the radio by his bed set to a rhythm and blues station, and as he settled back and closed his eyes, a song came on: "All I do is think of you."

He thought of Phillip and the last time the two were together. He remembered the red jacket and the fear Phil had of being alone in his new school and new neighborhood.

Batron started to cry. After a few minutes he turned the radio off and got up. He bounded down the stairs and rushed out. He didn't want to be alone or at home on this night.

———

Officer Luis Torres spent the day cleaning his yard, bagging leftover leaves from the previous autumn. Tuesday was his day off, and it felt good to be away from the department. After 10:00 P.M. he settled back on his living-room sofa and turned on the Channel 5 news. On this evening, as it had done for the previous two decades, Channel 5 began its newscast with a question that had become a New York cliché: "It's ten P.M. Do you know where your children are?"

The first item was about the Teaneck shooting. Luis Torres sat forward and listened as the live report came on.

The reporter didn't have much to go on—only that a black teenager had been shot by a white police officer and that residents of the Intervale Road neighborhood were angry. The name of the officer had not yet been released, but a man in a white jacket who claimed to be a witness was talking.

His name was Dexter St. Hillaire. Torres didn't know him but wasn't surprised. Teaneck was a large town; Torres knew many people in the black neighborhoods but couldn't be expected to know everyone. St. Hillaire said the boy who was shot had his hands up and was yelling, "Don't shoot."

"So you're saying the victim was begging for his life and the policeman shot him?" the Channel 5 reporter asked.

"Yes," said St. Hillaire. "Yes."

The newscaster mentioned the boy's name, Pannell, but it didn't register with Torres either. The report lasted only a few minutes, and when it was over, Torres's phone rang.

It was a former cop. "Did you hear the news?"

"Yeah," said Torres.

"Who do you think it was?"

Torres thought a moment. "Who's working tonight?"

The ex-cop ticked off the names. Murphy. Brennan. Lavigne. Blanco. Librie. Croonquist. Spath.

Torres felt numb. "I can tell you who it was," he said.

"Who?"

"I think it was Gary," said Torres.

━━━━━

Gary Spath sat in the basement locker room of the Teaneck police headquarters, waiting. On the second floor Officer Wayne Blanco sat across from an investigator from the county prosecutor's office, a Teaneck detective, and a court stenographer. It was 10:56 P.M., and Blanco had agreed to give a sworn statement about the shooting. The first question spoke volumes about the tenor of the interview.

"Officer Blanco," the investigator asked, "do you mind if I call you by your first name, which is Wayne?"

Blanco didn't object. Over the next forty-nine minutes, until 11:45 P.M., Blanco took the detectives through an account of the day. For the most part his story was essentially the same as his earlier versions given to Chief Burke and Lieutenant Hogan—except for several key alterations.

Unlike his statement to Hogan only a few hours earlier, now Blanco's explanation was that Pannell had reached into his left outer pocket for his gun as he turned toward Spath the first time. Blanco also said that

Spath's first shot was not a warning shot. When the shot missed, Blanco said Pannell withdrew his hand from his left coat pocket, ran another thirty feet, plunged his hand back into the pocket, and wheeled. At that point, said Blanco, Spath fired the fatal shot. The interview ended with the detective from Teaneck asking two questions about Phillip Pannell.

"Wayne, were you in fear for your life?"

"Yes," said Blanco.

"Did you believe he was going to shoot the gun?"

Blanco was unequivocal. "Yes."

It was 11:45 P.M. No one knew that Blanco had already told a different version of his story to Lieutenant Hogan at the hospital. Hogan was never asked to file a report, nor did he do it on his own. Investigators did not learn of his conversation with Blanco for another month. But that night one question was left unasked: If Blanco was in fear for his life and he believed that the boy in the red jacket was going to shoot, why didn't Blanco fire too?

Spath was sent home. Detectives from the prosecutor's office had concluded he was too distraught to give a sworn statement. Before he left, however, Spath dialed the lawyer whose name he had heard years before at the police academy, Robert L. Galantucci. The two spoke briefly, and Galantucci told Spath to call him in the morning. Galantucci, a former prosecutor who devoted almost a third of the time and resources of his private practice to the legal affairs of police officers and their families, didn't think the officer who telephoned him had much to worry about. It seemed like a justifiable shooting, Galantucci thought. Just the same, he was cautious.

"Don't say anything to anybody," Galantucci said. "Just go home. Rest."

———

Outside the police station clumps of residents stood under the shadows of the trees, drawn there by telephone calls, their children, or the television news. Reporters and cameramen also had come, and by midnight the crowd numbered more than a hundred, scattered in groups by the steps, the driveway, under the trees, and on the lawn. Here and there a television light from a hand-held camera scanned the area. Every few minutes a teenager entered the building, sometimes with a detective or two, to give a statement to investigators.

Inside, detectives were trying to sort through the versions of stories. Several witnesses were saying that Pannell was shot first in the leg.

One bystander said he was on his knees when he died. Others said he had his hands up. Still others said he was screaming, "Don't shoot," and never had a gun in his pocket.

Detectives knew two of those statements were untrue. Lieutenant Jack Terhune had gone to the hospital, checked Pannell's leg, and found no bullet wound. What's more, detectives had Pannell's gun, plus the sworn statement by Norman Brew that the boy had reached into his pocket and pulled the gun out on Gramercy Place. The other pieces of the story were mystifying. *Were Pannell's hands raised? Was he trying to surrender?*

Here the credibility of the teenagers was emerging as a key factor in how detectives weighed information. Most of the Teaneck detectives knew the kids to be street kids, not honor students. A few were members of the Violators. Some had been arrested before or were known as troublemakers. Officer Wayne Blanco had told such a different version of the shooting that one thing was clear: Somebody was lying. Detectives figured it was the kids.

There was another problem, however, and Chief Burke wasted no time in facing it. In his office he had gathered together as diverse a group as you could find at that late hour. When he first heard of the shooting, Burke called George Powell, the man who had spoken so highly of the police department ten days before, at the NAACP-B'nai B'rith awards ceremony. Burke had enough experience to know that blacks might be upset over the shooting. Perhaps Powell could act as a conduit for information or as a liaison to the black community. Already Powell was playing a role in the investigation along with a black lawyer, Franklin Wilks. Some black teenagers were reluctant to speak to police, and Powell and Wilks were offering to sit in on interviews. Chief Burke said okay.

Also in Burke's office was a tall man with a boyish face: John Holl, the acting prosecutor of Bergen County. Holl, an assistant state attorney general, normally worked in Trenton, but because Governor Florio had taken so long to appoint a new prosecutor, Holl had been ordered to fill in.

Powell knew Gary Spath. His daughter had gone to school with him. Franklin Wilks, whose law practice was centered in the suspicious world of the Bronx County Courthouse, had already voiced concern that the cops might have planted the gun on Pannell. Burke, hoping to put that rumor to rest and certify that Pannell indeed had a pistol, got up from his desk, went into another room, and came back with the silver pistol. After showing the gun to the group and putting it back in the evidence locker, Burke returned to the room and said he had something else to explain. This was not the first time Spath had fired his weapon, the chief said. Spath had fired before, the chief said, and had been reprimanded.

Powell suggested that Burke suspend Spath until the Pannell shooting was thoroughly investigated. Burke refused. John Holl explained the investigation had hardly begun and police didn't have enough information yet.

But Powell was insistent. Suspending Spath was one way to calm the community and send a message to black residents that the police would conduct a fair investigation. To let Spath go home, said Powell, without any evident consequence for his actions showed a lack of respect for blacks.

"You've got to suspend the man." Powell went on. "If you don't, it shows that the life of a black teenager is not important, that this guy just goes on, that his life is not disrupted in any way."

Burke shook his head no.

The phone rang. It was Mayor Frank Hall, and John Holl got on to speak to him about the need to calm the community. Powell and Wilks now left; the police needed more witnesses and asked if Powell and Wilks would go to the scene and coax some reluctant teenagers to come forward. Chief Burke walked downstairs. He had heard that a group of people had gathered on the front steps and figured he ought to speak to them.

As he stood on the steps of the police station, the crowd moved closer and quieted. The chief began by announcing that police would conduct a full investigation. He said the police had recovered a gun on Pannell—"a Saturday night special," he called it. He said both officers involved had been sent home. He mentioned that the shooting might have been in self-defense. He did not pass on what he had told Powell, Wilks, and John Holl: that Spath had fired his gun before under questionable circumstances.

The crowd was no longer silent. To some, Burke's comments hardly seemed impartial. A teenage boy rushed forward, pushing aside a knot of people. The boy lunged at the chief and slapped him in the face.

Burke seemed startled for a second. His face puffed and reddened. The boy disappeared into the crowd and the night. Burke wheeled and went back inside.

When John Holl saw Burke, he knew something was wrong. The chief had a red welt on his cheek. When the slapping was described to him, Holl decided he ought to go downstairs to the crowd. He worried that Burke had gone too far in explaining Spath's motive of self-defense. That sort of revelation was best left for a courtroom. He wondered if the chief not only had angered the crowd but might have prejudiced the investigation.

At that point Holl believed that Officer Wayne Blanco's version of events was holding up: The cops had confronted a boy with a gun, they had chased him, and Spath had fired in self-defense after the boy had reached in his pocket for a gun. But Holl was far from willing to lock in a final decision on Blanco's credibility, much less Spath's. Investigators hadn't even talked to Spath or all the witnesses yet. There were forensic tests to be conducted, as well as an autopsy. This was no time for conclusive decisions on the shooting; it was a time to appeal for calm.

As Holl opened the glass front door of the police department, he could feel the crowd's anger. Two police officers flanked him, and he stood on the front steps, wondering what, if anything, he could say to soothe them. He opted for a time-tested solution: He would tell them that investigators didn't know the full story yet.

"Calm down," Holl said. "We will give you the information as soon as we have it. Go home tonight, and we'll be releasing information tomorrow as we get it. But we're still trying to find out—"

A voice, angry, cut him off. "Is the officer arrested?" a black man shouted.

"No," said Holl.

"Why isn't he arrested?"

"Because we don't have enough information yet to know whether he should be arrested," Holl answered.

The man kept pressing, his questions aimed for effect—like a prosecutor in front of a jury. "Do you know the kid is dead?"

"Yes."

"And you know the officer shot him." The man went on. "That's all you need to know."

"We're still investigating," Holl said.

He wanted to find a way to assure the crowd that his investigators were trying to act fairly. From the moment he had heard the news that evening, of a white officer shooting a black teenager, he knew that race would make the case volatile. He had not expected it to happen so quickly, though. If anything, John Holl saw himself as diligent and fair, the sort of 1960s Catholic who went into government service as a calling, not just for a paycheck. But in dealing with the public, he had one unavoidable problem: a pronounced stutter that worsened under stress.

As he stood on the front steps and felt the crowd close in, Holl could feel his vocal cords tighten. Almost from the moment he opened his mouth, he started to stutter, badly. "I'm not a very good public speaker," Holl said, figuring the crowd might be sympathetic.

A middle-aged black man in front with a bald head would hear nothing of it. "Well, let's get somebody who can speak. You can't even speak."

"I have a speech impediment." Holl started to explain, the words coming from his mouth in short bursts as his stuttering worsened. "*I c-c-c-c-c-c-c-c can't sp-sp-sp-sp-sp-sp speak v-v-v-v-v-v-v very w-w-w-w-w-w-w well.*"

The middle-aged black man was angry. "You can't even talk," he shot back. "Why don't you get somebody out here who can talk?"

John Holl went back inside. The crowd backed away, forming into small groups again. By the trees, where the town set out a picnic table for its workers or anyone else to sit at in warmer months, black kids clustered around one another. Some were crying. Closer to the steps a group of mostly white middle-aged men and women huddled. A few later said they sensed the implications that the shooting might have on Teaneck's image as a continuing experiment in peaceful integration. They were fearful of what they were seeing: blacks confronting white cops on the steps of the police station while the media recorded everything. The group included several community leaders—or would-be leaders. Loretta Weinberg, the chairwoman of the town's community relations board and a candidate in the upcoming council election, was there. So was Annie Allen of the town's Rainbow Coalition and an organizer of the state's March Against Racist Violence the week before in honor of the anniversary of the assassination of Martin Luther King, Jr.

The group talked about finding a way to bring the town together, to allow people to express grief in a constructive way, to help mend what some thought could be the town's broken spirit and, at the same time, show the outside world a measure of Teaneck's integrity and idealism.

A few in the group were veterans of the 1960s and the antiwar movement. In those years one way to bring people together was to hold a vigil. Yes, someone said, that was it. A vigil—silent, reverent, peaceful, a moment to grieve for the loss of life without extending blame, a chance to heal whatever wounds had been opened, and an opportunity to show the television cameras that Teaneck still believed in its ideals. The others nodded. It would be a perfect blend of public concern and peaceful action. The group decided to spread the word. The vigil would be the next night, on the lawn in front of the police station and the town hall. People should bring candles.

Bill Crain worked until almost ten before heading home to Teaneck. Besides his work as a psychology professor at City College, Crain counseled mental patients at St. Luke's Hospital in Manhattan on Tuesday nights.

As he walked in the door, his wife, Ellen, greeted him. She'd had a free night from her job as an emergency room pediatrician at Jacobi Hospital in the Bronx and had been answering the phone for almost two hours. As word spread through town about the shooting, friends telephoned asking for news or just to talk. As much as the death of a teenager was troublesome, almost every caller seemed to focus on skin color, expressing the same concern: that it had been a white police officer who'd shot a black youth. Even though no conclusion had yet been reached on whether the shooting had anything to do with race, a mysterious power seemed to emanate from the phrase: White cop shoots black kid. The callers sensed that. But the callers expressed dismay too. *This happened in Teaneck?*

"Guess what happened?" Ellen announced as Bill walked in.

Bill didn't answer.

"Wait until you hear this," she said. "A black kid has been killed, and it was a white cop who killed him."

Bill and Ellen sat and talked over what she knew so far, including the plans for a vigil the next night. Bill wondered about the implications for the town he felt proud to live in, but one thought persisted.

"This is going to tear the community apart," he said finally.

Several blocks away Art Gardner had finished the Seder meal his wife had prepared. All through dinner his mind had wandered. He wondered what had happened to the boy on the stretcher. He wondered about the kids who seemed so angry.

As his wife put away the dishes, Art announced he was going out. He headed first to a bar where he knew he would find friends who were black, Carl's Corner. He had only the bare facts. But for Gardner that small kernel of news about skin color—that a white cop had shot a black kid—was enough to spark the engine of memory that he carried. He thought of South Carolina, his boyhood. He remembered the disdain white cops showed toward black youth, how one cop—white with reddish hair—once tried to order him around for no reason at all and how he felt humiliated afterward. He recalled the way blacks always tried to respond to cops with a "yes, sir." Always be polite, no matter what, his father had told him on more than one occasion. That was the southern rule. And then he thought of an interview he once heard. It was the early 1960s, and the nation seemed transfixed by the confrontation of white tradition and the new civil rights movement in the South, and on a television news program Gardner listened to a reporter ask a southern white politician what he thought of blacks. How dumb the answer seemed at the time, yet how painfully cruel it was. "I've always thought of niggers as superior pets," the white politician had told the interviewer.

As he drove to Carl's Corner, southern memories seemed to well up in Gardner as if they had been stored in some internal chamber and were now loosed by the news. He parked the car and saw some kids talking. Gardner walked over and asked if they knew anything about the shooting.

One boy announced, "He was shot in the back." Another followed with "He had his hands up."

Gardner was astonished. The two phrases—shot in the back, hands up—seemed far removed from what he had come to expect of Teaneck. They seemed so . . . southern.

He watched the group for a few more minutes. They were angry, and Gardner remembered how angry he'd felt when he'd wanted to integrate that lunch counter in Columbia, South Carolina, almost thirty years before. When Art Gardner was young and living in the South, black anger had been quiet, repressed, channeled. This was different. Gardner headed back to his car.

"Oh, no," he whispered to himself. "Here we go."

It was after midnight when the phone rang in a two-bedroom apartment on St. Mark's Place in Brooklyn. The Reverend Alfred C. Sharpton, Jr.,—Reverend Al to most—picked up the receiver.

Sharpton hated answering machines. Every year at Christmas he usually received an answering machine as a present from one of his admirers, but he never bothered to attach it to his phone. "I must have ten at the house that I don't use," he claimed. If someone needed to reach him, Sharpton wanted to take the call himself. The man loved the phone. It didn't matter what the hour, Sharpton insisted on answering it personally. Al Sharpton loved to talk. It was no surprise to him that his enemies—and a few friends too—compared him to a salesman.

Sharpton's attorney, Alton Maddox, was on the line. The two had been working feverishly in recent weeks on two court cases. The first, a murder trial of several white boys from Bensonhurst accused of killing Yusuf Hawkins, was scheduled to begin in a week in Brooklyn. Sharpton had befriended Yusuf's estranged mother and father and saw himself as the force that could galvanize the community. He wanted to be center stage for that trial—but not as a witness. He viewed trials as not simply the sedate domain of lawyers, judges, and juries. He saw them as a much wider stage, especially when race was a factor. In Sharpton's view, trials were not just examinations of isolated acts. When blacks were the victims of white violence, Sharpton saw trials as an opportunity to raise larger questions about bigotry and what he believed was a justice system that was too slow to respond.

Sharpton had some successes with this strategy, notably at the trials of several white men in the white enclave of Howard Beach, Queens, who had chased a black man onto a crowded highway where he was struck and killed by a car. But his record as an activist was hardly unblemished. And in some ways Sharpton, who six months before had turned thirty-six, saw Bensonhurst as his return ticket to respectability after the harsh criticism he had received for taking on the black teenager Tawana Brawley three years before. She claimed she had been raped by a gang of white men including a man she said was a police officer. Brawley said the rapists had scrawled "KKK" into her skin and smeared her body with feces. She was found crawling out of a plastic garbage bag. She was fourteen.

At first the story galvanized liberal whites and black activists. Bill Cosby promised to donate money. Boxer Mike Tyson lent his name to a list of supporters. But the girl's story just didn't stand up. There were too many holes, too many pieces that didn't fit. In time Tawana Brawley seemed more a faker than a victim.

Sharpton, along with Maddox and another attorney, C. Vernon Mason, would hear none of this, though. They claimed that for the authorities to cast even the slightest doubt on Brawley's story showed racism. The three called for a special prosecutor. They named a white auxiliary cop as the rapist and accused the New York State attorney general, Robert Abrams, of masturbating with pictures of Brawley. Sharpton eventually took Brawley and her family into what he called "protective custody" and refused to allow cops to interview them. After almost a year of circuslike demonstrations, charges, and counter-charges, the story of the confused fourteen-year-old girl in the garbage bag was exposed as a lie in a series of painstakingly researched articles in *The New York Times*. Sharpton, Maddox, and Mason were roundly rebuked, even within the black community. In Bensonhurst Sharpton saw the chance to make people forget the blunders of the Brawley case.

But Sharpton had another problem. The second case with which he was involved was smaller but far more serious. It was an investigation of his finances and taxes. Sharpton, a minister with no church, lived well, with new suits, a constant stream of limousines and drivers, and plenty of free time to show up at any confrontation in the New York metropolitan area that involved blacks and whites. His income, how-ever, was listed as only thirty thousand dollars. The feds had long felt he was skimming, and now they wanted him in court.

On the telephone Alton Maddox didn't want to talk about Benson-hurst or Sharpton's tax problems. Maddox, who lived in New York City but whose wife worked in the library at Teaneck High School, said he had just taken a phone call from a woman in Teaneck, Dorothy Rob-inson. The woman, Maddox said, had first called the black radio sta-tion WLIB and asked for Sharpton's home phone number. The station, accustomed to getting dozens of such calls each day, referred Robinson to Maddox's office, and when she phoned, she related the story about the black kid shot in the back by a white cop.

Maddox thought the story important enough to call Sharpton. He added that Robinson wanted Sharpton to come to Teaneck and speak. As he listened silently, Sharpton thought of his schedule and the one ahead. He was especially fearful of his tax case. That one could land him in jail. The last thing he needed, Sharpton thought, was another case.

Anyway, Sharpton believed Teaneck's troubles were far smaller than anything that could take place in New York City. He had been to Teaneck a few times, visiting friends he knew from his days as a music producer. Teaneck was the suburbs, he thought, and most blacks he knew there lived in nice homes. One friend of Sharpton's even had a backyard pool.

Sharpton hung up the phone, lay back on his pillow, and closed his eyes. Teaneck could wait.

NINE

BREAD OF AFFLICTION

SIX HOURS LATER

After 7:00 A.M. on Wednesday, April 11, breakfast television viewers in the New York metropolitan area were greeted by the sight of two young black men in Ray•Ban sunglasses, black leather jackets, and several layers of gold chains around their necks. The two stood under a maple tree on Intervale Road in Teaneck, New Jersey, and claimed to know the story of how Phillip Pannell came to be shot the night before. In truth, Charles Reyes and Irin Rivers had become intoxicated by the powerful elixir of exaggeration and rumor, which they served up as gospel truth that morning. Yes, Rivers and Reyes happened to be on Intervale Road when Pannell died. What they didn't explain to the interviewer from *Good Day New York*, the popular Fox television morning news show, was that they were some fifty yards away from the patch of grass where the shots were fired, and their view had been blocked by hedges and parked cars. That they spun their yarn on live TV sparked a chain reaction that is best depicted by a troublesome term that Teaneck had struggled for years to avoid: polarization.

Irin Rivers began the interview by describing how one cop shot Pannell first in the leg to wound and stop him and then finished him off with a fatal shot in the back. Pannell had not been shot in the leg even though it looked as if he had been when he tripped running into the yard. Sure of himself, Rivers plunged ahead anyway.

"He was laying on the ground," Rivers said, "screaming for his mother, and the other cop just shot him in the back for no reason."

Rivers's voice choked. "Phil was the type of person who would do anything for you," said Rivers, voice trailing off. As Rivers stifled a sob, Reyes picked up the story.

"He had no gun," Reyes said of Pannell. Rivers nodded in agreement. "I was with him all day." Reyes went on, even though none of the dozen other kids had seen Reyes in those last hours before the chase and the gunshots. "He had no gun. No weapon of any sort. At the time Phillip Pannell was still crawling and screaming for his life, saying, 'Mommy, please help me. Please don't shoot me.' The other cop walked over and shot him."

For Charles Reyes, one message he wanted to transmit was that the shooting was merely an extension of a larger pattern of harassment by white cops against young black men who happened to wear too many gold chains and drove sporty cars. "I always get pulled over and stopped," he said.

"I think someone should step up and help us fight. The kid was only fifteen." Rivers cut in, apparently unaware that the friend he claimed to be so close to was actually sixteen.

"I would definitely think they should prosecute him for murder," Reyes said of Gary Spath.

Rivers nodded. "Definitely."

Cops, who watched the interview or heard about it, interpreted the broadcast as the worst possible sign of things to come. Reyes and Rivers were well-known troublemakers. Now, however, they were being cast on television as credible witnesses, mixing rumors, lies, and facts—all framed by the allegation that white cops were targeting black males for harassment in Teaneck.

Reyes and Rivers were not alone. The night before, officers at Teaneck police headquarters watched the televised news accounts of Pannell's shooting and wondered what was happening in the town they thought they knew. Kids and some adults went on the air and told compelling versions of the story, unedited, unchallenged. After watching several broadcasts, cops tracked down the kids and adults and asked them to give sworn statements to verify what they had said on the television. But cops quickly discovered that in too many cases the stories by the kids didn't make sense. Either the purported witnesses weren't witnesses at all or they changed their story when confronted by police, telling something far more dramatic to the media and the outside world.

It was becoming increasingly clear to police that few people had actually seen the shooting. A boy named Jon, for example, claimed to have seen it. Cops later learned he was a block away and was merely repeating stories he had heard from others. He was only one of a half dozen such people who took to the airwaves and claimed to be eyewitnesses when they were not.

The first few hours of any police investigation, but especially a shooting, are the most important, and the reason has much to do with human nature. Over time most witnesses tend to change their stories as they speak to other witnesses or if they read about the incident in the newspapers and hear it discussed on the television. Experienced detectives say it's critical to talk to witnesses before they have the opportunity to compare their stories with anyone else's. Otherwise the investigation is tainted, and it's difficult to establish a foundation of truth that is essential to building a case. If the first witnesses tell versions that are exaggerated, another, more difficult problem evolves; Other witnesses who may know far more subtle versions of the tale—even contradicting earlier accounts—may be reluctant to come forward. It's one thing for a witness to provide facts for an investigation. It's something else to ask that witness to come forward and undermine what his neighbors have been telling the local TV station.

The first hours of an investigation are important for another reason that has little to do with the nuts and bolts of detective work and everything to do with the ebb and flow of public opinion. If the case has far-reaching public interest, the first reports in the media can frame how the public responds. In a murder case, if news is circulated about how brutal it was, the public often demands prompt and massive police response. The previous year in New York City's Central Park Jogger case the weight of grisly news coverage and public outrage prompted police brass to assign scores of detectives to the case. As a result, the gang of black youths who committed the crime were quickly arrested.

For police, the public response to a crime can be helpful. For one thing, it can sway politicians to free overtime funds for extra detectives. But if the incident involves a cop and accusations of racial prejudice, the initial public response often sets a tone that is impossible to erase. In Teaneck the tone on both sides was set early.

It is part of every cop's job to begin any investigation with a healthy dose of skepticism about the motives and truthfulness of each witness. After Phillip Pannell's death, ordinary police suspicion was quickly compounded by the fear that far too many blacks appeared to be lying and were hell-bent on railroading a white cop into a murder indictment. It didn't help that almost all the police who were investigating the shooting were white and almost all the witnesses were black.

———

As the doors opened to Teaneck High School that morning, students passed out a one-page orange flyer that had been hurriedly scrawled and photocopied by a group calling itself the Rainbow Youth Coalition that had managed to align itself with the white adults who had been outside the police station the night before. The flyer announced that the candlelight vigil the adults had suggested would be held that night "to protest the senseless slaying of Phillip Pannell by a police officer." The flyer continued three additional messages:

"End Racist Violence."

"Support Each Other's Human Rights."

"Unite for a better Teaneck."

Meanwhile, that morning the school administration was passing out its own one-page flyer to teachers and staff, entitled "Information About the Shooting on April 10." As much as the administrators were interested in disseminating information, they also worried about how the outside world would react to the story. The flyer warned teachers and staff that "this information is for internal purposes only, and is to bring you up to date. It is not to be shared with the press, but is to be used to present students and/or parents with the facts. Please note: No member is to speak with the media; no reporters are to be permitted on school grounds."

The flyer, typed on school stationery with the Teaneck school district motto, That Each May Learn, went on to list a "chronology of events" that had been assembled with the help of the police.

The flyer did not mention Phillip Pannell's name or Officer Gary Spath's. But in addition to stating incorrectly that the officers had "searched several teenagers," it contained a far larger error that sparked a series of arguments between teachers and students that morning and contributed to the mood of divisiveness. It said that the shot that killed Pannell hit him "on the side"—not in the back as students were already telling one another when they discussed the shooting in the hallways and in classrooms. It was not the last time people argued about the location of the bullet hole on Pannell's body or the last time that information from law enforcement authorities turned out to be wrong.

By 9:30 A.M. someone had already hung a sign in a high school hallway that said: THE POLICE WON'T GET AWAY WITH THIS ONE. WE PROMISE YOU. Outside the school's black door, students had posted another hand-scrawled sign: PHILLIP TODAY. THE BLACK RACE TOMORROW. By 11:00 A.M. someone had pulled the fire alarm and the school was being evacuated.

On the first-floor hallway near the physical education department, Art Gardner stood silently, transfixed by the flow of students that passed before him. Black girls walked by, convulsed in sobs, tears rolling down their cheeks. Black boys balled their hands into fists and banged lockers and cursed. Most of these students, Gardner noticed, were not troublemakers. They were kids he knew to be polite, quiet, studious. He had never seen them act this way. Gardner had heard that many of the known troublemakers—Phillip's friends mostly—were already upstairs in the library.

It was supposed to be a day when freshmen and sophomores took standardized tests to measure their academic achievement. But by the end of the first period it was clear that the school would have its hands full keeping students from roaming the hallways. Gardner pulled several kids he knew into his office to talk. He decided on a soft approach. "Hey, fellas, what's going on?"

A black boy glared at Gardner. "Hey, man, they always shooting the black man."

Another said: "They always killing black men."

The white students, Gardner noted, kept to themselves in silence or were nowhere to be seen. He wondered if they had gone home or were avoiding the hallways where the black students seemed to be congregating. He went up to a white boy he knew and asked him how he was.

"They shot this black guy," the boy said, "and now black kids are angry at me because I'm white."

In almost every conversation with a black student Gardner heard something he had never heard before: Black students told him how much they disliked the local police. Like many black adults with memories of the South, he found himself wondering if Spath would have been so quick to pull the trigger if Phillip Pannell had been white.

Such thoughts made him uneasy. He had always thought the police in Teaneck were far more sensitive than the South Carolina cops he had known as a boy. Gardner knew a few of the Teaneck cops; he had never suspected them of the kind of harassment the kids were now telling him about.

Gardner saw a white teacher who had spent much of the morning trying to allow her students to vent while trying to interject a word of advice here and there. Frustrated, the woman turned to Gardner. "I don't know anything about these kids," she said.

Art Gardner pondered the words for a moment and nodded. He had to admit he too didn't understand what the kids were going through.

———

As the Bergen County Courthouse in Hackensack stirred to life at 9:00 A.M. that day, a family court judge, Birger M. Sween, was handed an order headed "Work Release Review." Sween was a veteran of arbitrating the most personal of disputes. It had been his job several years earlier to untangle the gnarled custody arrangements in the Baby M case after the state supreme court had overturned a ruling by another of Breen's colleagues at the courthouse to legalize surrogate baby contracts. The order on Sween's desk that morning was far less complicated. It noted that Phillip David Pannell still owed $19,906.88 in child support to his family and that his future wages would be garnisheed to pay it off.

Pannell had not been out of the county jail since January, when detectives had found him hiding in his former home in Teaneck. But the real purpose of the order—and its timing—was left unstated. By affixing his signature to the piece of paper, the judge was giving permission for Phillip Pannell to leave his jail cell so he could prepare for his son's funeral.

———

Lelia Johnson had never heard her son cry like this. It was a deep waillike moan, from the gut. She looked at Batron as he slumped in a chair that he had pulled up to the heavy round wooden oak table in the high school library. She wondered what, if anything, she should say.

The night before, Batron had seemed in shock, as if the news of Phillip's death hadn't sunk in yet. When he spoke then, his tone was one of disbelief. The tone had changed now. Her son was in pain.

She had not wanted Batron to go to school that morning, fearing that his emotions would take over and he would get himself in trouble. After he had left for school, she and another mother drove to the Teaneck municipal hall to ask how the town planned to help teenagers deal with the shock of the shooting. She was angry. She had heard Phillip had been shot from behind. "In the back," she kept saying to herself. She couldn't understand how—or why—such a thing could happen. She also knew that if she were angry, certainly her son would be even more angry. "I didn't know whether to knock down buildings or get picket signs," she said. After a few minutes at the municipal hall and a brief discussion with the town manager, she decided to visit the high school.

As she entered the library and heard Batron's wail, Lelia Johnson walked over to him. She put her hand on his shoulder and took a seat next to him. But Batron didn't speak. A minute later he got up and walked into a nearby bathroom with several other boys.

Lelia Johnson listened. Inside the bathroom the crying grew louder and more intensely painful. She heard a hollow sound. Someone was kicking a door on a bathroom stall. She heard a thump. Someone was pounding the wall. None of the other adults moved, so she remained in her seat, listening.

A few hours later she drove home. She found Batron's address book and started dialing the numbers of other parents. Something had to be done to help the kids, she thought. If not, she feared what they might do. It was one thing to kick a wall in the bathroom. What would happen when the kids got out of school?

She phoned a dozen parents and asked them to come to a meeting that night, then headed out the door. It was 3:30 P.M.—time to get to her job at the beauty parlor.

That day CC's Cozy Cuts—the haircutting shop Lelia Johnson ran on Teaneck's northeast end—became an information hub for black women who reflected on the shooting of the young man the night before and how their sons and daughters might deal with it. Ever since she had gone to the scene the night before, Lelia Johnson had nursed her own sense of uneasiness about Phillip's death. She was upset that a boy so young had been shot. After seeing the yard by the house with the mustard-colored siding, she was bothered even more. The yard was enclosed, with a fence on one end and hedges on another side. "You could see Phillip was trapped," she told the women in the shop. "Why did the police shoot to kill?"

At the beauty shop she discovered other women shared her misgivings. CC's had four chairs, and that afternoon several customers showed up. A few didn't want to talk about the shooting at all, in part, they said, because they didn't know much about it and just preferred to listen. But others seemed to have strong opinions or strident questions.

"It shouldn't have happened," said one woman.

The others nodded. Lelia Johnson was silent as the women talked. As the day had progressed, she had become focused more and more on one uneasy thought: If the boy had been white, the police officer wouldn't have fired. She had nothing to base her belief on, only her instincts of growing up in North Carolina and the memory of her parents taking her brothers aside as they reached their teenage years and lecturing them on why they should be humble when confronting white police officers. She remembered how in the South blacks learned early from fact as much as legend that white officers were more likely to shoot first and ask questions later when dealing with black males. So, too, she recalled how her parents and other black adults had believed that the scales of justice were so weighted in favor of police and the white community that it was virtually impossible to make charges of police misconduct stick. As a way of avoiding any hint of trouble, many black parents instructed their sons in lessons in how to behave. "Don't talk back. . . . Always say 'yes, sir.' . . . Don't make any sudden movements."

Lelia Johnson had never sat Batron down and given him that lecture. Her move to New Jersey was more than a journey of physical geography; she believed she had left the legacy and legends of police mistreatment behind when she crossed the Mason-Dixon Line. The North was different, she figured, and Teaneck was different from most places in the North.

"They kept saying he had a gun," a woman said.

Lelia Johnson spoke up. On this question she had a firm feeling. "I don't believe he had a gun."

The woman persisted. "But they say he had a gun."

Another woman shook her head. "He was out playing basketball. How do you play basketball with a gun?"

Lelia Johnson agreed. She knew Phillip, and the notion of his carrying a gun seemed preposterous. "Where would he get a gun?" she asked. "Why would he have a gun out playing? Why would he be showing it around? I don't believe—"

Another woman interrupted. "It was a plant. Cops cover themselves, and they are known to carry throwaway guns. They planted the gun on Phillip."

To Lelia Johnson the idea seemed as plausible as anything else. The beauty shop was silent again. The conversation was going nowhere except in a great, mysterious circle.

"We left the city to get away from this," a woman said finally. "This is what we moved here to get away from."

"Yes," said Lelia Johnson. "That's the whole reason people bring children here, to bring their child up in a safe environment." She paused and pondered her words. "We can't stand for this," she said.

———

At the high school it had been a morning of tears, conspiracy theories, and the coming and going of adults to offer counseling. "I would urge all of you to hold on to each other for encouragement and support," a black teacher, Cheryl Miller-Porter, told the morning assembly of several hundred mostly black students. "I can't answer why this happened. Things of this nature are painful. We need to come together."

After she had spoken, a man most of the students had never seen or heard of rose and took the podium. Franklin Wilks had been working diligently to establish himself as a key player in the aftermath of the shooting. Other blacks questioned why a police officer would shoot a black teenager in the back, but Wilks was one of the first to hint openly that the killing might be a possible civil rights violation. Like the police, he understood the importance of the first twenty-four hours after a shooting. Earlier that morning, after helping police round up witnesses and sitting in on some interviews, he'd stood outside the police station and tossed off two remarks that were to resonate in the days ahead. Asked by David Voreacos, a reporter with the *Bergen Record*, whether Pannell was carrying a gun, Wilks chose his words carefully: "I did not interview anyone who said he had a gun." What he did not say was that Chief Burke had already shown him a gun that police claimed to have found on Pannell. Nor did he say that police had already been in contact with Norman Brew, who made the first phone call to police. Wilks then outlined what he believed might be the criteria for judging the shooting to be racially motivated. "Reasonable and justifiable use of deadly force" by Officer Gary Spath, he said. "That's the linchpin." Wilks believed only the grand jury could properly examine that question. And then he planted a seed that blossomed with great emotional force in the days ahead: "I don't have all the facts yet, but the facts I have point to that it was not a justifiable use of deadly force."

Wilks had begun to conclude that the shooting would evolve into a major case, involving race and police. Hours later, standing before the school assembly, he announced: "We are going to keep an eagle eye on this. There is a big discrepancy between what the police are saying and the eyewitness accounts."

As Wilks took his seat, a black student called out that he had something to say. He jumped up on the stage and took the microphone to perform a two-minute rap song about the shooting, ending with one line that touched off loud cheering: "I feel the need to explode."

As the cheering waned, the fire alarm rang again. Teachers rose and announced that the building had to be cleared. A black man stood to declare that the fire alarms were part of a white conspiracy to stop black students from discussing their feelings. Urged on by several teachers, the students evacuated anyway. But the incident was typical of what was taking place in one way or another all over school.

At lunch a hundred black students walked out of the high school and headed for the police station, followed by clumps of white stragglers. As they passed some of the stately Tudor houses in the mostly white neighborhood that adjoins the high school, they were quiet. There was no chanting, little of the anger of the night before, when groups of teenagers had massed on Intervale Road. An unsuspecting passerby might have even thought the group was on some sort of field trip. The only hint of fury came as the group walked up the driveway of the municipal complex. Joyce Venezia, the Bergen County correspondent of the Newark *Star-Ledger*, had been there that morning, trying to make sense of the unfolding story and its array of conflicting facts and sentiments. Before the students arrived, George Powell of the NAACP had told her, "This isn't Bensonhurst." Venezia now noticed the students marching up the driveway. Notebook in hand, she figured this might be a good chance to interview some of them and record their feelings. She spoke to two girls walking together. "Hi, I'm Joyce Venezia of the *Star-Ledger*. Can you tell me what's going on here? What are you guys doing here?"

One girl raised an arm and rammed it into Venezia's shoulder, stiff-arming her, as she walked past. "Out of the way, white bitch," the girl muttered.

At the police station the group gathered quietly by a dormant lily pond as reporters and photographers tried to penetrate their circle and talk to them. Some refused to talk to any whites. Others were more forthcoming, claiming they had seen the shooting, that Pannell had been calling out, "Don't shoot," and had been shot as he crawled on the ground. Still other students shouted their sentiments.

"They said he got shot once. They lied. They shot him twice."

"The police, they harass us for no reason. On the way home from school, on a Friday night, just for being together. They start to harass you. They push you and say, 'Go home.' They arrest kids for walking on the street."

"They're concerned with making Teaneck look good. The only difference between this, Bensonhurst, and Howard Beach is it's a cop who did the killing here."

"This is cold-blooded murder. They better move that cop out of town."

Detectives walked in and out of the police station. Police cars cruised by every few minutes. An occasional officer in uniform walked out of the building, but for the most part police stayed out of sight, keeping watch on the group from windows. Driving in his white 1984 Nissan 300 SX, Marinos Loukeris, twenty-eight years old and the coowner of a local fur store, decided to pull into the parking lot. Loukeris, who is white, later explained that he had wanted to "express support for the kid that died." He stayed for a few minutes. Then, deciding to leave, he pointed his car toward the driveway that ran past the lily pond and the group of black students.

The group swarmed around Loukeris's car and forced it to stop. Two black teenagers in leather jackets jumped on the hood. One of them lifted his foot and smashed it into Loukeris's windshield. The other jumped up and down on the hood, then spun and slid to the pavement, where he did a slight hip-hop step across the driveway to the crowd. The two were smiling, and the crowd cheered. For the second time that day Irin Rivers and Charles Reyes had managed to command attention. And once again their deeds were recorded on television.

Loukeris got out of his car, looked at his shattered windshield, and waved his arms at the crowd and asked them to move out of the way so he could drive away. He stood silently next to the car before getting back behind the wheel, his face sagging in sadness.

"I was with them a hundred percent," he said. "Now this."

———

Batron Johnson stood on the sidewalk with some of the other Violators as Reyes and Rivers stomped the windshield of the white guy's car. Batron didn't move, and the incident happened so fast that he didn't have time to consider whether he ought to join in or not. He felt numb.

After arriving at school, Batron sat on the steps outside, then went into the library, where he ran into his mother. He didn't want to speak to any adults, much less listen to them, so he avoided the assemblies that were taking place in the morning. So many adults had come to school, Batron thought, most of them offering advice. He wanted none of that.

A picture kept flashing through his mind. Batron had an eighth-grade yearbook photograph of Phillip that he had photocopied and carried with him all day. That afternoon TV news cameramen asked to see the photo, and they took pictures of it for their news broadcasts, gathering around Batron as he displayed the black-and-white portrait. It would be the first chance for the world to see the face of the boy who had died and now sparked so much anger, but Batron had no idea how controversial that photo would become among those who eventually sided with Gary Spath. The photo showed Phillip as Batron knew him: smiling slightly, his eyes wide and open for anything. He looked young. In the days ahead Phillip's photo and the image it projected—and who controlled that image—emerged as a flash point.

Batron thought he had done something worthwhile by showing the photograph of his friend to the news media. He thought now of the broken windshield. The stomping seemed to have set off something inside him. He was angry, deeply angry at the cops. Any cop. All the cops. It didn't matter. They murdered my brother, Batron thought as he stood on the sidewalk. As soon as he got home, he picked up the phone and dialed his mother at the beauty shop.

"They're going to have a vigil tonight at the municipal building," he said, "and I would like to march."

Lelia Johnson considered the possibilities. A march could mean trouble. But if she didn't let her son find a way to vent his frustrations peacefully, that could mean trouble too. Either way, it was a gamble.

"Okay," she said. "You can march, but I will meet you there."

"Okay," Batron said. He had another question. "Do you have any candles? We want to bring red candles." Red was Phillip's color.

━━━━

Art Gardner did not like what he was seeing or hearing now. The assembly had ended with a fire alarm and a man he had never seen before proclaiming the dangers of a white conspiracy. At the police station other young men had vandalized a white man's car. Adults he had never seen before—this lawyer from the Bronx, Franklin Wilks, for example—were passing out theories as easily as they passed out good morning greetings. Gardner could see the lines being drawn.

He decided to call together the students he knew best, the Black Youth Organization, which he had formed years before to sponsor cultural programs. A little after 3:00 P.M. the students crammed into a lecture hall with teachers and local politicians.

Frequently during the day Gardner repeated the same advice to students: "You have the right to feel angry, but you don't have the right to do something stupid." As he watched the students file into the lecture hall, Gardner felt better. He wanted the students to have the opportunity to express their feelings, and he wanted adults there to listen. "We've come together to state our view," he said as he stepped forward and looked over the gathering. "We want to know how you feel. I think you should talk about this, not just a venting of your anger, but it is important that all of us in authority know exactly how you feel."

Gardner had been wrestling for hours with the tide of fact and rumor. He had heard so often that Pannell had been shot in the back that he had already discounted the school memo that said he had been shot in the side. But what about the gun? Some students insisted Pannell was unarmed. But Gardner knew Pannell was no angel either. If anyone were carrying a gun, it might be Phillip Pannell. A girl rose and declared that she had felt for a long time that adults in the community did not listen to the complaints of students. Gardner knew the girl and trusted her judgment; she was college-bound and a well-known participant in the high school's extracurricular activities. He had never heard her speak this way before, though.

"We always knew something bad was going to happen at Teaneck High School," the girl said. "But nobody listens to young people."

Frank Hall stood to the side of the lecture hall as the students spoke. Hall was pleased. These were bright students, the sort that Teaneck was proud of. As long as people talked peacefully, he believed the town could manage. He worried about trouble from across the border. He had heard that a vigil was being planned, that people from New York were coming.

"If we can contain it in Teaneck," he said a few hours later, "we can probably deal with it. But I'm concerned about outside agitators."

———

In Hackensack, in his office on the second floor of the Bergen County Courthouse, Acting Prosecutor John Holl sat down with the two men he had met with the night before at the Teaneck police station—George Powell and Franklin Wilks—and a third man he had never seen but had heard much about, the Reverend Herbert Daughtry. The three had come to Holl with a request: They wanted him to join them in asking Governor Florio to appoint a special prosecutor to examine the shooting.

"What do you need a special prosecutor for?" Holl asked.

He was not so much angry as insulted. He had done nothing, he believed, to raise suspicions. Indeed, Holl thought he was going out of his way to conduct the investigation by the book. What's more, he had made a special effort to bring black citizens such as Powell and Wilks into the investigation, allowing them to sit in on some interviews with witnesses and briefing them on the information gathered. Holl wondered if the men sitting before him had any idea how unusual it was for ordinary citizens to be given such special treatment.

George Powell spoke. It wasn't so much a question of Holl's ability or his judgments so far, Powell said, as a matter of sending the right signal to the black community that the largely white law enforcement establishment would not play favorites. Powell believed that by calling in a special prosecutor, specifically tapped by the governor, blacks might feel a possible cover-up would be avoided.

Daughtry added that the black community was angry with the shooting, especially the widely circulated story that Pannell had been shot in the back. Holl knew of Herb Daughtry's work in Brooklyn, where he was pastor of a Pentecostal church and a civil rights activist. But for all his work in Brooklyn and his identification there, Daughtry was a suburbanite. He *lived* in Teaneck, his backyard bordering a golf course. Daughtry suggested that such a move might calm some of the hotheads in the black neighborhoods.

But Holl would not budge. Anyway, it was far too early to call for a special prosecutor. After a brief discussion in an adjoining office the three black leaders emerged with another proposal: If Holl would suspend Officer Gary Spath, they would back off on their call for a special prosecutor at this time. Holl told them that he could not in good conscience order Teaneck's police chief to suspend Spath. It was way too early for such a conclusion. There just wasn't enough evidence yet.

Holl had other worries. He had scheduled a press conference for 4:00 P.M., and he wanted to send out the positive message that his office was trying to conduct a full and fair investigation and that he had the support of some influential black leaders. He asked Powell, Wilks, and Daughtry to sit with him at the conference, promising to place no restrictions on what they could say. He said he would give a statement on the case, then the three could speak. Holl privately worried that the three men would use the press conference to call for a special prosecutor and place him in the difficult position of having to turn them down publicly. But he was confident he could deliver that message in a gentle way if he had to. His chief hope was that he would gain credibility by having them sit with him. Shortly before four, Holl left his office and headed for a larger meeting room. He walked in, took a seat, and looked around for the three men he had just spent the last hour talking to. The room was crowded with camera crews, reporters, and police. But Holl couldn't see the three and figured they were merely waiting in the back until he finished.

Holl opened with the promise of a thorough investigation of Pannell's shooting and the news that the evidence would be presented to a grand jury next week. "There is a lot of confusion in this case," he said. "There are more questions than answers. I am not prepared to say at this point that we know what happened." He explained what investigators knew so far about the foot chase and the gun that had been recovered, and then he asked for "patience and restraint."

As he finished, Holl looked for Powell, Wilks, and Daughtry but didn't see them. As he left the press conference, he asked what had happened to them. An officer from the Bergen County Sheriff's Department, the special force that guarded the county jail and the courthouse, told him they had been barred at the door. They didn't have the correct credentials to get in.

Holl was incredulous—and furious. He stormed out, fearing that whatever small measure of trust he had managed to build with the three black leaders had been damaged beyond repair, that they would return to the black neighborhoods in Teaneck and announce they had been double-crossed by the chief law enforcement officer in the county and blocked from expressing themselves. Holl ordered a squad of investigators to drop everything and head for Teaneck to find the three.

"Don't bring them in," Holl said. "Let me know where they are. I'll go to them."

If anything might be the final spark to touch tinder in the black community, Holl feared this might be it.

━━━━

Reverend Amandus Derr couldn't believe what he was hearing.

A vigil?

Marchers?

Mandy Derr didn't hear of the shooting until he walked into his office at Grace Lutheran Church that morning. The night before, he had conducted a Holy Week service. By the time he arrived home, he had missed the news.

Today, April 11, was Derr's forty-first birthday, and he wanted to get home early. When he heard of the shooting, he figured it might be a long day. When he heard about the vigil being planned for that evening, he figured it might be a dangerous day as well. Before Derr could even take a seat at his desk that morning, the township manager, Jack Hadge, was calling to invite him to an emergency meeting of the Teaneck Crisis Management Team, a group that had been organized the year before, after four teenagers in the adjoining town of Bergenfield had hatched a suicide pact and died together in a car they had left running in a garage. The crisis management team's goal was to bring together school counselors, clergy, police, firefighters, and other experts who might lend a hand if a similar problem developed in Teaneck. The Pannell shooting was the team's first real test.

That morning, in a meeting in the basement of the town hall, the team quickly went through a list of potential trouble spots. They had dispatched counselors to the high school. But the most worrisome issue before the group was the vigil. As the group learned after talking to contacts in the black community, there was to be not one gathering but two. White liberals—those standing outside the police station the night before, who had produced the flyers passed out at the high school that morning—planned to meet on the steps of the municipal building at 7:00 P.M. for a candlelight vigil. The second gathering was being organized by a group that called itself Concerned Black Parents and would march through town. The black parents planned to gather at the town's only black church, First Baptist, across from the Bryant School and within sight of the house on Intervale Road where Phillip Pannell died, then march down the middle of Teaneck Road at rush hour and converge on the municipal building a mile away.

Mandy Derr listened to the competing plans and responded with three words: "Oh, my God."

He thought how out of step whites seemed in planning a vigil. This wasn't the 1960s, when Martin Luther King, Jr., set the tone with his nonviolent marches and Peter, Paul, and Mary served up folk songs; this was the 1990s. If anyone set the tone and the beat of protest, it was the Reverend Al Sharpton. Ten months before, Sharpton had marched into Brooklyn's white Bensonhurst community. Hundreds of police were needed to keep his group separated from angry whites. Derr wondered if a similar scene might develop in Teaneck as two groups of marchers converged.

Derr's Lutheran colleague, Reverend Bruce Davidson, telephoned one of the white organizers of the candlelight vigil and asked her to cancel. She refused.

The crisis team discussed asking the marchers and vigil organizers to move to another place. If blacks and whites converged on a church, perhaps their peaceful instincts might overwhelm whatever violent urges they harbored. But it wasn't entirely clear who was organizing the black march. If anything, the crisis management team was learning the first lesson of a crisis: Once the furies are released from their box, calm management principles are about as useful as a broom in a dust storm. Derr got in his car and headed to the high school. He knew a half dozen students very well. All were white, and all were in his youth group at Grace Lutheran. That day all were fearful. From there he went to the local Catholic church, St. Anastasia's, for another meeting.

By now the crisis management team had given up trying to stop the vigil and the march. The issue now was how to provide security, and as Derr listened in silence, a black teenager who had been summoned to advise the group was making an incredible suggestion: to bring in members of Louis Farrakhan's Black Muslims as vigil marshals.

Derr knew the Black Muslims well enough. Their security force, the self-styled Fruit of Islam, was distinguished by trademark bow ties, porkpie hats, and dark suits. Derr shook his head. It was foolish to bring the Black Muslims and what many perceived as their brand of anti-Semitism to a town with such a large Jewish population. The teenager persisted. "The blacks won't respect you," he said, "but they will respect the guys with the bow ties."

To Derr's relief, the crisis management team politely rejected the notion. But to Derr the suggestion was warning enough; clearly the black community had different notions about what kinds of groups commanded respect. He wondered what the vigils would bring—and about the days afterward. Was there any group or person that could step forward as a leader respected by whites as well as blacks? He put the question aside for the moment. Time to call his wife and tell her he would not make his birthday dinner.

"Don't worry about me," Derr told his wife. "We're expecting a little bit of difficulty tonight, but I'm going to be at the police station. Nothing can happen to me there. I'm in the safest place."

TEN

CUP OF SUFFERING

Batron pulled the black hoodie over his head, then reached for a red bandanna. Red was Phil's favorite color, and in the months before he was killed he had begun to hang a red bandanna from a pocket of his baggy jeans and sometimes had wrapped it around his head. To the uninitiated, Phil Pannell might have looked like one more kid in over-size clothes with a piece of calico dangling from his pocket. But to those who knew how clothing had come to symbolize the lines being drawn by teenagers who fancied themselves members of street gangs, Pannell's bandanna had all the cachet of gang colors.

Batron knew the truth; Phil was somewhere in the middle, a kid who had gotten into his share of fights and ended up all too often in the police station. But Teaneck wasn't South Central Los Angeles, and the Violators weren't the Crips or the Bloods—in Batron's mind anyway. He wrapped the bandanna around his head.

At about 7:00 P.M. he left the house. It was almost a mile to the First Baptist Church near the Bryant School and the house where Phil had been shot. All morning in school and later at the police station Batron had listened as black kids talked about striking back at the police. Nobody mentioned a riot, but Batron heard friends talking about "messing things up" and, if not that, wearing red in memory of Phillip as a statement of defiance. Earlier that day one of the Violators had wrapped an inch-wide red ribbon around a pole outside the Mediterranean Deli. As he approached the church that evening, Batron was ready for anything, with his own compound of curiosity and anger. "I didn't really care," he said later. "We already lost. We lost somebody, Phil. We had to do something."

The sidewalks were crammed with people, black people mostly. Batron saw a few of the Violators, such as Otis and Steven and Chuckie. He felt good to be around them. But there were more adults here. Batron recognized a few teachers and parents. Mostly there were strangers, many with placards and banners. Some of the women pushed baby carriages. Must be two hundred people, Batron thought.

He saw Phil's father, bearded and tired-looking. "This is real," Batron said to himself, "real."

John Holl looked over the growing crowd by First Baptist. He did not like what he saw. All day, as he juggled and sorted through the facts of the case and tried to measure the reaction in the community, Holl had feared the worst: that the shooting of a black youth by a white cop would become inflamed by race and his job as prosecutor would become swamped by the tides of politics and mistrust. In a way this was inevitable, Holl thought. For politics to encroach on a criminal case was symptomatic of what race relations had become in America. Then again, Holl was enough of an optimist to hope that this episode might be an exception. The trick, he figured, was to establish some sort of trust between the black community and the cops. But how? The black man who had telephoned with the initial report of Phillip Pannell's gun had also told police that he was afraid of retribution from his community. Holl ordered that the cops not release his name. But that was a comparatively minor cause for concern. The problems seemed to grow with each minute. In the last twenty-four hours Holl felt like a weary salmon trying to swim against an uncontrollable current.

The night before, Chief Burke had been slapped on the face. Burke was no wordsmith, Holl thought, but he was no racist lughead either and didn't deserve such treatment. It was Burke who'd had the presence of mind to ask NAACP leaders to sit in on interviews with some of the black kids and adults who claimed to be witnesses. Holl privately admired what Burke was trying to do, but accustomed to guarding evidence with all the zeal of a soldier guarding gold at Fort Knox, he at first was angry with Burke's decision. Moreover, Holl wondered if

Burke might have prejudged the case by explaining to the crowd the night before that Pannell was reaching for a gun and that Spath had been acting in self-defense. Spath hadn't even sat down with investigators yet. It was too early for Burke to be offering opinions. These contradictory signs from Burke bothered Holl deeply.

Likewise, Holl noted disturbing contradictions among the black leaders. Powell, Daughtry, and Wilks seemed to want to conduct a fair, thorough, nonpolitical investigation—at least that was what they said—yet their first moves had been framed in politics. The investigation was barely under way, and the three men were already calling for a special prosecutor and demanding that Spath be suspended. They wanted a symbol, and Holl, a career prosecutor schooled in the assemblage of facts to build a case, thought symbols were part of politics, not criminal law. Suspending Spath would send a signal that the officer's actions might be wrong. Still, Holl understood why symbols were important to prosecutors, politicians, and the public alike. It was treading the line between politics and the prosecution that made him uneasy. To investigate properly, he needed community support. What's more, he sensed that the community, especially Teaneck's black community, had to believe in the credibility of the prosecution in order for a decision to have any lasting meaning. It didn't help that these leaders had somehow been barred from the press conference. A bad start. At the same time Holl wondered why none of the black leaders had found it a problem that the teenager was carrying a gun. He worried that each side was intent on seeing the story through the narrow lens of self-interest and was not recognizing the complexity of the case.

He still had not been able to talk to Daughtry, Powell, or Wilks about the press conference mix-up, and now he was obsessed with finding them before the vigil. The investigators he had sent out that afternoon had turned up empty-handed. Holl had driven toward the First Baptist Church, parked several blocks away, and walked along Teaneck Road.

He spotted Daughtry first. The minister was still angry. Holl apologized, but Daughtry seemed unmoved. He told Holl he would think about whether to accept his apology. Holl saw Wilks next. Compared with Daughtry, Wilks was a hissing pressure cooker. Wilks accused Holl of lying. Holl found himself in a locked box: denying that he was a liar but unable to prove it. Holl walked away, feeling even worse than before.

A few minutes later—*finally*, Holl remembers thinking—Powell appeared. Holl approached the older man.

Powell was not angry, but he wasn't friendly either. Of the three, Holl saw Powell as the best hope for building an alliance. But Powell shook his head at the prosecutor's attempts to apologize. Holl interpreted this as the worst sign: Powell had lost whatever confidence he felt in Holl. To the dejected Holl, it was as if Powell were saying, "You're in over your head."

Holl tried again to explain that there had been no conspiracy at the press conference to embarrass the black leaders. Ultimately Powell said he would accept Holl's apology. But he added that he planned to speak at the vigil and would announce that he was officially calling for a special prosecutor.

Holl walked away, eventually finding himself on the corner by the First Baptist Church, feeling more and more dejected as he watched the crowd assemble. His eye was drawn to an especially large banner that hung from two pieces of wood and was now being held aloft. IN THE NAME OF PEACE, THEY WAGE WAR. GENOCIDE NO MORE, said the banner in large letters. In smaller letters were the names of recently killed blacks, among them Yusuf Hawkins and Eleanor Bumpurs. Holl was drawn to the names of places on the banner: New York City, Bensonhurst, Soweto, . . . Teaneck.

The marchers started down Teaneck Road toward the police station. A black teenager held a white poster board with a hand-lettered message: UNITE TO FIGHT RACISM. STOP THE KILLING.

Behind the boy, two girls held their own piece of poster board with another message: RACIST COP KILLING.

The crowd moved onto Teaneck Road, stopping buses and cars in the southbound lane. Pannell's father was in front, his arm linked with Daughtry's. Wilks walked on the side, by the curb. As the marchers picked up the pace, they began to chant, louder and louder, "No justice, no peace. No justice, no peace."

Holl followed for a block, then got into his car. He was the man in charge of the investigation, the chief law enforcement officer of the entire county. Yet at that moment he felt powerless.

———

Reverend Derr heard the chant and remembers whispering under his breath, "Oh, my God." He had said this to himself several times already that day. Indeed, the phrase had become something of a mantra for him, much like the chant that was growing louder.

Derr, in his black suit and clerical collar, stood on the green in front of the town hall. The road sloped gently here, and he could take in the full size of the crowd. It was larger than he thought it would be. How would the police react? Minutes earlier he had stood on the front steps of the Teaneck Jewish Center with a rabbi and watched a yellow school bus pull up with a group of students from Fairleigh Dickinson University. Derr had gone to the rabbi to ask if the Jewish Center could be kept open as a place for vigil participants to discuss their feelings. Catholic and Episcopal churches planned to open their doors as well. Derr figured that if the town could keep the kids off the streets and in peaceful settings to discuss their feelings, trouble might be avoided. The rabbi promised to keep the center open. Derr was grateful, but as he eyed the bus with the university kids, he thought about the outsiders converging on the town.

Standing with the rabbi, Derr studied the signs the university kids carried. Derr wondered about Bensonhurst. Yes, a black kid had been killed there, but the similarities between Yusuf Hawkins and Phillip Pannell ended there.

Or did they? Derr wondered if there was something about being black in the 1990s that he, as a white man, didn't understand.

The university kids were on fire. As Derr watched, the students hopped off the bus as if they were football players running out of a locker room for a championship game. Almost as soon as their feet struck the pavement, they started chanting: "No justice, no peace."

The anger bothered Derr. Where did it come from? Whatever worries Derr had felt throughout the day were now increasing geometrically. These kids were not here to protest one shooting; they had a litany of complaints. He also knew Teaneck was suddenly vulnerable, and he wondered if other people with other agendas were taking advantage of the situation. Were his town and the shooting of one kid by one cop being used for something larger?

———

Holl took his place at the back of the crowd on the municipal green. Before him he could see the town hall with its commanding white columns and its sedate red-brick facade, topped by the steep slate roof and a cupola.

The front steps were crowded with speakers who jostled for the microphone. Both vigils had come together: the mostly white group that had gathered on the green and now the blacks who marched along Teaneck Road. Whatever schedule had been planned had been tossed aside. When the black marchers reached the lawn, the crowd of whites parted, and the blacks walked up to the front steps, chanting as the whites stood in silence. The FDU kids were some of the loudest, moving through into the crowd and calling out, "We're fired up. We're not gonna take no more." Other marchers chanted: "Teaneck, Teaneck, have you heard? This is not Johannesburg."

It was worse than Holl had feared. And as the sun went down, he began to feel for the first time not only uneasy but unsafe. Along the fringe of the crowd, black teenagers were running, some darting at him full speed, then veering off at the last second, flashing by like moths drawn by a porch light. It was as if the vigil had become several events at once: the speakers on the steps, the kids on the fringe, the quiet whites in the middle, the chanting blacks. "The crowd," Holl said later, "was about to burst."

He had to leave; he was due back at his office in Hackensack for a live television interview with a New York City station, and he wanted to impart a message to the outside world that the investigation was in good hands. But first he wanted to hear what George Powell had to say.

Powell took the microphone and addressed the crowd in his measured baritone. He talked of the seriousness of the case. (No problem there, Holl thought.) He mentioned the need for a thorough investigation. (Again, no problem.) Then Powell got to his point: He wanted a special prosecutor—along with one more demand. He was imposing a deadline. He would give the authorities five days to appoint the special prosecutor.

Powell didn't mention what would happen if such a prosecutor was not appointed. He didn't have to. Holl knew a threat when he heard one. He felt the anger rising inside him as well as the sinking sadness that a day's work at building harmony had gotten him nowhere.

The Violators were moving. Batron didn't want to listen to any more speeches. Neither did the others. After some of the adults—men Batron didn't know—spoke, his friend Kyle Alston walked up the steps, grasped the microphone, and began to cry and said, "I love you, Phillip."

Batron could feel himself angered again. Kyle's words suddenly personalized Phillip's death in a way that surprised Batron. He had never expressed his feelings that way: to say he loved Phillip. But Batron *did* love him—yes. And now Phillip was dead, shot down by a white cop.

Batron ran with the group to the side of the town hall, on the grass near the library. He could still hear the speeches and the crowd cheering. Phillip's father was speaking, and Batron stopped to listen. A few people in the crowd held candles and lit them. "My son would want this: nonviolence," Mr. Pannell said, his voice seeming to pause on each syllable. He seemed shy, uncomfortable in front of the crowd, but he continued in his halting manner. "There is no violence here, no violence, please."

The phrase had barely echoed across the green when Batron heard the crash of a window breaking. He spun around. One of the Violators had thrown a rock through a side window of the town hall, spewing glass into an office where the lights were on.

The Violators ran. Batron followed at the rear. Chuck was at the front, and the group took off around the fringe of the crowd, running in and out of the small knots of white adults. A few older boys were in the lead now, and the group, which included others besides the Violators, headed for the police station, where two officers flanked the front door.

As the kids approached, the cops moved inside. One of the older boys wound up and fired a rock; it smashed against the brick wall. Another threw a piece of concrete through the door, spraying glass into the station lobby. Inside, cops scurried to get out of the way. Others ran into the lobby from offices. The Violators paused for a second and looked at their handiwork. One of the older boys turned to Batron, Chuck, and the others. "Okay," he said, "you ready to do this?"

———

Paul Ostrow felt the mood change, as if a new weather front had blown through when the black marchers came down Teaneck Road. The group that had gathered on the town green beforehand was primarily white, with a smattering of blacks, too, and included many of the yuppie professionals whom Ostrow regarded as the backbone of Teaneck's middle class. A few had brought young children. He liked that. The group seemed intent on showing its concern and doing it peacefully. The black marchers, he thought, arrived with a far different demeanor. More than anything Ostrow noticed their faces, creased and twisted in anger.

It was getting dark. A few white parents took their young children by the hand and slowly gravitated to the back. Ostrow could see the parting of the ways: angry, younger blacks pushing toward the steps of the municipal building or running along the edge of the crowd, whites in their thirties and forties backing up. A cop he knew said: "This is gonna get ugly."

Ostrow eased himself to the back of the crowd. He didn't want to be here, but he figured he should be since he was running for the township council and the election was only a month away. Mostly he wanted to see how people would react to all the attention. He looked over his shoulder. Spectators gathered across the street by the Saints Café. A block away he saw kids on bicycles.

He examined the array of television cameras. Once again, he thought, Teaneck would be in the news. Ostrow worried: How would the media portray his town? He feared that it would be seen by the outside world as an angry place where the races were at odds. And if that stuck, Ostrow feared the chain reaction it would set off: Young white families would stop moving into town. The dream of Teaneck to remain middle-class and integrated would be a dream that had died.

Teaneck always drew some sort of attention, Ostrow thought, if only because it had set out to desegregate its schools voluntarily and market itself as a model town for racial integration. Now it seemed that it was under a magnifying glass, with all its faults on display for the evening news. It's like looking at an apple tree, he thought. From a distance it looks beautiful. But when you get close, you notice that even the healthiest trees have a few apples with worms and some branches with wilted leaves. Ostrow figured he had better leave. He had heard the town council planned to hold a special meeting at 8:00 P.M. It was 7:45.

All day Chief Bryan Burke had feared what he saw taking shape outside his police station. For all its good intentions, the vigil was also a gathering place for trouble. Some combination! The good white and black liberal adults of Teaneck standing on the same green lawn with kids who wanted to throw rocks at the cops. When the piece of concrete crashed through the glass door of the station, Burke ran downstairs from his second-floor office and ordered the dispatcher to broadcast a call to bring in the police who had been massed a few blocks away. "Get ahold of the county police," he commanded, "and get them over here."

Burke's plan had been simple. He'd keep most of his own officers near the station or inside. But except for some plainclothes undercover men who mingled with the crowd in front of the town hall and a smattering of cops in uniforms, he'd kept the majority of Teaneck officers in riot gear arranged in formation on a driveway behind the building. If he needed reinforcements, he had officers from other towns and from the Bergen County police force at various spots around town. Hackensack police were grouped in a parking lot two blocks from the Teaneck police station. Four county police cars were parked near Route 4.

When the call for help went out over the radio, three cars turned on their lights and sped south on Teaneck Road, around the rim of the town hall.

Mandy Derr was walking in the front door as Burke rushed down the stairs and issued his order. "They're coming around," Burke told Derr.

Besides his concern about trouble by the kids, the Reverend Derr had harbored a lingering worry all day about how the cops might react. Several officers he knew had mentioned earlier in the day their worries about running into trouble with the kids and whether or not the town had a plan to deal with the possible riot that had been rumored. Derr had noted that cops were shocked and even fearful after the black kids had descended on the police station that afternoon and cheered as two of their group smashed the car window.

Derr had heard a few officers mention that they feared the female dispatchers might be raped. Others talked of the police station's being burned down. One cop asked Derr if a temporary station could be placed inside a trailer on the parking lot of his church. The question was supposed to be a joke, but Derr suspected the humor masked deeper anxieties. At one point in the afternoon Derr had asked the Teaneck town manager about preparations for a possible riot.

"Yes, we have a plan," the manager told Derr.

"Well," said Derr, "tell your officers about it. These guys are scared to death."

Too late for that now. Derr heard a window break, then another. He headed out the station door on Burke's heels, toward the rear parking lot.

8:05 P.M.

Mayor Frank Hall took his seat at the center of the bench inside the Teaneck council chambers and called the meeting to order. He could still hear the speeches outside, but the voices seemed muted. The chambers were in the rear section of the town hall, with floor-to-ceiling windows that overlooked the lot where the police parked.

As Hall looked out, he could see Paul Ostrow sitting in the front row. The audience was small. Only a half dozen people had shown up, along with a camera crew from the local CBS affiliate. Even if Spath

had been justified—and Hall was by no means sure of that right now—
Hall realized that the bullet that had torn into Phillip Pannell's back
had ripped a hole in the community. The mayor did not know how
large that hole was, but he knew it was there and had to be patched.

"I would like to open with a short statement of how horrified and
upset I am and the rest of the council that these tragic events happened," said Hall, his voice wavering slightly. "I am convinced that it's
the council's obligation to make sure any investigation is fair and thorough, that when it is finished we will all be satisfied. . . . I am very
upset that the fabric we have put together is torn and wounded, and
we are going to do our best to put it together again and regain the
trust of all segments of our community."

Hall summed up what he had been told by the prosecutor's office:
that an autopsy was being performed on Pannell, that the state police
lab was being called in to help with the forensic analysis, that the
evidence would be presented to a grand jury. "I was pretty impressed,"
Hall said, hoping to inject a note of optimism.

But Hall decided to propose as an added measure an idea he had
been pondering for several hours. "I would like to suggest to this council that we monitor the investigation so that we can be sure that we
are satisfied that it is complete and honest and that there will be no
cover-up. And in light of that, I would like to suggest that the council
appoint a blue-ribbon panel of people, the spectrum of Teaneck, to
monitor the investigation for us."

Hall suggested several people: two black men, a white Orthodox
Jewish woman, a white Protestant man. It was the classic Teaneck
style committee, balanced by race, ethnicity, and sex. Councilwoman
Eleanor Kieliszek nominated the head of the League of Women Voters. Hall nodded. Good choice. But right there the discussion ended.

One of the most fiery council members, Lou Schwartz, took the
floor for the next five minutes to berate the town manager for not
having been at the police station the night before. When Schwartz
quieted, the deputy mayor, Peter Bower, spoke up. He had been outside on the steps a few minutes ago, propping up a guitar amplifier he
had borrowed from his teenage son to use as the sound system. He
too was angry. Bower, a Yale graduate, a veteran of the 1960s antiwar
movement, and now the chairman of the department of environmental
studies at Barnard College, knew the importance of a sound system at
a rally. It was a way of controlling the crowd and providing instructions,
and he and his wife, a first-grade teacher in New York City, had spent
most of the day trying to convince the town to set up its sound system

for the vigil. The town had refused, so Bower had improvised with his son's amplifier. In the crush of the crowd the amplifier would not stand up on its own, so Bower had been reduced to holding it on a railing on the steps.

Bower began by citing a vigil the previous year in memory of a Jewish resident whose lawn had had swastikas burned into it. For that vigil, attended mostly by middle-aged Jewish residents, the town had set up its sound system. Now he wanted to know why a sound system couldn't have been provided for the Pannell vigil. Bower, who was white and drew support from the town's white and black liberals, feared that this sort of oversight could be interpreted as evidence of institutional racism. His voice rose in volume with almost every word. "Now I wonder why it is that we can get a system for one event and not for this event? To me it is a sign of disrespect, and that's the best euphemism I can find for it. To have to sit in the cold out there, juggling the piece of equipment. We had no lights on the steps until we finally got in the building and found the switch to turn them on. This is contemptible. It is just an indication of some other problems that we haven't addressed in this town."

He never got the chance to say what those problems might be. The noise outside, much louder, seemed to be curling around the building and into the rear parking lot. Jack Hadge, the town manager, got up and looked out a window.

"The kids are bothering the police outside," Hadge said. "One of the police is being harassed. There's a mob outside. There is a fight over there and something starting over there. People are being bothered outside."

Mayor Hall asked for a motion to adjourn.

A rock crashed through the window.

———

Everything was coming out, and Batron could feel the energy surge through him as he moved with the crowd into the parking lot. Everything: all the hurt, all the anger. He looked behind him and saw a row of police in riot helmets. On Teaneck Road, several county police cars roared by, their lights pulsing.

The crowd seemed to panic at the sight of the flashing lights, their colors sparkling even more starkly in the dark. Many ran on the grass between the police station and town hall and into the rear lot. As Batron followed the other Violators, he saw more police in riot gear.

They must be out here for a confrontation, Batron thought. *Whom were the cops planning to confront?* This time, he figured, he would not take any pushing around. No more. *We have to do what we have to do,* he thought.

He heard the sharp crack of a two-by-four on a car window. Batron turned quickly. The kids were rocking an unmarked brown police car that two detectives had parked and gotten out of. Batron ran over and reached and lifted and pushed. The car rolled onto its side. The kids cheered.

———

"Fucking niggers . . ."

Mandy Derr spun around when he heard the words. The cops lined up behind him on the driveway seethed as the kids flipped the brown car and started to crack windshields on others. The cops stood in formation, nightsticks in their right hands, riot helmets atop their heads, their eyes focused on the kids.

"Let's go knock some heads," one said. Derr didn't recognize the face. The cop was from another town.

Another cop muttered, "Who the fuck do they think they are?"

Mandy Derr looked at Chief Burke, as did the cops, awaiting his command. The chief was not in uniform. Derr also saw he was not carrying a gun.

Burke worried that some of the kids in the crowd had guns of their own. If he turned the cops loose and attempted to round up the rowdy ones, he feared an officer might get shot. And if an officer were shot, other officers would respond with more shots. Also, there were too many nonrioters around. Burke had seen women pushing baby carriages. Suppose they were hurt in a police stampede?

After rolling the first car, the kids went after another one, then another. Derr saw someone lift a garbage can over his head and fling it into a car windshield. The screams grew. Spotlights beamed from the rise overlooking the lot, where the TV trucks were arrayed to broadcast the vigil to New York City studios. It was almost as if the parking lot had become a stage and the lights on the ridge were theater lights. The lights seemed to follow the kids from one smashed car to the next. Derr wondered if the TV lights were leading the kids or the kids were leading the lights.

On the ground around him, Derr heard the thump of rocks striking the pavement. He turned to face the kids, and a rock careered off his forehead. Derr staggered momentarily, then reached for his head. No blood.

He turned toward Chief Burke. He too had been hit by a rock. Like Derr, the chief wasn't bleeding.

Derr ran to the rear of the police formation. After collecting himself for a minute, he ran back to the front of the line, near the chief.

George Powell jumped into a Teaneck police car and turned on the bullhorn. "Please disperse . . . please disperse," he urged repeatedly.

The kids weren't listening.

The cops were clearly angry.

Derr heard an officer shout, "Coward!" at the chief.

"Yellow," blurted another.

A few officers wandered into the crowd. A lieutenant pulled a black kid off a car. Another officer was almost like a spinning top, his hands outstretched, his mouth agape as he yelled at the kids to stop. But Burke wouldn't let the formation march forward. And now even the calmer officers were calling out to the chief.

"Let's stop this," one yelled.

"Come on, Chief."

"Look what they're doing."

The chief whirled and yelled back, "Absolutely not! I don't want anybody doing anything. Just protect yourselves."

Mandy Derr looked again at the TV lights and the clumps of cameramen running after the rampaging kids. He wondered what the damage report would be: how many cars, how many broken windows. And then the thought occurred to him: This picture is being broadcast to the world.

———

Lelia Johnson was screaming, screaming louder than she had ever screamed. All around her she could hear the sound of turmoil, of breaking glass and girls and boys shouting and adults calling out for their children. She looked for Batron but couldn't see him and bolted into the crowd.

The kids seemed to be overcome by a power that was unnatural— out of control, she thought. They were like sheep too, stampeding in bunches from one wrecked car to the next, pulled along by the group. She saw one of Batron's friends jump onto the hood of a police car. She saw one with a large stick, another with a garbage can. Rocks flew. The windows at the library were breaking, as were windows in the municipal hall and the police station.

The vigil had gone well at first. Lelia Johnson especially liked the concluding prayer by a minister. She had carried red candles from home, and from her spot on the municipal green by the flagpole, she lit her candle and prayed silently for the Pannell family. But the scene at the rear parking lot was a paradox—and chilling. She knew the kids were angry. She had seen some of the anger ooze to the surface that afternoon at the high school. This was more serious. The cops wouldn't stand by forever and let their cars be vandalized. She ran farther into the crowd. *Where's my son?*

She felt herself starting to panic. No sign of Batron. "Don't do this," she yelled to no one in particular. "Don't do this."

None of the kids responded. *Could they even hear?*

"Stop," Lelia Johnson yelled. "Don't give them an excuse to beat you. Stop . . . stop . . . stop."

She couldn't scream anymore. Her voice, hoarse, gave out.

━━━━

Art Gardner wanted to grab a kid. But who? And how? There were too many to restrain, at least fifty in a full-bore riot and another hundred watching. Gardner stood in the middle of the parking lot, his head turning from side to side to watch the kids smash windows and flip police cars. He started to yell, then held his voice. It was useless, he thought. The kids were on their own.

He recognized many faces. These weren't outsiders, Gardner thought. Most were from Teaneck. And the ones he recognized had never shown much passion for anything before.

To his left he saw the flicker of lights. Gardner turned. It was a television cameraman, falling, being pushed and pummeled by kids, their shapes silhouetted by the camera lights. Gardner ran over and pulled the kids away. The camera crew ran toward the police formation by the driveway.

The depth of the kids' anger surprised Gardner. That day in school he had seen the emotions pour out. But now the anger had roared far beyond. These kids really *hate* the cops, he thought. *Why hadn't he noticed this before?*

Gardner stared at the police for a second or two. They too were angry, frustrated at being held back by their chief. Gardner saw other adults—black men mostly—trying to step between the cops and the kids and coax the kids away from the police cars. But nothing could stop them. It was as if the kids were an engine that had to run itself out of fuel. Gardner decided it was time to leave. If the cops started to move in, he didn't want to be around. He remembered the stories of Newark's riots in 1967. Too many innocent people had been shot. Anyway, he figured, you either joined a riot or escaped from it. It was no place for spectators.

The kids were moving away from the cops. Several had picked up a large plank, possibly from a wooden barricade that the police had set up to separate crowds. The kids held the plank like a battering ram and were running with dozens of their friends across the street to Marcia's, a dress shop with mannequins in the windows displaying sequined gowns for the upcoming prom and wedding season.

The kids rushed the shop as if attacking a castle and bashed in a plate glass window. Traffic along Teaneck Road slowed as the mob passed, and Gardner could see several kids scamper into the shop. Some came out with their arms filled with dresses.

The mob headed up the street toward a camera shop, the Mediterranean Deli, a real estate agency, and beyond. Who knew what might happen? Gardner felt numb. As a teacher, he wanted to stop this. He knew many of the kids as students. But he was a realist too. This mob had to run its course.

He looked across the parking lot and spotted three girls, all students at the high school, all black. The three seemed afraid, reluctant to follow the other students.

"Mr. Gardner," one of them said, "take us home. We don't want to be here."

Gardner felt oddly relieved. At least some of the kids didn't want to riot. At least some saw something wrong in taking out their anger this way.

"Hey," Gardner said, "let's get a Coke or something. Let's go somewhere and sit down. Let's talk."

———

Phil Lavigne listened to the stream of words on the police radio. What was happening at the station?

Lavigne and another officer were on the south end of town, checking a tip that a prowler was trying to break into a house, when the radio on the car dashboard jumped to life with reports of the rioting at the police station. The kids were moving up Teaneck Road, after looting the dress shop. They smashed the windows of the camera shop and the Mediterranean Deli. Someone had actually lifted an oil drum and thrown it through one of the deli windows.

The police dispatcher was calling for Lavigne's car. Get to the real estate agency next to the Mediterranean Deli, the dispatcher said. Two women had phoned the police that they were trapped inside and hiding in a closet to stay away from the kids.

Lavigne's partner gunned the car, taking a roundabout route to the agency, skirting the top of the ridge and rolling down a quiet residential street. At the bottom of the hill stood the deli, and Lavigne could see the mob of fifty or sixty kids on the corner. He figured they might scatter when the car pulled up.

But as the police car rolled to a stop, one kid ran out with a cinder block in his hands. The boy raised the cinder block over his head and brought it down on the windshield. From the passenger side Lavigne could see another boy, his hands wrapped around a plank from a wooden barricade. The boy whipped the plank back and aimed it for the passenger window. He hit the doorframe behind Lavigne's ear. As the car backed up, Lavigne noticed the doorframe was bent. Another boy raised a garbage can over his head and threw it at the car.

Lavigne grabbed the car radio. "We're under attack!" he yelled. "We need some help here."

Up the hill, safe in his house, Paul Ostrow listened to Lavigne's call on his portable radio. Ostrow had been following the radio traffic since he returned home an hour earlier. He listened as buses were rerouted around the riot area. He listened as the police called for help from neighboring towns. But when he heard Lavigne's voice, Ostrow's worst fears surfaced. He turned to his wife and muttered, "They're going to kill a cop. This is going on right down the block."

Lavigne's partner hit the accelerator and took off for the police station.

▬▬▬▬▬

Carol Ann Campbell, a columnist on the *Bergen Record,* had spent the evening at a Catholic church several towns away rehearsing with a choir. The next day she would have to write a column about Teaneck, and she wanted to get a start on the research. She left choir practice early and headed for Teaneck, hoping to make some contacts with people who had attended the vigil and might want to talk about the shooting.

Never one to dress down for an occasion, Campbell wore a cashmere coat and a pearl necklace. As she got out of her car, she realized something was horribly wrong. She heard a crash of windows and saw the kids in the middle of the street. Campbell took out a notebook and walked up to the group closest to the curb. She identified herself and asked if anyone would like to be interviewed.

As if on cue, the group turned on her, calling her a liar and accusing her—and the rest of the white press—of not being interested in printing the truth. Campbell tried to convince them otherwise but soon knew it was no use. Off to the side Campbell saw a black boy run up to the floor-to-ceiling plate glass windows of the real estate office and start kicking. The glass shattered and crashed down as the boy jumped back and out of the way. Campbell walked over and asked the boy why he had broken the window. She never heard his answer as he ran away. A piece of a steel pipe flew over her head, spinning like a propeller that had broken free of a helicopter. On the street a knot of black kids ran up to a car and smashed the windshield with a baseball bat. Campbell, alone, yet feeling remarkably calm at that moment, focused on the passengers of the car. Such panic in their faces, she thought. The car, which had slowed to avoid hitting the kids in the street, sped away.

Campbell walked over to yet another group. She had always believed that a journalist's notebook was the street equivalent of a hall monitor's pass, that if you flashed it even in a riot, you could navigate almost any barrier or group without getting hurt.

"What's going on?" she asked.

A teenage boy lunged at her. He grabbed her pearl necklace and twisted it around her neck. Campbell tried to jump back, but the boy tightened his grip, and for a brief moment she feared the necklace would break and her pearls would scatter along Teaneck Road.

"What are they worth?" the boy asked.

Another boy grabbed Campbell's notebook, ripped out the pages, and tossed them into the street. The first boy loosened his grip on her necklace, and Campbell broke free. For a moment she considered trying to go on and interview kids. She even asked for her notebook back. But a girl walked up. "I think you better leave," the girl said. "No more questions."

Campbell walked toward the police station. She tucked her necklace down into her coat, asking herself why she had worn it anyway. Coming her way on the sidewalk was a black couple in their thirties. They noticed that Campbell seemed to be upset and stopped to ask how she was.

She briefly recounted what had happened to her. The couple nodded, described their own experiences at the riot by the police station, then mentioned another fear that Campbell, as a white woman, did not feel, could not feel, at that moment. Because they were black, the couple worried they would be mistaken for rioters.

Several blocks north on Teaneck Road, Hoda Bakhshandagi focused his camera on the kids approaching him. *Click.* He pressed down on the shutter for another picture of black youths breaking windows on a suburban street. *Click. Click. Click.* These pictures would sell, he figured.

Bakhshandagi, twenty-nine, was a free-lance photographer, who drifted where the current of news took him. Iranian-born, raised on the rainy shores of Bremerton, Washington, and educated in America's heartland at Kent State University, Bakhshandagi had taken his passport and a sense of adventure to the Gaza Strip to photograph the Palestinian demonstrations and more recently to Bensonhurst for pictures of the racial rift that followed the murder of Yusuf Hawkins. He came to Teaneck on this night primarily because he had nothing else to do and he heard through his network of police sources that there might be trouble. He had been the target of rock throwers in Gaza and verbal taunts in Bensonhurst. His attackers had never drawn blood, though.

Bakhshandagi didn't know Teaneck, so he hooked up with two other photographers and walked the streets, a bulky camera bag slung over his shoulder and his sixteen-hundred-dollar camera dangling from his neck. It was after 10:00 P.M., and he had taken plenty of shots. Bakhshandagi was fishing for the keys to his Buick Regal parked on a side street when the kids jumped him.

There were about fifteen of them, all black teenage males. "Let's get the white boy," Bakhshandagi heard one of them scream as a punch slammed into his nose, shattering his glasses and staggering him. He wrapped his arms around his camera and tried to run, but the punches rained down on his head, against his ears, on his back, under his chin, into his forehead. His nose spurted blood. His right eye swelled. His camera bag ripped open, and he could feel the kids rifling it.

He held on to the camera, though, as he ran for safety. It later took three stitches at Holy Name Hospital to close the cut on his nose where his glasses had broken. It took six hundred dollars to replace the light meter, camera battery, and other equipment he lost from his bag. But he wouldn't make any money this night. His film with the shots of the riot had fallen out of his camera bag as he ran.

The mob worked its way slowly north on Teaneck Road, followed by a V-shaped formation of cops in riot helmets and some black ministers and other black men. At Jerry's Pizza kids threw rocks through the windows. At a Jeep dealership the plate glass windows didn't shatter, but thick fissures ran from top to bottom. At Carl's Corner a few patrons spilled outside to watch the mob pass and analyze the looting. The patrons, all black, stood on the sidewalk. None tried to stop the kids from throwing their rocks. To listen to them, one might think they didn't even mind that the breaking windows were in their town. On this corner, outside this bar, the looters had rooters. It was as if the shooting of Phillip Pannell were reason enough for everything that was taking place.

"They have pent-up anger, and they have to release it," said Rosiland McLean, watching the mob. "The kids in Teaneck have nowhere to go. We have to show them that we're unified. If the cop had been suspended without pay, it would have been different."

"This must stop," said Jerome McPherson, as he looked at the kids. But as if catching himself, he added a defense: "We have to stand up for ourselves."

"I don't think it's solely a looting thing," said Arnott Charles. "It's more of a disgusted feeling. People are very angry. This shooting is very bad. It's a very silly thing that happened."

"Yeah," said Ernest Carlos. "Why was a young brother shot when he was running away?"

Down the block the Reverend Mandy Derr took up a position by a hardware store. He knew the owner and had promised to try to protect his windows from the mob. After the rioting at the police station Derr had driven through side streets that paralleled the mob's march north, toward the town's black neighborhoods. The kids who were most angry headed north, and the police didn't try to stop them. The police, Derr noticed, marshaled their forces to block marchers from heading up Cedar Lane and into the town's main business district. Derr wondered if it was planned, and as he looked over the scene, he found himself standing next to a black teenager. The two were spectators but, as Derr quickly realized, with different points of view.

"Look at that," the boy said, motioning toward the police who were blocking Cedar Lane. "First it was the Hanukkah decorations. Now this. You see, all they're interested in is protecting the Jews in this town."

Derr was stopped by the remark, and not just by its bitter anti-

Semitic tone. Even in a riot a young man was drawing a sweeping conclusion about Teaneck race relations.

Derr had parked his car before the mob reached the section of shops where the hardware store was. In his black clergyman's suit with the white clerical collar, Derr walked along the sidewalk. As the kids approached from the opposite direction, he stepped out of the shadows and stood by the curb. "Please don't do this," he said as kids picked up rocks and broke windows at the stores around the hardware store. "Please stop."

The kids walked on. They hadn't broken a window in the hardware store. A small victory, Derr thought, but on this night he would take it. It was 10:30 P.M. He headed for home.

On the other side of town Art Gardner settled into a booth at Louie's Charcoal Pit with the three teenage girls he was driving home. He ordered sodas for everyone.

Gardner still could not understand what was bothering the kids who rioted. Had he missed something in them before this?

As he looked across the table, he realized he wouldn't find the answers to those questions on this night. The girls with him were as despondent as he was.

"Mr. Gardner," one asked, "why are those kids acting like that?"

"They're angry," Gardner answered, quickly realizing nothing he could say was really enough to explain it. "They're venting their anger through the wrong channel."

At that moment Gardner could feel the gap between his era and that of the girls with him. Thirty years before, grievances by black kids seemed so clear. Even the words of Martin Luther King reflected that clarity. But now . . .

Yes, a black teenager had been shot in the back. Gardner could feel the anger swell in him when he reflected on that. But the kid had been a troublemaker, with a gun in his pocket. And what's more, this was Teaneck, Gardner thought, not Selma, Alabama, or Jackson, Mississippi.

One of the girls seemed to read his mind. "Everybody is going to talk about our town," she said. "Whites are going to say, 'We knew blacks and whites couldn't live together. That's the way they are.' "

Gardner was silent. It had been a night of soul-searching, and right now Art Gardner couldn't find anything to say. In his heart he knew she spoke the truth. Too many whites in other, mostly white towns would now look at Teaneck and point fingers. It was almost as if white suburbia had wanted Teaneck to fail, he thought. And right here, in full view of the television cameras, was the evidence on display: rioting black teenagers flipping police cars.

Gardner could think of only one thing to say, and he knew far too many whites would repeat these words when they thought of Teaneck's grand experiment with integration. "When people think of us and see these pictures," he said, "they'll say, 'I told you so.'"

———

At the municipal building Mayor Frank Hall stood in the parking lot. The mob was far north, working its way back into the black neighborhoods, with the cops trailing. It would be a long night. Hall was hearing radio reports about looting at the Wonder bread store. A few kids had been arrested. Several officers who had been caught in the crowd when it moved north had been injured too. One cop had even been kicked in the groin.

The parking lot was a shambles. As Hall walked, he could hear the broken glass crunch under his feet. He stared at the police cars on their sides and wondered who all the rioters were. All day he had heard rumors of outsiders coming to Teaneck, but as he looked over the crowd earlier that evening, there were plenty of familiar faces, along with plenty of strangers. Were the instigators local kids? Were they from New York City?

By the curb he noticed a piece of paper, a leaflet with the headline STOP THE RACIST COP KILLINGS. Hall bent down and picked it up. In thirty-one lines of typewritten anger, he could sense what his town faced. The leaflet recounted some of the lies, rumors, and facts that surrounded Pannell's death: that he had his arms raised to surrender, that he was crying, "don't shoot," that "every single witness" said Pannell didn't have a gun on him, that a nurse was ordered not to perform CPR.

"Does this all sound very familiar?" the leaflet asked.

Hall read further, trying not to notice the misspellings or the fractured grammar.

Every week or two now it is roughly the same story—another young man is killed—almost always black or Hispanic by a racist mob or police officer. There are sharply conflicting stories by eyewitnesses an the cops. Then an investigation, maybe a prosecution, and, if it's a cop, a slap on the wrist, suspended with pay and given a desk job until things cool down. Then comes the next killing. It could be any of our kids. This racist violence must be smashed!

The intensely racist nature of this capitalist system is becoming much clearer through these attacks, which Teaneck is not imuned to. It's schools can no longer meet the needs and aspirations of many or most students. Its junk-food, junk-band, dead-end, low-pay, high-rent, high cost of living growing homeless economy has condemned a large percentage of our youth to PERMANENT UNEMPLOYMENT. George Bush's joke of a "war" on drugs guarantees the addiction of many youth, and the escalation of street crime—which cops use as their green light to harass, intimidate, and provoke young people—often now in DEADLY encounters.

More black cops is not the solution. We have plenty of them from Bushwick to South Africa, their job is to uphold this racist system and keep profits flowing. The solution is to organize young and old, multi-racially, students, workers, and unemployed to FIGHT FOR JOBS and schools that REALLY teach and AGAINST racist violence everywhere. To move this struggle forward. . . .

The leaflet went on to advertise a May Day march in Washington, D.C., and was signed by two groups Hall recognized as far to the left of the political spectrum, with touches of communism, the International Committee Against Racism and the Progressive Labor Party. Hall thought the groups had gone out of business years before, but apparently the death of Phillip Pannell had given them reason to emerge from hibernation.

The leaflet ended with a five-word message: "Avenge the death of Phillip Purnell."

For the first time that day Hall had reason to smile. These groups, he thought, couldn't even spell correctly the name of their newest victim.

———

The Reverend Al Sharpton was tired. It was another Wednesday, his night to preach and raise money for his cause at the converted movie house in Brooklyn known as the Slave Theater. As was his custom after sessions at the Slave, Sharpton led his entourage to Junior's restaurant for a post-rally feast. Sharpton was well over three hundred pounds, and his appetite matched his girth.

Around 11:00 P.M. he drifted into the bar to catch the first stories on the evening news, vaguely wondering if there would be anything more about the shooting in Teaneck.

Sharpton had scanned the papers and now knew the basics: A kid had been shot by a white cop. Sharpton was intrigued, but it was no longer unusual for a cop to shoot a black kid in America. He also knew Teaneck. One of his friends who lived there often bragged about Teaneck's long history of peaceful race relations. After Sharpton had visited, the memory he carried back to Brooklyn was of a black neighborhood with split-levels and two-car garages and middle-class incomes. For Sharpton, who grew up in housing projects and drifted from careers in religion to music to civic activism, Teaneck represented stability, a black man's promised land—if such a place could be found in America. Anyway, he figured, racial battles were the stuff of Brooklyn, not the suburbs.

The television in the bar was tuned to Channel 7, the local ABC affiliate, and as the first pictures came on Sharpton stood in silence. It was Teaneck, and the footage showed black youths jumping and flipping police cars. The reporter was calling this a full-fledged riot.

To no one in particular, Sharpton started speaking. "I don't believe this," he said above the din of the TV, locked on the screen and the footage. "This is Teaneck?"

———

Paul and Ricki Ostrow watched the eleven o'clock news in silence. Before sitting down, Paul had turned on all the lights outside the house and removed the special ambulance corps plate from his windshield. If the rioters came up his street, they might see the plate and mistake his car for a police car. In the distance he could hear sirens and horns. Neighbors came out and asked what was going on, but Ostrow didn't feel like talking. "Don't ask," he told one before walking inside.

Ostrow felt sickened as the footage of the kids jumping on police cars rolled across his screen. When it was over, he turned to Ricki.

"Our house. Our town," he said. "We grew up here. Do you believe this? This is like the inner city. This is just the beginning."

ELEVEN

"WE KNEW THE GUY HAD A PROBLEM"

A block away on the same street as the Ostrows' house, Officer Luis Torres sat alone in his living room. It was almost midnight, and most of the kids had stopped breaking windows. Torres, on the second of two days off, had not, to his surprise, been called in for emergency duty. But his mind and conscience were at police headquarters anyway. He was sickened. "I felt," he said, "responsible." But it was not the rioting that bothered Torres; it was the officer who had pulled the trigger and killed Phillip Pannell. For all his commendations, Gary Spath had another side to his police career: Spath had fired his gun three times in eight years on the force. The shot that killed Phillip Pannell was his fourth firing incident.

By every standard that measures police shootings in America, from cops who work suburbs like Teaneck to the roughest streets in cities, from studies by police agencies to academics, Spath's shootings were far above the average number for any officer, even those in careers of more than twenty years. To have that many shootings in so short a time was a statistical red flag.

Luis Torres thought his friend had a problem, but he had never been able to break the curtain of silence that Spath had wrapped around that aspect of his police career. Now, as Torres thought of the boy's death and the rioting, he recalled those hours several years before

on the midnight shift when he sat with Spath and talked freely about
so many personal subjects. But when Torres tried to bring up the
shootings, Spath had closed up. Back then, Torres had worried often
for his friend, but he had eventually given up trying to offer advice.
Now Spath had killed someone, and no matter what the other cops
were saying about the boy in the red jacket and his juvenile record,
Torres could not stop wondering if Spath had been too quick on the
trigger.

———

Despite Hollywood's and television's depiction of cops firing guns more
frequently than they take coffee breaks, most rarely pull their guns
from their holsters, much less pull a trigger. Almost all American police
officers go their entire careers without firing guns in the line of duty.
And even though studies by the Police Executive Research Forum
showed that the number of shootings by police increased slightly in
the late 1980s in New York City, Kansas City, Dallas, Los Angeles,
Philadelphia, Houston, Atlanta, St. Louis, and San Diego—a fact at-
tributed mostly to the rise in violent crime from the spread of crack
cocaine—the numbers were only half what they had been in the early
1970s, when assaults against police reached an all-time high and more
police fired back. A 1987 study of the New York City Police Department found that officers used physical force of any sort in less than
one tenth of 1 percent of all police-civilian encounters and that guns
were drawn in less than two tenths of 1 percent of all instances in
which any sort of force had to be used to subdue a suspect.

Yet in suburban Teaneck Gary Spath not only had drawn his gun
but had fired it three times before killing Pannell. Why?

Even Spath seemed to have trouble fathoming it. On those rare
occasions when he broached the subject, his words were terse, and his
explanation was to repeat the standard line that he had felt his life
was in danger. Beyond that, said other officers who spoke to him about
it, he would not add anything more. Since he didn't want to speak
about it, many of his colleagues had stopped prying. "We knew the
guy had a problem," said an officer. "But how do you confront him
with it?"

Even Fred Greene, Spath's former lieutenant and baseball coach,
couldn't break through. "I would bring it up, but he just didn't seem
to want to go into it," Greene said. "You couldn't force it."

Greene did remember Spath's volunteering a thought on another
police shooting. In New York City in 1984 cops had used shotguns to

kill a sixty-year-old overweight grandmother, Eleanor Bumpurs, who they said lunged at them with a butcher knife when they broke down the door to her apartment. Bumpurs was black, and her killing touched off a renewed debate on whether white police were likely to use force when confronting blacks who resisted arrest. Black leaders in New York openly expressed doubts about the police version, questioning whether the officers exaggerated the danger Bumpurs posed. Greene himself wondered why a *squad* of cops had to resort to shooting a grandmother. One evening at police headquarters Greene was holding an informal discussion about the Bumpurs killing and looked up to see Spath standing by Greene's office door, listening intently. The conversation waned, and as the others walked away, Spath spoke up in a tone that struck Greene as unusually harsh. "I'd rather be judged by a jury of twelve," Greene remembers Spath saying, "than be carried out by six pallbearers."

Frm 1971 to 1990 the two thousand police officers working in Bergen County's seventy towns reported firing their guns only thirty-six times, according to statistics compiled by the county prosecutor's office. Fifteen shootings were accidents, with guns fired as they were being cleaned or, in a few cases, with pistols going off when cops fell down while chasing criminals on foot or in struggles to make an arrest. In another five cases police shot and killed rabid or injured animals. Of the remaining sixteen shootings, three were by one officer: Gary Spath.

Of the thirteen shootings that Spath did not participate in, police killed four suspects and wounded another. One officer was killed during those years: a sheriff's deputy shot by an accused killer who grabbed the deputy's gun while he was standing guard. But Bergen County's police still had vivid memories of three brutal shootings of local officers in the 1960s: two in Lodi, who died execution style in a bar after they had been disarmed, and Captain Tom Pierson's partner in Fort Lee, who was shot as he checked out a suspected robber.

One reason Spath was never forced to confront the questions raised by his shootings, some police theorize, is that he never wounded or killed anyone. Nor, for that matter, had any of the people he shot at attempted to shoot him; none carried guns. But all of Spath's targets had one other common characteristic: All were black men. If this was just coincidental or evidence of a deeper problem, no one knew. As much as Spath was reluctant to talk, the Teaneck Police Department maintained what amounted to an institutional silence on his shootings, not covering them up as much as never really exploring whether the officer who managed to win so many commendations might also need help. One of Teaneck's town managers, Werner Schmid, who supervised all municipal workers, including police, during a career that began in 1955 and ended in 1988 (right before Spath's third shooting), had issued a standing order years before that he wanted to be informed any time a police officer even drew a gun. But Schmid says he was never told of any of Spath's shootings—and certainly not that one of his officers had three shootings on his record. "I never heard a thing," he said afterward. "I should have."

In a November 2, 1983, memo to the department entitled "Use of Firearms," Chief Burke raised two issues that followed Spath in the years ahead, even to the fatal shooting of Phillip Pannell. "I would not expect any officer to stick his neck out on an individual basis without at least taking that most important step of insuring that help is on the way," the chief wrote. He ended the memo with this line: "I again reiterate that warning shots are a no-no."

Gary Spath's first shots were warning shots. In that first shooting, on October 12, 1985, he not only broke the rules about firing his gun but tried to cover it up by filing a false report. The incident took place not in Teaneck but in Fort Lee.

Perched atop the Palisades cliffs that overlook the Hudson River and face Manhattan's Upper West Side, Fort Lee had evolved into an enclave that seemed part suburban, part urban, part highway cloverleaf. Those driving from the south on Route 95 to New England often knew it for a sign before the George Washington Bridge that seemed a perverse warning: *Last Exit in New Jersey.* Two centuries before, the town had been home to a Revolutionary War fortress that overlooked the Hudson. On an especially desperate day in 1776 and in the face of a surprise incursion across the Hudson by British troops, the Fort Lee garrison of 2,667 colonials, many tossing their rucksacks and bedrolls, beat a hasty retreat through Teaneck's marshland and eventually down the spine of New Jersey to Valley Forge, Pennsylvania. Beginning with the completion of the George Washington Bridge in 1933, Fort Lee was transformed into a bustling community that by the 1980s included high-rise condominiums, stately houses, and small duplexes. It was not uncommon to find several generations of Italian and Irish families on the same blocks as new immigrants from Japan and Korea. Fast-money corporate executives mixed with blue-collar expatriates from the Bronx and Jersey City—and an occasional Mafia lord. In the 1950s Albert Anastasia, the head of the Mafia's brutal Murder Inc. gang, settled into a thick-walled, creamy white Spanish villa with a red tile roof atop the Palisades cliffs, a short walk from the Palisades Amusement Park. After Anastasia had been gunned down in a New York City hotel barbershop, his house was bought by comedian Buddy Hackett. And if Hackett wanted to take a short walk, he could visit Frank Sinatra's mother, Dolly, who had moved to Fort Lee from Hoboken in the 1960s. People generally came to Fort Lee from someplace else. It was that kind of town, a place of transition.

On October 12, 1985, a Saturday night, Gary Spath found himself in transition. Only four months before, he had received the third commendation of his four-year career—a citation from his chief for his "restraint" and "professional behavior" in breaking up a fight at the Teaneck High School senior prom "that resulted in defusing what could have been a major incident." At 8:20 P.M. on October 12, Spath was on a routine patrol when he heard a radio message that Fort Lee officers were chasing a 1972 green four-door Pontiac along Route 4, down the Palisades and into the flatlands and Teaneck. The driver was suspected of robbing a gas station.

Spath headed toward Fort Lee, and as he drove east on Route 4, he noticed a string of police cars with flashing lights approaching from the opposite direction. The Pontiac, which had been zigzagging through traffic at more than 80 mph ahead of those police cars, had careened into a concrete divider and spun out of control. The driver was trying to make a run for it. Spath, who pulled off the highway, saw a black man run down an embankment from Route 4, flag down a red Toyota on a side street, and jump in.

Spath played a hunch: maybe the man was the driver of the Pontiac, escaping by commandeering another car. He turned on his flashing light, pulled the Toyota over, and called for backup help from the Fort Lee police. He was right; the man was the suspected robber. At this point it seemed like a routine arrest. The suspect, Martin Gourrier of Teaneck, was well known to local cops as a thief. Even the Pontiac had been stolen. Spath needed to fill out an arrest report, so when Fort Lee police handcuffed Gourrier and placed him in the backseat of a squad car, Spath slipped behind the wheel of his police cruiser and followed Fort Lee police to their headquarters to get more information.

The ride took no more than ten minutes. Then, when the car with Gourrier in it stopped at the Fort Lee police headquarters, Gourrier jumped out like a caged bull. Somehow he had managed to slip out of his handcuffs. He body-slammed two Fort Lee cops, then bolted through the parking lot toward a grocery store and a neighborhood of brick houses with postage stamp–size yards.

Three Fort Lee cops and Spath took off after the man. Spath was faster than the other cops and surged ahead by a few yards. He seemed to be gaining on Gourrier. As they reached the grocery store parking lot, one of the Fort Lee cops, shouted, "Halt!" Gourrier froze and turned for a second or two. He was no more than twenty yards away. The cop fired a warning shot in the air.

Spath heard the shot from behind him. He drew his gun and kept running after Gourrier. Spath said he saw Gourrier stop and turn in a crouch. Spath said afterward that he thought he noticed a flash from Gourrier's hand. *The handcuffs? A gun?* Spath wasn't sure, but he suspected the worst. He fired two warning shots in the air.

As Chief Burke noted in his memo two years earlier, police rules specifically prohibit warning shots. If officers believe they are in danger—Spath said he felt just that when he saw the flash in the man's hands—regulations are specific: Shoot to kill. Years later Spath could not explain what prompted him to point his gun in the air instead of at the man who was trying to escape.

When he heard the shots, Gourrier yelled, "Don't shoot me. Don't shoot me."

As Spath and the other cops closed in, Gourrier bolted again, this time cutting through a backyard. As the chase wore on, at least two other officers fired their guns. In all, police say, at least six shots may have been fired that night by a variety of police officers.

Spath wrote in his report that he became dizzy as he continued running. He was also lost. He wandered for another fifteen minutes, then heard shouting. He spotted a Fort Lee cop who told him the whole block was surrounded. Even a dog patrol had arrived from the county police. Another cop warned that Gourrier was running their way. Spath looked across the darkened yards. He heard muffled yells from behind a house, and he spotted Gourrier in the shadows.

Spath sprinted. His gun was now back in his holster. He chased Gourrier across one yard, then another, and finally caught him in the third, with a flying tackle in which Spath and Gourrier rolled to the ground in a sweaty mass of fists, kicks, and armlocks. Gourrier, who was a few inches taller and twenty pounds heavier than Spath, kicked him first in the groin, then in the chest and leg. Other cops now jumped on Gourrier. This time they handcuffed him more carefully and tightly. As for Spath, his back was killing him, and he feared his spinal cord might have been bruised in the tussle. As Gourrier was taken off to jail, Spath went to Holy Name Hospital.

In all, it had been a splendid night for Spath, except for two pulls on the trigger of his .357 magnum—the warning shots. "I knew that," he said later in recalling the story. No matter how heroic he had been in chasing down Martin Gourrier, Spath worried that he was in big trouble.

He erased any trace that his revolver had been fired. When a gun is discharged, the miniexplosion of gunpowder that propels a lead bullet through a steel barrel leaves behind a greasy residue. If you are firing a revolver, as Spath was, there are also empty shell casings left in the cylinder.

When shots are fired in an incident involving many cops, it's standard procedure to check all officers' guns if for no other reason than to determine how many shots were fired and by whom. So when the Teaneck police supervisor that night, Lieutenant Patrick Hogan, heard reports of shots fired in Fort Lee, he dispatched a sergeant to Holy Name Hospital to check on Spath and the condition of his gun. By the time the sergeant arrived and took down notes for a report he later typed, the sergeant noted that Spath's gun was clean of any residue, and all the bullets in the cylinder and in the ammunition pouch had been accounted for. The conclusion: Spath hadn't fired his gun.

Later that night, after he had been checked by a doctor at the hospital, Spath returned to police headquarters and typed a two-page report on the chase. He wrote that he had heard "what sounded like shots being fired" and that a Fort Lee cop had called into a radio, "We got shots fired." But he never mentioned he had fired his own gun, and he knew he had not been truthful. "I went home that night sick to my stomach," he said, recalling the shooting.

Two days later Teaneck police Captain Gary Fiedler read Spath's report. Chief Burke was away for a few days, so Fiedler, the next highest-ranking officer in the department, was in charge. He went through the weekend reports of arrests, burglaries, and complaints, and as he finished Spath's two-page description of the capture of Martin Gourrier, a thought came to Fiedler's mind: Spath deserves a commendation. Barely thirty minutes later as Fiedler was composing a commendation letter, the phone rang. It was the Fort Lee police chief. He wanted Spath at Fort Lee headquarters as soon as possible so detectives could talk to him. From the urgent tone in the chief's voice, Fiedler figured the chief wasn't inviting Spath to give him a medal.

Fiedler asked what was wrong. "He said there's a problem," Fiedler remembered, "something about Spath discharging his weapon."

Fiedler called Spath and got right to the point: Did you fire your gun? Spath said no.

It was Spath's day off, but Fiedler asked him to come in anyway and drive to Fort Lee. As he hung up the phone, Fiedler decided he would accompany Spath. "I was afraid," Fiedler said, "that they would try to pin something on him."

In Fort Lee, however, it wasn't a question of finding blame as much as finding truth. When they reached the Fort Lee police headquarters, Fiedler and Spath were seated across a table from several officers. A detective looked at Spath and didn't waste any words: Some shots had been fired on Saturday night. Several Fort Lee cops had come forward and admitted they had fired their guns. Others now said Spath had fired too.

Fiedler looked at Spath. But Spath was shaking his head. He hadn't fired his gun, he said.

Fiedler looked back across the table at the detective. The two had known each other from past cases, and Fiedler caught the man's eye and read the sort of unspoken message that experienced cops can send to each other when they're questioning someone. "I knew they had something on him," Fiedler said. "I knew that somehow Gary had fired his weapon."

But Spath stuck to his denials, and Fiedler decided it was time for a heart-to-heart talk. Fiedler, raised as a Jew in the Catholic heartland of New Jersey's Hudson County, had signed on with the Marines and served in Vietnam, before becoming a Teaneck cop. In his two decades on the job he had cultivated a reputation as one of Teaneck's most down-to-earth officers, with a track record of speaking his mind and an instinct for feeling at home with almost any of Teaneck's disparate groups, whether he was coaching a peewee football team or worshiping at his synagogue. On the ride back to Teaneck, he told Spath about the danger of falling into a trap of lies.

"I want the truth," Fiedler said, his tone harsh, then quickly turning softer and more personal as he drove. "Obviously these guys know something. They're looking at me as though I'm covering up here. Don't make me look bad. I have no idea what went on. If you fired your gun, I got to know. Because they must have some information that they're not letting on to."

The ride took no more than twenty minutes, and Spath sat in silence. Fiedler, sensing that the young officer was bothered, parked in the lot behind Teaneck police headquarters. He turned again to Spath. "You better think this over. I expect to hear something from you on this."

A day later Spath went to Fiedler with the truth.

The police department, meanwhile, was buzzing with gossip about the incident, and Fiedler was worried. Some of the other officers seemed to be a little too involved with covering up for Spath. But why?

It took Fiedler another day to understand. The answer lay in Spath's gun and that routine report by the sergeant who'd visited Spath in the hospital. Fiedler figured Spath must have known he was in trouble as he went to the hospital and had switched guns and ammunition pouches with another officer before the sergeant examined the gun and counted his bullets. But which officer? The department gossip mill was buzzing with names, and Fiedler had a hunch who had helped Spath, but he never pursued it. He later explained that he thought it was useless to try to force another confession and perhaps create a rift in the ranks. "They protect each other," Fiedler said. "Anyway, there was just no way to prove it."

Fiedler filed a report to Chief Burke, along with a supplemental report by Spath in which he admitted to the shootings but never explained why he had at first kept mum about it or how his gun had come to be so clean after being fired. When Burke read the reports, he suspended Spath five days without pay. He did not send him for special counseling or training on weapons. Fiedler then did something that even surprised Spath: He went ahead and submitted the commendation letter for Spath he had been writing when the Fort Lee chief had called. Fiedler cited Spath for his "observations and quick action" and "professionalism and diligence" that night in Fort Lee. He later explained he was trying to praise Spath for what otherwise was fine police work in tackling Martin Gourrier even on a night when the officer violated the rules. It was the first time anybody on the force could remember a Teaneck cop receiving a suspension and a commendation for the same incident.

Thirteen months later Spath fired his gun again. It was 5:34 P.M. Monday, December 1, 1986. A call came over Spath's radio of a prowler in a Teaneck neighborhood that bordered a golf course. The area was an occasional target of burglars. As Spath drove by the house in question, a resident flagged him down and said the prowler had run across the street a few minutes before.

Spath got out of his car and checked the front, then slowly walked into the backyard, trying to be quiet. He crouched, drew his gun, and looked around for signs that a window or door had been pried open.

He didn't have to look far. "Within a few seconds," he said in his report, "a darkened figure appeared at an open window." Spath was still in a crouch and kept his gun pointed at the ground. He guessed that the man in the window did not see him.

"*Freeze*. I am a police officer!"

The man hesitated a second. Spath says the man then stood on the window ledge and glared down. "He started yelling and jumped from the window, arms outstretched, directly at me," Spath wrote in his report. "Fearing for my own safety, I fired one shot at the suspect."

Spath missed.

If the burglar had any thought of trying to fight with Spath, he quickly changed his plans. "Oh, my God," he yelled at Spath. "Oh, my God."

Spath ordered the man to lie on the ground, then checked to see if he was hurt. He wasn't. Spath called for help, disclosing over the radio that he had fired a shot. Within minutes eleven Teaneck officers and detectives were on the scene. As the officers checked out Spath's story, the shooting seemed to some to be a bit of an overreaction, yet it wasn't against regulations either. Spath claimed he feared for his life, and under police rules of deadly force that's all he needed to justify pulling the trigger. The fear, of course, had to be reasonable. But in Teaneck's police department there would be no questioning of that. Chief Burke would say he "admonished" Spath for firing his gun, but there would be no formal note in Spath's personnel file to back up that claim. Spath's police union later singled him out in a letter in his personnel file for "meritorious service" and "dedication and perseverance" in subduing the burglar.

Spath went back to work as if nothing had happened. Unlike the FBI, which sends its agents through a special seminar any time they fire their weapons, Spath again was given no extra training, no special advice, no formal evaluation that might have shed light on whether he was too quick on the trigger. He was on his own.

The year before, the Bergen County prosecutor had issued special guidelines that required local police to file a report on every shooting even if it was accidental and no one was hurt. Years later, when they searched their files, investigators had no record from Teaneck's police department that Spath fired his gun on December 1, 1986.

Twenty-five months later—New Year's Day 1989—Spath fired his gun a third time. He was working the night shift, in plain clothes and with Officer Phil Lavigne, in an unmarked car. The two were on special duty, looking for possible drug dealers as part of a recent strategy by the state attorney general, the Statewide Narcotics Action Plan (SNAP). Lavigne was behind the wheel; Spath was riding shotgun. Soon after 6:00 P.M. they parked on a street near Englewood and spotted a beige 1980 Honda Accord pull off Route 4 with its license plate wired on and dangling.

To cops, a loose license plate is a signal that the car might be stolen. In this case they were right.

The man behind the wheel, Robert Callahan, was something of a one-man crime wave, with a two-page rap sheet dating back to 1979 with convictions for burglary, drug dealing, car theft, assault, bribery, and endangering the welfare of a child. Three years before, when the state police stopped him after a high-speed chase along the New Jersey Turnpike, they found his son, Keith—then only three years old—along for the ride. That night in Teaneck, Callahan was out of jail on parole for that earlier high-speed chase on the turnpike. Several hours before, he had smoked marijuana laced with angel dust. Driving into Teaneck, he had five dollars in his pocket, a carving knife under the front seat, a marijuana joint, a small plastic bag of cocaine, a teaspoon of angel dust concealed in a cigarette package, and his son, now five, sitting next to him in the passenger seat. The Honda had been stolen from a train station twenty-five miles down the highway, in Plainfield.

Spath and Lavigne called Teaneck police headquarters with the license plate number and were told that the plate had been issued for a red Plymouth. Spath and Lavigne turned on their siren and dashboard flashing light.

As soon as they turned on their siren, the Honda took off at 50 mph, winding its way on a six-mile course that ended up on a straightaway in Teaneck with the most sedate of names, Windsor Road. Callahan swerved around two police roadblocks. As he passed a baseball field, Spath and Lavigne pulled alongside Callahan on his passenger side to encourage him to stop. Callahan had other ideas. He swerved toward the cops, forcing them off the road. He then jumped the curb, wiped out a fifty-foot section of chain-link fencing, drove into the field, and spun around. Spath and Lavigne jumped out of their car and drew their guns.

Lavigne darted across Callahan's front bumper in an attempt to reach the driver's door, but he slipped and fell on the wet grass. Callahan floored the accelerator. "I could hear the engine racing," Lavigne said. "I realized the car was coming at me."

Lavigne, right hand gripping his 9 mm semiautomatic pistol, realized he had no time to get to his feet. "I looked up and saw the car upon me," he said. "I rolled over and fired a shot." The car missed him by less than a foot. The bullet from his gun passed through the Honda's fender.

On the other side Spath heard the gunshot, but he didn't know who had fired. Was it his partner? The man in the car? He couldn't see Lavigne, and he feared the worst: that the Honda had run him over or the seemingly crazed driver had shot him.

As the Honda went by, Spath fired a shot from his revolver at the back of the car. The Honda took off, passing a swing set, rolling over a curb, and heading down a residential street to Route 4. Spath spotted Lavigne in the grass.

"You okay?" he asked.

"Yes," shouted Lavigne. "I'm all right. Don't fire."

It took another chase by Teaneck cops to corral Robert Callahan and his stolen Honda—and his five-year-old son, whom neither Spath nor Lavigne knew was in the car when they fired at it. As for Gary Spath, it took a special board of inquiry and some deft interpretation of Teaneck's rules to exonerate him.

———

Of the three times Spath fired his gun, it was the third shooting that bothered Luis Torres the most. News of a shooting always spreads fast and quietly among cops, and often the reaction is a mix of sympathy and concern. When a cop fires his gun, it is one of those reminders to other officers of the power they hold in their hands as well as the danger they face. But this latest story was disturbing, and as Torres listened to the other officers talk, he wondered how such a shooting could take place. There was a kid in the car, Torres thought. And when Torres heard that Spath's bullet was fired at the rear of the car, his worries heightened. How could anybody feel his life was threatened if the car was already past? And if he kills the driver, the car becomes a thousand pound bullet that could hurt innocent bystanders.

Torres sensed this latest shooting bothered Spath too, perhaps more than the others. But as he looked around the police department, Torres found little outward concern. "That is what got me upset," Torres said.

"I wondered if the department thought he was developing a pattern. Whether Gary was right or wrong, I would have thought that as an administration the police department should have asked that question of whether Gary needed more training or whether he had a problem. Just because you have the right under the law to do something doesn't mean you should do it. I would have to feel really threatened to fire my gun."

But Torres had never felt he could say those words to his friend or to march into the chief's office and express his concerns. After each shooting Torres had gently tried to bring up the subject with Spath and been rebuffed. Torres felt duty-bound to dispense some advice, and he thought Spath needed to hear it, but he didn't want to break up their friendship either. "I didn't want to be too confrontational, to the point he gets defensive and mad at you," Torres said later. "So I dealt with it as lightly and as reasonably as I could."

Torres dropped hints. In their late-night talks he dropped a word or two about the shootings, noting his own concern about whether he could fire even if he felt justified. If Spath answered at all, Torres remembered, he blamed the police brass for having too many rules and not backing him up. Or he muttered that he had "done the right thing." Beyond that, Torres wondered if his friend ever thought much about the course he was on.

———

When he heard about the third shooting, Chief Burke had been furious, especially because Spath had fired at a car driving away from him. According to the chief one of the most serious mistakes an officer could make was to fire at a moving vehicle. "You can't kill a car," Burke often told officers. "Kill the driver, and the car could kill someone else." He had spelled out rules to his officers that they were not to fire at moving cars—or so he thought.

The kindest comment one might make about Burke's "General Order Twelve" about firing at cars was that it was well intentioned. The instructions were unclear, and as Burke was to learn when he tried to use them to punish Spath, they contained a loophole.

After the third shooting, the Teaneck police set up a four-member board of inquiry, made up of experienced officers who would examine the circumstances of the chase. It heard from Lavigne and Spath and examined Burke's order on firing at moving vehicles. What bothered the board was this statement: "No warning shots are to be fired in an effort to stop a fleeing person or for any other purpose such as shots

which endanger innocent persons and shots at or from a moving vehicle." It was confusing, the board ruled, explaining in a January 30,
1989, memorandum that "the statement first says no warning shots
are to be fired to stop a fleeing person and then goes on to describe
other types of unauthorized warning shots."

With such an ambiguous rule, how could Spath be charged? The
board exonerated him. But it also recommended a top to bottom review of the department's policy.

On February 10, 1989, Teaneck's police received a new weapons
statement from their chief. In response to Spath's latest firing and the
confusion about shooting at cars, Burke left no doubt about what he
wanted: There would be no shots whatever at or from moving vehicles.
"This is included," the chief wrote, "to eliminate the possibility of
injury to innocent persons in the event the driver lost control of the
vehicle. And in another part of the two-page memo, the chief spelled
out some general guidelines for weapons: "We must be continually
alert and ready to defend ourselves and the citizens we are sworn to
protect, and at the same time maintain uppermost in our thoughts
and actions not to overreact when it becomes necessary for us to remove our weapon from its holster."

Like Spath, the chief was raised in Teaneck. He graduated from
Teaneck High School in 1956, the same class as Fred Greene's. Before
joining the police force in 1962, Burke had been a mailman on the
northeast side of town where blacks first moved in the late 1950s. In
his twenty-eight years as a cop, he had fired his gun once: to
alert a hunter in the Teaneck marshes in the early 1950s that he was
poaching.

In Spath Burke saw an officer with the potential for a successful
police career, possibly even as a detective. "Anything that came down
the line, requiring police activity, he would be there," said Burke. "He
was a good sniffer." But the chief was troubled by Spath's three shootings in just thirty-nine months. This required more than just another
memo, so one day Burke called Spath into his office. Burke believed
Spath's first shooting in Fort Lee was flat-out wrong. That, and the
false report by Spath, was why he had suspended his officer for five
days. Burke believed the latest shooting at the back of the car was
wrong. The only shooting Burke could even remotely find justifiable
was Spath's second, when the burglar jumped out the window. But
even when Burke as a patrolman once surprised a burglar who had a
knife, he had resorted to his own hands (and a well-placed foot) to
trip and handcuff the man.

Burke looked across his desk at Spath. The chief had already decided to order Spath to a special two-day street survival firearms course at the county police academy. But that course wasn't set to begin until mid-March. First he wanted to talk to Spath. "What's going on here?" the chief asked.

Spath responded that he felt justified in firing. In this latest case, the car in the park, Spath said he felt he and his partner were in danger. "He definitely was gonna hurt me and my buddy," the chief remembers Spath saying.

Burke studied the officer for a second. What Spath was saying cut to the heart of all police work and the rules about firing a gun at another human being. If an officer feels his life is threatened, he has the right to draw his weapon and even pull the trigger. The officer's judgment, however, must be reasonable. The threat has to be real.

And here Burke thought Spath might be having some trouble. How could a threat be real when the car had gone by?

"I don't care," the chief said. "I don't want this to happen again."

PART III

TRIBES

TWELVE

TIDES

On the morning after the riot Paul Ostrow was out the door earlier than usual. He hadn't got much sleep anyway, having lain awake in bed until well after midnight, listening in the dark to the staccato chatter on his police radio. He learned that the mob had broken windows, that dozens of kids had joined in the vandalism, and that it had taken the police until well into the early morning to restore order, with the last report of vandalism at 5:30 A.M., when the windows went at a video store. With the sun rising, Ostrow wanted to survey the damage himself.

It was Thursday, Holy Thursday for Christians. For Ostrow, it was a hard day, regardless of the riot. Because of the Easter holiday, most businesses were closing early on Friday. For a salesman, an early quitting time on a Friday meant a long day on Thursday. At 7:00 A.M. he steered his year-old azure Pontiac Grand Am onto Teaneck Road. The Mediterranean Deli's windows had been shattered, but workers were already clearing away the broken glass and installing temporary plywood covers. Next door, at the real estate office, where the two women had remained safely in the closet until the rioters passed, the curtains and venetian blinds rattled and swayed as the morning breeze whipped through the opening where floor-to-ceiling windows had been.

The sun was out, clear and springlike; it was going to be a crystalline

April day. As Ostrow cruised north along Teaneck Road, the traffic coming toward him seemed slower than normal. Rubberneckers, he thought. People from all those white towns to the north getting a look at the damage, just as he was. Ostrow resented their leering and feared the worst: that the people from the neighboring towns would drive by and tell themselves that they were glad they didn't live in Teaneck.

The morning newspapers all carried stories about the riot. TEANECK IN SHOCK. VIOLENCE ERUPTS IN WAKE OF SHOOTING, roared a banner headline in the *Bergen Record* that ran atop color photos of a police car turned on its side, of Phillip Pannell's father tearfully hugging his daughter, Natasha, and of a white teacher comforting a black student at the high school. A smaller headline added: ROCKS THROWN AT COPS. The tabloid New York *Daily News* played the story on its front cover: VIGIL TURNS VIOLENT; COP SLAYING OF BLACK TEEN SPARKS RIOT IN TEANECK. Beneath the headline was a photo of teens flipping a police car. Another tabloid, the *New York Post*, printed more pictures of teens jumping on cars with COP'S KILLING OF BLACK TEEN SPARKS VIOLENCE. Even the staid *New York Times* published a large spread on its metropolitan news page with yet another photo of teens jumping on a police car and the headline YOUTHS ATTACK POLICE STATION OVER A KILLING. On an inside page, next to contradictory accounts of the shooting, the *Times* ran a six-paragraph story that paid homage to the town's past and mirrored the thoughts of many in Teaneck. DECADES OF PRIDE SHATTERED, said the *Times* headline, along with a comment from a local real estate agent that summed up the town's goals. "People who live in Teaneck are looking for diversity," the agent explained. "Teaneck is not for those who wish to live in a homogeneous community."

Ostrow didn't need to examine the newspapers or watch the television news to remind himself what was at stake that morning. CNN had broadcast the pictures across the United States. Later that day Ostrow got calls from friends in Scottsdale, Arizona, in Needham, Massachusetts, and in Baltimore, Maryland, all asking the same things: How are you? What's going on there?

As he drove north on Teaneck Road, Ostrow's mind was awash in similar questions. He wondered how much the town would change.

At least sixteen stores had been damaged in some way. A few, such as the dress shop and the film store, had been looted. Some of the rioters had been arrested as they ran from the Wonder bread store with loaves of bread. At the municipal complex—home of the police station, the library, and town hall—workers later covered the broken doors and windows with wood panels. In all, seventy-seven window-panes had been shattered at the library, twenty-three at the town hall, and twenty-five at the police station, with the main door, twenty-eight by seventy-four inches of quarter-inch-thick safety glass, needing to be replaced.

At the Mediterranean Deli the owner John Callas said it would cost ten thousand dollars to replace the plate glass windows and damaged equipment. All along Teaneck Road that morning trucks from area glass companies had swarmed to the damaged stores like birds in search of bread crumbs. One undamaged dress shop on Cedar Lane installed a two-story-high plywood facade as a precaution against possible looting in the upcoming weekend. Across town, closer to the black neighborhoods, the owner of a video store that had had its windows broken was already making plans to install an iron gate, the sort of urban symbol that the townspeople had feared. When the store owner applied for his construction permit, town officials tried to talk him out of it, fearing his action might set off a scramble by other stores to install iron screens. The store owner would hear none of it. He had five thousand videos, plus thousands of dollars in electronic equipment to protect. He had his iron gate within a week.

Around town the plywood quickly became billboards. WE ARE OPEN. USE REAR DOOR, proclaimed one store owner in white spray-painted letters. At Marcia's dress shop, as she swept up broken glass, the owner, Estelle Levine, was bitter over the looting. "Why did they do this to us?" she asked. "We didn't do anything to them."

Amid the debris small acts of kindness appeared. Up the street from Marcia's, as workers at the Film Lab tried to match piles of receipts with customers' films that had been developed, in order to determine what had been damaged or lost, they made a grim discovery. In breaking into the store and scattering piles of negatives, enlargements, and home snapshots, looters had somehow overlooked a stack of photographs of Phillip Pannell. The boy's family had dropped off his photo the day after he had been shot and ordered several enlargements. As workers cleaned up and sorted through records, Pannell's sister, Natasha, came by to ask if the enlargements were ready. One of the film lab technicians found the pictures, but when Natasha asked how much she owed, the technician handed her the stack. There would be no charge.

Ostrow knew that Teaneck's greatest natural resource was its people. Yet he worried that the night would bring more violence. He wondered if, in the long run, the riot would touch off more white flight. He remembered the commitment he and his wife made years before to return to the town where they were raised. He remembered the commitment he had made weeks before to run for the township council. He thought of backing out, then figured that would be a cowardly move. Perhaps he could instill some calm. This town still had many good characteristics, Ostrow believed. "We were a little island in the middle of Bergen County that people always pointed to and said, 'Look what they have. Look what they're able to do,' " he said. "But now it was as if a tidal wave had washed over the island. And we were all waiting for the waters to recede so we could see what was left."

Ostrow drove all the way to Teaneck's northern border. Police cars were positioned at the town's National Guard armory. Several cars with troopers from the New Jersey State Police sat by an elementary school. Ostrow knew the cops had to be there, but their presence was a reminder that the trouble could be far from over. He knew many Teaneck cops, and as cruisers drove by, he looked in the car windows at the men in the blue uniforms. The cops' faces were drawn—fearful, Ostrow thought. There were no smiles, no familiar happy waves. The cops who stopped to talk seemed subdued. Ostrow hadn't learned yet that police had already fielded several anonymous threats that one of them might be shot while on patrol.

Ostrow felt himself instinctively wanting to defend his town. But how? His first thoughts were of the police and what they'd had to contend with the night before. He thought of Phillip Pannell. Stories were circulating about his juvenile record. He wondered again why a teenage boy would be out in the rain at dinnertime on a school night. Where were Pannell's parents? Ostrow had already heard his father had been in jail the night of the shooting. What sort of family was this?

At the ambulance corps headquarters a black friend stopped Ostrow and talked about Pannell's being shot in the back. He was bothered by this, as was Ostrow. Why, the man asked, did a police officer shoot the boy in the back? But another black friend took Ostrow aside later and said the cop "did what he had to do."

Ostrow felt himself taking sides. "I didn't know Phillip Pannell," he said, "but I knew who Gary Spath was, and I knew where he came from."

━━━━━

Later that same morning Spath settled into a leather chair in an office in Hackensack and looked across the desk at a lawyer. Robert Galantucci eyed Spath for a moment. Galantucci—Bobby to his friends—

always studied his clients. First impressions, he often said, were the most important to him. He liked to have a gut feeling about a defendant before he stepped into a courtroom to plead his or her case. While Galantucci often gave the impression of being gregarious—listening to Louisiana zydeco music, throwing lavish parties, and bantering in the sort of backslap street talk of his native East Orange, where his high school classmates voted him class clown and his teachers had thought he would never amount to much and urged him to become a butcher rather than an attorney—he was a reflective man. As a defense attorney he tried to master not only the rules of law but the eccentricities of human behavior.

In Spath he liked what he saw. "Tell me what happened," Galantucci said.

The slender officer across from him began to speak, and Galantucci was touched. More than a third of his clients were cops or related to cops, and Galantucci had seen more than his share of police braggarts who prided themselves in landing an extra punch on a drug dealer or kicking in the door of a house while checking out a family fight. Spath showed none of those signs. He seemed devastated by what he had done. Galantucci, noticing the officer's puffy eyes, sensed he had been crying.

Galantucci started to interrupt Spath at one point, then stopped and rocked back in his leather chair, telling himself to be quiet. Galantucci glimpsed in Spath an asset lawyers covet almost as much as clients with million-dollar bank accounts. The young cop not only told a coherent story but told it with a level of sincerity that no lawyer could coach a client to display. Galantucci made a mental note: If this cop ever had to go on trial before a jury for this shooting, Galantucci would not hesitate to let him take the witness stand.

Galantucci had heard about the riots. He wasn't worried. As a former assistant prosecutor about to celebrate his forty-fourth birthday, he prided himself in sizing up a case quickly, and this one didn't seem all that much of a problem, even with the potential racial discord that seemed to be brewing. Yes, Spath had shot a teenager in the back, but the teenager had been carrying a gun. To Galantucci, Pannell's gun was the great equalizer. The officer had nothing to worry about. Galantucci had already heard that the prosecutor planned to suspend Spath formally from the police force if he didn't give a formal statement. As Spath finished, Galantucci reached for the phone and dialed the prosecutor's office to say Spath would like to talk.

"Don't worry," he told Spath after hanging up the phone. "Just tell them what happened."

▬▬▬

Thelma and Phillip Pannell had not seen each other since January and had hardly been in each other's company for most of the last twelve months. But their son's death had brought them together again. As Spath headed to the courthouse to tell his story to detectives, the Pannells walked out the front door of a wood-frame house four miles away in Englewood to hold their first news conference.

The house, owned by Thelma Pannell's aunt, was where Phillip's mother had taken refuge rather than return to River Edge. Her estranged husband arrived the next day from jail. As she walked down the front steps to face the wall of television cameras and the bouquet of microphones by the sidewalk, Thelma Pannell wore the same denim jacket she had taken when she dashed from her apartment two nights before. Unlike her husband, she had been too distraught to go to the candlelight vigil. This was her first time out in public, and as she stood before the cameras, her eyes welled with tears.

Phillip David Pannell spoke first. "My son is not here," he said. "There is no reason. All I want is justice for my son."

His wife interrupted. She had read and heard stories about her son for the past two days, and she was bothered by the way he was being portrayed, especially by the emphasis on his juvenile delinquency, gang membership, and status as a high school dropout. She said that she wanted her son remembered as a decent boy; he sang in a church choir, she added. "He was a regular kid," she told the reporters, her voice gaining strength. "He wasn't bad, but he stuck up for himself. He wasn't one to let anyone beat up on him. He was loved."

Her son's problems with the law, she said, were often provoked by the police. "There are some cops in Teaneck who told him to move along." She didn't know if Spath was one of them. "I hope he is not," she said.

She didn't need to be prompted by questions from reporters. As she spoke, it was almost as if she had a mental list of subjects to address. "He was not a dropout in school," she said. "The Englewood kids were threatening him with knives. He wasn't safe there." The reporters nodded and took notes. She was angry that the police claimed her son was running from them when he was shot. She shook her head. "The boy was blocked in," she said. "He couldn't run. He couldn't run nowhere. How could they shoot him in the back? In the back."

She started to cry.

A reporter asked if she thought the shooting was racially motivated.

Thelma Pannell paused, stifled a sob, then looked out over the group. "Yes, I do," she said.

Her husband spoke up, adding fuel to what was already a controversial rumor in the black community. Pannell insisted his son was unarmed. But even if he had been, he said his son had not tried to draw and fire at Spath and Blanco. "It wasn't life-threatening to them. He was shot in the back for no reason."

His wife was silent. Standing with the Pannells was a man who had worked long and hard for two days. Just before the press conference began, Franklin Wilks had convinced them to allow him to be their attorney. And now, as the television cameras whirred and stared at him, he had some announcements to make.

He began by saying that Phillip was never frisked by either officer, explaining that he had interviewed ten witnesses who said neither of the police officers ever got close enough to touch him, much less search him for a gun before he ran. Then Wilks fed the rumors. "The boy had no weapon on him," he said, ignoring again the fact that he had been shown the silver starter's pistol two nights before in the police station. But even if the police account was true and Phillip was carrying a gun, Wilks said, the boy never tried to threaten the police with it. "There was no weapon drawn at the time of the shooting, and there was no reason for the police to believe there was any danger of imminent harm to themselves or any third person. This was a classic violation of civil rights."

The last sentence hung there, as Franklin Wilks wanted it to.

Wilks paused, then went on with the announcement he knew would make headlines in the next day's newspapers. He said the Pannell family had decided to file a lawsuit against Teaneck. He had already drawn up the papers—the formal document known as a notice of claim that precedes the actual filing of a suit claiming wrongful death. "I wanted," he explained later, "to get ahead of the curve on this case" and "get off the mark quickly. I wanted to have impact." Wilks believed the shooting was, at least, a mistake by the officer and, at worst, murder or manslaughter. From his experience in New York City, with other cases in which the police were accused of misusing their power, Wilks understood it was important to send an early message. And the most effective message from any lawsuit was the demand for money.

"In New York they always use a hundred million dollars," he said later, recalling how he made his estimate. "This is New Jersey. They don't give as much money."

He scribbled out a number: thirty million dollars.

It made a great headline.

———

John Holl had been reading the headlines from his perch in the prosecutor's office. He too wanted to send a message: He was not a racist.
Holl not only wanted blacks to hear it but wanted them to have confidence in its truthfulness. "I was very much concerned that my background be gotten out," he said. "I want people to know that I have a
history in my life of being in favor of racial equality and racial justice.
And I had done things like that. I was trying to let them know if you
let me stay in charge of this investigation of this case, then you will
have a champion for justice, someone you can believe in. I was brought
up that way. My father instilled that in us, that we respect blacks. We
could not use the word 'nigger' in our house. We just didn't do it. It's
just not our style."

Holl had spent his early years in the same town as Bob Galantucci—
East Orange—but the two did not know each other. Holl, at forty, was
four years younger than Galantucci and later moved to South Orange.
And while Galantucci had attended public high school, Holl's education was grounded in Catholicism. After graduating from Seton Hall
Prep, he had gone on to Jesuit-run Fordham University. As a Catholic,
coming of age in the 1960s, he was impressed by the social activism
that had blossomed within the church in the wake of the Second Vatican Council. While Catholicism was still a conservative institution
when it came to matters of sexuality, the church's views on race relations and other issues such as workers' rights and poverty were becoming stridently progressive. Holl was drawn by Catholicism's
attempts to mix theology with social issues after Vatican II, and when
he became a lawyer, he had privately vowed to carry a sense of fairness
that he had learned in his religion to his work as a lawyer.

But now, Holl feared, that message wasn't getting out in the hot
mix of racial anger and politics that had steamed out of the fissures
in Teaneck. Holl's mostly white staff of detectives told him the black
community was shutting them out. Those who claimed to be witnesses
weren't cooperating, and those who had come forward a day or two
earlier with tips were suddenly mute. "The riot changed everything,"
Holl said. "Nobody would talk to us anymore. There was tremendous
tension. People clammed up."

That morning Holl took aside his chief assistant prosecutor, Dennis
Calo, to discuss strategy. Holl had already ruled out a racial motive in

the shooting. Spath, he figured, had not pulled the trigger out of some sort of hatred for blacks. But Holl was beginning to think that Spath's actions might be a possible violation of other laws. He was bothered by Spath's previous shootings and wondered if the officer was too prone to use his weapon without exercising proper—and legal—care for the rights of a suspect. Holl had reached no firm conclusions. At most, he figured, Spath's shooting might be a manslaughter offense— that is, if the story was true that Phillip Pannell's hands were raised and he was trying to surrender. If Pannell's hand was in his pocket and he was turning as if to draw or fire his gun, then Spath could have been justified in firing. Which version was correct?

As the two lawyers sat together, Holl laid out an option he had been considering: Why not just indict Spath and go right to trial?

Holl shocked himself by the directness of his suggestion. He said later he had raised the question, wanting to play the role of a devil's advocate and spark a discussion. Yet he also sensed in his gut that the community needed to hear the evidence in an open court.

Calo was incredulous. In his fourteen years in the Bergen County Prosecutor's Office he had earned a reputation as a tough-as-nails, by-the-book prosecutor. His specialty was murder, and his style was dead-pan serious, no tricks. He was absolutely opposed to indicting Spath unless the evidence led to that. And in Calo's mind, the evidence was far from conclusive. On the night of the shooting Calo had gone to the Teaneck Police Department and the shooting scene. He had directed investigators, organized the investigation, and decided that Spath was in shock and should not be forced to give a statement then. The next day he studied Spath's personnel file, in particular the three previous shootings, and wound up thinking that the officer might have had a nervous trigger finger but was far from a wanton murderer. Nonetheless, Calo had determined that Spath's nervousness was important. "I don't think any of us really felt that we were dealing with someone who was evil and actually wanted to kill somebody for no other reason than to just kill him," Calo said. "I think the real question boiled down to: Did he act reasonably? Did he use force, deadly force, in a reasonable fashion?"

Here Calo's experience as a homicide prosecutor pointed him to a fundamental problem: The boy was shot in the back. What's more, Pannell was running away and did not brandish his gun at the cops. "One of the material elements for justification for the use of force," said Calo, "is that before you resort to deadly force, you have to feel that you're in imminent peril."

Calo harbored doubts that Spath was in danger when he pulled the trigger, despite the story that Pannell was turning and reaching for a gun. Calo also questioned the stories of witnesses who claimed Pannell had his hands up. But more important to the strategy that he and Holl were pondering, Calo's experience told him something else about this case: It would be difficult, perhaps impossible, to indict Spath, even if everyone concluded that he had fired too soon. One factor nullified almost any mistake Spath might have made: Pannell's gun. Calo knew that few grand juries would be willing to indict a police officer for killing a kid who carried a gun—unless, of course, there was some other factor. So far Calo had not found that other factor.

Despite the statements by Wilks and the Pannells and the rumors in the black community, Calo was sure the gun had been in Pannell's pocket. He had investigated police cover-ups before, and this did not strike him as a case in which police had planted a gun in the boy's pocket. What's more, he had studied the reports of witnesses who claimed Pannell had a gun, from Norman Brew, who telephoned in the first report, to the group of teenagers who were now coming forward to say that they knew Pannell had been carrying a pistol and that they had seen him with it that day. Several teens had even identified the silver pistol as the one Pannell had carried.

Calo thought it would be wrong to push for an indictment of Spath merely for political expediency. "We can't sacrifice this guy's rights," Calo told Holl.

Holl knew Calo was right and felt embarrassed that he had even raised the question. But there was another option to consider: Why not suspend Spath from the force? Holl thought of what George Powell of the NAACP had said to him two days before. Suspending Spath would send a message to the black community that law enforcement authorities were taking the case seriously.

━━━━

Galantucci had not noticed Spath's hands before. But now, as the two sat in a windowless interview room in the prosecutor's offices on the second floor of the Bergen County Courthouse, Galantucci saw that Spath was holding a crucifix.

The lawyer was bothered for a moment. He believed in leaving religion at home, not parading it in front of prosecutors, and he feared they would see it as a showy ploy on Spath's part. He made a mental note to speak to Spath later about it.

It was almost 3:00 P.M., and Spath and Galantucci had been sitting in the room since noon with two detectives, Sergeant Robert Rehberg of the prosecutor's staff and Lieutenant Jack Terhune of the Teaneck Police Department. Galantucci knew both men and had been Terhune's lawyer when he was accused of assaulting a man he arrested in Teaneck (the case had been dismissed). Spath had answered question after question for three hours from the detectives, and at precisely 3:04 P.M., after a court stenographer had been summoned and Spath had taken an oath to testify truthfully, he began his formal statement.

With the first question Sergeant Rehberg set a familiar, friendly tone, addressing him as Gary. Over the next 103 minutes Spath took the detectives through an account of April 10, 1990, beginning with the series of fights and citing precise times and locations for each of his stops leading to the shooting. Lieutenant Terhune explained later that he had come because he was the chief detective for Teaneck's police and was still investigating the case. But from the outset he played another role, intended or not. If Spath couldn't spell the names of some of the Violators, Terhune was there to help him. If Spath mixed up some of the descriptions—a black hat instead of a red hat; a yellow T-shirt instead of a yellow sweatshirt—Terhune was there to correct him. At one point, when Spath was describing Rasjus and Shariff, Terhune jumped in: "Gary, is it fair to say you arrested or at least brought these two individuals to the Teaneck Police Department prior to April tenth?"

Terhune later said that he was a stickler for details and wanted the record to reflect not only the most accurate story Spath could tell but also the fact that some of the boys he encountered that day had arrest records. Terhune's critics put his actions in another light: that not only was he coaching Spath through a critical statement but that he was helping portray an atmosphere of danger on the streets of Teaneck that might eventually help Spath deflect any charge that he had been overzealous. If Spath was truly a suspect in a homicide investigation, these critics said, why would Terhune seek to help in any way with his statement? And would he do the same for any ordinary citizen?

It would not be the last time the police, or Terhune, were criticized for treating Spath favorably. When Spath was describing how he had drawn his gun after getting out of the car, Sergeant Rehberg interjected another important point that Spath had not mentioned on his own: "Were you in fear for your life at that point in time or for your safety?"

"I most certainly was," said Spath.

Minutes later, as Spath described firing as Pannell reached into his pocket and turned, Rehberg again interrupted. "At that point were you in fear for your life and your safety?"

"Yes, I was," said Spath.

It was a crucial point for Spath. In order to explain adequately why he had fired, he had to say specifically that he felt his life was in danger. Terhune then bore in even more, asking Spath to clarify what he meant. Did Spath mean to say, asked Terhune, "specifically that the individual had a gun in his pocket and was about to pull it out and turn to shoot at you?"

"I was concerned," said Spath, "that he was reaching into his pocket and he was turning so that he could shoot myself and my partner at that time."

There was one more important gap to fill in. How did Spath know Pannell had a gun in his pocket? Spath said in his statement that he did not actually see Blanco try to frisk Pannell but that he heard Blanco yell, "He has a gun," as Pannell bolted. Spath had not yet explained how he concluded that Pannell had a gun in the pocket. Unless Spath explained this, a sharp prosecutor would jump on him. Again, Terhune interjected a question. "And," he asked, "based upon the earlier statement made by you by Officer Blanco, you knew he had or you believed he had a gun in his jacket pocket?"

"Absolutely," said Spath.

The session ended with Rehberg turning to Spath's lawyer, in the same spirit of familiar congeniality that framed the interrogation. "Mr. Galantucci, do you have any questions?"

"I don't think it would be appropriate for me to ask any questions at this time," Galantucci said. "I would just note that Mr. Spath has been here for just about five hours, he's been here in an attempt to cooperate in every way possible and continue to cooperate. There have been disruptions with the telephones, with people knocking on the doors, it's been hot in here, but he's nonetheless tried to answer each and every question that has been posed to him. I just want the record to reflect that."

"Okay," said Rehberg. "Thank you."

It was 4:47 P.M.

———

Shortly after 4:30 P.M., as Spath was winding down his statement, prosecutor John Holl headed downstairs to announce to a press conference that he had decided to suspend Spath—but with one condition: Spath could still collect his paycheck. Actually Holl was not the man who signed the suspension documents; he had ordered Chief Burke to do it. And as the prosecutor took his seat in front of a half dozen radio and television microphones in the room where he had tried to hold a press conference the day before with the black activists, Burke, wearing a wrinkled maroon blazer and a face etched in a mixture of weariness from a lack of sleep and sadness at what he had just done, sat down next to him.

Holl began by announcing Spath's suspension, adding that it should not be interpreted as an indication that the police officer was guilty. Holl said that Officer Wayne Blanco had been placed on leave but was still a member of the police department. Spath's case was different. He had fired the shots. What's more, Holl reasoned, Spath would be tied up for weeks as the evidence was collected. Suspending him would give him the opportunity to cater to the demands of lawyers and detectives without having to dip into his vacation or sick leave to take time away from his job.

George Powell and other black leaders had called for Spath to be suspended without pay, but Holl couldn't bring himself to do that. He wanted Spath separated from the Teaneck police force, if only for symbolic reasons, but he didn't want him to suffer financially; he hadn't even been formally charged with a crime, much less convicted of one. "This is being treated as a homicide investigation," Holl told the assembled media, cops, and other onlookers. "I feel it is in the best interests of the community that this officer be suspended. I hope it will reduce tensions in the community."

He then announced that the grand jury would begin taking testimony the next week. "This," said Holl, "is not going to be done in a short period of time."

Chief Burke sat silently, rubbing his fingers on the blond oak table, occasionally looking into space. When Holl was finished, veteran TV journalist Gabe Pressman of WNBC, asked Burke whether he thought Spath was justified in firing even though Pannell had never drawn the gun from his pocket.

Burke paused and looked back at Pressman. "I don't know," he said, "what was going through the officer's mind."

———

As Holl and Burke fielded questions one floor below, Galantucci and Spath left the interview room. Spath was drained, emotionally and mentally. Galantucci was buoyant. Sure, there would be questions about Spath's actions, especially in light of the other shootings, but his lawyer believed Spath had told a convincing story.

Dennis Calo walked up and asked to speak alone to Galantucci. When Spath was out of earshot, Calo delivered the bad news: Spath had been suspended.

Galantucci felt the blood rise into his neck and through his cheeks. His jaw tightened. He had walked in with his client in what he believed was a genuine spirit of cooperation, hoping that if he allowed Spath to tell his story, the investigation would go no further. Galantucci didn't even feel the need to present evidence to a grand jury. But now he felt double-crossed. Not only had the prosecutors baited Spath into giving a formal statement but they were going to convene a grand jury.

"You motherfucker!" Galantucci exploded.

Calo asked him to understand Holl's reasoning.

"Understand? I understand perfectly," said Galantucci. Galantucci thought that by suspending Spath, prosecutors were sending a message that his client was guilty or at least that his actions were suspicious. And while Galantucci trusted the integrity of grand juries—and trial juries—to sort through evidence, he also knew that their members were human and were influenced by the outside political atmosphere and how a case was covered in the newspapers. A suspension would sit in jurors' minds. Galantucci also thought that Spath's suspension would play into the hands of the rioters: that if they broke windows and flipped police cars, then the authorities would cave in.

"Don't let them dictate what's right and wrong," Galantucci said. He hustled Spath out the door.

Back at his office Galantucci's phone was ringing with calls from the reporters. Did he want to comment on Spath's suspension? He decided it was time to draw the line. "Gary Spath," he said, "has been stabbed in the back."

LATER THAT NIGHT

Fred Greene sat in the mix of fluorescent light and darkness of his basement and wondered what he should do about the shadows he faced. As a black man he was angry that a young boy had been killed by a police officer's bullet. Shot in the back no less. But as a former cop—a Teaneck cop, who had been Gary Spath's friend and supervisor—he knew Spath wasn't a racist. If anything, Greene believed,

Spath was a victim of a system that did not offer police officers enough training on how to think fast on their feet when they were confronted by boys with guns. Teaneck was caught up in its past: a peaceful suburban town where races basically got along. Didn't anybody realize that the town was less than five miles from New York City and its problems? The number one problem wasn't race or the suburbs. It was criminal activity, coupled with the tendency for today's teenagers to carry guns. Greene believed many cops in the suburbs weren't being properly trained for that new reality.

Something else weighed on Greene's mind. A key to Gary Spath's story was Blanco's frisk of Pannell. By saying he conducted a frisk, Blanco had established that Pannell was indeed carrying a gun. Without such a frisk, Spath's actions, questionable anyway, were even more questionable. A cop is not supposed to fire his weapon unless he is sure of the danger facing him. Without Blanco's story, all Spath had to go on was the word of a resident who described a silver gun in the hands of a boy in red that a dispatcher had said "might be a toy." What's more, Spath had radioed that the boy in red seemed to be trying to get rid of the gun. If Blanco had never frisked Pannell, Spath wouldn't be absolutely sure that Pannell had a gun, toy or not. It was a technical point, Greene realized, but such technicalities were the heart of the law and police work. If Spath was not entirely sure that Pannell had a gun, his shooting could be judged as reckless.

Earlier that evening Greene received an emotional phone call from a cop who had been to a meeting with several other officers, including Blanco, to discuss strategy and to protect Spath from being railroaded by pressure from the black community and zealous prosecutors. The cop was upset.

Greene asked what had happened. The cop said Blanco had told other officers that there were problems with the story of the frisk. "The frisk never happened," the cop told Greene. "It never happened."

On the other end of the phone line the cop was ready to cry. Greene sat in silence. He had never liked Blanco. Greene thought he was too hard-nosed, too likely to play the tough guy. But if Blanco had not frisked Pannell and, therefore, never confirmed that Pannell was indeed carrying a gun, it was Spath who would suffer. And that is something Fred Greene did not want to see happen. What's more, he knew how prosecutors' minds worked. If they discovered one falsehood, they would suspect many more.

As a retired cop Greene felt obligated to report this news to the authorities. But he felt an obligation to his department too. He did not want to be a rat. For now, he would keep silent.

———

Thelma Pannell finally made it home to the River Edge apartment. There was much to do. She had to get her clothes ready for the funeral. She also had to check her mail. But first she needed to check the closet.

She went right to the cardboard box where she kept the silver starter's pistol. When she heard that Phillip had died with a silver gun in his pocket, instinctively she had feared the worst. She had kept silent, however.

She rummaged through the box: nothing. She opened other boxes, looked in closets, and went through Phillip's room. Her suspicions were turning into a nightmare. The gun in Phillip's pocket, she suspected, was her gun.

This was a secret that required careful guarding.

THE NEXT MORNING

It had been a long week for Officer Phil Lavigne. He had seen both sides, up close. On Tuesday his good friend Gary had shot a teenager at almost the same time that Lavigne expected Spath to arrive at his home for dinner. Lavigne had performed CPR on the dead boy in the ambulance and later at the hospital had taken a wet cloth and wiped Spath's distraught face and removed his friend's gun belt and shirt.

At Wednesday's riot Lavigne had been the target of a mob's vengeance near the Mediterranean Deli. On Thursday, the day after the riot, he worked the late shift and didn't punch out until almost 4:00 A.M., Friday.

Lavigne drove across town to his house on Teaneck's south side, but he was too wound up to sleep. The night air was cool, and he opened the door and took a seat on the porch. Lavigne had had little time to collect his thoughts all week. But now, as he sat on the porch in the predawn silence, he reflected on what had taken place. On his own and mostly for his own enjoyment, Lavigne wrote verse. He took out a pen and a notebook.

The shooting had brought into focus so many of the hazards of police work. It had also underscored another undeniable fact about police: that their decisions, good or bad, are not made after long deliberation. He scribbled one line, then another. The words poured out, and within an hour he had fashioned a five-stanza poem. At the top of the page he scribbled a title, "The Blink of an Eye."

The blink of an eye, much faster than light.
The blink of an eye, the decision of life.
How quickly it travels, how fast it must be.
To make that decision, Either you or me.

There's no time for thinking, it's all in high gear.
There's no time for anger, there's no time for fear.
In the blink of an eye, it happens that quick.
You never expect it, it's over—that's it.

They train you for combat, and so, so much more.
And with shield and gun, you head out for war.
You protect and you serve, and you work to your best.
And hope you never enter the enemy's nest.
But should you do so, and the ambush begins.
The guns must be drawn, and the blue shirts must win.

In the blink of an eye, the decision is made.
To go home at night, or be placed in the grave.
It will be judged by many, who have never been there.
For they don't understand the burden we bear.
They'll pick and they'll question.
Just how this was done.
In the blink of an eye, he used his gun.

I'll tell you, my brothers, just blink your eyes.
It takes just that long to be dead or alive.
Should you happen to step in the enemy's nest.
Don't blink your eyes. Just let God do the rest.

Phil Lavigne finished as the light in the eastern sky signaled another sunrise. The poem, he thought, said it all.

THIRTEEN

CROSSROADS

On the southeast border of Teaneck, where the land slopes into the marshes, two of America's most traveled highways intersect in a massive weave of overpasses and cloverleafs. Route 95, the superhighway that links Maine and Florida, meets Route 80, the cross-country interstate that runs from near New York City to San Francisco. It was this sort of crossing of roads large and small that once made Teaneck so appealing to the postwar suburban migrants in the 1950s. From Teaneck you could go almost anywhere fast, to Manhattan, Brooklyn, and Queens, to Newark, to all the area airports, even to the new corporate meccas of New York's Westchester and Connecticut's Fairfield counties. In the weeks after Phillip Pannell died, Teaneck discovered it had become a crossroads of another sort. So many of the emotions that the town once thought itself immune to suddenly made surprise appearances, brought there by paths that were either well disguised or previously nonexistent.

The first of these forays was actually a piece of paper, a leaflet that arrived on the streets of Teaneck on Friday the thirteenth, April 13, Good Friday on the Christian calendar. The leaflet was hand scrawled in pen-and-ink and photocopied from an original that appeared to have been drawn on yellow legal paper. No one claimed responsibility for it. At the top and bottom of the leaflet, in large print, were the letters

N-A-A-C-P. But these letters didn't stand for the National Association for the Advancement of Colored People. On this leaflet the letters had two meanings. At the top *NAACP* stood for "Nigers [sic] Are Actually Colored Pricks." At the bottom it spelled out "Nigers [sic] Are Actually Cotton Pickers." In the center, hand drawn, were four black male figures, all with bulbous Afro haircuts, puffy lips, and round eyes that seemed to bulge in terror. Each figure had a bone in his hair. Standing to the side was the figure of a white Teaneck police officer with a rifle and a sign that said: TEANECK POLICE PISTOL AND FIRING RANGE. WHITES ONLY. The officer was pointing the rifle at the blacks, one of whom wore a T-shirt that said "Troop Pannell."

Blacks accused whites of circulating the leaflet. Whites suspected it was a black conspiracy to drum up antipolice anger in the black community. Whatever the source, it had the immediate effect of contributing to polarization.

A day later another leaflet circulated through the black neighborhoods. Unlike the first, this one had a source and a targeted audience: "A message to the youth of Teaneck from the Revolutionary Communist Party, New York City Branch." Under a large headline—IT'S RIGHT TO REBEL!—the leaflet ran on for two pages, declaring "Justice for Phillip Pannell! Killer Cops to Jail—No Bail! No Peace for Racists!" In smaller type the leaflet said:

> No one should have to live the way Black people are forced to live in this country. What happened to Phillip Pannell was no mistake—honest or otherwise. This is Amerikkka . . . Gary Spath is a murdering hired dog for the system . . . He is a serious danger to the community . . . What is needed is to draw a hard line against white supremacy and to wage a bold, massive, non-stop and uncompromising struggle against this white supremacy and the system that upholds it . . . Revolution is the solution.

The leaflets, obviously the work of extremists, were symptomatic of the emotional trip wires, the color lines, that had been strung across the town. From the black community came a wave of fresh accusations about police harassment of black kids and that what some felt were the racist attitude of the town symbolized by Gary Spath's bullet. Even the news of Spath's other shootings—now publicly acknowledged by the authorities after being leaked to the press by cops who thought Spath too trigger-happy—fed the fire. More than a few blacks believed that Spath would have been disciplined earlier had his targets been whites. Reactions from the white community were far more quiet, but their sentiments and the lines some whites were drawing were reflected in private conversations. Phillip Pannell, many whites said, was a young criminal whose father was a jailbird. The Pannells were just the sort of problem Teaneck did not want. "He may have been a member of his church choir once," said one white woman in a sentiment repeated often by others, "but he was no choirboy."

The public response by Teaneck's establishment was something else entirely. In attempting to sound a reasonable tone, Mayor Frank Hall told the Washington *Post:* "If we were a model of integration, now we should be a model of the way we confront our problems." He made himself available to the major New York City television stations, telling one of them, WABC-TV, that the town still had much work to do before it achieved its goal of becoming a model integrated community. "We haven't finished writing the final chapter," Hall said. Later, on WNBC-TV, as Hall sat on a picnic bench outside the police station, he somberly noted that the riot "reminds us that we have more work to do" but that he "has confidence in the people of Teaneck," that local residents "don't want to trash the town," and that the riot was the work of outsiders. Finally, on WCBS-TV, he added: "We're shocked by what has happened. Obviously we have been out of touch with some feelings in the black community. We became complacent."

Teaneck was on the defensive. But now almost every comment about the shooting was framed in a racial context. At one point George Spath invited reporters to his home to declare that he feared his son would be made "a scapegoat." As for charges that his son was a racist, the senior Spath had a blunt answer that underscored the increasing anger among Spath's friends and family: "Never in my house was there anything racial—never." Councilwoman Eleanor Kieliszek also went public in defense of Spath. She had known the Spath family for years and was telephoned by Spath's mother in those first days for help in countering what she believed was a willingness by the press to portray her son as a trigger-happy racist. "Gary Spath grew up in this town," said Kieliszek. "Anyone who insinuates that he's a racist is just plain wrong. The racists moved out of Teaneck a long time ago."

Not everyone in the black community was willing to single out Spath as a racist, nor was every white resident critical of the Pannells. But in subtle ways the focus of the public debate had changed; what had been concerns over a police shooting on Tuesday had grown by Friday to embrace racism in general and Teaneck's image as a model town in particular. Gary Spath was no longer just a cop with a gun, and Phillip

Pannell no longer just a kid with a gun; both were becoming symbols of larger questions about how well integration was working in Teaneck . . . and beyond.

"I have two sons, two and four years old," said Annie Allen, the black chairwoman of the Bergen County Rainbow Coalition, including the Rainbow Youth Coalition, who had helped organize the ill-fated march and vigil. "I am frightened that ten years from now my kids can be shot in the schoolyard for being rowdy. Teaneck's still, in my opinion, one of the best models of integration in the country. But to say that it's integrated and that's where the struggle ends is a mistake."

Courtly Wilson, a fifty-five-year-old black postal supervisor, spoke of the racism he saw in white shopkeepers, a subject black adults mentioned frequently before the shooting but most whites had almost no feeling for. "They watch you as if you're going to steal something," said Wilson. "It makes me angry all the time."

Another black resident, Deirdre Baker, who had lived in Teaneck for more than ten years, said the shooting reminded blacks that despite their move to the suburbs and their embrace of a middle-class life, they still faced some of the same urban problems they thought they had left behind. "As a black parent, it frightens me," Baker said. "The homes in this community cost two hundred thousand dollars. We're not a large welfare community. This is not a troubled community. This community has good resources, and the people work hard. We should not see our children shot down."

Across town, Mark Zitter, an Orthodox Jew, said he thought far too many critics had jumped to the conclusion that Spath's shooting of Pannell was racially motivated. But the aftermath had caused him to reflect on some dynamics of his town that he never considered. "Maybe it's a little more polarized than I realized," Zitter said. "Maybe I don't understand what's going on in the black sections of town."

———

Officer Luis Torres could feel the change in his town and police force. On his first day back, after being off for two days, he was given a partner, a black officer, and assigned to patrol the black northeast neighborhood. The instructions were simple:

"Be careful.

"Watch out for false alarms.

"Don't get ambushed."

Since the shooting, especially in the days after the riot, the rumor that a cop would be shot in retaliation for Pannell's death had circulated through Teaneck. Torres was stunned when he heard the instructions and the warning, but as he and his partner set out in the black neighborhoods, he could see why cops felt that way. "You'd look at people's faces, and you could see the anger in them," he said. And in the car that night he could sense turmoil in himself that he hadn't felt before the shooting. As a Hispanic he knew he was in a minority in Teaneck and even more on the police force, which was still the domain of whites. Of the eighty-three officers in the department in April 1990, only five were black or Hispanic. In the days that followed, Torres and his black partner were often assigned to the northeast. He was never told why, but he suspected it had everything to do with skin color and little to do with competence. "I imagine that they felt maybe because he was black and I was Spanish that it might not be confrontational," Torres said.

Torres noticed a change in some of his fellow officers too. As more black kids spoke on television about feeling harassed, Torres could see that his white colleagues were seething. Many of the kids who spoke were troublemakers anyway, and the media seemed to care little about checking out their stories. Or so the officers said.

Torres knew another side to this issue. Some cops kept a close eye on black kids or looked to the black neighborhoods to hand out quick tickets on cars with broken taillights. It was also known among cops that the store owners along Cedar Lane did not want kids to congregate. Torres was savvy enough to understand the symbolism of a white cop approaching a group of black kids in the white business district and telling them to "move along." To the white cop, he was only doing his job. To the black kids, it was harassment. As Luis Torres came to understand, it was all a matter of perception.

One of the white store owners acknowledged this in an interview with *The New York Times*. "Was I surprised by this?" asked John Pandolfo, the owner of a fish store. "Well, as long as I've been here there's been pressure, tension between the police and the youth. There are always undercurrents of that. The kids will hang out, and as a service to the merchants the police will move them along. But it's taken as harassment when you have white police officers and blacks hanging out. It would be different if it were mixed."

Too late for that now, thought Torres. The lines were set. As he patrolled the black neighborhoods that night, he noticed more kids than usual on the street. The public schools were closed for the Easter holiday, so it was not unusual for teenagers to be out after dinner. But as he looked out the window at the clumps of teenagers who eyed his car as he cruised past, Torres felt the change. There were sullen, angry stares from the black kids. A few even turned their backs and raised their arms in mock surrender as the police car drove by. Torres knew what they were doing. The turned back and raised arms represented Phillip Pannell.

Torres did not feel angry. He understood why the kids felt the way they did, though he feared he would be drawn into the crossfire if the rumors that an officer might be lured into ambush were true. He decided to be careful. He knew his uniform, not his skin color or ethnicity, was his most noticeable badge now.

Yet he felt oddly distant from that uniform. On that first day it was only a faint feeling, but he was uneasy about it just the same. The watchword in the police department was "loyalty," and in those early days Torres could feel the pressure at work to line up support behind Gary Spath. Torres knew Spath wasn't a racist. Racism hadn't caused Spath to pull the trigger and fire a bullet into the boy's back. Torres was sure of that. But that wasn't the issue. It was competence and how a police officer reacts under pressure. Here, Torres found his feelings of friendship giving way to the knot in his conscience. Before he could be blindly loyal to his uniform, he had to settle the rumbling in his heart.

THE SAME NIGHT

Dorothy Marcus felt another kind of rumbling. Her community had changed in the course of a few days, and the meeting she had scheduled weeks before to discuss race relations and forge plans for a larger session with the League of Women Voters had become something else entirely. Almost four dozen people were now crowded into her living room. White middle-class Jews mixed with black adults. On the floor—thanks largely to her daughter's influence—sat a large group of teenagers, many of whom had known Phillip.

Over the next two hours the group voiced concerns about the high school, police harassment, black gangs, the lack of leadership in the town, the media's handling of Teaneck's reputation, and the shooting itself. Irked at something a white man had said, one black woman stormed out. But she was the exception. The group sat along the edges of Marcus's cozy rectangular living room. There was no firm agenda. The kids talked about harassment and the general feeling that black and white students were not mixing well. The white adults, Marcus noticed, not surprisingly seemed to be holding back. Whites always felt reluctant to speak out in mixed groups. She remembered it had been that way in the 1960s. In the 1990s things hadn't changed much.

Marcus was especially drawn to the sentiments of one black man. She had heard of Art Gardner before and knew him as the high school gym teacher. But she had never heard him speak. Indeed, despite her experience in race relations, Marcus was surprised by what Gardner had to say. He described himself going shopping. Gardner, large, imposing, but well known as a coach, a father, a husband, and a teacher, spoke of being followed as he walked through a store in Teaneck. Gardner said he thought salesclerks saw him as a shoplifter. It was a case of misplaced suspicions, but Gardner said he could not erase the belittling feeling from his memory. Art Gardner was a suspect only because of the color of his skin.

━━━━━

In Bergen County in April 1990 there were more than a hundred funeral homes. There were places that catered to the special religious requirements of Jews or Catholics or Buddhists. Others were magnets for mobsters. Still others catered to AIDS victims. In Hackensack the Conyers Funeral Home was known for something else: its almost exclusively black clientele. On Good Friday William Conyers, the funeral home owner, had begun to embalm the body of Phillip Pannell when the phone rang.

Conyers was late in preparing the body. It had been three days since Pannell's death, but with an autopsy by the county medical examiner, a partial autopsy by a state medical examiner, and another autopsy by a doctor hired by Pannell's attorney, Franklin Wilks, the embalming and other funeral preparations had been delayed. Conyers took the call and heard a voice that had become familiar. It was Dennis Calo of the prosecutor's office. He wanted to drop by to conduct just one more test on Pannell's body. Conyers stopped the embalming. Just before 3:00 P.M. Calo and six other white men walked into the funeral home. Among other items they carried a video camera, a steel probe, and Pannell's red parka. They also had one big question: Could they prove if Pannell's hands were up or down when he was shot?

Among experienced homicide investigators the tests for body movements by shooting victims are grounded in common sense. The tests are crude, yet they can be surprisingly accurate if done correctly and carefully. The fundamental premise is that bullets generally travel through clothing in a straight path. If you can line up a bullet hole in a coat with a bullet hole in a body, sometimes you can calculate body movements, especially of the arms. In Pannell's case the experiment revolved around a simple thesis: If Pannell's arms were raised, his coat would likely ride up on his back. And if that were the case, the bullet hole in the coat would be lower than the corresponding spot on Pannell's body when the coat was placed with the arms at Pannell's side. The methodology was not perfect science; Calo said it might not even be classified as science. The night before at the funeral home, he and the county medical examiner had tried to line up the bullet hole in the coat with the bullet hole in Pannell's body. Neither Calo nor the medical examiner thought he could draw any conclusion. But Calo was not satisfied, and the next morning he placed a call to Peter De Forest, a scientist who specialized in reconstructing crime scenes.

Quiet, bespectacled, and perpetually curious, De Forest worked out of a cluttered home laboratory in New York's Westchester County, and he had gained a reputation among prosecutors and defense attorneys as a man who could look at a murder scene and tell a story of what happened by analyzing such elements as the way blood splattered on a wall or the way a victim's hair burned in a fire. Forty-nine years old and California-born, De Forest spent much of his time teaching at New York City's John Jay College. When he wasn't in a classroom or consulting with prosecutors and lawyers, he was writing such articles as "Identification of Blood by Anti-Human Hemoglobin Serum" or "A Study of Refractive Index Variations Within and Between Sealed-Beam Headlines Using a Precise Method." Indeed, he was a man whose life was enveloped by the arcane elements of criminal investigations. His doctoral dissertation (at Berkeley) told much about the complexities of his profession: "Individualization of Human Hair—Pyrolysis-Gas Chromatography." In two decades of combining teaching and crime solving, he had been called by prosecutors to testify in more than one hundred cases, using his ability to analyze evidence to help reconstruct all manner of crime scenes—including the Central Park Jogger assault case and New York City's "Preppie Murder." And when public television produced a documentary on the assassination of President John F. Kennedy, De Forest was hired as a consultant to analyze autopsy findings.

Helping De Forest at the Conyers Funeral Home was the same man who had attempted to test Pannell's clothing the night before, Dr. Lawrence Denson, the Bergen County medical examiner. Denson was not a certified pathologist; he was something of a dying breed in American medicine, a doctor who dabbled in a variety of specialties. He still ran a family practice out of the house in Hackensack that he had grown up in. On any day you might find him in one room, impeccably dressed in a white shirt, a demure striped tie, and a pressed white doctor's coat, examining a patient and dispensing advice in friendly Norman Rockwell style. To step into his living room, where a piano with its collection of classical sheet music sat next to a table that often held a stack of *Foreign Affairs* journals, he had only to pass through a door. As a younger man Denson had befriended the county medical examiner. And what had begun as a curious hobby had evolved into a passion for performing autopsies. If he was known for anything, it was for not jumping to conclusions. Dr. Denson was no publicity seeker; there would be no television show about him on a par with *Quincy,* nor were there many features about him in the local newspapers. Larry Denson operated in anonymity, and that was how he preferred it. Many patients who came to him and asked him to cure sore throats, examine rashes, or listen to irregular heartbeats had no idea he spent so much time around autopsy tables with the victims of murders and car wrecks. And many patients, he found, were often shocked when he would shy away from making firm diagnoses. He took pride in remaining noncommittal. "I have a very favorite phrase I use: 'I don't know,'" he said. "It shakes up a lot of patients when you say that. But it's extremely important. I was taught to say, 'I don't know,' a long time ago. If I don't know, I don't know."

As the group gathered around Pannell's body on Good Friday, Calo hoped for a firmer conclusion. He already knew that the two versions of the shooting—that Pannell was reaching for a gun or that he was raising his hands in surrender—were playing havoc with his investigation. And he was enough of a newspaper reader to know that the conflicting accounts of the shooting were contributing to some of the turmoil on Teaneck's streets. If he could find an answer, perhaps Teaneck could find some calm and the investigation find direction.

The group placed Pannell's nude body on the funeral home embalming table. It was a tight room, ten by ten feet, with white walls and cabinets with glass doors that held the tools, fluids, and cosmetics of a mortician. De Forest set up his video camera on a tripod by the door that led to the funeral home's viewing room. At 2:59 P.M. he turned on the camera.

De Forest first examined Pannell's hands, noting abrasions on the boy's left hand from a fall when he tried to run from the Bryant School playground or perhaps when he fell after being shot. It was impossible to tell. Detectives then pulled Pannell's body into a sitting position. The boy's head slumped forward, and from behind De Forest looked over the wide sutures from the autopsies that seemed like stitching on a baseball and ran from the boy's left shoulder blade and down his back. The autopsy had been extensive. All of Phillip Pannell's internal organs, including his heart, had been removed. But in their search to determine if he had been shot in the leg—a rumor that turned out to be untrue—doctors had sliced muscles down his legs and arms. What's more, the doctor hired by Pannell's lawyer had sliced into the boy's shoulder blade in an attempt to see what bones had been nicked as the bullet passed through. After all the surgical cuts had been sewn up, Pannell looked like a rag doll in a toy repair shop.

The detectives dressed Pannell's upper body in clothes like those he had worn the night he was shot, starting with a black hooded sweat-shirt similar to the one cut away when paramedics had tried to save his life. Before putting Pannell's red parka on the body, Dr. Denson took a metal tube about the size of a Bic ballpoint and began to push into a spot on the boy's back where the sutures crossed.

"Hold it," a detective called out. "He's falling down."

Two other detectives reached for Pannell's armpits and propped him up.

Denson pushed again with the metal rod. Another detective called out, "Is that the right spot?"

Seemingly unaware of the question, Denson twisted and turned the probe. The detective called out again: "You better check because it's important that you are in the right spot."

Denson, shirtsleeves rolled up, was having trouble getting the probe past the thick thread that was used to sew up the autopsy cuts. "Damn thread," he mumbled. "That's killing me."

Denson moved back, and De Forest turned off the camera. Denson asked for a larger metal rod, which he then used to push into and widen the suture wound on Pannell's back. Denson said later he thought he had picked the correct spot, but he never double-checked. In the original autopsy the bullet hole in Pannell's back was noted on a chart with measurements—from his left heel and from his spine. But for the test Denson didn't take out a measuring tape. When asked later, he shook his head and muttered his familiar phrase: "I don't know."

Several minutes later, with the video camera back on, Denson was finally able to insert his smaller probe.

"Is that spot right?" Dennis Calo asked.

"That's about the spot," said Denson.

Peter De Forest said, "Okay, very good."

With the probe in place, the detectives and De Forest conducted a series of tests. They moved Pannell's arms over his head, in a surrender position; they let the boy's arms fall to his side; they held them in front at chest level. Only once, however, did the bullet hole in the coat line up with the metal probe in the spot Denson had designated as the bullet wound: when Pannell's hands were at his side, in a position that corresponded with his reaching for a gun in his pocket.

The tests were over within an hour. And as the group walked out of the funeral home into what was left of the Good Friday sunshine, Calo turned to De Forest and asked for a preliminary conclusion that might give detectives a theory around which to frame their investigation. Were Pannell's hands up in surrender, as blacks said, or were they down and possibly going for a gun, as Spath and Blanco said?

"Looks like the arms were down," De Forest said.

THE NEXT DAY

In a small room just off the sanctuary of St. Mark's Episcopal Church in Teaneck, a handful of police officers sat down around a table. It was 7:30 A.M., and from the room the police could look through windows and into the silent church and its rows of empty pews. On Sundays when the church is crowded, the room is the domain of parents who can watch the Anglican mass through the windows and not worry about their children making noise. On the morning that the police gathered there, church volunteers were arriving with flowers to place around the altar in preparation for the next day's Easter services.

Reverend Mandy Derr took a seat at the table along with several other members of Teaneck's clergy, including the pastor of St. Mark's, Reverend Lucinda Laird. Derr was glad to see the cops. A few police wives had come too, along with several children. In the days since the shooting and the riot Derr had met too many cops who seemed angry, confused, resentful, and afraid. He harbored great respect for police. Most were down-to-earth types who went about their jobs seriously, conscientiously, and carefully, with rarely an emotional outburst. Now it was as if someone had opened a valve on a steam pipe.

What the clergy heard over the next two hours was far more than they had expected. The cops were angry with the town, their superiors, politicians, whites, blacks, the media. It seemed to Derr that no group escaped. The cops thought liberals at the newspapers and on television had turned the shooting into a racial issue, emphasizing that Spath was white and Pannell was black. Pannell was a juvenile delinquent, one cop said. His record was well-known—even to the press. Why was he depicted as a martyr? The reports from the street portrayed more and more kids as carrying guns. Why weren't the media writing about that?

That morning *The New York Times* had carried an exclusive report on its front page that Pannell's friends claimed he did not have a silver .22-caliber revolver but was actually carrying a far less lethal BB gun. The implication of the story, written by one of the *Times's* most experienced reporters, was obvious: The silver revolver that police said they had found in Pannell's pocket might have been planted. If nothing else, the story served to undercut the police version. But what neither the police nor the *Times* knew at that point is that the story was half true: Pannell had played with a BB gun at Tryon Park before he was shot, while he was carrying the silver pistol in his pocket.

Another cop jumped in. "This isn't a black-white issue. This is a police officer dealing with a kid who was breaking the law. The kid had a gun."

"Yeah," said another. "He was a kid with a gun, not a black kid with a gun."

It was a good point, Derr thought. Few people seemed to be focusing on the fact that Pannell was carrying a gun. Derr gazed around the room as he listened. He had decided before he arrived that he would not challenge anything the cops said. This was a time to listen, not argue or even ask questions. Derr agreed with some of what the police were saying. Yet he was troubled by the unfolding reactions, not only in the room but all over town. None of the cops around the table was black, just as almost none of the people charging racism in the shooting was white. The stories and reactions from blacks and whites, Derr thought, seemed so different, so opposite, that it was as if there had been two separate shootings.

Derr saw some cops as so emotionally upset that they should be excused from their daily duties. While there seemed to be plenty of opportunities for blacks to express their feelings, there had been almost no opportunity for police to vent, in Derr's view.

Another cop was speaking now. Why, he asked, was there so little public support for the police? He believed that Teaneck's politicians were acting like those wooden dolls with bobble heads, nodding in apparent agreement with almost any accusation from black teenagers or others who charged police harassment. Why, the cop asked, was no one stepping out and showing more support for police? Why wouldn't anyone come out solidly behind Gary Spath?

One of the wives started to cry. She was worried about her husband and the rumors that a cop might be shot. She worried that her children might be harassed by rowdy black kids at school.

Another cop spoke up. The blacks, he said, should have been stopped from rioting. But now that they had been allowed to riot, who knew what would be next? It was just more evidence, he went on, of how do-good, liberal whites had caved in and allowed Pannell to become a martyr and had stood back while a riot took place. It was a double standard: The cops were criticized for unproved charges of harassment, but blacks were allowed to riot with no consequences. "You have to understand," an officer said, "that the only thing between you and them is the police department. And it's a thin blue line."

Derr got the message loudly and clearly. The police were unsure of how to act. Suppose a fight broke out at a black bar? Should the cops rush in and break it up? Would they be drawn into a racial issue? What might have seemed an odd question only a week before seemed an overriding concern now. For a moment Derr wondered if the entire Teaneck department should be put on leave and the state police called in to patrol neighborhoods for a week or two. Maybe everyone needed a breather.

Derr tried to accentuate the positive, mentioning how police had helped him in the past in checking out attempted robberies at his church. "You have supporters in this community," he said. "You have supporters among us."

But the shooting by Gary Spath had driven an invisible wedge into that relationship. For Derr, it was still possible to examine what Spath had done and raise questions about it without having to make a judgment about the whole police force. As he listened, though, he knew that more and more officers did not feel that way, that for many police Spath was becoming a symbol of many of their difficulties. If you questioned what Spath had done, then you were questioning the entire force.

It was almost 10:00 A.M. Mandy Derr had to leave for another meeting, this time with the town council at his church, Grace Lutheran. As he drove across town, the anger welled inside him. He parked his car, walked into his own church meeting room, and plugged in a coffeepot. The council had asked to meet at Grace so they might avoid reporters who gathered around the town's municipal building. Derr understood. This was a time for somber reflection, especially now, on Saturday, traditionally a quiet day before Easter.

As the council along with other community leaders took seats, Derr rose to greet everyone. He pointed out where the bathrooms were and where people could get coffee if they wanted. Then he paused to switch gears. There are a few times when a preacher's natural eloquence blends perfectly with the emotions in his heart. For Mandy Derr this was one of them. The words flowed, so fast and concisely and honestly that even he was surprised later. He painted a portrait of a Medusa-like town, with a leadership that had too many heads, each one intent on fighting all the others instead of working together. There had been too much bickering. There were too many groups being pitted against one another. They had been fighting over so many small issues that they had completely missed problems that had been brewing in the community between races, with cops, between ethnic groups. There were too many personality differences, with one council member hating another for insults uttered years before. There were too many people, Derr said, not mentioning names, who seemed intent on using the shooting of Phillip Pannell to push their own agendas, whatever they might be. "If you can't work together," he said, "you can't expect to bring this town together."

Derr left and went home. He was not hopeful.

THAT MORNING

Paul Ostrow went to his synagogue. He was not a regular each Saturday. He tried to go at least once a month to the Jewish Center, but today he felt he should be there. He wanted to hear what people were saying. He wanted a hopeful sermon.

He was troubled. He basically believed Spath had acted properly, but Ostrow was by no means happy with this position. A kid was dead, shot in the back. No matter how the shooting was explained, he was bothered by that. And now his town seemed to have lost the internal gyroscope that for so long had regulated its sense of balance. Ostrow was even more upset about that. He loved his town, but in the last week he had begun to question why he had moved back to Teaneck and whether his kids would be safe here.

In the synagogue Ostrow took a seat in the fourth row on the left side. He liked the spot. At a bar mitzvah he often sat there so that he could watch the face of the boy who was being honored in the rite of passage from youth to adulthood. On this day Ostrow remembered how his father had sat with him in the same place in this same synagogue the day after President John F. Kennedy had been assassinated. Ostrow had been preparing for his bar mitzvah then, and on that day he was especially touched when the ark was solemnly opened and the Torah was removed to be read at the service. It is a moment when the congregation offers prayers for the community and for the nation, including the President. On the day after Kennedy's assassination Ostrow was especially struck by how the congregation was already praying for the new President, Lyndon Baines Johnson.

Similar prayers were offered on the Saturday after Gary Spath shot Phillip Pannell. But this time Ostrow didn't find himself praying for his country or his new President, as he had on that Saturday in November 1963. On this day his prayers were for his town. The town was the subject of the sermon by Rabbi Dave Feldman. The time had come, said the rabbi, for Teaneck to reexamine itself. The loss of a life—rightly or wrongly—was an opportunity to consider larger questions. Was Teaneck really a model town? Was Teaneck really what it thought it was?

———

The next day, Easter, at another house of worship a preacher looked out over the black faces in his congregation. The Shiloh AME Zion Church, which drew its members from Teaneck and Englewood, was packed, and its pastor, the Reverend Stanley Dennison, had been up late crafting his Easter sermon on the meaning of resurrection—in the time of Jesus of Nazareth and now. But first Dennison wanted to comment on the death of Phillip Pannell. He began by asking all the children and teenagers to come forward and stand in the well of the church in front of the pulpit. The kids stood four and five abreast, from one side of the church to the other. Dennison knew many of them, and he assumed many had known Phillip Pannell.

Dennison found himself trying to read their mood. Some seemed angry and sullen. Dennison was worried about the wake that night and the funeral the next day. Rumors were circulating that the kids might try to march again, that they might even try to go after the cops. The minister wanted to encourage the kids to talk about their problems rather than resort to more violence. The next time he did not expect the police to hold back. The next time, he believed, would be very bloody.

"We owe you an apology," Dennison said at the outset.

He figured that would get their attention, and it did. Dennison remembered how kids mentioned before the shooting that they felt police in Teaneck harassed them and how most adults discounted such feelings as youthful complaints. Since the shooting Dennison and other black adults wondered whether it could have somehow been prevented if they had listened to the kids' concerns about harassment and had talked to the police about them. If nothing else, listening seriously to the kids would have forced adults to become involved more in their lives. Perhaps someone would have noticed Phillip's wandering and his troubled life.

"I want to apologize for not listening to your complaints before," Dennison said. "When you told us what kinds of things that were happening, about what the police were doing, we turned a deaf ear, and we didn't respond. We didn't follow up, and we were wrong, and we're sorry."

Some of the girls were crying. Dennison went on. He told the kids about the importance of talking about their feelings, about how adults should listen to them. "We love you," he said, "and we don't want anything to happen to you."

Throughout Teaneck's churches and synagogues similar messages went out to white and black congregations. It was as if the weekend had brought in a new batch of grace-filled elixir, as if the clergy recognized the need to extend a message to the people of Teaneck to remain calm and hopeful.

On Friday evening services at the Reform Jewish temple, Congregation Beth Am, Rabbi Allen Darnov had paid homage to Teaneck's past, recalling that it was the first community in the nation to voluntarily desegregate its schools through busing and that some of its residents had placed Not for Sale signs on front lawns in an angry retort to white flight. "We like our self-image, and when image and orientation were shattered in that night of broken glass, we found that we could no longer trust our world view, and we sensed a loss," Darnov told his congregation. "It was and is a loss that grieves us like a death."

Across town on Saturday morning at an Orthodox synagogue, Congregation Beth Aaron, Rabbi Ephraim Kanarfogel called for an open discussion of issues. "There are a number of people that feel they have been mistreated consistently by the police," he said. "Whether that is so, our sensitivity to our neighbors requires that we as residents allow and support some form by which these problems can be discussed and addressed."

Likewise, on Easter morning the Reverend Lucinda Laird took the pulpit at St. Mark's Episcopal Church and called for Teaneck to look beyond its problems and strive for solutions. "We know we have experienced death," she declared as television cameras from NBC News rolled. "We know Good Friday. We live in a Good Friday world. It is the Easter world that experiences resurrection."

"We can't deny there are wrongs," said the pastor of St. Paul's Lutheran Church, the Reverend Bruce Davidson. "We have to see that there are, in our community, instruments of healing and reconciliation. We must be agents of that hope that we celebrate on Easter."

At Teaneck's only black congregation, the First Baptist Church, where the vigil march had begun several days before, the Reverend Robert Merritt issued a clear call for nonviolence. "I stood there on Teaneck Road, watching our young people throw barriers through windows," he said. "The police department in this community were waiting for you to do it. They were expecting it. Why do you think they had that riot squad in here?" He paused for a moment to let the congregation take in what he had said. "But," he continued, "he who lives by the sword dies by the sword. Remember, Jesus didn't fight back."

The congregation answered with a loud chorus of "amen."

At Grace Lutheran Church the Reverend Mandy Derr did not preach a sermon that Easter Sunday. He was exhausted, and by a small stroke of luck he had invited another Lutheran minister weeks before to be a guest speaker. The Reverend Donald Larsen fitted the task perfectly. He had been in Detroit during the riots in 1967. "This isn't just Teaneck," Larsen told the Grace Church worshipers. "This is America."

Derr in his clerical robes sat on the side. Larsen's message was one of empathy; he had been there before. And while Derr felt calmed by his words, another part of Larsen's message stung. "This is not going to be easy," Larsen said. Instinctively Derr knew that was true. Although many of Teaneck residents were openly saying that the town would mend quickly and move on, Derr knew there were fundamental issues that needed to be confronted or they would merely go underground and emerge at another time.

He thought of the death of his first wife in 1981 after a twenty-month struggle with breast cancer. He had been exhausted after that, and he feared another long struggle now. For the services that day Derr had written special petition prayers for the Pannell and Spath families. (In the days ahead he mailed the church bulletin with those prayers to both families.) But as he went home after the Easter services to spend the day with his second wife and son, Derr was afraid. He was convinced there would be another shooting. "Absolutely convinced," he said later. And the probable victim would be a white police officer.

If that happened, Mandy Derr was sure of the result. It would be open warfare, he told himself. And then he remembered something that Don Larsen had said in his sermon: how so many of the stories of the early Christian Church were built around two words, "go" and "tell." Larsen's words had given Derr new inspiration. He decided that tired or not, he would get involved. The politicians were not capable of healing Teaneck, no matter how many scoldings Mandy Derr delivered, but he was hopeful about the clergy. The trick was to agree on a message. He knew that might be the most difficult task. To understand how difficult, all he had to do was pick up a newspaper.

THE SAME DAY

On page 22 of the weighty Sunday edition of *The New York Times*, on a page with a photograph of children in Weehawken, New Jersey, participating in an Easter egg hunt along the Hudson River, the Manhattan skyline as a backdrop, another preacher weighed in.

The Reverend Jesse Jackson had heard about Pannell's death and had already discussed it on the telephone with his friend, Reverend Daughtry. Jackson knew Teaneck and had stayed at Daughtry's Teaneck home when he campaigned for President in 1988. He didn't know all the facts in the shooting, but he was bothered that Pannell had been shot in the back, possibly with his hands up. Telephoned by a *Times* reporter at his home in Chicago, Jackson said the shooting was typical of what he saw as a growing number of confrontations between police and black males. "I have three sons," Jackson said, "and all three have faced gunpoint or handcuffs. And they were well behaved and drug-free."

Jackson called for a special prosecutor to examine the Pannell shooting. "This must be a national outrage," he said.

Then Jackson added a comment about Gary Spath that would remain for a long time in the minds of the police: "The full weight of the law must come down on this assassin."

FOURTEEN

"WE WON'T FORGET"

EASTER NIGHT

The Reverend Al Sharpton wanted to go to Teaneck. He had been planning the trip for three days, ever since he heard from Dorothy Robinson. He remembered her words and felt both pride and concern. "The local leadership out here is not going to do anything that would compromise their standing in the community," she told him. "We don't have any Al Sharptons out here." Sharpton had long thought there would be a riot somewhere in America by young blacks against police. He had monitored the tensions for years in New York City and had expected them to spill out on several occasions. Now Teaneck was the scene of a riot, and the media were covering it. Reporters telephoned Sharpton each day. What did he think? Was he planning to get involved? On Easter Sunday evening there was to be a wake for Phillip Pannell at a church near Teaneck. Sharpton looked at his schedule. He had nothing planned.

For Easter Sharpton had the use of a black Lincoln Continental stretch limousine, driven by a man he knew only as Captain Shah. The driver had been a Black Muslim leader, but in recent years he had earned his keep as the driver for boxing promoter Don King. The limo was King's Easter present to Sharpton, a one-day loan for him to take his message anywhere in the metropolitan area.

Before 10 A.M. Sharpton was at La Guardia Airport in Queens to pick up Chicago Congressman Gus Savage. Sharpton had invited Savage to speak to a gathering in Brooklyn on Monday. Now Sharpton and Savage had an entire day on their hands, not to mention the limousine. Sharpton ferried Savage from the airport to Easter services at Bethany Baptist Church in Brooklyn's Bedford-Stuyvesant. As the two walked out of the church, Savage turned to Sharpton. "Farrakhan's in town," he said.

"Really?" said Sharpton. "What's he doing?"

Savage knew Minister Louis Farrakhan from Chicago, where Farrakhan lived and operated the headquarters of his Nation of Islam. Farrakhan had come to New York City on the weekend to install a new head of the Nation's mosque in Harlem. Sharpton had convinced Savage to go with him to Pannell's wake, but that wasn't supposed to begin until 7:00 P.M. "Why don't we go by and say hello to Louis?" Savage suggested.

Sharpton nodded. *Why not?* He had known Farrakhan for years. Late in the afternoon, when Sharpton and Savage walked into the Black Muslim mosque at 125th Street in Harlem, Farrakhan greeted them and asked them to come up on the stage with him before the congregation. When the service ended, Sharpton mentioned he and Savage had to leave for Pannell's wake. "A black kid has been shot in the back by a white cop," said Sharpton.

Farrakhan had heard. He also knew Teaneck. His daughter-in-law had grown up there; her family had telephoned his office with the news. "If you wait twenty minutes, I'll go with you," Farrakhan told Sharpton.

A little before 7:00 P.M. a caravan of two black limousines and five other cars wove through the traffic across the George Washington Bridge and rolled west on Route 4. Captain Shah led the way, the backseat of his limousine occupied by Sharpton and Yusuf Hawkins's parents. In the limousine behind them were Farrakhan, Savage, and Alton Maddox. In the other cars were some two dozen of Farrakhan's bodyguards, the red bow tied Fruit of Islam.

The caravan pulled off the highway and into the neighborhood on the Teaneck-Englewood border where ten months before Officer Gary Spath had pursued the bank robber who had fired a pistol at some men. The cars turned down a block with wood-frame homes and stopped in front of the Community Baptist Church, where the body of Phillip Clinton Pannell lay in an open mahogany coffin.

It was dark now, and Sharpton could see the crowds of kids lining the sidewalks, waiting to get into the church. He didn't know it then, but more than a thousand people—all but a handful of them black— had descended on the small church for the wake.

Sharpton got out first, and across the street kids started to chant, "Al . . . Al . . . Al." Sharpton turned and waved. Farrakhan's bodyguards got out and lined the sidewalk at attention and in silence. As Farrakhan emerged finally from his limousine, the crowd cheered again. When the limousines pulled up and word spread of the new arrivals, Thelma Pannell was hustled out a side door by several friends who were concerned with Sharpton creating a scene. Phillip David Pannell walked out of the front door, tears rolling down his cheeks and calling out, "My son, my son. I won't have my son. They shot him in the back. Where is my son?" The Reverend Herbert Daughtry put an arm around Pannell and whispered, "Peace, peace."

Meanwhile, Sharpton was miffed. An older man had stopped him at the door and told him not to come in. "You guys are not welcome here," the man said. It had been years since Sharpton had heard that from another black man. He turned to Farrakhan, shrugged, and kept walking into the church, pushed along now by the Fruit of Islam. "Who is this guy?" Sharpton asked.

The man was George Powell. The two did not have a chance to meet. Nor did Powell have an opportunity to explain himself. George Powell wanted reason to descend on Teaneck and the shooting to be examined by a special prosecutor. He did not want activism—not now anyway. With Sharpton on the scene, Powell feared the atmosphere he was trying to create would evaporate. He also hoped to meet with Jim Florio soon. The last person Powell wanted by his side or with the Pannell family was Al Sharpton.

THE NEXT DAY

Phillip Pannell was buried in sunshine. During his funeral service his closed coffin was flanked by an arrangement of flowers in the shape of a heart and eight other arrangements of mums, roses, and carnations. Atop the coffin sat a blanket of white and red carnations with a blue ribbon. A choir sang "What a Friend We Have in Jesus," and the printed program for the service urged mourners to "honor his life and memory by continuing to strive for unity and justice for all people of all races." Phillip, the program added:

> was actively involved in the Inspirational Choir as a tenor. He was affectionately called "Clint" by his family members. He is loved and remembered as a young man who loved to sing, play basketball, football and spend time with his friends. He was very popular, well-respected and loved by everyone. Phillip was anticipating acceptance into the Job Corps so that he could positively and productively spend his time, while he obtained his high school diploma. Phillip's aspirations and dreams were to become a football player or a rap singer.

Throughout the entire service Thelma Pannell sat in the front pew, wiping away tears and biting her lower lip. Crowded into the pews around her and in the balcony were 350 people. Another 400 stood outside and listened to the service on loudspeakers. "When he was shot," said Jesse Jackson in a letter that was read to the congregation, "people who cared bled everywhere. In the shadow of the Statue of Liberty, the American promise has been shattered."

A Teaneck High School student, Theo Bolden, rose and mounted the pulpit. He wore a black shirt and suit with a white carnation and a red ribbon attached to the lapel of his jacket. The red was in memory of Phillip Pannell. "They come in our community with fear in their hearts," said Bolden of police, jabbing his index finger at his heart for emphasis. "No longer will we put up with public officials putting guns in the hands of people who are untrained to our needs."

"Amen," said a voice in the crowd.

"They come in our community, our homes, with fear in their hearts tempered by racial violence," Bolden continued.

"Amen."

But it was the Reverend Herbert Daughtry, the main speaker, who delivered the most caustic message to the mourners. "This has to stop," he called out, his voice rising steadily. "The people we pay to protect us kill us. Let the word go forth. Let it reach the White House. Let it reach the dignitaries across the country. We ain't going to take it no more." As he spoke, a girl in the balcony threw her head back and grasped the pew in front of her, tears streaming down her cheeks. In other pews adults put their arms around teenagers or placed hands on the shoulders of children near them. When Daughtry paused, he was answered as much with an "amen" as with a chorus of sobs. "I wonder what would have happened if a black officer had killed a fif-teen-year-old Irish kid," Daughtry said. "I wonder what would have happened if a black officer had killed an Italian kid or a Jewish kid. There wouldn't have been just a few broken windows down on Teaneck Road."

As he spoke, Daughtry pulled at the black robe that he wore for the service and raised his right hand, his index finger extended. "We are a mighty decent people," he boomed. "We are a mighty outgoing people. But let me say. We can't take it forever. Something's got to give. We must build a monument so that as long as the sun rises and sets and goes down, as long as life lasts, this city, this country will never, ever forget Phillip Clinton Pannell."

Outside, after the hearse with Pannell's body had pulled away and led a caravan to the Fair Lawn Cemetery, Batron Johnson stood by the curb and looked over the crowd. The night before, he had gone to the wake, and he thought the body he viewed in the coffin seemed too young and thin to be his friend. Interviewed on televi-sion earlier in the week, he had tried to hold back tears. "I always want Phil to know I love him. I'll always love him," Batron told WCBS. "I hope the man who shot him gets what he deserves. Half my heart is broken."

But now Batron was not crying. The funeral had tapped a bubble of anger he carried and left him numb. A reporter from *The New York Times* walked up and asked what he thought.

"We just can't cry anymore," said Batron.

THREE HOURS LATER

Three men, all wearing well-tailored suits, slid into a booth at Louie's Charcoal Pit restaurant on Teaneck's Cedar Lane and or-dered coffee. For all anybody knew, the three could have been suc-cessful businessmen putting the finishing touches on a deal. One of them, tall, with a wisp of a mustache caressing his lip, was an attor-ney who bore a striking resemblance to photographs of the young Thurgood Marshall. Until now Theodore Wells had remained in the background as the rage boiled up in Teaneck. Few knew him or were aware that he was one of the few black men in New Jersey who could pick up a telephone and reach some of the highest officials in the government, in Trenton as well as in Washington, D.C. If any-body wielded real power at that moment in Teaneck, it was Wells.

Governor Florio had asked him to step forward quietly and monitor the scene, but he had opted to remain in the shadows and avoid press conferences or interviews. Wells was to report back to the governor, with nothing on the record.

Wells had spent most of Easter Sunday with an official director of the state NAACP, Walter Fields, successfully negotiating bail for Kyle Alston, the teenager who had spit at Officer Wayne Blanco minutes after Phillip Pannell was shot and had been arrested later in the riot after speaking at the vigil. For days some segments of the black community had quietly seethed that Officer Gary Spath had been able to enjoy Easter with his family, while several teenagers accused of participating in the riot were in a county juvenile jail. A new rumor had spread that if Alston wasn't set free to attend Pannell's funeral, another riot might take place. Wells worked the phones all day Sunday, at one point reaching prosecutor John Holl on a car phone as he drove back from Easter dinner with his family on Long Island. Late in the day, at Holl's bidding, Wells found a judge who would turn Alston loose— with one condition: Walter Fields would have to accompany him to the funeral.

Now, on Monday, Wells faced a far more complicated task. Across the table from him that afternoon sat Fields and George Powell. Wells took out a pen, turned over the paper place mat, and began to scribble notes.

Wells's forte was strategy. Raised in Washington, D.C., he had learned some of his skill from the spiritual masters of strategy, the Jesuit fathers at the College of the Holy Cross in Worchester, Massachusetts. It was at Holy Cross that Wells met another black student, Clarence Thomas. The two were still close friends and talked regularly by telephone. But from Holy Cross, Wells and Thomas had gone in vastly different directions. Thomas went on to Yale Law School, Republican conservatism, a presidential appointment to head the Equal Employment Opportunities Commission, a federal judgeship, and later the United States Supreme Court. Wells went to Harvard Law School, on to liberal Democratic party politics, and, now back in New Jersey, in private practice with an annual income of almost a million dollars and a specialty of defending politicians and corporate officials accused of corruption. Politics was his love, and he had become a loyal adviser to Senator Bill Bradley and an effective fund raiser for the state Democratic party. It, in turn, named Wells chief counsel. Like another attorney in her mid-forties, Hillary Rodham Clinton, Ted Wells had been named as one of the hundred most influential lawyers in America by the National Law Journal. He was best known for his tenacious research, his eloquence in the courtroom, and his ability to take what many other lawyers believed was a losing cause and find a way to win. If anything summed up Ted Wells, it might have been the framed copy of a story about him in the *New York Post*: LEGAL WHIZ WHO PULLED A RABBIT OUT OF HIS HAT. As he sat in Louie's with the men from the NAACP, amid the aroma of coffee and bacon, Wells had thick files awaiting him back at his office for his biggest client, the Exxon company, and a case that demanded many long hours, the mammoth Arthur Kill oil spill in New York harbor.

In Teaneck, however, he was being asked to pull out another rabbit. Powell and Fields did not trust the local police or prosecution staff to investigate the Pannell shooting fairly. Both thought the case raised serious questions about police behavior—not only Spath's but the investigating officers as well. Powell and Fields had not yet learned of Teaneck Lieutenant Jack Terhune's sitting in on Officer Gary Spath's interview with prosecutors, but they had heard that other Teaneck detectives had monitored interviews by the prosecution. Some in the black community believed local cops had overstepped the bounds of fairness and were engaged in a tacit conspiracy to cover up any mistakes Spath may have made. Spath was well liked and had hardly been disciplined in his three previous shootings. With such a history, both Powell and Fields were questioning why anyone would trust Bergen County authorities to mount a serious case against him now.

But Powell and Fields saw a larger issue. The way the shooting was investigated could very well send a message in New Jersey and nationwide about the ability of blacks to get fair treatment in what Powell and Fields regarded as a landscape that was one of the white bastions of control—the suburbs. Powell was adamant; the only way to guarantee justice in this case was to appoint a special prosecutor. Also, there was something else to consider. Powell called it the Sharpton factor. If Phillip Pannell's wake was any warning, leadership in the black community might easily be wrestled away from calmer voices if Sharpton ventured into the scene. If Sharpton became involved, Powell figured, the white authorities would surely dig in their heels and not give in to requests for a special prosecutor.

Wells nodded as the two men described their dilemma. He had an idea. He believed that neither the governor nor the state attorney general would appoint a special prosecutor. New Jersey law, he said, was not set up to easily permit that. He could think of only two cases in which a special prosecutor had been appointed. And in those cases the conflicts of interest with local authorities were far more apparent than the conspiracy theories that Powell and Fields now discussed. In this case, the appointment of a special prosecutor would probably sink into unwieldy political arguments about who was best for the job.

What might be a possibility, said Wells, was for the attorney general simply to take over the investigation. This kind of option was rarely used because county prosecutors in New Jersey are given wide latitude. On paper they report to the state attorney general, but because they are appointed by the governor, they have more independence than prosecutors who are elected. But with the Pannell shooting, Wells explained, there was a chance that the attorney general could exercise his right to "supersede" a case. John Holl was the acting prosecutor of Bergen County, but he was still a deputy state attorney general. To transfer the investigation to the hands of the attorney general, and his staff in Trenton, would not be that sticky.

Wells knew he had to move quickly. That night he made a call to Trenton and spoke to Robert Winter, the state director of the Division of Criminal Justice and the second most powerful lawman in New Jersey after the attorney general. Earlier that day Winter and his boss, Attorney General Robert Del Tufo, had gone to Newark to be briefed on the investigation by John Holl and Dennis Calo. Del Tufo also wanted to discuss another idea he had been considering for a few days: that the investigation ought to be moved out of Bergen County to more neutral turf. Del Tufo worried about the possibility of further rioting and, if not that, marches by Sharpton on the Bergen County Courthouse. Del Tufo and Winter had not forgotten how Sharpton had manipulated public attention during the Tawana Brawley case. Holl said he opposed moving the investigation. He argued that this was an opportunity to prove that the system could work, even under difficult circumstances. Plus, said Holl, he had already scheduled grand jury proceedings to begin the next day. Del Tufo listened but made no commitment.

Calo spoke next. The early findings of the investigation were mixed, he said. The forensic test with Pannell's coat had indicated that the boy's hands were down, not in a surrender position, as black witnesses said. But Del Tufo was bothered about one aspect of the police account. "What about the frisk?" he asked.

"What about it?" Calo answered.

Del Tufo's concern centered on the legal issue of probable cause. If

Pannell had not been frisked, had Spath had enough probable cause to draw his gun and shoot the teenager? Calo understood the question. He too was concerned the story of the frisk might not be true. But a gun had been found in Pannell's pocket, Calo said. Even if the police had not frisked Pannell, he argued, no jury would indict or convict Spath. Pannell had a gun. That was enough for a jury.

FIFTEEN

THE GUV, JESSE, AND BIG AL

THE NEXT DAY

Governor Jim Florio quietly slipped into Teaneck. But he didn't come to talk about the riot or Spath or Pannell—not in public anyway. He came to talk about taxes. That morning Florio walked into the student union on the Teaneck campus of Fairleigh Dickinson University to speak at a forum that had been scheduled weeks before as part of his campaign to sell the ambitious agenda he had been shaping in the first four months of his administration. He was a driven man, a loser twice before—in the 1977 gubernatorial primary and in the 1981 gubernatorial election—as he tried to jump from his congressional perch to the coveted governor's seat in Trenton, where Woodrow Wilson had once ruled before moving on to the White House.

Florio's priority list as governor ran from reforming auto insurance to banning assault rifles. But it was school reform and the need to improve conditions in New Jersey's urban schools that had captured his political heart. Florio believed that the key to fixing the academic mess in city schools lay in finding a way to bring school spending in poor cities up to the levels of the wealthier suburbs. He also had a strong hint that the state supreme court was about to order that anyway by demanding that the state step in and fill the spending gap, and he wanted to get a head start. But proposing such a massive change was one thing; doing it in the political climate of New Jersey, where most whites lived in the suburbs and most blacks in the cities, was an entirely different matter. He knew he had to take some state aid from suburban schools and give it to urban schools, but he couldn't take it all. He proposed raising state taxes, especially income taxes for whites in wealthy towns. Some critics—among them the conservative columnist George Will—labeled this Marxism. Others, who admired Florio's ideas, called it a Robin Hood approach: taking from the rich to give to the poor. But for all his noble intentions, Florio had a problem: In his election campaign the previous fall he had made his own "read my lips" declaration and said that he saw "no need" to raise taxes. By April 1990 his staff had already drawn up the battle plan for a $2.8 billion hike in the state income tax. Florio knew he would have to coddle, pressure, snarl at, and finally twist the arm of almost every member of the state assembly and senate. He and his staff also knew that it would not help to become bogged down in the sort of quagmire that Teaneck seemed to be headed for just at a time when he was trying to transform a state school-financing system in which race was a largely unspoken but hugely important component. Still, he was the governor; it had been a week since the death of Phillip Pannell and the riot, and he had not yet visited the town.

On Tuesday, April 17, Florio arrived in Teaneck before 9:00 A.M., and as he stood before his audience at the student union, he was draped in the look of a confident politician, showing little hint of how sensitive he and his staff were to Teaneck. Trim and calm in a charcoal suit and red tie, the governor spent an hour singing the praises of his tax plan. It was a typical Florio performance; he had a scientist-like command of his facts but a delivery that was as exciting as a traffic jam on the New Jersey Turnpike.

As soon as the forum ended, Florio walked into a smaller room at the FDU student union for a closed-door meeting that had been hastily arranged the day before. Around a table, out of sight and earshot of the press, sat George Powell, Walter Fields, and Franklin Wilks. Noticeably missing was Ted Wells, but that was deliberate. Wells figured that if he dealt with Florio with others present in a meeting, his usefulness as a back-channel link between the black community and state officials would diminish. He also sensed that the hard decisions about Teaneck would be made in private, among men who trusted that their words would remain that way.

Florio had his strategy too. He had decided that he would leave the legal decisions in the investigation to Attorney General Del Tufo. Florio's staff had spent hours on the telephone with friends and sources in Teaneck to gauge the political climate and how the governor could become involved. But what neither Florio nor his staff anticipated was the symbolism a closed-door meeting with black leaders might convey to the largely white police force in Teaneck and their supporters. Florio left town after meeting with only one side. It was not the last time he was blind to such political pitfalls.

Powell, Fields, and Wilks were not without a strategy of their own. Before walking into the room, they had decided to drop their demand for a special prosecutor and propose that the case be moved to Trenton with a grand jury drawn from surrounding Mercer County, where 20 percent of the population was black. The idea had come straight from the politically expedient mind of Ted Wells. Without using the word, Powell, Fields, and Wilks essentially were asking that the state "supersede" in the case. Moving the investigation seventy miles away from Teaneck, they believed, would serve the obvious purpose of taking control away from Bergen County cops. Powell, Fields, and Wilks now played a trump card they had taken from Wells's deck. Moving the investigation, they said, might also deter "outside agitators" from disrupting the investigation and grand jury proceedings. Florio didn't need to be told who the agitators were; all week his staff had been worried about Sharpton and his unpredictable followers, who now seemed to include Louis Farrakhan. Florio's staff did not want their boss in the same mess that New York's Governor Mario Cuomo had found himself in three years before, when Sharpton and lawyers Alton Maddox and C. Vernon Mason used media hype, protest marches, and a continuing cry for a special prosecutor in the Tawana Brawley case to portray Cuomo as insensitive to the concerns of blacks. "There is a whole spectrum of outside people trying to exploit this situation," Wilks said. "These people tend to act when they see the perception that the system is not responding."

Unknown to Powell, Fields, and Wilks, however, Robert Del Tufo had already ordered John Holl to postpone the grand jury but not to explain why. That would come later. Holl's announcement that morning was brief and obscure. He said the grand jury that was set to meet at the Bergen County Courthouse had been delayed by "procedural reasons." If Florio knew about Holl's announcement, he didn't say. He left the meeting without making a promise or a public comment.

Florio's staff were aware of the pitfalls of not saying anything and thereby heading off any rumors. But they were steadfast in wanting to stick to their strategy. Let Del Tufo handle the Teaneck tangle, they said. Florio had bigger issues to deal with, such as taxes.

Later that afternoon in Trenton, in an angular glass building that looked over the Delaware River and was not far from where George Washington's troops rowed across on Christmas Eve and surprised the British garrison, Del Tufo sat with his advisers to plot strategy. Del Tufo had come to a decision: His office would take command of the investigation. The grand jury would convene in Trenton, not Bergen County. But the grand jurors would not be drawn just from Mercer County. Del Tufo decided to form a state grand jury, with members drawn from across New Jersey. And in an attempt to placate the fears of the Bergen County police that they were being viewed as untrustworthy, investigators from the county prosecutor's office would be allowed to stay on the case. In his statement Del Tufo noted that he was "mindful of the volatile and somewhat polarized nature of the situation" but nonetheless wanted "a calm, deliberate, incisive, and thorough review of the facts in an atmosphere somewhat removed from the tensions, pressures, and emotions of the local scene.

"We intend," he added for emphasis, "to be thorough and complete."

Within hours he had an earful of reactions. Ted Wells was on the phone with Del Tufo's deputy, Robert Winter, criticizing the decision to permit Bergen County detectives to stay on the case. Wells understood that Del Tufo was trying to fashion a King Solomon–like solution that would please all sides. But Wells was upset. He called it a "cut-the-baby" decision—a reference to Solomon's threat to slice a baby in half to please two mothers. Nobody was well served, said Wells.

Sharpton and his lawyer-activist ally Alton Maddox found a microphone in time for the evening news. Maddox referred to Powell, Fields, and Wilks as "smooth-talking Uncle Toms" for dealing with Florio behind closed doors. As for the grand jury's being moved to keep it away from demonstrators, Maddox promised not to let the seventy miles of highway that separated Teaneck from Trenton deter him and Sharpton. "We can get to Mercer County," said Maddox. "As long as they don't take it to the moon, we can get there."

Sharpton was insulted that Powell, Fields, and Wilks had said they did not want him involved in Teaneck. Sharpton saw the Pannell

shooting as more than just a solitary incident, one police officer killing
one youth. He wanted the shooting to be woven into what he saw as
the larger fabric of police brutality against blacks. And he saw himself
as leading the way. "I'm a nationally known activist, and as far as I
know, Teaneck is in the nation," Sharpton boomed. "This issue is
bigger than Teaneck."

Sharpton also had been in Teaneck that morning. He had wanted
to meet Dorothy Robinson and other blacks on Intervale Road. He
wanted to see where Pannell had died.

With Robinson in the lead, Sharpton walked into the yard with the
fence and came to the same conclusion that dozens of others had
reached: Phillip Pannell had been cornered. Listening to Robinson's
contention that Pannell had been raising his hands in surrender, Sharpton could feel himself becoming more angry as he stood there. But his
problem right then was not so much convincing himself of the righteousness of embracing Pannell's death as a cause as it was convincing
Teaneck's blacks to trust him.

Sharpton's political instincts told him that the incident at Pannell's
wake in which he and Farrakhan had been briefly blocked from entering was no aberration. Farrakhan was furious and had even telephoned
Sharpton before dawn the day after the wake to vent his fury about
Teaneck's blacks. Sharpton, for his part, was concerned how the rift
might affect his role on the scene. "The last thing I needed," he said,
"was a pissing contest with the New Jersey black leadership."

After looking over the yard where Pannell died, Sharpton walked
back to Robinson's house. He told her he wanted to become involved.
"Listen," he said, "the only thing I've learned is this: To keep the
pressure on a situation like this, you've got to keep it in the media."

He paused, pondering several plans, including a speech he was already scheduled to give to students at Fairleigh Dickinson University.
"We need to march out here," he told Robinson. "I'll—"

She interrupted. "Well, I don't know how many local people will
march."

Sharpton was unfazed. Teaneck wasn't the first community to keep
its welcome mat hidden when he showed up. What's more, he was
accustomed to middle-class blacks' being reluctant to march with him.
In those moments Sharpton saw himself for what he was: a professional
community protester. To be middle-class, Sharpton thought, was to
find peace and tranquillity. The lifestyle was the antithesis of the mood
of organized disorder that he wanted to create. He also knew Teaneck
blacks feared another riot. "I'll bring enough marchers," he said. "B

lieve me. You just organize this block, and we'll come through here Saturday, and we will make sure everybody in this country knows Phillip Pannell's name."

Sharpton had one worry, though. He still had not met the Pannells, and from what he had been hearing, they were not keen on marching. Sharpton did not want to be denounced by the very people he would claim to be marching for. He asked Robinson to reach out to the Pannells. "What you've got to do is find the family," he said. "Ask whether the family will march. If they don't march, ask whether they plan to denounce us. I don't need them to sanction it. I just don't want them to oppose it."

From there Sharpton met with several young men who had formed an activist group called the African Council. They included a physician, an engineer, and a college administrator, all in their late twenties and early thirties, and they had spent much of the last week trying to counsel Teaneck teenagers. When Sharpton proposed a march, several members of the group winced. Sharpton was talking about bringing in special marshals to ensure the march was nonviolent. The African Council, however, knew the kids; the kids wanted to fight the cops.

"If we can get these kids out, can we control them?" one man asked.

"You all probably can't," said Sharpton. "But we will."

THE NEXT NIGHT

In the same student union building at Fairleigh Dickinson that Florio had visited now were Al Sharpton and Alton Maddox. They brought with them a female rap singer from Englewood, Lisa Williamson, who later achieved some notoriety under the stage name Sister Souljah. Sharpton was nervous and worn. The day before, he had sat in the courtroom in Brooklyn with Yusuf Hawkins's parents for the opening of the trial of three white men accused of killing their son. In a few days he was due to be in another courtroom in Brooklyn to face charges that he had misappropriated funds from his own National Youth Movement and defrauded contributors by leading them to believe that the movement was a national network when in fact, it was run out of a single office and had only a few members and one goal: to promote the causes and activities of one man, Al Sharpton.

Standing before the students, Sharpton could feel the energy swirling through him. All but a handful of the students were black, and when he appeared, they applauded loudly. A good sign, he thought.

To those who knew him, Sharpton seemed to have a split personality. In a small group he could be remarkably reticent at times, a congenial conversationalist and listener, with a sharp sense of politics, a ward boss's mind for analyzing strategy, a knee-slapping sense of humor even about himself, and a photographic memory for times, dates, phone numbers, and addresses. But on the stump, before a crowd, another side of Sharpton often steamed forth, as if the presence of a microphone and a crowd caused a fissure to open and another personality to emerge. He rarely smiled or told jokes. His brow cemented in a perpetual crease, and his eyes bulged with a hard anger. His voice rose in power and depth, and when he spoke, he was prone to make outrageous statements that seemed totally out of character with the private person. Even Al Sharpton says he is surprised sometimes by what Al Sharpton has to say.

At Fairleigh Dickinson he had been invited, along with Maddox and Williamson, to participate in a forum to discuss the shooting, moderated by a reporter for WLIB-FM, a black radio station that frequently promoted Sharpton's causes and kept listeners abreast of his comings and goings. But Sharpton had another goal. It was time, he figured, to shake things up. For that, however, Sharpton didn't have to speak. Lisa Williamson, who announced she was the director of Our Children, Inc., in Harlem, took the microphone and declared: "You can fight or you can die. Racism in New Jersey is definitely not a new thing. Our community exists in a state of war!"

The students cheered. "White people," said Williamson, "are ignorant because they are miseducated. The system is designed to make you think you are better by virtue of the color of your skin, and white is the weaker color."

More cheers.

Maddox stepped to the microphone. He referred to whites as "honkies" and commended "the students for rebelling last week" at the police station and along Teaneck Road. Future protests in Teaneck, he said, should be for blacks only.

More cheers.

It was Sharpton's turn. "One of my brothers has been killed here," he said. "You should not let any peace come until justice comes. Do the right thing and make sure this brother is the last brother that goes down!" Sharpton did not learn until days later that Pannell had been found with a gun in his pocket. No one had told him that yet, he said, and he had missed it in his review of news reports.

The students were screaming even louder. Sharpton paused as the cheers rolled over him, then decided it was time to make an announcement: He was coming to Teaneck again, this time for a march on the police station. Would the students join him?

Yesssss.

"The only thing for you to do to bring justice is for you to stay in the streets and keep the tension high!" Sharpton shouted.

Moments later Maddox added his own command: "Leave here, and go down Teaneck Road."

Streaming out of the student union, many students were pumped up. "We should fight until we get what we want," said a freshman, Sharmee Brown. "This isn't happening only in Teaneck. This is happening all over the world."

Other students were chanting as they poured down the steps and into the night. "Down with Teaneck Road. . . . Fuck the police. . . . Fight the power. . . . Kill anything in uniform."

Then, as quickly as it had begun, the chanting ended. As a protest this one had made it across the parking lot and perhaps a half block farther. There would be no marchers on Teaneck Road that night. When Sharpton left, the students quieted as they returned to their dormitories or to their cars. But the next day Teaneck officials would not remember that Sharpton's and Maddox's calls for a spontaneous march had fizzled. They would remember his promise to return.

The battle of statements was in full swing. Even before Sharpton's visit to the FDU campus, Teaneck's council emerged from hibernation with a two-page manifesto on Phillip Pannell's death. The council believed it was in a difficult position, but it wasn't just racial politics that worried it. The news that the Pannells were seeking a thirty-million-dollar judgment against the town paralyzed the politicians. In addition, the council was well aware that the police and Gary Spath's family were angry at what they saw as a lack of support for their side. The town's attorney, Martin Cramer, advised council members to choose their words carefully, to keep neutral so as not to affect a possible lawsuit settlement. They did, in a way that managed to anger both sides.

The council's two-page statement did not refer to a shooting or a killing or even a death. The description of the shooting was reduced to two words: "tragic occurrence." The council said that it was "profoundly saddened," that "we believe that the prevailing mood in Teaneck is one of sadness and that the vast majority of Teaneck residents, regardless of their backgrounds and origins, share our passion for fairness and justice." It promised to appoint "an independent panel of Teaneck community leaders to monitor the judicial process" and report back to the town. Finally it issued a call for the sorts of ideals that Teaneck took pride in postulating: "Before we can resolve our problems, we must understand them. . . . We pledge to all of you that we will be vigilant about the judicial process, that we will seek to heal the wounds, and that, above all, we will seek light and reason in our efforts to bring our community back together again."

Hidden between the lines and in the ambiguous wording of the council's statement were deep divisions within the town that were mirrored in the differences between council members. Some believed the police—Spath, in particular—deserved more support. Others thought Pannell's death was a loud warning that Teaneck needed to reexamine itself. Deputy Mayor Peter Bower, an organizer of the vigil, thought that the council's statement focused too much on the riot and that his rivals were doing this to make him look bad. He also noted that he had been the only council member to visit Pannell's family and that his white colleagues had little understanding of how the shooting had tapped latent anger in the black community. "The grief among the youth," he said, "is just overwhelming."

Mayor Frank Hall tried to parry Bower. "We couldn't get too much into the shooting because of the lawsuit," the mayor said of the wording in the council's statement. "It's not all that I would have liked to have said to the family."

Within a day of the council's statement, there were responses from two distinct corners of the Teaneck community. The first came in the form of a four-page sheet distributed by black college students, listing a series of sixteen "facts," several opinions by "police experts," and ten "demands." The "facts" included a charge that Spath was driving recklessly in his car at speeds over fifty miles per hour as he approached Pannell in the Bryant School playground, that Pannell was never frisked, that Pannell's hands were in the air when he was killed, that Spath and Blanco held back residents "at gunpoint" and prevented them from providing first aid to Pannell after the shooting, that Blanco fired the first shot, that Pannell was actually playing with a BB gun when he died, that police questioned witnesses without advising them of their rights, that Spath and Blanco were not ordered to take drug tests after the shooting, and that Spath had fired his gun previously at a woman and a child in a car.

The demands ranged from the "immediate suspension and arrest" of Blanco and Spath on murder charges to drug tests for them, the suspension of Chief Burke, more recreation for teens, more summer jobs for youth, and a "storefront" city hall "to address the civic needs of the adult community at convenient evening and weekend hours."

The second statement came in the form of an ad in the weekly *Suburbanite*, from a group that called itself Concerned Citizens of Teaneck. It was signed by more than fifty Teaneck residents, a mix of black and white professionals and those who were active in politics or other town activities. Art Gardner's name was there. So was Bill Crain's. "We citizens and workers of Teaneck," the ad began, "are shaken and saddened by the killing of Phillip Pannell by a Teaneck police officer." The ad listed nine demands, ranging from a special prosecutor and public hearings to investigate charges of police harassment to sensitivity training for cops and teachers, a crisis team to work with children, improved recreation programs for teenagers, an affirmative action plan for town and school workers, multicultural courses at schools, and a special board of residents to handle complaints against the police. "Teaneck has faced difficult challenges in the past," the ad said. "Let's join together to face the challenges before us."

Mayor Hall refused to respond to the leaflet distributed by black students, a decision that again angered the police, who thought the town's mayor should have shown some support for its embattled officers. Hall also assumed that the ad from the Concerned Citizens was a personal attack on him and that its real motive was to drive him from office. He was not entirely incorrect. Many of the Teaneck progressives who signed the ad had begun to think that Hall, the last link to the town's integration fight, was a political dinosaur who should be retired.

———

Frank Hall didn't feel out of touch. Nor was he ready to leave office, not without a fight anyway. But he was feeling like a man with too many fires to extinguish. He had two visitors coming to his town, and each carried a share of potential problems. Jesse Jackson had announced he was coming to Teaneck on Thursday. Hall knew that Jackson already had referred to Spath as an "assassin." What's more, the local Jewish community distrusted Jackson for his remarks years before that New York City was "Hymietown" and for reaching out to PLO leader Yasir Arafat. But Hall figured that whatever difficulties Jackson left in his wake, they would be nothing compared with what Al Sharpton might do. On Saturday, Sharpton was planning to lead a march through town. Hall, who had hoped to reach out to the black community by going to Pannell's wake, had angered blacks by not going to the funeral. The mayor said he had had a commitment to work that day for his engineering firm and could not get time off. Hall scrambled to find his footing on the middle ground. But in the middle Frank Hall found few friends.

Jackson, Hall announced, would be welcome in Teaneck as a national leader whose message of peace might provide some consolation. Hall tactfully didn't mention Jackson's assassin comment. "I think if Jackson came, it would be a wonderful thing for the Pannell family," Hall said. "I consider him a healer."

As for Al Sharpton, Hall refused to condemn him, as many whites hoped he would. On the other hand, the mayor didn't lay out a welcome mat either, as some vocal blacks hoped. "The best thing Teaneck could do is ignore Sharpton. Don't show up," said Hall. "That would be the best thing to happen in Teaneck in two weeks."

The Next Day, Thursday

The sun hadn't risen yet, but the phone next to Al Sharpton's bed was ringing. He didn't mind. Friends, and even journalists, understood that to reach Sharpton, it was best to start early, preferably before dawn. The caller was familiar. Reggie Harris, an anchor with WCBS-TV and a Teaneck resident, had known Sharpton for years. The two admired each other. Sharpton saw Harris, one of only a smattering of black anchors in the nation, as a tough but fair newsman, unafraid to ask difficult questions, even of black leaders. Harris, successful and suburban and middle-class, liked Sharpton's urban swagger. Harris had come to see Sharpton beneath all his bloated polemics as a man who was inherently concerned with the welfare of his people. On many occasions, as the two became more comfortable with each other, Harris urged Sharpton to reach out to the growing—and affluent—black middle class, many of whom, like Harris, agreed with many of Sharpton's goals but found his tactics wanting. "I always thought he had a core of disaffected people whom he could get out immediately for a march," said Harris. "But there was a lot of support for him from middle-class blacks who could fund that movement. He wanted to build a movement. And if he asked for thousand-dollar checks from contributors, he could get them if he would broaden his base and sort of soften his rhetoric. Not change what he's saying, just how it's said.

Don't be crazy. Just be angry. I had always been needling him about that."

Harris had similar hopes for his town. In Teaneck he had found a vibrant middle-class black community. Raised in St. Petersburg, Florida, and a graduate of Florida State University, Harris, the son of a construction laborer with a seventh-grade education and the grandson of a midwife at a whites-only hospital, had gone on to television jobs in New Haven, Connecticut, and Dallas, Texas, with comfortable suburban homes. His friends included entertainers and athletes, but as a black man in the white suburbs he had never felt comfortable until he moved to a black neighborhood in Teaneck. "I wanted to buy a house from a black person, and I wanted to live in a black neighborhood, a nice black neighborhood," he said. "I found that."

He was enough of a realist to know that Teaneck wasn't perfect. "It's a misnomer to call this a melting pot because it's not," Harris said. "There is no racial utopia, but for me this worked." Harris could afford the wealthier white neighborhoods, "but I like being with my folk," he explained. And despite his success—or perhaps because of it—he understood police harassment all too well. In ten years in New Jersey, Harris had been stopped and pulled over in his car five times by police. Never in Teaneck, though.

He could not find much sympathy for the lifestyle Phillip Pannell led. Harris and his black friends set rules for their children and did not allow them to get into trouble. "He [Pannell] was not a typical black Teaneck kid. We have kept our families together. Our kids aren't going to be carrying guns because the first time the kid is in trouble, we're going to break his freaking butt. You don't wait for the problem to grow." Nonetheless, Harris had major problems with the way Pannell had been killed, especially the shot in the back. Harris also didn't trust the local police to investigate the shooting fairly. A rumor was floating that Spath and Blanco had been told on the night of the shooting to smooth out some of the inconsistencies in their explanations. Harris understood how difficult it was to verify such a rumor. But he believed that the rumor, true or not, was grounded in mistrust. The only solution, he thought, was for the investigation to be handled by the state attorney general. So far such a plan seemed well under way, except for one large variable: Al Sharpton.

Ted Wells had quietly approached Reggie Harris with a request: Could he set up a secret meeting with Sharpton?

On the phone Harris told Sharpton that Wells wanted to meet that morning. Sharpton, worried about his support among blacks in New

Jersey, agreed. When Harris hung up, Sharpton immediately phoned
C. Vernon Mason with a question: Who is Ted Wells?

Sharpton had never heard the name, but Mason knew Wells and
vouched for him. An hour later, at a diner on Cadman Plaza in Brooklyn, Ted Wells slid into a booth with Reggie Harris and C. Vernon
Mason. Across from him, his eyes examining Wells with a healthy dose
of suspicion, sat Al Sharpton.

Wells spoke first, explaining that he had established a channel for
off-the-record contacts with Governor Florio and Attorney General Del
Tufo. Wells had managed to gain support behind the scenes in the
black community for the decision the day before to move the case out
of Bergen County. But he was concerned Sharpton might undermine
his efforts. Wells knew Sharpton had met with some potential witnesses, and, considering Sharpton's reputation after the Tawana Brawley case, Wells thought prosecutors would have a difficult task in
establishing the credibility of any witness who had dealt with Sharpton.
As a defense lawyer himself Wells could foresee legal problems if
Sharpton tried to play a role in controlling witnesses as he had in the
Brawley case or in letting some witnesses hold public press conferences
before they testified in court. It appeared to Wells that Sharpton had
established too close a relationship with Dorothy Robinson; she had
told investigators that she would not speak to them without Sharpton's
advice. The attorney general's staff in Trenton was hard at work pulling
together a team of black investigators and lawyers to lead the investigation, if for no other reason than the fact that black faces might be
more comfortable to black witnesses. For prosecutors, Wells thought,
the prospect of Sharpton's advising any witnesses was a nightmare,
while for Spath's defense attorney, such news would be a welcome gift.
"Some defense attorney," said Wells, "is going to use that against the
prosecutors."

He mentioned another worry. If Sharpton marched, would there be
violence? He explained that Florio and Del Tufo were concerned that
Teaneck could become another riot zone—but not necessarily with
blacks throwing the rocks. This time, cops were worried that local
whites would stage a counterdemonstration. Police had even received
a few threats on Sharpton's life. The scenes of Sharpton's marches the
previous year in Bensonhurst, with angry whites holding up watermel-
ons as Sharpton passed by with armed police guards, were all too fresh
in Wells's mind.

"How do we know it's not going to get out of control?" Wells asked.
Sharpton was chagrined. As diplomatic and soft-spoken as Wells

was, the message was all too clear: Sharpton felt he was an unwanted interloper. He turned to Reggie Harris. "You know my whole career," he said. "I've never led a violent march."

Wells knew Sharpton's history too. Sharpton was loud and confrontational. But he did not advocate violence. "Yes," Wells said, "but you can't control the other side."

Privately Sharpton was worried about this too. Teaneck was not his turf. He worried about how whites would respond to him, but he was even more worried about the black teenagers and friends of Phillip Pannell who had joined in the riot. For now, however, Sharpton decided to keep his worries to himself.

"Well," said Sharpton, "I think you ought to start working on the other side. Because I'm marching. They can talk to Mario Cuomo, and he'll tell them nobody tells me what to do."

Wells had not expected Sharpton to back down. He wanted to deliver his message but not in such a way as to cut off all ties with Sharpton. If Wells left with anything, he wanted Sharpton as an ally, not an enemy. Wells suggested the two sides could help each other— with Wells working on the inside circle of power and Sharpton as a milder activist to drum up public support.

Sharpton nodded. He did not want a confrontation with Ted Wells either. He found himself trusting Wells. Sharpton said he would not prevent any witness from talking to investigators from the attorney general's office, but he would not cancel his march on Saturday. Instead he promised to remind blacks in Teaneck that any protests ought to be nonviolent. Still, he couldn't let the meeting end without a warning. "I will help," Sharpton said, "but if the investigation isn't fair, they will have me to deal with. I will be the gorilla at their doorstep."

Wells smiled. He felt he had established a rapport with Sharpton and found himself admiring the man somewhat. Wells casually mentioned that Jesse Jackson was scheduled to visit Teaneck that afternoon and that some local leaders were hoping that Jackson's visit would overshadow the upcoming march by Sharpton and even cool some tempers.

Sharpton laughed loudly. "Do you know who taught me confrontation?" he asked. "Jesse Jackson."

LATER THAT MORNING

Jesse Jackson pulled his lanky frame into the front seat of the charcoal gray Lincoln Town Car and asked for the portable phone. To ride with Jackson in a car is to watch a man frenetically in search of a voice on the other end of a cellular line. By April 1990, after three decades as a civil rights activist and two presidential campaigns, Jackson had come to see himself as America's racial traffic cop and ambassador. All racial crises seemed to flow eventually to Jesse Jackson—as he preferred. If they didn't, he often flowed to them. On this day, Thursday, Jackson had flown the shuttle from Washington, D.C., to New York's La Guardia Airport. From there he hopped a helicopter to a pad in Secaucus, New Jersey, and settled into the Lincoln for a twenty-minute trip up the New Jersey Turnpike to Teaneck.

At Jackson's side for the entire trip would be the congressman for Teaneck and its surrounding area, Robert G. Torricelli. Only thirty-eight, Torricelli was bright, ambitious, and talented. He had already established himself as an expert on foreign policy, especially Latin America and Cuba. On race relations, however, he was a neophyte. Thinking that the facts of the investigation were still not known and that he might be making a political mistake by rushing in too soon and appearing to take sides, he had briefly considered not accompanying Jackson.

By contrast, the shooting bothered Jesse Jackson deeply. "Shot in the back? Sixteen years old? It kinda spoke for itself," Jackson said later, recalling his feelings. He thought of the stories he had heard of blacks being shot in South Africa and of how black men had sometimes been killed in the American South before the 1960s civil rights movement. If a southern police officer shot a black man, rarely were questions asked—except, of course, where to bury the victim, said Jackson, who had grown up in North Carolina and quarterbacked his college football team.

Then there was the setting: Teaneck. Jackson admired the town's history of integration, but in the days following Pannell's death, Jackson was disturbed by reports he was hearing from black friends in town that the police were acting defensively and might be withholding information. Jackson saw Teaneck as an important symbol for the nation. If a town that was a model of integration was the site of such a divisive incident, what did this mean for the rest of America? In the days after the shooting, this question plagued Jesse Jackson. One of his reasons for coming to Teaneck was to try to find an answer.

That morning's newspapers carried a story that the Pannell family attorney, Franklin Wilks, had finally conceded publicly that young Phillip was carrying a gun the night he was shot. But Wilks was quick to say that the gun should not be an issue in the investigation. "It's a distraction," he said. "It's not a factor in the equation."

Jackson had not yet met Wilks, but he shared his views about Phillip's gun. It didn't matter what Pannell was carrying; as long as the boy was not trying to draw the gun, Jackson believed, there was no cause for police to shoot. "The police who were involved didn't even seem to show remorse," he said. "There seemed to be more interest in the image of Teaneck than in the moral act. This was not down south in Mississippi, where you could just dismiss it as a regional thing. This was way up north, next to New York City. And now the community drew lines rather defensively, in most instances along racial lines. It seemed like morally the circumstances were rather substantial that something wrong had taken place, but no one wanted to face it."

That week Jackson and his staff had received a half dozen phone calls from Teaneck blacks, all asking him to come and focus national attention on Pannell's death. In each call Jackson heard a common theme: They did not trust the local police to conduct an impartial investigation. He was struck by what he was hearing about the case and wondered if it was an indication of deeper racial divisions in Teaneck that mirrored those of far more segregated towns he had visited. "I know that many blacks who live in Teaneck have a huge sense of racial division, racial rejection, oppression by the political order, by the economic order, by the cultural order," said Jackson. "They experience this first hand in school—a rather white apparatus. That's why there was so much distrust early on."

Bob Torricelli had been boxed in. If he refused to accompany Jackson, he would seem aloof and in danger of facing the nightmare that all white Democratic politicians feared: anger from blacks. Jackson— and local black voters—would sharpen their swords and flay him as insensitive to minorities. But if he went, Torricelli knew he risked alienating whites, especially Jews, who were a powerful cornerstone of his constituency, or, worse, getting sucked into a debate over race in which the sides were still undefined. A few white supporters, in fact, told him not to come.

Torricelli had not spoken to the Pannells or to the Spaths, but friends of both families had phoned his New Jersey staff. In each case the sentiments underscored the divisions that the congressman thought were developing on Teaneck's streets, with the Pannells fearing a police cover-up and the Spaths fearing their son would be railroaded. Torricelli's allies in the New Jersey Democratic party, including Matty Feldman, told him that the town seemed awash in racial propaganda. Torricelli was especially miffed that Jackson had jumped into the fray using the term "assassin." When Jackson phoned, Torricelli mentioned the comment, saying that the situation in Teaneck was becoming polarized and that "assassin" would not calm things.

Jackson explained that he believed his words had been taken out of context. "He didn't apologize," Torricelli said, "but he did back off." Still, the congressman wondered: What message was Jackson trying to send? In private Jackson seemed to call for healing; in public he tended to toss verbal grenades. Either way, Torricelli saw the Teaneck trip with Jackson as a no-win situation—with the least dangerous option to go and listen and say as little as possible. Anyway, Jackson was planning to meet with Governor Florio in Princeton afterward. If Jackson was able to provide some peace, Torricelli wanted to be there. "Well, it may not be a good idea to come," he told friends. "But it's a reality. Let's try to make the best of it." It was his staff car that would ferry the group to Teaneck.

As the car took him from the helicopter, Torricelli was in the backseat with the Reverend Herb Daughtry and one of Jackson's young staffers. In the front Jackson chatted on the telephone with an aide in Washington about a future visit to a midwestern city. After fifteen minutes and several other calls, Jackson hung up and turned to the man behind the wheel, Torricelli's aide, Adam Crain, Bill Crain's older son.

Crain, a year out of college and a graduate of Teaneck High School, admired Jackson. The night before, Crain stayed up and wrote a lengthy letter to Jackson, explaining what Jackson's visit might mean to Teaneck. Crain sensed that the shooting and the riot had so strained race relations in Teaneck that it would take months, perhaps years to repair them. He was hoping for an opportunity to present the letter to Jackson and perhaps talk to him about his town. But before Crain could speak, Jackson had a question for him: "Who are the people we're visiting?"

Adam Crain was startled. Didn't Jackson know the *names* of the Pannells?

"This is the Pannell family," Jackson's staffer said from the back. "You're going to visit them."

"What's the mother's name?" Jackson asked.

"Thelma Pannell."

Crain saw an opening and ventured into the conversation. He said that Thelma and Phillip Pannell were separated and no longer living together. He did not mention that Pannell had just gotten out of jail.

Jackson asked the name of the dead teenager. Crain told him. It was clear to him that Jackson knew there had been a killing, but he knew little else, certainly not the crucial details. Crain thought: I know more than he does. Here is Jesse Jackson coming into a community to play a role in the process, yet he still hadn't been thoroughly briefed.

Crain got back to the business at hand. He was off the highway and driving through Englewood. When he reached the corner of the street where Thelma Pannell's aunt lived and pulled up to the curb, blacks were calling out Jackson's name and swarming around the car. "Reverend Jackson . . . Reverend Jackson." It was like a god arriving, Crain thought.

Jackson got out and hugged a woman, then walked into the house, with Torricelli, Daughtry, and Crain trailing. Jackson gathered the Pannells—Thelma, Phillip, and Natasha—in the living room and asked everyone, including Torricelli and Daughtry, to form a circle and hold hands. Crain remained by the stairs but within earshot. Crain thought that Jackson seemed at home with the Pannells and comfortable in what he was about to do. Jackson bowed his head. He prayed for God's help for those who were grieving. He noted how unfair it was for a boy so young to be shot down. He asked for God's help in seeking justice. Afterward Jackson chatted with the Pannells for another ten minutes, hugged them, and left.

On this day Jackson was the political version of a stone skipping across the top of a racial pond. In some ways, he said later, he saw this as his forte, landing in a trouble spot and bouncing from meeting to meeting, all the while hoping for a singular message to get out: He had come to extend the hand of calm. His next stop was St. Paul's Lutheran Church in Teaneck. There Jackson would comfort the community or at least meet with it. But as the visitors walked into St. Paul's fellowship hall, one thing became instantly and ominously clear to Bob Torricelli: This was not the Teaneck community he knew. The audience included men from Louis Farrakhan's Nation of Islam, and there was also present a black man in a floor-length white robe and matching turban who called himself Rabbi Yahvah Yasraal and said he represented one of the twelve tribes of "African Hebrews." His message: Violence against the police involved in the shooting was entirely proper. Asked where he was from, Yasraal volunteered one word: "Florida."

In the front sat a group of younger Teaneck blacks, slouched in chairs, their faces frozen in glares. Torricelli spoke first. He had decided before he stepped to the podium that he would try to give a pep talk of sorts for the justice system. And so Bob Torricelli, former student of the John F. Kennedy School of Government at Harvard, launched into a proper civics lesson, declaring that the system was working, that "justice will be done," that the slow process of investigations was fair and was proceeding. "My typical civics speech" was how Torricelli described it. "In retrospect that was rather naïve."

Within a half minute of the start of his remarks a man in the audience shouted. Torricelli paused. He was not accustomed to being cut off. The man's voice spit out the anger. "Want to deal with this?" he yelled. "Let's find the child of a white police officer and kill him."

Some of the kids in the front cheered. "Eye for an eye," one cried out.

"Yeah."

Torricelli tried to continue, but it was too late. Jackson stood up and took the podium, and Torricelli sat down. Jackson waited for the crowd to quiet. He told them that he understood their anger but that they should mount a nonviolent protest campaign, not one grounded in retribution. He told them that the black community needed to organize, that it should march again if necessary, and that ultimately blacks should register to vote. The ballot box, not the rock, or the bullet, changed society, Jackson believed.

Some of the Black Muslims were now shouting from one corner. It was almost as if Jackson were a commercial interlude between wrestling matches. The Muslims were angry that their leader, Louis Farrakhan, had been stopped at the door to Pannell's wake. Like Torricelli before him, Jackson seemed taken aback; he hadn't known about the Farrakhan incident. A Black Muslim man, yelling louder, was upset that Herb Daughtry had been at the wake and was blaming him for shutting out Farrakhan.

Jackson had seen this before, blacks fighting among themselves over leadership. In the past he had watched such petty rivalries divide some of the most powerful civil rights groups. He tried to talk more about nonviolence. But the room clearly was not his. Jackson, the preacher, had a congregation he could not dominate. Thelma Pannell got up from her seat and walked out, tears rolling down her cheeks. A few minutes later Jackson, Torricelli, and the others followed.

It was now becoming a habit in Teaneck. Community activists and politicians met in private, then walked out the door to tell the world what they had discussed. "There were some radical voices, not for justice but for revenge," reported Rabbi David Feldman of the Teaneck Jewish Center who was inside with the group. The rabbi gestured toward Jackson. "He was the voice of sanity and calm and peace."

Torricelli was still shocked by what he had heard inside and did not want to say much. Mrs. Pannell had composed herself. Her message was twofold. She was angry that some whites were trying to justify the shooting of her son because he was carrying a gun. "Even if he had anything, they could have come and picked him up at home," she said. But she also was bothered by the calls for violence she had heard inside the church. "Black, white, or yellow," she said, "we've got to come together."

Jackson stepped forward, his six-foot-three quarterback's frame towering over the group. "The voice of rage is frightening," Jackson said. "To watch that baby lowered into the ground was frightening." Inside St. Paul's Jackson had not spoken about whether racism was at the heart of Pannell's death. In public now he said that "circumstantial evidence" indicated that the killing was motivated by racism and that the grand jury should indict Spath. Pannell's death, he said, demonstrated how police departments are riddled with racism that translates into violence against blacks. "Police fear and paranoia is translating into violence," Jackson added. "That process must end."

A reporter mentioned Sharpton's march.

"He has the right to come," Jackson said. "The issue must be mass, disciplined, direct action to change the environment of young men getting killed on the streets."

Mayor Frank Hall, who had been inside St. Paul's, was crestfallen. Now Jackson was calling for marches on Teaneck's streets and even declaring that Sharpton ought to get involved. "I would have hoped he would discourage Sharpton," Hall said, "but in general I didn't expect him to repudiate other black leaders."

Off to the side Bob Torricelli also was surprised. Inside the church, in the face of other black men openly calling for violence, Jackson had stepped forward with an appeal for nonviolence, to allow the system to take its course. What's more, in an earlier conversation with Torricelli, Jackson had described Sharpton as something of a charlatan who took advantage of tense racial face-offs and used them to draw attention to himself. Torricelli had told Jackson that Sharpton's up-

coming march in Teaneck had all the potential for inciting more violence. Jackson acknowledged that, but also conceded there was
nothing he could do to stop Sharpton.

Not only did Jackson back away from criticizing Sharpton in public,
but his words—especially his call for an indictment and his assessment
that the shooting was racially motivated—had a sharper edge. It was a
side to Jackson that Torricelli had only heard about and not seen before
in person, the difference between public and private rhetoric. He wondered: Who was the real Jesse Jackson? Torricelli decided he would keep
his misgivings to himself. The less said, the better on this day.

Jackson turned toward the gray Lincoln, which would take him to
the helicopter and another flight to his meeting with Governor Florio.
As he walked along the sidewalk, Jackson's eye was drawn to a very
young black boy who had come with his mother to watch the press
conference. Jackson stopped and took the boy's hand. "Who am I?"
Jackson asked the boy softly, looking down.

"You're Jesse Jackson," the boy answered.

"No," said Jackson. "Repeat after me: Who am I? I am somebody."

It was a standard Jackson line, repeated often at appearances with
children and with adults, from small church groups to political con-
ventions. When Jackson was in full tilt, the lines flowed in a poetic,
repeat-after-me cadence. It had become his trademark on the stump,
a political prayer of sorts.

"I am somebody.

"Respect me.

"Protect me.

"Never neglect me.

"I am somebody.

"Keep hope alive."

To have pride, Jackson believed, blacks had to recognize their self-
worth: that they could control their own lives if they set their minds
to it, that they were not inheritors of what white society told them to
be, that they were "somebody."

The little boy slowly said the words. "I . . . am . . . somebody."

Jesse Jackson smiled and got into the car.

TRENTON

At Jim Florio's office it had been an edgy week. The governor's staff
had kept a close watch on Teaneck, but the town was not familiar

territory. With the exception of the governor's press secretary, Jon Shure, who had lived in Teaneck for several years while working as a reporter for the *Bergen Record*, most of Florio's inner circle were from South Jersey. The shooting had sobered the governor's staff, but the rioting and the possibility that it could erupt again worried them more. For the first week some members of the staff met twice a day to exchange information. "We all wore beepers," said Brenda Bacon, Florio's chief of policy and planning and one of four black members of his cabinet and senior staff. "We were constantly keeping tabs on things. The situation seemed to be changing constantly, and we were monitoring it hour by hour on some days. We knew we had little control over the situation in Teaneck. And we were using any avenue we could to keep the town calm."

The staff took calls from friends on police forces, from black leaders, such as George Powell, and from younger black leaders, like Larry Hamm of the state Rainbow Coalition. It was a wide-net style of research: Throw out the net and see what information you can draw in. Jackson's arrival, the staffers hoped, would encourage calm in Teaneck and allow investigators time to examine the shooting without another riot breaking out. As for himself, Florio still feared being dragged into a political brushfire; he had decided not to tour Teaneck to examine the riot damage.

"The situation in Teaneck was thrust on us," said Florio's chief of staff, Steve Perskie, "and obviously no one wanted it." Like most of the members of the governor's staff, Perskie had little experience in the complicated social maze of race. He was white and from the most famous piece of barrier island on the Jersey shore, Atlantic City. In Trenton his best-known accomplishment had come almost two decades before, with sponsorship of the legislation that legalized gambling in his hometown. He had never before dealt with a race riot or even this sort of face-off between blacks and police. Also, like most of Florio's staff, Perskie was a policy man, at his best analyzing staff reports and meshing the complicated wheels of bureaucracy with the ideals of law and legislation. He had worked in several diverse levels of government—from the state legislature to a judgeship and now to the executive branch as Florio's right-hand adviser. His job, as he viewed it, was to monitor the situation and keep his boss safe from political shrapnel. But Jackson's decision to go to Teaneck and his request to visit with Florio posed a challenge

Like Torricelli, the governor was cornered with the political aftershock. If Florio snubbed Jackson, black voters in New Jersey's big cities would surely notice and perhaps snub him in the voting booth. On the other hand, if he met Jackson, Florio risked the anger of white suburbanites and middle-class moderate Democrats who had formed the core of his landslide election victory six months before.

Beyond politics there was another factor. It was not the governor's job to dictate how the attorney general should manage a criminal investigation. "The governor was a purist in this sense," said Perskie. "Florio did not want it to appear that the Jackson meeting had any effect on a decision to move the case to Trenton." Florio had already been briefed by Attorney General Del Tufo about taking the investigation from Bergen County, and the governor supported the decision. But with Jackson asking for a meeting, Florio's staff faced another dilemma: If it announced the decision to move the investigation after Jackson's visit, it would appear that Jackson had played a role in orchestrating the change. Florio's staff figured it would beat Jackson: It announced the venue change two days before Jackson came.

Florio had still more worries. The mere fact that he was sitting down with Jackson to talk about Teaneck—and the investigation—would be an event unto itself. It was important to control the message, Perskie and the others thought. It was one thing to speak privately with Jackson. But what would Florio tell the outside world? And where would they meet?

"From cops we were hearing that this investigation is going to be a police lynching," said Perskie. "The cops were telling us, 'If you tie our hands on this, no cop will feel safe on the street.' On the other hand, the blacks were telling us that there is going to be a cover-up by the cops and the Florio administration better deal with it."

Florio's staff figured it would be a mistake to meet in the governor's office in the Trenton Capitol building, the brick-and-mortar symbol of state government, where the governor issued official decrees, signed bills, and greeted dignitaries who had official business with the state. Florio's advisers, especially Perskie, believed it was important to frame the Jackson meeting as a personal visit, an opportunity for two powerful Democrats to discuss a potential problem. Florio could demonstrate his concern, Perskie felt, but he should not do anything official and certainly not seem to cave in to a request from Jackson to appoint a special prosecutor. The meeting would have to be private, in a place where the press could be kept far away. "We didn't want," said Perskie, "a media feeding frenzy at the statehouse."

For New Jersey governors, there is one such place where privacy and grandeur converge comfortably, the governor's private mansion, twenty miles away from the pragmatic office buildings of Trenton, on the rolling hills of Princeton. The Greek Revival mansion, white, with Doric columns and thirty-three windows with black shutters across the front and overlooking a circular driveway of red stones, is called Drumthwacket, a Scottish word that means "wooded hill." Built in 1833 and a ten-minute walk across farm fields to a stone bridge and a meadow where Washington's ragtag colonial army beat back several British regiments on January 3, 1777, and where soldiers from both sides who were killed in the battle are buried, the Drumthwacket mansion actually had a far more intimate impact on the lives of twentieth-century Americans, especially those who liked tight clothes. The mansion once housed the laboratory where spandex was invented. For almost three decades, before it was taken over by the state of New Jersey and refurbished as the governor's mansion, it was home to Abram Nathaniel Spanel, a chemist and inventor who founded the Latex Corporation and made millions selling bras, dishwashing gloves, and other rubber items under the trade name Playtex. What had once been the room where he and his scientists labored had now become a light-filled, airy music room with a baby grand piano, an 1810 grand-father clock, and a sedate landscape painting of a house that Napoleon's brother once owned in central New Jersey. At the south end of the room a door led into another room that was almost opposite in color, tone, and character, the Drumthwacket library. Florio would meet Jackson there.

Jackson's helicopter landed in Princeton after 4:00 P.M., and he and Torricelli were driven directly to Drumthwacket, stopping for only seconds to greet the press by the main gate, some two hundred yards from the front door.

On the flight down Torricelli was still shaken by the anger he had witnessed at St. Paul's. As the helicopter floated over the thick ribbons of highways that had carved up the central Jersey fields that were once vegetable truck farms for New York City and Philadelphia, Torricelli turned to Jackson. "Did that ever happen to you before?" he asked.

Jackson nodded. He was exasperated. "It happens all the time," he said. "You have no idea what's going on out there, and if you had been in a major city in America, it would have been worse."

Torricelli knew what the black man across from him was implying: that even Bob Torricelli, congressman and student of American politics, did not understand how leadership in the black community was no longer the domain of a few national leaders, as it had been in the days of the Reverend Martin Luther King, Jr. Black leadership was fragmented, with all manner of agendas and rhetorical styles and with a power that tapped into the persistent distrust among blacks for white America. It was no longer out of the question for blacks to jeer Jesse Jackson. As for jeering a white, liberal congressman, well, that was par for the course.

Torricelli asked about the Black Muslims. Jackson said they were a rising force and well respected by blacks. "You only deal with the leadership of the black Christian Church," Jackson said. "You have to understand the alternative leadership that is taking up a place in the black community."

Before reaching Princeton, Jackson had phoned Al Sharpton. Jackson said he had noticed the unusual concern in Teaneck about Sharpton's upcoming march. He also wanted Sharpton to know he had given his blessing. "These people," said Jackson, "are more worried about you coming out here than the kid getting killed."

As the car pulled up to Drumthwacket, Florio stayed inside the main foyer with its red carpet and a painting by William T. Ranney of George Washington, flag in hand and atop a white stallion as he rode through dust and smoke to rally his troops in the Battle of Princeton. Jackson could not remember when he had last met Florio; Florio's staff struggled to recall when the two had even met. They were not close. Florio had not supported Jackson in his ill-fated attempts to win the Democratic presidential nomination, and while they shared many of the same liberal political views, they had little contact. Florio led Jackson and Torricelli through the parlor and the music room into the library. The governor enjoyed the library and often chose it over larger rooms in Drumthwacket for meetings with friends or advisers. Of all the distinctive features in the library, perhaps the most unusual was one that couldn't be seen: The entire room was encased in cement to protect it from fire. In the center of the south wall, above a fireplace, was a Latin inscription, "In tempestata floresco," that seemed suited to the bare-knuckle politics on which Jim Florio prided himself: "I flourish in the storm."

Jackson and Florio sat down, with Florio settling into a floral print sofa. To Florio's right, resting on shelves, were the bound papers of Woodrow Wilson and Thomas Jefferson.

Jackson took a seat across from Florio. To Jackson's left, keeping a silent, symbolic witness as the two men discussed the legal rights of a police officer and the civil rights of a dead teenager, stood a narrow candlestand that had been made two centuries earlier by James Madison as a student at Princeton. Torricelli sat next to Jackson, and two Florio staffers, Brenda Bacon and Jon Shure, took the remaining chairs. Jackson leaned forward, his elbows resting on his knees. He had already vowed not to try to push Florio into a corner, although he had two specific requests: a special prosecutor and a change of venue. But he was not going to ask Florio to make a decision that day. Anyway, he had already won one victory. The investigation was being moved to Trenton.

Jackson thought of Emmett Till, the black teenager killed in Mississippi decades before. He remembered the killings of blacks in other towns in the South that local police had not responded to seriously. If Jesse Jackson walked out of that room with anything, it was going to be with the confidence that he had drawn attention to Phillip Pannell's death as a point on the historical road that blacks traveled and that government needed to focus on police brutality against blacks. "When I come into a situation like this," Jackson said, "it is to draw attention to it. It's a positive use of one's persona, to put light in darkness and heat in cold places. That's what you're supposed to do."

Once he started speaking, he didn't stop for five minutes. His voice was deliberate, not the rising Baptist preacher's style that he uses on the pulpit. As Brenda Bacon remembers it, he began with a time-honored politician's gimmick: He stroked Florio.

"Governor," said Jackson, "I've told people that Jim Florio is going to do the honest, right thing. I know you're not going to be intimidated." From there he cut right to the point: He asked Florio to appoint a special prosecutor.

Florio, likewise, got right to the point. No, there would not be a special prosecutor. Florio spoke quietly but firmly. He had a pugilist's face, square-jawed and scarred from his boxing days in the Navy when an opponent's punch had crushed his cheek. His eyes, however, were soft and friendly. And despite his tendency to be direct in conversations, Jim Florio had a subtle capacity to convey warmth in the way he looked at the person across from him. He told Jackson that Attorney General Del Tufo had already taken a hand personally in the case, that command of the investigation had been taken away from Bergen County authorities and would be handled by the attorney general's staff in Trenton, that there would be a full investigation, that the evidence would be presented to a grand jury, that the state would try to resolve some of the conflicting testimony about where Phillip Pannell's hands were, and that the investigation had already brought in forensic experts to study autopsy reports.

Torricelli spoke. Teaneck, he said, had a long history of peaceful integration. It was known for neighborly relationships between blacks and whites. Teaneck was the last place, Torricelli said, that he had expected this sort of racial face-off to occur. He said the fabric of the town had been badly torn, and he was concerned about what would happen now to the tradition Teaneck had worked so hard and so successfully to forge.

Torricelli did not know Jim Florio well either, but he thought the governor was trying to send a message of his own to Jackson and to those on both sides with his direct tone and succinct answer that there would be no special prosecutor. On this day Florio was not in a compromising mood, and Jackson knew enough not to press him. After ten minutes the group devoted the next half hour to small talk about Florio's legislative agenda and national politics. Jackson praised Florio at one point for taking the initiative in trying to increase funding for inner-city schools. It was clear Jackson had done his homework on Florio and was impressed by his tax plans aimed at improving city schools and in building bridges between what Florio himself had called the "two New Jerseys," the cities and suburbs.

Florio seemed pleased. "I have to clean up a budget mess," he said finally.

Jackson got up to leave, saying that he didn't know how involved he would remain in Teaneck's troubles but that he planned to keep abreast. He didn't ask Florio to appear with him before the press; the governor and his staff had already decided that they would not do that. It was a risk, of course. By keeping silent about their meeting, Florio would give up an opportunity to define his role—and that of the state attorney general—in the investigation. Nevertheless, the governor and his staff were concerned with how it would look if he were in front of cameras with Jesse Jackson by his side. But Florio had not anticipated one thing: By not speaking in public, he was opening the door to conspiracy theorists on both sides.

He also hadn't counted on what Jackson might say. As he was driven through the main gate of Drumthwacket, Jackson stopped and answered a few questions from the reporters who had waited. By this point Jackson had expanded his array of targets beyond Jim Florio. He began by calling on President Bush to take action against what he said was a national "epidemic of violence against young African-American males.

"Because it is national," said Jackson, "the President and the U.S. Attorney General must likewise assume some responsibility. This cannot be addressed by just the governor alone. I would think the kind of aggressive action taken by this governor must be pursued and expanded across this country." Governor Florio was "wrestling with a tough situation," Jackson continued. "The first step of getting a grand jury of jurors made from around the state is a step in the right direction. Getting a deputy attorney general to handle it, as opposed to a local prosecutor, is a step in the right direction." And bringing the investigation under the umbrella of the state Attorney General's Office, said Jackson, is "in effect" the same thing as appointing a special prosecutor. Jesse Jackson hadn't won his case with Jim Florio. But when he spoke to the world, while Florio stayed inside and remained silent, it certainly seemed as if Jackson had won.

To some police officers, especially Gary Spath's friends, the conspiracy stories were rolling in high gear. It was as if Jackson and Florio had hatched a pact along the lines of Hitler and Stalin, a secret agreement to make an example of Gary Spath, to bring down the full weight of the state and drag him into court.

The afternoon that Jackson met with Florio, Spath's parents met with the press at their home in Teaneck. It had been ten days since the shooting, and they had become increasingly frustrated at the way their son and the shooting of Pannell was being portrayed. Gary, they said, was in seclusion, devastated and deeply worried that he would not be treated fairly by investigators. What bothered him most, they added, were the media. "It's like a faceless monster," Elaine Spath said of the press coverage of her son. "I can see the pain in him. It's just a horror to see him so down." George Spath said his son had felt bolstered by the hundreds of supportive letters and calls he was receiving. Gary was now seeing a doctor, had gone out of town for the past weekend, and had been ordered by his attorney not to talk to the press. "Everybody is talking about the media taking this kid [Gary] over the hurdles," Spath said. "It's getting to the point where we don't even turn on the news anymore because we don't even know if what they're saying is accurate."

His son, he explained, had been "crucified" in some reports, especially from blacks who said the shooting was racially motivated. "Why can't it be reported just the way it went down and what happened and leave it go at that, instead of always looking at the racial element, which did not exist?" Spath asked. "He's concerned, and we're concerned, about whether he will get a fair shake or whether he will get railroaded because of political pressure."

———

Within hours of the first news reports about the meeting between Jackson and Florio, a petition was circulating around police stations, town halls, malls, and other public places throughout Bergen County. It was sponsored by a heretofore unknown group that called itself the Taxpayers of the State of New Jersey. It could also have taken the name Supporters of Gary Spath. The petition, addressed to Florio, named two targets: the Bergen County Prosecutor's Office and the media for circulating incorrect allegations about the shooting of Phillip Pannell. The petition did not specify what those incorrect allegations were, but it left no doubt who the victim was.

"Why is your office sitting back and letting a dedicated police officer's life be ruined?" the petition asked. "Win or lose the damage caused by the media and lack of cooperation from your office toward this police officer will be irreversible."

In his basement Fred Greene sat at his desk with four leaflets he had collected, each one a vehicle for wild allegations about Spath, blacks, Pannell, and the police. Greene had not seen this sort of hatred in his town, not even after Martin Luther King, Jr.'s, assassination, or when neighboring Englewood had rioted. During the most raucous debates before Teaneck had voted to integrate its schools, there had been some shameful allegations, Greene remembered, but nothing like this.

He figured it was going to get worse. In two days Al Sharpton was going to march through town. Greene turned on his computer and started typing.

Dear Rev. Al Sharpton and attorney Alton Maddox Jr.:
If you were quoted correctly, then my greatest fears could be realized on Saturday, the day of your planned march in Teaneck.

I suggest that while you have every right to speak your mind, when you want to and where you want to, I would ask you to consider that your words do have impact. I would ask you to recognize that while talk is cheap, life is precious. I would ask you not to get caught up in your own rhetoric, for your words will most certainly be misinterpreted. Finally, I would say to you that if you are truly bent on starting a revolution in Teaneck, realize that many good and decent people—young and not so young, black, brown, white, yellow, and red, government and non-government—will likely be victims.

Why do I get the feeling that you have different agendas, that young Phillip Pannell's death is simply a vehicle for people like you to promote yourself? In Teaneck, this past week has brought visitors ranging from militants to skinheads to revolutionaries, and none was being escorted by a real estate agent.

This tragedy has awakened a dichotomy of feelings, both positive and not so positive, but we, the community as a whole, will have to work it out. There are problems, serious ones, but we have to deal with them. If conflict does arise on Saturday, you, Mr. Sharpton and Mr. Maddox, within hours, will be safe in your homes while we're trying to put ourselves back together.

We are a vulnerable community. During the march, no residents will be standing on the curbside angrily demanding that you or other visitors go home. No racial epithets will be forthcoming. No confrontationists waiting at the next corner. There'll be mostly people of many ethnic groups, full of fear, concern, and confusion, wondering whether the wounds will ever get an opportunity to heal.

While at this very moment, some are humming the tune "Memory," others are foolishly committing hubris, praising themselves for who they are and the hours they've committed "to the struggle." Still others, including myself, are bristling at the suggestion that we are incapable of addressing our problems, of speaking for ourselves, of purging our very souls if necessary. We are no longer talking of Teaneck; we are talking of life.

My greatest desire would be that we, the herd, not attend the rally, and that you, our "leaders," be left to feed off each other. May your rhetoric fall on deaf ears. Let peace on earth begin with us.

Fred Greene mailed the letter to the *Record*, which published it on Friday morning, the day before Sharpton's scheduled march. A few hours after the Friday paper arrived on his doorstep, Greene said, two black men visited him. He knew them, and when they asked if they all could take a ride somewhere and talk, Greene got into their car.

The men drove Greene to a secluded spot several blocks from his house and pulled over. The two men were angry with Greene for writing to the newspaper—the white newspaper, they said. They explained they had heard other blacks wanted to pay a more violent visit to Greene's house. They wanted to pass on some advice first and head off any trouble: Shut up.

SIXTEEN

HOME FIRES

April 21, 1990, Midnight

Frank Hall sat alone in his apartment. It had been a heady evening, full of laughter. Amid all the tensions, Hall had taken a few hours away from his mayor's job to go out to dinner with his family and celebrate his sixty-seventh birthday. But as the last hour of one day flowed into the first hour of the next, he was back at work. A New York City radio station had called and wanted Frank Hall for an interview.

At precisely 12:08 A.M. Hall was connected on the air to Barry Gray, host of a call-in show. Urbane, well read, politically conservative, and possessed of a intimate baritone that appealed to those who liked to keep late company with a radio voice, Gray had been a staple of New York City broadcasting for more than two decades, with callers who ranged from the lonely to the loony, with occasionally star bursts of insight on the human condition too. On this morning he got all three.

After reading a commercial for a Brooklyn-based firm that offered loans with "no income or credit check" to "stop foreclosure and bankruptcy," Gray turned to Teaneck. "We are on WOR, and on the newsmaker line is the mayor of Teaneck, New Jersey, Francis Hall. Mr. Mayor?"

Hall sounded tired. Gray began by asking why Hall ever ran for office in the first place.

"Oh, gee," said Hall, his mood lightening with Gray's unexpected tone. "I got involved twenty-four years ago. I think once I met some of the leaders of the town at the time, and I said, 'Oh, boy. I better get involved.'"

Gray laughed. "What's happening today that's so special?"

"Well, ah, special, I guess, is the word for it," said Hall. "Al Sharpton is supposed to come in with his busloads of people from New York or Brooklyn or somewhere and march and demonstrate in Teaneck."

"Why?" Gray asked.

"I don't know," Hall said. "As far as I'm concerned, what he's trying to do is his own agenda and polarize people. Because in Teaneck we've been trying to live Martin Luther King's dream of working things out together and living together and have been fairly successful, I must say. But what Sharpton wants to do is, it seems to me, just the opposite."

Hall then did something he had not done before: He expressed a measure of sympathy for the Pannell family. He referred to the "family of the tragic victim," mispronouncing Pannell as "Parnell," as Jesse Jackson had done in a TV interview two days earlier. Hall said he was "sorry" for the Pannell family. "I'm still grieving myself," he said, "and it's a terrible shock."

Gray asked whether Sharpton needed a permit to march.

"He's supposed to have a parade permit, yes."

"Did he get one?" Gray asked.

"Not that I know of."

"And what do you plan to do, Mr. Mayor?"

Hall knew he could not stop Sharpton without calling in a large force of police. If he did so, he also knew Teaneck would again look foolish on television.

"I'm gonna be . . ." Hall began. Then he spoke haltingly. "I live on Teaneck Road. I'm going to be watching and I'm going to be in touch, constant touch with the chief of police and the township manager—"

In that instant Frank Hall realized he sounded helpless. But considering his options, he saw no other choice. In the ten days since Phillip Pannell had been shot Hall had come to understand that few of the old rules applied anymore and that men like Sharpton set their own schedules . . . and agendas.

Barry Gray interrupted. "Mr. Mayor, do you find that this has brought the black community and the white community together? Or driven then apart?"

Hall said he had heard from several young families that had told him they had moved to Teaneck long after integration was set in motion because they wanted their children to grow up in a diverse community where kids of different skin colors "really do play together." For emphasis, he added, "And that was from black and white families that I heard from."

Barry Gray cut to a commercial. When he returned, he asked listeners to phone in comments to Hall. He took four calls: a woman who wanted to denounce all racism in the world; another who was angry about conditions in Haiti; another whose only point seemed to be to wish Frank Hall a happy birthday; and another woman who wanted to give Barry Gray the home telephone number of Al Sharpton so he could invite him on the air. (Gray said that he had extended an invitation several years before but that Sharpton never showed "at the appointed time. That only happens once.")

Gray then went to a commercial for a diet plan. When he returned, he introduced a woman caller, Gary Spath's mother, Elaine. "Mrs. Spath, it is your son I believe who is charged with the killing of the young man?" said Gray.

Elaine Spath paused, seemingly to draw a breath. Her voice was laden with fatigue and exasperation. "Well, I don't believe there's been a charge yet, but I'm sorry. I apologize for my hoarse voice. I'm exhausted. I haven't slept in nights. And I was about to turn the radio off when I heard what your topic would be and who your guest is."

"Ahuh," said Gray.

"And the reason I'm calling," she said, "is, of course, I do not want to and I cannot speak of the incident. I am speaking to Mr. Hall, who has lived in Teaneck for a long time, as we have."

Elaine Spath's voice had been reduced to a near whisper. As each slow syllable emerged, the anger and hurt in her voice seemed to swell ever so slightly. As Barry Gray and Frank Hall were soon to realize, this call was no dispassionate analysis or even a partisan view. This was something else entirely, a window into the wounds of a family that felt forgotten in the racial swirl and, rightly or wrongly, was angry because of that. Gray and Hall fell silent as Elaine Spath continued.

"We have always supported Mr. Hall through his years in our town politics," she said, "and I need to say that I have been seriously hurt and disappointed that Mr. Hall has never found the time or reason to contact us and express any kind of his feelings about the grief that we are going through because our son has been shattered. Thank God he's alive. But his life has been completely shattered, ah, mostly due to something that has nothing to do with Mr. Hall."

Elaine Spath explained that a newspaper—it was the *North Jersey Herald & News*—had printed her son's home address. As a result, she said he and his family had been forced to leave town and go into seclusion with relatives. "They remain in hiding for their own safety," she said. "My main reason for calling tonight is that I don't understand why Mr. Hall has made no contact with us, made no gesture toward us, because we are grieving just as well as the mother who gave birth to a child and lost a child. It's not meant to be that way for any of us. And I'm grieving for a son who we raised as a hundred percent all-American. The only grief he ever gave us in his whole life was to fail a few grades occasionally in school. And other than that, he's just been the most wonderful kid a mother could hope to have, and we're watching him be persecuted, crucified, absolutely bashed by the media, and we are not able to respond. I know we will have our day in court, and I have no worry at all about my son's vindication because the truth always surfaces. If I didn't believe that, I wouldn't be able to stand up."

Barry Gray broke in, his tone soft. "Tell me about his wife and family," he asked.

"Ah, a dream," said Mrs. Spath. "A dream. A beautiful wife. The most lovely children any man could have. They are . . ." She seemed to choke up. "They're just wonderful. They attend church. He's a wonderful dad. He spends a lot of time with his children. And he's just a devoted family man."

"I shan't ask you about what took place," Gray interjected. "It would obviously be unfair. Ah, how is he taking his suspension?"

"Very badly," said Elaine Spath. "Because it rings of connotation of guilt to him."

Gray continued: "What has he done with himself all day, every day?"

"Prayed a lot," she said. "He tried to do a little fishing to keep his children out of harm's way, to keep his family from being too depressed. He's a very up guy and usually cheers everyone else up, and it's very difficult for us to watch him."

Gray asked about calls and letters.

"Entirely supportive," she said. "And not just from friends in our community but throughout the world. And that's not an exaggeration. Throughout the world."

"And what of the black community?" Gray asked.

"We do have—we do have support," Elaine Spath said. "We could not have lived in this town all our lives without having dear black friends, and they are with us and support us and have made the calls to us. They're very upset and hurt that their community has been taken from their hands and expressed to us that these so-called leaders really are not representative of their feelings."

Gray asked how her husband was taking this. She drew a long, tired breath. "Terribly," she said. "Terribly. It's what we call in police families the second worst thing that can happen. The first worst thing is, of course, the unspeakable."

From the moment Elaine Spath came on the air, Frank Hall had listened in silence. He felt awkward, tense, a little saddened at the predicament in which he found himself.

"Mr. Mayor," Gray said, "you want to make any comment?"

"I'm chastened," Hall said, "and humbled by Mrs. Spath. And I must say that George Spath is an old friend from way back. I've admired him as a police officer. I knew him quite well and admired his work, and ah, well, I guess you know where the road is paved with good intentions, and that's true. I've been caught up with all kinds of things—the media and the council and a million details—and never got around to something which should have been first. And I apologize."

Gray asked Elaine Spath for her response.

"Yes, I know the problems he's been dealing with for the past week," she said. "But, ah, our needs are also to be reassured that we still have the same kind of support. If anything, my husband passed on a legacy to his son of integrity and honesty, and of course, that is what will see him through this."

"Mrs. Spath, thank you very much for being with me," said Gray, "and for having the courage to make this call. I am most grateful."

"Well, I'm thankful to you for giving me the chance to be heard," she said.

"I hope all is well. God bless you," said Gray.

"Oh, it will be," said Elaine Spath. "Thank you."

FOURTEEN HOURS LATER

Al Sharpton's marchers arrived in Teaneck in seven yellow school buses that rolled off Route 4 like packages on a conveyor belt. Sharpton was delivered in slightly more comfortable accommodations, a chauffeur-driven maroon Chrysler Le Baron, courtesy of his chief financial backer at the time, Lenora Fulani and her New Alliance party. The man and his buses were almost two hours late.

A march by Al Sharpton is a time-tested but unpredictable extravaganza, with all the planning of a parade and the serendipity of a stroll through the park. The basic script is set. The group gathers in one spot and marches to another, with Sharpton at the front, his arm linked with someone who claims to be a victim and his expression set in purpose. But there is plenty of room for all sorts of improvisation by the various people who show up and no strict attention paid to the clock. As for Sharpton, those who know him say he never arrives on time. If he's an hour late, he's early.

Like most of Sharpton's major marches, the one that descended on Teaneck on April 21—the day before the nation celebrated Earth Day—began in Brooklyn, at the Slave Theater, with Sharpton holding a pep rally for black pride, where the door guardians announced to anyone interested that the theater was off limits to whites. From there some four hundred marchers boarded buses and set off on their journey to Teaneck. "If you get violent," Sharpton told the crowd before they left, "we're going to kick you out."

Cops have claimed for years that Sharpton pays his marchers as much as ten dollars apiece or provides vouchers for meals at Brooklyn restaurants in return for their participation. He denies it. "I don't need to pay anyone to march," he said. Nevertheless, in Teaneck that day the police, including Chief Burke, circulated the rumor: Sharpton's marchers were being paid to come. When asked how they knew, police resorted to the ambiguous vocabulary of people who are not entirely sure of their information. Some cited "New York City police intelligence." Others said they heard it through tipsters. No one could name a credible source, but the rumor floated anyway. It was that sort of day.

In Teaneck few caravans of marchers were more unwelcome. For a town where busing to schools played such a historical role, the buses that bore Sharpton's followers were a symbolic wedge driven into its image. And for blacks and whites alike, it forced this question: Who in Teaneck would march with Sharpton?

Sharpton had other worries. He had not yet heard from the Pannell family. Would they endorse or oppose the march? And as much as that lack of contact bothered him, the prospect of marching through Teaneck concerned him more. He was confident that he and his marshals could control the 400 Brooklynites he brought on buses. He was not so sure about the 250 people in Teaneck who waited to join him. Some of the local marchers, he figured, surely would be the kids who had rioted ten days earlier. Even when he marched in Bensonhurst ten months before to the taunts of white residents, Sharpton had had no worry about his people remaining nonviolent. But Teaneck was not his turf. As much as Al Sharpton seems to be a man without schedule or script, he is also a control freak. In Teaneck he felt his grip had loosened.

"My whole strategy is on the line if one kid throws a brick," Sharpton said. "The question then becomes: Can Al Sharpton deliver a peaceful march? Can he keep control? See, your career's on the line. People don't understand the risks in any of this. They would ruin me if I had a march that turned into a riot. All I needed was one kid to go crazy."

Lelia Johnson had the same worry. But in her case her focus was on one person: her son. When Batron Johnson told his mother he planned to join Sharpton's march, she decided she would go too to keep an eye on him. She feared that his anger and hurt might get the best of him. "I hate all white police," he had told her. "If this was a black cop, this shooting wouldn't have happened."

Batron was especially drawn to the chant "No justice, no peace." He had heard it during the vigil that led to the riot. As Sharpton's marchers began their walk from the Bryant Elementary School to the police station, Batron heard the chant again. The words pushed and prodded his conscience and his anger. "There will be no calm," he said, "until there is justice." And for Batron, justice was nothing less than the arrest, conviction, and jailing of Gary Spath for murder.

When she could step outside the worry she felt for her son, Lelia Johnson found herself with many of the same feelings, though not as intense. Phillip's death was wrong. She had already reached that conclusion. She also had come to believe that the white police officers in Teaneck not only harassed black boys but had no idea how to communicate with them. The result, she feared, was an explosive mix of fear, frustration, and anger at the inability of the two sides to understand each other. As for Al Sharpton, she thought that Teaneck's black community was far too timid to focus attention on sensitive questions

about the police department. The day of the Sharpton march she had called a meeting of other parents of black teenagers at her home to talk over what steps they could take to protect their children from their own vengeful urges and from what they worried might be police retaliation. As a first step she believed that going to Sharpton's march in person would be enough in the short term to protect Batron. When she announced her plans, someone asked how *she* felt about marching with Sharpton. Lelia Johnson had never attended a civil rights march before. As a girl in North Carolina she wanted to march once with Martin Luther King, Jr., but her parents persuaded her not to, fearing that King was too radical and would cause trouble. But now, with her concern for her son and with the anger that welled in her, she believed it was time to take to the streets.

"It doesn't bother me at all," she said of Sharpton and the misgivings other black friends had for his style. "Somebody has to fill the void."

———

Dorothy Marcus faced a similar dilemma. Her teenage daughter told her she planned to march. Though Marcus believed attention should be paid to Pannell's shooting and the questions of Teaneck police harassing blacks, she thought Sharpton was the worst possible catalyst. To her Sharpton had taken America's civil rights movement down a dangerous road that cloaked itself in violent rhetoric embodied in the chant of "No justice, no peace" but claimed to be part of the legacy of Martin Luther King. To Marcus, King was the great unifier; Sharpton pulled people apart. Her daughter would march; Marcus would stay home.

———

Paul Ostrow couldn't stay home, but he couldn't bring himself to march. He opted to be a spectator. But as much as he wanted to see what Sharpton would do, Ostrow did not want to be seen. In part he worried how his appearance would affect his candidacy for the council, especially among police supporters who tended to favor him because they knew him as the president of the ambulance corps. On the other hand, Ostrow believed that as a would-be leader of his community he had an obligation to view any possible havoc the march might create.

So he went—in disguise. He pulled his Pittsburgh University baseball hat low over his brow, donned sunglasses, and wore a shirt with its collar turned up. He monitored Sharpton's arrival on his police radio at home, and as the march began, he walked to a gentle hill that overlooked Teaneck Road and the police station. This is just what we need, Ostrow thought as he considered his predicament: spending part of a Saturday afternoon in disguise watching Al Sharpton march through his town. He turned to a friend. "This is an embarrassment for Teaneck."

A mile away, in a parking lot next to the Bryant Elementary School, where the march was beginning, another son of Teaneck was making his own unique contribution to the day. For Charles Webster, thirty-one years old, the journey that had taken him to this day and this spot of Teaneck asphalt had been long and meandering. His roots were in the black neighborhood around the Bryant School; he had grown up only a few blocks away in a brick Cape Cod house. But Charles Webster was never entirely comfortable in his black world—or in the white world, for that matter. Through no fault of his own, he often found himself somewhere in the middle.

Webster's mother was blond and white, a nurse; his father, a former Army sergeant who went on to become a New York City police captain, was black. Webster spoke with the rhetorical energy of a black preacher—with even a southern accent at times. But his appearance conveyed an entirely different message. His eyes were blue, his skin honey pale, and his hair light brown and straight. When he was a boy, his locks often turned blond in the summer. "The police used to tell me I was on the wrong side of town," said Webster. "I told them I lived here, in the black neighborhood. They couldn't believe it."

At Teaneck High Webster captained the cross-country team and was selected as the first student representative to the Teaneck school board. After graduating from Fairleigh Dickinson, he remained on campus as a recruiter for minority students. Teaneck was a place to grow up, but he had set his sights on living in another town. When Pannell was killed, the angry memories flooded back. He had struggled for years about how to embrace his black heritage, even volunteering a decade before to help search for the bodies of black children along riverbanks outside Atlanta during a series of murders there. But far too often Charles Webster had to face facts: He was from two worlds.

The shooting of Phillip Pannell changed all that. It was as if a dormant electromagnet had snapped to life inside Webster's soul, and the anger and memories and resentment became pointed. Webster came to realize that the black world accepted him far more readily than the white world did. And if anything symbolized the perceived misuse of power by whites for him, it was the police.

As he stood on the parking lot waiting for Sharpton, Webster could feel his anger from the past blend with his fears of the present. In the days after Pannell's death he had decided to step forward as one of the founding members of the loose-knit alliance known as the African Council. He had already spoken to Sharpton about strategy and the fears of more violence. Like Sharpton, Webster believed more rock throwing by the kids would be disastrous. But as much as Sharpton feared that more rioting would sour the credibility of the demand for an impartial investigation of the shooting, Webster feared that more violence by black teenagers would result in an even more violent reaction from whites.

Meanwhile, Teaneck seemed to be attracting its share of those who wanted to take advantage of the unsettled scene to promote their own agendas. On the parking lot a group from the Communist party and another group calling itself the War Resisters League huddled together. Nearby, members of the ecology group Greenpeace gathered.

Webster walked over. He wore a white shirt, neatly starched, and a thin brown tie, knotted at his neck and pleated brown dress pants. The Communists and the others, he said, could not join the march. They would distract from the message. Webster turned to a group from the black fraternity Phi Beta Sigma. He had brought them from FDU to serve as parade marshals, asking them to wear their fraternity jackets. "Gentlemen," he boomed, "there are going to be mounted policemen out there. I want you to walk between our citizens and the officers on these horses. Protect our women and children!"

He paused and looked over the group. The two hundred-odd marchers awaiting Sharpton's arrival started to line up behind the fraternity boys. Webster was pleased.

"We're standing on moral ground, gentlemen," he said. "Our message is very important. The issue is Phillip's murder, nothing else."

———

Al Sharpton could not stay focused. As he stepped out of the car and watched the marchers emerge from the yellow school buses, he could feel his nerves jumping. A soft spring drizzle was falling, and Sharpton put on a long gray raincoat over his blue satin jogging suit. Someone handed him another newspaper article in which local black leaders denounced his march. Not good, Sharpton thought.

"If they were not going to march, fine," he said. "If they don't want to support me, don't say anything. This was my first confrontation with suburban America. Compared to where I usually go, in Bensonhurst and Howard Beach, this was like Andy Griffith and Aunt Bea and Mayberry RFD."

Sharpton was convinced that the riot ten days before could ultimately prove disastrous if it were the only image of black anger allowed to persist in the wake of the shooting. To force a thorough investigation by law enforcement authorities, there had to be a nonviolent follow-up. "A march would signal to the police department and the state authorities that there was going to be a consistent effort to see justice here. It wasn't just going to be a brief explosion of anger and then everything could go back to business as usual. If there were no follow-up marches—and there were none planned at the time—I felt the case would have been over and Spath would walk away," he said.

Another issue bothered Sharpton. He had his pride, and no one was going to tell him where he could not march. He believed his reputation was on the line in Teaneck. "Anytime people start publicly saying that you can't come into an area and you submit to that, then that kills your whole future."

Sharpton wrapped his hands around an orange and white bullhorn: "No justice, no peace . . . no justice, no peace . . . no justice, no peace . . . no justice, no peace . . . no justice, no peace."

The crowd followed along, as he repeated the phrase five times before switching to another chant.

"What do we want?" Sharpton screamed.

"Justice," yelled the crowd in reply.

"When do we want it?" he cried.

"Now," said the crowd.

Sharpton kept going. "Teaneck, Teaneck, have you heard? This is not Johannesburg."

The chanting continued as the marchers left the parking lot and walked onto Teaneck Road, trailed by the seven school buses. Thirty minutes later, on the front steps of the Teaneck municipal hall, Sharpton again looked out over the marchers. Successful. No one had thrown a rock. Even the police on horses had remained out of sight. By the curb the school buses waited to take the marchers back to Brooklyn.

Sharpton again raised the bullhorn to his mouth. "To the Pannell family," he said, "we give our condolences. But they killed a black boy regardless of his name. It's not about one family. It's about all black boys."

The crowd roared.

"To Teaneck," Sharpton said, "we say this is not a one-night stand. We don't need violence. Our presence is disturbing to the power structure." The crowd cheered again, and Sharpton handed the bullhorn to Alton Maddox.

As in the appearance earlier in the week at Fairleigh Dickinson, it was Maddox who spouted some of the most incendiary rhetoric. As officers listened in the police station next door or from their positions as parade monitors, Maddox mentioned Gary Spath and the fate he hoped for him. "It is only the life of Gary Spath that we want," Maddox said. "We want him to be subjected to the harshest criminal punishment. Our anger or hatred should be directed at him, not the merchants on Teaneck Road. What we want is a life for a life, the life of Gary Spath."

Charles Webster rose. He had come prepared with a handwritten speech, with lines underlined and in capital letters for emphasis. And from almost the second he opened his mouth, his body shook with energy, his voice rising like a preacher's, the rhetoric spilling out like a football coach exhorting his players.

"We are here today for the children both living and dead," he declared, "those who have had the *ultimate human right of life* denied to them and those who will continue to have that right denied to them if we allow our judicial system to perpetuate this *madness* . . . black, yellow, red, and, yes, even white, we are all African. The true blood of all mankind flows from the same river of living. I say to you all: know your *history*. But that will not be enough to turn back this *hate and fear* based upon color. We must all, as a people, come together on a moral ground and demand justice for Phillip and all of the Phillips that will continue to be slain in ours and all of the backyards of America. . . . For Teaneck, I say *dare*. Have the *guts* again to be first in sending the nation a message, that these incidents, cowardly acts against our children of color, will not be tolerated here or anywhere."

As the group began to file away, one Teaneck marcher tugged on Sharpton's sleeve and motioned him aside. Sharpton walked down the steps of the municipal hall to a spot on the grass where he was introduced to a short black man with a beard, Phillip David Pannell.

Sharpton was relieved. He had finally met someone from the Pannell family.

Pannell thanked Sharpton and pledged his support. Sharpton shook Pannell's hand. Within weeks the two were frequent companions, with Sharpton visiting Pannell each week to drop off an envelope with several hundred dollars in cash. "It was our little allowance for him," Sharpton explained later. "We needed to keep him going. I felt sorry for the guy."

SEVENTEEN

"IT'S LIKE A
MARITAL SPAT"

The western wall of the William Cullen Bryant Elementary School stands like a silent sentry against the ribbon of traffic that passes on Teaneck's northeast end. Carved into a cement swatch that augments the school's brickwork and classroom windows is an inscription.

Deeply hath sunk the lesson thou hast given,
And shall not soon depart.

The lines, from Bryant's nineteenth-century poem "To a Water-fowl," are meant to celebrate nature and how humankind can draw meaning from it. In the months following Phillip Pannell's death, few phrases seemed more appropriate in depicting Teaneck's mix of angst and anger. It was as if Teaneck had been placed on a giant examining table.

In the early years after Teaneck's public embrace of integration, the town's complicated demography became a magnet for academics in search of a living laboratory in race relations. But that seemed ancient history and benign now. The Washington *Post* dispatched a writer to examine what had happened to the community. The New Jersey PBS affiliate sent a film crew for two months to produce a documentary. *The New York Times* ran a "special report" entitled "The Races of

Teaneck" with this headline: KILLING REVEALS RACIAL DIVIDE BENEATH MODEL COMMUNITIES.

In Teaneck itself certain facts of life—some well known to residents but not talked about—were coming to light and appeared to contradict, or at least to raise questions about, the town's image. Why, for instance, did most blacks still live in only one section of town? Why did so few blacks shop on the town's main business street, Cedar Lane? Why was the town's private swim club overwhelmingly white even though it advertised itself as having an open membership policy? Why did so few blacks utilize the town's summer recreation program? Why were most of the students in high school honors courses white even though the school claimed the courses were open to any student who cared to sign up? Why were the majority of students in special education programs black? Why had 20 percent of the black students at the high school been suspended for one reason or another in 1990?

Was Teaneck a model of integration? The question had been asked, but never with such volume and force as now. Several demands—the call for expanded recreation, for more minority police officers, and for sensitivity training—had even been made before. If Teaneck needed a blueprint—or a foreshadowing—of the problems of the 1990s, all it had to do was look back at a brief period of its own history that had been largely forgotten by the time Phillip Pannell and Gary Spath met on the playground of the Bryant School. On a balmy series of September evenings in 1968, in the months after Martin Luther King, Jr., and Robert F. Kennedy had been assassinated, and after a summer of protest marches in black ghettos around the nation and at the Democratic National Convention in Chicago, groups of black students in Teaneck had taken to the streets to protest a range of problems, notably the lack of recreation facilities in their neighborhoods, the lack of black studies courses at the high school, and what they described as harassment by police. One evening two hundred students marched up Teaneck Road and broke a few store windows.

That series of marches by black students and the brief flurry of vandalism had been largely pushed onto a dusty shelf of the community's collective memory. By 1990 few talked about it anymore; most didn't even know about it, in part because almost half the town's residents had moved in after 1970. But even for those who had lived in the town in the 1960s, the protests were not viewed as a warning. "I barely remember it," said Paul Ostrow—and he was a Teaneck High senior in 1968.

Why the protests were relegated to the dim snapshots of Teaneck's

past had as much to do with human nature as with the town's reputation. Teaneck preferred to talk about the integration of the mid-
1960s because that was a triumphant moment, said Mayor Frank Hall.
Whatever difficulties followed in the years afterward were viewed as
another story. If 1968 was remembered as notable for anything in Teaneck, it was for the publication of a book that chronicled the town's
integration efforts, Reginald Damerell's *Triumph in a White Suburb*.
But for those who cared to look back on the marches by black students
in 1968, the record was available. Resting on a shelf in the Teaneck
Public Library was a fifty-six-page report, issued on May 1, 1969, by a
ten-member task force of clergy and other town residents, appointed
by the Teaneck township council. Against the backdrop of the Pannell
shooting and the riot, the findings were prophetic. The task force reduced the town's difficulties in 1968 to two areas of concern—"a
black-white problem and a youth-adult problem"—and both were
exacerbated by a police force that had been inadequately trained to
deal with Teaneck's diversifying population. According to the report:

> The black-white problem stems from a philosophical, geographi-
> cal, economic, social, and religious division of the community.
> Though the community prides itself on having made strides along
> lines of integration, the fact remains that clear-cut divisions exist
> in all of the above categories. Teaneck is caught in the passion
> resulting when forces of integration tending to fuse the commu-
> nity clash with forces of separation tending to pull the community
> asunder. . . . The township police force, which, at times, is caught
> in the human emotions of black-white tensions and may not re-
> spond with the restraints necessary, only intensifies conflict.

The forty-three recommendations of the task force included improved recreation facilities, police sensitivity training, the recruiting of
more black students for honors courses, the hiring of more black teachers, and the establishment of more black studies courses. The report
continued:

> Teaneck is a changing community. This change must not be
> looked upon unfavorably or negatively. Indeed, the interplay of
> distinctly different forces can give greater strength and character
> to the township of Teaneck. But it is in the kind of leadership
> given to these forces, and the fusion which results from such lead-
> ership, that Teaneck will truly find itself. Teaneck is among the

communities going through the experience of a change that will someday engulf the totality of American life. In this regard, Teaneck has a headstart and, would it succeed, it will serve not only its own purpose for being, but would become an exemplar for others to follow. The fulfillment of this promise rests in Teaneck's hands.

In the years that followed, more black studies courses did find their way into the high school and more black teachers were hired, though some critics said not enough. In the 1970s a school task force was formed to integrate more black students into honors courses, but the results were mixed. Most black students stayed away from honors classes, even though the school had adopted an open enrollment policy. Recreation improved somewhat, with the construction of an indoor basketball center and small swimming pools in parks around town to augment the private club that was erected largely by residents frustrated that politicians could not agree on building a large centralized municipal swimming pool. The pool debate during the early 1970s featured charges and countercharges of racism, with critics claiming that the town's reluctance to build a large central pool stemmed from a hidden fear that black residents would dominate it. The charge, while largely unsubstantiated opinion, was nonetheless bolstered when anonymous cartoons depicting blacks jumping into a pool and chasing whites out circulated through town.

But in all of Teaneck's changes—or attempts—the one institution that remained largely untouched by postwar transformations that swept through Teaneck was the police department. By 1990 it still had no central computer system; its detective bureau kept records on a coffee-stained out-of-date IBM personal computer that had been donated. Its operations manual dated back to 1947. Records were stored in a basement that was once designated as a bomb shelter and now was subject to floods and leaks from pipes. Street officers had no ongoing program of training to help them deal with the variety of ethnic groups in town. Weapons training consisted largely of going to the pistol range twice a year and shooting at a paper target. Perhaps most controversial of all to black activists and others, considering the fact that a white officer had shot Phillip Pannell, was that few black or Hispanic officers had been hired. In a town that prided itself on—yes, bragged about—its history of integration, how had the institution that protected its citizens remained so white, with only 6 percent of the force black or Hispanic? In neighboring Englewood, one third of the police officers were nonwhite, largely because of stepped-up recruiting efforts.

The most noticeable and enduring change from the 1968 protests was a set of lights around the basketball courts at Tryon Park. Two weeks after Phillip Pannell died and the call for improved recreational facilities was sounded again, the Tryon Park courts received a gift: new nets on the baskets. Throughout the rest of the town another more subtle change took place. Dozens of public trash cans were removed from sidewalks, in the wake of the riot, trash cans were viewed as potential weapons. As for any examination of the larger issues behind the riot, of the shooting, and of race relations in general, it would have to wait. Despite pleas from Mandy Derr and others, the township council remained incapable of curtailing its tradition of petty bickering; it could never agree, for instance, on how to form a task force to analyze the shooting and riot. Into the void stepped a variety of others. One of them was the Reverend Herbert Daughtry.

Before Pannell's death, Daughtry had purposely kept a low profile in Teaneck, viewing the town largely as a place to sleep and gather strength before returning to his ministry in Brooklyn. Born in Georgia in 1931 and the son of a Pentacostal minister, Daughtry served four years in prison in the early 1950s on charges of armed robbery and forging government checks before becoming a minister. In Brooklyn his church became a model for a variety of programs, including counseling for drug addicts and AIDS victims, after-school tutorial sessions for wayward teenagers, even a system for helping poor families obtain mortgages. But as much as he loved working in Brooklyn, Daughtry found it too dangerous a place to raise a family. In the early 1970s the Daughtrys had moved to a house on the edge of a public golf course in Teaneck. In the following years Daughtry's children typified the sort of middle-class success that Teaneck was proud of. One went to Dartmouth; another to the University of Michigan. Daughtry, meanwhile, straddled two worlds. In Teaneck he was the proud father of college–bound children; in Brooklyn one of his abiding concerns became blacks who had been killed by police. In speeches he often recited a list of a dozen young men who had been shot by police in what he considered suspicious circumstances.

In April 1990 Daughtry added a name to his list: Phillip Pannell. He also decided it was time to focus more attention on his town. In a lengthy essay in the *Record*, entitled "Teaneck at a Crossroads," Daughtry dismissed a theory, raised by some middle-of-the-road whites and blacks, that a nervous, jumpy Officer Gary Spath, with a questionable record of using his gun in the past, had fired his revolver because he mistakenly thought Pannell was a danger to him. Daughtry believed this theory missed the point and wrote that Spath's action symbolized how whites reacted to blacks when they felt in danger: They shot first and asked questions later. What some whites found to be the action of a cop with emotional problems that caused him to use his gun, Daughtry saw as the actions of a racist. Daughtry had found this to be the case in the dozens of police shootings he had studied. "The accident theory is equally difficult to accept," he wrote, "since we're told that accidents are often unconsciously contrived." The message was that Spath—and many other white cops—are more fearful and less respectful of blacks. "For blacks," said Daughtry, "these police killings are rooted in the value placed on African humanity. For 400 years, African people have been negated, emasculated, and decimated."

In his essay he went on to play down the riot damage. "Surely, this was not your classic riot," said Daughtry, who insisted that the damage amounted to "only 12 broken windows, a few smashed cars, and a little looting." He offered ten suggestions, including "some immediate, tangible expression of concern to the Pannell family," "a massive march for justice, unity, and a future together," and "something to perpetuate the memory of Phillip Pannell, such as a youth center named after him and an annual conference in his name to discuss issues and relationships.

> Teaneck must acknowledge its shortcomings. While Teaneck is a beautiful town with decent, well-meaning people, it is not without its problems of race and religious prejudice. . . . As difficult as it is, Teaneck should not rush the healing process. Generally, whites, along with some blacks, want to hasten healing and reconciliation. But that may not be wise. Most African-Americans, especially the youth, want to move slower. They want to mourn longer. They want to talk about Phillip, racism, and police harassment. To shut that off too abruptly could prolong the tension and lead to more serious consequences. Teaneck should take great care that in its desire to show impartiality it doesn't forget that a young man is dead.

Such analysis became common. At parties, over coffee at Louie's Charcoal Pit, by the tennis courts at Votee Park, and in more formal settings such as town council meetings, it seemed that scores of residents were dissecting Teaneck. On some days it was as if the town had been thrust into a mass therapy group. "It's like a marital spat," said a white woman who had volunteered to counsel teenagers. "You don't like to fight, but you don't want to walk out either."

"My phone just keeps ringing off the hook," said Paul Ostrow as he lamented his inability to keep consoling neighbors. Councilwoman Eleanor Kieliszek spent so much time listening to complaints and fears and soothing hurt feelings that she nicknamed herself the Mother of the Municipality. Art Gardner and the Reverend Stanley Dennison left their homes each night to spend several hours walking the streets and parks of the northeast section and talking to black teenagers. "I just want to keep them out of trouble," said Gardner.

In several ways such efforts quickly bore fruit, some of it bittersweet. At Tryon Park a gang from Englewood declared a unilateral truce in Phillip Pannell's memory and vowed to stop picking fights with the Violators. As a measure of their sincerity the Englewood boys took black Magic Marker and left a graffito message on a green electric meter box the size of a tombstone that overlooks the park's basketball courts. It read:

PEACE
Englewood Posse

Such victories were rare, however. As soon as one potential fire was quelled, another seemed to flare, sometimes fueled more by rumor than fact. Charles Webster, the African Council member who helped organize local volunteers at Sharpton's march, told a meeting of black leaders in Englewood that teenagers were buying .32-caliber pistols "at fifty bucks a pop." When he spoke to the *Village Voice*, he was even more ominous. "Everybody's strapped," said Webster, using a street term that meant teenagers were carrying guns. "Everybody's ready." Weeks later he explained that he was reciting a rumor that he had not thoroughly checked out. He had decided to go public with the story, however, because he wanted to warn parents that their kids might be in danger.

Amid the elastic combination of rumor, fear, and analysis, some in Teaneck tried to go on with life, however worrisome it had become with the news that more protest marches were on the way and that cops feared guns on the street. At the Mediterranean Deli owner John Callas stood outside one morning and smilingly proclaimed that he would not place protective bars on the new plate glass windows that he had installed. "I refuse to board up," he said. "I do not want to live in a prison. I like the sun to shine in my store. I won't put bars on my windows. The minute I have to do that, I'm out of here." He walked inside and surveyed his deli, now operating again as if nothing had happened. The sign over the counter announced the day's specials: chicken salad, cucumber salad, and Greek salad. Callas stepped into the back room and leaned against a shelf that held sweet red pimientos, bottles of caramel sauce, jars of strawberry jam, and boxes of raisins and looked around. He seemed weary, forgiving. "They trashed me," he said, "but it wasn't vengeful. I was just in the wrong place at the wrong time. Sure I got hit. I got hit hard. But I got to go on with things. They say time heals all wounds."

By a meat counter that had been ransacked in the riot—the salami ended up in the real estate office next door—Callas's wife, Stacey, said the couple's emotions wandered somewhere between steadfast determination and heartsickness. "We spent two hundred thousand dollars to get this place going," she said. "Some kids came in and said the riot wasn't the right thing to do." Such words are comforting, she commented, but the memory of the deli's being ransacked by dozens of kids, many of them customers, was difficult to lose. "Some days, I have to tell you, we're very depressed," she said. "Sometimes we just come here and stare at each other."

Outside, a black teenager who went by the street name O.J. walked by, stopping briefly to look at the new windows. O.J., a regular customer, conceded he had participated in the riot and stood by as one of his friends threw an oil drum through the windows that night. "This place shouldn't have gotten trashed," he said. "These people are cool here. They're nice. But how do you feel about justice for the black man? Why does a cop go shooting a person in the back? That's the reason this place was trashed. If we could have gotten to the cop, this place wouldn't have been damaged. There's no justice, no peace."

His cheek muscles tightened; his eyes narrowed. He spun on his heel and walked away. "Damn," he muttered.

MONDAY, APRIL 23

At Teaneck High students returned to classes after a week's vacation for Easter and Passover. That morning the flag that flew from the hundred-foot-high pole on the school's front lawn was lowered to half-staff by students. In the main lobby Batron Johnson and some of the other Violators converted a trophy case into a memorial to Phillip

Pannell. On one shelf rested an eight-by-twelve blowup of Pannell's yearbook photograph from the previous year—his freshman year—his red bandanna, a red candle, and a typewritten statement that paid homage to Phillip's birthplace (Englewood) and his brief tenure at Teaneck High School. It listed his "best friends," beginning with Batron and including Zeke, Chuckie, Steven, and the other Violators. It ended with a message that Batron and the others directed as much to themselves as to all teenagers. It said nothing about his juvenile delinquency or the fact that he died with a gun in his pocket. And even though members of his gang signed it, the note did not contain the name Violators. The gang signed off with a new code: "V Posse." The note read: "Everyone who knew him loved him and this is the way we should remember him: By not taking his death in vain. By not committing violent acts. But instead, coming together in unity to create a positive change for racial justice in Teaneck. Phillip Pannell—2 young 2 die."

In his office across the lobby from the trophy case principal James DeLaney turned on the public-address system. Students were gathering in homerooms, and DeLaney asked for attention. For days he had worried about how students, especially the Violators, would behave when they returned and how he might restore an atmosphere of academics yet still permit his students to reflect and grieve. At that moment he was faced with the dilemma facing so many of Teaneck's leaders: how to talk about what happened and remain optimistic.

"No one can deny the fact that this community has suffered the tragic loss of a popular teenage life," DeLaney said. "No one can deny the fact that this is a community which is reeling from the result of unrest in the form of a riot. And no one can deny the fact that this school cannot succeed as a house divided against itself. We cannot lose sight of the fact that our differences have always been and continue to be our greatest strength. Right now we need to have each student, staff member, secretary, custodian, and cafeteria worker assume a leadership role to help make things better in Teaneck. We cannot and will not forget or avoid what has happened here in the past thirteen days. We can commit ourselves right now to care for each other with sensitivity and concern. Now is the time for each person who can hear my voice to agree that the time has come to start the healing process. It is time to exert that extra effort—that discipline and that involvement which has always made Teaneck a special place."

DeLaney announced plans for forums with police and with students in Hackensack and Englewood "whose occasional outward hostility belies their deep roots of commonality" with Teaneck. "The forces and lessons of history are being played out right now in Teaneck, New Jersey. We need to provide answers and actions that will have a positive message. We need to face head-on someone who is different rather than turn our backs. We need to say to this person today, 'Welcome. Can we talk?' Teaneck High School, this is the ultimate challenge you have faced so far in your sixty-year existence. Be sure that you meet the challenge today and tomorrow and every day in the future. May each strive for peace, understanding, and equity."

Afterward one of the juniors, a white girl, told reporters who converged on the school that Teaneck High was returning to normal. "We've moved from the violent stage to the logical stage," she said. But for at least one other student, DeLaney's message of hope, reason, and healing fell flat. That day Batron Johnson skipped most of his classes. It was to become a new habit for him, one that would be hard to break. "I just couldn't bring myself to go," he said. "I just kept thinking of Phil."

SEVERAL HOURS LATER

Across town in the American Legion hall members of Teaneck's police force gathered for their monthly union meeting. At the front of the room stood Gary Spath's attorney, Robert L. Galantucci. Like the police officers there, Galantucci had quietly fumed for the past thirteen days. Accusations of police harassment had made headlines in all the New York area newspapers. Police maintained that the charges were unfounded, but the denials seemed to do nothing to stem the tide. "Show me any situation, and we will investigate it," said one captain, reciting a theme that others adopted.

But in addition to such charges, what angered police were the photographs of Phillip Pannell in newspapers and on TV. One showed a wide-eyed Phillip with short hair, taken when he was fourteen and in the eighth grade, two years before his death. The other, depicting Phillip with the high hair look that rap singers were popularizing, had been taken when he was fifteen years old and a freshman—the year before. Police believed the photos were inaccurate. Pannell, they said, looked too young.

Galantucci had already set about obtaining from police sources the mug shot of Pannell that had been taken three months before his death, after he and other Violators had been arrested for beating up and stabbing the man at the Hackensack bus stop. It depicted Pannell with angry, glowering eyes and a stubborn expression. "That was the Phillip Pannell that Gary Spath saw the night he had to fire his gun," said Galantucci. "Pannell wasn't the choirboy in those yearbook pictures."

Spath, in seclusion since the shooting, had shown a renewed devotion to religion. He told his priest, Father Bart Aslin, that he had received a message in a vision only a few days after the shooting that "things will be fine." After talking with several relatives, he concluded that the message was delivered by a long-dead relative of his wife. Later, Aslin said, Spath had another vision with a similar message. "I took it as being Jesus who spoke to him," the priest explained.

Spath was said to spend portions of each day in deep prayer. But to the outside world—and to the black community—he had virtually disappeared. He had given no interviews and made no appearances, leaving it to friends and relatives to explain his side of the shooting. After combative WABC radio talk show host Bob Grant commented on the case, Spath's mother called to say thanks and enlist his support. Grant, who lived in New Jersey, was more than happy to oblige; he had a long history of supporting police, not to mention an abiding dislike of Al Sharpton, Jesse Jackson, and Jim Florio. Grant saw them as engaging in a cynical pact to improve relations in the black community by dispatching a cop to prison. Grant figured that the decision to move the investigation to the state attorney general was proof. "I saw in this case the same type of dynamics that were let loose in other cases," he said. "Suddenly it's the police that are on trial, where the black community is intimidating public officials who know there is a lot of demagoguery, but they don't challenge the blacks because they don't want to be called racists. That word just paralyzes people. I've seen this happen for years and years."

Elaine Spath told Grant that she felt her family was under siege from the press, politicians, and the black community. "If it wasn't for you, we would feel totally lost," Grant remembers her telling him.

When Grant hung up the phone, he felt sorry for the woman he had just spoken to. He wanted to help. "She felt the media were totally unsympathetic," Grant said. "She felt the portrayals of her son in newspapers were wrong. She felt there was no attempt to be even-handed, that a lot of people in the media were trying to curry favor with the black community by opposing the Spath side in stories.

"That's why the record and character of Gary Spath were important," Grant explained afterward. "If he had a reputation of being quick with the trigger, the kind of cop who fired his gun before, then it would have been different."

What Grant didn't know when he stated these views was that Spath had indeed fired his gun before—three times. Elaine Spath didn't tell Grant. Other police officers who phoned or wrote to Grant were equally mum about that sensitive subject. Grant did not know about Gary Spath's previous shootings until more than two years later, when he was interviewed by a journalist. Such selective silence about Spath's past—and Pannell's—was part of an odd personal and psychological curtain that draped over the larger questions Teaneck wrestled with. Just as Sharpton, Jackson, and other black activists didn't want to discuss Phillip Pannell's juvenile crime history, school problems, family discord, or even the source of the gun he carried in his pocket, preferring instead to portray him virtually as an innocent victim of a trigger-happy cop, so Spath's supporters were equally unwilling to talk about the officer's history of firing his gun, preferring to portray him as a deeply religious cop doing his job and facing the danger of a gun-toting thug who left him no choice. A battle of images had shaped up, with each side portraying the other in the most negative terms.

Privately some cops were bothered by Spath's history. It was cops who leaked the story of those shootings to the press. It was done anonymously, of course; to criticize Spath openly was viewed as disloyal. On one occasion reporters interviewed a prominent chief in a neighboring town who spoke unwaveringly and on the record in support of Spath. Privately and off the record, the chief sang an entirely different tune, questioning why Spath had been allowed to continue as a cop after the first shooting. "Something was wrong," the chief said. "He has too many shootings."

Meanwhile, the *Record* was targeted for a variety of telephone calls from Spath supporters, leaking information about Pannell's juvenile record and his parents' troubled marriage. One friend of Spath's had taken the trouble to go to the county courthouse and make copies of the Pannell marriage records. Another friend, a police officer, telephoned the newspaper to give a lengthy sermon on Pannell's being shot "in the side," not in the back. Yet another cop, in an effort to counter claims from blacks that Spath was a racist, telephoned with what became a widely circulated but entirely false story: that the boy Spath had taken home from Carl's Corner two months before was black. Other supporters complained so much about the use of the phrase "shot in the back" that *Record* editors told reporters to substitute a less provocative "shot from behind" in stories.

Many days Spath took his family out of town, fearing that blacks might vandalize his house, even though volunteer cops kept a round-the-clock guard. Father Aslin said that for weeks afterward Spath seemed in shock. Cops described him as a broken man. "Is he heartbroken? Yes," said his lawyer, Robert Galantucci. "If remorse carries the connotation that he's done something wrong, then he's not remorseful, because he's not done anything wrong. The only way he speaks to the Pannell family is through the Lord. He has offered many prayers to the family. He's aggrieved, like the good Lord would be aggrieved. He'll repose with Phillip's soul."

Privately Galantucci worried about the young cop he was defending. Spath seemed to be sinking into an inner realm of despair. Galantucci was concerned that if this continued, Spath would not be capable of stepping into a courtroom and explaining his actions in a convincing way. Galantucci figured it was time to give Spath a pat on the back and demonstrate to the press that his client was not emotionally destroyed. Looking over the cops who had assembled for the union meeting, Galantucci began to speak:

"It's been a tough time for Teaneck and for some people who have really been pushed in the background on this thing. It's been a tough time for you people. I think that all good, thinking people—people that are going to listen to everything that occurred in this particular matter—are going to have to come out with an abiding respect for what it is that you do for a living. There were some questions: 'Gee how come we're not fighting back and slugging it out in the paper?' I think when we think about it, we know that the right way to fight this is not in the press. I assure you that we attempted to speak to the press on many different occasions. Some of the information, some of the statements that we made to the press were, in fact, reported. Only some of the information. That's what the problem will be. I think that all of you people know Gary; you know what kind of a person he is. I know that each one of you had to, over the past thirteen days, put yourself in his position. You're trained to do a job. It's not something you do by choice. But you're trained to make hard decisions. You're trained to look at half a second and what you have to do in that half a second period of time, and you do it and do it the best way you can. You all know that he's a decent person and a person who cares. He's a person who cares about you and a person who cares about other young people. He's taken a hell of a beating, and it's because of the support that you people have offered to him that Gary's going to be okay. . . . There is no question but that Gary acted as any good police officer would have acted. . . . Gary didn't chose to do what he did do. It's something that he had to do to protect not only his own life but the lives of the people that were in the neighborhood. Yes, even the kids that are now talking about him. . . . I can tell you there's going to come a time when the police department in Teaneck is going to be respected by the public after the public has had an opportunity to know what the facts of this case are. And they're going to know it. They're going to know it soon. We trust that the politicians will now stay out of the way, and we trust that the grand jury will not accept the nonsensical sensationalism that has been bred by the press. The emotionalism that has been stirred by certain people, some from the community and some not from within the community. These people, frankly, are going to have to take a backseat when we get to the facts. You see, the facts can't be dumped in this case. You can't stick your head in the sand, and even the members of the press are not going to be able to stick their heads in the sand."

Galantucci, a natural talker, could feel himself in the midst of a ramble. He paused and looked toward the back of the room. "There is one person," he said, "who has come here today to say thank you." Gary Spath walked in.

The cops had been quiet during Galantucci's speech, but now they were on their feet and cheering, clapping, and whistling. Spath seemed embarrassed and shocked as he shifted his feet and waited for the room to quiet. Galantucci had already instructed him not to talk about the shooting. He seemed unsure of what to say. He looked at the floor for a few seconds, and when he spoke, the words fell out haltingly. "I just want to tell everybody here in this room, not just you people here in this room but all my brothers throughout the state and throughout the country that your prayers and your support have just been incredible. It's just incredible. The appreciation that my family and I extend toward you—we'll never be able to thank you for that support and your prayers. I pray that you'll be able to keep up the support and the prayers. Thank you."

Then he left, clutching a stack of cards and letters, as several officers embraced him. The cops stood again, applauding, several of them wiping away tears. You could hear the cheers on the street.

Tuesday, April 24

At 7:00 A.M. Mandy Derr walked into the fellowship hall in St. Mark's Episcopal Church carrying boxes of doughnuts. He arranged them on a table, then plugged in the coffeepot. A priest, a rabbi, and several other ministers walked in a few minutes later. The group arranged folding metal chairs in a semicircle and waited.

That morning the clergy again had invited Teaneck police officers to come for counseling. The session was scheduled for an early hour in the hope that some members of the night shift might come along with officers who had time to drop in before starting their day patrol.

Ten minutes passed.

Fifteen.

Twenty.

Derr heard a door open and a single set of footsteps, echoing off the walls of the otherwise empty and silent hall. A lone officer walked through the door at the far end of the hall and strutted toward the group. He stopped about eight feet from the circle of chairs. Derr looked up. The cop seemed rushed, nervous. He looked over his shoulder. Another officer stood near the door to listen.

"I've been sent to tell you that none of us are coming to see you until there is some evidence that you and the rest of the community are going to support us," the cop said.

The officer didn't give his name. The clergy didn't answer. Not knowing whether to interrupt and challenge the officer or let him vent, Derr could feel his mouth drop open. He thought the officer had probably memorized what he was saying. The cop folded his arms across his chest, still standing, feet apart.

"There is no direction from above," the cop continued. "We don't know what we're supposed to do now when we hear of kids making trouble. We're angry and we're afraid and we're not being issued any kind of riot gear. Another march is being planned, and there is no plan of action." As for the clergy, the officer said he and other cops were upset that several ministers, including Mandy Derr, had gone to Pannell's funeral. By doing that, the clergy had taken sides, the cop said.

Lucinda Laird, the Episcopal priest and rector of St. Mark's, spoke. She said that her fellow clergy had not taken sides by going to the funeral and that some clergy believed they could be helpful in listening to the concerns of officers and speaking to the police brass or political leaders. A Catholic priest followed up. "Look," he said, "your families are hurting. Your children that go to school are scared. We want to be at least able to listen to you."

The officer glared for a moment. "People are making a racial issue out of this, and it's not," he said. "There's not a racist bone in Gary's body."

Derr studied the man before him. The officer seemed to have a litany of complaints, statements, and frustrations. The media, he said, were biased and publishing or broadcasting numerous falsehoods. The black community was totally wrong in portraying the police as harassing kids. Spath's life had been wrecked. "You know that choirboy picture in the *Record*? Well, that was taken when he was only a little kid. You got to see what he looks like now. We have a mug shot of Pannell."

"Mug shot?" asked one of the ministers, surprised.

Yes, the cop replied, Pannell had a criminal record.

Mandy Derr's mind raced. The Teaneck situation was now bordering on information overload. He had basically found himself supporting Spath—but with the reservation that Spath might be trigger-happy. He knew about Pannell's juvenile problems. But the way the cop before him was speaking crystallized the paradoxical nature of questions the town faced: Even though Pannell was a bad kid, did he deserve to die? Even though Spath might have been threatened, was he right to shoot Pannell? Was this whole story being portrayed wrongly by the media? By the blacks? By the cops?

The policeman turned to leave, then stopped to make another point. His body seemed to tremble. "There's no way this could be racially motivated," the cop said. "He was just doing his job. . . . Do you know that Gary found a black kid wandering around? He was four or five years old. He took him to the station, and Gary stayed with that kid and treated him like his own son. It was a black kid. In the end Gary took him home for the night.

"And another thing; we have a picture hanging up in the locker room, where Gary is giving a turkey to a black woman. . . . There's no way this could be racially motivated. He was just doing his job. . . . And we need people to say that. . . . Has anybody been in touch with the Spath family? You've probably been in touch with the Pannells, but I don't think anybody has called the Spaths."

Mandy Derr interrupted. The clergy council had not called on the Pannells or the Spaths, he said, assuming both families had their individual priests and ministers. "But we're gonna be here to listen to you," Derr said. "You can tell the other officers that we're gonna be here."

"We're not coming to talk to you," the cop told him, "because we don't know how these words will be used against us."

Derr listed times and dates for other counseling. One minister got up and handed the cop a printed sheet with the times of the counseling sessions. The cop wheeled and walked out. The clergy sat in silence for another minute or two.

"Oh, my God," someone said finally.

Two Hours Later

In Newark the team of investigators and lawyers tapped by Attorney General Del Tufo to investigate the Pannell shooting gathered around a conference table. Del Tufo was not there; he had been called to Washington to testify before a congressional committee about the dangers of semiautomatic assault rifles. The group was nonetheless formidable. The meeting was chaired by Del Tufo's deputy, the head of the state Criminal Justice Division, Robert Winter. John Holl and Dennis Calo were there, and the team had two noteworthy additions: Robert Carroll, a former cop who had become a lawyer and a state prosecutor, and Peter Harvey, Alabama-born, the son of a preacher, a graduate of Morgan State University (with Walter Fields) and Columbia Law School. Harvey, a former federal prosecutor, had been recruited by Governor Tom Kean's Republican administration for the state Attorney General's Office. For several months now he had been holed up in an office in Trenton, carefully crafting Governor Florio's legislation to ban assault rifles. Not an assistant of Del Tufo's, Harvey was surprised when he was asked to join the Pannell case. He quickly understood why. Harvey possessed an asset none of the other lawyers had: He was black. He was a realist too. The group needed a black face. "I was their man," he said.

For the next two hours the team outlined its plans. The twenty-three member grand jury was to assemble the next day in Trenton to hear evidence, and the strategy was simple: The team would keep a virtual open door to witnesses; anyone who believed he or she had information would be invited to testify, even if his or her credibility had been questioned. The group was keenly aware of Sharpton and the political problems resulting if he led protests or called press conferences to introduce witnesses who had never been invited to testify. Almost all the black teenagers who had been with Pannell that day would be subpoenaed whether or not they'd seen the shooting. After the kids, as many as a dozen or more Teaneck police officers would be brought in, in part to document how the early part of the investigation had been handled.

Then forensic evidence would be introduced. The first issue was Pannell's gun. Investigators had not been able to learn how Pannell obtained it or converted it from a starter's pistol. But the state police laboratory had found physical evidence that left no doubt that Pannell had the silver .22-caliber pistol in his pocket when he died. The lab had discovered in the left outside pocket of Pannell's red parka tiny metal filings that matched the gun. Such evidence would be enough to dispute the witnesses who said he was unarmed. The filings indicated that the gun had been carried in the pocket for some time.

Finally the team discussed how to examine the question of where Pannell's hands were when he was shot. The forensic expert Dr. Peter De Forest had indicated that Pannell's hands were down and possibly reaching for a gun in his pocket, not up in a surrender position, contradicting the teenagers' claims. De Forest had a video of the test he had performed on Pannell's body at the funeral home. The team agreed that De Forest would be one of the last witnesses to be called and that his testimony would probably seal the conclusion that the team had come to believe: that Spath might have shown better judgment and more patience in firing at Pannell, but that there was not enough evidence to indict him for a crime. Pannell had not appeared to be surrendering; his hands were down, possibly going for the gun in his pocket.

There was one problem: Spath's backup, Officer Wayne Blanco. No one in the group that day, even those who believed Spath should not even be investigated by a grand jury, much less considered for indictment, thought that Blanco was telling the whole truth about frisking Phillip Pannell and calling out to Spath that the boy had a gun on him.

This was not a small point. If Blanco lied about the frisk, what else were he or other cops trying to cover up? Small lies lead to big lies— or so the prosecutors believed. Even though he was not at the team meeting, Del Tufo's prosecutorial eye had already focused on Blanco. "We had a question about a cop lying at a fundamental moment in the case—the pat-down," the attorney general explained later. "Yes, we were concerned that this was evidence of other lies."

Before driving to Newark that morning, Peter Harvey had studied Blanco's statements, then compared them with Spath's. He noted that Spath said he did not see the frisk but did hear Blanco's warning of the gun. How odd, Harvey thought. None of the dozen teenagers or handful of adults on the scene had seen the frisk or heard Blanco's warning. Yet some of those same teenagers were not blindly loyal to Pannell; several had come forward to corroborate that he was carrying the silver pistol.

Next Harvey was drawn to the inconsistencies in Blanco's statement to Teaneck Lieutenant Patrick Hogan at Holy Name Hospital—that Pannell's hand was never in his pocket—and Blanco's formal sworn statement to the prosecutor's investigators hours later in the police station in which he said that not only was Pannell's hand in the pocket but that he was turning in a threatening manner as if to shoot. Harvey discovered that in the hours between those statements Blanco spoke to Teaneck Detective Lieutenant Jack Terhune. And as Harvey read Spath's statement of several days later, here was Terhune again, this time asking leading questions and, in Harvey's view, appearing to coach Spath. *Had Terhune instructed the officers to get their stories straight?*

Harvey was suspicious. Spath's description that Pannell ran, turned, and reached for his gun—even after the officer had fired a first errant shot—didn't make sense. As described by Spath, Pannell's movements seemed downright illogical to Harvey. As a federal prosecutor Harvey had befriended his share of FBI agents and other law enforcement officers who had confronted people with guns. "You're not gonna tell me," he said, "that a kid running at full blast across the wet street and wet grass jumps a hedge, turns, tries to outdraw the cops, is shot at, turns around, continues to run, and does the exact same thing again that just got him shot at seconds before."

In his own mind Harvey had one word for Spath's version of events: "bullshit." And if Spath was not telling the truth, what could he be hiding?

Harvey then learned that Spath had fired his gun before and had been reprimanded for filing a false report. Harvey had a bad feeling in his gut. This is wrong, he thought. This is a bad shoot.

Del Tufo, who shared Harvey's reservations about the police versions of the shooting, still wasn't ready to accept that the killing was illegal. On the basis of what he knew at that point, the state attorney general didn't think Spath would even be indicted. "I would have found it unlikely," he said. But he was aware of the political need to investigate the case in a credible manner and even to produce a record of testi-

mony in the grand jury of as many witnesses as possible. "In fairness
to the deceased," he said later, "there has to be a perception of legit-
imacy in the law enforcement process."

He was bothered that Pannell had been shot in the back. But that
was outweighed, he thought, by the facts that Pannell had a gun and
that the initial conclusions on De Forest's forensic tests supported
Spath and Blanco's story. "The hands-down version, which is what we
were operating on, suggests the officer was in jeopardy," said Del Tufo.

Bob Winter concurred. "The overwhelming factor in this case from
beginning to end was the presence of a weapon on Pannell," he said.
"The presence of a loaded weapon inherently taints the credibility of
the victim."

But the possibility that Blanco lied was as bothersome. As Winter
sat with the other lawyers that morning in Newark and looked over
the conflicting statements, he also thought Blanco had concocted the
story of the frisk as a way of bolstering Spath's actions. "If there was
no pat-down of Pannell," said Winter, "there is a prima facie case
[evidence to raise suspicions] of unjustifiable homicide, which gives us
a reason to proceed with an investigation."

Bob Carroll was even more emphatic. "If the story of the pat-down
is fabricated," he said, "then everything else the police say is suspect.
It's a legal point, but Spath has to establish that the kid had a gun
and where the gun is before he can use deadly force. . . . Without the
pat-down, Spath is on thin ice."

The group discussed options. It might not be murder that Spath
could be targeted for, but there were several other charges that might
apply, from reckless manslaughter to dereliction of duty. "The pat-
down goes to the state of mind of Spath," said Del Tufo afterward,
and whether Spath could legally say his life was threatened if he was
not entirely sure Pannell had a gun. If Spath was not sure Pannell had
a gun and where it was hidden, his actions could be deemed reckless.

Bob Carroll had already met with Blanco at the Bergen County
Courthouse and warned him about the danger in not telling the truth
about the frisk. "The truth is going to come out," Carroll recalls saying.
"If you are not telling the truth, I'm telling you it could crush you.
Your policeman's career and your partner's career will go down the
drain."

Blanco didn't budge. He stuck to his story.

Jesse Jackson came back to Teaneck. When he passed through before, Teaneck High School was not in session. Jackson wanted to spend time with students, and as he entered the high school gymnasium, thirteen hundred students rose from seats in the bleachers and from folding chairs set up on the basketball floor and cheered as if a rock star had just walked in. Jackson waved as he mounted a stage that had been placed under a basketball net and approached a podium flanked by two potted palms. He stood for a moment and, feet apart and shoulders back, looked around the gym. Camera strobe lights flashed. The ovation went on for another minute. When the gym fell silent, Jackson asked the students to join their hands and bow their heads as he prayed: "Our Father, forgive us for our sins and foolish ways. Search our hearts. If you find anything, take it out . . . malice . . . racism . . . sexism . . . anti-Semitism . . . anti-Hispanicism . . . anti-Arabism . . . anti-Asian–bashing. . . . If you find anything that should not be, renew us, revive us, lift us. Let us today draw the line. No more hatred."

Jackson looked up. He asked the students to repeat after him "I am somebody. Respect me. Protect me. Never neglect me. Teaneck is number one."

The students did—and cheered again and clapped. Jackson asked them to sit down.

"A crisis has been visited upon you," he said, his hands outstretched, fingers apart, his voice rising. "The question is, What do you do in a crisis when the lights go out? One option is to panic and surrender. It's dark, and so turn on each other."

He paused, his eyes scanning the crowd, shaking his head from side to side.

"It's not a redemptive option. When the lights go out, don't turn on each other. In the dark, turn to each other and not on each other, and then wait until morning comes. This crisis in Teaneck is not limited to here, but it is here. . . . So here we sit in a house divided. We were brothers and sisters who now look at each other in strange ways. . . . The crisis of Phillip's death has now given us the opportunity of reassessment. . . . Death has challenged us to come together and assess the value of life. What is the challenge of your age? Learning to live together. There is no solution in an eye for an eye or a tooth for a tooth. An eye for an eye is at best short-term gratification. An eye for an eye—that only leaves you blind and ugly. No more shooting.

No more families torn apart. Break the cycle of violence."

He went on for almost forty-five minutes, scolding, pleading, commanding, begging, and inspiring, as his voice journeyed through a symphony of tones. Here was Jesse Jackson, the Baptist preacher, not the would-be politician trying to talk about foreign affairs or economic policy. He was personal and pastoral, speaking of how he had been arrested in 1960 as a college student in North Carolina while trying to integrate an all-white lunch counter.

From his seat on the side Art Gardner felt himself smile. He recollected his own attempt to integrate a lunch counter and was glad now that Jackson was teaching some history. The kids needed that, Gardner thought.

Jackson noted that Martin Luther King was only twenty-six years old when he staged the bus boycott in Montgomery, Alabama. He called out the names of the Freedom Riders who had died in the civil rights movement of the sixties. He reminded the crowd that twenty years ago four students protesting the Vietnam War at Kent State University had been killed by Ohio National Guard soldiers. He paid homage to the ethnic, racial, and religious mix that had become the hallmark of Teaneck. "You represent the hope of the whole world. There are few schools in the whole world with this multiethnic mix."

He turned to the boys in the crowd. "You're not a man because you can make a baby. You're a man because you can raise a family. A child brought into the world desires a father who cares." The students clapped loudly, as did the adults, who included Thelma and Phillip David Pannell.

Jackson took out a handkerchief from his suit pocket and wiped his brow. "There's not a problem in Harlem," he said, "that's not in Teaneck. Do you want to get well? If there's hatred between the races, do you want to get well?"

"Yes!" the students answered.

Three boys, each wearing a baseball cap backward, walked into the gym from a rear door and hip-hopped down an aisle to the bleachers. Jackson stopped and looked them over.

"Please take your hats off," he said, his voice lowering. "It's so basic and civil."

The boys removed their hats. Several other boys got up to leave. They seemed disgusted. "Young brothers," Jackson said, "please stay."

They sat down.

Next Jackson directed his comments to anyone who was a witness to Phillip's shooting or the other events that day. "Protect your credibility."

He asked anyone who had tried drugs such as heroin, cocaine, and crack to come forward to a spot in front of the lectern. Several students walked forward, huddling together in the front, their heads bowed. Others squirmed in their seats. The crowd started to murmur. Another two dozen students rose and went forward. Jackson asked anyone who had tried marijuana to stand by his or her seat. Half the students got up. He asked whether anyone had drunk alcohol. Everyone stood.

A baby cried. "Let the baby stay," Jackson called out, smiling. "I can talk over a baby."

Jackson looked over the group for a moment, then asked them to hold hands. He bowed his head and asked the crowd to repeat his words. "This is my life. . . . I want to use my life to make a difference. . . . I want to be an instrument for peace and justice."

The students sat down, and Jesse Jackson switched gears. He turned to the two dozen TV and newspaper reporters sitting on folding chairs to his left and said he would like to hold a press conference and take questions. But he asked the students to stay in their seats, so they could observe "the way we communicate."

"Ordinarily we have a press conference in a side room," said Jackson. "You'll learn something."

A reporter's hand shot up. The grand jury was meeting that morning in Trenton. Did Jackson have any thoughts on what the grand jury might do?

"There is a need for an indictment," said Jackson, "and a need for a conviction."

The students applauded.

A reporter mentioned Jackson's reference to Spath the two weeks before as an "assassin." Jackson nodded.

"Do you still stand by that comment, and, if so, why?"

Jackson looked down at the lectern, then scanned the gym. "That was an unfortunate term," he said, measuring his words. "I should not have said the man who killed Phillip Pannell was an assassin." He paused. "He was an executioner. When the state kills someone, it's an execution."

Jackson didn't stop there. "If there is no indictment, it is a signal that justice has collapsed. If there is no conviction, it suggests that the system isn't fair."

━━━━━

Sitting with his fellow clergy, Mandy Derr felt numb. Jackson's speech to the students had been hypnotic. As a preacher himself Derr had been amazed at Jackson's control of the crowd, his use of language, and the ebb and flow of his speaking style. But the press conference portion was a disaster, Derr thought. As Jackson said the word "executioner," Derr looked around him and could feel an emotional bottom fall out of the room. What has he done? he thought. This is awful. We're back to square one.

━━━━━

In the bleachers Batron Johnson was cheering. Yes, he thought, Jackson was right. Phillip had been executed, and Spath was the executioner. It was time for justice, Batron thought. Batron felt strong in his anger.

Jackson took another question, then announced he had to leave. He waved to the crowd and walked into a hallway, as students crowded around and asked for autographs. He went into a classroom to speak briefly to a group of students who claimed to be witnesses. "Those of you who are witnesses need to be credible witnesses," he said as a dozen boys and girls slumped in chairs or leaned against desks. "When you get into a courtroom situation, what you may say on television or in the mass media may be used against you. . . . All of the people who are involved must remain very disciplined and clear. The point is really that we have lost one of our children. . . . Do not allow anyone to take your eyes off what the goal is."

Jackson thanked them and headed for the school library to meet with another dozen student leaders, who took seats at round tables. Jackson sat atop an empty table, his feet dangling over the side. He asked if anyone had a question.

A sixteen-year-old girl raised her hand. Kiran Malavade, whose parents had come to Teaneck from India, was nervous. Her voice seemed to crack, but she went on. She wanted to know why Jackson was calling for a conviction before all the evidence on Gary Spath was collected. Several students hissed. Jackson raised his hand. "No, let the sister speak."

Malavade's voice rose in volume. The brief interruption seemed to give her confidence. "How can you call for a conviction?" she asked. "The most we can call for is a fair trial."

Jackson started to answer, but a black senior, eighteen-year-old David Kent, jumped in. "It's an assumption of prejudgment and a bias," he told Jackson.

For a half second Jesse Jackson seemed stunned. Then he shook his head from side to side. "When the state pulls the trigger," said Jesse Jackson, "that's called an execution."

———

At the hour that Jesse Jackson stood in the gymnasium, ten men and thirteen women assembled for the first time in a windowless room on the fourth floor of the Richard J. Hughes Justice Complex in Trenton. The group, which included four blacks, had been drawn from all corners of New Jersey. It was known as State Grand Jury 252-90-5, but it came to be known simply as the Spath grand jury.

The group was asked to take seats at a series of oak tables that had been arranged in a U shape and faced a judge's bench and a witness box. A court stenographer took a seat and started typing as Assistant Attorney General Robert J. Carroll began to speak. He introduced two colleagues: Dennis Calo, who raised his hand, and another deputy attorney general, Lawrence Monaco. The group and others, explained Carroll, "will be presenting to you, over the next several weeks, a case which we will formally title 'In the Matter of the Death of Phillip Pannell.'"

He spelled out Pannell's last name and said that Pannell had been shot by Teaneck Police Officer Gary Spath on April 10, 1990, at approximately 6:20 P.M. "Our responsibility in presenting this case to you," Carroll went on, "is to basically marshal all the evidence, bring it in here, and allow you to eventually make a decision, and at the conclusion of the case, we will, of course, charge you as to the appropriate law and the principles that have to be applied to your consideration of the evidence in the case."

Carroll sat down, and Monaco took over. Whenever a grand jury meets, the prosecutors take time to explain their role and the responsibility of the grand jury. Part of the reason is common sense—to inform the grand jurors of their duties and limitations—but the other reason is legal: to plant within the jurors' minds, as well as place in the court transcript, the fact that the final judgment on the evidence is left to the twenty-three men and women selected to hear it, not to the prosecutors.

"We will be presenting to you testimony and evidence in a case in a matter which has generated a substantial amount of media attention, to say the very least," Monaco began. "The press coverage has, quite frankly, consisted of, among other things, statements and comments by witnesses and purported witnesses; statements and comments by people who do or may have a legitimate interest in this investigation and its outcome, and it also has included comments and statements by people who have no real legitimate interest in the investigation, except their own self-interest. You're not to consider any of that, except as it may be presented to you here in the grand jury room, while you're in session.

"Basically, ladies and gentlemen, the question that's ultimately going to be presented to you is whether or not the shooting of Phillip Pannell was a criminal homicide; whether it was excusable or justifiable under the law.... You should not assume that we, myself, Mr. Carroll, and Mr. Calo, are seeking any particular result for any reason whatsoever.... Nor should you assume that we seek a particular result because we're prosecutors. The role, the ethical, professional responsibility of a prosecutor, is to see that justice is done. We do that in this case, as in all other cases, by seeking the truth.... Ultimately it's your job, your responsibility, to judge the credibility of the witnesses, and to weigh all of the evidence that's presented to you. The role of you, as a grand jury, is sometimes described by some people, and you may have heard it before, as being the bearer of the sword and the shield within our criminal justice system.... It's your duty and responsibility to return the appropriate indictment, and in that manner, you wield the sword. On the other hand, and equally important, you as an independent body stand between those who may be falsely accused, whether private citizen or public official, and their accusers.... In that way, you bear the shield."

THAT EVENING

In the junior high school auditorium where Teaneck's black and white leadership had gathered on April 1 to honor two men who led the fight for integrated schools twenty-five years before, the town's clergy conducted an interfaith Service of Reconciliation for the People of Teaneck.

The ceremony featured readings from the Old Testament, the New Testament, and the Koran. A woman and a man with a folk guitar sang the old sixties anthem made popular by Peter, Paul, and Mary "If I Had a Hammer." A minister read Martin Luther King's "I Have a Dream" speech—words that caused the crowd to stand and join hands. The Reverend Lucinda Laird, the Episcopal priest at St. Mark's, read a Litany for Justice and Reconciliation:

"Almighty God . . . we have turned away from you, broken your laws. . . . and violated our relationships. . . . We admit uncharitable thoughts toward our neighbors and prejudice and contempt toward those who differ from us. . . . We admit to blindness to human need and suffering. . . . We admit to complacency and smugness and a lack of desire to change our ways. . . . We admit that injustice flourishes in our lives. . . . We come together this night as a wounded and broken community. . . . Lord, hear our prayer."

Rabbi Kenneth Berger noted that "despite the pride that we've taken in Teaneck, we have not been immune to the social problems." Since Pannell's death, the rabbi said, "feelings of sorrow, pain, and even fear have been experienced by everyone here tonight. It is time to begin the process of healing and reconciliation."

He was followed by a Lutheran minister, the Reverend Bruce Davidson, who somberly began: "No matter what the circumstances may be, the death of a sixteen-year-old is always a tragedy."

Davidson paused and asked for a "moment of silent prayer and reflection for Phillip Pannell." After a minute he continued: "We must indeed acknowledge what brings us together tonight. Among some young people and their parents there is fear, intense fear." He said, "Police officers feel they are unfairly stereotyped as violent and racist," and there is "concern for Officer Spath."

"Yeah," said a black woman on the side near the front, "a killer."

If Davidson heard her, he didn't show it. He looked over the crowd and asked everyone to pause again in silence to pray for Gary Spath and "all those whose lives have been touched by the tragedy."

A minute later Davidson offered a postscript. "This may not be a simple process," he said. "We have to look at some wounds that we have not seen. We are here to combat the cynical misperception that racial and religious harmony is not possible." He quoted Thelma Pannell's wish that she had expressed the week before with Jesse Jackson for "black, white, yellow—we all have to get together." For Teaneck, he said, "I hope that tonight we can make that dream a reality."

The evening ended with the crowd holding hands, swaying, and singing "We Shall Overcome." For the organizers it also ended on a note of sadness. Of the three hundred people who were there, fewer than fifty were black. Most were white and middle-class. Two distinct groups were virtually unrepresented: black teenagers and the police.

LATER THAT WEEK

Lelia Johnson noticed something changing about her son. He was qui-
eter around the house, seemed withdrawn and lonesome, often not
saying more than a few words for days.

"When he didn't talk, that bothered me," she said. "I knew he was
thinking."

But what? She suspected Batron cried at night to himself. Some
nights she threw her arms around his broad shoulders as they sat on
the red cushioned sofa in the living room. She pulled him tighter to
her and rocked him back and forth as she had when he was a baby,
while the TV flickered across the room. But Batron wouldn't say anything. "After he felt sleepy, he would get up and head upstairs," said
his mother.

One evening she followed him into his room and sat on his bed and
hugged him again. Batron started to cry, at first just a whimper as tears
rolled down his cheeks, then a constant sob.

"Why, Mommy?" Batron asked. "Why did this have to happen?"

Over the next few minutes she couldn't find an answer. Nor did she
have to. Batron had cried himself to sleep.

SUNDAY, APRIL 29

Mandy Derr stood at the pulpit of Grace Lutheran Church. It was the
last Sunday in April. He had not mentioned the troubles in Teaneck
in his sermon the previous week, preferring to let some of the emotional dust settle. Now he knew he could not avoid them. Derr felt a
sense of unreality descending on Teaneck. He considered the two main
characters in the drama—Spath and Pannell—flawed, a mix of good
traits with problems. Yet each side had turned them into extremist
symbols, either all good or all bad. To blacks, Spath was an executioner; to whites, he seemed almost saintly. Derr was enthralled by the
story that Spath had tried to adopt a black child. (He did not yet know
it was false.) As for Pannell, to blacks, he had become a martyr; to
white cops and their supporters, he was a criminal.

The town, meanwhile, continued to be a rumor engine. After Jackson's speech and the reference to Spath as an executioner, Derr had
driven to a restaurant for a meeting of the Teaneck Rotary Club. As
he walked in the door, the crowd knew about Jackson's appearance.

But instead of "executioner," the crowd had heard that Jackson had called Spath a "murderer."

Derr corrected them. It was a small point, he knew, but important. Then he considered the further irony: Mandy Derr, the white Lutheran minister, who had been appalled at Jesse Jackson, had come to Jackson's defense. Teaneck *was* becoming surreal.

The day after the clergy service of reconciliation, the township council had taken over the Ben Franklin Middle School Auditorium to conduct a meeting. Hundreds of residents showed up, and Derr had watched a nervous Frank Hall try to steer the mood of the room toward some sort of calm. "We want to hear what the town has to say, about putting ourselves back together," the mayor said. "I must say we must see that justice is done in the tragic shooting of Phillip Pannell, and we must see that it never happens again. We must determine the root causes of the following night of violence, including the depths of anger and frustration of black youth of Teaneck."

Hall looked at the television crews that had set up cameras in the auditorium. "We want to hear what you have to say, and unfortunately we're on television, which I didn't want," he said. "I'll tell you what is my experience with television. There are always people, one or two, who would like to put on a show on camera if they are unhappy. So I was hoping this would be an ordinary council meeting where we can have a free exchange of ideas."

Those hopes were quickly dashed. Dozens of people lined up at a microphone. Many called for the firing of Chief Burke or the formation of a special board to monitor reports of police harassment. One speaker called for Spath to get the death penalty. Another said a monument should be erected to Phillip Pannell. A few called for reconciliation and peace. Others came in with long lists of requests: an improved affirmative action program, better recreation, more seminars on black history, and neighborhood meetings to discuss racial and ethnic differences.

Lelia Johnson was in the crowd. Besides her son, she worried for her town. As she listened to the other speakers describe how their children had been stopped by police for no apparent reason, she became more angry and approached the microphone.

"I hope the council is truly listening to the complaints of the people of Teaneck," she said. "Our kids should not be afraid to walk our streets. . . . We should not stand by and allow this to happen. The kids have a saying, 'No justice, no peace.' And I support them."

The crowd cheered.

That night Mandy Derr had wondered at the amount of anger that had been stored and stirred. As he stood now, on Sunday, in his pulpit, Derr surveyed the congregation. They were like him, he thought: unsure of what was happening in their town and searching for some sort of answer to get them through. Derr was most afraid for the teenagers. After Jesse Jackson had left Teaneck High School, Derr made a point of talking to the students he knew there. Whites, especially white boys, were fearful. Jackson's visit had not calmed the school; if anything, students said it seemed even more tense. Derr looked down at the two-page sermon he had typed out. "These have been the most difficult of days. Recent events have dashed the hopes and dreams, even the feelings of well-being of many people. Many people are afraid today. Many more are hopeless. Still more are just plain angry. They know an innocent young man has been unjustly accused—persecuted, tried, and condemned with no semblance of justice in sight. They know a young man has been killed—whatever promise his life held is now permanently snuffed out. Political leaders have postured and then washed their hands of the incident. All sorts of people are in pain and sorrow and at a loss. People are choosing up sides. No one trusts anyone else; not one another, not the politicians, not the police who did the awful deed. Things are a total mess. There is no end in sight. . . ."

Derr told the congregation that he had just described not only the past few weeks in Teaneck but the uncertainty that many early Christians felt after the death of Jesus of Nazareth. "For the township of Teaneck," Derr went on, "for every part of the community, and for me, these have been the most painful and difficult of days." He said that only once before in his life had he confronted "a situation so enormously difficult as this": the death of his first wife to cancer in 1981. "There are times," he said, "when I see no solutions. To be perfectly honest with you, I had not been this tired and worried and personally involved with unjust suffering and pain since I had to care for my Bonnie in the days of her illness and her dying."

He could think of only one balm: God and the refuge of faith. He asked the congregation to stand, as he read the first lines of a hymn written by Martin Luther and Johann Sebastian Bach.

Here the true Paschal Lamb we see,
Whom God so freshly gave us;
He died on the accursed tree—
So strong His love to save us.
See, His blood now marks our door;

Faith points to it; death passes o'er,
And Satan cannot harm us. Hallelujah.

"And not just sing it," said Mandy Derr as the organist began to play, "but mean it!"

EIGHTEEN

"RACE WAS ON THE TABLE NOW"

ELECTION NIGHT, MAY 8, 1990

Paul Ostrow wanted to be alone. The polls were closed now, and he wanted time to collect his thoughts before the votes were counted for the town council election. He opened the front door of his campaign manager's home, where he had gone to wait for the results, and walked out.

It was after 8:00 P.M., and the sun had already sunk into a fuchsia haze beyond the trees. Ostrow felt proud. He had vowed to run a dirt-free campaign, and miraculously he had managed to do that. "Principles, not politics" had been his slogan, and he believed he had stuck to it.

He walked up a hill. The neighborhood was like his, Ostrow thought. The houses had been built in the 1930s and 1940s, and each seemed different, each displaying an individual sense of character and presence. A Tudor, with turrets and leaded glass windows, stood regally next to a colonial. Overhead, strong, stately oak trees commanded the sky. This was the Teaneck that Ostrow valued, unique yet well ordered, traditional yet home to a polyglot of peoples. It was one reason he had decided to run for the council. Four seats were open, and eight candidates were running. In his most idealistic moments Ostrow believed he could give something positive back to his town. When the pragmatic part of him took over, though, he thought that he could bring a sense of reasonableness too. Ostrow didn't want to lose. He wasn't looking forward to winning either.

He could feel the difference in town. It wasn't easy to identify. People in Teaneck often didn't talk about race in public; the small campaign get-togethers that were set up—the town called them cottage parties—were dominated by talk about the high cost of collecting garbage. Ostrow could hardly remember anyone talking about Phillip Pannell or Gary Spath. He knew the silence was deceptive. His phone lines had been filled with worried voices for the past month. He paid as much attention to what was spoken in private by his friends as what was proclaimed in public. Private truths often differed substantially from public truths. Ostrow suspected other towns were like that. It was human nature, he thought.

Some friends talked of moving, others of removing their children from the public schools, still others of rumors they had heard. Was Sharpton coming back? How many marches were being planned? What kind of juvenile crime problem had Pannell had? And if he had had a problem, why was he now depicted as a martyr? Just the same, was Spath trigger-happy? If so, why had he been on the police force for eight years?

Ostrow was especially worried for the public schools and, in the long run, for his children. His son wasn't due to go to the high school for another three years. In the meantime, Ostrow wondered if the high school would become awash with race problems. Lowering the flag to half-mast in memory of Phillip Pannell was not a good sign, he felt, nor was the memorial to Pannell in the trophy case by his gang members. To Ostrow, it seemed that the school authorities were trying to appease black kids to keep them from going on a rampage.

Local politics seemed as steeped in intrigue. Ostrow was well versed in the complicated formula of tradition and unwritten rules that local politicians followed. Long before, the town had openly eschewed traditional partisan lines, and no one ran as a Democrat or a Republican. People formed ad hoc groups with names such as Committee for Responsive Government or they just ran as individuals. Teaneck even deliberately scheduled its municipal elections in May so as to avoid the coattails—or sinking anvils—of Democrats and Republicans in the November elections. The most significant ingredient in the Teaneck political mix, however, was race and ethnicity. Since the 1960s the unwritten rule of Teaneck politics was that candidates for local offices did not try to cater to racial groups and marshal forces into voting blocs—not overtly anyway. Ostrow knew the truth: that people were intimately aware of which candidates were Jewish or liberal or conservative or moderate . . . or black. Over the years the various coalitions even tried to balance their groups with a few whites, a Jewish candidate, and a black. But like a country club that never talked out loud about the groups it kept out, Teaneck's political leaders did not speak overtly of their ethnic and racial balancing acts when choosing candidates. As much as Ostrow regarded the tradition of not openly discussing race, but remaining privately fixated on it, as somewhat phony, the results were generally positive. An all-black slate would never win, nor would an all-Jewish slate. Nor should either win. Ostrow believed in his heart that mixed coalitions were best for Teaneck. Unlike cities where political parties had marshaled voting blocs, Teaneck had adopted an open approach. The unspoken rule in town politics was to try to win with a broad coalition, with support spread evenly throughout black and white neighborhoods.

This campaign had a different feel to it, though. It seemed more ominous than those in the past. A few days before the election an ad appeared on black radio stations. "The winds of change are blowing through Teaneck," it proclaimed repeatedly. The ad went on to attack Mayor Frank Hall as the man who supplied the police with riot gear. "What will Hall do next time?"

Ostrow knew the ad targeted black voters. A group of white liberals—including some in the Concerned Citizens, which was one of the first with a list of demands on the town after the shooting—were attempting to round up black voters. If that happened, Ostrow knew, it would set off a chain reaction, with each side retreating into itself. Teaneck would be vulnerable to bullet voting, in which ethnic groups vote only for candidates like them.

A few nights before, at Fairleigh Dickinson University, a college professor who lived in town but worked at City College of New York, Leonard Jeffries, had spoken to a black audience and declared that he had been stopped "thirty to forty" times by Teaneck police. "I've been stopped two or three times in front of my house," said Jeffries, the chairman of the black studies department at CCNY. When police asked him what he was doing there, Jeffries told the audience he'd replied: "I'm going into my two-hundred-fifty-thousand-dollar house. Do you have any questions?"

Jeffries went on to state that God was black and Africa the birthplace of humankind. "We've got to get back to our African center," he declared. "The most important thing on this globe, the most important thing in the human family, is that which is African."

Ostrow knew such rhetoric could split Teaneck. "Race was on the table now," he said later. He thought it was not unlike a corporation that had been tarnished. "From a business point of view we had an image problem, we had an advertising problem. You have to regain your credibility in the eyes of those that utilize your product."

What he didn't know is that the slate that had put together the radio ad had hired a political consulting firm that had conducted a poll of Teaneck residents. Indeed, race was a worry to many whites, the poll found, but not as great a worry as crime and garbage collections. Among blacks, race relations were clearly more important but still not an overwhelming worry. The consultant who conducted the poll, Rick Shafton, was amused and amazed at the zeal with which the whites sought to exploit this. They saw this as an opportunity to knock out Frank Hall, said Shafton. What they didn't see is that only the black section of the town supported them and that by trying to appeal to blacks with their message, they ran the risk of polarizing the town along racial and ethnic lines.

Ostrow had finished his walk around the block and stepped back inside his campaign manager's home. The phone rang. It was one of his supporters at the town hall, keeping tabs on the election tally. "It looks good," the man said. "The first two districts came in, and you came in first in both."

White, Jewish districts, Ostrow observed. He expected to do well there. He had many friends there.

A few minutes later the phone rang again. The black districts near the William Cullen Bryant Elementary School were sending in results now. Ostrow was running in seventh place there.

The pattern began to develop, and Ostrow saw it all too clearly. He was running well in the white districts and in those on the south end that were integrated. But in the black neighborhoods of the northeast section of Teaneck he was far behind. By the end of the night he had received more votes than any other candidate, with more than forty-five hundred votes. Hall retained his seat but by only ninety-eight votes. More worrisome was the way the votes were cast. Whites favored whites; blacks favored blacks. For the first time in as long as local politicians could remember, a Teaneck election had signs of bullet voting. But while ethnic and racial groups in cities use bullet voting to flex their political muscle, in Teaneck it had the opposite effect. Both black candidates lost, as did all but one of the white liberals.

Bullet voting in the black neighborhoods had failed. What's more, Ostrow suspected a white backlash had been mounted to defeat liberals and blacks—another form of bullet voting. The new council would have only one black (an incumbent who was not up for reelection), an Asian, and five whites.

Ostrow smiled as friends congratulated him. Deep inside he knew the celebration would be short-lived. "The town wasn't going from the frying pan into the fire," he said. "We were going from the refrigerator into the fire."

THREE DAYS LATER

At the Teaneck police station cops were lighting a fire of their own. In a show of support for Gary Spath and to raise money for what could be a long legal battle, the police union sold gray T-shirts emblazoned with the words "Never a Doubt" and Spath's police badge number, 195.

The shirts had been the idea of Officer John Hyland, Spath's brother-in-law. For several days until they were told by Chief Burke to stop, the police sold the shirts openly from behind the main radio desk at the police station for ten dollars each.

By the end of the week the police said they had taken a thousand orders for the shirts. It was left to Spath's lawyer to explain what the message, "Never a Doubt," meant. "There is never a doubt that what he did was correct," said Robert Galantucci, "never a doubt that what he did was in perfect conformance with his training and experience, never a doubt that he's going to be vindicated, and never a doubt that all of Teaneck's police officers will walk with their heads high real soon."

It was left to Phillip Pannell's attorney to respond. Franklin Wilks said the shirts were "insensitive" and "inflammatory," then added: "There's never a doubt in any right-thinking person's mind that this young's man's civil rights were violated. There's never a doubt in anyone's mind that there was an injustice here, and never a doubt that the police are acting irresponsibly here."

The head of the police union, Officer Steve Librie, said the message on the shirts was "nothing more than a show of support for Gary Spath. There's never been a doubt that we support him. That's what it means."

Whatever the meaning or the interpretation, two weeks later supporters of Phillip Pannell were selling their own T-shirts, with the countermessage, "Never a Chance." Pannell's name was spelled "Pannel."

By the end of the month T-shirts had become a fashion statement. Police in Dumont, a neighboring town whose officers had been summoned to help quell the riot, sold a shirt to commemorate their role with this message:

RIOT BUSTERS
I SURVIVED TEANECK
APRIL 11, 1990

On the back of the shirt, the cops had their own message for the Reverend Al Sharpton. Like the Pannell shirt, the version by the Dumont cops had a misspelling. "Reverend" was "Reverand."

REVERAND AL, THE COP'S PAL
THANKS FOR THE OVERTIME.

There was one additional problem: Sharpton had not been in town when the riot occurred. The Dumont officers who designed and sold the shirts explained that it was "just a fun-type thing" and a "goof." But to many in Teaneck the T-shirts symbolized how the most extreme or irresponsible voices seemed to dominate. "We don't need people to be aroused now emotionally," said Mayor Hall. "We're trying to heal this town. Whatever the T-shirt slogans mean, if it is interpreted or perceived by people to set up one group against another, I think it's absolutely wrong."

By mid-May the Teaneck council announced that it would form a commission similar to the Kerner Commission of the 1960s that investigated American race relations and urban riots. "We need to know the answers to these simple questions," said Hall. "The shooting of Phillip Pannell, the rioting the following night, what happened and why." The council authorized the commission to hold hearings and examine further the general state of race relations in the town and the accusations of police harassment. One councilman even suggested the commission look into the origins of the T-shirts. But the council couldn't agree on who should sit on the commission or when to form it. Several members feared it would be used to target the white liberals who organized the vigil as those causing the riot. Two weeks later the idea was tabled, never to be resurrected.

A week later the council voted to create a special board to hear complaints from residents about possible harassment. Council members liked the general idea of a civilian complaint review board but worried about its aftereffects. One concern was legal: that the board might uncover information that the Pannell family could use against Teaneck in its thirty-million-dollar lawsuit, which had not yet been filed. Another worry was political. The police board would placate blacks and white liberals but would alienate police and their supporters. The police had already quietly signaled their anger toward the town by cutting back on the numbers of tickets they wrote, thus cutting the town's revenue, while according to the town manager, the riot had cost the town $390,000, with expenses ranging from property damage to overtime for police to replacement of three damaged police cars, to the purchase of new riot gear, as well as doctors' bills for three officers who had been injured.

On the evening that the police board was formally debated, Walter Fields of the NAACP stood at a microphone in the middle of the council chambers at municipal hall. Before this, he had resisted going to council meetings; he was not a Teaneck resident, and he felt far more effective playing the background role with Ted Wells and others close to the Florio administration. But Fields now thought Teaneck was at a critical juncture, especially with the decision to form a police board. "It will go a long way in building confidence in the police department," Fields declared. "We need to bring the police department back into the community."

After Fields finished, Theo Bolden, the Teaneck High School senior who had spoken at Pannell's funeral, rose from his seat. "When I try the system, the system doesn't work for me," Bolden said. "Who protects me from the police? The police are out there and beating up on me."

Intended or not, it was left to Mayor Hall to sound a cautionary note. He was still trying to straddle a middle ground, pleasing few, angering many. "You are using me for an instant solution," Hall told Bolden. "I can't give you an instant answer. We don't want to start beating up on the police department either. We shouldn't stereotype anyone."

By June Pannell supporters were marching through the town's business district every Saturday afternoon, with chanting that had taken on a personalized tone. No longer were marchers yelling, "No justice, no peace." As the group walked past Louie's Charcoal Pit one Saturday and the movie theater where *Total Recall, Torn Apart,* and *Pretty Woman* were featured, a new chant resounded.

"What's the charge?"

"Murder."

"What's the verdict?"

"Guilty."

"Spath is a murderer,"

"Put him in jail."

———

Bill Crain heard the chants. It bothered him that the anger in people's hearts had found its way to the street in such ugly tones. As much as he was troubled by Spath's shooting, Crain believed firmly that everyone was innocent until proved guilty. Spath might well be a murderer, Crain thought, but a jury, not a mob, should decide that.

Crain could see divisions forming in his town. The police T-shirts were like an emotional punch in the nose, and he wondered what sort of mind-set could come up with the slogan Never a Doubt. The cops either possessed a level of insensitivity bordering on the pathological or had no idea how deeply the shooting had angered even the most moderate of blacks. He knew too that Sharpton's command to "keep the tension high," his reputation from the Tawana Brawley case, and his willingness to draw publicity from racial trouble had turned off white liberals. If there were any whites who were even thinking about marching, they had been discouraged by the angry chants. Crain had felt the urge to march but had managed to squelch it. By June the marches had become a regular Saturday activity, but they were notable for their monotone. No whites marched.

In those early weeks Crain attended dozens of meetings. He had gravitated toward the Concerned Citizens group because it included many of the white liberals who had helped elect him to the school board. By June he had become frustrated, though. It wasn't the politics; it was the inability to embrace a course of action. The group had been handcuffed by the marches, Sharpton's militancy, and the chants. Crain also thought that many liberals, while believing the shooting was wrong, still questioned whether they could wholeheartedly support a cause that centered on a juvenile delinquent, a gang member who carried a gun. Crain himself had problems with this.

If he was moved in his heart, it was from conversations with blacks. At several meetings he had been touched by the level of anguish in many blacks. He heard how some white leaders whom he viewed as fair-minded were considered racist by blacks, that the town's attitude toward blacks (which Crain generally thought was enlightened) was regarded as demeaning and condescending. Blacks told him that far too many whites acted as if they had done blacks a favor by integrating the schools. As Crain learned, many Teaneck blacks wondered why it had taken Teaneck ten years after the U.S. Supreme Court had outlawed segregation to integrate its schools. Crain was proud of the integration, but as he began to look at it from the black perspective, his pride seemed tarnished. The more he tried to understand Teaneck as a black, the more he realized that the railroad tracks that divided the town geographically also divided racial perceptions. "The dirty laundry of the town started to come out," said Crain.

What moved him more than anything were the stories of harassment by police—or the perception of it. To be black and young, he realized, was to wonder about any police car patrolling your street. "It was the deep secret of the town," said Crain. "Some of us who were white had been blinded. These black kids could not be kids. They could not hang out on the street corner like kids. Anytime there was a couple of them standing in front of a drugstore, the police would come and move them along. Anytime they were driving in a car that looked at all modern, it was pulled over by the cops. The humiliation and the intimidation they felt and the rage that started to emerge after Pannell was killed—that came out so fast."

Crain wondered why more white liberals were not as bothered as he by this. He suspected it had to do with the Violators. In mid-May, for instance, Pannell's friend, Leslie Johnson, and several Violators had been arrested for gun possession in Jersey City. Another problem, according to Crain, was the inability of many whites to find common ground in the humiliation blacks faced. Most white drivers had never been stopped for no apparent reason or suspected of being a shoplifter, as respected black adults told Crain they had. He remembered an incident from his own childhood when he had been falsely accused of stealing candy from a Los Angeles grocery store. "I wanted to bust the supermarket up. I was so mad. The more I shouted, the more they told me to calm down. I wanted to talk to somebody, but they just told me to go home. I finally returned with my parents, and the manager admitted that maybe someone made a mistake. 'But that's life,' the manager said."

Crain admired Martin Luther King, Jr., to the point where he saw him as a spiritual leader as much as a civil rights leader. Of all of

King's speeches, Crain was drawn to one in 1961 in which King commented on accusations that he was disturbing the harmony between whites and blacks. For that speech King coined the term "negative peace," and in those weeks after Pannell's death Crain picked up a book of King's speeches and turned to the passage that explained it: "We've had a negative peace in which the Negro patiently accepted situations in his life, but we've never had true peace. We've never had positive peace. And what we're seeking now is to develop the positive peace, not merely the absence of some negative force, not the absence of tensions, but the presence of justice and brotherhood. I think this is what Jesus meant when He said, 'I come not to bring peace but a sword.'"

Crain had come to understand the power in King's words. Peace often had to be achieved by making people uncomfortable, not by being gentle. But how could Bill Crain be a sword, as King referred to it?

One Sunday evening Crain found himself at a gathering of the Concerned Citizens at the Teaneck Ethical Culture Society meetinghouse. The discussion was a carryover from others: more strategy about local politics and more talk about how to convince the town to improve recreation, set up police sensitivity training, and rekindle the commitment to affirmative action hiring. Crain was tired of this.

The group numbered only about twenty people, all sitting in a circle of chairs. Crain noticed a black woman who had not come before. As the discussion waned, the woman introduced herself. "I'm Lelia Johnson. I'm scared for my son and his friends."

If anyone in the room was nodding off, this opening was enough to wake them. She went on to explain that her son, Batron, had been friendly with Phillip Pannell and had been deeply distressed after the shooting and riot. She suspected that Batron and his friends might retaliate against the police.

She had brought her son and several of his friends to meet with Fred Greene, but the boys had walked out of the meeting, angrily pushing chairs away. She had come to the Concerned Citizens because she did not know where to turn. She knew her son was falling behind in school, that he was not going to all his classes. She also knew he had attended some of the Saturday marches but had become frustrated. Batron, she said, wanted action. "The kids are out there getting angrier and angrier," Lelia Johnson said. "I'm afraid of what they might do."

She sat down, and after the meeting Crain and another white man,

Jim White, walked over. How could they help? She asked them to meet Batron and his friends.

Four Days Later

Crain looked across the table into Batron Johnson's dark eyes.

The group had been able to get a room at St. Paul's Lutheran Church. As he scanned the room, Crain felt oddly detached. Next to him sat Jim White, who was a lawyer and, like Crain, Harvard-educated. Crain had brought along his other son, Tom, who had just come home after completing his freshman year at Brown. Across from them sat Batron and several of his black friends. If what Lelia Johnson said was true, none was on the fast track to the Ivy League.

In one way Crain felt comfortable. Several black men had come, among them William David-El, who had coached Tom Crain in a youth football league.

Lelia Johnson sat next to Batron, and Crain sensed that mother and son had a close bond. As Batron spoke, she placed her hand on his shoulder.

"I'm gonna go out there," he said. "I'm gonna go out in the street and we're gonna . . ." His voice trailed off, then picked up seconds later. "The kids are talking, and I don't know what we're going to do. Kids are getting guns."

Crain studied Batron. The teenager seemed not to want to be talking to these white men. It was as if he had been forced to come, probably by his mother. Batron shifted, turned to the side.

The boy spoke of how angry he felt, that Pannell's death was unjust. Crain admired his passion and the way he articulated his feelings. Here was a young man laying out his humanity. He was angry and worried for himself, unsure of what he was going to do. To admit that, Crain thought, was powerful.

"You can't think that violence is the only way," Crain said. Batron seemed to bristle, but he went on anyway. "In fact, you're gonna get killed. If you go out there with guns, you're going to be considered a ruffian."

Batron glared back at Crain. He didn't appreciate being called a ruffian.

"I'm not saying that you're a ruffian," Crain added. "But this is what you're going to be accused of. Listen . . . listen . . ."

Crain asked Batron if anything could convince him that violence was not a good strategy.

"The only thing that would stop me is my mother," Batron answered.

Batron looked again at Lelia Johnson. Crain thought Batron was trying not to upset her and admired him for this. As angry as Batron seemed to be, his anger was not enough to overwhelm his love for his mother.

Crain felt energized. It was as if Batron's threats of violence and his own unsettled feelings about how best to become involved in the town had crystallized. "What about nonviolent protest?" he asked.

"Bullshit," said one of the boys who had been silent.

"That won't get anything done," Batron replied.

Crain felt he was on to something. He had marched only a few times in his life for any cause, the last occasions being almost a quarter century before, when he and his wife joined in several protests against the Vietnam War. Other than that, primarily concerned with completing college and graduate school and raising a family, Crain had taken only a modest role in political protests in the intervening years. He thought of Martin Luther King and King's spiritual mentor, Mohandas Gandhi.

"No," Crain said to Batron. "Nonviolence is a powerful weapon. Gandhi drove the British out of India without firing a shot. Don't underestimate the power of nonviolence. Don't underestimate the power of what you can do."

Batron quieted.

David-El spoke next. More marches were being planned, and he wanted more adults. "We got to watch out and take care of the kids in our town," he said.

Batron said he would be there.

Crain got up to leave, then turned to Lelia Johnson. "Will you be at the marches?" she asked. "Maybe this has some hope."

Crain said he didn't know. He had to work on Saturdays. As a psychologist he augmented his teaching at City College in Manhattan with Saturday morning counseling for mental patients at St. Luke's Hospital that usually ran well into the afternoon. She thanked him just the same.

As he drove home in the car with his son, Crain was silent. The issue was justice, he thought. *Yes.* Pannell had been shot, and it was important to have a fair, unblemished examination of the facts. To ensure that would take far more than sanctimonious words. Politicians understood protest marches. And if Crain was suggesting that other people march in a nonviolent manner, why wasn't he marching?

He thought of Batron's hurt and anger over his friend's death. He also remembered David-El's words: "We got to watch out and take care of the kids in our town."

A Saturday in June 1990

Officer Luis Torres recognized their faces from newspaper pictures: Phillip and Thelma Pannell. Torres, who had the day off, was walking the mile and a quarter jogging path around the rim of Votee Park. As he passed the park's picnic area that afternoon, he noticed the Pannells. Another Saturday march by activists through Teaneck's business district had ended, and Torres figured they were relaxing with supporters. He kept walking.

Torres had thought of the Pannells many times since the shooting. At the police station they had been depicted in the worst possible light: bad parents of a bad kid. His son had told him that the younger Pannell had been a continuing source of trouble at school, though often his actions were more prankish than criminal.

Among fellow cops Torres could see the lines of exaggeration being drawn. He knew the truth was somewhere in between: that a troubled son had died and a cop's life now lay in ruins. It was the human tragedy of both sides that plagued him. Yes, Phillip had been a bad kid, but Torres had known plenty of bad kids when he grew up in Harlem. They all didn't deserve to die. By the same token, he knew Gary Spath was a decent man, but he had problems as a cop.

At the police department middle ground was dangerous territory. The police union was intent on showing a unified front to the public. It bothered Torres that few cops showed the slightest inclination of expressing any sorrow that a young son of Teaneck had died; the emphasis was on surrounding Spath with a cocoon of support that protected him from what Torres believed was the single most important and damaging question: Spath's earlier shootings. Torres generally remained quiet, however, keeping his misgivings about Spath and his distress over the harsh portrayal of Phillip Pannell to himself. As he walked along the track, he wrestled with these thoughts. Luis Torres was a man who prided himself in speaking his mind, but in the last two months he had become a man in a shell. *Should he say something?*

Twenty minutes later he had completed the circle around Votee with his daughters in tow and was again passing the Pannell group by the picnic tables. He stopped and asked to speak to them. He was not in uniform; he was in shorts and a T-shirt.

"Hi," he said, "I'm Officer Torres. I'm on the Teaneck police, and I just want to have a couple of words with you."

Torres strolled with the Pannells to a spot where the three of them could talk privately. He knew he was speaking as a police officer, but he wanted to emphasize something else: He was a private citizen too.

"I realize that no one has come up to you and said anything from the police department," Torres said. "I'm doing this on my own. I'm not speaking for the Teaneck Police Department, but I want to tell you I'm very sorry your son was killed."

Torres paused and looked at the Pannells. They eyed him in silence. He went on. "I don't know the facts of the story, but I just want you to know one thing: Gary Spath is not a mean person. Gary has been made out to be a bad guy. I just want you to understand that he isn't the kind of guy that he is being played up to be."

At the mention of Spath's name, Pannell bristled. "No," said Pannell, "he killed my son."

He began to ramble as he spoke. To Torres, he seemed in deep pain. "He shot my son in the back. . . . He shot my son in the back." He kept repeating the phrase several times and calling Spath a racist.

Torres shook his head. "No," he said. "Gary is not that kind of cop. He's not the kind of cop who is racist in any way whatever."

Torres nodded toward his daughters, standing nearby. "I have children too," he said. "I can understand how you feel. It's your flesh and blood. I also want you to know the cops aren't here to hurt people."

He turned to leave and wished them well, hoping that his last words might soften Pannell's anger. Thelma Pannell had not said anything as her husband and Torres talked. But as Torres walked away, she spoke up. "Thank you," she said.

NINETEEN

MARCHING TOWARD JERUSALEM

FRIDAY, JUNE 29, ARDSLEY, NEW YORK

Dr. Peter De Forest sat at a desk in his home laboratory and opened a folder of papers from the test he had performed on Phillip Clinton Pannell's body almost three months before at the Hackensack funeral home. Something wasn't right.

It had been a busy spring for De Forest. He had flown to the Netherlands for a conference of forensic scientists and returned to conduct a series of seminars at the FBI Academy in Quantico, Virginia. This day he had managed to piece together a few hours to compose a final report on Pannell's movements in the seconds before he was shot. De Forest's initial conclusion seemed sound. When he, Dr. Lawrence Denson, and the detectives had placed Pannell's coat on his body and lined up the bullet hole in the fabric with the wound in the boy's back, Pannell's hands fell easily to his side. When the hands were raised over the head, the hole in the coat fell out of alignment with the wound. The conclusion seemed obvious: Pannell must have had his hands in a downward position, possibly with his left hand reaching for a gun, as the police suspected.

De Forest spread his notes on his cluttered desk. Behind him sat a large Macintosh computer that he planned to use to type his report.

Overhead, long fluorescent lights bathed the room in a gray-white brightness. De Forest turned on his VCR, slipped in the videotape he had made during the funeral home test, and sat back to watch.

The tape had run only a few minutes when De Forest hit the stop button. He reached for his file and pulled out the notes from Dr. Denson's autopsy, performed a few days before De Forest had been called into the case. He looked at the measurements that had been taken on Pannell's body. He checked the description of the location of the bullet wound on Pannell's back, then played the video again, closely studying the portion where Denson had marked the bullet wound on Pannell's back.

De Forest went back to the autopsy notes. He double-checked the measurements. He switched off the VCR.

Dr. Denson had made a mistake.

SATURDAY, JUNE 30, MANHATTAN

Attorney General Robert Del Tufo settled back into his seat in Lincoln Center's New York State Theater. He had maintained a subscription to the New York City Ballet and had decided to take in the afternoon performance before the company left for its summer home in Saratoga, New York. On the bill was a ballet that paid tribute to the music of Charles Ives. In *Ives, Songs,* the dancers, choreographed by Jerome Robbins, took the audience through a tour of life, from childhood innocence to youthful dreams to the reality of marriage and families, and finally to old age. It is a subtle ballet, evoking some of the passion of Robbin's best-known choreography in *West Side Story.* But to understand its meaning, the audience must pay attention to its details.

Del Tufo felt relaxed as he walked out of the theater into the late-afternoon humidity. The grand jury examination of the Pannell shooting had gone smoothly. Sharpton had backed off and had not flooded Trenton with marches, in part because he was tied up with his tax problems and the trial of the whites accused of killing Yusuf Hawkins. Yes, Teaneck had been the scene of smaller marches, but no further rioting had occurred.

New Jersey's attorney general was unhappy with Officer Wayne Blanco's story about the frisking of Pannell. Del Tufo thought that Blanco had probably doctored his story, but he considered it a small point amid the widening pile of evidence. He was also bothered by Blanco's grand jury testimony only a few days before that he could not even remember speaking about the shooting to Lieutenant Patrick Hogan. It had been Hogan who claimed that Blanco initially said at the hospital that Pannell's hand was never in his pocket. Del Tufo trusted Hogan and suspected that Blanco had changed his story and claimed Pannell's hand was in his pocket as a way to protect Spath. Even if Spath was correct in firing at Pannell, Del Tufo didn't like being lied to. Finally there were the worries about Teaneck Lieutenant Jack Terhune. Del Tufo thought Terhune had been far too protective when Spath gave his first and only statement on April 12. Detectives were supposed to be dispassionate investigators; they should not coach the subjects of investigations. What's more, Terhune had seemed evasive when questioned the week before in the grand jury about why he had never filed an official report about his trip to Holy Name Hospital to examine Pannell's body and his discussions with Blanco and Spath. Some on Del Tufo's staff, in mock tribute to Terhune's cool, polished manner, had nicknamed him Smilin' Jack.

But the worries about Blanco and Terhune seemed secondary now. Del Tufo believed that his staff's investigation was rock solid and would probably not result in an indictment of Spath. True, Terhune's behavior was suspicious, and Blanco's testimony was hardly credible, but Del Tufo also thought that the black adults and teenagers who claimed to be witnesses had not told the whole truth either. They said Phillip Pannell had his hands up and was trying to surrender, but Del Tufo knew what the tests on the boy's jacket by Peter De Forest and Dr. Denson had shown: Pannell's hands were down.

If Del Tufo felt any solace, it was in his staff's ability to slowly sort through the intricate case. In two months the grand jury had met ten times and heard testimony from fifteen police officers (ten from Teaneck); nine Teaneck adults, who described how they saw Pannell either brandish his gun or run from Spath; three ambulance technicians; one emergency room doctor; and thirty-four teenagers. The grand jurors had traced Pannell's movements the day he died. They had watched prosecutors expose some of the kids as liars. They had heard some kids admit that Pannell had a gun and others give conflicting accounts of what color the gun was and whether Pannell had kept it in his pocket or in his belt. They had visited Teaneck to look over the route on which Spath had chased Pannell. The grand jurors would not hear anything about Spath's prior shootings, nor would they learn about Pannell's juvenile delinquency except for vague references to the Violators. That was fine, Del Tufo thought. The law gave wide latitude to prosecutors, but it also protected the targets of the law from being judged by every past misdeed. Del Tufo could live with that. He believed in the system and its ability to remain fair to the truth.

Del Tufo knew the Pannell case, like the ballet he had just watched, was complicated. He also believed its subtle details would be the key to the truth. After finding his car in the Lincoln Center garage and getting on Manhattan's West Side Highway, Del Tufo reached for his cellular telephone to check his messages.

Bob Winter had phoned. He wanted Del Tufo to call him. It was urgent.

Del Tufo dialed, and Winter got right to the point. "You won't believe this," he said. "De Forest called and thinks he's made a mistake. He did some further tests and thinks the boy's hands were in the air."

On Monday, July 2, 1990, Peter De Forest was scheduled to make his way to the angular green glass and steel justice complex in Trenton and the room on the fourth floor where the grand jury was meeting. But after two witnesses that day the jurors were sent home. The next day Robert Del Tufo left his home early in Morristown, made his way over the Tappan Zee Bridge that spanned the Hudson River, and followed the back roads to De Forest's home laboratory in Ardsley. He wanted to see the tests himself. Bob Carroll and Bob Winter pulled up just after Del Tufo.

Inside, they watched as De Forest played the tape of the test with the jacket on Pannell's body. De Forest slowly explained the mistake.

That day in the Conyers Funeral Home—Friday, April 13, 1990— the group that handled Pannell's body had not referred to the measurements from the autopsy that could pinpoint the fatal bullet wound. Dr. Denson had not even brought a measuring tape; he had estimated where the bullet wound was and apparently been badly sidetracked by all the stitching on Pannell's back from the two other autopsies. From what De Forest could see on the video, Denson's estimate was off— possibly as much as ten inches. Instead of marking the bullet wound by Pannell's shoulder blade, Denson had chosen a spot by the boy's waist.

De Forest knew the implications. If the bullet wound on Pannell's body had been marked correctly—by his shoulder—the jacket would have had to be raised in order to line up the hole in the fabric with the wound. And if the jacket was raised, Pannell's hands could have been up, not down, when he was shot. To drive home the meaning of such a mistake, De Forest had invited a young man approximately the same height as Pannell to the laboratory and had him put on Pannell's red jacket. De Forest marked a spot near the model's shoulder blade that corresponded to Pannell's bullet wound and guided the young man through a series of arm motions as he tried to line up the bullet hole in the jacket with the bullet wound. The only time the bullet hole in the jacket lined up with the wound was when the model's hands were over his head, in a surrender position.

Del Tufo, sitting in a chair against a wall, could barely talk. "It was a really chilling experience for me to see the boy with the hands in the air," he said later. "Because if this young man was trying to surrender and was shot, it just made everything that happened so much more horrible and suggested that the person who fired that shot shouldn't have. If the boy's hands were in the air, it increased in my own mind the possibility that the officer made some sort of tragic mistake."

He knew he would have to explain this to the public. It would also mean changing the strategy of the grand jury presentation in midstream.

Over the next few days Del Tufo sat down with Carroll and Winter. The entire investigation—indeed, many of the questions that were aimed at undercutting the testimony by the teenagers and other black witnesses—had been based on the assumption that the forensic test of April 13 had been correct. Now it appeared the black witnesses might have been correct and the police wrong. The prosecutors could not say for certain that Pannell was trying to surrender, but it seemed less likely that he was trying to outdraw the cops. The boy's hands had been up.

Del Tufo and the others figured they had two choices. They could dismiss the grand jury and start over or they could bring in De Forest, let him explain the mistake, and hope the jurors were able to come to some sort of reasoned judgment about Spath's actions.

Del Tufo was concerned that the investigation had dragged on for a long time. To stop it now and start over might send a wrong signal about the credibility and competence of the Attorney General's Office. "The various interest groups were looking at it and expecting some kind of determination," Del Tufo said, "and I guess people's blood pressure was rising."

He decided to go ahead.

6:30 A.M., JULY 27, 1990

Bill Crain decided it was time to put some action behind his words. The morning sun was already above the trees as he stood on the Teaneck municipal green with fourteen adults and teenagers. He looked around him. Everyone except him was black.

He felt oddly alone. But his conversation with Batron and later talks with his sons, Adam and Tom, had convinced him that it was one thing to speak about justice and nonviolence, but something else to put it into practice. For weeks Crain had felt the pull of his conscience to join the marchers. Today, he figured, was an appropriate time to act. The group had decided to march to Trenton, seventy miles. Crain admired the scope of the march. The sheer distance made it seem like a pilgrimage, not unlike the long march that Martin Luther King, Jr., once made across Alabama.

The Reverend Herbert Daughtry dropped by to see the group off. He asked them to join hands and form a circle for a short prayer. "God, protect these people on their quest for justice, and let them be guided by you."

Crain was not a regular churchgoer, but he had admired the spirituality of Martin Luther King, Jr., and other civil rights activists. As the prayer ended, Crain felt sure of himself. He knew his white friends, even fellow liberals, would have difficulty accepting his decision to march. But he had come to believe in the essential righteousness of the marchers' cause and the larger issues that blacks believed were represented in the Pannell case. He had been touched by the stories of blacks being harassed by police or just feeling inferior in the white-dominated world, even in Teaneck. At times, as he listened to the tales, it was almost as if there were another world in Teaneck, one hidden from whites. Bill Crain had come to believe in the need to satisfy the thirst by blacks to find they could trust the justice system.

He was still bothered by the militant chanting, though he also thought liberal whites were using the chanting as an excuse to stay away from the marches or to avoid facing the concerns of blacks. But Crain had come for his own reasons too. He believed his presence was a statement in favor of nonviolence. He wanted teenagers such as Batron to understand that nonviolence could work.

Crain had heard Charles Webster talk about Gandhi in some of the meetings he had attended. And when Webster mentioned the idea by members of the African Council to march to Trenton and attempt to resurrect some of the moral energy that King had galvanized during his march from Selma to Montgomery in 1965. Crain felt pulled to join. The length of the march, down the spine of New Jersey, through the black urban core of Newark, through the white, blue-collar sections of New Brunswick, through the leafy streets of Princeton, would put the group in touch with almost every population group in the state.

The marchers wanted to meet with Governor Florio at Drumthwacket. What they didn't know is that Florio's staff had already arranged for him to be out of town.

TWENTY-FOUR HOURS LATER, PRINCETON

Dawn. The group had marched all night. Sometime after 2:00 A.M. Al Sharpton pulled up. He had just gotten out of jail in New York City after a weeklong sentence for a protest march he had led there. Crain had never met Sharpton. Seeing him, in the early hours of the morning, with no television cameras around, on the lonely stretch of Route 27 in New Jersey, Crain was impressed. Sharpton marched two hours with the group, then left.

In Princeton now the group rested at the police station, slouching against the brick walls of the lobby. Crain could look through floor-to-ceiling windows and see a monument to another long march. Two centuries earlier George Washington had led his ragged troops from Valley Forge through Trenton and finally to Princeton, in the series of victorious battles against the British that built morale and confidence throughout the colonies.

Crain felt ragged too. At one point he had gulped white grape juice from a bottle and remarked, "That's the best apple juice I ever tasted."

"Ah, Bill," someone said, chuckling, "that was grape juice."

It got a big laugh, and the other marchers were still teasing Crain about it. On the road Crain felt a closeness to the other marchers. Webster had lost several toenails during the long hours of walking. Some of the women had blisters so large that they couldn't walk anymore and had to ride in a van. One of the marchers, Bill Jones, a physician, had said he was too sick to march. He marched for long sections anyway, Crain noted.

Walking the entire route was Phillip David Pannell. Crain knew him only from news photos. As he walked with Pannell, he had come to admire him too. Yes, Pannell might have had his troubles with alcohol and drugs, but Crain found a fundamental decency in the man. When Pannell attempted to deliver a letter to Florio's mansion and could not get in, Crain felt saddened. Pannell had walked so far, yet the most he could accomplish was to hand the letter through the iron gate at Drumthwacket.

One of the other men looked across the lawn to the white columned governor's mansion. "Looks like a plantation," he said.

It was meant as a sarcastic remark, but Crain sensed it came from a deeper place that most whites could not understand. Along the march it had been white onlookers who asked why they were marching, and when told, often turned away in silence. Among blacks, however, Crain noticed a different reaction. In neighborhoods of Newark blacks had come out of their houses as the marchers passed and cheered when told the cause. The shooting of Phillip Pannell had sparked an entirely different feeling among blacks, Crain realized.

If only whites understood.

———

De Forest worked most of July to complete his tests on Pannell's jacket. In the meantime, Del Tufo called in another expert, Dr. Michael Baden, a former New York City medical examiner with a well-regarded reputation for taking on high-profile cases. It was Baden who had been summoned in the 1970s to analyze complicated autopsy findings, when a congressional committee reexamined the assassinations of President Kennedy and Reverend Martin Luther King, Jr.

Baden looked over Dr. Denson's notes and the autopsy findings of the doctor who had been hired by the Pannell family and determined that at least Pannell's left hand was raised above his shoulder. The fatal bullet, Baden discovered, passed through a fleshy muscle mass by Pannell's left shoulder blade. If the arm had been down, the bullet would have damaged those muscles and nicked the shoulder blade, the scapula. But because the arm was up, the shoulder blade and muscles around it were untouched.

On July 30—four weeks after De Forest discovered the mistake— the grand jury was called back to session in Trenton. It had been twenty-eight days since it had last met, but the prosecution team had decided ahead of time not to explain the interlude. The witnesses would testify as if nothing had happened.

De Forest went first, laying out his findings, then enduring a series of skeptical questions from jurors. Unlike trials, at which juries remain silent, grand jurors are permitted to raise questions. Next came Baden. He too was met by a barrage of doubt.

In his office four floors above, Del Tufo was getting frequent reports from the grand jury. The skeptical tone of the jurors bothered him. It wasn't just natural curiosity they displayed; it seemed to border on disbelief. It indicated the grand jurors, while they wanted to probe for the truth, may have been locked in to the earlier versions of the shooting: that Pannell was reaching for a gun. De Forest and Baden were thrust into a role of having to contradict evidence that had already been presented, notably by the police. Del Tufo was worried.

The next day prosecutors showed the video of the error-filled appearances of Irin Rivers and Charles Reyes on *Good Day New York* on the morning after Pannell had been killed. Weeks before, when Rivers and Reyes had testified, grand jurors had asked to see the video, which the prosecutors had mentioned, but until now they hadn't been able to find time to play.

The timing couldn't have been worse. If De Forest and Baden, suggesting that Spath's version might be less than truthful, had unsettled the grand jury the day before, the showing of the video with Rivers and Reyes propelled the jurors in another direction, suggesting that the testimony by blacks might be exaggerated.

After the tape ended, a member of the prosecution team, Boris Moczula, began a long explanation of what charges might be considered. Slowly he described how and why the grand jury might consider charges of murder, aggravated manslaughter, manslaughter, or provocation manslaughter. He explained the concept of self-defense that Spath and Blanco had raised. Finally Moczula reviewed four "factual issues": what happened before Spath and Blanco reached the Bryant School and confronted Pannell, what occurred at the school and whether a frisk took place, what took place in the side yard on Intervale Road and whether Pannell was reaching for a gun, and what Spath and Blanco told other police officers after the shooting.

At the end Moczula reminded the jurors of the task they had undertaken three months earlier. "As part of that oath," he said, "you swore to make diligent inquiry into the presentation of matters before you and not to be influenced by envy, hatred, fear, affection, the hope of gain, or any other personal prejudices. What that oath means is that your decision in this case should be reached after a careful evaluation of the evidence presented to you and that personal biases should play absolutely no part in your deliberations. You have a duty to follow that oath."

The prosecution team walked out, leaving the jurors to themselves. In the hallway outside, Bob Carroll and the others could hear raised voices as the jurors debated.

An hour passed, and the door opened. The jurors wanted the charges of murder and manslaughter reexplained. They also wanted to hear more about self-defense as a reason for a police officer to fire his gun.

Bob Carroll walked in. He explained that if the jurors found De Forest and Baden's testimony believable, they could reject Spath and Blanco's claim that Pannell had to be shot in self-defense. "Under the facts of this case," said Carroll, "the law would allow Officer Spath to use deadly force only in self-defense or in defense of another. In other words, Officer Spath does not have the right to use deadly force in order to arrest Mr. Pannell or to prevent Mr. Pannell's escape."

A juror interrupted. "Excuse me. Would you repeat that again? I think a lot of people need to hear that part again."

Upstairs Del Tufo had deliberations of his own. He suspected the jurors were having trouble coming to a conclusion. He had also switched his view of Spath. Whereas only a month before he thought Spath probably should not be indicted, now he thought he should be.

Just before 5:00 P.M. the grand jury took a vote. By a fifteen to six margin, the jurors decided not to indict Spath.

Del Tufo sat on the news as he wrote a statement and talked with his aides. Two hours later, around 7:30 P.M., he called a press conference. Del Tufo announced the grand jury vote not to indict Spath, then said he was calling a new grand jury. "The interests of justice require that the matter be presented to another grand jury," he said.

He went on to describe what he had concluded was Dr. Denson's mistake. "Errors of major significance had been made by the Bergen County medical examiner in his postmortem examination of the deceased. The errors included a faulty forensic study and an inaccurate autopsy analysis, both of which led to an incorrect conclusion concerning the possible actions of Mr. Pannell at the time he was shot. The mistake permeated and distorted the investigation and the grand jury presentation."

The attorney general did not go into details about the tests on Pannell's jacket, nor did he specifically describe how the mistake by Denson had tainted the grand jury analysis of the case. The "process was contaminated by the faulty information," said Del Tufo. "It was virtually impossible to overcome this taint" even by introducing correct forensic test information. "Our conclusion is fortified by the fact that the grand jury which heard the case was seriously divided. In addition, a full panel was not available." Two jurors had dropped out because of sickness or family commitments.

"The case is of utmost importance to the family of the deceased, to the accused, to the integrity of law enforcement, and to the community in general," Del Tufo said. "The interests of justice can be served only by a properly structured, fair, and impartial presentation to a grand jury whose judgment is not in any way affected or clouded by the misinformation."

As a final measure, Del Tufo ordered the state medical examiner to step in and oversee Dr. Denson and operations of the county medical examiner. Del Tufo also announced that he was notifying federal authorities in case there were "potential civil rights violations" against Phillip Clinton Pannell.

━━━━

In Hackensack Gary Spath walked into the lobby of his attorney's office and faced a bank of television cameras. He wore a blue blazer, gray slacks, and a blue tie, but from the way his clothes seemed to hang on his frame, he seemed to have lost weight. Spath folded his hands in front of him and eyed the floor. Before arriving at Galantucci's office with several off-duty Teaneck officers, he had made a stop at a church.

"I'd like to thank the Lord Jesus Christ for carrying me on his shoulders. I don't think he's going to let me down," Spath said haltingly, his voice trembling. He did not look up and seemed to want to leave. Galantucci had asked him to say something, however.

"We've been praying for the Pannell family," Spath said. "We will continue to pray for the Pannell family. I pray that Phillip Pannell walks with Jesus Christ right now."

As he stood next to Spath, Galantucci seemed calm, even soft-spoken, but inside, he was steaming. He had yet to learn about Peter De Forest's tests, but it didn't matter. For Del Tufo to call another grand jury confirmed his worst fears: that the case was being driven by politics, not by constitutional principles. He believed Del Tufo—and, by extension, Governor Florio—were trying to placate the black community, not just with the Spath case but by aggressively pursuing allegations that state troopers had harassed black motorists on the New Jersey Turnpike.

"These guys are headhunters," Galantucci said of the attorney general's team. "They've done it with the state troopers, and they're trying to do it with Officer Spath."

Galantucci turned and walked back into his office to ponder the next step. Steve Librie, the president of the Teaneck police union, had already issued a vague threat. "I think Teaneck officers are going to be outraged that they're going to be dragged through this again," he said. "It's going to hurt morale, obviously. The more morale is down, the less service and protection they can give to the citizens."

Galantucci was fed up. For weeks he had been thinking of taking a more aggressive stance, as cops and others had telephoned him to ask how to counter the weekly allegations from the marches in Teaneck. It was time now, he believed, to go on the offensive.

In Teaneck, news of the new grand jury seemed to stir what had been a calm summer pond. Four days after Del Tufo's announcement the African Council led two hundred marchers up Cedar Lane, the largest gathering in two months. The group met in a municipal parking lot, next to a Sunoco gas station that had gone out of business, its windows boarded up with large sheets of yellow plywood. The night before, on the plywood, someone has scrawled a message to the marchers: NEVER A DOUBT.

Behind the scenes the clergy council and others set up a series of community dialogues. But as much as the dialogues were supposed to be open discussions for all residents, the clergy kept a tight rein on invitations. One reason was to bar known agitators or would-be politicians who would use the sessions as a soapbox. But another was to limit press attention. Teaneck wanted to go through its therapy in private.

The political scene had also changed. Despite being reelected to the council, Frank Hall was voted out of his mayoral job by council colleagues. In Teaneck the mayor is not selected by voters; after each election the council selects the mayor, and often the highest vote getter gets the nod. Paul Ostrow didn't want the job; he felt too inexperienced. But the council thought Hall had been too much of a lightning rod for criticism. Few had managed to anger black activists and the Spath family, but Hall's attempts to walk a line in the center had done that. As a compromise and for her experience, the council tapped the eighteen-year council veteran Eleanor Kieliszek, outwardly mild-mannered but a skilled and occasionally crafty behind-the-scenes player with wide support from older whites and a motherly concern for the town's reputation. In the 1970s, when Kieliszek was mayor the first time, she had achieved a small reputation throughout the state for promoting the concept of open public meetings. At the time her support for sunshine laws was considered somewhat risky, especially in the Jersey Democratic party where backroom discussions were not just a time-honored tradition but were considered a requirement in some towns since the politicians would have been thrown out if the public had known the sorts of featherbedding and sweetheart deals they engaged in.

But Kieliszek's progressive roots would not help her now in Teaneck. Within weeks one black critic rose from the audience at a council meeting, pointed a finger at her, and called her "the face of racism." Why such venomous rhetoric was directed at Kieliszek was very much tied to the odd politics and racial theories of one man, Leonard Jeffries.

The new mayor knew a lot about Jeffries. He lived in town and was noted for wearing African garb, but in recent years Jeffries had become much more widely known for his statements on race. As the chairman of the black studies department at City College, where he had been recruited for the top job in the early 1970s despite his not having completed his doctorate or published any scholarly writings, Jeffries often laced his lectures with theories about whites' being inferior to blacks. Whites, he said, were "ice people," who had stolen many achievements in mathematics, architecture, medicine, and astronomy from African civilizations. Blacks, he said, were "sun people"—far more creative but victimized by European whites. Of all the white ethnic groups, Jeffries reserved his greatest scorn for Jews. It was the Jews, he said, who had directed and financed the slave trade. In recent years he had said it was Jewish educators who had blocked efforts by him and others to create an Afrocentric education curricula, in which Africa was seen as the point from which almost every aspect of human life had evolved.

Teaneck's Jewish community was well aware of Jeffries's theories. During the summer of 1990, when a group of black residents approached the council and asked for money and permission to hold a Unity Day with Jeffries as the keynote speaker, Kieliszek and council members balked, believing that any official township-sponsored program with Leonard Jeffries would be anything but unifying.

Five days after Del Tufo's announcement Jeffries took the podium in the auditorium of the Ben Franklin Middle School. When the Teaneck council dragged its feet, Jeffries's supporters used their own money to rent the auditorium. Jeffries wasted little time in referring to Phillip Pannell. He said that the shooting was murder and that it would occur again, in part because of the white-dominated educational system built on institutional racism that cast blacks as inferior.

"We have an opportunity, a tremendous opportunity," said Jeffries. "In the death of this young black man there is new life, new hope, potentially."

What he proposed was nothing less than a revolution in the Teaneck school curriculum, a proposal not unlike that being proposed on campuses and in some school systems around the nation. "The war for control of the minds of our people is what it's all about," Jeffries told the crowd. "Agitate, educate, organize, and make some serious change. . . . Africans created civilization itself and gave it to the world. We cannot run from the truth."

What Jeffries's speech symbolized was a subtle shift in social activism. No longer were blacks campaigning merely for a fair investigation of Pannell's death. In the future their focus would include education too.

A week later Mayor Kieliszek moved the regular weekly council meeting from the meeting room at the municipal hall to an auditorium at an elementary school. She said she had been asked to make the switch by residents who wanted to voice a different opinion from that of black activists who had dominated much of the public debate portions of meetings since Pannell's death. All week calls had gone out from local Spath supporters and others to flock to the auditorium. When the mayor called the meeting to order, the auditorium was packed with almost two hundred people, most of them white. After dispensing with some routine business, Kieliszek asked if anyone wanted to speak.

Grace Borowitz, who taught chemistry at a nearby state college, got up from her metal folding chair, her hands clamped around a letter she had written to Governor Florio. "Teaneck is not perfect, but it is the best in this area," she said. "Things should not be seen only in terms of black and white. We want Teaneck the way it was before. We don't want to be dictated to by outsiders."

Among the list of "outsiders," Borowitz cited Al Sharpton and Jesse Jackson. As for Phillip Pannell, she believed not enough attention had been paid to the fact that he was carrying a gun. "Any person brandishing a gun asks for trouble," she said, "and such activity should not be condoned or tolerated." But she aimed some of her most bitter scorn at Leonard Jeffries—a "black racist" she called him.

The room erupted, with blacks standing and shouting and several walking out. Police were summoned, and Kieliszek threatened to end the meeting. As Borowitz spoke about the gun Pannell carried, Thelma Pannell stared at her, her eyes welling up with tears. Thelma's husband was not with her that evening. The week before, he had fallen on the sidewalk outside a liquor store and hit his head. He had been stone drunk. A Teaneck police officer gave him mouth-to-mouth resuscitation.

After Borowitz sat down, Thelma Pannell stood and asked to be heard. "I have sat back for four months waiting for justice," she said. "If that was a black cop who shot a white boy, he would not be out walking the street. I have a black face and I'm black, and I'm proud to be black."

A tall black man stood up. Curtis March, who directed the black studies program at Teaneck High and had marched on several occasions, thought that whites in Teaneck were living with a false pride over their integration efforts in 1964. He felt the town's integration had lagged even then. But as he looked at the school system and other municipal departments, especially the police, he wondered how a town that claimed to be integrated could have so few black faces on its municipal payroll. Borowitz's words sparked his anger.

"Maybe if the adults would take a lesson from the youth in this town, we would not have this name-calling and mudslinging," March said. He turned to Borowitz. "She said she wants Teaneck to return to the community it used to be. How long did it take this town to allow blacks to integrate into its school system? It took ten years to implement the Supreme Court's 1954 decision."

As the night wore on, the voices of moderation all but disappeared— with one notable exception: "We talked about being black, white, Jewish," said Jim Reilly, white, Bronx-born, and a manager with Shell Oil. "Not once did I hear 'Teaneck resident.' Until we start thinking like that, this town is going to have a problem."

A WEEK LATER

Spath's supporters had a new plan to make money for his legal defense. Unlike the "Never a Doubt" T-shirts, the message on the blue and orange bumper stickers that the police and others were now selling on his behalf left no doubt who was being singled out for disdain.

WE SUPPORT LAW ENFORCEMENT.
IMPEACH FLORIO. DUMP DEL TUFO.

By week's end five thousand stickers had been sold, with another five thousand on order. One of them had found a place on a car owned by Chief Burke. "I think the general consensus is that the attorney general does not represent law enforcement in this state," Burke said. "It appears he is just out to hang Officer Spath."

Bob Galantucci had a trump card. A man claiming to be a member of the first grand jury had called. He was outraged at Del Tufo and told Galantucci that the attorney general was wrong. The jurors had understood just fine De Forest's evidence and explanation about the mistake in the autopsy test. But the man said the jurors believed Spath was correct in shooting Pannell. The deliberations had not been "clouded by misinformation," nor was it "impossible to overcome this taint," as Del Tufo had said in his press conference. Del Tufo, the man went on, had essentially exaggerated the problems in the grand jury in an effort to find an excuse to call a new grand jury and get an indictment.

Galantucci, initially nervous that he would be severely reprimanded by a judge for talking to a member of a grand jury, felt euphoric. "I have a problem talking to you," he told the man. "But I don't want to let you go." He asked the man to call him back in a few hours.

In the meantime Galantucci called together the lawyers in his firm to weigh the options. *This* was clearly big news. If what the juror said was true, Galantucci could use it to go to court and stop the new grand jury from going ahead. He was willing to bet a paycheck that the second grand jury would serve up an indictment; the prosecution team would make sure of that. If he could throw a wrench into that process, maybe he could save Spath from a painful and unpredictable court trial . . . or win another battle in the public relations war.

This is pretty hot, thought Galantucci later. What are we going to do with it? I've got a client, and I want to make sure that justice prevails. But I also don't want to step over a line where I'm not gonna help myself or my client.

He had a possible solution. He would ask the juror to write to the judge in Trenton in charge of the grand jury. That way the man's complaint could be put on record, and Galantucci could use it in a legal motion.

The man called back. Galantucci gave him not only the address of the judge's office but also the address of the attorney general. Meanwhile, Galantucci phoned the judge and told him of his conversation and that the man was writing a letter. Galantucci offered to do the judge a favor: He would send a courier to pick up the juror's letter and deliver it.

A few days later the man called again. He had more jurors who wanted to sign his letter.

Galantucci asked how many.

"A dozen."

AUGUST 22, 1990, HACKENSACK

They came by bus and by car, and when they were gathered, nearly three thousand police officers had converged in the dog day humidity that enveloped the Bergen County Courthouse. Some had traveled from Pennsylvania and Connecticut.

Galantucci sat on the steps of a nearby office building and watched. The PR offensive touched off by Del Tufo's call for a new grand jury was now in full swing. A police officer from a town near Newark who moonlighted as the host of a radio show called the *Police Desk* had taken up Spath's case, devoting show after show to it. Sergeant Steve Rogers of the Nutley police force not only was adept on the radio but could hold his own in front of a live audience too. The week before, Rogers had phoned Galantucci to talk about the police rally at the courthouse. He wanted to know what message to send.

Galantucci mulled over the question for a second. For months Galantucci had thought that the media had not focused enough on the fact that Pannell was carrying a gun, often referring to it as the gun that Pannell "allegedly" carried or that "police say" he had a gun. Such precise phrasing bothered him. His experience with the case had taught him one lesson: Television news reporters looked for pithy statements, sound bites.

"Make sure they know that this kid had a gun," Galantucci said.

Rogers had already discussed that issue extensively on his radio show. The fact that Pannell was carrying a gun, Rogers believed, had thrown a whole new light on the boy's confrontation with Spath. But it was one thing to hold a lengthy debate on the radio; it was something else to speak about it at the rally. Rogers needed a slogan.

At the courthouse now the police formed up in front of the sun-washed steps. Some of the cops were in uniform; many came in civilian clothes with their pistols strapped to their hips in disregard of regulations in most police forces that off-duty guns be concealed. Hundreds wore the gray "Never a Doubt" T-shirts. But the most overwhelming characteristic of the crowd was its color. All but two or three cops were white.

The week before, in applying for a parade permit, members of the Teaneck police union had said their purpose was an "exercise of public opinion" and that the crowd would be only 150 to 200 people. Soon after the permit was granted, a message was sent from Teaneck police headquarters on the statewide police crime teletype to spread the news of the rally. A later follow-up message was blocked electronically by state authorities who believed the teletype system should not be used to publicize rallies.

Rogers, a deeply religious evangelical Christian who had organized a prayer service for Spath a few months earlier at a local Catholic church, stepped to the microphone and looked out on the crowd. He had expected a few hundred police officers, but when he saw three thousand faces looking back at him, he was moved. The Spath case had touched him deeply. He believed black activists, notably Sharpton, had used it for their own agendas, and Rogers had wondered if other officers felt that way. Now he knew.

"The thin blue line has risen from the ashes of silence!" he declared.

But Rogers drew his largest applause and loudest cheers when he invoked the names of Sharpton, Jackson, Florio, and Del Tufo. "The gang of four" he called them.

"Governor," he continued, "you've lost the largest voting bloc in the state of New Jersey. We want you out of office, and we want you out of office now. I've concluded that most politicians are prostitutes."

The police, some carrying printed placards reading NO GUN, NO PROBLEM or JUSTICE IS BLIND, NOT DEAF AND DUMB, were ready to march into Teaneck. But Rogers had one last message. "The most important factor in this case is that Phillip Pannell had a gun," he said. "He had a gun . . . he had a gun . . . he had a gun."

Rogers repeated the line, and the crowd picked up the chant. "He had a gun . . . he had a gun . . . he had a gun."

And the march began.

The group was led by Bergen County sheriff's deputies on horseback and by Spath's priest, Father Aslin. Behind them the cops lined up ten abreast. As they passed the offices of the *Record*, they chanted, "Print the truth." And as they passed a restaurant where several black teenagers turned their backs to them and raised their hands above their heads as Pannell allegedly had done, the cops again took up Rogers's chant: "He had a gun."

When the march reached Teaneck, the owner of a deli set up a table on the sidewalk and passed out iced tea and cookies. From another corner Chief Burke waved and gave a thumbs-up sign. White homeowners came out to the sidewalks. "We're behind them a hundred percent," said one woman with her children. "It's about time." An elderly man, standing with his wife, said the black marchers of the last few months belittled the town. But his remarks could have just as easily been directed at the cops as the black activists. "We're sick and tired of people coming from out of state, and they're wrecking our town," he said. "This is a happy town. We want justice, peace. Blacks and whites always lived here together in peace."

Galantucci was happy now with the message being sent. Rogers's chant was brilliant. He could feel the tide starting to change. "We were playing politics," he said. "It's almost like we held it back until the right moment, and then we popped it. We popped it at exactly the right public relations time. I don't consider myself a PR genius, but we hit them at the right time. It was a turning point. We knew that we were not out there alone."

The next week, when black activists resumed their weekly marches, they too had a catchy new chant, directed at the Police Benevolent Association: "PBA . . . KKK. PBA . . . KKK. PBA . . . KKK."

September 25, 1990

Along with a new team of prosecutors, a new grand jury convened in Trenton to examine Phillip Pannell's death. Assistant Attorney General Robert Carroll was still supervising the team, but the evidence would be presented primarily by two lawyers who had recently handled cases against police officers, Charles Waldron and Wayne Forrest. The witness list had been trimmed substantially—to just twenty-five names— and among the first to testify would be Peter De Forest and Michael Baden. This would be no wide-open grand jury investigation, with evidence swept into the grand jury room in huge loads. This time the strategy had changed dramatically, to another common method of channeling evidence into a grand jury. The prosecution would present only its strongest evidence and its most credible witnesses, for prosecutors now had a single goal: an indictment of Gary Spath in the killing of Phillip Pannell.

First, however, they had one major obstacle: Robert Galantucci and the angry members of the first grand jury. A group of jurors had met with a judge in Trenton on the same day as the police march into Teaneck. Galantucci had filed a special motion to halt the second grand jury, claiming that Attorney General Del Tufo had acted improperly by throwing out the no-bill decision by the first one. In a legal brief the defense team had inserted a footnote at the bottom of a page with a vague reference to the letters sent by angry members of the first grand jury. The footnote was more than just a legal maneuver. Galantucci wanted the press to read the court papers and pick up on the news that grand jurors were upset. But it was now almost October, and no one in the media had shown the slightest curiosity over the footnote. "That footnote," Galantucci explained later, "was a red flag to the media and to other lawyers. I thought it was dynamite news."

Galantucci had also dropped all sorts of hints, telling reporters who called him frequently to take a close look at the court papers. But he feared being too specific. His aim was to generate numerous news stories about the anger among the first grand jurors in the hope that members of the second grand jury would read them. Like many defense attorneys, he believed that jurors read the newspapers even when told not to. If he could plant a message with them, even a subtle one, Galantucci believed he might be able to head off what he believed was going to be a full-court press to indict.

His efforts finally hit pay dirt. On November 8, 1990, the New Jersey Law Journal broke the story of the letters.

Galantucci had never read the letters, three in all. When he did, he was elated. It was as if he had written them himself. In the first letter, written only three days after Del Tufo had called for a second grand jury, thirteen former grand jurors called its formation "an injustice to the Pannell family, Officer Spath, and all of the people of the state of New Jersey." Fifteen of the twenty-one grand jurors who voted ended up signing one or all three letters. But as emphatic as the letters were, several grand jurors interviewed by the Law Journal or other newspapers, went further and accused Del Tufo of being less than truthful. "We don't want to come right out and say Del Tufo is a liar, but that's what he is," said one juror. "I just pray that the governor of the state of New Jersey does not realize the truth of the matter, because I don't want to believe that my governor would go along with a lie for political reasons, when that lie affects so many people in so many ways."

Said another: "At one point we realized it's no more a matter of justice. It's a matter of hanging a cop."

And another: "We knew what was expected, but we weren't going to do it."

Still another: "I believed in our justice system before I was called on this grand jury. After I went through the experience of seeing how it works firsthand, I no longer believe in it."

As for race and its effect on the case, several jurors said the grand jury did not think the shooting of Pannell was racially motivated. "Death," said one, "has no color."

For all the attention they stirred, the letters had no effect on the second grand jury. On November 28, 1990, the jurors voted to indict Gary Spath for reckless manslaughter.

Earlier in the day Al Sharpton had held a press conference at the Apollo Theater in Harlem. Rumors were already flying about a grand jury vote, and Sharpton issued a threat: "We have no choice but to turn Teaneck upside down if they come back with anything less than a murder indictment. We're calling on all students to stay home from school if a no-bill is announced. We want to penalize the area for the death of Phillip Pannell."

Sharpton didn't confine his threat to Teaneck or the justice system. He had a message for blacks too. "When this verdict drops," he said, "my assignment is I will put a necklace on any Uncle Tom that jumps on television or radio talking anything other than justice."

In Trenton Attorney General Del Tufo had heard enough of Sharpton's threats. He called a press conference of his own and let loose with what seemed to be months of pent-up anger. "The conduct of Mr. Sharpton in calling for turmoil and even worse is outrageous, but assuredly, neither untypical nor unexpected," Del Tufo proclaimed. "He is, as he has demonstrated so vividly in the past, a pariah, a piranha who feeds on human misery, who exploits tragedy, grief, and racial difference for his own self-aggrandizement.

"The grand jury has acted," said Del Tufo in announcing the indictment. "But we should all be mindful that an indictment is but a charge. Without acrimony, but rather with compassion and understanding, let us endeavor to have the further operation of democratic processes take their course."

THAT SAME NIGHT

Gary Spath drove to Galantucci's office with his wife to hear the news. As with the first grand jury, he expected to be indicted. He walked into the hallway outside Galantucci's suite of offices, the same place where he had last spoken to the press. He drew a deep breath up through his nose and pressed his lips together as he looked into television cameras. He seemed like a man who was working hard to hold back whatever he was feeling. He looked down as he spoke.

"I'm very hurt, and I'm disappointed," Spath said. "The one good thing about this is that the truth will come out. Everyone will find out the truth. I know the truth in this matter."

Galantucci was angry, but unlike his previous comments, this time he focused his thoughts on race. He said the attorney general had tightly controlled the evidence in the second grand jury by limiting the number of witnesses and what they testified about in order to secure an indictment and "throw a bone to a segment of the community." That segment, he said, was "the black segment."

Spath has been "thrown to the wolves," Galantucci went on. "What has happened here is Mr. Del Tufo and Mr. Sharpton have accomplished their political objective."

THREE WEEKS LATER

Gary Spath was formally arraigned in a first-floor courtroom in the Bergen County Courthouse. Waiting for him was a familiar face. In the nine months since the shooting Jack Terhune had run as a Republican for Bergen County sheriff and won. Phillip David Pannell also saw a familiar face. Judge Charles R. DiGisi, the judge who invoked a small measure of compassion five years before and allowed Pannell to go free after a drug arrest, was selected to handle the case.

The Pannells arrived first, accompanied by Al Sharpton, Herb Daughtry, and members of the African Council, all of them passing through metal detectors. The press was next and led to an empty jury box.

This would be the first time Spath had seen the Pannells—and vice versa. And as Spath walked through the metal detector and into the courtroom with his wife, his parents, his priest, and other police officers, Thelma Pannell gulped and let out a long sob. "My baby," she cried, "my baby."

Sharpton placed his hand on her shoulder as she slumped forward.

Spath took off his camel overcoat and sat down at a defense table to face the judge's bench. He bowed his head and made the sign of the cross.

He pleaded not guilty. He was given no bail and released on his own recognizance, with Judge DiGisi taking note that hundreds of officers from across the state had written letters promising to ensure that Spath would show up for trial. Seventeen sheriff's deputies stood guard at various points around the room.

The process took less than twenty minutes. Spath's group left first, then the Pannells. And if anything stood out in the entire procedure, besides the minimal amount of talking, it was the stark arrangement of the color in the room.

Blacks sat on one side, behind the Pannells. Whites sat on the other, behind the Spaths.

PART IV

TRIALS

TWENTY

THE GODS OF
IDOLATRY

There are few occasions in Teaneck for its mixture of racial, ethnic, and religious tribes, subtribes, and cross-pollinated tribes to gather under one roof and celebrate their common ground without treading on spirituality, pride, history, or tradition. One of those times is Thanksgiving.

With its secular roots and its universal impulses toward sharing and family ties—not to mention a place on the calendar that did not interfere with any major religious, ethnic, or racial holidays—Thanksgiving in Teaneck had been viewed as an invitation to bring people together. The week before Gary Spath was indicted, the Reverend Mandy Derr stood at the pulpit of the Teaneck Jewish Center. He was proud of what he saw. Here, as two hundred people were gathered in a synagogue, he could see the flesh-and-blood evidence of what made Teaneck great. Jews sat with Christians, who sat next to a few Muslims, who in turn sat near a smattering of Baha'is and agnostics and atheists and Ethical Culturalists. It was an amalgam of shades: whites, blacks, Asians from India, Pakistan, the Philippines, Latin Americans, and the various blends that come from marriage. On that night many of the emotional currents that had crossed Teaneck during the last seven months had found their way into the synagogue. Spath supporters, who thought there shouldn't even have been a grand jury investigation, much less an indictment, sat with blacks and a few whites who were campaigning for a trial and vast changes in the police department and school system. The ceremony had been conceived years before by the clergy council as an "interfaith" service to celebrate Thanksgiving, but often the keynote speaker tiptoed around religion and instead dwelled on the generalized themes that the holiday evoked.

On this evening Derr decided he would not sidestep religion and instead make a point of mentioning three great traditions. He began with the Shema, the Jewish prayer from the Book of Deuteronomy: "Hear, O Israel! The Lord is our God, the Lord alone." Next he read from the Christian New Testament and St. Paul's letter to the Ephesians: "There is one God and Father of all mankind, who is Lord of all, works through all, and is in all." Finally he quoted the Koran: "There is no God but Allah."

Derr wanted to remind the crowd that the three religions had some things in common: a belief that there is a supreme being and a central moral code. But the readings were merely an introduction to the real point he wanted to make: that America, in its need to emphasize differences and individualism, was creating idols of selfishness, self-indulgence, and self-importance. In Teaneck, Derr thought, the idols had taken on a grotesque form.

For months he had watched the bile that seeped from the town's racial corners into its main stream. Lately the self-righteousness of the most extreme sides—the Spath and Pannell supporters—had seemed to worsen. Black activists had staged almost three dozen marches through town, with the chanting of "Murderer" banging into the town's stability like a sledgehammer on concrete. Likewise, the massive police march a few months earlier, with its provocative chant of "He had a gun," had been pulverizing. Not only had the demonstration angered blacks, but many whites, especially liberals, had said afterward that in showing off their unity (and numbers), the police had exhibited the same sort of arrogance for which they criticized black activists. It had not helped that the police had used a town garage to store placards and had publicized the march over the statewide police teletype. For Derr, the council meetings had become less a reasoned debate than a meanspirited verbal circus, where some residents used the open-microphone "good and welfare" segment to spout accusations and conspiracies. On one evening Professor Leonard Jeffries had stepped to the microphone, turned his back on the council, and lectured the audience for twenty minutes about racism, African civilization, and the need to revamp the nation's education system. Derr had stopped attending the meetings because he had gone home too many times depressed and upset, wondering why a town with so much reverence for differences between peoples had declared war on itself in such a contemptuous way. Chief Burke had been forced into retirement, a move Derr supported, thinking that it might calm some of the most extreme voices and open a door to reforming the police department. Derr also knew that many whites, including those supporting Spath, considered Burke's forced retirement a political bone that had been thrown to blacks. At the same time Derr had begun to hear a new and disquieting message: that whites had done enough in desegregating schools in the 1960s and what blacks wanted now was too much.

But what exactly did blacks want? Derr was puzzled in part because it was difficult to pinpoint who spoke for the majority of blacks in Teaneck. Was it the marchers on Cedar Lane each Saturday? The stormy orators at council meetings? The men like Art Gardner who had walked Teaneck Road at night trying to keep black teens from getting into confrontations with cops? Derr had heard that some black families were taking their children—especially their boys—out of the high school because they feared gang violence or peer pressure by fellow blacks to stay out of white-dominated honors courses so as not to "act white." Derr wondered if anyone listened to concerns of those families. Within the year two black families were to file a lawsuit asking Teaneck to pay their school tuitions elsewhere because of their fears for their sons' well-being.

On November 1, 1990, All Saints' Day, a series of gang fights had broken out at Teaneck High School, and for Derr it underscored how vulnerable the town was. Indeed, school authorities were now saying publicly that a group of thirty students had been continually disrupting the school since Pannell had been shot. The fear of ongoing trouble had prompted the school to cancel its annual homecoming bonfire, usually held on the same night as the Thanksgiving interfaith service. And before Spath's indictment, administrators sent home a letter advising parents to keep their children inside when the grand jury rendered its decision. What school officials and others weren't saying was that all but a few troublemakers were black. Derr knew that, as did almost anyone who plugged into the town's gossip network; the color of the combatants had become a central part of nearly every conversation about school violence. That so many white people gossiped about this, but that few would speak about its implications publicly, was ample evidence to Derr of how fearful and divided the town had become. In-his view, neither side seemed to understand the damage being done. Extremists had come to believe that the turmoil was necessary to prove a point, private and public.

By Thanksgiving Derr believed that self-righteousness was beginning to take a destructive toll on Teaneck that would be difficult to repair. When he began his sermon in the synagogue, Derr wanted to remind the town of the damage already done.

"In Teaneck we burn incense to that particular idolatrous trait gratuitousness, when some of us claim, 'We have given them so much since 1964, what more do they want?' as if we are the bestowers of rights to others, rather than receivers of equal rights and equal privileges from the one God we claim. This false god is contentious, encouraging us to see our own agendas rather than the common good. Most of all, this god is self-congratulating. It is invoked every time we are pleased with what we've done, usually in the past. And unwilling to see the need for further action, for change, even for repentance for today and for tomorrow. We find a hymn to that idol, which sounds an awful lot like an old nursery rhyme and is accompanied by extensive back patting. This year, in particular, you can hear it all over town: 'Little Jack Horner sat in a corner, eating his Christmas pie. Stuck in his thumb, pulled out a plum, and said, "What a good boy am I." ' "

Derr did not feel particularly hopeful, but he wanted to leave a hopeful message.

"We celebrate Thanksgiving this year in an America whose communal morality is adrift. . . . We celebrate Thanksgiving this year in a world where nationalism and ethnicism and sectarianism are on the rise and community is in retreat. We celebrate Thanksgiving this year in Teaneck, a town that is a microcosm of nearly every diversity on the face of the earth, and precisely because we are that microcosm, we must together resolve to make community work. . . . Together we must move from that first tenet of our faith—the oneness of God—to the second, common to us all: to love our neighbors as we love ourselves. . . . Then Thanksgiving in Teaneck will be what Thanksgiving was designed to be: the common sharing of brothers and sisters of all the gifts our God had given."

———

In all his years in Teaneck Batron Johnson had hardly ever ventured into the white neighborhoods on the northwest side where Gary Spath had been raised. On the days when he did, he came away with the feeling that he was not merely in another neighborhood but in another world. "When I was seven or eight, my friends and I would ride our bikes all over town," Batron said. "We noticed that the majority of the colored people lived over here, in the northeast. Over there, on the white side, it's separate. They have more money than we do. Even the black people on that side have more money. They don't know what we have to go through here, especially the rivalries with Hackensack and Englewood. They don't have to worry about when they get outside about looking behind to see who is behind them. Here you have to worry about that."

Batron had biked to the Cedar Lane business district, but those trips also had been rare and, on one occasion, filled with a painful experience. A summer day a few years before, he had gone to a five-and-dime store to buy a squirt gun. But as he roamed the aisles, he sensed the white manager was following him.

Batron, in junior high school at that point and on the cusp of his teens, had known already that black kids were treated with a measure of suspicion. On some days when he rode his bicycle to the Thomas Jefferson Middle School and passed through white neighborhoods near the golf course, he felt the presence of police patrols, not stopping him but watching nonetheless. "I felt that if I was a white kid over there, the cops would have kept going," he said later. "I knew they were keeping an eye on me. I didn't know if it was harassing. I didn't tell my mom."

On that day at the five-and-dime Batron became upset with the manager. He felt the urge to say something but stopped himself. He bought his squirt gun, then left. He never went back. "This is my neighborhood," he said years later, pointing to the block in front of his house. "This is what I call Teaneck. I don't know the other part of town. Don't need to."

The feeling was common among black kids in Teaneck, but many adults were largely unaware. Art Gardner didn't notice it until he took a group of black students to a hamburger joint one evening. He happened to drive through the northwest side of town, on a shortcut, taking Winthrop Road, one of the wealthiest streets in Teaneck. As he listened to the boys marveling at the colonial and Tudor mansions that sit on Winthrop's wide and deep lawns, Gardner realized they had never been to this part of town before.

Gardner wondered why. Kids today had bicycles. And certainly they could walk; Winthrop Road wasn't that far from their homes. Only railroad tracks separated the two neighborhoods. But the more he talked to the boys, the more he realized that one reason blacks stuck to their side of town was that they felt comfortable there.

Jackie Smith knew that feeling. In 1990 he was a detective with the Englewood Police Department, but as a black kid growing up in Englewood in the 1960s he often cut through Teaneck's white northwest side on the way to visit friends in Hackensack. Invariably he remembers police stopping to ask what he was doing. Smith would say he was just passing through, but he got the message.

During the summer after Phillip was killed, Batron was out joyriding one night with two other boys, Jimmy and Raheem. They cruised down Cedar Lane and headed toward Hackensack on the way to a Burger King. As they passed the Sunoco station where the "Never a Doubt" graffiti had been painted, Batron noticed a group of students in a parking lot. Raheem wheeled the car on a U-turn. The boys drove by the lot, noticing two Teaneck police cars who appeared to be watching the students. They drove another block, pulled into a parking lot at a grocery store, and made another U-turn to head back toward Hackensack and the Burger King. As they passed the Sunoco station, a Teaneck police car waited to join the Cedar Lane traffic. Officer Wayne Blanco was behind the wheel.

Jimmy looked out and gave Blanco the finger. The boys laughed and drove on. Two blocks later Blanco was on their tail, the lights atop his police cruiser flashing. The boys pulled over.

Blanco got out and walked to the driver's window and asked for Raheem's license and registration. Batron sat in the back. Like the others, he was silent. As Blanco looked at Raheem's license and registration, Batron noticed something move on the passenger side of the car. He turned to see another police officer, a backup. Batron looked at the cop's hand; he had drawn his pistol.

"He's got a gun out," Batron yelled. "He's got his gun out."

The boys turned around. The cop had taken his .357 magnum from its holster and was pointing it at the ground. Batron didn't know what to think; he didn't move. The others also stayed still. Blanco handed back Raheem's license and registration and told the boys they could go. The other officer holstered his gun.

Now, in late November, Batron had his own guns. In the days just before Thanksgiving Batron Johnson received a gift from a friend, a .25-caliber pistol. Two weeks later the same friend gave Batron a .32-caliber pistol. "I didn't take them to parties or to school," said Batron.

"I took them when I was by myself on the street." But he didn't think he needed protection from the cops even though the incident with Blanco still bothered him. Cops, in turn, feared making stops because of the rumor on the street that black teenagers were carrying guns and looking to shoot an officer.

Batron had no such intentions. It was black kids from Hackensack and Englewood he really feared. His guns were protection from them.

He was a junior now, but just barely. After Phillip's death Batron hardly went to class, and when he did, he didn't always complete his homework. He caught up by going to summer school.

His junior year had been an academic roller coaster so far. By some stroke of luck and happenstance, Batron was not involved in the November 1 series of fights, but some of the other Violators were. He wondered now if he would need protection at his own high school.

On weekends the streets seemed more foreboding. Batron was alone often when he ventured out. The Violators had broken up somewhat. Rasjus and Shariff had left town; their parents sent them to Virginia to be with relatives and to keep out of trouble. Jimmy had gone to Texas. Lelia Johnson had considered sending Batron away too, then figured she would worry too much about him. And if that was the case, she would rather worry where she could see him in person.

With a gun in his belt or in his pocket, though, Batron felt as if he had a layer of protection he'd never had before. At parties with the other Violators he had known he was safe; if there was a fight, he would have someone to back him up. But when he was on the street alone, he had no backup.

Until now.

"I knew then that life is for real," he said. "Anybody could die at any time. And I'm not going to give anybody the chance to get me. If I got a chance to get somebody before they get me, I'm gonna get them. That's how everybody lives."

One evening, as he walked along Teaneck Road by Mackel Park, a car with Englewood kids stopped. The kids glared at Batron, a silent signal he had come to know well. The stare-down was meant as a challenge. Whoever backed off first was the loser—and the wimp. Batron was furious . . . and frustrated.

"If you got a beef, let's settle it," he called out.

He had the .32-caliber revolver in his pocket but hadn't shown it. The Englewood kids said they'd be back and peeled off. Batron yanked out the pistol, aimed at the rear of the car, and squeezed the trigger twice. He never found out if he hit anything. The Englewood kids didn't return.

Not long afterward Batron was driving alone in his mother's car through Hackensack. A carload of Hackensack kids, their facial expressions fixed in the macho stare, pulled up next to him.

Batron looked at the stony glares. He had his .32-caliber revolver with him. He reached for his waistband, wrapped his fingers around the grip, and raised the pistol, pointing it. The stone faces cracked, and Batron caught a glimmer of surprise and fear. The car with the Hackensack boys sped off. Batron jammed the gun back in his belt and smiled to himself.

In his house he had hidden the guns in a bag behind his dresser. Most days between Thanksgiving and Christmas Batron selected one of them to carry. Just before Christmas Batron's year-old brother was crawling on the floor. He reached behind the dresser and pulled out the bag.

And showed it to Batron's mother. It was the .25 caliber.

Lelia Johnson yelled at Batron that night, scolding him. Batron was silent. He still had the .32 caliber. She felt she had been closely monitoring him. She decided it wasn't enough; she would keep a closer eye on him.

Several weeks later, as she carried Batron's coat upstairs, she checked Batron's pockets and found the .32 caliber.

She hid both guns, then threw them out. But what she couldn't get rid of were the worries she felt about her son and the road he seemed to be on. It had been eight months since Phillip's death, and Batron seemed more and more like an asteroid with no prescribed orbit, floating and unstable. Lelia Johnson had vowed she would not let her son end up like Phillip. But then there had been the confrontation with Blanco and the officer who drew his gun. She stormed into the police station to complain after Batron had told her the story and was told the officers had been following proper procedures, that under circumstances they deemed dangerous, the police were allowed to draw their guns.

Soon after, she sat Batron down and gave him that lecture she had thought she would never have to give when she moved north. "Be polite around police," she said. "Always answer yes, sir and no, sir. Don't make any fast movements. Don't argue."

THAT SAME MONTH

At the Teaneck police station a white envelope without a return address arrived in Officer Luis Torres's box. Torres opened it and pulled out a "Ziggy and Me" card with a drawing of a man and a dog atop a hill at night watching a falling star. He opened the card. It was from Gary Spath.

Torres had felt more and more isolated. He had not kept his doubts to himself about the Pannell shooting, and he knew the other officers, especially the union leaders, resented his questioning attitude. By nature Torres was a devil's advocate. Among fellow cops he had wondered aloud whether Pannell had his hands up and why Spath had to shoot the boy in the back. He speculated about whether Spath had chased the boy into a corner, forcing him to act in a dangerous way. He asked why Spath and Blanco sped up to the schoolyard in their police cruisers as if they were going to a fire from which people needed to be rescued.

Torres didn't like Blanco. Like Fred Greene, he thought Blanco had a fiery temper that was easily torched. The year before, Torres remembered, Blanco had chased a car driven by a black man. The car had spun out of control and smashed into a tree, killing the man, and afterward Torres remembered thinking that Blanco had seemed nonchalant about it, as if the chase and the death were part of the job. The incident had confirmed in Torres's mind what he felt about Blanco. A few years before, Torres had pulled over a car with several blacks that had been driving recklessly. In such a case it was Torres's style to approach the car slowly, partly to size up what he was getting into but also because he was aware how blacks feared cops. If he was calm and deliberate, he might put a damper on the driver's adrenaline. Speed not only kills but can cause tempers to explode.

That evening, unknown to Torres, Blanco also had been watching the car. Before Torres could get out of his car, Blanco had pulled up, jerked his car to a halt, and bolted out with his gun drawn. He was screaming.

Torres couldn't understand what Blanco was saying, and he could understand why the officer was hot, but he just couldn't condone it. To Torres, one of the worst tendencies of any cop was to let his or her anger boil over. And now, as he thought more about the shooting of Phillip Pannell, Torres had a theory about what might have taken place: Blanco's temper and Spath's tendency to fire his weapon were too dangerous a mix. Torres wondered if that combination had played a role and if another officer might have calmed Spath. On many occasions Torres wished he had been there with Spath when the radio call went out about the boy with the gun.

Other officers took Torres aside when he spoke this way and told him to stay quiet. On two occasions, when Torres responded to a call, he noticed that his backup officers took their time to get there. One of the officers, a close friend of Spath's, had even told Torres that he didn't want to back up an officer who wasn't backing up Spath. Torres had thought about telling the chief or a captain, but he stopped himself. The officers already viewed him as a traitor. "I was the Judas," he said. "They saw me as the one who was not loyal." The issue of his loyalty had come to a head when the union announced plans for the August police march. Not all the Teaneck officers, especially the black officers, supported it. Union leaders had passed the word that officers who did not support the march for Spath might not get support from the union if they were ever in trouble.

Torres complained, openly asking whether the union was clamping down on freedom of choice. And he voiced more concerns about Spath's actions. "How do we know the kid was turning?" he asked. "Gary never saw the gun. How did he feel his life was in danger?"

Cops were openly hostile now to his questions. One officer yelled at Torres in the station locker room. Others who might have exchanged a few words now walked past him without saying anything. It was becoming standard practice to give Torres the silent treatment. He had not spoken to Spath, but he suspected that others had told Spath about him. He opened the card.

DEAR LOU,

How are you? You may think that it's odd for me to write to you. However I felt I had to, from some of the many things I've been hearing.

Louie, I don't know what is going through your head. I don't know why you think the way you think or say some of the things that you've said, but I want you to know that I have always thought of you as a friend and I always will—no matter what your opinion may be or no matter what things you talk about from the past.

Yes, Lou, I've had a tough 7 months, and God knows what's in store for the next 7, but I'll never forget our friendship—no matter what. Louie, I only want to live my life with my family in peace. They don't need anymore hurt. Haven't we all had enough?

Take care, Lou,
I still love ya!!
GARY

After the indictment Torres was tempted to pick up the telephone
and call his old friend, but he never did. In the weeks after the indictment he stopped talking about the shooting and his doubts. He
thought about quitting the force, then decided against it; he had too
much seniority. He also thought about moving from town, but he now
had a roomy house near the high school. Luis junior was in the high
school too and doing well.

When he thought of his son, Torres was reminded of Spath and the
personal kindness his friend had displayed. When Luis junior needed
a ride home each day from a Catholic grammar school and neither
Torres nor his wife could be there to pick him up, Spath had volunteered to do the chauffeuring. Also, the new house had needed work,
and in years past Spath had helped Torres with painting or bathroom
remodeling. But now Torres felt uneasy about even telephoning his
old friend to say hello. He let the work go on his house.

On his days off Torres got into the habit of driving two hours south
to Atlantic City, to be alone with the cards and a drink. In six months
he lost ten thousand dollars.

———

The Reverend Stanley Dennison was getting an education. On many
weeknights, beginning in the summer and running into the winter, he
made a point of driving to Teaneck Road after a day at his Englewood
church. He parked his car and got out to walk, up one side and down
the other. He passed Mackel Park and Carl's Corner, the liquor store
where Phillip David Pannell collapsed in a drunken stupor, and the
Wonder bread and Jobber auto parts stores and CC's Cozy Cuts,
where Batron's mother worked. Sometimes Dennison's trek took him
all the way to Tryon Park, where the kids still played basketball against
a backboard that bore graffiti signed "Violators." Sometimes he walked
on Intervale Road, where Phillip Pannell had died.

Stanley Dennison was born and raised in Opelika, Alabama, near the
Georgia border, and he never forgot where he came from. The town
got its name from a Cherokee word for "great swamp," and to live
there—even after Martin Luther King, Jr., and the Southern Christian
Leadership Conference had won their share of battles against segre-

gation—was to tread lightly. Even in the 1960s, when Dennison grew up, color was the barometer of where you stood in the Opelika pecking order. Blacks had their neighborhoods; whites theirs. Blacks addressed whites with "yes, sir" and "yes, ma'am." In some stores blacks used the back doors. In some restaurants blacks always ordered takeout. Blacks were not allowed at tables.

It wasn't the law as much as it was tradition. And one of the earliest traditions Stanley Dennison understood was the one about crossing borders. If you were black and you walked in the white neighborhoods, you'd better have a good explanation. Chances were you were going to be stopped by a police officer. Dennison, who had summer jobs mowing lawns on the white side of town, knew the routine well. A cop would first ask where he was going; Dennison would give the name of the white family who hired him. The cop would ask the address; Dennison would give it. Then the cop might throw in a question to startle him: "What did you steal?"

On the way home the routine was slightly different. Dennison would have to explain where he had been and give an address. And then, as a parting shot, a cop would often tell him, "It's too late for you to be over here. You need to be in nigger town."

Dennison was called "nigger" often. If you were black and grew up in Alabama, "nigger" was part of the white vocabulary. But it was more than just a description or an epithet. In the South the word "nigger" was a verbal line that was drawn through life, a border between peoples. And "nigger town" was the other side of the line from white society. Dennison felt at home there. When he ventured out, he knew there were rules to abide by.

Up north he rarely heard "nigger." As for boundaries, yes, there were separate neighborhoods. Englewood had its poor section that was mostly black. Teaneck's black middle class had the northeast side. But he also saw blacks and whites going to school together, side by side in restaurants and movie theaters. It wasn't perfect, but it wasn't the Alabama of his boyhood either.

On his walks, however, Dennison had come to an uneasy conclusion that something was lacking in Teaneck's black neighborhoods. The black kids, he realized, needed black adults to help them navigate their way in what still was a white world, the way his parents and other adults had helped him navigate Opelika. Some Teaneck kids had absentee parents simply too busy with jobs or personal problems. Some had no parents. Others were too wild for parents to control. Still other kids were followers, too naïve to know what sorts of problems they attracted by their behavior. The black kids hated the police. It was a near-universal feeling, Dennison discovered. In recent years the hatred had worsened, but Pannell's death had taken the lid off. If a police car passed through the neighborhood, chances were that a black kid would yell something nasty.

The cops seemed befuddled. Dennison knew they had stopped telling large groups of black kids to "move on." The new acting chief, Donald Giannone, who had replaced Burke, acknowledged that. "In the past," he said, "if we saw a large group of kids, we would tell them to get off the corner. The merchants wanted us to do that. Now we just let the kids stay."

But not confronting the kids was one thing; not talking to them at all was something else. Dennison was perturbed by the line that no one seemed willing to cross. Most cops, he noted, seemed just as hardened as the kids. On his walks he discovered that he rarely spoke to the police. They knew who he was, of course. He made a point of wearing his collar when he walked the streets, and on occasion he introduced himself to officers. But as he observed the scene more, Dennison believed that as much as the kids needed to be counseled, cops needed someone to talk with too.

One evening, months after Pannell's death, he spoke briefly with an officer who had parked his car by the curb near the Bryant School playground.

"This is where we staged some of the marches," Dennison said.

The officer nodded. He said he had been assigned to several as an escort. Dennison thought he seemed tired.

"What do you think of the situation?"

"I don't like the atmosphere in the community," the officer said. "I didn't harass anybody. I didn't shoot anybody. I'm just doing my job. I'm not prejudiced. I'm not biased. I haven't done anything to anybody, but I'm feeling all this hostility."

Not long afterward, as Dennison walked south on Teaneck Road, past Carl's Corner and a fish market, he saw a police officer sitting in an unmarked sedan. Dennison had parked his car in the same lot. It had been warm that day, but after the sun went down, the air had turned crisp and he wanted to get home. The cop sat on the passenger side, with the door open and his legs dangling out.

Dennison walked over. "Nice night out, isn't it?" he said.

The officer nodded. "Are you out for a walk?"

"No," said Dennison, "I'm probably doing the same thing you're doing. Just watching the streets."

The cop laughed.

Dennison mentioned that the summer had generally been quiet, with little of the violence that Dennison feared might follow the riot. The cop nodded and reminisced about how he had enjoyed working in Teaneck before Pannell had been shot.

"Teaneck is a nice town," the cop said.

"Seems to be," said Dennison.

"Especially before this," the cop said. "I enjoyed working here, but now I'm not crazy about riding. . . . I'm looking over my shoulder. There's a lot of tension in the air. A lot of tension in the neighborhoods."

"Well," said Dennison, "once we can keep the kids quiet, things will quiet down."

"Well, I hope so," the cop said.

Dennison liked the cop. He seemed approachable, friendly. But in their conversation they had skirted the central issue that had drawn them to their patrols of Teaneck Road.

"What did you think of the shooting?" Dennison asked finally.

"I can't talk about it," the cop said.

"What do you mean, you can't talk about it?"

"I just can't talk about it."

The easy conversational tone had changed. The cop seemed tense, defensive. Dennison sensed the officer was under orders, official or unofficial, not to talk about Spath. He also felt the cop was uneasy having to respond so bluntly. Dennison turned to leave, feeling it was not the right time to press the issue. "Well," said Dennison, "It's been nice chatting with you."

Dennison took a step toward his car, then turned at the sound of the officer's voice.

"One guy fucks up," the cop said, "and we all have to deal with it."

TWENTY-ONE

HEARTS AND MINDS

APRIL 1991

Paul Ostrow counted the friends who had moved out of town. One family had left for Woodcliff Lake. Another to Closter. Another to Tenafly. Another to Saddle River. Another to Hillsdale. Another to Glen Rock. He didn't have to be told why. Whites were fearful of their future in Teaneck. The migration had not yet turned into a deluge; so far it was just a slow trickle. But Ostrow could feel it. He wondered if it was just a temporary thing.

Some of his neighbors would have gone anyway. They wanted larger houses or more land or lower taxes. But the shooting of Pannell, the marches, and the other turmoil had sprung the latch. "I had the feeling some whites were tiring of the Teaneck experience," said Ostrow. "People wondered what kind of anchor they had in town."

One of his friends who left—white, an Italian-American man with a wife and children—felt left out by the increasing focus on race, not only in the town's politics but in the stepped-up efforts by the school district to design a multicultural curriculum for all grades. "I don't see anybody doing anything for my culture here," the man said.

Ostrow didn't think the man wanted an increased focus on Italians; he was tired of the spotlight on blacks. A month after Pannell's death the Teaneck school district had decided to increase its efforts to develop a multicultural curriculum. A committee to revamp courses had been formed two years before, but the Pannell shooting prompted the school district to move faster. At the same time black parents and activists had used the shooting and its aftermath as a reason to renew the call for more courses in black history and a greater emphasis on teaching about black role models. With so many black kids in special education classes and so many being suspended—while whites flooded honors courses and all but shut blacks out of the top thirty places in the high school graduating class—some local black educators believed black students would perform better if the curriculum emphasized their heritage more.

Among some whites Ostrow was hearing increased frustration over the proposed curriculum, especially the stated goal of the curriculum committee first to focus on the needs of black students and then to move on to other ethnic groups. At the heart of discussions were the same issues that were emerging nationwide: Whose history is taught and which culture's achievements are emphasized?

In Teaneck, as elsewhere in America, whites wondered if the accomplishments of Greek philosophers would be lost to studies about heretofore obscure Africans as courses emphasized black civilizations. It didn't help that some black scholars acknowledged they had difficulty proving what had actually existed and what was legend. Ostrow worried that Galileo's theories would be discussed in context with theories from African mathematicians whom black scholars were now touting as important too. Would evolution now focus on the belief of many black scholars that all life began in Africa? Would there be an endless debate over who had invented architecture, astronomy, calculus, and even the concept of monotheism? For years American schools had taught a Euro-centered curriculum, emphasizing the music, mathematics, science, writings, and philosophies of Europeans. If the accomplishments of Africa in a more Afrocentric curriculum were thrown into the educational mix, whites wanted to know what would be lost. And in satisfying black scholars, would students be shortchanged in the competition for spots at prestigious colleges? As one white man put it to Ostrow, "It's fine if my kid knows about African kings. But what will get him into a good college is his knowledge of calculus and physics." Another friend told him, "I don't want my kids in Patrice Lumumba High School."

Ostrow knew that beneath the insulting humor was a serious concern. What was happening to one of Teaneck's greatest assets, its public school system? Would the curricula now be swept up in the politics of race? "I felt like the Teaneck that I remember as a child was no more, nor would it ever exist again," Ostrow said. "That doesn't mean it's something to run away from. It's just different."

The difference gnawed at Ostrow. In the Teaneck he had grown up in, there were no violent gangs, no need to notify the police if the high school was having a dance, no need to worry about letting children ride bicycles by themselves. In the aftermath of the Pannell shooting, however, Ostrow worried about such things, especially about his children's safety.

His son and daughter were not yet in the high school. But in the fall of 1990 the fighting at the high school was not comforting to Ostrow. When he heard from school officials that a core group of three dozen students was responsible for most of the trouble, he was surprised. It was only a fraction of the twelve hundred students who attended the high school. Ostrow valued the legacy of going to school with students of different colors and ethnic backgrounds. At college he'd noticed how whites who had never gone to school with blacks felt uncomfortable around black students. Ostrow had been especially close to three black students in high school. One was now a Broadway producer. Another was a doctor. The third, Walter Braxton, was back on the scene in Teaneck. Braxton, a standout wrestler at Teaneck High School despite having an artificial leg, was now an investigator for the state Attorney General's Office and assigned to the Spath case. Ostrow ran into Braxton one afternoon at the ambulance corps headquarters. "Some way to return for a reunion, huh?" Ostrow joked.

Ostrow now pondered over his children's chances to make friends with black students. In his younger days he had come to admire what he called Teaneck's "rainbow of flavors." On paper the rainbow was still in Teaneck. But the flavors . . .

It was for this reason that Ostrow and his wife discussed leaving Teaneck. Spring was here, the best time to sell a house. They worried that if they stayed too long amid the troubles, their house would decline in value. And suppose there was another riot?

In the summer of 1990, For Sale signs had popped up like daffodils on Teaneck's lawns. Real estate agents tried to dismiss the rumors, but facts were facts: Few buyers were looking at homes—unless they were Orthodox Jews wanting to move to a well-defined community. Even blacks seemed reluctant to move in. At one point a homeowner was so desperate to sell his home that he placed an ad in the newspaper that began "Terrified in Teaneck." The Teaneck council issued a formal protest over that ad, which was withdrawn, but it was enough of a scare to cause some to remember the early 1960s, when whites in the northeast section sold their houses in a panic and in a few years almost the entire neighborhood became a black ghetto.

As he and his wife weighed their options, Ostrow saw much good in his town. He still had a lot to value here: his home, his friends, his synagogue, his walks to the library or the ice-cream store. He thought of the summer before and the community dialogues he had participated in. Blacks, whites, Jews, Christians, and other ethnic, racial, and religious groups formed small groups to discuss their differences and similarities. There had been anger and sorrow and occasional misunderstandings, but the discussions made Ostrow appreciate the town he lived in even more. He couldn't duplicate the diversity here. Yes, there was friction, but he believed it was worth it—most of the time.

"Why should I move?" he asked. "Because there are blacks in my kids' classes? That's a crazy reason to leave. Some people would do that, but I consider integration a healthy experience. But if the school became predominantly minority, then I would feel uncomfortable for my child." He knew most whites felt that way, but Ostrow wasn't afraid to admit it. None of the whites wanted to be the last ones to leave.

By himself, and without telling his children, Ostrow looked at a few houses in other communities and liked what he saw. He could get a larger house with more land and lower taxes. But the towns were all-white, with few Jews. He decided to stay put.

NOON, APRIL 10, 1991

At Teaneck High School one hundred students walked out and headed toward Cedar Lane. It was the first anniversary of the shooting of Phillip Pannell. No memorial was planned at the high school, so students took to the streets. They were led by Batron Johnson.

Three months before, Batron had joined a new discussion group at the high school. It began in secret, with a dozen or so black boys being ordered to sit down and talk about why they were fighting so much. The initial reason was to explore the gang fight that took place on November 1, 1990. A black guidance counselor, Charles Cobb, and a black psychologist, Gordon Presley, were the group's directors. In several early meetings Cobb and Presley spent as much time stopping arguments and potential fights as they did counseling. But as the group met more often, the boys branched off to other topics. They discussed violence and how they might avoid it to settle their differences. They discussed racism and how blacks are affected by its most subtle forms. They discussed leadership and responsibility and the need to succeed in school.

Batron didn't want to join in at first. He had missed the early meetings. But when he eventually came, he found a power that he had never found in any school activity before. The group met weekly, and everything that was discussed was confidential. Batron had never had such an outlet before. In February, when Cobb and Presley decided that some of the boys should be discussion leaders, the other boys voted for Batron. They also chose a name: Young Black Gentlemen.

Batron liked it. It was time, he felt, to move beyond the Violators.

The first anniversary of Phillip's death was Batron's first real test. He knew it. So did Cobb and Presley.

As a condition of joining the Young Black Gentlemen, Batron and the other boys had pledged to stop getting into fights. Several weeks earlier a man named Rodney King had been beaten by police officers in Los Angeles. Batron had seen the videotape and felt his fury rise again. Another example of police brutality, he thought. Only this time it was on tape.

Batron could not put his feelings about Phillip's death behind him. He decided he had to mark the anniversary of the killing in some way, but he didn't want a riot to break out. The group left the high school and walked toward the Acme grocery store. Some of the students pushed the large plate glass windows, but nothing broke. Batron felt good. He had told his friends not to throw rocks.

The group passed the Wigwam Tavern, where the police hung out after hours. During one of the summer marches Batron and several other Violators had jumped a white man outside the tavern who called them niggers. Today, though, the group slowly walked by, chanting, "No justice, no peace."

At the police station the students milled about on the lawn—much as they had on the afternoon after Phillip's death. Batron told them to keep moving. They walked up Teaneck Road, heading toward the high school. On the side streets Teaneck police gathered in riot helmets but stayed out of sight of the kids. A Teaneck police cruiser rolled down a street as the kids were passing, and one of the boys threw a rock and broke the windshield. But that was the extent of the damage.

The kids returned to class. In Teaneck that day it was considered a small victory. In the life of Batron Johnson it was a huge step. "I liked being a leader," he said. "I felt we were accomplishing something."

August 1991

Spath stopped by Galantucci's office one afternoon to review the case and just to say hello. He had been at home most of the summer, playing Mr. Mom to his two kids while his wife worked as a dental hygienist. In his spare time he pitched for a team in an amateur adult baseball league.

Galantucci wanted Spath to meet a journalist. Spath had little or no contact with reporters. On one occasion Joyce Venezia of the Newark *Star-Ledger* had run into him in the aisle of a hardware store. Spath put his head down and started to back away like a cornered animal. Venezia had to assure him, "I'm not working right now, Gary."

On other occasions when Galantucci had tried to introduce Spath to newspaper reporters at the courthouse, he seemed glum and tight-lipped. Galantucci knew the trial would be coming up and figured it would be good for Spath to have at least some familiarity with the journalists who would be staring at him from the other side of the courtroom.

When the journalist walked in, Spath stuck out his hand. He wore a white T-shirt and jeans. He was thinner than at his arraignment. His hair seemed thinner too.

The journalist asked how he was. He smiled.

"Okay, considering," he said.

The journalist asked whether he thought the coverage of him was fair.

"The one thing I resent is being called a racist," Spath said. "I'm not a racist, but people I don't even know have been calling me that ever since the shooting. I did what I had to do that night. I didn't want to do it, but I felt my life was in danger. To be called a racist for that is really unfair."

He paused.

The journalist mentioned that the newspapers hadn't called him a racist but that his accusers had been quoted as referring to him that way.

"I'm not a prejudiced person." Spath went on. "Anybody who knows me could tell you that. The only things I'm prejudiced against are the designated hitter and AstroTurf."

SEPTEMBER 1991

On a Saturday morning after Labor Day an Orthodox Jewish psychologist named Emanuel Landau walked up the steps to a black man's home in Teaneck and knocked on the door. It was the Sabbath, but what Landau had to say couldn't wait.

Art Gardner opened the door. "Manny!" he said in a booming voice.

The two had known each other for several years. Landau lived around the corner. One summer Gardner had placed a sign on his garden: FREE TOMATOES. Landau, who had strolled by, had taken home several beefsteaks, and a friendship had been born.

Gardner often felt uncomfortable among his Orthodox neighbors. On one occasion he heard that some of the neighbors didn't want their children playing with his son. Gardner made a point of saying hello to the Orthodox adults whom he saw walking to and from the synagogue. More often than not he found he was the one who initiated any conversation.

Manny Laudau was the exception. When the two met, they talked about their families, their work, the garden, the neighborhood. In Manny, Gardner felt he had met someone who was interested in going beyond polite hellos. The year before, Gardner had joined Landau in the town-wide dialogues. From those large groups Gardner, Landau, and a handful of others decided to form a small ad hoc group concentrating on the relations between blacks and Jews. The meetings began slowly. The group participants spoke of why they had moved to Teaneck and found an immediate commonality. Jews liked Teaneck because they felt comfortable there. Even in the 1990s many suburban towns had few Jews. Gardner said virtually the same thing. He had moved to Teaneck because he wanted to be comfortable in a town where being black and in a mixed marriage was not unheard of.

Gardner realized that it was the first time he had ever sat down with Jews and talked about his heritage and theirs. At first the conversations were careful. "No one wanted to insult anyone," said Gardner. Slowly the group touched various hot buttons.

Jesse Jackson was one of the first. A Jewish woman wanted to know why blacks admired him so much. She didn't care for his

"Hymietown" remark, his friendship with Black Muslim head Louis Farrakhan, or his meeting with PLO leader Yasir Arafat. Gardner asked, somewhat in exasperation, when Jews were going to forgive Jackson for labeling New York City as "Hymietown" seven years earlier. "It appeared that no matter how many times Jesse apologized," said Gardner afterward, "the Jewish people wanted his hide."

The issue was never resolved, but Gardner regarded the group as a forum for Jews and blacks to discuss the sorts of differences they didn't usually have an opportunity to talk about. After several months they had brought up the Pannell shooting. "We didn't know what the other was thinking," said Gardner. "Whites saw it as a cop doing his duty and not a racial thing. They saw the kid as a criminal. But many blacks felt that race played a large role in the shooting and certainly in the pain blacks felt."

In the summer the group came face-to-face with an issue that had virtually fallen upon them. On July 20, 1991, Leonard Jeffries left his Teaneck home for Albany, New York, where he spoke for three hours to college students. The speech was videotaped, and when portions were played on newscasts around the nation, Jeffries became synonymous with two seemingly distinct subjects that had become fused: black pride and anti-Semitism.

In his speech Jeffries repeated many of the themes that had become the center of his lectures at Manhattan's City College: that Africa was the center of civilization. But in the Albany speech he seemed to single out Jews for special criticism. Jews, he said, had financed the slave trade and engaged in a twentieth-century conspiracy in Hollywood with the Mafia to depict blacks in movies as not intelligent. Now, in the 1990s, Jeffries had found a new Jewish conspiracy. Jewish academics, he said, were behind the attempts to block efforts to expand public school curricula to include multicultural theories and courses.

The uproar was instantaneous, and Jeffries was front-page news for weeks. Gardner had remained patient with the black-Jewish dialogue group, deliberately not mentioning Jeffries. One evening, however, he asked the group to discuss Jeffries and what he meant to blacks and Jews. The conversation was strained, Gardner thought. He took over, explaining that he had met Jeffries and admired his knowledge of African history. A Jewish woman spoke up, saying that Jeffries might be right in saying some Jews were involved in the slave trade but that the way he had spoken it seemed as if he were saying all Jews condoned slavery. As with Jesse Jackson, the group could reach no firm conclusion. But it was a beginning, and Gardner would not know how valuable a beginning until Manny Landau knocked on his door on that September Saturday.

A radical Jewish group known as Kahane Chai was planning a march past the homes of Jeffries and the Reverend Herb Daughtry. Kahane Chai was named after the Jewish radical Meir Kahane, who had been known for two things: His statements that all Arabs should be thrown out of Israel and his founding of the Jewish Defense League. Kahane had been murdered the year before,* and the group that bore his name had vowed to take to the streets at the slightest hint of anti-Semitism. Jeffries's remarks caught their attention. So had the actions of Daughtry during a week of rioting by blacks in August 1991 against Hasidic Jews in Crown Heights, Brooklyn, after a car in a caravan with a Hasidic leader had gone out of control and killed a black child. To Kahane Chai, Daughtry seemed too ready to excuse the violence by young blacks against Jews.

In response to Kahane Chai's planned march, the Teaneck African Council was planning a countermarch past several town synagogues on the Sabbath that fell between the beginning of the Jewish New Year (Rosh Hashanah) and Judaism's most solemn day, Yom Kippur. If the blacks disrupted Jewish services, Landau thought that fights might break out. He also thought blacks might go after Jewish radicals who marched past Jeffries's and Daughtry's homes. Landau wanted Gardner to set up a meeting with the African Council.

Gardner knew one of the council members, Bill Jones, who had played football for him several years earlier at Teaneck High School and had just completed medical school. It was Jones who had driven Jeffries to Albany for the infamous speech. Landau wanted to tell Jones that most Jews in Teaneck did not support Kahane Chai's strategy.

The dangers in the planned marches were obvious to Landau and Gardner. If fighting broke out between blacks and Jews, the Pannell-Spath case would seem like a minor argument. "It was a tense time," said Reverend Mandy Derr. "If anything happened in those marches, the town would fall apart."

Several days later Landau and several other Orthodox Jews met with the African Council in Art Gardner's living room under a portrait of Martin Luther King, Jr., and drew up a modest truce. Teaneck's Jewish community would issue a formal condemnation of the Kahane Chai

---

*The man convicted and serving a life sentence for Kahane's murder was charged in 1993 with other Arab immigrants in a scheme to blow up bridges, tunnels, and buildings in New York City.

march. In return the African Council would not march.

A few days later the Kahane Chai group, fifty strong, came to Teaneck aboard a school bus from Brooklyn, following the same path of highways and exit ramps that Sharpton had followed seventeen months earlier. They chanted: "We are Jews, we couldn't be prouder! If you don't like it, we'll yell a little louder!" They marched, first past Leonard Jeffries's home and then past Herbert Daughtry's. At the town hall they gathered on the front steps and issued more condemnations, as specially trained sheriff's officers stood by with Teaneck police in riot helmets and night sticks. Then the group got back on its bus and headed to Brooklyn. Except for some verbal jabs, back and forth, between the marchers and a group of black teenagers, there was no trouble.

"I'm sure glad I'm Manny Laudau's friend," Gardner declared.

"Without Art Gardner," said Landau, "this town would have been in trouble."

THAT SAME MONTH

Bob Galantucci was finally getting to see the evidence. It had been ten months since Gary Spath's indictment. His trial was scheduled to start the week after Labor Day, but it had been delayed in the deluge of motions and countermotions. At one point Galantucci threatened to ask that Phillip Pannell's body be exhumed so another autopsy could be performed. But for the most part the case had inched ahead quietly. One of the few exciting moments had been in August, when in the midst of a routine hearing Al Sharpton had fallen asleep in court with his mouth open.

Attorney General Del Tufo had chosen yet another prosecutor, Glenn D. Goldberg. In twenty years with the Essex County Prosecutor's Office in Newark, Goldberg had earned a reputation for taking on difficult, complicated cases and winning them. His most recent victory was in the ten-month trial of a day care worker, Margaret Kelly Michaels,* who had been accused of molesting several dozen young children. Goldberg, an amateur magician and devout Orthodox Jew, was well known for his gimmicks and tricks to get the attention of jurors. For

*In 1993, a New Jersey appeals court overturned Michaels' conviction, citing prosecutorial abuses, including the questioning of the children that tainted their testimony by planting suggestions of sexual abuse. In June 1994, the New Jersey Supreme Court upheld the appeals court ruling.

the trial of the day care worker, he had brought in children's magnet-ized letters, scrambled them on a board, then arranged them in order to spell G-U-I-L-T-Y.

For the Spath case, Goldberg had already brought in a new forensic expert to duplicate Peter De Forest's tests on Pannell's parka. What's more, he had achieved in a few days what dozens of investigators and a psychic brought in by black activists had been unable to do: He had located the first bullet that Spath fired at Pannell and missed. To do this, Goldberg reached out to a former FBI agent from Utah with an expertise in metal detection who found the slug buried in under an inch of soil in a yard adjacent to the one where Pannell died. With the bullet in hand, Goldberg was now able to analyze fibers still at-tached to its nose and prove that it passed through a portion of Pan-nell's jacket while the boy was facing Spath. Goldberg believed this scientific evidence bolstered the testimony of Dorothy Robinson, Mel-vin DeBerry, and Jennifer Bradley, who said Pannell faced Spath with his hands up when the cop fired his first shot and missed. Spath had contended that Pannell with his hand in his left pocket only turned his shoulder at the first shot. Goldberg believed that by showing the direction of that first errant bullet and scientific analysis of the order of coat fibers on the bullet that acted like a cookie cutter as it tore through the fabric, he could prove that Pannell couldn't possibly have had his hand in his pocket. If he had, that first bullet would have struck his hand or wrist. Goldberg planned to couple this with the evidence on the second, fatal bullet hole in the back of the parka and how it lined up with the bullet wound in Pannell's back when the boy's hands were raised, and he was confident he could prove Spath had fired recklessly.

Meanwhile, Galantucci was secretly working on his own surprise. On September 12, 1991, he had driven to the attorney general's offices in Trenton with his private investigator, Michael Struk, and a ballistics expert for a special session to examine all the evidence in the case. Piece by piece the three men looked over what had been collected: Pannell's coat, his gun, Spath's gun, the photographs of the death scene, the contents of Pannell's pockets, and the bullets to Pannell's gun. Galantucci's expert noticed a tiny nick on the edge of one bullet.

The three had agreed not to speak to one another in the evidence room at the attorney general's. But outside, in the lobby, Galantucci pulled the two men off to the side. "What do you think?" he asked.

"I didn't see anything special, except for the nick on the bullet. I think it might be a light hit," said the ballistics man.

"What does that mean?" Galantucci asked.

Struk, a former New York City homicide detective who had solved the murder of a violinist at the Metropolitan Opera—the Murder at the Met case—and recently completed work as a consultant on the movie *Sea of Love*, knew what it meant. He broke into a wide smile. "It means somebody tried to fire the gun, but it didn't go off," the expert said.

The meaning of this didn't hit Galantucci until the ride home with Struk. The bullet with the nick had been in the firing chamber of Pannell's gun when the boy died. The nick wasn't conclusive proof, but it could provide some measure of leverage for the defense in court; if there was a light hit on the bullet, it meant that someone tried to fire it and the gun didn't go off. *Suppose Phillip Pannell tried to fire it in that split second before Spath shot him?*

Galantucci planned to ask that question in court. He might not be able to prove Phillip had tried to shoot or that Pannell was trying to outgun Spath, but he didn't need to. All he needed was to plant a seed of reasonable doubt.

He decided to keep the news secret. He wouldn't even tell Spath.

FOUR MONTHS LATER

Galantucci and Goldberg finally had a trial date. The Gary Spath trial would begin on January 2, 1992, in a courtroom before Judge Charles DiGisi. In the week before Christmas the judge called Goldberg and Galantucci into his court for a final hearing. As the attorneys were ready to leave, the judge mentioned that the list of the jury pool had been completed. It should be large enough, DiGisi said. There were more than two hundred names. By law the lists of names in jury pools were available to both sides in the case. Galantucci dispatched Mike Struk to get a copy.

Struk, who was moonlighting as a consultant on the television show *Law and Order*, knew what to do. He had already assembled a volunteer group of cops from throughout Bergen County for the task ahead. One cop put the names into a computer. From there other cops took handfuls of names. Each potential juror was checked in the town he or she lived in. *Had they ever committed crimes? Did they ever express any anti-police sentiments? What sorts of bumper stickers were on their cars? How did they vote? Did the neighbors know them? Did they have any quirks?*

The most important people in the trial of Gary Spath would be the citizens selected to sit in the jury box. Robert Galantucci desperately wanted a favorable cast. Over the next few weeks the jury pool was computerized, and a page of information on each potential juror was printed out and placed in a three-ring binder for Galantucci to refer to quickly.

"We checked criminal records," he said. "We checked whether people were known in the community, who were troublemakers or who were solid citizens. I was looking for an edge. That's all. Just a sign of what these people might be like. If I rode by and saw a bumper sticker 'Impeach Florio and Dump Del Tufo,' that was a guy for my jury."

But there was one factor Galantucci couldn't measure. When it came to the jury, his concerns came down to one question: Had any of the jurors read about Gary Spath's prior shootings?

It had been a long wait for the trial, but Galantucci had wanted it this way. It had been many months since the newspapers carried stories about those prior shootings, and he wanted to keep it that way. The last thing Galantucci wanted was for Gary Spath to be known as a trigger-happy cop.

TWENTY-TWO

NEW JERSEY V.
GARY SPATH

The Bergen County Courthouse, with its copper dome looking down on a pocket park and a statue of an obscure Revolutionary War general, Enoch Poor, can be a swirling, cascading white-water hub of unpredictable humanity. Most days, however, it is a slow river of pedantic legal routine where habits die hard. Several thousand people pass through the courthouse doors each day, many seeking some sort of resolution to their tangled lives. Some bring delinquent kids who have stolen hubcaps or spray-painted graffiti or murdered. Many come to get divorced. Others arrive to fight the hardened demands of bill collectors or landlords. Some declare bankruptcy or claim injuries from car accidents. Some arrive in handcuffs after robberies or drug sweeps. A few come to plead mercy. Others bear the arrogance of silence, confident that the connections of their high-paid lawyers in elegant suits and soft loafers and sweetened vocabularies will be enough to help them escape jail or fines . . . or both. Hundreds come for jury duty or to deliver legal documents or coffee for a judge who arrives early and expects to work late. Dozens come to get their shoes shined in the lobby or to listen to the latest scuttlebutt from politicians who wish they were higher on the pecking order. A handful come just to watch.

In this maelstrom of movement most things remain unchanged.

Schedules and staffing are cemented by tradition, and despite the masses of people that whirl through the courthouse, much of life there continues just as it always has. That is why a change in routine on the day the Gary Spath trial began caused people to sit up and notice.

Around the corner from the main lobby and down a granite-walled corridor, a glass door that was usually locked and rarely used except for deliveries had suddenly been converted into a special private entrance. The door was for Gary Spath and his family.

Whereas Phillip Pannell's family entered the courthouse through the main door like everyone else, passing by the thick line of spectators, which included dozens of police officers and activists on both sides, Spath was allowed to come and go through the side door, which was unlocked by a court officer when the contingent arrived. Spath saw no lineup of spectators, walked no gauntlet of glares. No one else used the door. The guards were courtesy of the sheriff's department, run by Spath's old colleague on the Teaneck police force Jack Terhune. Legally, Spath was the defendant in a manslaughter trial and the Pannells were the family of the victim. But if a stranger had happened to stumble upon the courthouse that first day, he might have thought Spath was the victim and the Pannells were the defendants.

For months Spath's lawyers had portrayed him as a victim of an overly aggressive attorney general, a governor whose foremost concern was to pacify blacks, and a liberal media so intoxicated by self-importance that they refused to recognize the dangers faced by cops, even in the suburbs. If the mood in the courthouse that day was any barometer, Spath had won the first battle in what became a war of perceptions.

The prosecution team had tried and failed to change the venue of the trial, citing Terhune's position as Bergen County sheriff and titular head of courthouse security as a sure conflict. Prosecutors had been suspicious of Terhune ever since he positioned himself in Spath's first and only interview with detectives, serving up leading questions, they said, and correcting his colleague numerous times. In applying to move the trial, lawyers for Attorney General Del Tufo argued that because Terhune was a potential witness—and a controversial one—he should not be allowed to take charge of trial security. Del Tufo lost his bid for a new venue, but in deference to the attorney general's worries, Terhune assigned his undersheriff, Jay Alpert, to supervise the courtroom guards for Spath's trial. Del Tufo and his prosecutors didn't know that Alpert had a faint connection

to the case. As a detective with the Hackensack police force before
joining the sheriff's department, he had played a role in the arrest of
Phillip Pannell and several Violators two years before, when Aaron
Johnson was beaten at a bus stop. Nor did the attorney general know
that Spath's lawyer, Robert Galantucci, had represented Terhune in
an unrelated case several years before. To Del Tufo's staff, who discovered these connections after the trial had begun, the courthouse
scene was little more than an old boys' network that had small regard for ethics and questions of conflicts of interest. To courthouse
regulars it was the way things were done.

Galantucci called Del Tufo's efforts to change the venue a "conspiracy" and a "disgrace." In a court brief aimed at keeping the trial
in Bergen County, Galantucci's law partner Philip DeVencentes
summed up the widespread disgust that many police felt upon hearing
of Del Tufo's distrust of the popular Terhune and his guards: "The
specter of this lurking conspiracy among sheriff's officers bears as much
substance as the phantom which stalks the nightmares of those who
sleep with troubled consciences."

For the people of Teaneck, who could watch from across the Hackensack River with a mix of relief and dread, the trial embraced almost
any meaning that they wanted to place on it. The mayor tried to sound
a note of optimism. "I think the trial will reveal the truth and the
truth will be very healing," Eleanor Kieliszek told the *Record*. "The
verdict will be anticlimactic."

Elsewhere in town the trial was seen as a funnel into which poured
all the racial divisiveness and rumor that had dominated its politics.
That the trial was also seen as the best way to answer the questions
of what happened the night Spath shot Pannell—and why—only
added to the pressure Teaneck placed on it, with blacks and whites
seeming to have opposite opinions on a verdict of guilty and both sides
worrying if trouble would break out. "If Mr. Spath is convicted, elements of the African-American community will be able to move on
with more of a sense of comfort, but some white people will not," said
Stanley Dennison. "If he's not convicted, then there will be anger in
the African-American community, especially among younger people.
Some hotheads will want to act recklessly, but cooler and calmer heads
will prevail."

Batron Johnson studied his school schedule in search of a day he
could leave early and go to the trial. He was a senior now and didn't
want to jeopardize his grades and chances of graduation, but he wanted
to be in the courtroom if only to see the man who killed his friend.

Paul Ostrow thought again of Teaneck's image; he resigned himself to expecting it to be trashed. Luis Torres planned to watch each day's televised proceedings on Court TV before going to work. Art Gardner formed a group of adults who would patrol the streets and keep teenagers from getting out of control. He called it the Verdict Night Committee.

Mandy Derr heard that a few white shop owners on the northeast side had quietly armed themselves with guns in case another riot erupted. "The shooting brought out that we hadn't solved all the problems between races and ethnic and religious groups that we thought we had," said Derr. "If there's anything good that can be said about the Pannell shooting, and not much can, it's that those problems were all on the table."

At the courthouse it was more than ironic that after months of pronouncements by prosecutors and defense lawyers that race had nothing to do with the case, the first issue as the trial began was the skin color of the jury.

DAY ONE, JANUARY 2, 1992

Of the 261 residents of Bergen County called to be members of the jury pool, 7 were black. As small as the black population was in Bergen County, the percentage of blacks in the jury pool was even smaller. Of the county's 825,380 residents, only 40,031 were black, about 5 percent of the population. The percentage of blacks on the jury pool for the Spath case was 2.7 percent, in part because the pool was drawn from lists of registered voters and licensed drivers. In Bergen County, like America, black representation was low on both those lists.

Bob Galantucci generally wanted a jury of working-class people, with more women than men if he could swing it. He said he was most concerned with anyone who might harbor a "prejudice to cops." Privately he acknowledged that he wanted at least one black juror "just for credibility." Publicly, however, he tried to minimize color. "Race," he said, "has never been an issue in this case and never will be."

Prosecutor Glenn Goldberg said he wanted a jury of smart people. The core of his case was an array of scientific evidence and complicated facts that he planned to weave into a circumstantial quilt that he hoped would prove that Spath acted recklessly. He yearned for a jury of college graduates. Privately he also wanted a black juror or two, but he didn't expect to be so lucky. In public he echoed Galantucci's comments. "I have no concern about the race of the jurors," Goldberg said.

One black juror, ABC-TV weatherman Spencer Christian, begged off, citing job commitments and scheduling conflicts. Judge DiGisi set him free. Another 98 white jurors, who cited similar excuses, were allowed to go too. For the remaining 162 people in the jury pool, what remained was a process of elimination, all of it beginning with Judge DiGisi asking questions: "Have you heard of the case? Have you formed an opinion? Do you know the defendant or the victim or their families?"

One white man admitted he had formed an opinion about the case by talking with a police detective; he was dismissed. A woman had read about the case and conceded she had preconceived notions about the way it should be judged; she was excused. Another woman had graduated from Teaneck High School years before and knew a member of Gary Spath's family; she was excused. Another woman was let go after she said the Court TV cameras would make her nervous.

Goldberg sat at a wooden table with a chart depicting positions in the jury box. As prospective jurors took seats, he made notes on scraps of paper that he pasted on the chart. At an adjacent table Galantucci sat with a yellow legal pad, penning notes to himself. By law Goldberg, as the prosecutor, could excuse twelve jurors. Galantucci, as the defense lawyer and, by law, given more leeway, could dismiss twenty.

Goldberg dismissed a woman whose niece had been murdered twenty-six years before and a widow who had testified in a child custody case. Galantucci dismissed a single woman who was studying finance in night school and a retired teacher who once taught one of the black teenagers listed as a possible witness. The judge dismissed a postal worker who delivered mail to Spath's house, a woman who knew Spath's brother-in-law, and a construction worker who had put a new roof on the home of the medical examiner, Dr. Lawrence Denson.

On the third day of jury selection, a Monday, a black bus driver asked to be excused. He reported to the judge that over the weekend, as he was making a run to Newark, a man who said he was related to the Pannells got on the bus and said he recognized the driver from court. "If Spath isn't convicted, Teaneck's gonna burn," the bus driver quoted the man as saying. Judge DiGisi asked the driver if he felt threatened. The man nodded. DiGisi excused him.

By midday on Wednesday, January 8, two black women sat among the fourteen potential jurors. One of the women—her first name was Harriet—had lasted all week. She was an executive secretary at an insurance corporation in Manhattan and was married to a vice-president for Blue Cross Blue Shield, the health insurance conglomerate. The other woman, Anita, was older and lived in Teaneck, not far from the Bryant School. She described herself as a devout Christian who worked for a church.

Galantucci didn't feel good about Harriet. She worked in New York, was younger than Anita, and seemed more opinionated, he thought. By the end of Wednesday Galantucci had excused her. He could live with Anita as the only black juror.

At his office that evening Spath's father took Galantucci aside. He had a hunch about Anita. George Spath remembered her from his days on the Teaneck police force, but he couldn't place her. Galantucci was worried. With Spath's help, Galantucci placed several phone calls to veteran cops, who, in turn, checked records. Yes, they knew Anita. Twenty-five years before, her son had been arrested for shooting out streetlights with a BB gun.

Galantucci was in a box now. He wanted Anita on the jury, but not under these circumstances. She should have disclosed her son's criminal background. But when the judge had asked if anyone in her family had ever been arrested, she had said no. *Why hadn't she spoken up?* Galantucci had a bad feeling about her.

DAY SIX, JANUARY 9, 1992

That morning Goldberg and the prosecution team asked to speak privately to Judge DiGisi with Galantucci and a court stenographer. DiGisi led everyone into his chambers and closed the door.

The prosecution believed that Galantucci had violated a state regulation that prohibits defense lawyers—and prosecutors—from dismissing blacks from juries with no apparent reason. Galantucci's dismissal of Harriet seemed to be without good reason.

Anticipating that there might be a challenge such as this, DiGisi had kept careful count of the black jurors and why they left. He turned to Deputy Attorney General Catherine Foddai, who was speaking on behalf of the prosecution team, and ticked off the list: Of the seven original black jurors, five had asked to be excused. He cited Spencer Christian's busy schedule, a black woman who worked as a maid and couldn't get time off, and the bus driver who felt threatened. The judge asked whether it was fair to deny black jurors the right to be excused or to hold them to a higher standard than whites merely to ensure that a black person sat in the jury box.

"I'm going to say to a black, 'I don't care what your reason is'?" DiGisi asked. " 'Because you're black, you've got to stay here no matter what'?"

Anyway, said the judge, Galantucci had dismissed only one black juror.

"There's only two," said Foddai.

"So what?" said DiGisi. He was feeling impatient. "Suppose there was none? Suppose there was one? . . . How do we decide that? . . . What you're saying is that he can't challenge one black person?"

Galantucci stepped forward. "I have something I want to bring up—"

DiGisi cut him off. "It's almost as ludicrous as saying that the Italians were being systematically excused," the judge said.

Galantucci started to chuckle. "There were a lot more Italians excluded than anyone else," he interjected.

DiGisi turned serious. "You know, you're supposed to have a jury of your peers. Now what are we supposed to do, go out and handpick a jury?"

Foddai said that Galantucci should have had substantial reasons for dismissing Harriet. It seemed to her that he hadn't.

DiGisi wouldn't accept that. Galantucci had the right to dismiss jurors without explaining himself. If he had dismissed ten black jurors, perhaps that would have been suspicious, the judge said. But so far Galantucci had asked only one to leave. There was still the other black woman, Anita.

The judge turned to Galantucci. "Now, what did you want to tell me?"

Galantucci spoke slowly. He began with a complaint about the size and cramped conditions in the courtroom, seeming to be leading up to something.

"Go ahead," said DiGisi.

Galantucci got to the point. He said he had been advised that members of the attorney's staff had been making undue eye contact with jurors. He specifically cited a black detective nodding toward Anita.

"I saw him nod to her, and she nodded in return," Galantucci said. "I saw that, Your Honor. That gives me tremendous concern."

He then explained that Anita's son had been arrested years before for shooting a BB gun in Teaneck. The boy, said Galantucci, "was processed in the Teaneck juvenile bureau at a time when George Spath was in that bureau. That gives me tremendous concern."

Glenn Goldberg was fuming. No one on his staff, he said, was deliberately making eye contact with jurors. As for George Spath's remembering that Anita's son had a juvenile problem, Goldberg believed a law had been broken in revealing that information since juvenile records are generally not made public. Goldberg asked his assistant Wayne Forrest to fetch a lawbook and quote from the state statute: "If the police officer in the course of his police duties obtains information on a juvenile and discloses that, then he shall be guilty of a disorderly persons offense."

DiGisi said he wanted to see Anita. A minute later the door opened, and a sheriff's officer escorted Anita into DiGisi's chambers. He asked her to sit down. The other lawyers listened as he questioned her.

The judge asked how old her children were and whether they had ever been in trouble with the police.

"Yes," said Anita.

She went on to explain that her son had been caught years before with a BB gun. She hadn't disclosed that information, she said, because she didn't understand she was supposed to. She explained that she couldn't remember all the details, but that her son had gone before a juvenile judge.

"Do you feel that would prohibit you from judging Mr. Spath in this?" DiGisi asked.

"Oh, no, no," Anita said.

"Would you have any feeling of hostility to any policemen in Teaneck?" he asked.

"No, no. I don't," Anita answered.

"Would you blame them for inflicting this charge on your son?"

"No, no."

"You're certain of that," DiGisi asked.

"I'm certain of that," Anita said.

DiGisi told Anita she could go back to the jury. After the door closed behind her in his chambers, he turned to Galantucci and said he wasn't worried.

But Galantucci wasn't satisfied. He wanted DiGisi to remove her from the jury, a deft request that would place the responsibility on the judge, not on the defense. "What does concern me is the kind of sympathies that could potentially flow to someone like Phillip Pannell, who also is alleged to have had a gun in this instance," the defense lawyer said. "For those reasons I think this woman should be excused, Judge."

DiGisi refused. If Galantucci wanted her off the jury, he would have to do it himself.

Galantucci had another card to play. His volunteer police investigators had combed the records in Teaneck and discovered that Anita had received a traffic ticket from the Teaneck police and had not disclosed it to the judge.

DiGisi called for Anita again.

The judge asked her if she ever had a traffic ticket. She said that she had, that she had been stopped by a cop for passing a stopped school bus, that she had pleaded guilty. It was five or six years ago, she thought.

DiGisi asked if Gary Spath had given her the ticket. She said no, that she couldn't even remember who the officer was who stopped her. The judge asked her if she had argued with the cop.

"No," she said, "I didn't have any argument with him because I knew that I was wrong."

DiGisi told her she could go. He saw no problems with her. After the door closed, Galantucci announced he would exercise his right to dismiss her.

DiGisi took a few minutes to study the law, then asked Galantucci to state for the record why he was dismissing both Harriet and Anita. Galantucci then cited Anita's failure to disclose the traffic ticket and her son's arrest. As for Harriet, Galantucci cited the same problem he initially had mentioned about Anita: He had been told by his staff and members of the Spath entourage that Harriet appeared to be making suspicious eye contact with blacks in court, in this case the Pannell family.

DiGisi turned to the prosecutors. "He has given his reasons," the judge said.

He paused, then went on. He cited again the census statistics showing how few blacks lived in Bergen County. "Now there's nothing further that I can do," DiGisi said, seeming to speak to himself as much as the others. "We didn't make the rules of the game. . . . We don't make the playing field. . . . The sod has not been planted by us."

Moments later Galantucci returned to the courtroom and formally dismissed Anita.

Gary Spath's case would be heard by sixteen jurors, twelve to be named to the jury after all the evidence had been presented and four alternates who would stand by in case anyone had to drop out. Eleven were men; five were women. They included a science researcher whose father had been a New York City cop, a man who worked in a Sears hardware department, the retired president of a mortgage investment firm, a purchasing agent for a securities firm, an unemployed commodities trader who now worked at an ice rink mopping floors, a personnel manager with two relatives who were police officers, and a retired trucking executive. All were white.

Later that day the Concerned Citizens of Teaneck issued a statement condemning the jury selection: "To a large extent, the justice system itself is on trial in the Hackensack courthouse. We could only react with disbelief and anger when learning that the jury will not reflect the multi-racial character of Teaneck. It is an outrage that not one African American will be on the jury. To claim that race is not an issue in this case is to stick one's head in the sand."

DAY TEN, JANUARY 15, 1992

It had taken six days to choose a jury and another three days to argue over what evidence could be presented. Galantucci was relieved about one thing, however. The prosecution had not mentioned Spath's prior shootings in the hearing on evidence. Galantucci hoped the issue had slipped from the public's memory. As the formal part of the trial began, however, the defense lawyer feared the shootings would be the subject of more newspaper stories and thereby poison the jury. Galantucci had even written a letter to Judge DiGisi asking him to order Goldberg not to mention the shootings in the presence of the jury. Goldberg promised not to, but Galantucci figured the prosecutor would eagerly talk about them when the jury was out of the courtroom so he could tickle the media's interest. Galantucci had long thought jurors read newspapers and watched TV news during a trial, despite judges' stern warnings not to. "He thinks he can control the jury," Galantucci confided to a journalist one day in discussing Judge DiGisi. "I have my doubts."

Bob Galantucci wanted no holes in his plan to portray Spath as a cop doing his duty. For that reason Galantucci had asked to introduce Pannell's juvenile record into evidence and then backed off. He wanted to plant a story of his own that the jurors could read in the newspapers or watch on television. The prosecution was livid.

"He wants to denigrate the victim's character in front of the jury and make him look like a less worthy victim," said Assistant Attorney General Catherine Foddai. "All he's trying to do is poison the jury's mind."

While the trial had officially begun almost two weeks earlier, it wasn't until today—Martin Luther King, Jr.'s birthday—that the jury would finally have an opportunity to listen to opening arguments by lawyers for each side. It had been 645 days since Spath had fired that fatal bullet at Phillip Pannell.

Spath arrived first, walking slowly. Courtroom 138, on the first floor of the courthouse, was cramped and intimate, with a pitched floor that gave it a theaterlike quality. The clock was broken, the fire alarm tended to go off for no reason at all, and heating pipes clanged, warbled, and hissed as steam passed through them. Only eighty people could squeeze into the room. But with an entire section of fifteen seats set aside for reporters and another ten for the Spath and Pannell families, open seats were at a premium. At 6:00 A.M. the first spectators were already lined up.

Spath's wife, Nancy, took a seat in the front row next to an off-duty Teaneck officer. On the other side of her a woman who had befriended the Spaths wrapped a rosary around her fingers and eyed the room, her forehead creased in tense worry.

The Pannells arrived shortly after 9:00 A.M. Pannell wore a knee-length black leather coat. His wife wore a purple dress. Their daughter wore a red parka. "For Phillip," said Natasha, who had received permission to leave school for the day.

As with the arraignment the year before, the room was divided by an unofficial color line: most blacks on one side; most whites on the other. Only this time another prominent color was present: the blue uniforms of police officers. The Pannell and Spath families could almost touch elbows in the front row. But neither side acknowledged the other. Before Judge DiGisi entered, Spath's brother-in-law and fellow Teaneck cop John Hyland planted himself in an empty seat between the woman with the rosary and Thelma Pannell. He folded his arms and stared straight ahead. Phillip's mother tapped her right leg.

For opening arguments, the prosecution speaks first. At 9:32 A.M., after seating the jurors and admonishing them not to speak about the case to one another or anyone else or to read anything about it, Judge DiGisi nodded to Prosecutor Glenn Goldberg.

Goldberg sprang out of his heavy wooden chair and paced around the well of the courtroom, behind the defense table and back to a spot in front of the judge's bench. He raised his arms and declared: "Forget it.

"Forget it," he repeated. "Forget it. Forget everything you have heard about this case. Forget everything you have ever read about this case. Forget everything you've ever heard."

He let his words sink in.

"Everything you've ever heard is wrong. Everything you ever saw is wrong. Everything you've ever read is untrue. It's all inaccurate, mistaken, untrue, and incorrect."

He picked up an eraser and rubbed it against a blackboard that he had brought into the courtroom. "Basically you have to erase everything from your minds about this case. . . . Erase every little dot from your mind. So we can start out with a clean slate.

"Before I tell you what this case is about, let me tell you what it is not about. First, this is not a murder case. No one from the state is suggesting to you that the defendant woke up and decided he was going to kill someone. This is a reckless manslaughter case. Second, the police are not on trial in this case. Nor is this a trial of the Teaneck Police Department. This is not a trial of police procedures. Nor is this a sympathy contest where you are here to weigh and evaluate whether the suffering of the victim outweighs the suffering of the defendant. Nor is this a therapy session where you are going to be asked to restore people to what they were before the case. Nothing you can say or do will ever take away the pain and hurt and suspicion of any of the families in this case."

Like most good lawyers, Goldberg was supremely interested in controlling the ebb and flow of the courtroom and hence the pace of the story he would lay forth. Whichever side managed to do that best would have a head start toward winning the case. The day before, Goldberg had lectured the press, pulling a group of reporters around him in a circle in the hallway and warning them that if they quoted him incorrectly, he would never speak to them again. He was already furious at the *Record* for printing a front-page analysis of the case with the headline A DEFENSE ATTORNEY'S DREAM and the subhead EXPERTS FIND ODDS HEAVILY STACKED AGAINST CONVICTION. Goldberg knew he would have a tough time convincing any jury to convict a police officer, especially in this case, where the victim had a gun. But he didn't want the press reminding the world of that. Lecturing the press at the start of a trial was a tactic he had used before, and it generally worked for him. Goldberg believed that journalists were essentially dependent on the goodwill of the people they wrote about, and most good reporters go to great lengths to keep doors open. On that day, though, he didn't score many points. More than one reporter interpreted Goldberg's words as a petulant threat.

With the jury in opening arguments, Goldberg wanted a fresh start too. He took the jurors over the highlights of the case, beginning with the complaints about teenagers fighting along Teaneck Road, the confrontation at the Bryant School playground, the chase, and the shots. Goldberg contended that scientific evidence would prove that the bullets fired by Spath were like the "pop of a flashbulb" that would document Phillip's movements. He referred to the teenagers that day as "children in the playground" and Pannell's pistol as "a garbage gun."

"The victim, unfortunately, did have a gun that day," said Goldberg. "It was a starter's pistol that someone had changed into a weapon that could fire bullets. Some kids were passing it around. It was attractive to them. It shouldn't have been. It was wrong for them to have it. They should not have had it. Unfortunately Phillip ended up with it. Phillip wasn't intending to hurt anyone with it. He wasn't intending to die."

Goldberg knew little about the gun, except that it was real and that Pannell had it. In nearly two years of investigating, his staff had never been able to trace how Pannell got it. As he spoke about the gun, Thelma Pannell looked straight ahead, seemingly focused on some far-off spot.

Goldberg pointed at Spath, his voice rising. "Phillip Pannell was not shot at because he was black. The defendant did not shoot at him because he was white. The shot was fired because this defendant was engaged in a reckless course of conduct. . . . He shot him dead, shot him in the back, literally destroying the boy's heart and killing him."

Goldberg turned to the jury and lowered his voice. "No criminal case is pleasant. When a law enforcement agency prosecutes a law enforcement officer, this is particularly sad and very unpleasant. But when the evidence is here and when it is clear, this type of prosecution is absolutely necessary. . . .

"A trial, as you know, is a search for the truth. We are about to embark on a mission—you and I and the rest of us—just as astronauts embark on a mission. You will be aided by the most modern and scientific and technological advances and by your own good common sense . . . to go where no trial juror has ever gone before."

Goldberg walked to his chair and sat down. He had spoken for precisely fifty-two minutes. DiGisi nodded for Galantucci to begin.

If Glenn Goldberg had tried to separate Gary Spath's actions from those of other police officers and portray Spath as a maverick cop, Robert Galantucci's strategy was to cast Spath as an ordinary cop on the beat who was confronted with a decision he didn't want to make. The day before, Galantucci's law partner James Patuto had hinted at the strategy of trying to humanize Spath. "I think the jurors, through the course of the trial, will get the sense from the defendant of who he really is, and they're going to see that Gary Spath is a nice guy," said Patuto. And if Gary Spath was a nice guy, Phillip Pannell was something else.

Galantucci walked from his seat at the defense table to the rail of the jury box and looked at the fifteen faces before him (one of the jurors had already been excused because of the flu). He was capable of loud histrionics, but at this moment the tone of his voice sank as if he were inside a confessional.

"Tragically, on April tenth, 1990," Galantucci began, "Phillip Pannell found that it was necessary to carry and threaten with a gun. Those actions, ladies and gentlemen, set into motion a set of circumstances that bring us here today."

He explained that the burden of proof was on the prosecution and that it was a very high burden. Then he turned to Spath. "Gary Spath believed that it was reasonably necessary to protect himself in the line of duty."

Galantucci stopped and let the sentence hang there.

"That's the issue in this case," he continued. "That is what I ask and beg that you consider as the evidence is presented in this case. How would you behave at that second in time? You're not talking about a moment in time. You're talking about a split second in time.

"The issue in this case is not whether Phillip Pannell had his hands up or was reaching in a pocket for a gun. That is but one issue. . . . It's a policeman's job to get loaded guns off the street. That's what this case is about. Put yourself in his position."

Galantucci's voice was contemptuous now. He mentioned Pannell's gun again. "Call it what you will. It is a gun with bullets that kill. This is not a story hour. . . . They're young people—fifteen, sixteen, and seventeen. But they're old enough for one of them to be carrying a gun that kills."

He told the jurors that Pannell was on probation. "If it wasn't for the untimely death of Phillip Pannell, Mr. Goldberg and the attorney general would not be calling him an alleged victim. They would be calling him a defendant."

As Goldberg had done minutes earlier, Galantucci took the jurors through the series of fights and radio calls to which Spath responded on April 10, 1990. But his version differed so much in tone and point of view it seemed as if he and Goldberg were describing separate events. Galantucci's rapid-fire cadence slowed. "He didn't choose to respond to the call," he said of Spath. "That's his job. That's his duty. That's his obligation. . . . You hear a gun call and you have to take precautions. You have to be careful. . . . It's a gun call. Be careful so that you don't die, so you don't take a hit."

Gary Spath had kept his eyes locked on Galantucci. But as the lawyer described the chase, Spath dropped his head and started to weep silently. A court clerk handed him some tissues, and he wiped his eyes.

"It was not a choice that Gary Spath wanted to have to make," Galantucci said. "It was a choice he had to make. He didn't have a moment in time to consider. He didn't have experts to talk with and discuss. He didn't have a prosecutor there. Gary Spath had a split second to make a decision. Put yourself into Gary Spath's shoes at the second, the split second, that he had to make a determination. He didn't have a courtroom. He didn't have a grand jury to discuss it. He didn't have lawyers to advise him."

Galantucci turned, as if to walk away, then stopped. He ended his thirty-minute talk as he began it—with a reference to Phillip Pannell: "You can say Phillip Pannell was shot in the back. Let's clear this up once and for all. Phillip Pannell was shot from behind."

DAY TWELVE, JANUARY 17, 1992

In the previous two days Goldberg had elicited testimony from Dorothy Robinson, who demonstrated how she thought Pannell's hands were raised—to ear level. But Galantucci had won small victories of his own, portraying Robinson as being too far away—a hundred feet—to have a good sighting and getting her to admit that she had spoken to Al Sharpton. Galantucci implied that Sharpton had advised Robinson on how to craft her testimony. She shook her head back and forth. "I have no connection with Mr. Sharpton. I never took advice from Mr. Sharpton. Mr. Sharpton has nothing to do with my statement."

With another prosecution witness, Detective Anthony LaPlaca, Galantucci had sprung his surprise. Goldberg had summoned LaPlaca, a ballistics expert, to the witness stand merely to identify formally Pannell's and Spath's guns, as well as the bullets. It was a routine move by the prosecutor. Before the story of the shooting could be told, the guns had to be identified and described.

On cross-examination Galantucci asked LaPlaca if he would care to reexamine the bullets from Pannell's gun. LaPlaca took out a magnifying eyeglass, not unlike that used by jewelers. He seemed momentarily stunned and looked up. One of the bullets, LaPlaca said, seemed to have a "light hit" on it.

Galantucci was ecstatic. The gamble had paid off. He asked LaPlaca what he meant. One of the bullets, LaPlaca explained, had been struck by the hammer. Someone had tried to fire the gun.

Goldberg was in a fury. He later asked Court TV for a copy of the videotape of the exchange between Galantucci and LaPlaca and studied it. It was his feeling that LaPlaca was not surprised by Galantucci at all, that in fact, this was another conspiracy by Bergen County law enforcement to come to Gary Spath's aid. Goldberg implied that Galantucci or someone close to him had warned LaPlaca to expect the question about the light hit on the bullet. Galantucci denied it, claiming neither he nor anyone else had spoken to LaPlaca beforehand. Likewise, LaPlaca said he had not been alerted to the light hit.

Goldberg wouldn't back down. When he heard that Galantucci had once represented LaPlaca's son in a legal matter, that was enough for him. It was a plot.

On this day Goldberg's suspicions would be fed even more.

He called Melvin DeBerry to the stand and asked him to recount how he had been strolling down Intervale Road on the evening of April 10 with Jennifer Bradley and watched as Phillip Pannell raised his hands in surrender when Spath fired. DeBerry wasn't an especially adept witness. He slurred his words and changed his small descriptions of the scene from one minute to the next. But his significance to the case was to come outside the courtroom.

As he walked out, DeBerry was met by sheriff's deputies, who slapped handcuffs on his wrists and led him away in full view of television camera operators, who had been alerted that an arrest was about to take place. The deputies claimed they just happened to have found a two-year-old warrant in their files that entitled them to arrest DeBerry for failing to visit his probation officer after a conviction for being under the influence of the drug PCP. A police dispatcher in a northern Bergen County town had been watching the trial on Court TV and thought DeBerry looked familiar. The dispatcher punched DeBerry's name into the county computer system that lists active arrest warrants and discovered DeBerry was a fugitive. The dispatcher phoned the sheriff's department, which was more than happy to clear its files of an old warrant. As for Jack Terhune, he quickly announced that he had been out of the courthouse all morning. He had a previous appointment for a seminar at the police academy.

Prosecutors were livid. Goldberg's assistant Wayne Forrest asked Judge DiGisi to remove the sheriff's officers from security for the courtroom and the jury. Forrest said the sheriff's department had been engaged in a "continuous course of misconduct" during the first days of the case. He had heard reports of black spectators' being searched more closely than whites as they entered the courtroom and passed through metal detectors. He had also believed that Spath's use of a special door was wrong. But the DeBerry arrest was an escalation. "A perversion of the process," Forrest said, wondering if the arrest was a none-too-subtle message to other witnesses that they might be subject to scrutiny if they testified against Spath. "If they will intimidate the state's witnesses," said Forrest, "it is clearly an obstruction of justice."

But DiGisi refused to change the security lineup. The sheriff's guards stayed.

DAY FOURTEEN, JANUARY 22, 1992

Glenn Goldberg had been waiting for this day for months. He had long believed that he could not rely on the testimony of eyewitnesses to convict Spath and prove that Pannell's hands were up. The witnesses were too unreliable and, in a few cases, too inarticulate. None told a perfect, convincing story. Each had flaws. Galantucci would tear into them like a lion going after a wounded antelope. Goldberg's secret weapon was science.

As a prosecutor he had come to believe that as compelling as eyewitnesses could be, some of the most devastating evidence in a court case came from a science lab. It was unvarnished, unblemished, and, most important to Goldberg when it came to the Spath case, not tainted by race.

What Goldberg wanted to do was ambitious. Using scientific analysis and testimony by two experts, he planned to prove there was no doubt that Phillip Pannell was trying to surrender when Spath shot him. To Goldberg the conclusion was simple yet complicated: Pannell's hands were in the air. On the basis of scientific evidence, said Goldberg, that was the *only* position they could have been in.

He brought in Dr. Michael Baden first. As he guided Baden through a daylong analysis of the position of Pannell's shoulder blade, Goldberg was confident, his measured, methodical questions balanced by his matter-of-fact tone. Baden had long believed that Pannell's arms had to be up in a surrender position because his shoulder blade had moved in such a way as to avoid being nicked by Spath's bullet.

The second part of Goldberg's equation of proof was to be Dr. Peter De Forest, the forensic expert who had participated in the botched test with Pannell's jacket two years earlier. Goldberg had been upset for months with De Forest, who did not seem to want to take a 100 percent conclusive position on Pannell's hands. "He kept wanting to perform more tests, and finally we grew tired of him," said Goldberg. Also, there was the problem of the mistake during the forensic tests three days after Pannell had been killed. Even though De Forest discovered the mistake and in turn helped convince the attorney general to reopen the investigation into the shooting, Galantucci could use that mistake to poke holes in anything De Forest said, Goldberg thought.

He was right. Galantucci had spent weeks feverishly preparing to attack every shred of credibility in Peter De Forest. Goldberg decided on a counterattack. He switched experts. Instead of De Forest, Goldberg brought in another forensic expert, Lucien Haag, to discuss how the bullet hole in Pannell's parka lined up with the bullet hole in his back and how that proved the boy's hands were in the air to surrender, not going for a gun in his pocket.

Haag's style was somewhat the antithesis of De Forest's: the cool confidence of Haag against the nervous qualifications of De Forest. And in Haag, a forensic criminalist from Phoenix, Arizona, Goldberg believed he had a man who would make a concrete decision and stick to it in the face of withering cross-examination.

Haag did just that. He had concluded that Pannell's hands were up. Galantucci attacked, prodded, and pressed him on every point. Haag would not concede. The best evidence, he said, was that Pannell's hands were up. He wound up his theory with a key phrase: His findings, said Haag, had "a reasonable degree of scientific certainty."

At least one member of the jury was already having doubts. "It looked like Haag was trying to force the prosecution theory [that Pannell was not going for his gun] onto his experiment," the juror said later. "It seemed as if he was trying to find the proof for what the prosecution said what happened. It just didn't look real."

Galantucci had no idea what the jury was thinking. He feared

Haag's testimony greatly. He eventually won a small point: that Pannell's hand could have been in his pocket and pulling out a gun with his elbow raised over his head. The position was so extreme that when it was demonstrated in court, it brought muffled chuckles from the black spectators. To demonstrate it, Galantucci dipped his head down and cocked his elbow over his head, pointing upward, his hand in the pocket of his suit jacket, pulling it up, as if he were draping himself in a cape. Goldberg later referred to it as "the Batman position."

Galantucci had done much better with Dr. Baden. For his testimony Baden had decided to demonstrate his theories by using a live model, in this case a black detective who worked for the Attorney General's Office and whose body was thin like Pannell's but, at five foot nine, was an inch shorter. The detective stripped to the waist and lay facedown on a table as Baden took an orange pen and marked a spot near the bottom of his left shoulder blade (about 4.3 inches from his backbone) to demonstrate the location of the bullet wound on Pannell's back. The jurors seemed transfixed and sat forward in their chairs to watch.

But in his cross-examination Galantucci lit into Baden as if the doctor were prescribing useless medicine. Galantucci scoffed at Baden and finally got him to concede that Pannell's shoulder blade might have moved out of the path of the bullet if Pannell had hunched over.

For Bob Galantucci it had been two long days on the attack. He had won some concessions, but they were small, and he knew it. Goldberg's scientific evidence was not just tantalizing but strong too. Galantucci needed something to bring the jury back to what he called the central issue of the case: Phillip Pannell and his gun.

DAY SEVENTEEN, JANUARY 28, 1992

Bob Galantucci got his wish, and it came from the mouth of one of Phillip Pannell's closest friends.

That morning the prosecution had rested its case. By afternoon Galantucci was well into his defense presentation. At 3:00 P.M. he called Leslie Johnson to the witness stand.

Two days before, Johnson, the former Violator, had been arrested for firing a .32-caliber revolver through the front door of a house in Hackensack because, he said, he had been angry with one of the men who lived in the house. When he was arrested, police asked Johnson about his gun and if he had used it before. Johnson said he hadn't carried it "since the day Phil Pannell was killed."

Hackensack detectives were startled. This was real news. They knew Pannell had a gun with him on April 10. But Johnson had never said anything, even when he testified before the grand jury. No one had ever asked him.

The story broke in the newspapers, and when Galantucci heard about it, he knew he had stumbled upon one of those lucky pieces of evidence that wallop jurors where it counts—in their souls.

Johnson was a dangerous witness for other reasons. He had already claimed to investigators and to the grand jury that he had unloaded Pannell's gun moments before Spath and Blanco arrived at the Bryant School. But Galantucci was willing to take the risk that the jury would disregard that part of the story. In Leslie Johnson—and especially in his demeanor—Bob Galantucci hoped to present a living, breathing image of what Phillip Pannell was like the night he was shot.

Unlike the teenagers who had already testified, Johnson did not wear his Sunday go-to-church clothes when he was called to the stand. He wore baggy jeans, a T-shirt, and a sullen, hardened look that made him seem much older than his seventeen years. But Galantucci believed the key to conveying a firm message to the jury about the dangers Spath faced when he pursued Pannell was to get Johnson to talk about the gun he carried.

"Did you have a gun on April tenth, 1990?" Galantucci asked almost nonchalantly.

"Yes," said Johnson, seemingly shy.

Galantucci proceeded step by step. He asked Johnson what kind. Johnson described it as brown.

Galantucci nodded, then referred to Pannell's gun and the pistol Johnson had. "Were they the only guns there that day?"

"There were other guns there," Johnson said. "But they weren't from Teaneck. . . . Two boys from Englewood."

Galantucci had his opening, and he was not about to let it pass without exploiting it. "So there were four guns that day," said Galantucci, noting with emphasis, "when Officer Spath arrived."

He didn't wait for Johnson to answer.

DAY EIGHTEEN, JANUARY 29, 1992

Blanco was Galantucci's next challenge. And if Galantucci had leaped on Leslie Johnson with legal glee, prosecutor Goldberg was practically salivating as he prepared to cross-examine Officer Wayne Blanco.

Technically Blanco was a witness for the prosecution. He was an officer of the law and would normally testify on behalf of the prosecution. But Goldberg didn't trust Blanco. The officer had refused to report for a pretrial interview and had gone to a Christmas party at Galantucci's house in the days before the trial began. What's more, there was the lingering suspicion that Blanco had fabricated all or part of the story of his frisking of Phillip Pannell.

Goldberg figured he could present his case without Wayne Blanco, and he did. What he secretly hoped was that Galantucci would be forced to call Blanco as a witness in support of Spath. If Galantucci did that, Goldberg could cross-examine Blanco.

Galantucci was not pleased with Blanco as a witness. He was not notably articulate, and his story of the frisk seemed shaky. But Galantucci believed in him. And Blanco, the backup officer, had come to court to back up everything Gary Spath said.

Galantucci knew the biggest problem would be Lieutenant Patrick Hogan's testimony that Blanco had told him at Holy Name Hospital that Pannell's left hand never got to his coat pocket. A few days before, Galantucci had stopped at the Teaneck police station to say hello to Hogan, whom he knew in passing. Galantucci didn't ask him to change his testimony. He wished him well and tried to leave the impression that there would be no hard feelings if Hogan took the stand with the story contradicting Blanco.

Galantucci led Blanco through an almost minute-by-minute recitation of the events of April 10, 1990. Only now Blanco offered two new elements to the story. Unlike his grand jury testimony, in which he said he had not been in position to fire his gun at Pannell, Blanco changed his story to say that he was about to fire but that "Gary beat me to it." And when describing Pannell's motions, Blanco added to his earlier version, told to prosecutors, investigators, and two grand juries. Blanco was not merely saying that Pannell had placed his hand in his left pocket and turned. He now described Pannell as pointing the gun in his pocket *toward* him and Spath as if to fire it.

Goldberg was astonished. He called Blanco's hand-in-the-pocket-and-gun-pointed description the "bank robber position" and asked why Blanco hadn't volunteered it before.

"You didn't say anything about him lifting his hand up in his pocket and thrusting it at Officer Spath?" Goldberg asked.

Blanco acknowledged he hadn't.

Goldberg pressed. "When you were asked what happened, you left out a detail?"

"No," said Blanco. "He put his left hand in his coat pocket, and he turned."

Goldberg asked again: Why had Blanco not also mentioned that Pannell had done much more than just turn, that the boy had pointed his gun too? It was an important point. Pannell's turning motion could be interpreted as not being a threat to police. But pointing the gun constituted a real threat that could not be denied.

Goldberg was skeptical. He saw this new version of Blanco's story as an attempt to bolster Spath's case further. To Goldberg this was the same problem the cops had been facing since the beginning: changing their stories in ways that didn't seem truthful.

He asked Blanco why he hadn't mentioned it when the prosecutor's investigators sat him down in the Teaneck police station the night of the shooting or when he went before two grand juries.

"I wasn't asked that," said Blanco. "We were sitting in an office. He didn't ask me to demonstrate. He just asked me what happened."

And so it went. Blanco seemed distant, unconcerned each time Goldberg uncovered another inconsistency or imprecision. When Goldberg questioned him intently about how he frisked Pannell and attempted to describe the pat-down, Blanco gazed back aloofly. "Yeah," said the cop, "that's about right."

Goldberg, grabbing a sheaf of transcripts, referred to Blanco's grand jury testimonies, ticking off the changes in the officer's story. Blanco snapped back: "The grand jury is a kangaroo court as far as I'm concerned."

Judge DiGisi told the jury to disregard that statement. But blanco's testiness would not be corralled. "You just can't understand it sitting in a nice courtroom," he said after Goldberg continued to press him. "It's a dangerous situation."

Goldberg asked him why he hadn't put his gun in his holster when he ran after Pannell.

"Mr. Goldberg, this all went like that," said Blanco, snapping his fingers. "There was no time to be holstering and jerking around."

Galantucci rose from his seat. Goldberg had beaten up on Blanco's inability to remember some specifics and change others. Galantucci wanted to interject some emotion. He asked Blanco to describe the danger he felt that night.

"You really had to be there, I suppose," Blanco said. "Gary felt he had to do what he had to do."

Day Nineteen, January 30, 1992

A few minutes after 9:00 A.M. Spath left his seat at the defense table and walked to the witness stand. He seemed relieved, anxious, impatient. Besides his wife in the front row, Spath could look out and see his priest, Father Bart Aslin, who had been coming regularly for days, devoting evenings to his work in a Catholic parish forty miles away. In those early months after Pannell had been shot, Galantucci had treated Aslin warily. But as the trial date had grown closer, he asked the priest to come as often as possible in his black suit and Roman collar. Aslin knew why: He was helping convey a message to the jury that Spath was a spiritual man.

For the next three days Spath told his story. Actually he spent the first twenty-five minutes answering questions from Galantucci. The rest of the three days was spent under the unrelenting rhetorical spotlight of Glenn Goldberg, one of its most intense scenes coming as Spath explained why he fired: "I shot because this guy was going to shoot me. He was reaching. He went into his pocket, and he was going to shoot me."

Spath's voice rose and almost cracked as he spoke. Goldberg turned and walked to a table that held pieces of evidence. He picked up Spath's .357 magnum. He walked deliberately to the witness box and asked Spath to take the gun and hold it.

Spath froze. He stared at the gun in silence for a second or two, then turned away, his eyes focused on a spot on the floor in front of the judge's bench. Goldberg tried to lead him through a series of other questions about his movements as he followed Pannell into the yard before firing, but Spath seemed preoccupied, as if he wanted to say something.

Goldberg paused and walked to the prosecution table. Spath started to speak. "I think about this every day—"

Goldberg cut him off. As much as Galantucci wanted to portray Spath's humanity and vulnerability, Goldberg wanted to focus on what he thought were Spath's inconsistencies, his tendency toward snap judgments, and his shaky emotional state. Goldberg had been frustrated. He had been blocked from asking Spath about the other times he had fired his gun; to do so would cause a mistrial. But before setting off on his cross-examination, Goldberg, without the jury present, had tried one last time to question Spath about the report he filed after his first shooting in Fort Lee in which he did not initially disclose that he had fired his gun. Goldberg wanted to show that Spath had a pattern of altering his account of events, a pattern, said Goldberg, that continued after he shot Pannell. Spath had other ideas. Throughout the morning it had become a battle of wills, with Goldberg poking, prodding, and searching for holes to exploit and Spath seeking to portray to the jury the emotions he felt.

"When you are dispatched on a gun call, Mr. Goldberg, you're in a different world," said Spath. "When you get a gun call, your heart pounds faster, your adrenaline pumps faster—you're different."

As he listened from his seat, Galantucci was pleased. Spath wasn't cracking. Galantucci was starting to feel confident about the case.

And then he went to lunch.

Outside the courthouse several members of the Nation of Islam were holding a press conference with relatives of blacks in New Jersey who had been killed by police. Galantucci felt his spirits plummet. Once again the outside world of racial politics was intruding on what he wanted to be the antiseptic world of the courtroom. He wanted a counterpunch. He had an idea.

The next day, at 10:05 A.M., the doors at the back of Courtroom 138 opened, and a man in a wheelchair was rolled in. Spath was on the witness stand at the time, but Galantucci, Goldberg, and DiGisi were talking about a diagram of the shooting scene, and their attention was diverted. To anyone who had kept abreast of police news in New York City, the man's pained face was familiar as the area's most prominent example of what a gun-toting teenager could do to a cop. Officer Steven McDonald had been shot in the neck several years earlier in Central Park by a teenager with a gun. He was paralyzed from the neck down.

Several weeks earlier McDonald, who often showed up at police events in his wheelchair, including New York City's St. Patrick's Day parade in his blue dress uniform, had passed the word that he wanted to come to Spath's trial. Galantucci had nixed the idea, fearing it would create a backlash of criticism that Spath was trying to manipulate public opinion to underscore the danger he felt that day with Pannell. But when the Black Muslims appeared outside the courthouse, Galantucci turned to an off-duty cop who was with him and asked him to call for McDonald.

DiGisi heard the hiss-harrumph of McDonald's respirator and turned to see McDonald being wheeled down the aisle by the Spath family to a spot near the front row and just behind the defense table. He was in full view of the jury. Walking by McDonald's side was a woman carrying rosary beads.

DiGisi turned to the jury and in as calm a voice as he could muster announced that it was a good time to take a break. The jurors rose from their seats and filed into the jury room for coffee. As the door closed, DiGisi turned and glared at McDonald. The judge's face reddened. He threw up his hands.

"This is an outrage!" DiGisi barked, his voice rising as he snapped off each word. "We are in the middle of continued, long cross-examination of Officer Spath. All of a sudden somebody is rolled in. . . ." DiGisi shook his head, side to side. "That to me, is mind-boggling. . . . It is something I cannot comprehend at this time. . . . I will guarantee you that it will not happen again."

Goldberg stood up. He too was dumbfounded, though he was trying to hold back his temper. For days he had become increasingly frustrated at the conditions in the courtroom and what appeared to be the deference that guards showed toward Spath and his entourage. But this was the ultimate affront.

Goldberg had enough. He asked DiGisi to move the trial to a new courthouse, claiming that McDonald would never have been allowed to enter the courtroom without the complicity of pro-Spath sheriff's deputies. The prosecutor was now convinced that the sheriff's department was actively trying to control the outcome of the case or, if not that, at least to make Spath feel as comfortable as possible. There was the special door for Spath; then Melvin DeBerry was arrested, now this. "The intent behind this is so obvious," Goldberg said. "If the state had done something like this, there is no question in my mind that the trial would have ended in an immediate mistrial."

Outside, as he was wheeled away from the main courthouse doors, Steven McDonald was asked why he had come. "I was just concerned," he said.

In Trenton Attorney General Del Tufo had been bothered for days about the sheriff's deputies. To him the use of a disabled officer in this manner was "an affront to the dignity of the court" and "an outrageous attempt to influence the jury. . . . The continued actions of the sheriff's department are particularly unfortunate because it is a law enforcement agency consorting with others in an attempt to undermine the jury process."

DiGisi called a recess. He phoned the New Jersey State Police, then talked with the county's chief judge. Two hours later he emerged with a plan. The sheriff's officers were reassigned—partly. DiGisi was calling in state police to guard the outside doors to his courtroom. But so as not to disrupt the jury or hint at the security concerns outside, he would allow sheriff's officers to remain in the courtroom.

It had been a contentious week, and it wasn't over yet. After the McDonald ruckus had been cleared up and state troopers arrived, Spath took the stand again. He had wept when McDonald was wheeled into the courtroom. Now he was starting to grow impatient with Goldberg's questions.

"I'm trying to be helpful here," he said at one point as Goldberg bore in, asking him to go over his actions again and again. "Sir, you have me here all day. I'm trying to be as helpful as I can to help you understand and help the jury understand what happened on April tenth, 1990. I've answered every single one of your questions. You can keep me here three weeks if you want."

In the audience the Reverend Herb Daughtry turned to the person sitting next to him. "He reminds me of Oliver North," said Daughtry.

Goldberg walked to the witness box and handed Spath a 1983 memo to Teaneck cops, reminding them to call for backup officers in dangerous situations. Spath scanned the page quickly, then testily quipped: "That was typewritten in someone's office. That didn't happen in the street."

Spath's strategy, with Galantucci's guidance, was to attempt to portray the unpredictable dangers that cops face on the beat, even in a suburb. Goldberg had believed Spath was deliberately exaggerating, trying to leave the impression that Teaneck's Bryant School neighborhood was akin to a drug alley in the South Bronx. At times Goldberg had even thought that Spath might be delusional. But how to explore this? The day before when Spath had described going on a gun call as slipping into a "different world," Goldberg saw an opening. *Different world?* Goldberg asked Spath to describe it.

Spath seemed ready for the question. He eyed Goldberg for a moment, a glimmer of contempt appearing to slip from his otherwise stolid expression. "It's something you'll never understand," Spath said, "unless you are a police officer on the street and you respond to the call of somebody with a gun."

Goldberg's equally impassive face seemed creased by a tinge of momentary contempt. To Goldberg, Spath seemed to want to speak only in generalizations, not specifics, when asked about his emotional state and how he framed his decisions about what constituted a dangerous situation. But Goldberg knew that cases of this sort, in which the jury might be prone to feel empathy for a police officer, were won on specifics and a prosecutor's ability to prove how a defendant did not think through his actions. Goldberg had noticed earlier that Spath seemed to chafe when asked to break down the shooting into a frame-by-frame analysis. Goldberg decided it was time to push.

"Since we'll never understand it, we have to rely on you to tell us. Let me break it down. Are you scared?"

"That's just it, sir," said Spath, his voice rising decibel by decibel, as each frustrated syllable slowly fell out. "You're trying to dissect the situation, piece by piece, frame by frame, inch by inch, and you are trying to dissect this into little, tiny pieces. This is something that took a split second. This guy was going to shoot me. I had no choice but to shoot at him to save my own life. . . .

"I couldn't believe it," said Spath. "I couldn't believe what I was hearing about Pannell's arms in the air and that I shot him for no reason or just because he was playing basketball."

Goldberg kept up the attack for most of three days before stopping. He had scored a few points, but not many. Spath had not cracked. As Goldberg sat down and assembled his notes, Galantucci jumped up.

"Did you express yourself as best you could?" Galantucci asked.

Spath seemed exhausted. "To the best of my ability," he answered softly. "There are two things that are with me every day," he said. "When I go to bed at night and I close my eyes, I see—"

"Objection!" boomed Goldberg, hopping to his feet.

But Spath continued. After three days he had felt blocked in by Goldberg's cross-examination, forced to confine his answers to specific questions. It seemed he needed to get out one final sentence.

"I remember the suspect reaching into his pocket and spinning on me, and I'll never forget it."

The room fell silent. There were no further questions from Galantucci . . . or Goldberg. Spath rose from the witness box and paced across the well of the courtroom. As he took his seat at the defense table, he bowed his head in his hands and prayed.

Day Twenty-four, February 6, 1992

Goldberg had a hot tip. Fred Greene had told friends about his secret: that another officer had told him that Blanco had admitted never frisking Pannell. Goldberg got a hint of the story and put out the word: Get Greene. Time was short.

It was nearly 10:00 P.M. when detectives from the attorney general's staff brought Greene to a room in a hotel near Hackensack where Goldberg and the other prosecution lawyers were holed up with transcripts and notes and strategy. Greene was hardly shy about telling his tale: In the days after Phillip Pannell had been shot, a Teaneck officer had come to Greene and told him that a group of officers had held a meeting at which Blanco conceded that he had never conducted a frisk. It had been almost two years, and Freddie Greene had never told prosecutors about the story. He said he had no independent proof that it was true; still, he was deeply bothered by it.

Goldberg's detectives asked if they could contact the Teaneck officer who spoke to Greene that day, but Greene balked. He felt his loyalty was being tested. The officer had shared the story with him in private and had since left the force and moved out of town. Greene didn't want to cause the man any trouble. Just the same, he knew how important the story could be, if true.

Several hours later, after detectives had coaxed the name out of Greene, they got the officer on the phone. He couldn't remember ever having a conversation with Blanco . . . or Fred Greene about Phillip Pannell or a frisk.

THE NEXT MORNING

Goldberg was now in full gear, trying to stall. He had worked thousands of hours to prove that Gary Spath was reckless, but he believed deep inside he had not done enough, that the puzzle of circumstantial evidence he had tried to assemble still had holes. If he could find credible evidence of Blanco lying . . .

Goldberg knew what it meant. He could score a tactical victory and force the trial into a whole new phase, possibly even re-calling Spath and Blanco to the witness stand.

Goldberg ordered his detectives to bring in another Teaneck officer who Greene said might have been present when Blanco made his revelation. The cop couldn't remember any meeting.

Goldberg's detectives bore down, warning the cop that his career was on the line. He sat in a second-floor office in the courthouse. Downstairs reporters, spectators, and Spath's defense team waited, unaware of what Goldberg was up to. The cop shook his head. He couldn't remember.

Goldberg and his staff headed back downstairs to the trial. "I wish," he said, "we knew about this earlier."

SATURDAY, FEBRUARY 8, 1992, TEANECK

Al Sharpton was back. He had come to the Spath trial just one day and had fallen asleep. But on this Saturday he had broken free of the legal troubles in Brooklyn that had tied him up for weeks, and he brought two buses of supporters to link up with marchers in Teaneck.

The group, about three hundred, gathered first at the Bryant School, then set off for the Bergen County Courthouse, four miles away. Except for the trek to Trenton, this was the most ambitious march yet.

A cold rain fell as the group set out, Sharpton in the lead, clad in a long leather coat and a blue jogging suit. One of his followers held an umbrella over his head. Another wore an exact copy of the red parka of the one Phillip Pannell had died in. Halfway into the march several reporters noticed a blue Ford Tempo with what seemed to be a four-man TV camera crew. A *Record* reporter walked up to one of the men when they stopped and noticed the name on his press badge: "Daily Planet." The plates on the car were from California.

It wasn't until a day later that the full story of this "camera crew" was finally pieced together and revealed. The four turned out to be Bergen County sheriff's officers; they had created false press passes and gone to the rally to videotape the marchers. The plates on the Ford Tempo had been stolen by the officers from a video transmitting truck from California that Court TV had parked at the courthouse for its broadcasts of the Spath trial.

TWO DAYS LATER, COURTROOM 138

Robert Galantucci stood before the jury again. It had been six weeks since he had addressed them in this way, pleading for his client. There had been many sideshows in the trial, from the arrest of Melvin DeBerry to the arrival of the Black Muslims to Steven McDonald's entrance into the courtroom to the news of sheriff's officers posing as a TV crew. Privately Galantucci worried that the jury had heard about those events and would hold them against Spath.

After Spath had testified and Galantucci had called several expert witnesses of his own to punch holes in the testimony by Dr. Michael Baden and Lucien Haag, Goldberg came back with two days of rebuttal witnesses, including the man he believed could be his trump, Patrick

Hogan. Since the shooting, Hogan had been promoted from lieutenant to captain on the Teaneck police force. Unflustered and clad in his uniform, he told what Goldberg had believed was a convincing tale that could sway the jury against feeling sympathy for police: that Blanco had said Pannell had never reached into his pocket for a gun.

Goldberg was pleased. He rested his case.

As Galantucci stood before the jury for final arguments, he had come to realize that the end was much like the beginning. There were two distinct stories to this case. Either Pannell's hands were up or they were down. Either Gary Spath felt danger or he was reckless.

Galantucci stretched out his hands and spoke in a voice barely audible. "There is so much to say."

Galantucci had sensed that the jury liked his style. He talked with his hands and used the shortened, clipped phrasing of his working-class roots. He had even made jurors chuckle at times. That was a good sign, he figured. But he had no sense of how they felt about his client.

He walked forward and placed a hand on the rail of the jury box. "If there is an honest doubt, you must return a verdict of not guilty," he said. "The state must prove that Gary Spath did not have the right to use force to defend himself."

He mentioned the discovery of the light hit on the bullet in Pannell's gun. "I do not suggest to you for one moment when it was that light hit was put on that bullet," he said. "All I can tell you is that at some point that trigger was pulled." He described how Phillip Pannell was taller and bulkier than Spath even though he was sixteen years old. He encouraged the jury to "not be fooled" into thinking the teenagers who hung out with Pannell were just ordinary "boys and girls." He asked that one of the jurors try on Pannell's coat when they went into their deliberations room and test out Lucien Haag's theories.

Then Bob Galantucci asked: "Did Gary Spath reasonably believe that he had the right to protect himself?" He eyed the jurors for a second. "Even if his judgment was wrong," he continued, "that doesn't mean he didn't have the right to protect himself. . . .

"When Gary Spath came to work, I don't think he chose to get involved in this thing. . . . When you close the door, Gary Spath had less time than that to make his decision. . . . He had a blink of an eye. . . . I ask that you return a verdict that is consistent with the facts, consistent with common sense and logic, consistent with the law, consistent with the truth and justice, too. . . . I pray for nothing less. Nothing less, please."

Galantucci sat down. He had spoken for seventy-one minutes, longer than he wanted. He took out a handkerchief and wiped his brow.

Goldberg spoke now. "Remember . . . remember . . . remember what you have heard," he asked the jury. "Just as I told you at the beginning of the trial to forget, I ask you now to remember."

So began the slow tracing of the facts.

"This is Teaneck," Goldberg said. "This is Teaneck. When the defendant refers to the streets and you don't know what it's like, ladies and gentlemen, we're talking about the streets of Teaneck. We're not talking about Fort Apache in the Bronx."

He said there was "absolutely no question" that Phillip Pannell should not have had a gun. But Goldberg said that Pannell deserved a trial and that Spath's "reckless course of action" denied him that right. The prosecutor implied that Blanco and Spath had enhanced their story of Pannell's movements by inventing what Goldberg called the "bank robber position" of Pannell's hand in his coat pocket. He pooh-poohed the story of the light hit on the bullet, implying that Detective LaPlaca had conspired with Galantucci to reveal that. He questioned Jack Terhune's ethics. "Never in my mind did I imagine that during the course of this trial we would be entering the twilight zone," Goldberg said.

As for Phillip Pannell, he said: "I can't offer any consolation. What Phillip Pannell did was wrong. He shouldn't have had a gun. He is certainly no hero."

But such faults, said Goldberg, should be ignored. Concentrate on the evidence, he urged the jury.

"Justice, justice shalt thou follow," he said. "Justice in this case requires, unfortunately, that you find the defendant guilty of reckless manslaughter."

THE NEXT DAY, FEBRUARY 11

Judge Charles DiGisi took three hours to instruct the jury on their duties. Midway through, he picked up on a topic that Galantucci had mentioned the day before in final arguments.

"Even if you believe Gary Spath made a mistake," DiGisi said, "as long as you feel that mistake is reasonable, you can accept his explanation of self-defense" in shooting Phillip Pannell. And, the judge added, if the jury agreed that Spath had rightly felt his life was in danger and used self-defense to protect himself, then the jury could acquit him.

NINE HOURS LATER, 8:00 P.M.

The jurors walked into the courtroom. They had eaten lunch and dinner and talked over their doubts most of the day. One of the jurors had tried on Pannell's parka. In the course of examining Pannell's gun, another juror had broken its handle.

DiGisi asked if they had reached a verdict. The foreman nodded yes.

Spath stood up with Galantucci. Both stared straight ahead. In the family seats Thelma Pannell was without her husband.

"We find the defendant not guilty."

One side of the room erupted in cheers: the Spaths.

Thelma Pannell slumped to the floor. "My Lord . . . my Lord," she cried over and over.

Her sister Dale Monroe pointed a finger at the jury and began to scream, "What the hell are you doing? . . . *What the hell are you doing?*"

Galantucci grabbed Spath in a bear hug, not letting go for several minutes, rocking slowly back and forth, as Thelma Pannell was led out, her cries echoing off the granite walls in the corridor.

Ten minutes later the Spath contingent walked into the night, with the television lights blinding them. An hour later Gary Spath stood in the lobby of Galantucci's office.

"I feel like the winning pitcher in the seventh game of the World Series," he said.

His mother passed a group of reporters and quipped: "The truth will set you free."

"It wasn't a fair fight," said Galantucci, smiling. "We had truth on our side."

In Teaneck Lelia Johnson got the news on the telephone. Batron was at the high school, meeting with several other boys. She put on her coat and got in the car.

She found her son by the black door, quiet in a way he had not been in two years . . . since those months after Phillip had been killed.

She opened the door of the car. Batron got in and went home.

On Teaneck Road Art Gardner was on patrol, cruising north and south, trying to find any boys in search of trouble. The streets were empty. Teaneck was quiet.

It was fifteen degrees outside.

TWENTY-THREE

BY THE WATERS
OF BABYLON

THE NEXT DAY, BERGEN COUNTY COURTHOUSE

Professor Bill Crain heard the chants, curving, floating, pushing, swaying, and rising across the empty sidewalks of Hackensack. The sound,
jarring, dull, and persistent, broke the winter stillness, seeming to overwhelm everything else.

"No justice, no peace . . ."

Crain looked up, wondering. He stood outside the main door of the
courthouse with Herb Daughtry, Stanley Dennison, and a half dozen
reporters. Crain shuffled his feet to keep warm on the cold granite
steps. The sun was out, orange and hopeful, casting long stick-figure
shadows as it shone through the leafless tree branches above. Crain
jammed his hands into the pockets of his jacket, hunched his shoulders, and looked across the square at the statue of General Enoch Poor.
Nothing but the sound "No justice, no peace."

Crain had not given as much thought as he hoped to preparing for
this moment, this morning after the verdict. He had felt sad and unsettled when he got out of bed. It all had ended so quickly, so unre-
solvedly, Crain thought. The verdict wasn't the community and
personal healing he had hoped for. If anything, the jury's judgment,

amid the cheering by Spath's people and the cursing by Pannell's, had seemed to pull the emotions farther apart.

Crain had felt sorry for Spath as he watched him throughout the trial, his psychologist's antenna telling him that the officer had suffered deeply and seemed remorseful for the bullet he had fired. But Crain also believed Spath was guilty and should be punished. Simple justice required it, as did the larger, more complicated need to demonstrate to blacks that they could get a fair hearing. The scientific testimony had convinced him that a reckless act had been committed. His own marching for the past eighteen months had caused him to believe in the need for a message for the black community.

"No justice . . . no peace."

The chant was rising, drawing closer. Crain had come to the courthouse with Daughtry and Dennison to protest Spath's acquittal and call on the federal government to take up the case. Crain had long thought there were larger issues at stake, for Teaneck as well as the nation. But the trial, with its all-white jury and the actions of the sheriff's deputies, had convinced him that the civil rights of the Pannell family had been grossly violated. Crain was now the only white person who regularly marched with black activists or attended their meetings to plot strategy. He had grown to admire many of them, often repeating to his white friends their stories of discrimination. Too often, though, Crain had felt lonely after those conversations. *Why did he seem to understand the pain in the black community and his white friends seem so hardened to it?* Today, on Abraham Lincoln's birthday, the answer seemed just as elusive and painful as it had in the months leading up to the trial.

Daughtry stepped to the TV microphones, holding a typewritten statement in his hands. "The result of this trial has proven that the system has failed us once again. In spite of the fact that Phillip C. Pannell was shot in the back with his hands in the air, the universal sign of surrender, in broad daylight, an all-white Bergen County jury has seen fit to find Teaneck Police Officer Gary Spath not guilty. The system failed us here in Bergen County, it failed for blacks and whites alike. . . ."

"No justice . . . no peace. No justice . . . no peace. No justice . . . no peace."

Daughtry stopped and looked across the square. Kids, hundreds of them, poured around the corner and crossed the square, their uneven lines curving around the dormant flower beds. Must be at least two hundred of them, Crain thought. He did not recognize anyone, though.

The kids walked through the press conference, as if they were a tidal wave and the adults on the courthouse steps were mere atolls in the ocean. They kept walking into the courthouse parking lot.

"No justice, no peace. No justice, no peace. No justice, no peace."

Dennison ran after them, then Daughtry. And Crain.

"Where are you going?" Dennison yelled. "Heyyyyyyy. Hold on. Stooooooop. STOOOOOOOOP."

After a hundred yards the kids halted. Dennison grabbed several leaders and pushed them back to the courthouse steps. The others followed.

"We are angry that Spath got off," said a girl.

"The death of Phillip Pannell cannot be forgotten," said a boy.

"Where are you from?" Crain asked.

"Hackensack."

"We want to go to Teaneck," one boy said.

Crain felt the press of time and priorities. At City College a psychology class waited. Yet there were these kids. For Hackensack kids to go to Teaneck usually meant one thing: a fight. Crain looked over the crowd, worried. This was exactly what he feared: kids marching on Teaneck. It was a prescription for a riot. Only this time the cops would not hold back.

One of the girls said she was president of her class. Several others said they were in the National Honor Society. A few, in dark hoodies and with stony faces, seemed like fighters. A girl, who seemed to have taken charge of the group, said that students had been upset all morning at Hackensack High School over Spath's not guilty verdict. The students wanted to do something, she said. When their lunch period began, they left the school and marched to the courthouse, hearing a rumor that Daughtry and other adults might be there.

It was a mixed group, Crain thought. But leaderless too. Daughtry was lecturing them about putting their energy to good use and not getting caught up in violence. The kids seemed to calm and listen. Daughtry's was a face they knew; many had seen him on television.

Daughtry asked the group to congregate by a corner. He too had appointments back in Brooklyn. He turned to a journalist: "But I don't want these kids walking alone into Teaneck. There'll be trouble."

Standing at Daughtry's side, Bill Crain nodded.

"Let's march," yelled Daughtry. "But remember. We're proud black men and women. We march without violence. . . ."

His last words were drowned out. "No justice . . . no peace."

TEANECK HIGH SCHOOL

Batron Johnson felt the old anger and loneliness coming back. He had gone to school the morning after the verdict, partly out of habit, partly in search of comfort. His mother had lectured him about not getting into any fights. Batron knew the cops would be waiting for him to make a false move. Still, he wanted to strike something . . . anything.

A teacher saw him in the hall and asked how he was. Batron could feel his face tighten. "There's no justice for the black man," he said. The teacher nodded and walked away. Batron figured no one really wanted to hear him.

"We need to call a meeting," Batron said.

He thought of getting the Young Black Gentlemen together. But in some ways a meeting inside a room seemed insufficient. Batron wanted to *do something*. It was almost noon, and he wanted to leave.

He heard a voice, one of the old Violators.

"What's up?" Batron asked.

Hackensack kids were marching to Teaneck, the boy said.

Batron decided to get the old gang together. In his pocket he still carried his red bandanna.

IN HACKENSACK

As the kids were marching to Teaneck, Gary Spath held another press conference at his lawyer's office. His exuberant, thankful tone of the night before had disappeared. Spath was angry. "I'm the one whose civil rights have been violated," he declared. "I'm the victim here."

His anger was not enough to stop him and his family from praying, he said, for the Pannell family. "That's the kind of people we are," Spath explained.

An hour later he went on the radio with his staunch supporter, talk show host Bob Grant. Spath was still piqued about prosecutor Glenn Goldberg's gibe three days earlier in closing arguments that Teaneck was not the Bronx. Spath thought Goldberg was trying to imply that cops in Teaneck did not face the same dangers as officers in the Bronx. To Spath, it was a cheap shot that needed to be answered. City-style violence, he believed, had seeped into the suburbs long ago.

"We have," said Spath, "a lot of garbage overflow."

IN TEANECK

The Hackensack kids were marching up the hill on Cedar Lane now, approaching the top of the ridge that ran through Teaneck. The Teaneck police had met them at the border, and a rumor had swept through the group that the cops would block them from entering the town. But the Teaneck cops announced they would escort the marchers, stretching now several hundred yards along the street. A police car, lights flashing, positioned itself in the lead. Another slipped in behind. Cops were stationed at each corner.

Along the Cedar Lane business district, store owners and shoppers came out and stopped, drawn by the chants and the numbers of kids. Near a drugstore a white man held up the morning's edition of the *Record* with its banner headline SPATH NOT GUILTY. The man stood triumphant for a moment, a smile across his face as the students walked by. The students seemed to pick up the chanting as they saw the man and the headline, but two boys broke from the crowd and ran at the man. They tore the paper from his hands and stomped it on the sidewalk. Teaneck cops were on their heels. They grabbed the boys and handcuffed one of them. The crowd, meanwhile, resurrected a chant that Crain hadn't heard in a while: "Teaneck, Teaneck, have you heard? This is not Johannesburg."

Crain had decided to cancel his classes at the college. He felt moved and energized by the kids. He worried for them too. They had been touched by Phillip's death, as he was. But they seemed unsure of what to do with their feelings now that the verdict had come so fast. Crain had thought the jury would deliberate for a few days at least. The amount of evidence, and the need to go through it, required that, he believed.

It felt good to be marching. But Crain could feel eyes watching him too. White people resented him for marching all these times. He had known this for months. There had been calls to his house, sometimes from well-meaning friends, advising him to stop and consider what he was doing. But Crain had said no. This time he knew people would gossip more about him. But of all the marches Crain had participated in—and there had been dozens now—today's seemed to hold a meaning the others had not. In the other marches Crain had taken his place at the rear. Today he was needed in front. What Daughtry had said was true. These kids shouldn't walk alone today.

TEANECK HIGH SCHOOL

Art Gardner feared trouble was coming, but he had no idea where or how.

At the high school the day seemed oddly calm. Half the kids hadn't even come to school. Many whites stayed home, and Gardner knew why: If the black kids went on a rampage, whites wanted to be far away.

Gardner believed the whites' fears were unfounded. If the kids got violent, they would go after the cops.

As he had done on that morning after the shooting almost two years before, he patrolled the halls, trying to listen for meaning in the sentiments he was hearing. Some of the kids were surprisingly quiet. A few just mumbled the expected taunts or chants.

He had noticed Batron. The boy seemed unusually agitated, Gardner thought. But at least Batron stayed in the school building all day.

After 3:00 P.M. Batron left the high school and walked down the hill toward the police station with some of the old Violators. Gardner followed at a distance. So did other black adults.

━━━━━━

The Hackensack kids had already walked by Teaneck High School, chanting and pleading with the Teaneck kids to come out and join them. A few Teaneck kids had poked their heads out windows, but no more than one or two had left, their teachers warning them that there might be trouble if the two old rivals mixed together.

Daughtry and Crain needed a destination. *How about the Teaneck municipal hall?* So many of the other marches had ended there with speeches.

The Hackensack kids left the Teaneck High campus, wound down a hill, and meandered along Teaneck Road. Twenty minutes later they reached the town hall. Their leaders mounted the steps and crowded together. Daughtry spoke first. He thanked them and praised them for remaining nonviolent. "You have sent a message," he declared. "What you have done today is important. We will not forget you. This town will not forget you. Give yourself a hand."

The students clapped and cheered.

Crain was relieved. He stood by a tree on the lawn that separated the town hall from the police station. He smiled at the kids. They seemed excited they had walked so far.

A girl was speaking. "What we have done today will help make peace," she said. "Our towns can come together. We don't need to be rivals. We can be together. . . ."

Crain looked to his right.

The Violators.

Batron saw the Hackensack kids on the front steps as he walked at the head of the Violators. The Hackensack students were congratulating themselves, and Batron was sickened. *What's to feel good about?*

"My friend is dead," he said. "There's no justice."

Batron had no plans, no destination. He felt the energy of the day moving him, however. When the Violators gathered at Teaneck High School, they naturally seemed to head in the direction of the town hall, on the heels of the crowd from Hackensack.

When Batron saw the Hackensack kids, however, he wanted no part of them. He led the Violators through the fringe of the Hackensack marchers . . . toward the police station.

Art Gardner was worried now. He knew what Batron was capable of, but he also knew Batron was just another kid.

He felt sorry for the boy. Batron seemed so saddened, his face pulled and creased, his shoulders hunched as he walked. He wasn't saying anything. Neither were the other Violators.

One of the boys with a red bandanna pushed a photographer from the *Record* and knocked him down. Another took a swing at a reporter in a trench coat who was holding a tape recorder.

Gardner looked toward the police station. Cops were streaming out now, all of them wearing riot helmets and holding nightsticks in their palms. A dozen cops formed a skirmish line in front of the police station.

Crain was talking with William David-El when he too noticed the cops. David-El ran over, furious, telling a lieutenant that the police line would cause trouble.

"We have to show presence," the lieutenant barked back.

Batron saw the cops and started to cry. He started to walk toward the street, appearing to leave. But at the sidewalk he wheeled. Several other Violators grabbed for his shoulders, but he broke free and headed back toward the police line, his head down.

He wanted to punch a cop. Yes, flatten one of them. "Take one of them with me," he said. "For Phillip . . ."

Batron stopped.

Before him stood Art Gardner. And Charles Cobb, the guidance counselor and adviser to the Young Black Gentlemen, and Curtis March, the high school teacher. And other black teachers and adults. The men stepped between the Violators and the police. "Come on, boys, no trouble," Gardner boomed.

His voice seemed to stop them. Batron's friends had caught up with him now. He brushed off an arm that had draped around his shoulder and rushed the cops.

Gardner and Cobb and March and the others stepped forward. "Go home, Batron," shouted Curtis March. "Go home to your family."

Batron stopped . . . and turned away. His hands were balled in tight fists. Tears still rolled down his cheeks.

He walked home.

TWENTY-FOUR

LAST RITES

EARLY MARCH 1992

Batron looked out on the crowd in the strange auditorium. He had been selected to travel with a group of a dozen Teaneck High School students to speak to a high school in South Jersey that was just starting to go through the strains of integration. Like Teaneck in the late 1950s, the area had become a magnet for nonwhites who were moving from the cities, and the high school had asked Teaneck students to come down for the day and advise them on how they might get along with one another.

Batron felt shy about speaking to a large group. Riding south in a bus with the other Teaneck students that morning, he did not know what he would say.

As he sat on the edge of the stage in the auditorium, he thought of Phillip. Batron felt himself start to cry, but he held himself back. No tears today, he said to himself.

After the verdict the month before and the march the next day on the police station Batron had felt a change in himself. In a private way he felt proud of himself. He had gone to the police station, fully intending to get into a fight, hoping to punch a cop. But something had held him back. He remembered Art Gardner and Curtis March and

Charles Cobb placing themselves between him and the police line. *Black men.* Batron wanted to be like them, with a good job and a reputation in the community for doing good things. He wanted a family too. And college.

But first he had to graduate. More than anything he wanted that. Batron did not want to be left behind in school as his class moved on. He didn't want to drop out either.

"I want to make something of myself," he said. "But I'm a black man in a white world. Ain't nobody gonna give it to me."

He had felt that way ever since he had read *The Autobiography of Malcolm X.* Spath's trial had solidified his feelings. It was a white world, and to be black was to risk having someone stomp on you—or so he had come to think. As he gazed on the auditorium of students, he wanted to say something he had never said publicly before. He stopped a moment to collect his thoughts.

"My best friend was killed," Batron said. "I almost went over the edge, but I didn't, thanks to my mother. I'm here to tell you that I've dedicated my life to the memory of my friend. He didn't make it, but I will."

The crowd cheered.

April 5, 1992

On the first Sunday in April Paul Ostrow was honored as the "Man of the Year" by one of Teaneck's most prestigious groups, the B'nai B'rith. Ostrow had invited some two hundred of his friends to the banquet hall at his synagogue, the Teaneck Jewish Center. He was being cited for his work with the ambulance corps and with his synagogue and for his devotion to his family and his community.

The year had been hard, with all the personal clashes in local politics, not to mention his private concerns. This was one of Ostrow's happiest moments in months. He looked around the room, at his friends and the professions they represented: bankers, lawyers, doctors, teachers, shop owners.

"This is why I stay in Teaneck," he said. "This is my community."

April 23, 1992

On a clear spring night Gary Spath drove to a dinner in his honor in the town of Little Ferry, which lies just south of Hackensack. If he looked up and to the east, as he walked into Vecchiarello's restaurant, he could see the Empire State Building against a navy blue sky, its needle point gleaming in soft white and blue spotlights.

More than 150 police officers and their families had gathered for a meal of fruit cup, salad, baked ziti, roast beef, string beans, and white cake with white frosting. Among those receiving awards were an FBI agent who had had his life threatened, a narcotics detective who had made several major busts, and the entire Nutley Police Department for its innovative work in community policing. In accepting the award on behalf of his police department, the mayor of Nutley paid tribute to Spath. "What happened to you shouldn't have happened to a dog. I have no sympathy for criminals. I'm very proud when you blow them away."

The group that sponsored the banquet, the Detectives Crime Clinic, had been divided about giving an award to Spath. One of the group's members had nominated him, but the board, composed of detectives from New York City and New Jersey, was far from unanimous in its support. That night, as the officers ate dinner and awaited the awards portion of the banquet, a board member walked into the bar, spotted a journalist, and shook his head. "We debated it for twenty minutes," the cop said, "and those who were opposed to Spath just abstained." The majority favored giving Spath an award—"Policeman of the Month"—for April 1992.

When it came time for Spath to receive his award, the crime clinic president, William Fitzmaurice, walked to the podium.

"Now comes the moment of truth," Fitzmaurice said. He held up the plaque for Spath and read from the citation: "for your ability, courage, and understanding which have won the respect, confidence and admiration of your colleagues in the law enforcement profession."

Fitzmaurice paused. He seemed about to cry.

"I've had the privilege of meeting this young man a couple of times," Fitzmaurice said. "I think back to my twenty-eight years as a cop, and I never had to go through what he's gone through in the last two years. It tears me four ways from loose. As you can tell, I'm old enough to know what it is to shoot at somebody. But I did it in a war that was a declared war. Gary did it in a war that has not yet been legally declared. It's a war between law enforcement and the criminal element. I am in no way saying that what he did was right or was wrong. Gary did what he was trained to do. He reacted to a situation in the way he was taught to react and the way I was taught to react. I might be wrong. I don't think I am. I know that if it had been me, I probably would have done the same damn thing.

"This award is not made for what happened two years ago. This award is made for the ten years Gary Spath put his life on the line. He earned it ten years ago when he took the oath. He upheld the ideals that he was taught to revere."

With the "greatest of privilege," Fitzmaurice introduced Spath and asked him to come forward. The officers leaped to their feet, clapping loudly.

Spath walked to the podium. He posed for a photograph, shook Fitzmaurice's hand, then turned to the microphone.

"I hate to use clichés, but I'll just say one thing," said Spath. "It's a lot better to be judged by twelve than to be carried out by six."

JUNE 23, 1992

Batron graduated with the Class of 1992 at Teaneck High School. A month before, he received word that he had been accepted to Shaw University in North Carolina. He had gone to his senior prom, wearing a tuxedo, with a girl from Hackensack.

"I'm so proud he's going to college," said his mother. "It's been a long road, and it's been hard for him. I know."

As he received his diploma, Batron waved his arms over his head. Later he sat in the stands as his classmates offered a moment of silence "for one of us who didn't make it here tonight, Phillip Pannell."

Batron bowed his head. He thought of Phillip, of the red parka, of the girls they liked, of the squirt guns they used to buy, of the occasional fights they got into, of the bicycle rides they took together, of the Nintendo games they played, of that night in April 1990 when the phone rang and a friend had said Phillip had been shot . . . by a cop.

"I started to get angry," said Batron. "And then I just felt it go away."

JULY 20, 1992

Batron sat in the passenger seat of a station wagon, heading west on Route 4. He pushed the buttons on the car radio in search of a song. The air was thick with summer humidity, and Batron opened a window and turned to Steven and Otis and Eric in the backseat. "When did we go to the cemetery last?"

"Just after the trial?" said Steven. "Sometime then. It was at night, and it was cold."

Batron nodded.

In two weeks he was scheduled to leave for Shaw, but first he wanted to say good-bye to Phillip. The car eased into the Fair Lawn cemetery, well known over the years for accepting blacks. Edmund Perry, the prep school student who assaulted a plainclothes New York City detective and was shot to death, was buried there.

The radio came to life, with a song the boys knew.

Can I talk to you?
Can I talk to youuuuuu?

Batron started to hum, then fell silent. "Over there," he said, pointing to a patch of lawn that had dried out in the July heat. "It's over there."

The boys got out of the car and walked.

"Where is it?" Steven asked.

"It's over here," Batron said.

"No," Otis said, "over here."

Batron pointed to the cemetery office. "They'll tell us where Phil is buried."

In the car ride over, Batron said he felt bad that Phil didn't have a grave marker yet. The Young Black Gentlemen were going to sponsor a dance to raise money for a headstone, said Batron, but with the end of the school year nothing could get organized. Plus, some of the younger black kids were getting into fights. The school got nervous about holding a dance, and it was canceled.

"There were many things we wanted to do," Batron said.

He walked into the office. A white woman looked up as he asked where Phillip Pannell's grave is.

"There's a marker on that one now," she said, pointing to a map.

In Englewood Stanley Dennison's church had held a gospel festival to honor the Pannell family. Thelma Pannell took the thousand-dollar donation that was given to her and bought a grave marker.

On the way across the cemetery, Batron hardly waited for the car to stop before jumping out. "Over here," he called out to the others.

He led the group to a patch of grass, and they stared down at a flat granite rectangle.

Phillip C. Pannell
Beloved son and brother
1973–1990
Rest in Peace

"Do you suppose they moved it?" Otis asked. He seemed to want to make conversation. The others stood in silence.

Eric bent over and cleared away some crab grass. Batron lay down, his thick legs spread out over the grave, his left arm wrapped around the grave marker as if he were caressing it.

He stared at the headstone for a minute. The others walked back to the car one by one. Batron, the last, got up and followed.

"I was just thinking about how I miss him," Batron said. "We've been through so many things, and I just miss him a lot. We all have our own memories of him, so we keep it like that."

The car pulled out, and Batron looked back at the grave one last time. He flicked on the radio and turned up the volume.

You belong to me.
I belong to you.

The car rolled out of the cemetery and headed back on to the highway and Teaneck.

"It's real now," Batron said.

EPILOGUE

"I like it there," the young man said. "I like being around my people."

They were words I was hearing more now, from both sides of the color line. *My people.* The young man who spoke them sat across from me in a diner on a January afternoon in 1994. It had snowed a few days before, and as the traffic outside our window negotiated the streets made narrow by the curbside piles of snow-turned-to-ice, the young man's thoughts turned to the dream of integration that his hometown had embraced thirty years before.

Teaneck, he said, seemed old. He felt he had outgrown it. In his free time, the young man said, he would get in his car and drive across the Hudson to Harlem.

"It's like a black planet there, a black universe," he said. "Yeah, Harlem."

What the young man was expressing, in some ways, symbolized one fundamental change taking place in American race relations, a drift from the dreams embodied by towns such as Teaneck to more separate states of life and perception. Indeed, by 1995, American race relations seemed to be characterized by the pressures of polarization—not the dreams of integration—with Teaneck no longer held up as a model but the exception to the rule, attempting to preserve some measure of integration in the face of separatist impulses. Some called Teaneck and its dream an anachronism. A few harsher critics wondered if it was a dream at all. Still, others felt the dream lived on.

Nationwide, life in black communities seemed to have its own set of polarizing factors. Since 1966, the percent of black Americans in white-collar jobs had more than doubled, to 45 percent of all black workers. The black poverty rate also had plummeted somewhat, from 45 percent to 30 percent of families. More than 11.5 million black men and women worked in careers classified as managerial, professional, and technical. In two decades, the number of black police officers had tripled and black health officials—nurses and doctors alike—had risen fourfold. And while only 1 in 17 black families in 1967 were considered affluent, by the nineties one in seven families had reached that rung on the economic ladder.

And yet, for every gain, there seemed to be a significant downside, with crime at the top of many lists of negatives. While blacks make up only 12 percent of the population, by the nineties they were committing almost two thirds of all robberies and more than half of America's murders—with most of the victims being black. At the same time, blacks had come to have a three times greater chance of dying in a police shooting. Perhaps most tragic of all, by the 1990s, one in four black men under thirty was either in jail, on probation, or on parole. In some cities such as Washington, D.C., the figure was even higher. Entire black urban neighborhoods were ruled now by crime.

The economic effects of this are devastating, with young black men earning on average one third less than their white counterparts and with black unemployment in that age group hovering at 13 percent, whereas only 5.5 percent of young white men were out of work. In this crucible of self-destruction, the black family seems more threatened than ever, with more than half of all black children nationwide being raised by single mothers.

Such trends seemed to contribute to separatism, not integration. Perhaps because of the widening fissures, brought on by crime, economic hardships, and family breakdown, it was not surprising that attitudes about race seemed to be worsening among young people. A survey by Peter D. Hart Research Associates found that half of all American youth describe the state of race relations as "generally bad." Almost half of all white youth—49 percent—say whites are denied opportunity by discrimination, whereas more than two thirds of black youth—68 percent—say it is they who are discriminated against.

———

In the months immediately following the trial of Gary Spath, the public outrage stopped in Teaneck. Several smaller marches followed the large one with Bill Crain and the Reverend Herbert Daughtry, but by the spring of 1992, Teaneck was quiet, even when riots erupted in Los Angeles. Al Sharpton had spent most nights and weekends in a rented town house in Englewood, but nonetheless was focusing his energies across the Hudson in New York City where he still maintained his primary residence and where he had dreams of elective office. He would lose in the Democratic primary in 1992 and again in 1994 for U.S. Senate. But he did not plan to give up. When I visited him at his Harlem office in late 1994, he was no longer wearing his trademark medallion of Martin Luther King that Hosea Williams had given him. His hair was graying. He had lost 60 pounds and was down to (for him) a svelte 240 pounds. He talked of wanting his daughters to see him as a respectable father and not "just another guy in a jogging suit yelling 'no justice, no peace.'" He said he had mellowed. His dream, he told me, was to be mayor of New York City.

By 1995, the Teaneck Police Department, had fourteen blacks, seven Hispanics, and one Asian officer on its ninety-seven-member force. Of the five female officers, two were black. A few weeks before the fifth anniversary of Phillip Pannell's death in April 1995, the department dedicated a new headquarters, and the department's Community Police Task Force, organized after the Spath trial, was being praised throughout the state for its efforts to forge links with Teaneck's disparate neighborhoods. One officer who had helped distribute the "Never a Doubt" T-shirts, which had been sold from the front desk of the police station during the spring of 1990 to raise money for Spath's defense and had been so controversial and divisive as a result, was now one of the task force's most active members. Much seemed forgotten and changed—or was it? Officer Luis Torres was assigned to Teaneck High School, where he spent his days mingling with kids. On one afternoon as I rode by, he was throwing a baseball with several boys by the black door. He smiled when he saw me. "I'm happier here. This is what I do best," he said.

"How is the department?"

Torres's face fell. "Same old thing," he said. "I'm still thought of as a traitor by some of the diehards."

"Traitor for what—that you asked questions?" I asked.

Torres nodded. "You know how it is. Some things don't go away overnight."

Bill Crain took his protests to the site of the new police station, arguing that the construction would destroy a grove of one-hundred-year-old trees. On the day construction was to begin, Crain placed himself in front of a truck in a show of nonviolent protest and was arrested. When he appeared in town court, he read a two-page type-written statement that ended with this sentiment: "If we lived in a society that had a deep respect for nature, we would have saved those venerable trees. Let us hope we can develop such a respect for all of nature that is within our custody."

A year after the Spath trial, a small group of activists, including Crain, had met in Tryon Park to hold a memorial service for the third anniversary of Pannell's death. After meeting by the basketball courts where Pannell had flashed his gun on that fateful April day in 1990, the group walked across the field to a corner where they had planted a maple sapling in Phillip's memory a year before. But the tree was gone. Vandals had cut it down and burned the stump. A year later—on the fourth anniversary of Pannell's death—police received a call about a boy with a gun at another park. A team of officers arrived, and the boy made a sudden move for a gym bag. But no shots were fired. The boy had a BB gun and was said to be taking it out to show police. "He's lucky he didn't get shot," said Lieutenant Paul Tiernan, the head of the community police task force. "These kids have no idea how dangerous they can be."

In Paterson, eight miles west of Teaneck, in February 1995, another black youth was not so fortunate. During an attempted drug bust, a sixteen-year-old high school sophomore, who dreamed of one day playing professional basketball even though he had never bothered to try out for his high school team, ran from a white rookie undercover narcotics officer. The youth stopped by a fence, where the officer, his gun drawn, grabbed him. As the officer was switching the gun from one hand to another, it fired, sending a bullet into the back of the young man's head. The Paterson Police Department called the shooting "accidental." Two days of window-breaking followed in downtown Paterson. Al Sharpton led a peaceful march. The narcotics detective hired Robert Galantucci as his defense attorney and in May 1995 a grand jury voted not to indict the officer. Several weeks after that grand jury decision a nineteen-year-old Colombian immigrant, who was reportedly brandishing an air pistol that resembled a 45-caliber semiautomatic, was shot by a Paterson officer.

At Teaneck High School, the Young Black Gentlemen seminar group, which had been so instrumental in helping Batron Johnson and others cope with their tendency to fight, quietly disbanded. By 1995, the high school instead became the focus of a new protest campaign by activists who charged the school district with institutional racism. At the heart of the argument were cold, indisputable facts—that white students, on the whole, did better than black students and dominated honors courses, whereas blacks were the majority in special education classes. Much of the energy for the campaign—not to mention the activists—came from the protests over the Pannell shooting. And in addition to student academic performances, the activists called upon the school district to examine the way black students were disciplined. If the white community became outraged initially, however, it was over a proposal to change the name of Thomas Jefferson Middle School. Michelle March, the wife of the high school's head of black studies, charged that because Jefferson had owned slaves that his name should be taken off the school.

With all three issues seeming to boil at once—the name change, the charge of institutional racism, and discipline—the school district formed three ad-hoc committees, one for each of the separate concerns. By the summer of 1994, each committee had submitted reports, but the one that drew the most attention was from the Committee on Institutional Racism, which charged that black students were systematically shortchanged within Teaneck's schools, that while the schools seemed integrated on paper that the academic paths of whites and blacks were far different, with whites being guided into more challenging courses and blacks pushed toward mediocre tracks.

The school board and school officials harshly criticized the report, claiming that forces other than racism, such as socioeconomic differences in black and white families, contributed to differences in student performances. The activists countered that such comments were, by nature, inherently racist. By late fall, school superintendent Harold Morris had cited another criticism. He charged that the black activists and their white liberal colleagues were aligned with the controversial Afrocentric professor Leonard Jeffries. Privately, Morris worried that the activists were bent on driving whites from the public schools, and on a sunny afternoon in late 1994 as we talked about those worries, he pulled out a piece of paper and pointed to some numbers. Forty percent of the white students, he said, had achieved at least the ninetieth percentile in standardized tests. Black students at Teaneck High, meanwhile, were hardly doing poorly; Morris said that while they had not achieved the same scores as whites, black students did better than 75 percent of black students throughout New Jersey.

It was testimony, said Morris, to Teaneck and its diversity—not to mention its emphasis on educational excellence. He then spoke of the future. It was grim, he said. In 1983, said Morris, 53 percent of Teaneck High's students were white. By 1990, the year Pannell died, the figure had dropped to 44 percent. For the 1994–95 school year, Morris said, the figure was 35 percent. In January 1995, the U.S. Department of Education announced that it would study Teaneck's schools to determine if there was any merit to the charge of institutional racism. Harold Morris looked upon the study—even if it vindicated Teaneck—as a body blow to the model of integration. "People are leaving with their feet," he said. "We are experiencing tremendous white flight. We are going to be an integrated town with a segregated school district."

The thought was very much on the mind of Paul Ostrow. Indeed, Ostrow thought about it, spoke about it, and worried about it almost every day. "We are becoming," he said one day in early 1995, "like Englewood—a mostly black school in a town that is mostly white."

Ostrow seemed saddened when I saw him that day. And yet, he still dreamed things would be okay. He had gone ahead, despite his fears of gang violence, and enrolled his son, Michael, in the high school. His daughter was scheduled to follow in September 1995. "My kids get to go to school with a wide variety of kids," said Ostrow. "Yes, there are problems, but there are problems everywhere. And where else can you find this?"

One dream of Ostrow's had faltered, however. He had wanted to become Teaneck's mayor. But while he was elected again to the township council in May 1994, he did not have enough votes to become mayor. In that same election, Frank Hall was defeated in his quest for another term on the council. He had been there a quarter century, arriving as one of the liberal mouthpieces of integration and leaving in bitterness, called a racist by some blacks for his own criticism of Leonard Jeffries. When I spoke to him in February 1995, his thoughts were on another battle he had survived fifty years before, Iwo Jima. But at the mention of Teaneck, Frank Hall became saddened. He said he had been badly misunderstood, that much of the work he had tried to do seemed futile. He remembered that late-night radio conversation he had with Gary Spath's mother and how she had refused to accept his apology for not having time to stop by their home and offer comfort. "I tried to walk in the middle and speak the truth," he said. "I especially wanted to focus on crime and violence. But people don't want to hear it now. The only people who get heard are the most radical. The voices of reason just aren't listened to. I'm probably one of the few guys around who fought at Iwo Jima and marched with Martin Luther King in Washington, D.C., in 1963. I guess that doesn't mean much anymore."

The Reverend Amandus "Mandy" Derr went back to devoting the bulk of his energy toward Grace Lutheran Church. He did not stop worrying about Teaneck, however. On his jaunts through the town's business district, he had noticed that white shopkeepers had become even more defensive in the years after the Spath trial. More than a few had confided in him that they kept guns under the counter.

"We haven't learned anything," said Derr, when I met him one morning. "We've just brushed it under the carpet."

Arthur Gardner started the 1994–95 school year, still in mourning. His wife, Susan, had died of brain cancer during the summer of 1994. The funeral, held at a Jewish funeral home, had symbolized to Gardner much of what he had come to love about Teaneck. An Orthodox rabbi, who had been a neighbor of the Gardners as a youth, led prayers. A young black man sang a spiritual. Eulogies were delivered by black and white men and women. The congregation was half black, but there were no discernible lines of seating arrangements as there had been at the Spath trial or other events in Teaneck in the wake of Pannell's death. Blacks and whites sat together.

"This is what it's all about," said Gardner that day, as he wrapped me in a bear hug. I again saw him in January 1995, at a community forum to discuss institutional racism charges in the school district. He was shaking his head. "You know the problem," said Gardner, "is that some whites don't see black folks for what we are. Sometimes we are invisible. We need to get over that. We need to remember that we are one people, that we're all alike."

As part of the concerns about institutional racism and its effect on the town, Dorothy Marcus resumed her role as a coordinator of community dialogues. By February 1995, she was hard at work assembling lists of people to invite for group discussions about race. Marcus also was selected to be a member of Teaneck's Civilian Police Review Board. By early 1995, the board had received seven complaints about the behavior of police officers in Teaneck, and dismissed five of them as frivolous. The other two were referred to the county prosecutor.

The Reverend Stanley Dennison was elected to the city council in Englewood. Walter Fields became political action director of the New Jersey NAACP. By 1994, he had become a regular commentator on television on racial issues. In the fall of 1994, he led the call for a boycott of conservative talk-radio host Bob Grant after Grant joked that Haitian refugees should be allowed to drown and that Martin Luther King, Jr., was a "scumbag." In 1995, Fields also led calls for the resignation of Rutgers President Francis Lawrence after Lawrence said blacks lacked the "genetic hereditary background" to perform as well as white students on standardized tests. Lawrence later apologized and said he misspoke.

In the summer of 1992, Phillip D. Pannell, Sr., was arrested twice— first in a stabbing incident and a week later for cocaine possession. Pannell spent almost two years in court-ordered rehabilitation, then was released. On January 5, 1995, he was arrested again and charged with making terroristic threats to his estranged wife, who had told him she no longer wanted to live with him. The police reported that Phillip told Thelma that he "was going to kill her with his Uzi submachine gun, putting Thelma in fear for her life." Weeks later, Thelma moved, telling friends she should no longer live with the painful memories of Teaneck, New Jersey.

In March of 1992, a month after his partner was acquitted in the shooting of Phillip Pannell, Officer Wayne Blanco was named Police Officer of the Year by the Teaneck Police Union. He was later moved up to the detective squad.

In the summer of 1992, Gary Spath officially retired from the Teaneck Police Department on a psychological disability, judged unable to resume police work because of emotional trauma from the Pannell shooting and its aftermath. As part of his disability, he was awarded a pension of two thirds of his salary—roughly $28,000—for the rest of his life. In March of 1993, the Teaneck Police Union gave Spath the Police Officer of the Year award, but dated it 1990 and cited Spath "in recognition of your courage and dedication to duty, for the strength to stand tall and persevere as well as your loyalty to your fellow officer." In that same ceremony, Spath was awarded the union's Medal of Honor "for actions taken in the line of duty on April 10, 1990, when you confronted an armed adversary. Your courage and perseverance resulted in the saving of yours and your partner's life, as well as protecting the community which you serve."

Six months later, Spath told me he wanted to move away from New Jersey to "someplace like North Carolina," but that his wife wanted to stay put. He pitched in an amateur adult baseball league, and earned extra money working as a landscaper and carpenter.

By 1994, the civil lawsuit that the Pannell family filed against Teaneck and Gary Spath—with the original damage claim for $30 million—was settled out of court, with the Pannell family receiving $195,000 from the town's insurance company.

After the not-guilty verdict in Spath's manslaughter trial, the United States Department of Justice said it would examine the shooting of Phillip Pannell and the investigation and trial of Gary Spath to determine whether Pannell's civil rights had been violated. FBI agents focused months of attention on trying to document Fred Greene's story that Blanco had exaggerated his story about frisking Phillip Pannell at the Bryant School playground. But the FBI was never able to prove the story. When the Clinton administration took over the federal government in 1993, the investigation was stalled by an unexpected problem: the delays that President Clinton had in finding someone to head the civil rights division of the department of justice after his first nominee, Lani Guinier, was forced to withdraw. According to Michael Chertoff, the U.S. attorney for Newark, the lack of a director of the civil rights division caused the investigation to be delayed for months. In the spring of 1994, more than two years after Spath was acquitted of manslaughter, the federal government announced that it was dropping its investigation. Spath has not left the shooting behind, though. In February 1995, during an appearance on Court-TV, he said that the shooting is often the first thing he thinks about each day when he awakens and the last thing he remembers before falling off to sleep. He has told friends he would like to become a police officer again. If not that, he says he would like to counsel officers involved in shootings. In the summer of 1992, Spath's parents sold their home in Teaneck and moved to a town in northern Bergen County. A few months before they left, their car was stolen one night by three black juveniles, one of whom had been at the Bryant School playground on the day Gary Spath met Phillip Pannell. After settling into their new home, Spath's mother, Elaine, wrote a note to Bob Grant, the talk-radio host at WABC radio in New York City, enclosing clippings about the stolen car and noting: "We have sadly parted with our cherished home of thirty-six years, but we could no longer feel safe in Teaneck. These recent months have been very difficult, both physically and emotionally."

In 1995, Teaneck celebrated the one-hundredth anniversary of its founding. The celebration began on New Year's Eve, with concerts, dances, a parade, and a midnight fireworks display. One man who was not around for the celebration was Matty Feldman. In April 1994, the man who led Teaneck's integration fight in the 1960s, collapsed and died from a weakened heart.

When I saw him again, Batron Johnson was still talking of Harlem. "It's a black universe," he said, "I like being around my people."

Across from me in the diner where we had come on the January afternoon, Batron locked his deep, mahogany eyes on me. He was twenty now, a sophomore at the predominantly black Shaw University in Raleigh, North Carolina. He had grown a beard and seemed thinner. He ordered a cheeseburger, and told me about two friends that had died recently from gunshots.

The first was a friend from college. It had been the previous September, and, as Batron later learned, the young man had been in his room one afternoon playing with a gun when someone had suggested a game of Russian roulette. Batron was returning from a biology class when he saw the crowd outside and the police and the ambulances. A friend walked up and explained what had happened, and Batron walked away. "I wanted to be by myself," he said. "I just couldn't be there."

A few months later, in December, Batron's cousin had been killed in an apartment building in Yonkers, New York. As Batron learned, he had walked into an elevator. Another man followed. A struggle followed. A shot rang out. Batron's cousin was eighteen.

Batron punched out his descriptions of the shootings with short, to-the-point descriptions, then fell silent, looking down into his plate as a waitress walked up and asked if we wanted anything else. Batron stabbed a french fry, stirred it through a pool of catsup, then washed it down with a gulp of Coke.

"My goal," he said, as the waitress walked away, "is to survive. . . . When I think of them, I think of Phil."

Phil.

The word seemed to fall from Batron's lips like a prayer. Batron explained how he had taped newspaper articles from Phillip's shooting and Spath's trial to the wall of his college room. Friends would walk in and ask if Batron knew Phillip Pannell. And Batron would tell the story of the boy with the gun and the chase by the police officer with the questionable shooting record and the shot in the back and the marches through the town called Teaneck.

That afternoon, as we drove home from the diner, I swung the car past the house on Intervale Road and stopped by the curb. We sat for a moment and looked in silence. The backyard was snow-covered now, and the forsythia bush was bare. The garage had been torn down and a basketball court had been built where the iris garden was. But the fence still stood, as it had been the day Phillip Pannell died there.

"Do you come here much?" I asked.

"Sometimes," Batron said, his voice flattening out and barely audible. "Sometimes I just come and sit . . ."

He stopped.

"Sometimes I come and just sit and cry. Phil was one of my best friends. I still don't understand this. He'll always be in my heart."

A Year Passed

It was 1995 and Batron Johnson was now a college junior. He had worked the previous summer in a medical laboratory, but because family finances were pinched, he had left Shaw to return home, working a full-time job at an auto parts store by day and attending classes at night at a local community college in northern New Jersey. His mother, Lelia, graduated from nursing school, and, when she reflected one spring afternoon on the road she and her son had walked these past five years, she had this to say: "I was determined that the streets weren't going to take him. When I look at him now, I'm very proud. He has grown so much."

As for Batron, he holds on to a dream he would like to fulfill one day. If he marries and has a son, he would like to name him Phillip.

NOTES ON SOURCES

PROLOGUE

2   Reference to Thomas Paine and Teaneck: Paine's *The American Crisis*, augmented by research by Teaneck historian Robert Griffin.

CHAPTER ONE: TURF

9   Cafeteria scene: Interviews with Batron Johnson, Steven Jowers, Charles Easter.

12   How Violators were named: Interviews with Batron Johnson, Charles Easter, Steve Jowers, Muziki Stewart, Otis Saunders, Jim Davis.

13   Fight at high school: Interviews with Batron Johnson, Steve Jowers, Charles Easter, Muziki Stewart, Otis Saunders, Jim Davis, Sean Honegan, James DeLaney, Jim White, and written reports from Teaneck Police Department.

17   Robbery in Englewood and arrest of suspect by Gary Spath: Teaneck police reports, commendation letters to Spath, interview with Spath.

18   Background on pattern of robberies: Chief Bryan Burke and Sheriff Jack Terhune.

CHAPTER TWO: "WE ALL LIVE IN A VERY SPECIAL TOWN"

21   Description of significance of ridge: Teaneck historian Robert Griffin.

22   Demographic information: U.S. Census Bureau.

24   Background on strategy for 1964 school desegregation: Interviews with Matthew Feldman and Frank Hall.

25   Reference to poor status of New Jersey cities: *Bergen Record*.

25   New Jersey school segregation: Harvard Project on School Desegregation.

26   Black migration to suburbs: *Bergen Record*.

27   Diversity Day: Author's observations, augmented by committee files and interview with Loretta Weinberg.

28 Arthur Gardner recollection: Interviews with him and his wife, Susan Gardner.

32 Account of fight at end of Diversity Day: Teaneck police reports.

37 Problems at lip sync concert: Teaneck police reports, interviews with Arthur Gardner and Teaneck police officers, news accounts in *Bergen Record.*

38 Fights at St. Anastasia carnival and reaction: Teaneck police reports, interviews with Batron Johnson, Lelia Johnson, Muziki Stewart, Charles Easter, news accounts in *Bergen Record.*

39 Educational issues and demographics: Interviews with Hal Morris, James DeLaney, Martin Cramer, Paul Ostrow, Tasha Morton, Lloyd Houston, Bill Crain, Art Gardner; demographic information from U.S. Census Bureau, Teaneck Board of Education, and New Jersey Department of Education, augmented by news accounts from *Bergen Record.*

46 Conversation of woman with Dorothy Marcus: Interviews with Dorothy Marcus.

CHAPTER THREE: THE BOY IN THE RED PARKA
47 Significance of black door: Interviews with Jim DeLaney, Tasha Morton, Art Gardner, Paul Ostrow, Jack Terhune, and Batron Johnson.

48 Phillip Pannell's back injury: Interviews with Thelma Pannell and Natasha Pannell.

49 Account of fight outside black door: Interviews with Batron Johnson, Charles Easter, and James DeLaney; reports by Teaneck High School and Teaneck Police Department.

51 Pannell family history: Documents obtained from Bergen County Probation Department and other civil court files, including financial records, augmented by interviews with Phillip and Thelma Pannell.

53 Naming of Phillip Clinton Pannell and scene with Phillip on roof: Interview with Thelma Pannell.

54 Phillip D. Pannell's criminal record: Documents obtained from Bergen County Courthouse and Bergen County Probation Department, including police reports from Englewood and Northvale police departments.

57 Pannell marriage problems and domestic disputes: Documents obtained from Bergen County courts, augmented by interviews with Thelma Pannell.

58 How Thelma Pannell had silver starter's pistol: Interviews with Thelma Pannell.

59 Phillip C. Pannell's fears: Interviews with Batron Johnson, Muziki Stewart, and Thelma Pannell.

59 Phillip C. Pannell's criminal record: Documents obtained from Bergen

County Courthouse and the county probation department, augmented by interviews with Thelma Pannell, Lieutenant Robert Adomilli, and police officers in Teaneck, Englewood, and Hackensack.

60 Scene at Pannell home during fight and later meeting with Violators: Interviews with Charles Easter, Batron Johnson, and Steve Jowers.

61 Meeting of Violators at Teaneck High School: Interviews with James DeLaney, Lelia Johnson, Batron Johnson, and Charles Easter, augmented by letter from DeLaney to parents.

67 Phillip D. Pannell's drinking: Documents obtained from Bergen County Sheriff's Department and other court documents.

67 Phillip C. Pannell's leaving Teaneck High School and his reaction: School files and interviews with James DeLaney, Thelma Pannell, and Batron Johnson.

69 Phillip C. Pannell's first day at Englewood's Dwight Morrow High School: Interviews with Richard Segall, Bill Mack, Thelma Pannell, and Batron Johnson, augmented by school records from Englewood.

CHAPTER FOUR: THE COP

78 Scene with Gary Spath comforting doctor: Interview with Paul Ostrow and Captain Patrick Hogan, augmented by Ostrow's letter to *Bergen Record*.

79 Spath family background: Interviews with *Bergen Record*, augmented by author interviews with Chief Bryan Burke, Werner Schmid, and other Teaneck residents.

80 Elaine Spath's recollections on Teaneck: Program for reunion of her high school class.

81 Demographic and socioeconomic analysis of Spath and Pannell neighborhoods: Study of census blocks and tracts, based on information supplied by U.S. Census Bureau and Bergen County Department of Planning and Economic Development.

82 Account of Gary Spath's involvement with mostly black baseball team: Interviews with Fred Greene and Leo Wielkocz.

83 Fred Greene background: Interviews with Greene and Bryan Burke, augmented by information in Teaneck High School yearbooks.

84 Gary Spath's school history: Information from court investigative file, supplied by state attorney general, augmented by Springfield College and Bergen Catholic High School.

85 Spath's high school sports history: Interviews with Norm Dermody and Chris Donfield, augmented by Bergen Catholic High School yearbook.

86 Spath's decision to become a police officer: Interview with Lieutenant

Robert Adomilli, augmented by interviews in *Bergen Record* with George Spath.

86 Spath's police training: Records from Bergen County Police Academy, investigative files of state attorney general.

87 Spath's commendations: Information supplied by Robert Galantucci and Gary Spath, augmented by Teaneck police reports and news accounts.

88 Teaneck police ticket quota problems: Interviews with Fred Greene, Chief Bryan Burke, Chief Donald Giannone, Lieutenant Paul Tiernan, and other Teaneck officers.

90 Torres family move to Teaneck: Interviews with Luis and Alma Torres.

91 Luis Torres's concerns for Spath's use of gun: Interviews with Torres.

92 Gary Spath's misgivings about police work and fear of drawing his gun: Interviews with Father Bart Aslin.

CHAPTER FIVE: "THIS TOWN IS A POWDER KEG"
94 Scene at Teaneck clergy meeting: Interview with Reverend Amandus Derr.

95 Background on Teaneck farming during colonial era: Interview with Robert Griffin.

99 "Mischief Night" gun incident: Teaneck police reports and author's interviews with police and synagogue members.

100 Conversation between Phillip C. Pannell and Bill Mack: Interviews with Bill Mack, augmented by interviews with Richard Segall and Thelma Pannell.

102 Phillip D. Pannell's troubles at Bergen County jail: Reports from Sheriff's Department and Teaneck police.

103 Violators' attack in Hackensack: Reports by Hackensack Police Department, sworn statements by Phillip Pannell, Leslie Johnson, Malik Burns, and Aaron Johnson to police, augmented by interviews with Thelma Pannell and other Violators and news accounts.

105 Phillip C. Pannell's wanderings during winter of 1990 and "Philly Blunt" nickname: Interviews with Lieutenant Robert Adomilli, Lelia Johnson, Thelma Pannell, Muziki Stewart, Batron Johnson, Englewood Police Sergeant Michael Blischak and Detective Jackie Smith.

107 Phillip C. Pannell fight in Englewood: Interview with Thelma Pannell.

108 Scene with Gary Spath and young boy and mother at Carl's Corner: Interviews with Lieutenant Robert Adomilli, Sergeant Phillip Lavigne, Officer Luis Torres, and Teaneck police reports.

113 Scene with Phillip C. Pannell confiding concerns about family: Interview with Muziki Stewart, augmented by interviews with Thelma Pannell.

115 Phillip C. Pannell obtains gun from family closet: Confidential interview with source close to Pannell family, augmented by interviews with Thelma Pannell and Investigator Quinton Collins of state attorney general's office.

CHAPTER SIX: MOURNING DOVE

116 Scene at Benjamin Franklin Middle School: Interviews with Martin Lasky, Matthew Feldman, George Powell, Paul Ostrow, Frank Hall, and Chief Bryan Burke, augmented by news accounts.

120 Account of shots fired in River Edge: Reports from River Edge Police Department.

121 Letter mailed by League of Women Voters: Copies of letter supplied by Dorothy Marcus, augmented by interviews with Marcus and other records from her files.

122 Description of Phillip C. Pannell's gun: Interviews with Muziki Stewart, augmented by interviews with Steven Jowers, Otis Saunders, Batron Johnson, James DeLaney, and Lieutenant Robert Adomilli.

124 Scene with Gary Spath delivering a mourning dove: Interview with Fred Greene.

124 Thelma Pannell learns of Phillip's placement in Job Corps. Interview with Thelma Pannell and with Job Corps, augmented by news accounts.

CHAPTER SEVEN: THIS DIFFERENT NIGHT

127 Description of weather on April 10, 1990: U.S. Weather Service, augmented by author's observations.

128 Morning scene at Pannell apartment in River Edge: Interviews with Thelma and Natasha Pannell.

129 Contents of Phillip C. Pannell's pockets, including job application: Evidence and reports compiled by state attorney general's staff and examined by author.

130 Gary Spath's desire to go fishing: Interview with Father Bart Aslin, augmented by testimony by Officer Wayne Blanco.

130 Scene with Phillip C. Pannell at Mediterranean Deli: Interview with Steven Jowers, augmented by grand jury testimony by Leslie Johnson and Jowers.

131 Spath's shooting scores: Records compiled by Teaneck police.

131 Blanco going for coffee: Testimony by Wayne Blanco.

131 Spath at Teaneck High School: Interview with Sergeant Phillip Lavigne.

132 Pannell on Teaneck Road: Interviews with Steven Jowers, augmented by grand jury testimony by Jowers, Leslie Johnson, Rasjus Jackson, Shariff Cameron, Carl Thrower, Jayson Bennett, Melissa Curry, Michelle Ortiz, Sylvia Curry, Raheem McNeil, Gail Chung, Jamil Graham, Tomisha Autry, Tyrell Autry, Bernard Pearson, Corey Goodall, Durell Jackson, Shawn Robinson, Jonathan Owen, and Omas Fisher.

132 Background on Spath's father as police officer: Interviews with Chief Bryan Burke, Chief Donald Giannone, and Frank Hall.

134 Calls to Teaneck police dispatchers: Dialogue taken from transcripts compiled by defense and prosecution and submitted as evidence in Spath trial.

134 Times: Radio transcripts or approximations based on interviews.

134 Spath's observations and statements: Radio transcripts, his statement to prosecutor's investigators on April 12, 1990, and his trial testimony.

135 Shariff Cameron's observations: His grand jury testimony.

136 Blanco's observations and statements: Radio transcripts, his statement to prosecutor's investigators on April 10, 1990, grand jury testimony, and trial testimony.

137 Delano McLawin's observations: His grand jury testimony.

138 Background on Tryon Park and juvenile problems there: Interviews with Chief Donald Giannone, Lieutenant Robert Adomilli, and Fred Greene, augmented by Teaneck Task Force Report on youth problems in September 1968.

141 Observations of various guns by teenagers at Tryon Park, on Gramercy Place, and in recent weeks: Grand jury testimony, augmented by interviews with Muziki Stewart and Steven Jowers, and trial testimony by Leslie Johnson.

144 Observations by Norman Brew: His grand jury, trial testimony, and interview with author.

149 Observations by Dexter St. Hillaire: His grand jury testimony.

150 Account of police cars driving across Bryant School playground: Grand jury testimony, sworn statement, and trial testimony of Blanco, trial testimony and sworn statement by Spath, grand jury testimony by Steven Jowers, Leslie Johnson, Ellen Dixon, Dexter St. Hillaire, Norman Brew, Calvin Dixon, and Melvin Dixon, and other teenagers present, augmented by interviews with prosecutor's investigators, grand jury testimony and trial testimony of Sergeant Robert Rehberg, and interviews with Steve Jowers and Jonathan Owen.

152 Blanco's frisk: His sworn statement to prosecutors, his grand jury and trial testimony.

152 Actions by Phillip Pannell at Bryant School: Grand jury and trial testimony by Blanco, sworn statement and trial testimony by Gary Spath, grand jury testimony by teenagers, and interviews with Steven Jowers and Jonathan

Owen, augmented by grand jury testimony by Norman Brew, Ellen Dixon, and Dexter St. Hillaire.

154 Police foot-chase Pannell, shots fired, and observations: Grand jury and trial testimony and sworn statement of Blanco, statement and trial testimony of Spath, grand jury and trial testimony of Melvin DeBerry and Dorothy Robinson, grand jury testimony of Jennifer Bradley and Dexter St. Hillaire, augmented by grand jury testimony of Sergeant Robert Rehberg, trial testimony of prosecution and defense experts, and grand jury testimony of Natalie Williams, Jocilyn Rostin, and Randolph Rostin.

CHAPTER EIGHT: BITTER HERBS

161 Observations by Arthur Gardner of scene on Intervale: Interviews with Art Gardner and son, Jerry, augmented by interviews with Kyle Alston, and grand jury testimony of Alston and Teaneck police officers.

163 Phillip Pannell in ambulance: Grand jury testimony of Officers Phillip Lavigne and Wayne Blanco, augmented by interviews with Lavigne and grand jury and trial testimony of ambulance technicians and paramedics.

164 Spath's words in car: Grand jury testimony by Sergeant Fred Ahearn.

165 Paul Ostrow's observations on hearing news of shooting: Interviews with Ostrow.

166 Thelma Pannell's activities and thoughts: Interviews with Thelma Pannell, Natasha Pannell, Steven Jowers, and Kyle Alston.

167 Time of Pannell's death and description of efforts in hospital to save him: Grand jury testimony of Dr. Glenn Birnbaum, augmented by grand jury and trial testimony of Dr. Michael Baden and Dr. Harold Adelman, autopsy records, and autopsy photos and videotape of forensic tests seen by author.

167 Spath's statements and demeanor in hospital: Grand jury testimony of Phillip Lavigne, Wayne Blanco, and Fred Ahearn, Bryan Burke, Patrick Hogan, augmented by interviews with Lavigne, Burke, Hogan, and Jack Terhune.

168 Conversation with Blanco and Lieutenant Patrick Hogan: Grand jury and trial testimony by Hogan, augmented by interviews with him.

169 Batron Johnson and Charles Easter go to hospital: Interviews with Johnson and Easter.

170 Meeting with Spath and Captain Tom Pierson: Interviews with Pierson, augmented by grand jury testimony of Teaneck police officers.

172 Scene with Thelma Pannell in hospital: Interviews with Thelma and Natasha Pannell.

175 Batron Johnson goes from hospital to Intervale Road: Interviews with Batron Johnson, Steve Jowers, Lelia Johnson, and Charles Easter.

176   Thoughts by Officer Luis Torres and phone call about Spath: Interviews with Luis Torres and his wife, Alma.

177   Blanco's sworn statement to prosecutor's detectives: Copy of statement obtained by author, Blanco's grand jury and trial testimony, augmented by grand jury and trial testimony of Sergeant Robert Rehberg.

178   Scene outside police station: Interviews with Alfred Egenhofer, Loretta Weinberg, Annie Allen, Fred Greene, Frank Hall, John Holl, and Chief Bryan Burke, augmented by Burke's grand jury testimony.

178   Scenes in Burke's office: Interviews with Burke, George Powell, Franklin Wilks, Frank Hall, and John Holl, augmented by Burke's grand jury testimony.

181   Scene with Holl outside police station: Interviews with John Holl, Loretta Weinberg, Alfred Egenhofer, augmented by news accounts.

183   Bill Crain's observations: Interviews with Bill Crain, augmented by his wife, Ellen.

183   Observations by Arthur Gardner: Interviews with Gardner.

184   Observations by Al Sharpton: Interviews with Sharpton, augmented by trial testimony and interviews with Dorothy Robinson.

CHAPTER NINE: BREAD OF AFFLICTION
187   Scene on WYNW broadcast of *Good Day New York* with Irin Rivers and Charles Reyes: Tape of broadcast viewed by author. Police reaction to broadcast: Interviews with Robert Galantucci and Jack Terhune.

190   Flyers at Teaneck High School by activists and school officials: Material obtained by author.

191   Scene at Teaneck High School: Observations by author, augmented by interviews with Arthur Gardner, James DeLaney, Batron Johnson, Lelia Johnson, Bruce Davidson, Jacqueline Flowers, Frank Hall, Charles Easter, Steven Jowers, Jeff Carroll, Jay Wolff, Franklin Wilks, and Charles Cobb, augmented by news accounts.

192   Phillip D. Pannell's release from county jail: Court documents obtained by author.

192   Batron Johnson's reactions in school: Interviews with Batron Johnson and Lelia Johnson.

193   Conversation at beauty salon: Interviews with Lelia Johnson.

196   Scene at police station, midafternoon: Author's observations, augmented by interviews with Joyce Venezia, Batron Johnson, Jonathan Owen, Jack Terhune, and Marinos Loukeris.

198   Scene in lecture hall at Teaneck High School: Interviews with Frank Hall and Arthur Gardner.

199 Scene at prosecutor's office: Interviews with John Holl, George Powell, Herbert Daughtry, and Franklin Wilks, augmented by interviews with Dennis Calo.

201 Concerns expressed by Reverend Amandus Derr: Interviews with Derr, augmented by interviews with Reverend Bruce Davidson, Reverend Lucinda Laird, Joe Chuman, and Chief Bryan Burke.

CHAPTER TEN: CUP OF SUFFERING

204 Batron Johnson at vigil and later riot: Interviews with Batron Johnson, augmented by interviews with Steven Jowers and Charles Easter.

205 John Holl at vigil and observations: Interviews with John Holl and George Powell, augmented by author's review of TV and newspaper accounts.

207 Mandy Derr's thoughts: Interviews with Derr, augmented by author's review of TV and newspaper accounts.

210 Paul Ostrow's thoughts: Interviews with Ostrow.

211 Scene inside police station: Interviews with Chief Bryan Burke, Mandy Derr, and Chief Donald Giannone.

212 Scene at Teaneck Council Meeting: Interviews with Frank Hall, Paul Ostrow, Peter Bower, Eleanor Kieliszek, and Reggie Harris, augmented by author's review of transcript of the meeting and TV videotape.

214 Accounts of riot at police station and up Teaneck Road: Interviews with Batron Johnson, Mandy Derr, Chief Bryan Burke, Frank Hall, George Powell, Charles Webster, Officer Phillip Lavigne, Carol Ann Campbell, Hoda Bakhshandagi, Reverend Herbert Daughtry, Reverend Stanley Dennison, Kyle Alston, and Lelia Johnson, augmented by news accounts, TV videotapes, and police reports.

223 Art Gardner at Louie's Charcoal Pit: Interview with Gardner.

224 Observations by Frank Hall upon finding leaflet: Interview with Hall and leaflet from his files.

225 Observations by Al Sharpton: Interview with Sharpton, with TV footage reviewed by author.

226 Observations by Paul Ostrow: Interviews with Ostrow, with TV footage reviewed by author.

CHAPTER ELEVEN: "WE KNEW THE GUY HAD A PROBLEM"

227 Thoughts of Officer Luis Torres: Interviews with Torres and his wife, Alma.

228 Frequency of police shootings: Interview with James Fyfe and review of material from Police Executive Research Forum and book *Deadly Force: What We Know* by Geller and Scott.

229 Fred Greene's observations on Spath's prior shootings: Interviews with Greene.

229 Police shootings in Bergen County: Obtained from prosecutor Jay Fahy in study compiled by investigators upon request of author.

230 Spath's first shooting, in Fort Lee, October 12, 1985: Author's review of police reports, department commendation to Spath, and news accounts, augmented by interviews with Captain Gary Fiedler, Captain Patrick Hogan, Captain Thomas Pierson, Chief Bryan Burke, Jack Terhune, and Gary Spath.

235 Spath's second shooting, in Teaneck, December 1, 1986: Author's review of police reports, PBA commendation to Spath, and news accounts, augmented by interviews with Captain Gary Fiedler, Captain Patrick Hogan, and Chief Bryan Burke.

237 Spath's third shooting, in Teaneck, January 1, 1989: Author's review of police reports, report of departmental hearing on shooting, and news accounts, augmented by interviews with Captain Gary Fiedler, Captain Patrick Hogan, Chief Bryan Burke, Jack Terhune, and Officer Phillip Lavigne.

238 Description of police department reaction to Spath's shootings: Interviews with Chief Bryan Burke, Chief Donald Giannone, Officer Luis Torres, Captain Gary Fiedler, Captain Patrick Hogan, Lieutenant William Broughton, and other officers who spoke off the record.

239 Reaction to third shooting: Police departmental report, augmented by interviews with Chief Burke, Captain Hogan, and Captain Fiedler.

CHAPTER TWELVE: TIDES

245 Description of riot damage: Documents obtained by author from Teaneck municipal files, augmented by author observations, police reports, news accounts, and interviews with Paul Ostrow, Gary Saage, John Callas, Frank Hall, Eleanor Kieliszek, Chief Bryan Burke, Chief Donald Giannone, Reverend Herbert Daughtry, and Reverend Stanley Dennison.

248 Spath's meeting with Robert Galantucci: Interviews with Galantucci, augmented by Spath's trial testimony.

250 Thelma and Phillip D. Pannell's news conference: Author's review of news accounts and TV videotape, augmented by interview with Thelma and Phillip D. Pannell and Franklin Wilks.

252 John Holl weighing options on Spath: Interviews with Holl and Dennis Calo.

254 Spath's statement to prosecutor's detectives: Copy of statement obtained by author, augmented by interviews with Robert Galantucci and Jack Terhune, Terhune's grand jury testimony, and grand jury and trial testimony by Sergeant Robert Rehberg.

256 Spath's suspension: Interviews with John Holl, Dennis Calo, Robert Galantucci, George Powell, Franklin Wilks, Chief Bryan Burke, and Reverend Herbert Daughtry, augmented by accounts of Holl's press conference and TV videotape.

258 Conversation between Fred Greene and a Teaneck police officer on Blanco's frisk of Pannell: Interviews with Fred Greene, augmented by interviews with Deputy Attorney General Glenn Goldberg, Deputy Attorney General Wayne Forrest, and investigators John Farley and Quinton Collins.

260 Description of Thelma Pannell searching for silver starter's pistol. Interviews with Thelma Pannell.

260 Officer Phillip Lavigne's thoughts behind writing poem "The Blink of an Eye": Interview with Lavigne and copy of poem given to author by Lavigne.

CHAPTER THIRTEEN: CROSSROADS
262 Flyers distributed in Teaneck: Copies obtained by author.

263 Variety of opinions in Teaneck: Author's observations and interviews with random residents at the time, augmented by news accounts.

265 Luis Torres's observations on tension in black neighborhoods: Interviews with Torres, augmented by interviews with Teaneck police.

267 Meeting at Dorothy Marcus's house: Interviews with Marcus, augmented by interviews with Arthur Gardner and Loretta Weinberg.

268 Forensic tests on Phillip C. Pannell's body at Conyers Funeral Home: Author's review of videotape of test, augmented by interviews with Dr. Peter De Forest, Dennis Calo, Dr. Lawrence Denson, and William Conyers.

272 Meeting with police at St. Mark's Episcopal Church: Interviews with Reverend Amandus Derr, augmented by interviews with Reverend Lucinda Laird and Joe Chuman.

274 Meeting with Teaneck officials at Grace Lutheran Church: Interviews with Reverend Amandus Derr, augmented by interviews with Frank Hall and Eleanor Kieliszek.

275 Scene at Sabbath services at Jewish Center: Interviews with Paul Ostrow.

276 Easter services at Shiloh AME Zion Church: Interviews with Reverend Stanley Dennison.

277 Descriptions of other religious services: Primarily from news accounts, except for St. Mark's Episcopal Church, which is based on interviews with Reverend Lucinda Laird and review of her sermon, and Grace Lutheran Church, which is based on interviews with Reverend Amandus Derr.

279 Jesse Jackson calls Spath an "assassin": News account in *The New York Times*, augmented by author's interviews with Jackson.

CHAPTER FOURTEEN: "WE WON'T FORGET"

280 Reverend Al Sharpton at Pannell wake: Interviews with Sharpton, George Powell, and Thelma Pannell, augmented by news accounts.

282 Phillip C. Pannell's funeral: Author's review of TV videotapes, augmented by news accounts and interviews with Reverend Herbert Daughtry, Charles Webster, Reverend Bruce Davidson, Batron Johnson, Reverend Amandus Derr, Walter Fields, Loretta Weinberg, and Peter Bower.

284 Scene at Louie's Charcoal Pit and strategy plans by black leaders in asking for special prosecutor: Interviews with Theodore Wells, George Powell, and Walter Fields.

287 Meeting with prosecution team: Interviews with Robert Del Tufo, Robert Winter, Dennis Calo, and John Holl.

CHAPTER FIFTEEN: THE GUV, JESSE, AND BIG AL

289 Governor Florio meets with black leaders in Teaneck: Interviews with Jon Shure, George Powell, Franklin Wilks, Walter Fields, and Theodore Wells.

291 Decision to move grand jury investigation to Trenton and political and legal ramifications: Interviews with Steve Perskie, Jon Shure, Brenda Bacon, Theodore Wells, Robert Del Tufo, Robert Winter, John Holl, Dennis Calo, Reverend Al Sharpton, and George Powell.

292 Decision by Sharpton to get involved: Interviews with Sharpton.

294 Scene at student union at Fairleigh Dickinson University: Interviews with Al Sharpton, Jeff Carroll, and Laurie Merrill, augmented by news accounts.

296 Legal concerns of Teaneck: Interviews with Frank Hall, Eleanor Kieliszek, Peter Bower, and Martin Cramer.

297 Strategy of Concerned Citizens: Interviews with Bill Crain, Loretta Weinberg, Frank Hall, and Peter Bower.

299 Meeting in Brooklyn with Reverend Al Sharpton and Theodore Wells: Interviews with Sharpton, Wells, and Reggie Harris.

303 Reverend Jesse Jackson's arrival in Teaneck and meeting with Pannells: Interviews with Jackson, Adam Crain, Congressman Robert Torricelli, Reverend Herb Daughtry, and Thelma Pannell, augmented by news accounts.

306 Jackson goes to St. Paul's Lutheran Church: Interviews with Jackson, Frank Hall, Congressman Robert Torricelli, Adam Crain, Reverend Bruce Davidson, and Thelma Pannell, augmented by news accounts.

309 Florio's planning for meeting with Jackson: Interviews with Steve Perskie, Jon Shure, Brenda Bacon, and Robert Del Tufo.

312 Description of Drumthwacket: *Drumthwacket: A History of the Governor's Mansion at Princeton, New Jersey*, augmented by interviews with mansion staffers Camille Amadio and Daphne Pontius and author's tour of mansion library and other rooms visited by Jackson.

312 Conversation between Jackson and Torricelli on helicopter: Interviews with Jackson and Torricelli.

313 Meeting between Jackson and Florio in Princeton: Interviews with Jackson, Congressman Robert Torricelli, Jon Shure, and Brenda Bacon.

316 Police reaction to Florio-Jackson meeting: Interviews with Sergeant Steve Rogers and Robert Galantucci, augmented by news accounts.

317 Fred Greene's thoughts on Al Sharpton: Interviews with Greene and copy of his letter in the *Bergen Record*.

Chapter Sixteen: Home Fires
320 Frank Hall on Barry Gray radio show with Elaine Spath: Interviews with Frank Hall and author's review of tape of the show and conversation with Elaine Spath.

325 Reverend Al Sharpton's march in Teaneck: Interviews with Sharpton, Paul Ostrow, Charles Webster, Frank Hall, Chief Bryan Burke, Batron Johnson, Lelia Johnson, Dorothy Marcus, and Ka-Pri Marcus, augmented by news accounts.

Chapter Seventeen: "It's Like a Marital Spat"
333 Mood of Teaneck: Author's observations and reporting, augmented by interviews with Frank Hall, Paul Ostrow, Eleanor Kieliszek, Charles Webster, augmented by news accounts.

334 Teaneck youth problems in 1968: Task Force Report, May 1, 1969, augmented by interviews with Fred Greene, Bryan Burke, and Frank Hall.

337 Herb Daughtry's observations: Interviews with Daughtry and review of his op ed article on Teaneck in *Bergen Record*.

339 Scene at Mediterranean Deli: Author's observations.

340 Scene at Teaneck High School and Pannell memorial in trophy case: Author's observations, augmented by interviews with James DeLaney and copy of his statement to students provided to author.

343 Bob Grant's reflections on Spath: Interview with Grant.

343 Conversation with Elaine Spath and Bob Grant of WABC: Interviews with Bob Grant, augmented by interviews with Robert Galantucci.

345 Spath at the PBA meeting: Author's review of tape of session provided by David Voreacos of *Bergen Record*, augmented by author interviews with Robert Galantucci, Teaneck police officers, and news accounts.

345   Spath's mood that time: Interviews with Robert Galantucci and Father Bart Aslin.

347   Scene at St. Mark's Church: Interviews with Reverend Amandus Derr, Reverend Lucinda Laird, and Joe Chuman.

349   Meeting of prosecution team in Newark: Interviews with Dennis Calo, John Holl, Peter Harvey, Robert Carroll, and Robert Winter.

350   Prosecutor's doubts about Blanco's story of frisk and its significance: Interviews with Robert Del Tufo, Robert Winter, Robert Carroll, Dennis Calo, John Holl, and Peter Harvey.

353   Visit by Reverend Jesse Jackson to Teaneck High School: Author's observations, augmented by review of videotape of event provided by Teaneck High School video department and interviews with Reverend Jesse Jackson, James DeLaney, Reverend Amandus Derr, Frank Hall, Reverend Herbert Daughtry, Thelma Pannell, and Batron Johnson.

357   Convening of grand jury in Trenton: Author's review of grand jury transcripts.

358   Meeting at Benjamin Franklin Middle School by Teaneck clergy: Author's observations, augmented by interviews with Reverend Bruce Davidson, Reverend Lucinda Laird, Reverend Amandus Derr, and Joe Chuman.

360   Batron Johnson's state of mind: Interviews with Batron and Lelia Johnson.

361   Meeting of Teaneck council at Benjamin Franklin Middle School: Author's review of transcript of meeting, augmented by interviews with Frank Hall, Eleanor Kieliszek, Lelia Johnson, Charles Webster, Bryan Burke, and Reverend Amandus Derr.

362   Sermon by Reverend Amandus Derr: Interviews with Derr and author's review of copy of sermon provided by Derr.

CHAPTER EIGHTEEN: "RACE WAS ON THE TABLE NOW"
364   Election night: Interviews with Paul Ostrow, augmented by interviews with Frank Hall, Loretta Weinberg, Peter Bower, and Rick Shafton.

368   T-shirt sales: Author's observations, augmented by interviews with Robert Galantucci, Bryan Burke, Teaneck police officers, Dumont police officers, black activists, and review of news accounts.

370   Chants at marches: Author's observations, augmented by interviews with Charles Webster and Bill Crain.

374   Bill Crain meets with Batron Johnson: Interviews with Bill Crain, Tom Crain, Jim White, Batron Johnson, and Lelia Johnson, augmented by interviews with Fred Greene.

376 Luis Torres meets with Pannell family: Interviews with Torres and Thelma Pannell.

CHAPTER NINETEEN: MARCHING TOWARD JERUSALEM

378 Peter De Forest discovers mistake: Interviews with De Forest, augmented by his grand jury testimony, and author's review of autopsy findings and videotape of forensic test.

379 Robert Del Tufo learns about mistake and reaction to it: Interviews with Del Tufo and Robert Winter.

381 Meeting in Ardsley to discuss mistake: Interviews with Del Tufo, De Forest, Winter, and Carroll.

383 March to Trenton: Interviews with Bill Crain, augmented by interviews with Reverend Al Sharpton, Steve Perskie, Jon Shure, Brenda Bacon, members of the Princeton Police Department, and news accounts.

387 Robert Del Tufo's decision to call a new grand jury: Interviews with Del Tufo and Robert Winter, augmented by author's review of final day of grand jury instructions and official statements by Attorney General's Office.

393 Reaction by grand jurors: Interviews with Robert Galantucci, augmented by accounts in the *New Jersey Law Journal* by Tracey Schroth and Kathleen Bird.

394 Police march on Teaneck: Author's observations, augmented by review of private videotapes by Sergeant Steve Rogers and Richard Kunath, news accounts, and interviews with Rogers, Father Bart Aslin, Robert Galantucci, Bryan Burke, and numerous other officers.

396 Strategy for second grand jury: Interviews with Robert Del Tufo, Robert Winter, and Wayne Forrest.

CHAPTER TWENTY: THE GODS OF IDOLATRY

403 Reverend Amandus Derr's Thanksgiving sermon: Copy of sermon provided to author.

407 Arthur Gardner's observations of kids: Interviews with Gardner.

408 Detective Jackie Smith's experience with Teaneck police: Interview with Smith.

408 Batron Johnson stopped by Wayne Blanco: Interviews with Batron Johnson, Raheem McNeil, Jimmy Davis, Lelia Johnson, augmented by Teaneck police reports and interviews with Chief Donald Giannone.

408 Batron Johnson obtains two guns: Interviews with Batron Johnson.

412 Gary Spath's card to Luis Torres: Obtained by author from Torres.

413 Reverend Stanley Dennison's conversation with Teaneck police officer: Interview with Dennison.

CHAPTER TWENTY-ONE: HEARTS AND MINDS
417   Paul Ostrow's state of mind: Interviews with Paul Ostrow.

420   First anniversary of Pannell's death: Interviews with Batron Johnson, Arthur Gardner, and various Teaneck police officers, augmented by news accounts.

422   Gary Spath's reflections on his case during meeting in Galantucci's office. Interview with author and author's observations.

423   Kahane Chai crisis in Teaneck: Interviews with Emanuel Landau, Arthur Gardner, Dr. Bill Jones, Mel Henderson, Reverend Bruce Davidson, Reverend Amandus Derr, Michael Kates, Loretta Weinberg, Barbara Shapiro, and Lieutenant William Broughton, as well as members of Kahane Chai.

423   Black-Jewish dialogues and other Teaneck dialogues: Interviews with Art Gardner, Loretta Weinberg, and Emanuel Landau.

427   Significance of first bullet: Interviews with Glenn D. Goldberg and Wayne Forrest.

427   Discovery of "light hit": Interviews with Robert Galantucci and Michael Struk.

428   Galantucci's strategy for investigating backgrounds of prospective jurors: Interviews with Galantucci.

CHAPTER TWENTY-TWO: *NEW JERSEY* v. *GARY SPATH*
430   Much of this chapter comes from author's own observations of the trial, augmented by a video transcript of the public proceedings, obtained from Court TV.

435   Discussion of black jurors in Judge DiGisi's chambers: Transcript of proceedings obtained by author from court stenographer, augmented by interviews with Robert Galantucci, Glenn D. Goldberg, Wayne Forrest, and Judge DiGisi.

445   Arrest of Melvin DeBerry: Interviews with Jay Alpert, Jack Terhune, WCBS-TV camera crew, Glenn D. Goldberg, John Farley, and Louis Braxton, augmented by news accounts and author's review of videotapes.

447   Reaction of jury to scientific testimony by prosecution: Author's off-the-record interviews with jurors.

453   Strategy behind entrance of Officer Steven McDonald: Interviews with Robert Galantucci and James Patuto.

454   Concern with courtroom security: Interviews with Judge Charles DiGisi.

456   Doubts about Blanco's frisk of Pannell: Interviews with Fred Greene, Robert Carroll, Glenn D. Goldberg, Wayne Forrest, John Farley, and Quinton Collins.

461 Reaction to verdict: Author's observations at Spath press conference and comments to author by Elaine Spath.

Chapter Twenty-three: By the Waters of Babylon

463 Scene in Hackensack: Interviews with Bill Crain, Reverend Herbert Daughtry, and Reverend Stanley Dennison, augmented by author's observations.

465 March to Teaneck: Interviews with Crain, Daughtry, Dennison, augmented by author's observations.

466 Spath's comments on Bob Grant radio show: Tape obtained by author from WABC radio.

466 Batron Johnson's thoughts as he left Teaneck High School and marched to police station: Interviews with Batron Johnson and Lelia Johnson, augmented by author's observations.

469 Scene at police station: Author's observations, augmented by interviews with Arthur Gardner, Batron Johnson, Lelia Johnson, Bill Crain, Reverend Herb Daughtry, William David-El, and Lieutenant William Broughton.

Chapter Twenty-four: Last Rites

471 Batron Johnson speaks to students at South Jersey high school: Author's review of videotape of speech, augmented by interviews with Batron Johnson, Charles Cobb, Gordon Presley, James DeLaney, and Lelia Johnson.

472 Paul Ostrow's feelings for Teaneck: Interviews with Ostrow, augmented by author's observations at banquet to honor him.

472 Gary Spath honored by Detectives Crime Clinic: Author's observations, interviews with William Fitzmaurice and member of board of directors for clinic.

474 Teaneck High School graduation: Author's observations, augmented by videotape of event and interviews with Batron Johnson, Lelia Johnson, and James DeLaney.

474 Visit to Phillip Pannell's grave: Author's observations while accompanying Batron Johnson and other teenagers, augmented by later interviews with Batron Johnson.

Epilogue

478 Reference to blacks in white-collar jobs and decline in black poverty: *Fortune* (June 1, 1992).

478 Number of black police officers: Unemployment and Earnings, U.S. Bureau of Labor Statistics, 1991.

478 Black family breakup: Population Reference Bureau, 1992.

478 References to black crime: Hacker, *Two Nations*.

484 Gary Spath's awards: From citations to Gary Spath.

484 Reference to arrest of Phillip Pannell: Court records and Teaneck and Englewood police reports.

SELECTIVE BIBLIOGRAPHY

For perspectives on race relations, suburban integration, police shootings, and views on Teaneck and accounts of the death of Phillip Pannell and the trial of Gary Spath, hundreds of articles found their way into my files from the following publications: The Amsterdam *News*, the *Atlantic*, the *Bergen Record*, The Boston *Globe*, the Chicago *Tribune*, the Cleveland *Plain Dealer*, *Commentary*, the *Connection*, *Emerge*, *Essence*, *Fortune*, the Gannett News Service, *Mother Jones*, *National Review*, the Newark *Star-Ledger*, the *New Republic*, *Newsweek*, the New York *Daily News*, *New York* magazine, New York *Newsday*, the New York *Post*, *The New York Times*, *The New York Times Magazine*, the *New Yorker*, the *North Jersey Herald & News*, the Philadelphia *Inquirer*, the *Suburbanite*, *Time*, the *Wall Street Journal*, the *Village Voice*, and *U.S. News & World Report*.

Research was augmented with television news footage from WABC, WCBS, WNBC, WNET, WNJN, WNYW, WPIX, and WWOR and with radio broadcasts from WABC, WBAI, WLIB, WNYC, and WWOR.

Following are books and other useful publications:

Anson, Robert Sam. *Best Intentions: The Education and Killing of Edmund Perry*. New York: Random House, 1987.

Appelbaum, Joy Zacharia. *The History of the Jews of Teaneck*. Teaneck: Appelbaum, 1977.

Auletta, Ken. *The Underclass*. New York: Random House, 1983.

Biskup, Michael. *Youth Violence*. San Diego: Greenhaven, 1992.

Branch, Taylor. *Parting the Waters: America in the King Years, 1954–63*. New York: Simon & Schuster, 1988.

Cone, James H. *Martin and Malcolm and America: A Dream or a Nightmare*. Maryknoll: Orbis, 1991.

Cose, Ellis. A *Nation of Strangers: Prejudice, Politics, and the Populating of America.* New York: Morrow, 1992.

Damerell, Reginald G. *Triumph in a White Suburb: The Dramatic Story of Teaneck, N.J., the First Town in The Nation to Vote for Integrated Schools.* New York: Morrow, 1968.

DeSantis, John. *For the Color of His Skin: The Murder of Yusuf Hawkins.* New York: Pharos, 1991.

Edsall, Thomas Byrne, and Mary D. Edsall. *Chain Reaction: The Impact of Race, Rights, and Taxes on American Politics.* New York: Norton, 1991.

Geller, William A., and Michael Scott. *Deadly Force: What We Know.* Washington, D.C.: Police Executive Research Forum, 1992.

Glazer, Nathan, and Daniel Patrick Moynihan. *Beyond the Melting Pot: The Negroes, Puerto Ricans, Jews, Italians, and Irish of New York City.* Cambridge, Mass.: MIT Press, 1963.

Greene, Melissa Fay. *Praying for Sheetrock: A Work of Nonfiction.* New York: Addison-Wesley, 1991.

Hacker, Andrew. *Two Nations: Black and White, Separate, Hostile, Unequal.* New York: Scribner, 1992.

Kotlowitz, Alex. *There Are No Children Here: The Story of Two Boys Growing Up in the Other America.* New York: Nan Talese / Doubleday, 1991.

Lukas, J. Anthony. *Common Ground: A Turbulent Decade in the Lives of Three American Families.* New York: Knopf, 1985.

Malcolm X. *The Autobiography of Malcolm X* (with the assistance of Alex Haley). New York: Grove, 1965.

McFadden, Robert D., Ralph Blumenthal, M. A. Farber, E. R. Shipp, Charles Strum, and Craig Wolff. *Outrage: The Story Behind the Tawana Brawley Hoax.* New York: Bantam, 1990.

New Jersey Attorney General. *Report of Task Force on the Use of Force in Law Enforcement.* Trenton: April 1992.

New Jersey Supreme Court. *Report of Task Force on Minority Concerns.* Trenton: 1989.

————. *Survey of Perceptions of Bias in the New Jersey Courts.* Trenton, 1989.

New York State Division of Criminal Justice. *A Report to the Governor on the Disturbances In Crown Heights.* Albany: 1993. 2 vols.

Salmore, Barbara G., and Stephen A. Salmore. *New Jersey Politics and Government: Suburban Politics Comes of Age.* Lincoln: University of Nebraska Press, 1993.

Schlesinger, Arthur M., Jr. *The Disuniting of America: Reflections on a Multicultural Society.* Knoxville: Whittle, 1991.

Sleeper, Jim. *The Closest of Strangers: Liberalism and the Politics of Race in New York.* New York: Norton, 1990.

Steele, Shelby. *The Content of Our Character: A New Vision of Race in America.* New York: St. Martin, 1990.

Taylor, Mildred. *The History of Teaneck.* Teaneck: Teaneck American Revolution Bicentennial Committee, 1977.

Teaneck Board of Education. *Report by Committee on Institutional Racism.* May 1994.

———. *A District Response to the Report of the Committee on Institutional Racism.* September 18, 1994.

———. *Report by Advisory Committee on School Names.* June 1994.

———. *Addendum for Advisory Committee on School Names.* June 14, 1994.

———. *Discipline Task Force.* June 22, 1994.

Teaneck Task Force. *Report on Youth Disturbances.* Teaneck Town Council, May 1, 1969.

Touche Ross & Co. *Teaneck Police Department: Operations Review.* November 1984.

West, Cornel. *Beyond Eurocentrism and Multiculturalism.* Monroe, Maine: Common Courage Press, 1993.

———. *Race Matters.* Boston: Beacon Press, 1993.

Wiley, Ralph. *Why Black People Tend to Shout: Cold Facts and Wry Views from a Black Man's World.* New York: Birch Lane Press, 1991.

ACKNOWLEDGMENTS

This book would never have been written without the love and support of my wife, Judy Kelly. Every page reflects her graceful touch as my sounding board and ad hoc editor. Our daughters, Michelle and Anne, endured many evenings as I ran out the door with a notebook, stared at a computer, or slumped in a chair with notes. I thank them for reminding me to come up for air.

Sam Vaughan was not just a pencil editor; he was my muse, passing on earnest advice and integrity over long talks in diners. He pushed me to reach for the best in myself and in this story. His presence in my life, along with his wife, Jo, who took many a phone message, is a cherished gift.

Morrow's senior editor, Paul Bresnick, was the strong hand on the tiller that brought this book home. He found loose threads that needed trimming amid fabric that needed preserving, always with a sense of fairness.

Also at Morrow, Lisa Drew spotted the importance of this story and was a source of upbeat enthusiasm. Jon Moskowitz kept track of details and deadlines, always with immense patience and kindness. Pearl Hanig did an expert copyediting job and Ann Cahn assisted in fact checking and devoted hours to pulling together the endless details.

My agent, Tim Hays, nurtured the seed of this idea, with an unwavering belief for what was important.

Jim Wright of the *Bergen Record* brought his sharp eye to early drafts and lent an ear to my meandering yarns.

Former *Record* editor David Hall, now at the Cleveland *Plain Dealer*, spotted an uncertain fire that burned in me and urged me to explore the depths of this story in columns and later in a book. Also at the *Record*, David Voreacos and Bill Sanderson shared insights and files, Peter Grad solved computer mysteries, and Neil Reisner rescued lost pages in the dark corners of a fickle hard drive.

Adam Hirschfelder put in long hours as my research assistant, shaping a mountain of statistics into a demographic portrait of Teaneck.

Dana Conklin and Aaron Elson transcribed miles of taped interviews. Sean Sexton took my files of crime statistics and meticulously broke them into patterns. TV producer Joe Vargas copied boxes of trial videotape.

Bergen County Clerk Kathleen Donovan and others at the courthouse, especially Geraldine Hrazanek, Frances Riley, and Michael Biamonte, brushed the dust off valuable files.

Judge Charles R. DiGisi, Dr. Lawrence Denson, U.S. Attorney Michael Chertoff, and Bergen County Prosecutor Jay Fahy freely offered hours of background.

New Jersey Attorney General Robert Del Tufo and his deputy Robert Winter endured scores of requests for information. In particular, Deputy Attorney General Wayne Forrest never failed to surprise me with his encyclopedic command of facts and reverence for legal precision. Others in Trenton or elsewhere who offered background on the prosecution include: Dr. Michael Baden, Louis Braxton, Dennis Calo, Robert Carroll, Quinton Collins, Dr. Peter De Forest, John Farley, Glenn D. Goldberg, Lucien Haag, Peter Harvey, John Holl, and David Schratwieser.

Robert L. Galantucci patiently walked me through the defense strategy, and the emotional side of police officers. His partners, Philip DeVencentes and James Patuto, filled in gaps, as did chief investigator Mike Struk and his secretary, Joanne Kenny.

Theodore Wells and Congressman Robert Torricelli supplied hours of insight into political decisions, as did Brenda Bacon, Steve Perskie, and Jon Shure of Governor Jim Florio's staff. Carl Golden of Governor Christine Todd Whitman's staff opened doors at the Drumthwacket mansion, with the help of Camille Amadio and Daphne Pontius.

At the New Jersey Department of Corrections Patricia Mulcahy arranged interviews with prison inmates. At the New Jersey Department of Education, Anthony Scalzo, Ed.D., and James Anzevino sped access to Teaneck school records.

The Police Executive Research Forum provided extensive analysis and advice with Temple University's James Fyfe on police shootings.

The staff of the New Jersey Supreme Court turned over research on bias in courts, with the help of Jerome Miller of the Augustus Institute and William Chambliss of George Washington University.

Harvard University's Project on School Desegregation and Gary Orfield provided additional and needed perspective on the educational and political dilemmas of race relations in New Jersey and the rest of America.

The Bergen County Police Academy opened its classrooms, permitting me hours of insight and instruction on firearms tactics and deadly force. Special thanks to Director Ronald Calissi, Chief Robert Re, Lieutenant Steven Babiak, Lieutenant Alan Grieco, Lieutenant Paul Ortenzio, and Sergeant Jean Rothenberger.

Other law enforcement officials who kindly steered me through the complexities of police work, the Spath trial, the Pannell family, and Teaneck include: Captain Tom Pierson of the Fort Lee Police Department, Sergeant Steve Rogers of the Nutley Police Department, Bergen County Sheriff Jack Terhune and Undersheriff Jay Alpert, and Detective Jackie Smith and Sergeant Michael Blischak of the Englewood police juvenile bureau.

The Teaneck Police Department was extraordinarily professional in discussing a variety of sensitive issues and providing hours of insight into crime in Teaneck and police-community relations, while also permitting me to review hundreds of pages of crime statistics and police reports. Some officers preferred to speak only on a confidential basis. Others, who spoke openly and provided a wellspring of understanding, were: retired Chief Bryan Burke, Chief Donald Giannone, Captain Gary Fiedler, Captain Patrick Hogan, Captain Walter Pinches, Lieutenant Robert Adomilli, Lieutenant William Broughton, retired Lieutenant Fred Greene, Sergeant Phillip Lavigne, and Lieutenant Paul Tiernan.

Jim Hulsizer of the Bergen County Department of Planning and Economic Development assisted in assembling Teaneck's census files. Historian Robert Griffin opened my eyes to Teaneck's past and census information from the eighteenth and nineteenth centuries. Teaneck Librarian Mike McCue gave me the run of his extensive collection and was gracious about my late returns.

Teaneck's schools were an invaluable source of information on racial issues, youth violence, and the psychological and educational issues in the aftermath of the Pannell shooting. Among those who walked an extra mile were Superintendent Harold Morris, high school Principal James DeLaney, former guidance counselors Jay Wolff and Charles Cobb, and psychologists Joel Baskin and Gordon Presley.

Teaneck municipal officials who assisted my search for records include: township manager Gary Saage and former clerk Elizabeth O'Brien.

Martin Lasky, along with Joseph Chuman, Reverend Lucinda Laird, and Reverend Bruce Davidson of the Teaneck Clergy Council, helped unveil the meaning of the township dialogue meetings.

The Reverends Al Sharpton and Jesse Jackson eagerly submitted to challenging questions, while also supplying important details.

The family of Phillip Pannell, especially Phillip D. Pannell, Thelma Pannell, and Natasha Pannell, willingly provided hours of background, even on difficult issues. Likewise, Gary Spath answered questions into his career, including his shooting record. For added perspective on the pressures Spath was under, I am indebted to Father Bart Aslin.

Generous colleagues in journalism, near and far, who provided help or advice, great and small: Steve Adubato, Jim Ahearn, Steve Auchard, Kathleen Bird, David Blomquist, Carol Ann Campbell, Bob Grant, Bob Hanley, Reggie Harris, Melinda Henneberger, Ralph Johnson, Elizabeth Llorente, Bruce Locklin, Steve Marsh, Jim McGarvey, Laurie Merrill, John Mooney, Beverly O'Shea, Al Parisi, Len Reed, Glenn Ritt, Don Rouse, Tracey Schroth, Rochelle Sharpe, Duane Stoltzfus, Kathy Sullivan, Bill Turque, Joyce Venezia, and Vivian Waixel.

Others, whose information and insight helped frame my research: Kyle Alston, Marlene Aravjo, Annie Allen, Vince Basile, Peter Bower, Bernard Brooks, Jeff Carroll, Stephanie Cheatham, William Conyers, Hartwell Cornelius, William David-El, Reverend Herbert Daughtry, Jim Davis, Norm Dermody, Chris Donfield, Charles Easter, Harold Eatman, Alfred Egenhofer, Matthew Feldman, Bernard Finnigan, Joseph Fleming, Jacqueline Flowers, Charles Grady, Mel Henderson, Sean Honegan, Lloyd Houston, Salaam Ismail, Carter Jackson, Reverend Gregory Jackson, Harold Jenkins, Dr. William Jones, Steven Jowers, Michael Kates, Jacqueline Kates, Ray Kelly, David Kent, Eleanor Kieliszek, Dennis Kohler, Richard Kunath, Emanuel Landau, Frank Lucianna, Bill Mack, Curtis and Michelle March, Rosemary McCain, Gerald Mohamad, Brother Keith Muhammad, Tasha Morton, Barbara Ostroth, Jonathan Owen, Jasmine Pomes, George Powell, Robert Robinson, Franklin Robinson, Otis Saunders, Richard Segall, Werner Schmid, Rick Shafton, Michael and Joan Sloser, Muziki Stewart, Jeal Sugarman, Charles Webster, Loretta Weinberg, Jim White, Leo Wielkocz, and Franklin Wilks.

Finally I am most grateful to those (and their families) who spent scores of hours with me and through whose eyes I have elected to explore the emotional and personal depths of this story and the racial questions it raised: Bill Crain, Reverend Stanley Dennison, Reverend Amandus "Mandy" Derr, Walter Fields, Arthur Gardner, Frank Hall, Batron and Lelia Johnson, Dorothy Marcus, Paul Ostrow, and Luis Torres. It was their sharing of personal insights—even painful memories—that forms the foundation of this story.

INDEX